PHILOSOPHICAL
DILEMMAS

PHILOSOPHICAL DILEMMAS

———————●———————

A PRO AND CON INTRODUCTION TO THE MAJOR QUESTIONS

SECOND EDITION

Phil Washburn

New York   Oxford
Oxford University Press
2001

Oxford University Press

Oxford   New York
Athens   Auckland   Bangkok   Bogotá   Buenos Aires   Calcutta
Cape Town   Chennai   Dar es Salaam   Delhi   Florence   Hong Kong   Istanbul
Karachi   Kuala Lumpur   Madrid   Melbourne   Mexico City   Mumbai
Nairobi   Paris   São Paulo   Shanghai   Singapore   Taipei   Tokyo   Toronto   Warsaw

and associated companies in
Berlin   Ibadan

Copyright © 1997, 2001 by Oxford University Press, Inc.

Published by Oxford University Press, Inc.
198 Madison Avenue, New York, New York 10016
http://www.oup-usa.org

Oxford is a registered trademark of Oxford University Press

Library of Congress Cataloging–in–Publication Data

Washburn, Phil.
    Philosophical dilemmas : a pro and con introduction to the major questions / Phil
    Washburn.--2nd ed.
       p. cm.
    Includes bibliographical references and index.
    ISBN 0-19-513496-6 (pbk. : alk. paper)
    1. Philosophy--Introductions.   I. Title.
BD21.W36 2000
   100--dc21   00-039934

Printing (last digit):   10 9 8 7 6 5 4 3 2 1

Printed in the United States of America on acid-free paper.

For my parents,
Dr. W. Wyan Washburn
and Emily Davis Washburn

BRIEF CONTENTS

Chapter 1. God, Immortality, and Faith   15

1.1   Does God Exist?   16
1.2   Is God Like Human Beings?   29
1.3   Can God Allow Innocent Suffering?   41
1.4   Is the Soul Immortal?   52
1.5   Is Faith an Answer?   62
1.6   Current Controversy: Is Buddhism Philosophy?   75

Chapter 2. Liberty, Equality, and Justice   95

2.1   Is Society Based on a Contract?   96
2.2   Is Liberty the Highest Social Value?   109
2.3   Is Equality the Highest Social Value?   123
2.4   Is Capitalism Just?   135
2.5   Should We Establish a World Government?   149
2.6   Current Controversy: Is Race Essential to Identity?   163

Chapter 3. Happiness, Obligations, and Values   187

3.1   Is Pleasure the Only Value?   188
3.2   Can We Understand Happiness?   203
3.3   Is Morality Relative?   213
3.4   Is Happiness the Standard of Morality?   226
3.5   Is Society the Source of Values?   241
3.6   Current Controversy: Should Doctors Ever End People's Lives?   251

Chapter 4. Free Will, Mind, and Human Nature   275

4.1   Are We Free?   276
4.2   Are We Responsible for Our Actions?   290
4.3   Is the Mind Nothing but the Brain?   301
4.4   Can Computers Think?   313
4.5   Are We Always Selfish?   325
4.6   Current Controversy: Are the Differences between Men and Women
      Philosophically Significant?   336

Chapter 5. Knowledge, Science, and Truth   359

5.1   Can We Know about the External World?   360
5.2   Does Science Give Us Real Knowledge?   371
5.3   Is Experience the Source of All Knowledge?   382
5.4   Is Certainty the Standard of Knowledge?   396
5.5   Current Controversy: Does Truth Exist?   410

CONTENTS

Preface to the Second Edition   xvi

Preface   xvii

Historical Parallels   xx

Introduction   1

Chapter 1. God, Immortality, and Faith   15

1.1   DOES GOD EXIST?   16
   Yes: Causal Theist. "In the Beginning"   16
      Critical Questions   19

   Yes: Design Theist. "Design or Chance?"   19
      Critical Questions   22

   No: Atheist. "The Retreat of the Gods"   22
      Critical Questions   25

   Methods and Techniques: Arguments   25

   Understanding the Dilemma   26

1.2   IS GOD LIKE HUMAN BEINGS?   29
   No: Abstractionist. "God Is Love"   30
      Critical Questions   34

   Yes: Personalist. "The Projection Theory"   34
      Critical Questions   37

   Methods and Techniques: Meanings of Words   38

   Understanding the Dilemma   39

1.3   CAN GOD ALLOW INNOCENT SUFFERING?   41
   No: Contradictor. "There Is No God"   42
      Critical Questions   45

   Yes: Reconciler. "Character and Contentment"   45
      Critical Questions   48

   Methods and Techniques: Consistent Beliefs   48

   Understanding the Dilemma   49

1.4   IS THE SOUL IMMORTAL?   52
   No: Terminator. "Immortality"   53
      Critical Questions   55

Yes: Survivor. "For and against an Afterlife"   55
    Critical Questions   58

Methods and Techniques: Facts and Concepts   58

Understanding the Dilemma   60

1.5 IS FAITH AN ANSWER?   62
    Yes: Believer. "Accepting Limits"   63
        Critical Questions   67

    No: Questioner. "Faith and Its Consequences"   67
        Critical Questions   70

    Methods and Techniques: Consequences   71

    Understanding the Dilemma   73

CURRENT CONTROVERSY

1.6 IS BUDDHISM PHILOSOPHY?   75
    Yes: Buddhist. "The Philosophy of Buddhism"   76
        Critical Questions   80

    *No: Specialist. "The Difference between Religion and
    Philosophy"*   81
        Critical Questions   84

    Methods and Techniques: Definitions   84

    Understanding the Dilemma   86

    Connections: Transcendentalist or Naturalist?   90

Chapter 2. Liberty, Equality, and Justice   95

2.1 IS SOCIETY BASED ON A CONTRACT?   96
    Yes: Contractor. "The Social Contract"   97
        Critical Questions   99

    No: Organicist. "The Social Organism"   99
        Critical Questions   103

    Methods and Techniques: Models   103

    Understanding the Dilemma   106

2.2 IS LIBERTY THE HIGHEST SOCIAL VALUE?   109
    Yes: Libertarian. "Liberty, the Supreme Social Value"   110
        Critical Questions   114

    No: Paternalist. "Empty Phrases"   115
        Critical Questions   118

    Methods and Techniques: Goals   118

    Understanding the Dilemma   120

2.3 IS EQUALITY THE HIGHEST SOCIAL VALUE?   123
    Yes: Egalitarian. "Society and Property"   123
      Critical Questions   127

    No: Elitist. "What Elitists Believe"   127
      Critical Questions   131

    Methods and Techniques: Means and Ends   131

    Understanding the Dilemma   132

2.4 IS CAPITALISM JUST?   135
    Yes: Capitalist. "Capitalism, Democracy, and Justice"   136
      Critical Questions   140

    No: Socialist. "Capitalist Society"   140
      Critical Questions   144

    Methods and Techniques: Thinking and Emotion   145

    Understanding the Dilemma   146

2.5 SHOULD WE ESTABLISH A WORLD GOVERNMENT?   149
    Yes: Internationalist. "Choosing a Peaceful Future"   150
      Critical Questions   154

    No: Localist. "The Politics of World Government"   155
      Critical Questions   158

    Methods and Techniques: Comparing   159

    Understanding the Dilemma   160

CURRENT CONTROVERSY

2.6 IS RACE ESSENTIAL TO IDENTITY?   163
    Yes: Essentialist. "The Meaning of Being Black"   164
      Critical Questions   168

    No: Nonessentialist. "Race and Identity"   169
      Critical Questions   174

    Methods and Techniques: Identity   174

    Understanding the Dilemma   176

    Connections: Individualist or Relationist?   179

Chapter 3. Happiness, Obligations, and Values   187

3.1 IS PLEASURE THE ONLY VALUE?   188
    Yes: Hedonist. "Hedonism"   189
      Critical Questions   191

    No: Pluralist. "A World of Values"   192
      Critical Questions   197

Methods and Techniques: Facts and Values   198

Understanding the Dilemma   199

3.2 CAN WE UNDERSTAND HAPPINESS?   203
   Yes: Definer. "Happiness"   204
      Critical Questions   206

   No: Muddler. "The Elusive Dream"   207
      Critical Questions   209

   Methods and Techniques: Essential Properties   209
   Understanding the Dilemma   211

3.3 IS MORALITY RELATIVE?   213
   Yes: Relativist. "Moral Relativism"   214
      Critical Questions   218

   No: Absolutist. "Right for You, Wrong for Me?"   218
      Critical Questions   222

   Methods and Techniques: Ad Hominem   222
   Understanding the Dilemma   223

3.4 IS HAPPINESS THE STANDARD OF MORALITY?   226
   Yes: Utilitarian. "Utilitarianism"   227
      Critical Questions   232

   No: Formalist. "The Principle of Morality"   232
      Critical Questions   237

   Methods and Techniques: Moral Theories   237
   Understanding the Dilemma   239

3.5 IS SOCIETY THE SOURCE OF VALUES?   241
   Yes: Functionalist. "An Objective Basis for Morality"   242
      Critical Questions   244

   No: Moral Theist. "The Current Crisis and Its Solution"   245
      Critical Questions   247

   Methods and Techniques: Necessary Conditions   248
   Understanding the Dilemma   249

CURRENT CONTROVERSY

3.6 SHOULD DOCTORS EVER END PEOPLE'S LIVES?   251
   No: Protector. "Having Reasons for Moral Decisions"   252
      Critical Questions   257

   Yes: Euthanizer. "The Complex Issue of Euthanasia"   258
      Critical Questions   261

Methods and Techniques: Justification   262

Understanding the Dilemma   264

Connections: Humanist or Objectivist?   268

Chapter 4. Free Will, Mind, and Human Nature   **275**

4.1 ARE WE FREE?   276

    No: Hard Determinist. "One World, Not Two"   276
      Critical Questions   279

    Yes: Metaphysical Libertarian. "Free Will and Common Sense"   279
      Critical Questions   281

    Yes: Soft Determinist. "Verbal Disputes, Facts, and Free Will"   281
      Critical Questions   285

    Methods and Techniques: Introspection   285

    Understanding the Dilemma   287

4.2 ARE WE RESPONSIBLE FOR OUR ACTIONS   290

    No: Excuser. "Rejecting Responsibility"   291
      Critical Questions   293

    Yes: Judge. "No Excuse"   293
      Critical Questions   296

    Methods and Techniques: Infinite Regress   297

    Understanding the Dilemma   298

4.3 IS THE MIND NOTHING BUT THE BRAIN?   301

    Yes: Materialist. "Body and Soul"   302
      Critical Questions   305

    No: Dualist. "The Inner Life"   305
      Critical Questions   308

    Methods and Techniques: Possible and Impossible   308

    Understanding the Dilemma   310

4.4 CAN COMPUTERS THINK?   313

    Yes: Mechanist. "Can Computers Think?"   314
      Critical Questions   317

    No: Mentalist. "People vs. Machines"   317
      Critical Questions   320

    Methods and Techniques: Analogies   321

    Understanding the Dilemma   322

4.5 ARE WE ALWAYS SELFISH?   325

    Yes: Psychological Egoist. "No Free Lunch"   326
      Critical Questions   328

No: Psychological Altruist. "Is Love Selfish?"   328
   Critical Questions   331

Methods and Techniques: Generalizations   331

Understanding the Dilemma   333

CURRENT CONTROVERSY

4.6 ARE THE DIFFERENCES BETWEEN MEN AND WOMEN
     PHILOSOPHICALLY SIGNIFICANT?   336
        No: Unifier. "Men, Women, and People"   337
           Critical Questions   341

        Yes: Complementer. "Who's Afraid of Difference?"   341
           Critical Questions   346

        Methods and Techniques: Classification   346

        Understanding the Dilemma   348

        Connections: Reductionist or Spiritualist?   353

Chapter 5. Knowledge, Science, and Truth   359

5.1 CAN WE KNOW ABOUT THE EXTERNAL WORLD?   360
        No: Internalist. "Knowledge of the External World"   361
           Critical Questions   363

        Yes: Perceiver. "The Limits of Ignorance"   364
           Critical Questions   366

        Methods and Techniques: Philosophy and Imagination   367

        Understanding the Dilemma   368

5.2 DOES SCIENCE GIVE US REAL KNOWLEDGE?   371
        Yes: Positivist. "Science as Knowledge"   372
           Critical Questions   375

        No: Romantic. "What Kind of Understanding?"   375
           Critical Questions   377

        Methods and Techniques: Making Assumptions   378

        Understanding the Dilemma   380

5.3 IS EXPERIENCE THE SOURCE OF ALL KNOWLEDGE?   382
        Yes: Empiricist. "The Source of Knowledge"   383
           Critical Questions   387

        No: Rationalist. "The Strange Case of the Mathematician"   388
           Critical Questions   391

        Methods and Techniques: Analysis   391

        Understanding the Dilemma   393

5.4 IS CERTAINTY THE STANDARD OF KNOWLEDGE?   396

    Yes: Foundationalist. "Certainty"   397
      Critical Questions   401

    No: Pragmatist. "The Test of Knowledge"   402
      Critical Questions   405

    Methods and Techniques: Observation   406

    Understanding the Dilemma   407

CURRENT CONTROVERSY

5.5 DOES TRUTH EXIST?   410

    Yes: Representationalist. "True Beliefs and False Beliefs"   412
      Critical Questions   415

    No: Postmodernist. "Ten Theses on Language"   415
      Critical Questions   418

    Methods and Techniques: Proving a Negative   419

    Understanding the Dilemma   420

    Connections: Intuitionist or Externalist?   424

Glossary of Contrasting Positions   429

Index   433

PREFACE TO THE SECOND EDITION

The main change I have made is to add several sections on "Current Controversies." By discussing the philosophical issues in Buddhism, race, euthanasia, gender, and postmodernism, I hope to attract students' interest and show them that philosophy is engaged with the important questions of our time.

Part of a teacher's job is to motivate and excite students. Some teachers are so enthusiastic about their field that their excitement is contagious and they do not need to do anything special to get students involved. Some teachers are enthusiastic about philosophy and assume that their enthusiasm is contagious when it isn't. They can't understand why students aren't more excited about what excites the teachers so much. I have tried to make this book interesting to students in every way I can, without distorting the nature of philosophy. Not only are these current controversies current, but they raise questions that students have probably raised in their own minds, perhaps about themselves and their own lives. Some teachers regard these issues as distractions from the traditional problems of philosophy. But if students see that philosophy can help them make sense of their own lives, then they will want to learn more about other areas of philosophy that aren't so directly connected with their daily concerns.

Many people have made suggestions for improving the book. I could not adopt every suggestion, since different teachers want incompatible things, but I have learned a great deal from my colleagues who used the book in their classes. In particular, I would like to thank Prof. Ralph Forsberg of Delta College, Prof. Don Habibi of the University of North Carolina at Wilmington, Prof. Gail Linsenbard of New York University, Prof. Tim Moses of Lake City Community College, Prof. Andrew Pessin of Kenyon College, and Prof. Paul Tibbetts, Jr., of the University of Dayton.

PREFACE

I teach philosophy in a university. When I meet people—in airplanes, at weddings, or through friends—and tell them what I do for a living, there is always an awkward pause. Sometimes people say, "How nice," and change the subject. They don't know what to say. Hardly anyone knows what philosophy is or what philosophers do. Most people don't know why anyone would spend time on philosophy. Sometimes I feel a little envious of nurses, plumbers, and insurance sales people, because they have jobs that everyone understands.

Rather than switch careers, I have written this book to help people understand what philosophy is all about. I hope it will help people see what philosophers do, how they do it, and maybe why they do it. I have tried to keep the writing simple, without taking anything for granted. I use plain language and everyday examples. On the other hand, I take philosophy seriously, and so I have not oversimplified matters either.

When I tell people what I do, I usually mention some of the ideas in this book. After the initial surprise, many are curious. Often they ask, "So, what is *your* philosophy?" All of my fellow philosophy teachers have had the same experience, and many of them think this question is hopelessly naive and simplistic. I disagree. I think it is an important question. Most people want to find a set of beliefs and values that they can live by, and philosophy should help them find it.

That is the second main goal I have in writing this book (besides telling people what philosophy is about). The second goal is to help people develop their *own* philosophy. Throughout the book I have used the word "worldview" to refer to a person's philosophy of life, general outlook, or basic beliefs and values. To build a worldview, people must know where to begin. They should know what choices they have, and why anyone would adopt one basic belief rather than another. They should know the consequences of adopting one worldview rather than another.

To explain the choices available to us, I have described the fundamental philosophical *questions* that people have always asked and still ask today. And I have described the most common *answers* that philosophers have given, in the past and the present, as well as the reasons they have for accepting those answers. The heart of the book is the questions and answers. But instead of simply describing answers, I have organized them in the form of debates, or "pro and con." I have formulated the questions so they can be answered yes or no (such as "Does God exist?" and "Is morality relative?"). Following each question are two brief essays, one defending a yes answer to the question, and the other defending a no answer. (The essays do not refer to each other, so they can be read in any order.)

The advantage of organizing the book this way is that it presents the problems and solutions most clearly. When people ask me about my philosophy, they are assuming that I have a philosophy, or worldview, that I can briefly explain. And they are assuming that if I explain my philosophy, they can more easily decide where they stand, by agreeing or disagreeing with my point of view. I think they are right. The best way for a person to decide what he or she thinks about some topic is to hear someone else present his views, and then react to them. It is even better to hear two people with conflicting points of view explain their ideas.

Of course it is impossible to present every possible answer to a question. There may be a third answer or a fourth answer. But the two answers in each section have convinced many people. They are the most famous, widely accepted positions, in my opinion. Each answer is usually based on the views of one or more well-known historical figures. I have not summarized these historical positions, but I have provided references and suggestions for anyone who would like to look up some historical precedents for the point of view of the essay.

The table of contents reveals the structure of the book. One can see the yes and no essays in each section. I have written each essay from the point of view of a person who believes a particular answer. The labels, like "abstractionist" and "personalist," are conveniences. They make it easier to talk about different answers. But the label isn't as important as what the label stands for. Building a worldview means deciding what you believe about God, society, values, human nature, and so on. It doesn't mean finding the most descriptive label for a belief. Furthermore, philosophers do not agree on the meanings of many of these terms. In another book, the writer may use the word "abstractionist" in a different way. In fact, people waste a lot of time arguing over the meanings of the labels instead of discussing the real questions. So the labels are merely useful shorthand, or containers, in which the ideas are stored. Readers should look beyond the containers and think about the ideas themselves. (I have provided a glossary at the back of the book, which includes brief definitions of each position.)

Many people have helped me with this book over the years. Several friends were kind enough to read through the manuscript and make helpful suggestions. I wish to thank Jim Colaiaco, Evan Goldstein, Marcus Hester, John Moran, Nada Popovic, and Mike Shenefelt for their generosity and insight.

Doug Ehring deserves a special word of thanks for his extensive, detailed, and penetrating comments. The book is not as good as he would like it to be, but it is better for his criticisms.

Gary Seay not only read the manuscript, but he also listened to my evolving, amorphous ideas in countless conversations. His stubborn good sense and keen ear for hidden assumptions and fallacious reasoning brought me back down to earth on many occasions.

This book was inspired in part by my Columbia buddies (the CDs). John Phillips and Ed Whittaker, as well as the aforementioned CDs, taught me more than they realize (although probably less than they hoped). Perhaps all those hours in the Ninth Floor Lounge weren't a total waste after all.

I used preliminary versions of the book in my classes at New York University. The hard-working students in the School of Continuing Education deserve extra credit for spotting flaws and obscurities in the text.

I am also grateful to the reviewers for Oxford University Press. Their high standards and even-handed observations were very helpful. Robert Miller, Senior Editor, offered some excellent advice as well.

Mrs. Jane Condliffe has helped me (and other educators and students) in many ways. She not only believes that education is vitally important, as many people do, but she also works energetically and creatively to support it.

Finally, it is a real pleasure to thank my best friend, Marianne—who is also my wife—for her ideas, her patience, her cheerfulness, and her companionship. I have been lucky in many ways, but my greatest stroke of good fortune was in finding her.

A Note to Instructors

I have written an **Instructor's Manual** which includes brief summaries of each section, answers to questions in the text, objective test questions for each section, writing assignments and essay topics, ways to use the text in either a history of philosophy or critical thinking course, and other suggestions to promote student involvement and discussion. You may request a copy of the Instructor's Manual by writing to the publisher.

HISTORICAL PARALLELS

For a brief introduction to the issues discussed by the historical figure, you may read the corresponding section in this volume.

Socrates on the examined life 1.5 Is Faith an Answer?
the good life 3.1 Is Pleasure the Only Value?
obeying the law 2.1 Is Society Based on a Contract?
morality and religion 3.5 Is Society the Source of Values?

Plato on the theory of Forms 5.3 Is Experience the Source of All Knowledge?
justice 2.4 Is Capitalism Just?
social classes 2.3 Is Equality the Highest Social Value?
immortality 1.4 Is the Soul Immortal?

Aristotle on happiness 3.2 Can We Understand Happiness?
the unmoved mover 1.1 Does God Exist?
free will 4.1 Are We Free?

Stoics on self-control 3.4 Is Happiness the Standard of Morality?
natural law 2.5 Should We Establish a World Government?

Epicurus on pleasure 3.1 Is Pleasure the Only Value?

Skeptics on perception 5.1 Can We Know about the External World?
knowledge 5.5 Does Truth Exist?

Cicero on natural law 3.3 Is Morality Relative?

Lucretius on atomism 4.3 Is the Mind Nothing but the Brain?
mortality 1.4 Is the Soul Immortal?

Augustine on the two cities 2.5 Should We Establish a World Government?
evil 1.3 Can God Allow Innocent Suffering?

	foreknowledge	4.2	Are We Responsible for Our Actions?
	belief	1.5	Is Faith an Answer?
Aquinas on	the existence of God	1.1	Does God Exist?
	the nature of God	1.2	Is God Like Human Beings?
	natural law	3.3	Is Morality Relative?
	God and morality	3.5	Is Society the Source of Values?
Thomas More on	Utopia	2.3	Is Equality the Highest Social Value?
Machiavelli on	politics	2.5	Should We Establish a World Government?
	human nature	4.5	Are We Always Selfish?
Descartes on	the external world	5.1	Can We Know about the External World?
	doubt	5.4	Is Certainty the Standard of Knowledge?
	mind and body	4.3	Is the Mind Nothing but the Brain?
Spinoza on	freedom	4.1	Are We Free?
Leibniz on	mind and body	4.3	Is the Mind Nothing but the Brain?
Hobbes on	the social contract	2.1	Is Society Based on a Contract?
	egoism	4.5	Are We Always Selfish?
	free will	4.1	Are We Free?
Locke on	the social contract	2.1	Is Society Based on a Contract?
	natural rights	2.2	Is Liberty the Highest Social Value?
	property	2.4	Is Capitalism Just?
	experience	5.3	Is Experience the Source of All Knowledge?
Berkeley on	perception	5.1	Can We Know about the External World?
	ideas	5.5	Does Truth Exist?
Butler on	altruism	4.5	Are We Always Selfish?
Hume on	knowledge	5.1	Can We Know about the External World?
	free will	4.1	Are We Free?

	the existence of God	1.1	Does God Exist?
	the problem of evil	1.3	Can God Allow Innocent Suffering?
La Mettrie on	materialism	4.3	Is the Mind Nothing but the Brain?
Rousseau on	the social contract	2.1	Is Society Based on a Contract?
Holbach on	egoism	4.5	Are We Always Selfish?
Kant on	synthetic a priori	5.3	Is Experience the Source of All Knowledge?
	duty	3.4	Is Happiness the Standard of Morality?
	perpetual peace	2.5	Should We Establish a World Government?
Burke on	tradition	2.2	Is Liberty the Highest Social Value?
Smith on	free markets	2.4	Is Capitalism Just?
Hegel on	society	2.1	Is Society Based on a Contract?
	the spirit of history	3.5	Is Society the Source of Values?
Bentham on	hedonism	3.1	Is Pleasure the Only Value?
	utilitarianism	3.4	Is Happiness the Standard of Morality?
Schopenhauer on	pessimism	3.2	Can We Understand Happiness?
Mill on	utilitarianism	3.4	Is Happiness the Standard of Morality?
	happiness	3.2	Can We Understand Happiness?
	liberty	2.2	Is Liberty the Highest Social Value?
Marx on	class conflict	2.1	Is Society Based on a Contract?
	capitalism	2.4	Is Capitalism Just?
Nietzsche on	values	3.3	Is Morality Relative?
	truth	5.5	Does Truth Exist?
James on	belief	1.5	Is Faith an Answer?
	free will	4.1	Are We Free?

Durkheim on	society	2.1	Is Society Based on a Contract?
Bergson on	free will	4.1	Are We Free?
	intuition	5.2	Does Science Give Us Real Knowledge?
Dewey on	instrumentalism	5.4	Is Certainty the Standard of Knowledge?
Wittgenstein on	meaning	5.5	Does Truth Exist?
Russell on	acquaintance	5.4	Is Certainty the Standard of Knowledge?
Positivists on	knowledge	5.2	Does Science Give Us Real Knowledge?
	artificial intelligence	4.4	Can Computers Think?
Sartre on	choosing values	3.5	Is Society the Source of Values?
	freedom	4.1	Are We Free?
	responsibility	4.2	Are We Responsible for Our Actions?
de Beauvoir on	freedom	4.1	Are We Free?
Buber on	God as Thou	1.2	Is God Like Human Beings?
Austin on	perception	5.1	Can We Know about the External World?
Rawls on	society and justice	3.5	Is Society the Source of Values?
Foucault on	truth	5.5	Does Truth Exist?

INTRODUCTION

What is philosophy? This book is intended to help you understand philosophy and to develop your own philosophy. Where should you begin? Perhaps the best way to start is with the word "philosophy." What comes to mind when you hear that word? What do you think philosophy is? To some people, "being philosophical" means being very steady and self-controlled in the face of disappointments. It means accepting loss or pain without becoming emotional about it. "They didn't hire him, but he was philosophical about it," someone might say.

At other times people use the word differently. They say, "His philosophy is 'Eat, drink, and be merry.' " Or "Do unto others before they do unto you. That's my philosophy." In these cases the word "philosophy" means a slogan or maxim that people hold, which sums up their beliefs about the world or their values. Other examples of such principles are "Live and let live," "Che sera, sera" ("What will be, will be"), or "The world is a crazy place."

Sometimes people involved in a discussion will say, "That's a philosophical question," where they mean that the question is about semantics, fine shades of meaning, or splitting hairs. For example, scientists disagree over whether animals can learn a language, and some say it depends on what we mean by the word "language." Often the reply is, "Well now the question is merely philosophical," or "You are making a philosophical distinction."

Finally, you may have heard someone say, "Oh he is something of a philosopher," where the speaker meant he is a crackpot or a crank. If a person is a vegetarian, or has a scheme to eliminate all government, or tries to communicate with aliens from outer space, others might say, "Don't pay any attention to him, he's just a philosopher."

These examples show that the word "philosophy" has various connotations and images associated with it. Thinking about these uses of the word "philosophy" is valuable because it makes us aware of what many people already believe about philosophy. It reveals *common assumptions* and things people take for granted about philosophy. You should be aware of your own preconceptions as you try to acquire a more complete understanding of philosophy.

Which of the meanings is correct? Is any of these the true meaning of the word? Probably not. Philosophy is too large and complex to be summed up in one or two phrases or uses like these. And while common expressions reveal people's assumptions, they are not the best way to understand what philosophy is. (The word "astronomy" might call up certain images or beliefs in people, but those widespread beliefs would not give us a good understanding of what astronomy is.)

On the other hand, these usages may contain a grain of truth. For example, most philosophers would probably agree that philosophy is a search for general principles that explain the world and guide our lives (like "Eat, drink, and be merry"), although it is more than that. So the second common meaning of the word has some truth in it. Philosophy also requires very careful analysis of key ideas and general concepts (like the concept of language), and therefore the third sense is partially correct. Moreover, if you study philosophy and take it seriously, you will probably find yourself set apart from others, who may regard you as a little strange. And finally, if you study philosophy, you will probably gain some tranquillity and peace of mind. But each of these four ideas is too sketchy and superficial to convey a reliable picture of philosophy.

Let's try a different approach. Instead of surveying ordinary expressions and assumptions, let's look at the *origin* of the word "philosophy." The word comes from two Greek words, *philo* and *sophia*. *Philo* means love, and *sophia* means wisdom, so originally "philosophy" meant the love of wisdom. A philosopher is one who loves wisdom or wants to be wise. But what is wisdom? Well, wisdom is a kind of knowledge, or understanding. So philosophy is the pursuit of wisdom, a kind of knowledge. In this way it is similar to other subjects taught in colleges and universities. Those subjects are also pursuits of different kinds of knowledge. So if we compare philosophy with other subjects that are more clearly defined we may reach a better understanding of what philosophy is.

PHILOSOPHY AND OTHER SUBJECTS

Biology is the pursuit of knowledge about living things. It is knowledge of life, or living organisms. (This word also comes from Greek, *bios*, which means life, and *logos*, which means word or speech.) Geology is the study of the earth, and it sums up all the knowledge we have of the earth. Sociology is the study of society, psychology is the study of the "psyche," or mind. All these subjects pursue knowledge about different aspects of the world.

But while a philosopher seeks knowledge (i.e., wisdom), it is a different kind of knowledge. For one thing, philosophy is the study of *all* of life as we live it and all of human experience. It is not limited to living things, or the earth, or society. Philosophy wants to understand the *whole* of life, not one aspect of it. A philosopher might ask, for example, how our knowledge of living things is *related* to our knowledge of the mind, and how they are both related to society, and in fact, how everything we see and do is interconnected.

Another difference between philosophy and these other subjects is that these subjects pursue factual knowledge, whereas philosophy pursues something different. A biologist wants to learn and discover facts about plants and animals. If you read a book about biology you will learn a lot of interesting facts about what cells are made of, how organisms grow, how they get food, and so on. But philosophy does not consist of facts like these. Instead, philosophy tries to make sense of the facts, especially the basic facts about our lives. It tries to understand what the facts mean and how they fit together; it does not try to discover new facts.

For example, it is a well-known fact that we all die. What does that mean for us? Is it very important, or not so important? How is that fact related to other parts of our lives? Does death mean that everything I do is ultimately meaningless? Biology will tell us about the physical and chemical changes that occur when a person dies, but those facts won't answer the philosophical questions. The basic facts of human experience are already known. Philosophy tries to put the facts together in a way that makes sense.

It is also a fact that some people are deliberately cruel. They intentionally cause an innocent person to suffer or to be unhappy. That is a fact, but what does it mean? How is it related to other parts of our lives? Moreover, when we read about cases of cruelty in the newspaper, such as abandoned children or beaten wives, we feel a strong revulsion and maybe anger. That is a fact, but what does that fact mean? How should we understand the cruelty, and our reactions to it? Should we say cruelty is morally wrong, and we know it is wrong because we feel so strongly about it? Maybe, or maybe not. Should we say the cruel person should be made to suffer in the same way he or she makes others suffer? Maybe, or maybe not. But the facts from sociology and psychology are not going to tell us what is morally right or wrong, or what we should do about it.

Philosophy is a search for knowledge, but the knowledge it seeks is different from other kinds of knowledge. Philosophical knowledge, or wisdom, is more inclusive than the knowledge of biology, sociology, or other subjects. It is about life as a whole. Moreover, the example about cruelty and morality shows that philosophers try to find knowledge about values as well. Philosophers want to understand how we should live. The basic facts about life are known, but the best way to live is not so clear. And in asking how we should live, philosophy is not asking for more facts. It is asking how we should respond to the facts.

The knowledge that philosophy seeks is wisdom, and wisdom is different from other kinds of knowledge. Furthermore, the *search* is different from the other subjects like biology or sociology. These subjects are sciences, and what makes a subject a science is the *method* it uses. Biologists try to learn about organisms by following the scientific method. That means, first, that they carefully observe something, such as a seed that grows into a plant. Second, their observations lead to questions in their minds, and they think of possible answers, which they state as hypotheses. Third, they perform an experiment to test the answer, to see if it is correct. Wherever possible biologists try to measure what they observe. Geology, chemistry, sociology, psychology, and all the sciences follow the same basic steps of the scientific method.

Philosophy does not follow the scientific method, because that method would not lead to the kind of knowledge philosophers want. What method does philosophy use? It isn't easy to say. Philosophers use many different methods. They try to understand human experience in many different ways. Different philosophers have said that a person can gain wisdom in different ways, and they disagree among themselves about the best way.

So far we have considered only the sciences. But we can get a better focus on the methods of philosophy if we compare it with other subjects that are not sciences.

PHILOSOPHY AND THE HUMANITIES

Philosophy is not like the sciences: it does not seek facts and it does not follow the scientific method. But is it like the *humanities*? The humanities include art, literature, and history. Those subjects try to understand human experience as a whole, as philosophy does. Educators sometimes say that the humanities try to understand what it means to be human. In other words, they seek to understand human experience in general. But their methods are different from those of the sciences. Artists and writers do not conduct experiments or try to quantify things. So in both these ways (i.e., in studying the whole of human experience, and in using nonscientific methods) philosophy is closer to the humanities than to the sciences. But the methods of philosophy are different from the methods of other subjects in the humanities.

For example, philosophy is different from art. Artists try to express or explain aspects of human experience through sights and sounds. Painters use colors and shapes, composers use sounds and rhythms, choreographers and dancers use movements, and other artists use other media. Artists respond to the whole range of life as we live it and try to make sense of it. If you know how to "read" their works, you can learn a lot about human experience. But philosophers try to put their ideas into *words*, not images. They try to explain human experience by describing what we can see or what we do, rather than painting it. And they try to put their results into general concepts and principles, rather than images or musical themes.

Literature is another subject in the humanities, and writers do put their ideas into words. They tell stories about all kinds of people and places, such as the story of the wandering hero Odysseus. Or, in dramas and films, they write dialogues that actors speak on a stage. But while philosophy uses language, it is different from literature because philosophers do not tell stories. They do not describe characters like Odysseus or what happens to them. Instead, they try to understand what experiences mean in general terms. They might use certain incidents and individuals as examples, but the examples are only means to understanding a general truth about life. For example, Odysseus' wife, Penelope, remains faithful to her husband for twenty years while he is away. Homer tells the story beautifully. But the philosopher is more interested in the significance of the event. Is Penelope admirable for being so loyal, or is that degree of loyalty unreasonable? Is love that strong? Can it last for twenty years with no contact between the lovers?

In other words, a writer like Homer wants to understand one example of love in detail, but philosophers want to understand love in general, based on many different examples. That is, they want to understand the concept of love. They want to find the truth about love, which they can state in general principles, like "Love is the strongest motive humans know," or something like that.

Another difference between literature and philosophy is that writers tell stories that are not strictly true. A writer invents characters and events, because writers want to entertain readers as well as enlighten them. Philosophers, however, seek only the truth. They are not interested in "a good story" for its own sake. But that brings us to another part of the humanities, namely history. History is also truth, not fiction. It must be based on known facts. A historian may try to organize his or her information in the form of a story, maybe even with a main character, but the story must be completely true, down to the last detail. And many historians do not tell stories at all, but describe a period of time, or one aspect of a past society. Not only do historians seek the truth, as philosophy does, but they also try to understand all of human experience. While historians have usually concentrated on political events, some also investigate the history of religion, the history of science and knowledge, past societies' moral beliefs and practices, social classes, agriculture, and other parts of life. How is philosophy different from history?

One obvious difference is that historians study the past, while philosophers are interested in all of human experience—past, present, and future. And philosophers do not try to determine the facts about some period or event, like the American Revolution, or even why it happened. They are less interested in the facts than in the judgment of the facts, or what the facts mean. For example, a historian might ask how Thomas Jefferson's contemporaries responded to the Declaration of Independence when they first heard it. On the other hand, philosophers might ask if the ideas expressed in the Declaration of Independence (equality, liberty, self-determination, the pursuit of happiness) are really the best guidelines for society. Or they might ask what historians mean when they say that the American Revolution was *caused* by the desire for self-government. Can historians really find causes in the past? How can the historian know that something was a cause of the Revolution? Is there a universal law that says that when a desire for self-government exists, then a revolution will occur? If not, then how can the historian know that the desire caused the Revolution?

These philosophical questions are at a higher level of generality than the historical questions about specific facts and causes. That is the difference between philosophy and history. Philosophers think about the broadest, most inclusive aspects of human experience, and about how the different aspects are related. A philosopher wonders about the nature of knowledge in general, and asks how a historian can know about the past. Or she wonders about the idea of cause and effect, and asks how some events in history can cause other events.

BUILDING A WORLDVIEW

Philosophy is like other subjects because philosophy seeks knowledge. But it is different from other subjects in the kind of knowledge it seeks and in the way it seeks knowledge. Philosophy is the love of wisdom. Another way to put this is to say that the goal of philosophy is to build a coherent, adequate worldview. A worldview is a set of answers to questions about the most general features of the world and our experience of it. In trying to build a worldview, philosophy attempts to answer the following questions:

1. What kind of being am I? What does it mean to be human?
2. What is the best way of life? What goals should I have?
3. How am I related to people around me? How should society be organized?
4. How can I find answers to these questions? What can I know with assurance?
5. Does religion provide the answers? Does God exist?

These questions indicate the most basic, fundamental aspects of human experience: (1) human nature, or self and identity; (2) moral values and action; (3) society and one's place in it; (4) knowledge and understanding; and (5) transcendence. Philosophers try to answer each of these basic questions, and put the answers together into a unified outlook, or point of view, that makes all of experience understandable. The goal of philosophy is wisdom, and wisdom means knowledge of the basic features of the world and your place in it. It means knowledge of who you are, how you should live, how society works, and how you can find out these things.

There are many possible answers to these questions, and thus many possible worldviews. The answers that you accept make up *your* worldview. They make up the beliefs and values that define you as a person.

The concept of a worldview raises many interesting questions itself, and throughout this book you will be thinking about various aspects of worldviews. For example, how do you acquire a worldview? Do you simply adopt the worldview of your parents, or your teachers, or your friends? Do you take one part from one source and other parts from other sources? Does everybody have one? How do you judge a worldview? What makes a good worldview or a bad worldview? Does it matter what my worldview is, or what my girlfriend's or boyfriend's worldview is? Can I change my worldview? You will think of additional questions as you work through the book.

One thing to notice about worldviews is that they are not simple. Each of the basic questions above can be broken down into more specific questions. For example, to answer the first question (what kind of being am I?), you need to answer some other questions included in it: am I free, or are all my actions caused by something outside of me? Will I survive the death of my body, or am I a physical machine which breaks down at death? Can I know myself better than others, or do other people see my real traits better than I do? Am I basically self-centered, or basically giving and self-sacrificing? Each of the other questions also includes more specific questions.

As you read about different answers to these questions, you will often have difficulty deciding what answer is best. For example, one difficult question is "Does God exist or doesn't he?" Some people struggle for years with this question. Was the world created for a purpose, or did it just appear, accidentally? How can you decide? Shouldn't you decide what God is like, or what kind of God we are talking about, before you decide whether or not he exists? These are not easy questions to answer, and it will get more complicated when you read different, conflicting answers, each of which may seem plausible.

Shaping and refining your own worldview is not something you can do in an hour. It takes some effort. At least it does if you want a satisfactory, mature worldview. In building a worldview you can live with there are some commonsense guidelines you should follow. The guidelines are based on the nature of philosophy itself. They will help you gain an understanding of who you are, how you should live, how society works, what is real and what isn't, and how you can find answers. One guideline is that your worldview should be based on *human experience* in the widest sense. Your beliefs and values should make sense of your experience and the world as you encounter it. It would be very frustrating (and irrational) to hold beliefs and values that are in conflict with your ordinary life and the things you see around you.

Nevertheless, many people do hold beliefs that are out of date, or expected of them, or flattering to their ego, but are not based on their real day-to-day lives or experiences. Voltaire portrays a perfect example of such an irrational worldview in his great classic, *Candide*. Candide's friend Pangloss, the philosopher, maintains that our world is "the best of all possible worlds." Meanwhile, Candide is shipwrecked, betrayed, tortured, and almost killed in an earthquake. It is very difficult for him to accept the idea that the world cannot be improved. So your experience is your starting point and your standard for building your worldview.

But of course you cannot ignore other people and their experiences either. Obviously you can learn and benefit from other people's experiences, since they can do things and go places you cannot. They may have thought about things more thoroughly and more deeply than you have. So you should step back and look at your own experiences, and listen to others, when you try to answer these philosophical questions. The whole point of philosophy is to find answers that make sense of life and human experience.

Another guideline you should follow is to think about how the parts of your worldview fit together. Your answers are *interconnected*. For example, how does your answer to the question "What kind of being am I?" relate to your answer to the question "How should I live my life?" Think about this example for a moment. One traditional answer to the first question is that you are a combination of two things, a soul and a body. Bodies live about seventy years on average, but souls live forever. And this traditional answer also says that the quality of your soul's eternal life depends on the way you live now, while you are still inhabiting this body. If that is true, then of course you should live your life the right way now, since this life is relatively short compared with your soul's life after it leaves your body. The point to see in this example is that the different parts of your worldview are interconnected. The answer to the question "What kind of being am I?" influences the answer to the question "How should I live my life?" and vice versa. In fact, all the questions are interconnected. Your answer to one will have an impact on your answers to the others.

That is why you should think about how the parts of your worldview fit together. They depend on each other. If you accept an answer to one question, and another answer to another question, but the answers are *incompatible*, then your worldview will be unstable and very difficult to hold. For example, a person might answer the question "What can I know with assurance?" by saying that we know what we can see. The test of knowledge is to see something with one's eyes. If you can see it, then you know it, and if you can't see it, then you can't be sure about it, according to this theory.

But the same person might answer the question "What kind of being am I?" with the traditional answer mentioned above (i.e., I am a combination of body and soul). This person would have a problem, because no one can *see* a soul. We can see a body, but we cannot see a soul. But if I can know only what I can see, then I cannot know that I have a soul. This person would have no good reason to believe his answer about being a combination of body and soul. In other words, two parts of his worldview are in conflict. His worldview does not make sense of things, but only adds one more layer of confusion to his beliefs. He should give up one of these answers and replace it with another that fits in with his other answers.

A third guideline you should follow is to accept answers that are clear and *understandable*. After all, the purpose of developing a worldview is to understand the basic features of human experience. You should try to state your answers in words that you and others can understand. A vague feeling, a gesture, a grunt, or a simple slogan is not an answer.

Finding clear, explainable answers can be difficult. For example, you could say that the foundation of society is each individual's unalterable human rights. Human rights should be the guiding principle of all government. That is your answer to the question of how society should be organized. Now this sounds very noble. But do you really understand this part of your worldview? Can you explain what rights are? What is a human right anyway? Can you explain what rights people have? Does everyone have a right to a job? To the best medical care? To make remarks that may offend someone? Can you explain why people have rights? What is it about me that gives me certain rights? Is it my intelligence, my moral sense, my ability to make choices, or something else? If I do not know the answers to these questions, then I do not know what you mean when you say people have human rights.

There is no doubt that *some* people can answer these questions clearly. They can explain their views. But if *I* cannot explain *my* answer—if I just say I know people have rights and that's the end of it—then I do not really have an answer. A mere slogan, like "Each individual has human rights," is not an answer, because I do not understand what it means. Unfortunately, many people who write about philosophy use words and phrases that they cannot explain. They might talk about "seven levels of consciousness," or "cosmic harmony with the World Spirit," or "being open to the aura of the other." I have no idea what any of these phrases mean, and the writers who use them do not explain what they mean. They are not related to any experience of mine, nor do they help me understand any experience I have had. The main purpose of phrases and sentences like these is to make the reader feel better, not to help him or her understand anything. These words have an emotional effect. They inspire feelings of awe and mystery, of tremendous importance, and perhaps of secret, privileged knowledge. But they are not answers. They are not part of a worldview, because they do not help anyone understand anything.

WHY BUILD A WORLDVIEW?

Constructing your own worldview is a long, challenging process. First you must discover what you believe about these important matters now. Maybe you never asked yourself seriously, "What can I know with assurance?" or "What kind of being am I?" Or if you asked yourself, you may not have worked out a complete answer. As you begin to think explicitly about your beliefs, you must try to formulate them clearly, so they are more than just vague phrases, like "human dignity," or "for the people," or "hard facts." Then you must test your answers against your experience. Do you have good reasons to accept your answers, reasons based on what you have seen, or done, or learned from others? Or are you accepting some answers just because they sound impressive, or your friends accept them? Next you must compare the answers to different questions, to see if all the answers fit together. Your basic beliefs about human nature might be in conflict with your beliefs about society, or knowledge, or something else. If that happened, you would have a kind of philosophical "split personality." You might be a kind of Dr. Jekyll on questions of transcendence, and a Mr. Hyde on questions of knowledge. But don't worry. It's very common, and it can be cured. The cure does require some effort, however.

Why should you take the time and make the effort to build a coherent worldview? There are many reasons. One is that the process is a lot of fun. People are curious. We all want to know more about the world and ourselves. And we want to know not only the facts but how the facts fit together. We are curious about the big picture. One of the most satisfying things you can do is understand something, especially if you have been puzzled by it for a long time.

Another reason to build a worldview is that people have a strong desire to define themselves and to know themselves. Everyone needs a sense of identity. People want to know who they are, and how they are like and unlike other people. The most important element of the sense of identity is one's beliefs and values. I may have light or dark hair, I may be tall or short, but those things are not what makes me who I really am. I may own a sports car or a pickup truck, I may wear designer jeans or cotton work clothes, but those things do not define me either. What makes me the person I am is what I *think*. Do I believe in God or not? Do I think people are basically trustworthy or not? Do I want to own fine things or do I want to improve the world? Do I get angry at rich people spoiled by wealth, or at poor people living off others' labor? Some people answer these questions one way and others answer them another way. The answers make you the person you are. These basic beliefs and values, and the actions based on them, are the core of one's identity. In a real sense, building your worldview is building yourself.

You can see how important beliefs and values are if you simply imagine the following case. Suppose you want to get to know a person, such as a new coworker or a new neighbor. What do you need to know before you can say you really know that person? Her taste in clothes? That might be a small clue, but it certainly isn't enough. The car she drives? Another clue perhaps, but it could be completely misleading. What you really need to find out is what she thinks. How does she answer these basic questions? What are her fundamental beliefs and values, about people, goals in life, right and wrong, God, society, and herself? If you can find out what she believes about those things, then you will really know her.

Some people say that philosophy is not practical. Nothing could be further from the truth. Philosophy is an attempt to find credible answers to the basic questions about life, and the answers a person accepts will have a tremendous impact on his or her life. Think for a moment about the different parts of a worldview. What kind of being am I? Your answer to this question will influence your self-image, and your feelings about yourself. What goals should I have? Obviously your answer to this question will virtually determine the direction of your life. How should I relate to others, or society? Your answer here will influence the kind of citizen you will be, your participation in political affairs, or lack of it, and the kind of changes you will work for. What can I know with assurance? Can I be sure about what I believe, or are most beliefs just shots in the dark? The way you answer this question will influence your confidence or doubts about your beliefs and worldview. What kind of world do I live in? Is it hospitable or hostile, predictable or chaotic? Your answer will certainly affect your outlook and feelings about your surroundings, and might even influence your choice of a career (if you are impressed enough to become a scientist and study the natural world). Does God exist? If you say yes to this question, your fundamental attitudes toward everything—yourself, other people, the natural world, death, morality, belief, everything—will be different from the attitudes you will have if you say no. If "practical" means it helps you to succeed in life, then philosophy is the most practical subject there is.

Philosophy helps you achieve success in your life as a whole, not necessarily in your pursuit of money. It is a very rewarding activity, and it may give you peace of mind, or inner strength, or confidence. Or it may not affect your feelings at all. The purpose of philosophy is not to make anyone feel better. The goal of philosophy is wisdom. It is motivated by curiosity and the desire to understand, not the desire to be happy. Sometimes knowledge is actually painful, but philosophers want to know the truth anyway.

Philosophy is not the same as "self-help." Everyone has seen or heard about self-help books. They are very popular. They have titles like *The Power of Positive Thinking*, *How to Overcome Stress*, *Slay Your Own Dragons*, and *The Cinderella Complex*. These books all have the same basic pattern. First they describe one or more personal problems that people have, such as loneliness, procrastination, too much stress and anxiety, low self-esteem, obesity, feelings of powerlessness, and so on. They recount specific case histories of people with these problems. Next they offer advice on how to solve the problem, often in the form of several steps you can take. For example, one book on feelings of powerlessness says that to overcome these feelings you should practice being honest and open, practice taking control, practice being your own person, and practice changing your habits.

Some people turn to philosophy because they expect philosophy to solve their problems for them. Studying philosophy *is* very rewarding, in a special sort of way, and it may change a person. But philosophy is different from self-help in two fundamental ways. First, self-help books are aimed at people with emotional and behavioral problems, problems that interfere with their normal lives or that make them unhappy. In other words, the problems self-help books discuss are problems in a person's feelings or behavior. The solution lies in changing the behavior, or perhaps in changing some beliefs that lead to bad feelings. Thus, in self-help books the answers are valuable only if they help a person stop procrastinating or stop feeling lonely or whatever. The answers are valuable for their effects on behavior or emotions.

The priorities of philosophy are different from self-help. In philosophy, convincing answers are valuable for their own sake, whether or not they change a person's behavior or feelings. Whereas self-help books place the emphasis on bad feelings, and look for answers to change those feelings, philosophy places the emphasis on answers themselves, regardless of people's emotional reactions to the answers. The only "feeling" philosophy tries to satisfy is curiosity. The test of an answer in self-help books is "Does it make me feel better?" The test of an answer in philosophy is "Does it explain human experience, is it consistent with other things we know, and is it clear and understandable?"

There is a second fundamental difference. Self-help books are about problems that only some people have. Most people are not so anxious or lonely that they seek help. But philosophy is about questions that apply to everyone. Philosophical problems are universal. They are not limited to one group or another group. The questions about the existence of God, human nature, the organization of society, and so on, are questions about human experience in general, not your experience or my experience or one group's experience. Moreover, the solutions in self-help and philosophy are different as well. A self-help book offers solutions that apply only to the individuals with the emotional problem. Usually the solution is to change one's feelings or one's behavior. But philosophy looks for solutions that are acceptable to everyone. It seeks answers that are convincing to any reasonable person.

This contrast between philosophy and self-help books is a little abstract, and mainly negative. It says philosophy is not self-help. In fact, much of this introduction has been negative in the same way. I have talked about how philosophy cannot be summed up in common catchphrases, how it is different from science, literature, and history, and how it is not the same as self-help. I have only indicated in very broad outlines what philosophy is all about. It is about constructing an adequate worldview, and finding answers that make sense of our lives and that fit together. But you cannot understand philosophy by reading a description of it, like the description in this introduction. You must get involved in philosophy to understand what it is. You can read a definition of philosophy, but that will not give you much of an understanding of what philosophy is all about. You can even read about great philosophers and what they have said, but that is not enough either. It is better than reading a definition, but it does not give you a real grasp of the subject matter or the methods of philosophy. Understanding philosophy is like understanding tennis, cooking, mountain climbing, or anything else: you have to try it yourself before you can understand it. To understand philosophy you must get involved with philosophical problems, you must weigh different solutions or theories, and decide which are convincing. You must *do* the same things that philosophers do. Reading about it isn't enough. The only way to understand philosophy is to practice it.

This book is designed to help you practice philosophy, that is, think about philosophical problems, try to understand the questions, examine the alternative answers, consider the pros and cons, and decide which answer is best.

GOD, IMMORTALITY, AND FAITH

1.1 DOES GOD EXIST?
THEIST OR ATHEIST?

———————————————————————•———————————————————————

All the questions that philosophers ask are important, but of all their questions, this one is probably the most important. Think of the consequences. If there *is* a God in the traditional sense, then He created you, He is watching you, He knows all your thoughts and feelings, He expects a great deal from you, and He will judge you at the end of your life. He will give you tremendous rewards or punish you severely (according to Western religions). He is also able to help you now in many ways, since He is able to do anything. Every human being was created by God, and therefore everyone deserves an absolute respect. It also means He created the world. The world is not an accident, but was planned. The world as a whole and everything in it has a design and exists for a purpose. We can understand that purpose by understanding God's plan. The world in a real sense is our home, built for us by a loving parent.

On the other hand, if there is *no* God, then we are alone in the universe. We cannot look to any transcendent source for help. Our destiny is entirely in our own hands. If we want moral standards, we will have to make them ourselves. If we choose to disobey them, nothing guarantees that we will regret it. Wicked people prosper and good people suffer; the world is not just. There is nothing divine or special about human beings; we are merely highly evolved animals. We have very strong, competitive instincts. The world around us is often hostile and dangerous. There is no reason behind things, nothing has any purpose. We cannot understand the meaning of nature because it has no meaning; it just is. So our whole outlook on life, and the way we live it, depends on how we answer the question "Does God exist?"

This section includes three essays. The first tries to prove that God exists based on the causal connections among events. What caused the things we see around us, and what caused those causes, and what came even before that? Mustn't there be a beginning? If you think this essay is convincing, then you are a causal theist. The second essay argues that the world is wonderfully ordered, like a complex machine, and therefore must have been designed by an intelligent creator. If you think the second essay is persuasive, then you are a design theist. Finally, the last essay tries to show that there are no reasons to believe in God. If you do not believe in God, then you are an atheist.

YES: CAUSAL THEIST
"In the Beginning"

Most people who believe in God believe on the basis of faith, or on the basis of a personal experience of Him. But aside from faith or experience, it is perfectly reasonable to believe in God on the basis of what we all see around us. In fact, rational considerations show that God *must* exist.

Two simple facts, taken together, show that God exists. First, it is a fact that everything in the world has a cause. Nothing just happens for no reason whatever. We see causes and effects all around us. For example, the rain causes the plants to grow, accumulation of moisture in the air causes the rain, the heat of the sun causes the evaporation and accumulation of moisture in the air, and so on. If you catch a cold, it was caused by germs in your body. The germs grow rapidly because you are tired from lack of sleep. They entered your body because they were floating in the air and you breathed them in. They were in the air because someone sneezed.

So whenever we think of anything in the world, we can always ask, "What caused it?" And when we find the cause of something, we can then ask what caused the cause, and what came even before that. In other words, we can trace the causal chain further and further back in time.

But this leads to the second important fact. We cannot imagine the causal chain going back forever. Our minds stumble when we try. We cannot grasp it. Try to imagine a chain that extends infinitely, without end. You cannot. Of course, you can think of it going very, very far, but when you think of the chain, you think of a definite object, with limits. You cannot think of an unlimited chain.

The same applies to the "chain" of causes going back in time. You can think of your parents, who caused you, and their parents, who caused them, and so on. But the line had to begin somewhere. You cannot imagine the list of your ancestors going back infinitely, without end. There had to be a beginning.

Some people maintain that we *can* imagine an infinite chain of physical causes. We simply say it is a chain "without end." But what kind of chain is that? "Without end" is a purely negative characterization, and negative characterizations only tell us what something is *not*; they do not tell us what something *is*. Therefore they do not help us understand anything. Suppose I say that I can imagine a new color. What sort of color? Well, it's not green, not yellow, not red, not blue, etc. Now do you know the new color I am thinking of? With that description, you have no idea what I am imagining. That kind of negative characterization does not give you a concept of a new color. Neither does "without end" give you a concept of an infinite chain.

It is true that mathematicians work with "infinity." But all they are doing is laying down some rules for manipulating abstract symbols (numerals), and then seeing what one can and cannot do within the boundaries of those rules. For example, an infinite series defined by one operation is said to "converge" toward its "sum," while an infinite series defined by a different operation is said to be "divergent." But these terms do not describe real series. They are artificial constructs. Mathematicians do not claim to be talking about the material world when they apply their rules.

The fact is that the series of causes we see around us must have a beginning. We cannot imagine it going on forever. And there is another reason to believe in a beginning. The great Catholic philosopher of the thirteenth century, Saint Thomas Aquinas, explained it this way:

> Now the series of finite causes cannot go on to infinity because in every series of causes the first cause is the cause of the intermediate cause, and the intermediate causes cause the last cause, whether the intermediate causes are many or one.

In other words, if A causes B, and B causes C, then A is the first cause, B is the intermediate cause, and C is the last cause (or last event). For example, (A) a salesperson presses a button beside the front door, (B) the button sends a current to the doorbell, and (C) the doorbell rings. Aquinas continues:

> However, if you take away the cause you also take away its effect. If there is no first cause among the efficient causes, there will be no last or intermediate cause.

He is saying that if (A) does not occur (e.g., no one presses the button), then neither (B) nor (C) will occur. The electric current will not flow, and the bell will not ring. He concludes:

> But if we proceed to infinity in the series of causes there will be no first cause, and therefore no final or intermediate effects would exist—which is obviously not true.

If the causal chain extended infinitely, there would be no first cause. But if there were no first cause, the later effects would not occur (just as the doorbell would not ring without a cause). But obviously we see effects happening all around us. So the causal chain cannot extend backward infinitely. There must be a beginning.

Now we are ready to put our two facts together. The first fact is that everything in the world is caused by something. The second fact is that the series of causes cannot extend back in time infinitely. Therefore, there must be a First Cause. And that is God. God is the source and origin of the world. He created the world, and therefore He created you and me. All rational people must accept the existence of this First Cause. They may not call the Creator "God," at first. But if they meditate on the true meaning of this conclusion, they will begin to acquire a more religious attitude.

Key Concepts

universal causation	causal chain	infinite series
imagine	negative characterization	First Cause

Critical Questions

1. What two facts, when combined, prove that God exists, according to the essay?
2. What is a negative characterization? Can you give an example of a negative characterization of something?
3. Do you think we can imagine an infinite chain of causes? Can we think of things that we cannot picture in our imaginations?
4. If we cannot think of something (maybe because it is self-contradictory, e.g., a square circle), does that mean the thing cannot exist? Could square circles exist?
5. The essay says we cannot imagine the causal chain going back without end. Why does Aquinas believe the chain cannot go back infinitely?
6. Does a causal theist believe God is caused or not? Does he or she believe God is infinitely wise, infinitely powerful, or infinitely good?
7. Has the essay proven that God exists, in your opinion?

YES: DESIGN THEIST

"Design or Chance?"

Like many people, I have often felt the overwhelming majesty of the world. Looking at the stars at night and thinking about the vast numbers and spaces, hearing a newborn's cry and thinking about her miraculous arrival, sitting by a lake and seeing the incredible harmony of multitudinous animals, plants, and environment are all enjoyable experiences. But the powerful feelings I had were more than merely emotions. They were an intuition of something more profound. I gradually realized that what affected me so deeply was the *order* of the world. It is magnificently ordered, like an incredibly vast machine. I think the strong feelings were a perception of an important truth. It is important because it convinces me that the world was created by a wonderfully wise and powerful Designer.

Some people do not see or feel the order of nature. To them, the world is more like a junkpile than a fine Swiss watch. They see nature as a heap of unrelated objects, jumbled together helter-skelter rather than a carefully constructed machine, with parts that mesh and support each other.

The different perceptions are very important, and not just a matter of aesthetics. If the world is like a heap, then it could have appeared by chance. It doesn't present any special problem in understanding why it works the way it does. It doesn't have any particular order, so there is nothing to be explained. It just happens to work that way. (There is still the problem of why there is any kind of world at all, why there is something rather than nothing. But that is a different question. The question here is "Why does the world exhibit *order*?")

On the other hand, if the world is like a *machine*, then it is impossible to believe that it appeared by chance. Swiss watches do not spring up out of the ground, or appear randomly like seashells on a beach. Every machine, without exception, is made by an intelligent *designer*. The parts of a machine must be deliberately assembled in a particular way, not thrown together haphazardly.

In other words, if the world is more like a machine than a junkpile, then we must suppose that some Designer put it together. I believe that the world is wonderfully ordered, regular, and harmonious, and that the order is evidence that it was created by an intelligent Designer.

Nature is like a machine in many ways. For one thing, all the manifold diversity we see is made up of only ninety-two basic parts—the ninety-two natural elements (hydrogen, helium, etc.). Every substance, whether natural or manufactured, every mineral, plant, and animal, is composed of these few "nuts and bolts." The only differences are due to the proportions. Machines, too, can be disassembled into their component parts, which are usually some type of metal, plastic, or rubber.

Another machinelike feature of the world is the interdependence of the parts. In an organism, for example, every part depends on every other part. If the heart or nerves malfunction, every other part will soon malfunction, too. In an ecosystem, like a forest, or a bay, all the plants and animals interact and depend on each other. If humans interfere and feed the deer in the winter, for example, or catch all the lobsters, then the balance is upset and severe problems appear. The parts of machines are interdependent in exactly the same way.

The interactions in nature are incredibly complex and precise. Your brain continuously monitors your body. It maintains a constant temperature of 98.6 degrees Fahrenheit. It keeps you balanced so you don't fall. It uses the liver, the kidneys, and the lungs to regulate the precise levels of sugar, water, and oxygen in your blood. It keeps you alert during the day and puts you to sleep when you need rest. All of these processes depend on extremely minute chemical changes, either in the blood or in the nerves. The precision is like the hundreds of electrical pathways and switches on a tiny computer chip, but much more exact.

When we think of machines, like watches, cars, or typewriters, probably the first thing we think of is repetition. Machines operate in a repetitive, regular way. The wheels go round and round in the same pattern over and over, the spark plugs fire one after the other, the typewriter carriage slides across and returns. And we see exactly the same regularity in nature. The lawfulness of the world is perhaps its most remarkable feature. Night follows day, season follows season, children follow parents. In our own bodies, the heart contracts and pumps blood into the arteries, it flows through the parts, and eventually returns to the heart to start all over again. The more we learn about the world, the more lawful, orderly, and regular it appears. It looks more and more like a vast, complicated machine.

Nature is like a machine in being orderly, exact, and made of interdependent, interchangeable parts. Since every machine is created by an intelligent designer, I conclude that the natural world was created by an intelligent Designer as well. The world is inconceivably more complex, precise, and grand than any machine. But that shows how much more powerful and intelligent than us the Designer of the world must be.

The heart of the argument is the resemblance between the world and a machine. But someone could challenge the other part of the argument, which is the connection between machines and intelligent designers. Today many people say that nature is lawful and made of interdependent parts, like a machine, but it *could* have grown up naturally. It could have evolved. They say that the regularity, the precision, and the interdependence do not require a Designer to be explained, but are the result of chance. Random combinations of elements, plus natural selection, can produce the admittedly astonishing precision and harmony that is so evident in the world.

But this seems illogical. It is surely obvious that no machines can occur by chance, not even the simplest ones. Can openers do not grow on trees. So how could the marvelously complex natural world, so much like a machine, spring up by chance? People say "evolution." But if that were enough, we should see machines grow up through evolution.

It isn't sensible to think that random combinations of atoms could produce the human body and mind. Do people *understand* or merely believe it because the present authorities say it is true? I for one do not understand it, although I have studied the theories. And I dare say that those who profess to believe it do not really understand it either, because it is too far-fetched. It is like believing that if the waves pound the beach long enough, they will eventually recombine the elements to produce a fine watch. A person might *believe* in miracles like this, but he or she would not *understand* how it happened.

We can add the idea that some combinations are more adaptive than others. But that isn't enough. The theory of evolution still holds that the end result—humankind—is the product of pure chance, one accidental change after another. Some changes work better than others. But that doesn't explain how the process of random combinations would produce such a complex being as a person. No one believes machines could be produced this way. But people are much more intricate than machines. Therefore, no one should believe people could be produced this way. The growth of the world might have taken millions of years, but it must have been guided by intelligent choice.

If the world is like a machine, and all machines require designers, then the world requires a Designer. Now, if the two premises are true, as I have tried to show they are, and if the inference is correct, then perhaps our attitude toward the natural world should change. We should show a little more respect for God's handiwork. Many people today see plants and mountains and birds as accidents, mere matter, or monstrous agglomerations, without plan or reason. Instead, perhaps we should try to appreciate the ingenuity of their design. If we look at nature in the right way, we might get a glimpse of infinite wisdom.

Key Concepts

machine	interdependence	evolution
lawfulness	designer	random combinations

Critical Questions

1. The essay says that if the world is like a machine, then God must exist. Why? How can one go from the first statement to the second statement? What is the intermediate step (or steps)?
2. In what ways is the world like a machine, according to the essay?
3. A design theist admits that the world is incomparably more complex and precise than any machine. Doesn't that prove that the world could not have been designed?
4. Can you think of any other similarities between the world and machines? Can you think of any differences between the world and machines?
5. Why does a design theist think the theory of evolution cannot explain the order in the world? What is wrong with the theory?
6. Does a design theist assume that humanity is the goal, or purpose, of biological change? If one rejects that idea, and believes that humanity is not the goal, but is only an accident, only the most complex species to appear so far, could one then accept evolution as an adequate explanation?

NO: ATHEIST

"The Retreat of the Gods"

People fear what they do not understand. Religious belief is a response to such ignorance and fear. It is an attempt to cope with a capricious, unpredictable, and potentially hostile environment. It teaches people to bow down, submit, beg for forgiveness, give gifts, and make sacrifices to try to appease the inscrutable gods. But fear is a self-defeating response. It encourages resignation and fatalism. Who could stand up to the gods themselves? Better to submit. But such passive attitudes perpetuate ignorance, and therefore fear, and therefore religious belief, in a futile cycle.

Since religion feeds on ignorance, religious belief has declined steadily over the centuries as knowledge has increased. Today the grounds for religious belief have disappeared completely. In our day there is no reason for anyone to believe in God. We can trace the decline of religion through six stages. In each successive stage the gods retreat farther and farther from ordinary life, they diminish in number, and they lose their recognizable, human characteristics.

1. Before the dawn of history, our primitive ancestors believed in countless "spirits" all around them. Primitive peoples today, who are at the same stage of development as those prehistoric ancestors, believe that trees, animals, the sky, springs, magic herbs, weapons, and other objects possess spirits of their own. Everywhere they turn, they see or hear a spirit. And they try to influence the spirits by offering gifts or promising service of some kind. Such an attitude is an understandable response to ignorance. If a fruit tree bears abundant fruit one season but little fruit the next season for no apparent reason, the primitive farmer might decide that the tree has a will of its own. It seems as unpredictable as people are. Since he couldn't influence the tree through natural methods, he might be able to influence it by flattery, gifts, or promises.

2. As civilization advanced, people learned more about the natural world and the causes of things. By the time of the ancient Greeks (500 B.C.E.), the spirits, or gods, had retreated to one place—Mt. Olympus—and they had diminished in number. There were only a dozen or so major Greek gods, plus various nymphs, naiads, sprites, and so on. The Greeks still regarded the gods as humanlike beings, and the gods controlled the important natural processes, like the seasons and the movement of the sun across the sky. But not every object or place was inhabited by a spirit, according to Greek religion. They understood how bees fertilized flowers, for example, so they did not need to believe in a "spirit of the flowers."

3. A further advance took place with the appearance of monotheistic, Western religions. The idea of one God probably originated with the ancient Hebrews before 1300 B.C.E., and evolved over the centuries in Judaism, Christianity, and Islam. The one God differs from polytheistic gods in several ways. He is not to be found anywhere on earth, but resides in a distant, transcendent heaven. He guides history in a general way, but rarely intervenes directly. We can see the contrast in Homer's *Iliad*, representing Greek religion, and the Jewish Scriptures (or Christian Old Testament), representing monotheism. In Homer's *Iliad*, the Greek gods frequently appear and talk to the heroes, they hide their favorites in a cloud, or turn aside a threatening spear. In early books of the Scriptures, the one God is similar to the Greek gods, in that he walks on the earth, appears directly to people in a bush or a whirlwind, and performs miracles. But as the monotheistic tradition evolved, God appeared less and less in human form. People realized that there were better explanations of why a spear failed to hit its mark. They did not need to evoke God to explain every little event.

4. Around 1600 the Scientific Revolution began, and within two hundred years the human race discovered more about the natural world than it had in the previous two thousand years, or two hundred thousand. Sir Isaac Newton, building on the mechanics of Galileo, systematized a set of precise laws that explained virtually all motion, from the distant planets to a flying cannonball to a clock's pendulum. Consequently religious attitudes changed. Educated people of this period adopted a form of religion known as "deism." They removed God even further from human affairs. God was now conceived to be a rational Being who designed the great world-machine and set it in motion, but who then retired and let it run by itself. People explained events by reference to prior causes, not by imagining that a supernatural God continually watched and interfered. There was no need for such a belief. Furthermore, since the Divine Being was less involved with human events, he might be less human himself. Deists still believed that God was rational (a sort of super-Newton), but he did not exhibit all the changing emotions of the Judeo-Christian-Muslim God, such as jealousy, anger, pity, and so forth. There was no reason to believe in such characteristics.

5. Newton's triumph was in physics. The next development was in biology. In 1859 Darwin published his *Origin of Species*, wherein he explained how the human species had evolved from simpler types of animals. We now understand why we have the human shape and human capacities that we have. They are adaptations to the environment, slowly built up over the eons by the blind process of natural selection. This new understanding has undermined religious belief even further. Deists had believed that a God was required to design the human body and human mind. Since they conceived of God as a kind of Divine Intelligence, they still believed that the human intellect was "in God's image." But now we know that the human mind and body grew up naturally, accidentally, through random mutations and natural selection, like other species. No one drew an original blueprint for humanity. There is no reason to believe that our human intelligence is a copy of God's nature. There is no reason to believe that God is intelligent or has a mind. Thus as we learn more, the need for God becomes smaller and smaller.

6. The last chapter in this story occurred in the twentieth century. As humanity has progressed throughout history, the idea of God has shrunk and receded. Educated people no longer believe that God is present, guiding physical objects like automobiles. They no longer believe God has emotions as we do. In fact, Darwin's discoveries removed the need for any human qualities of God at all. But if God was not human, religious people asked, then what was he (or it)? Maybe God is a "force" or "energy" that flows through all things, or maybe it is Being itself. Physicists believe in forces and energy, but what made the God-force different, in the minds of religious people, was that God was *good*. Whatever God was, it worked for the best, they insisted. But the horrors of the twentieth century have undermined that last characteristic. The pain and suffering of the wars, famines, and tortures, culminating in the Holocaust, have made it impossible to believe in a good God. A good God could not permit such things. But if we take away that last characteristic, what is left? Nothing. The idea of God has finally disappeared.

It has disappeared along with our ignorance and has been replaced by knowledge. The knowledge of physics, biology, and history may be difficult to accept, but it has the virtue of being based on reality rather than imagination and fear. Moreover, it leads to further progress rather than fatalism and stagnation.

The long retreat of the gods is one aspect of humanity's maturation. The story of spirits replaced by gods replaced by a distant God and so on is really the story of the childhood and adolescence of the human race. It shows our growing acceptance and mastery of the real world. With the final disappearance of God, we have reached adulthood. We no longer need fabulous stories to comfort us. We can face the world in a more mature way.

Key Concepts

spirits	monotheism	intelligence
polytheism	Deism	the Holocaust

Critical Questions

1. How was the evolution from primitive tribes to the ancient Greeks a decline in religious belief, according to the essay? How was the evolution from the Greeks to monotheistic religions a decline?
2. Do you agree that these changes were *declines*?
3. In what two ways did the idea of God change after the Scientific Revolution (i.e., in stage 4)?
4. What impact did Darwin's theory of evolution have on our image of ourselves, and on people's conception of God?
5. Do you think it is possible to believe in God but believe he or it is nothing at all like humans? Could we call a galaxy, or heat, God?
6. Do you think it is possible to believe in God but believe he or it is evil, or neutral, i.e., not good?

Methods and Techniques

ARGUMENTS

These essays are all philosophical because of the question they address. But they are also philosophical for another reason. They are intended to *persuade* you, the reader, to accept a certain conclusion. They are not telling a story, or describing anything, or trying to entertain you. Instead, each essay presents an argument. In philosophy, the word "argument" has a special meaning, different from the ordinary meaning. Ordinarily, an argument is a dispute or disagreement or fight. But in philosophy an argument is a set of reasons to believe something. "In the Beginning" and "Design or Chance?" both present reasons to believe that God exists, while "The Retreat of the Gods" tries to persuade people that God does *not* exist. Other philosophers propose reasons to believe that the highest goal in life is pleasure, or that we can never be certain of anything, and so on. They give reasons to accept their conclusions, and you must decide how strong the reasons are. Philosophers want to know what they should believe about these general topics, so they study reasons for holding one belief or another. Therefore, to a large degree philosophy is about arguments.

Writers could try to get you to accept their conclusions in a variety of ways. They could threaten you. They might say that if you do not agree with them they will come to your house and shoot your dog. Or they could plead and beg you to accept their conclusion. They might say that otherwise they will lose their jobs. Or they could try to bribe you. They could say that people who agree with them are more popular and have 23 percent fewer cavities. But of course these writers don't stoop so low. Like all philosophers they base their conclusion on well-known facts that anyone can observe. The first essay emphasizes the fact that events have causes. The second describes a number of established facts about the physical world. The third describes historical changes. In other words, they try to come up with objective evidence to support their conclusion. They think that the evidence should convince anyone that they are right.

These writers' appeals to facts illustrate an important point about arguments. All arguments have two parts, called "premises" and "conclusions." The facts are the premises. They are the reasons that the writer uses to try to make you believe something. The belief that the writer wants you to accept is the conclusion. For example, in the first argument, the premises are that everything has a cause, and that the chain of causes cannot go back in time forever. The conclusion is that God exists. The premises of the second argument are that the world is like a machine, and all machines are created by intelligent designers. The conclusion is that the world was created by an intelligent designer, i.e., God. You should enjoy isolating and stating the premises and conclusions in the other essays in this book. If you analyze a person's point of view very carefully in this way, you will be surprised at how sloppy some people are. Their writing may sound very eloquent and persuasive, but if you actually state the premises and conclusion, you often find a big gap: the premises don't support the conclusion at all. You may find gaps even in these essays.

With practice you will get better at picking out premises and conclusions, and seeing flaws in people's arguments. Of course the point of doing this is not to criticize people. The point is to make sure your *own* beliefs are based on good, solid reasons.

Understanding the Dilemma

THEIST OR ATHEIST?

Does God exist? If you answer yes, then you are a *theist*. If you answer no, then you are an *atheist*. "Theist" is a general word for a person who believes in some kind of divinity. A monotheist is a type of theist who believes in one god (monotheism), while a polytheist believes in many gods (polytheism). There are other variations, but for now you should concentrate on the basic division between theism and atheism. Is there a God or isn't there? Are you a theist or an atheist?

The essays in this section should help you decide. The first two support theism, and the third supports atheism. Which point of view is more similar to your own? You do not have to agree with everything a writer says. The essays simply present contrasting ideas to help you think about your own beliefs. If you found yourself nodding in agreement as you read "In the Beginning," then you are a theist. The second essay also supports theism. If you answered the study questions about "Design or Chance?" and, after reflecting on the various things in it, you decided that the observations and the conclusion were likely to be correct, then you are a theist.

On the other hand, if "The Retreat of the Gods" seemed accurate to you, then you are an atheist. If you agree that all the reasons for believing in God or the gods have disappeared and have been replaced by scientific explanations, then you are an atheist. The essay doesn't prove that there is no God. It only shows that the reasonable conclusion is that God does not exist.

There are different types of atheists and theists. In this section you have read about two types of theists, *causal theists* and *design theists*. Anyone who accepts the first essay and believes that facts about causes and the causal chain prove that God exists is a causal theist. People who accept the second essay are design theists because they look at the order and design in the world, and those facts convince them that God exists. A causal theist and a design theist agree with each other that God exists, but they have different reasons for believing in God. Both, however, disagree with the atheist. The main choice you face in this section is between theism and atheism.

Throughout this book you will be presented with choices between two alternatives, like theism and atheism. The decisions you make will determine your worldview. They will form a kind of network of your basic beliefs and values. It is difficult to make these choices. It is difficult to decide what you think. So most people try to avoid making a choice. They put aside the whole subject and ignore it. Or they try to find a middle ground, so they do not have to choose one side or another. In some cases a middle way may be possible. In other cases it isn't.

Is there a middle way between theism and atheism? The answer depends on what we mean by the word "God." In other words, the atheist says there is no being who created the world, who knows everything, can do anything, and watches us. A theist says there is a God, but some theists might define "God" differently from the atheist. One theist might say he or she believes in God the Creator but does not believe God knows everything, or can do anything whatsoever, or watches us. Is this a middle way? Could an atheist and a theist agree that such a being exists? To answer these questions you should read Section 1.2, "Is God Like Human Beings?"

Many people say they have found another middle way between theism and atheism. They say they are "agnostics." An *agnostic* is a person who believes that no one can *know* whether or not God exists. If you ask them "Does God exist," their answer is "I don't know." But an agnostic is *not* a person who cannot decide, and it is not a person who hasn't studied the issue or thought carefully about it. Real agnostics understand all the evidence and reasons theists and atheists give, but they have another theory about knowledge. They have studied the different ways of knowing (science, direct experience, logic, art, intuition, etc.), and have concluded that none of them gives good enough reasons to believe or not to believe in God. (You will read about knowledge in Chapter 5.) Is this a middle way between theism and atheism? Not really. It is more like giving up on finding any answer, rather than finding an answer that lies between the two sides.

So the issue for now is theism vs. atheism. Does God exist or doesn't he? Is the first essay right, or the second, or the third? If you are unsure about your answer, then you should make a tentative decision for now. Later, of course, you can change your mind. Making a decision will help you understand what it really means to hold a particular belief, because you will be personally involved. It will force you to think hard about the ideas because they will be your ideas.

The following statements may help you make up your mind. The first set consists of statements that a theist might make. They are beliefs that many theists hold. The second group includes statements that atheists might make. Of course not every theist believes every statement listed here under "theist," and the same is true for atheists and the other list. But these beliefs are generally characteristic of the two positions. Which statements do you agree with? Which sound true to you? Are you a theist or an atheist?

THEIST

1. Everything must have started somewhere, or must have come from something, and that beginning source of everything is a Supreme Being.
2. Everything that happens is observed and guided by a mind or power beyond the natural world.
3. The world was created for a purpose and is fulfilling that purpose.
4. I am not just an animal; instead, I am related to a higher being outside the material world.

ATHEIST

5. The world may not have a starting point, and if it does, that point is not God.
6. What we can see, touch, and investigate scientifically is all there is; belief in God is just prescientific superstition.
7. The world is completely comprehensible; everything that happens can be explained by circumstances and prior causes.
8. Human abilities are more developed than animals' abilities, but are not different in kind.

FOR FURTHER STUDY
Historical Examples

THEIST: Thomas Aquinas. *Selected Philosophical Writings*, edited by Timothy McDermott. Oxford University Press, 1993. Thirteenth century. Aquinas offers five famous proofs for the existence of God.

ATHEIST: David Hume. *Dialogues concerning Natural Religion*. Many editions. Originally published posthumously in 1779. In part 5 Hume presents several arguments against the design theist's position.

OTHER SOURCES

John Hick. *The Philosophy of Religion.* 4th Edition. Prentice-Hall, 1990. An excellent, even-handed discussion of all the issues. Chap. 3 is an examination of arguments against God, based on sociology, Freud, and modern science.

Brian Davies. *An Introduction to the Philosophy of Religion.* Oxford University Press, 1982. Chaps. 5 and 6 present the pros and cons of the causal argument and the design argument, and Davies concludes that both arguments are persuasive.

Bertrand Russell. *Why I Am Not a Christian, and Other Essays.* Allen and Unwin, 1957. A witty, lucid demolition of the causal and design arguments, a skeptical appraisal of Christ's teachings, and a rejection of the moral value of religion.

George H. Smith. *Atheism: The Case against God.* Prometheus, 1979. Clear discussions of faith, arguments for God, and the consequences of atheism.

Lecomte du Nouy. *Human Destiny.* Longmans Green and Co., 1947. Famous statement of the design argument.

Frederick C. Copleston. *Aquinas.* Penguin, 1955. Readable, sympathetic exposition of Aquinas' philosophy, including his arguments for the existence of God.

Richard Swinburne. *Is There a God?* Oxford University Press, 1996. Argues that the existence of God is a simpler explanation of the world than the existence of material objects by themselves.

J.J.C. Smart, J.J. Haldane. *Atheism and Theism.* Blackwell, 1996. Smart criticizes the standard arguments, while Haldane defends religious belief.

1.2 IS GOD LIKE HUMAN BEINGS?
ABSTRACTIONIST OR PERSONALIST?

A large majority of people in the United States say they believe in God, but I would guess that many of these people have never examined their concept of God very carefully. How should we describe God? What do we know about God? Did he walk in the Garden of Eden with Adam and Eve? Did he allow Moses to see his back? These descriptions from the Bible make God sound almost human, even to the extent of having a humanlike body. But most religious people would probably deny that God has a body. If he has no body, does he have a personality? Is he an introvert or an extrovert? Is he primarily a thinker, a feeler, or a doer? This doesn't sound right either. It is very difficult to say *what* God is like. Often the most that religious people can say is what God is *not*: he is not physical, not male or female, not limited by personality traits, not conscious in the way we are, etc.

But if a person cannot say what God is like, then it may be impossible for that person to believe that God exists. If a person knows very little about the nature of God, then there is very little for the person to believe. Consider an analogy. Suppose you visit a friend at her house, and she tells you that behind one door, which is always locked, is a wonderful gliptor. You have no idea what a gliptor is, and your friend cannot answer any questions about it. Is it alive, is it large or small, what is it made of, what does it do? Your friend cannot say. All you know is the name. Can you believe the gliptor exists? There is no question that your friend uses the word and says she believes in the gliptor. But can you believe the gliptor is behind the door?

The following essays are about the ways people think of God. The first takes the idea that *God is love* and tries to develop and defend it. It defends an abstract concept of God. The second examines the idea of God as a *father-figure*, and asks if it is reasonable to think of God that way. Is it reasonable to believe that God has personal, humanlike qualities?

NO: ABSTRACTIONIST

"God Is Love"

Karen McAlister, age 14, was angry. I had just begun teaching my regular Sunday School class for young teens when Karen raised her hand. "You keep saying God is wonderful, and we ought to thank Him for everything. But He doesn't sound so wonderful to me," she said. The other kids fidgeted and looked embarrassed. Karen went on. "We started this year with Genesis and God's creation of the world and Adam and Eve and everything. That's all fine. But later when God keeps sending plagues to the Egyptians and wants total obedience from the Hebrews, He just looks like a big baby who has to have his way."

Karen was clearly upset, and a few of the other kids began to agree with her. We spent the rest of the class period talking about the way that ideas of God change and evolve in the Bible. Karen's feelings are not unusual. Many thoughtful young people outgrow the simple, mythological picture of God, but cannot find a more mature, adult conception to take its place. Karen was in this transitional phase. She wanted to believe in God, but she could not accept the stories about a bearded grandfather-God that she had been told all through her childhood. And she was put off by the stern, violent God of the Old Testament. Now, at 14, she was searching for a more spiritual way of thinking about God.

Many people—not just children—have literal, cartoonlike images of God as an old man sitting on a throne, dressed in a white robe. When they think of God they think of Michelangelo's wise father-figure on the ceiling of the Sistine Chapel reaching over to give life to Adam. But that picture is much too limited. Other people cannot believe such a being exists. But since they cannot conceive of God in any other way, they stop believing in God altogether. And that's even worse. They need a deeper, more challenging, "mind-stretching" concept of God.

As we grow older, and live through more complex experiences, we can grasp deeper, more subtle ideas of God. When young children hear words like "wise" and "powerful," they understand them in terms of their own experiences. Their father is "wise" because he knows the entire multiplication table, or he knows the four food groups, or the answers to other questions. He is "powerful" because he can carry them in his arms, or open windows that are stuck. Wisdom means factual knowledge they can understand, and power means physical strength they can see. But when these children grow up, they go through a number of transforming experiences. They make friends, lose friends, fall in love, get rejected, get married, have children, and sometimes get divorced. They struggle with a career, succeed, fail, bend their principles, grieve over deaths, and watch their children grow. During this process, words like "wise," "powerful," "beautiful," and "love" take on whole new levels of meaning they didn't have before. Now, as adults, they are able to understand powerful emotions of ecstasy or anguish, and subtle shades of feeling. They understand the complexities of relationships, the wonder of free choice, the solemnity of commitment, the burden of responsibility, and a range of other ideas that children cannot grasp. They understand those parts of life that are profoundly moving, vitally important, and above the intellect. They become aware of the inner, non-physical, *vital* part of life. It is not automatic or guaranteed, but if they work at it, their spiritual lives become much richer. They become capable of experiencing multitudinous aspects of life that are far beyond the physical concepts and feelings of children.

If they work at it, they can develop a more spiritual way of thinking about God. I believe that all the things we tell children about God are basically true, but we must know how to understand those truths. God is not a grandfather in the sky. Instead, God is love. The true essence of God is love—pure, absolute, unconditional love. We say that God is love often enough, but we don't take it seriously. If we take the time to think about the characteristics we usually attribute to God, we will find that they all add up to love. Let's consider them one by one.

1. "God is the creator." Some people think of God as a kind of magician who can make objects appear suddenly out of thin air. But that is literal, childlike thinking. The real creative force in the world is love. Love inspires a man and a woman to create life. There is nothing more miraculous and wonderful than that creation, an act of love. Love of others brings people together to cooperate and create new ideas, new ways of living, new discoveries. Human creativity of all kinds derives from love, whether it is love of another person, or of a group.

We can even think of love as a metaphysical principle, if we stretch our minds a little. Love is a kind of attraction. And in a way, attraction is the most fundamental force in the universe. It explains all the galaxies, planets, continents, plants, and animals that make up the world. All that order and structure is the result of the attraction of some elements for others. Over the eons, matter and energy became more organized, more complex, more structured, through the combinations of more and more structures. Everything that exists is a group of atoms bonded together by mutual attraction. Materialists see only the atoms and decide that the world is a lifeless mass. But if we step up to a more spiritual level of thinking, we can see the *process* at work with the material, and the *pattern* in the matter, which is just as real as the matter. We can see the force of attraction that weaves through all things, creating order out of chaos and life out of lifeless particles. At a higher level we can recognize that it is the same mysterious force that draws us to other people, and generates all that we create.

2. "God is eternal." Some people think of God as an old man, because He lives for such a long time, namely, forever. So He is incredibly old. But it makes more sense to think of God as love. Love is eternal. We can know this in two ways. First, the force of love is not limited to you or me or any couple or any group of people. Even if love in one person ceases to exist, it continues in other people and other places, and even in the natural world. It is the source of all the structure in the world, so it will continue forever. We can know this in a second way through our own experience. When we are in love, we are drawn beyond our selfish, individual concerns toward something more important. We sacrifice our personal desires for the sake of the beloved. We transcend ourselves. In that experience we get a glimpse of eternity. We move closer to something—pure love—that is so much greater and stronger than any single person and his or her momentary desire. We begin to understand how love is not limited to any single person's feelings, but is infinite and eternal.

3. "God is all-powerful." In Exodus God is able to part the Red Sea, turn the Nile to blood, and perform other miracles. He is represented again as a kind of magician. But if we are looking for a more spiritual power, we can find it in love. "Love conquers all," people say. A man who is in love will climb mountains, cross deserts, and face all kinds of terrors in order to be reunited with his lover. And love gives him the strength to do it. When Gandhi wanted to liberate India from British rule, he could have tried to organize an armed rebellion, but he believed nonviolent resistance would be more powerful. He counted on people's decency and love of their fellow man, and he was right. Love proved more powerful than empire, greed, and fear.

4. "God provides guidance." Some people believe God gives them signs, like a book falling open to a certain place, or missing a train, or some other striking event. Or they think God talks to them. Most people, however, do not hear God's voice, and they regard the "signs" as coincidences. But we can find

guidance in love. If we are confused and don't know what to do, we can stop and reflect on love. For example, a man quarrels with his wife and then notices how sympathetic his young, attractive coworker is. Should he sleep with her? Or a woman feels bad for the homeless in her town, but she wants to work extra hours to get a promotion at her job. Should she devote some time to volunteer work? Love shows the way. If the man really loves his wife, he will recognize a brief, sexual infatuation for what it is, and remain faithful to her. If the woman really loves her neighbor, she will make some sacrifices to help him. People have always said God is the source of morality, and they were right. God is love, and love is the highest and truest morality.

5. "We are made in God's image." In other words, we are similar to God. Some people think this means God has two arms and two legs, or at least a face. But others cannot believe that God has a body or a face. On the other hand, if God is love, then we could be made in the image of God. Love is what makes us fully human. Animals mate and raise offspring, but they do not consciously, willfully feel love. The real center of our human nature is our ability to love. And the more we are filled with love, the more like God we are. When we give love to people, we are expressing the divine, God-like part of our nature.

6. "God is within you." God is not waiting for us in some distant heaven. He is not removed from the world, "above" us, or watching us, like Orwell's Big Brother. God is part of each of us, residing within our own hearts. God is as close to us as our own thoughts and feelings. He is the love that we feel inside ourselves. If you wish to know God, look within your own heart. Look at the unselfish, beautiful love that you find there, and you will begin to understand. Look at the pure devotion you see in a new mother, or in the cheerful social worker at the soup kitchen, or the nurse in the cancer ward. God is all around us, as well as in our own heart. We only need to know how to look.

People say all these things as they grow up, but too often they continue to think like children. The ideas are all true, but we must try to understand them in an adult way. We must give them a spiritual meaning. If we do, then we will have a more mature concept of God.

It took a long time for Karen, the teenager, to get over her anger. She felt that her religion was trying to spoon-feed her fairy tales. She even decided that if God is a vengeful, violent magician in the sky, then He does not exist. We have talked many times about the nature of God, and I've tried to explain that God is love. God, or love, is not simple or easy to understand, and Karen is still learning and growing. But there is one thing she understands completely: there is no doubt whatever that love exists.

Key Concepts

God	love	spiritual
identical	human nature	moral guidance

Critical Questions

1. When you think of God, do you think of a powerful, wise old man? How would you describe God?
2. Do you think children are incapable of understanding many things that adults understand, like love, commitment, responsibility, or betrayal? Can 16-year-olds understand all these things?
3. Abstractionists claim that their concept of God is more spiritual than most people's concept. What do they mean by "spiritual"?
4. Does love really provide answers to moral questions? For example, in the cases the abstractionist mentions, suppose the man says he loves his young coworker, or the woman says she loves her work. Then what guidance does love provide?
5. In general, how does someone prove that one thing, X, is identical with another thing, Y? For example, how does a scientist prove that lightning is identical with electricity? How could Lois Lane prove that Superman is really Clark Kent?
6. The abstractionist claims that all the beliefs people have about God are also applicable to love. Can you think of any beliefs people have about God but do not have about love? For example, do people believe God hears their prayers?

YES: PERSONALIST

"The Projection Theory"

One of the oldest and most common critiques of religious belief in God is the assertion that the concept of God is a projection of idealized human qualities onto nature. God, it is claimed, is imagined to be all that frail, frightened humans would like to be themselves—infinitely powerful, aware of the future, morally confident and irreproachable, and above all, immortal. There is no such being, the critique claims, just as there is no Santa Claus who will bring children whatever they ask for. Both characters are products of wish-fulfillment. That is, in both cases people want something to exist so strongly that gradually they decide that it really does exist.

As old and familiar as this critique is, the majority of people still believe in God. Are all these believers stubbornly irrational? Or is the critique flawed or inconclusive in some way? Does the theory undermine belief in the traditional God? This theory, which can be called the projection theory, needs to be evaluated. Is it true, and if it is true, what does it prove?

The projection theory has taken different forms over the centuries. As long ago as 520 B.C.E., the Greek philosopher Xenophanes said:

> If oxen and horses had hands and could draw and make works of art as humans do, then horses would draw their gods to look like horses and oxen like oxen.

But the projection theory was elaborated in more detail in the mid-nineteenth century by the German philosopher Ludwig Feuerbach. He based it on the psychological assumption that human beings strive to reach self-consciousness, but that they can do so only by seeing themselves reflected in their environment, in their art, their manufactured goods, their tools, and especially in other people's reactions to them. In a sense, they project themselves onto their environment, and then read the results to gain self-knowledge.

But a high level of development is required before a culture realizes that parts of the environment reflect our own selves. And it is very difficult to know which parts of the environment are reflections of ourselves, and which parts are independent of our effects. For example, primitives believe that a tree or river has thoughts and intentions of its own. They mistakenly project their own intentions and feelings onto inanimate objects without realizing that they do so.

According to Feuerbach, the modern concept of a single deity is another form of the primitives' projection. The believer's own thoughts and feelings are not projected onto particular trees or the wind, but are focused on a single Being who is not localized in a particular place. However, the monotheistic God has entirely human characteristics and emotions. Therefore, Feuerbach inferred, it was not God who created humans, but on the contrary, humans who created God. Humans created God in our own idealized image, as omnipotent, omniscient, and immortal, without realizing what we were doing. After the image was formed, it seemed—like Pygmalion's statue—to take on an independent life, issuing commands and making promises.

Feuerbach also concluded that religion prevented humans from fulfilling our potential. We worship the power and creativity of God, when we should realize that we possess all the magnificent qualities ourselves. Not as individuals, but as the species, humankind. The species is potentially omnipotent, omniscient, and even immortal. Humans should worship ourselves.

The most famous form of the projection theory is due to Sigmund Freud. While Feuerbach proposed some psychological assumptions as the basis of his critique, Freud developed a comprehensive, complex theory of the mind as the basis of his view of religion. First, he established that a large part of the mind is unconscious, but still effective. People have unconscious memories and desires that nevertheless affect their behavior. He further explained that the desires or memories are unconscious because the individual cannot bear to admit them consciously; they are too painful or embarrassing. A neurosis results when the individual attempts, indirectly or symbolically, to act on the desire or memory. An example might be obsessive hand washing, which could be an indirect expression of an unconscious desire to atone for sins. In addition, Freud discovered that a man's or woman's childhood experiences often exert a strong influence over their later lives, even though the adults do not remember the earlier events.

These aspects of mental functioning explain humankind's belief in God. As a young child, each person feels completely secure, protected, and provided for by a supremely capable father. But as people grow older they recognize that their fathers are not perfect, or infallible, or immortal. They face the terrifying prospect of being alone, of dealing with the hostile and threatening world by themselves. For most people, this possibility is too frightening. Most people unconsciously decide to remain children, if not physically, then psychologically. They are determined to hold onto the feeling of security and being cared for, even if they have to invent a surrogate father. As Freud says:

> The psychoanalysis of individual human beings teaches us with quite special insistence that the god of each of them is found in the likeness of his father, that his personal relation to God depends on his relation to his father in the flesh and oscillates with that relation, and at bottom God is nothing other than an exalted father. (*Totem and Taboo*)

People imagine an ideal father who is in complete control, who knows all, and whose favor can be won by obedience and devotion. Their real fathers appeared to have these qualities when the children were very young. As adults, their powerful, unconscious desire to be watched over by such a father leads them to believe, consciously, that such a supernatural Father actually exists.

How persuasive is the projection theory? Does it prove that religious belief is irrational, or even that God does not exist? How should the theory be evaluated? First notice that, even if the claims are true, and a theist's concept of God is nothing more than an enlarged concept of his father, the theory does not prove that there is no God. The theory (if true) describes only the way some people think about God. It says nothing about whether or not some sort of God—like a father or not—really exists. It is possible that God really *is* like a perfect father. The fact that people want very badly for such a father to exist does not rule out His existence. It is also possible (even if the projection theory is true) that God exists, but that He/She/It is not like a perfect father.

Notice in the second place that the theory does not apply to people who conceive of God in some way other than as a perfect father. It is true that Western religions (Judaism, Christianity, and Islam) describe God in anthropomorphic terms. But if other religions conceive of God as nonhuman, and not possessing fatherly wisdom, compassion, and strength, then the theory does not apply to them.

In the third place, the projection theory does not apply to people who have objective evidence that God exists. The thrust of the critique is that belief in God is irrational. Freud assumed that religious believers have no other reason to believe in God besides their childish desire for a perfect father. Their real reason for believing in God is merely their wish that He exist. They may talk about theology, miracles, philosophical proofs, or evidence from history, but these are all embroidery, according to Freud. These ideas do not move people. The real basis of their belief is not evidence or facts or any conscious knowledge at all.

The real basis is their unconscious desire to remain in a state of childish dependency.

This is the crux of the issue. Is Freud's assumption correct? Do people who believe in God have any objective reason to do so? Is their belief based on any real evidence? Or is it only wishful thinking? The strength of the projection theory as a critique depends on the answers to these questions. If believers have some independent evidence that God exists—such as a direct encounter, or a philosophical argument—and base their belief on that, then the projection theory is not a serious criticism and proves very little. If they can point to sound reasons for believing in God, then their belief is not irrational.

However, if they do not have any evidence, independent of their personal desire to believe in God, then it would seem that the projection theory applies to their particular case. And then their belief in God *is* irrational. Believing something solely because one wants it to be true is the epitome of irrationality. It is a flight into a dream world and a failure to accept reality. It is confusing one's own subjective feelings with the objective world, like a person who believes he is Napoleon because he wants to be powerful and respected. Believers certainly may want God to exist. There is nothing irrational about that. But they must have some reason, beyond their desire, to believe that He exists.

Therefore the projection theory proves nothing by itself, *even if it is true*. It does not prove that there is no God. It does not apply to those believers who conceive of God as nonhuman. And it does not necessarily prove that the belief in God is irrational. If the believer has good reasons to believe in God, in addition to a strong desire, then the belief may be perfectly rational.

Key Concepts

projection theory	anthropomorphic	infantile
critique	unconscious	irrational

Critical Questions

1. On what psychological assumption is Feuerbach's projection theory based?
2. Why is belief in God harmful, according to Feuerbach?
3. In Freud's view, why do people believe in God?
4. Freud probably developed his theory with monotheism in mind. Does it also apply to polytheism, in your opinion?
5. The essay states that, even if the projection theory is true, it is still possible that God exists. How? If God is a projection of our minds, doesn't that mean he is imaginary?
6. Do you know of any religion in which God does *not* resemble humans, and does not have human qualities?
7. How does the essay define irrationality? Does a personalist think that believing in God is irrational?

Methods and Techniques

MEANINGS OF WORDS

Philosophers want answers to important questions, such as "Does God exist?" They realize that an essential part of discovering good answers to these questions is understanding the terms or concepts in the question. They realize that before they can know whether or not God exists, they must know something about what God is like, or what it is that does or does not exist. In fact, it may not be going too far to say that philosophers are just as interested in figuring out what the questions and answers *mean* as they are in knowing which answers are correct.

Many of the questions philosophers ask are explicitly questions about the meanings of terms or concepts. What is happiness? What is a person? What is justice? Just as many people say they believe in God, so many people say their goal in life is happiness. But they cannot say what happiness is. The same is true of justice. Everyone says it is a good thing, but no one knows exactly what it is. Furthermore, two people can argue for hours about the justice or injustice of a policy if neither person has a clear definition of justice. Often what people call "philosophical" arguments are arguments over the meanings of abstract words. But while some think these arguments are a waste of time, in reality they are extremely important. People cannot have any solid beliefs about God, social justice, happiness, or other important issues, without having clear definitions of the key terms. Getting clear on what the words mean is a necessary precondition for finding any answers.

Both these essays try to explain what people mean by the word "God." The abstractionist's approach is to say that one thing—God—is really identical with another thing—love. In other words, two things that everyone thought were separate and distinct are actually the same. This one thing was merely looked at from two different points of view, so to speak. This is progress, because it reduces the number of problems we face. It simplifies our outlook. We no longer have to understand (1) God, which is very vague and confusing, *and* (2) love, which is clearer and easier to understand. If God *is* love, then we only have to understand love, which is already clearer than the traditional concept of God.

Other philosophers may use the same procedure. For example, one could survey many examples of happiness and propose that they all amount to pleasure. Happiness is really just pleasure. The idea of happiness is vague and hard to pin down, but the idea of pleasure is more specific and easier to understand. The experience of pleasure is simple and familiar to everyone. Now this is a controversial theory. Is it really true that every case of happiness is really a case of feeling pleasure, and nothing else? (You will read about this issue in Section 3.2, "Can We Understand Happiness?") The point of this example is not to define happiness. The point to see is that philosophers often try to explain a puzzling idea by showing how it is really the same as a simpler idea.

The second essay also tries to explain how people think about God, but it uses a different method of clarifying the idea. It emphasizes the *origin* of people's idea of God. And it points out that people may not realize what the origin is, because the origin is unconscious. The essay says people may imagine a powerful, protective Being, who is a substitute for their fathers. It not only asks *how* people think of God, but also *why* they think that way. Why do we define the concept the way we do?

One can ask the same question about other concepts, such as the concept of justice. A person might propose that our concept of justice begins in early childhood when we play games with other children. Maybe the first thing that very young children learn when they play with others is "be fair." If I may do something, then others may do it as well, and if I do not want others to do something, then I should not do it either. Philosophers might try to explain why we learn this rule. Here philosophers are trying to explain our concept of justice by uncovering its origin. That is one way to understand important concepts.

Understanding the Dilemma

ABSTRACTIONIST OR PERSONALIST?

Theists are different from atheists in so far as theists believe in God. But there are different kinds of theists. I have already mentioned monotheists and polytheists, causal theists and design theists. Besides the questions of one or many, and cause or design as evidence, part of believing in God is deciding what God or the gods are like. If you are a theist, what kind of God do you believe in? If you are an atheist, what kind of God do you deny exists?

The essays in this section present opposing views. An abstractionist believes God is an abstract, universal power, the power of love. Love is real, of course, and an abstractionist claims that love has most of the properties theists usually associate with God. But love is not a person. It is not conscious, it does not have thoughts or feelings, it does not listen to us. When speaking of love, we say "it" rather than "He."

The personalist describes a more traditional concept of God. According to this "personal" view, God does have human qualities. He makes plans and then carries them out, he feels approval and disapproval, he communicates with people, talking and listening, he knows about the world (in fact, he knows everything), and so on. Abstract powers or processes have none of these characteristics. Theologians may argue over which human traits God has. (For example, is God male, female, or neither? Does God feel anger, jealousy, regret, and other negative emotions? If God thinks, does that mean he can change his mind? But if he is omniscient and perfect, why would he ever change his mind?) Although they may argue among themselves, these theists are convinced that God is like people in some ways.

How can you choose between abstractionism and personalism? One thing to consider is why you believe in God. The kind of God you believe in is related to your reason for believing in God. For example, if you believe in God because you see evidence of divine power all around you, in the creation of the world, in the infinite power that creation required, in the direction of history, and elsewhere, then you may be an abstractionist. You may think of God as the power that created and organizes all of existence.

On the other hand, you may believe in God for different reasons. You may have had a personal encounter with God. Some people say they have heard God's voice, or felt his presence, and they are certain that it wasn't just their imaginations. If you have had such a life-shaking experience, then you probably believe in a personal God.

Both the essays contrast mature ways of thinking and immature ways. For an abstractionist, the very idea of a personal God is immature. An abstractionist says that theists need a more spiritual concept of God. A personalist says that the idea of a personal God is not itself immature, but some people's *belief* in a personal God is immature, because it is only a wishful projection of a father figure. No one wants to be immature, but the two essays have slightly different views of what is immature.

Which of the following sets of statements are you inclined to accept? Which describe the kind of God you believe in? Of course if you are an atheist, none of these statements seems true to you.

ABSTRACTIONIST

1. God cannot be visualized.
2. God is more like a force, a spiritual magnetism, or energy, or a pattern, than a person.
3. There are good people, and there is the quality of goodness itself, and God is more like goodness itself than like a particular good person.
4. We should try to enlarge and stretch our idea of God, and go beyond the concrete images we had as children.

PERSONALIST

5. God knows about me and cares what happens to me.
6. God is like a father-figure, but much greater.
7. Some things make God happy and other things make him sad.
8. Without emotions and thoughts and plans, God would not be comforting, would not give hope, would not be a being you could talk to.

FOR FURTHER STUDY

Historical Examples

PERSONALIST: Martin Buber. *I and Thou*. Macmillan, 1978. Originally published in 1923. Buber argues that a relation with a "thou" is fundamentally different from a relation with an "it," and that relations with finite, limited "thous" make us want a relation with an eternal, infinite "Thou."

ABSTRACTIONIST: Paul Tillich. *The Courage to Be*. Yale University Press, 1952. In the last two sections of the book, "Theism transcended," and "The God above God," Tillich tries to explain his more abstract conception of God.

OTHER SOURCES

Sigmund Freud. *The Future of an Illusion*. Norton, 1989. Originally published in 1927. A brief, clear analysis of religion as a form of self-delusion and dependence on an all-powerful father-figure.

John F. Haught. *What Is God? How to Think about the Divine*. Paulist Press, 1986. An attempt to explain some difficult, abstract ideas in comprehensible terms.

C.S. Lewis. *Beyond Personality: The Christian Idea of God*. Macmillan, 1945. Fireside chats in plain language about the Trinity and other Christian ideas about God.

Sallie McFague. *Models of God: Theology for an Ecological, Nuclear Age*. Fortress Press, 1987. Discussion of various metaphorical ways of thinking about God, from a feminist perspective.

J.B. Phillips. *Your God Is Too Small*. Macmillan, 1953. Easy to read critique of immature concepts of God, and defense of the Christian, personal conception of God.

James D. Collins. *God in Modern Philosophy*. H. Regnery, 1959. Broad-ranging history of philosophical thinking about God from the Renaissance to the present.

Philip L. Quinn, Charles Taliaferro, eds. *A Companion to Philosophy of Religion*. Blackwell, 1997. Short, readable articles on a wide range of topics.

1.3 CAN GOD ALLOW INNOCENT SUFFERING?

CONTRADICTOR OR RECONCILER?

—————————————— • ——————————————

The problem of evil is a standard, traditional problem in philosophy. But for many people it isn't an academic, theoretical problem at all. It is an urgent, emotional cataclysm in their lives. When something terrible happens, people naturally ask why. We try to understand why a loved one died, or why a natural disaster devastated a whole community. To understand means to put the tragedy into some larger context. We try to see how it fits in with our other beliefs and values regarding the goals we should have, human nature, society, or God. This question probably brings more people to philosophy than any other question.

The issue is usually called the problem of evil. But what most philosophers mean by "evil" is innocent suffering. When a child contracts a lingering, fatal disease, that is evil because the innocent child suffers. When one man kills another for his money, that is evil because the victim and his friends and relatives suffer.

Anyone can ask why these things happen. Is there any reason for them? Do they serve any purpose? What do they tell us about the kind of world we live in, or the nature of human beings? But the question is particularly pressing for people who believe in God. If God knows about the suffering, and if he can do whatever he wants, then why does he stand by and let it happen?

In the first essay below, the author claims that there is no answer. The only explanation of evil is that God does not exist. In other words, the existence of evil "contradicts" the existence of God, so to speak. Since we see evil all around us, and it is incompatible with God, we must conclude that God does not exist. The second essay says that evil is compatible with the existence of God. Evil can exist and God can exist, too, because God has a reason to allow evil to occur. God and evil can be reconciled.

NO: CONTRADICTOR

"There Is No God"

I am continually amazed by religious people. They remind me of contortionists who bend their bodies into weird, unnatural shapes. Religious people go to great lengths to bend and twist the facts to try to support their beliefs. But facts are stubborn. They won't go away. Eventually we have to learn to live with them, whether we want to or not.

To a normal person (not a mental contortionist) a few facts demonstrate that religion is misguided. Think for a moment about the world that standard religions say God created. It is obvious that the world is not a perfect place. In fact, it's pretty lousy. Suffering, pain, and tragedy fill every newspaper. War, famine, disease, and crime are so common that we hardly notice them; we take them for granted. I could go on and on, but it's too depressing. Some of this evil and suffering is caused by people. One man murders another, a woman abandons her family, we hate and torment each other. Other suffering is caused by the natural world. Disease strikes a young child, floods and fires destroy families and whole regions. Natural disasters cause just as much pain and sorrow as human faults.

How can all this evil occur, if there is a God? No one denies that people suffer, but *why* do they suffer, if there is a God? God is supposed to be all-powerful. He can do whatever he wants. And he is said to be benevolent. He loves his creation. If he is all-powerful, then he *can* eliminate suffering. And if he loves us, then he *wants to* eliminate suffering. But suffering occurs. How is that possible? If God wants to eliminate it, and he can eliminate it, then why does it still happen?

Look at it this way. Imagine a person who is walking along the street and decides he wants to buy a newspaper. And imagine that he is able to buy a paper. He has fifty cents in his hand and he is standing beside a busy newsstand. He really does want the paper, and he really can buy it. If these conditions exist, then what are the chances that he will buy a paper? It's a sure thing. There is nothing to prevent him, so long as he really wants to, and he has the means. Why wouldn't he go ahead and buy it, if he does want to and he is able to? The same question applies to God. How is it possible that he does not eliminate suffering?

It is possible only if (1) God does not *want* to eliminate it, or (2) he is not *able* to eliminate it. If he wanted to, and he were able to, then suffering would not occur. But it does occur. So either (1) or (2) must be true. (In other words, either there is no being who wants to eliminate suffering, or there is no being who can eliminate it.)

But if either (1) or (2) is true, then there is no God. A being who does not want to eliminate suffering is not loving and merciful, not God. Likewise, a being who is not able to eliminate suffering is not all-powerful, not God. Since suffering occurs, there cannot be a being who is both benevolent and all-powerful. We must give up belief in one of those traits, and that means we must give up belief in God.

Someone might continue to believe in a supernatural being who is able to make a better world, but who doesn't care about us, or who even takes delight in our anguish. Such a person would be like the character in Shakespeare's *King Lear* who says, "We are to the gods as flies to young boys: they kill us for their sport." But a being who is able to kill people for sport, or who even watches impassively and coldly as people suffer, is not God. That is more like a monster.

Or someone might believe in a supernatural being who cries out at the pain in the world, but who is just as powerless to prevent it as we are. That isn't God either. God is supposed to be the creator of everything. Surely if there were a being who created the world from nothing, then he could modify a few of the parts. So if the Deity is not able to eliminate suffering, that being is not God.

Of course apologists for religion have tried to squirm out of this bind in various ways. The standard maneuver is to claim that God is certainly able to eliminate suffering, and wants to, but he wants other things even more, and those other things require suffering. For example, they say God wanted human beings to be free, so we could freely choose to worship him. But if we are really free, then we have the capacity to do evil as well as good. Regretably we misused our freedom; we have chosen to kill and torment each other. And that is why evil occurs. It isn't God's fault; it's ours. This is "the free will theory" of evil.

But it is a very poor theory. There is other evil besides human evil. Who is responsible for earthquakes? Earthquakes (not to mention dozens of other natural calamities) cause tremendous suffering of innocent people, and earthquakes have nothing to do with free will. The free will theory fails for another reason. God must have *known* that people would misuse their free will when he made us. He is supposed to be all-knowing. He must have foreseen the hatred, violence, deception, and cruelty that people would spread around the world if he gave us a free rein. If he knew it would happen, and he created us with free will anyway, then he bears responsibility for the consequences.

Others offer a different theory. They say that suffering tests us and teaches us to be humble. Like Job in the Bible, our faith is being tested, and the purpose is to teach us how insignificant we are and how great God is. But this is absurd. Imagine a baby who is born with a horrible disease and who dies in convulsions after six weeks of pain. Suppose the parents and relatives do learn to be humble. Does that lesson justify the child's suffering? Is the parents' humility that important? Can a loving God use children like laboratory demonstrations to teach his lessons? This theory makes no more sense than the free will theory.

To be perfectly fair to believers, let's consider an additional point. They say that innocent people who suffer will be rewarded by God with unimaginable blessings in heaven. And that makes up for the suffering. Does it? Suppose the child who dies in agony is later rewarded in paradise. Does that really give God the right to torment the child in the first place? Does it prove that God is a loving father? If the answer isn't perfectly clear to you, then apply the same standards to a human parent. Here is a (human) father who beats and abuses his child. But he says he has a good reason. He wants to teach his other children to be humble and submit to him. And besides, after beating the child senseless, he rewards her with toys and chocolate and a vacation. Is the beating justified? No one with a sense of justice can say it is. If this kind of behavior by a human parent is brutal and vicious, then the same kind of behavior by God would be brutal and vicious.

Religionists are grasping at straws. There is no way to hold on to the idea of an all-powerful, benevolent God in the face of the suffering we see around us. The reasonable conclusion is not that there is a powerful but indifferent being out there, and not that there is a compassionate but weak being mourning with us. The reasonable conclusion is that there is no God at all. Some events are simply tragic. No one is pulling the strings, no one planned it all, no one is trying to teach us anything. There is no God.

Key Concepts

evil	dilemma	free will
suffering	omnipotent	humility
benevolent		

Critical Questions

1. What are the two main types of evil that the essay describes?
2. What are the two most important characteristics of God?
3. The essay describes a dilemma facing theists (people who believe in God) that is created by the existence of evil. What are the two sides of the dilemma?
4. A contradictor says that if we accept either side of the dilemma, then we must give up our belief in God. Why? Do you agree?
5. Why doesn't our free will explain evil, according to the essay?
6. If God wanted to teach us not to value this life and the things of this world, but to live for the next life, how could he do it? Wouldn't he have to make us suffer?

YES: RECONCILER

"Character and Contentment"

In every society and every age, some people believe in God and some do not. The proportions change, with first one side in the majority and then the other side. But the division is always with us. Though I cannot prove it, I feel sure that when cave men huddled around their campfires at night, some professed their faith in a Divine Creator, and others scoffed at their primitive superstitions.

Not only is the debate part of the human condition, but the sources of the disagreement are perennial and universal as well. Part of the human race is convinced of God's existence by the majesty of the world around them, and by the insistent voice within the inner chambers of their hearts. The other part denies that God exists because they say the world is horribly flawed. They see the catastrophes that take uncounted lives every year: the disasters of flood, fire, famine, pestilence, and quaking earth. No God worthy of the name would create such a botched, toilsome world, they believe. These disasters have always seemed, to part of the human race, incompatible with belief in a wise Creator. Thus the debate continues.

I will not end the debate with these few remarks. But I would earnestly appeal to you, the reader, to think carefully about your allegiance to one side or the other. In particular, I urge you to weigh on a just scale the alleged evidence against God. The nonbelievers are making a serious error. They rail against the pain and suffering of the world as if they would remove it altogether. They say that if they could make the world over again, they would eliminate all the hardships that we endure in this world. But they are shortsighted and see only the surfaces of things. Pain is a necessary part of life. It is part of what makes us human.

Is this mere fatalism, the exhausted resignation of the battered and defeated? No. My thesis is life-affirming, a plea for human dignity. I say pain and struggle and even loss are necessary for men and women to realize their true humanity. The greatest good that an individual can create is *character*. Strength of will, unflinching acceptance of the truth, determination to go on, to prevail, rising above the petty and the trivial, above all, disdaining self-pity: these virtues have been recognized in all ages as the components of character. They are the bones and sinews of a mature personality. They are not all of a person, but they are the sturdy framework, without which nothing else can hold up or last.

Everyone has character to some degree, but not everyone possesses it in the same degree. Some individuals are more reliable, more steadfast, more responsible, than others. Some people are the kind of people you would want to have with you in a crisis, such as being lost in a forest, or stranded in a lifeboat. And you undoubtedly know others whom you would *not* want with you at difficult times. But character isn't only valuable in emergencies. We all enjoy and admire integrated, stable people at other times as well. We trust them. We look up to them. We try to emulate them. In fact, they embody the ideal of human nature: the fully developed, self-possessed, strong personality. How do these integrated personalities acquire character? How would you try to instill character in your growing child? There is only one way. An individual must face challenges and overcome them. He must go through difficult tests, in which he draws upon all his personal resources, and discovers abilities of which he was not aware. He must sometimes fail, and learn from the failure, so he will not fail the next time. He must acquire a wide variety of experiences, so he can face a new situation with the confidence that he has worked through something like it before. He must learn about frustration, about pain, about the dejection following long, persistent efforts that come to nothing, so these feelings will not overwhelm him in the future. Therefore, suffering is necessary to form character.

Those embittered people who complain about the tragedies of life, and say that God should have eliminated them, do not realize what they are asking. Try to imagine a world in which there is no suffering at all. No one is ever hungry, no one ever falls and gets hurt, no one cuts a finger or breaks a bone, no one gets a headache or the flu or indeed any kind of illness. It never rains too much or floods crops, there is no drought, there are no quarrels, no anger, no jealousy, no crime, and finally, no death. Would this be an ideal world? I do not think so. The nonbelievers seem to think it would, but they are making a mistake about values. They are assuming that contentment or continuous pleasure is the highest value in life. But they are wrong. This pleasure-world would leave out the most important thing. The highest value is character, and in this world no one would have a chance to develop character. The necessary challenges are missing. No one would learn to extend himself, to strive, to be resourceful, or to be patient. Since all desires would be satisfied, no one would be forced to meditate on human limitations or on what is most important above all in life. No one would be wise.

A moment's reflection will bring to mind many examples to illustrate these general ideas. Abraham Lincoln is, of course, one of the most loved and admired figures in American history. Why? Because of his gentle, unbreakable soul. His beautiful Second Inaugural Address is perhaps the best expression of character in the English language. But the words and the personality behind them can be understood only in historical context. Lincoln had lived through the Civil War. He had seen the hospitals in Washington, he had made frightfully difficult decisions, he had searched almost desperately for a competent Union commander. And besides these matters, during the same years he had lost his young son to illness, and his wife was increasingly unstable. The photographs of the man from the 1850s to 1865 tell his story more eloquently than words. In spite of the tragedies, he maintained his perspective and his determination to bring good out of evil. In 1865 he was able to write:

> With malice toward none; with charity for all; with firmness in the right, as God gives us to see the right, let us strive on to finish the work we are in; to bind up the nation's wounds; to care for him who shall have borne the battle, and for his widow, and his orphan—to do all which may achieve and cherish a just and lasting peace among ourselves, and with all nations.

Lincoln shows us, by example, the very best that humanity can be. Few reach his stature, but all can aspire to the standard he set. It is not his intelligence, or even his compassion, that shines so brightly down through the years. It is his character. And his character would not exist without the soul-wrenching challenges that he met and mastered.

In the sharpest possible contrast to Lincoln, some people lead pampered, protected lives. They or their parents are well-off, they live in nice homes, drive expensive automobiles, buy gadgets and trinkets on a whim, order others about, and generally get what they want. In my experience, people from such backgrounds are spoiled. Beneath the surface, they are arrogant, insensitive, and utterly bored. They have never learned what is really important in life. Sometimes they not only lack character, but they even lack all moral sense whatever. The young man who strangled his girlfriend in Central Park in New York City a few years ago went to private schools and enjoyed a privileged life, but he never learned what is important in life.

Please understand me. I am not trying to persuade you that all suffering is good. It isn't. Nor am I advocating the popular idea that pain is a "test," and that when bad things happen God is trying to see if our character will hold and if we will remain faithful to Him. The "test" idea assumes that God is a suspicious, cruel being, and it assumes that we already have the quality of character *before* we are tested. I believe both assumptions are obviously false. Pain is not a test but an *opportunity*. Tragedy makes it possible for an individual to grow and learn and be stronger. In struggling to carry on, to rebuild, or to find purpose, an individual can discover within himself a clear vision, a center of gravity, and a focus that he has never known before, and that adds up to character.

Pain, then, is a complex and subtle gift. It is not good in itself, but it makes a genuinely human life possible. Moreover, it is only an opportunity, not a guarantee. The decision is up to us to take advantage of the opportunity. We must choose to face the challenges, to wrestle with them, to make our mightiest efforts, before we can grow and reach a higher level. It is a gift, but it is one we must have courage to use. Character is not a trait like eye-color, or dyed hair. It is not inborn and it is not easy to get. A person can only acquire real character through long, difficult experience. It is the result of experience and could not exist without experience. Thus a world that had no pain or suffering in it would also have no strong, complex men or women in it. I believe a world where character is possible is infinitely more valuable than a world of mere contentment.

Key Concepts

character	nonbeliever	contented life
suffering	value	opportunity

Critical Questions

1. What is nonbelievers' evidence against God?
2. How does one acquire character, according to the essay? If God is omnipotent, why couldn't he simply create people who are born with character?
3. A reconciler says nonbelievers are making a mistake about values. What is their mistake?
4. Do you agree with the essay that a world without pain is *not* an attractive world? Would you prefer to live in a painless world, or in our world?
5. What is the "test theory" of evil? Is there any difference between the reconciler's theory of God's plan regarding suffering and the test theory? If so, what is it?
6. Do you think God was being kind and generous when he created cancer and earthquakes? Is tremendous suffering compatible with belief in a loving, all-powerful God?

Methods and Techniques

CONSISTENT BELIEFS

Everyone has seen a movie or TV program about a trial. At some point in the program a lawyer will cross-examine a witness, looking for *inconsistencies* in his story. For example, Smith, the witness, might say that he met Brown on Thursday. "But wait a minute," the lawyer replies. "Brown was in New York on Thursday, but last week you said you stayed in Miami until Friday. You could not have met Brown on Thursday." In other words, the witness has made two inconsistent statements. He stated that he met Brown on Thursday (in New York), and that he stayed in Miami until Friday. He must be lying about Brown or about Miami.

Lawyers look for inconsistencies in a person's story because they are strong evidence that the person is not telling the truth. Two statements are inconsistent if they cannot both be true at the same time. For example, (*a*) "I was in Miami all day Thursday," and (*b*) "I was in New York all day Thursday" are inconsistent. If one is true, the other must be false. The following pairs of statements are also inconsistent [i.e., (*a*) is inconsistent with (*b*)]:

a. Brown is over six feet tall.
b. Brown is under six feet tall.

a. Green is single.
b. Green lives with his wife.

a. Black is an ardent tennis player.
b. Black never enjoys playing tennis.

a. White is a sincere democrat.
b. White opposes equality of political rights.

In each case, if (*a*) is true, then (*b*) must be false, or if (*b*) is true, then (*a*) must be false. In everyday language, we can say that (*a*) and (*b*) are *contradictory*, and that a person who stated both had contradicted himself. (In logic, the word "contradiction" has a more narrow meaning. Two sentences are contradictory if they cannot both be true, and cannot both be false. But we need not worry about that here.)

Consistency and inconsistency are very important in philosophy for the same reason that they are important in a courtroom. If two of your beliefs about God or human nature or society are inconsistent, then one of them must be false. So philosophers try very hard to eliminate any inconsistencies or contradictions among their answers to important questions. The most common criticism of philosophical theories is to show that in some way they involve a contradiction.

That is just what the contradictor tries to do in "There Is No God." He claims that statement (*a*), "God exists," is inconsistent with statement (*b*), "evil occurs." If one is true, the other must be false. And it is obvious that (*b*) is true. So (*a*) must be false. In contrast, the reconciler tries to show that the two beliefs, "God exists," and "evil occurs," are consistent, not inconsistent. They are consistent because a loving, all-powerful God could *want* evil to occur. It is an opportunity for us to build character, the most valuable thing we can have.

Understanding the Dilemma

CONTRADICTOR OR RECONCILER?

A reconciler believes that evil can be reconciled with the existence of God, and a contradictor believes it cannot. In other words, a reconciler says we can believe in God *and* recognize evil in the world at the same time, while a contradictor says that God and evil cannot exist at the same time. One "contra-dicts" the other. Furthermore, since evil obviously exists, the contradictor says, God must not exist.

So the question in this section is the following: "Are God and evil reconcil-able?" Is it possible to believe in both at the same time? Could anything explain how God could create evil? The reconciler represented here argues that God could allow evil because evil enables humans to achieve their greatest good, the creation of character. We can admit that evil occurs, but also believe that God loves us, because the evil is a sort of blessing in disguise; it makes growth and maturity possible. Suffering is a sort of necessary evil. A world without evil, the reconciler claims, would actually not be as good for us as our present world, so the present world is an act of love by God.

A contradictor claims that making innocent people suffer cannot be an act of love. A greater good might require inconvenience, perhaps, or a little pain, but the kind of grotesque, monstrous evil we see in the world could not be jus-tified by anything. The beliefs in God and in evil contradict each other.

The contradictor says the issue is like the paradoxical question some people ask: "What happens when an irresistible force meets an immovable object?" The only thing that can happen is that one has to give way. Either the force is not really irresistible, or the object is not really immovable. They cannot both exist in the same universe. If the force really is irresistible, then the object cannot be immovable, and vice versa. To say that something is irresistible is just to say that there are no immovable objects. Therefore you cannot believe in both at the same time.

The reconciler, however, says the issue is more psychological. Could God love us, but at the same time make us suffer? What purpose could God have in allowing evil to occur? What could his motivation be? What is he trying to accomplish by making us suffer? There are several possible answers. The rec-onciler says God's purpose is to give us a chance to build character. Does this make sense psychologically and morally? Reconcilers believe it does.

The key issue is consistency. Do your beliefs fit together intelligently? Or do you say one thing at one time, and something else, in conflict with the first state-ment, at another time? Both theists and atheists might have inconsistent beliefs. A contradictor claims that the theist's belief in God and evil are incompatible. But a theist might say that the atheist's belief in scientific laws and harmony in the world is incompatible with her belief that there is no God to create the or-der.

Similar conflicts exist in people's personalities and behaviors. Some men be-have like dependent children when they are with their parents; like experienced, confident playboys when they are with their girlfriends; and like disciplined machines when they are at work. Which is the real person? Most people strive to integrate and unify their personalities, and decide which basic attitudes make up "the real me." Philosophers try to do the same thing with their beliefs, which are an important part of one's personality.

CONTRADICTOR

1. Nothing could justify the creation of a world in which innocent people suffer the way they do.
2. Even if suffering built character (which is doubtful), the character is not worth the cost in pain and anguish.
3. The universe does not exist for our sakes; it is beneficial in some ways and harmful in others, but the universe doesn't care at all.
4. Reconcilers are emotionally dependent on the idea of God, and they will believe and say illogical things to keep that idea.

RECONCILER

5. Suffering is a terrible thing, but in the long run it makes us better human beings.
6. God expects a lot from us; we should not think that he treats us like fragile children.
7. A life of challenges and accomplishments is better than an easy life of pleasure.
8. God is not a complete mystery; we can understand why he allows people to suffer.

FOR FURTHER STUDY

Historical Examples

CONTRADICTOR: David Hume. *Dialogues concerning Natural Religion*. Many editions. Originally published posthumously in 1779. Part 11 contains Hume's classic formulation of the problem of evil.

RECONCILER: John Hick. *Philosophy of Religion*. 4th Edition. Prentice-Hall, 1990. In chap. 4 Hick presents a version of reconciliation based on the views of Irenaeus, a Christian theologian of the second century.

OTHER SOURCES

Nelson Pike, ed. *God and Evil*. Prentice-Hall, 1964. A collection of classic and contemporary pieces on both sides of the issue.

C.S. Lewis. *The Problem of Pain*. Macmillan, 1962. Argues that pain is God's way of getting our attention and making us aware of our dependence on him.

Brian Davies. *An Introduction to the Philosophy of Religion*. Oxford University Press, 1982. Chap. 3 is a defense of reconciliation on the grounds that God is neither moral nor immoral.

Fyodor Dostoyevsky. *The Brothers Karamazov*. Many editions. Originally published in 1880. Book 5, chap. 4 is a vivid, fictional statement of the problem of evil, together with two contrasting responses to it.

Carl Jung. "Answer to Job." In Joseph Campbell, ed. *The Portable Jung*. Penguin, 1971. Jung proposes that Job's God is so vast, powerful, and unreflective that he encompasses both good and evil.

Marilyn Adams, Robert Adams, eds. *The Problem of Evil*. Oxford University Press, 1990. Very detailed, sophisticated essays for and against reconciliation. Difficult.

1.4 Is the Soul Immortal?
Terminator or Survivor?

———————————————————— • ————————————————————

If you want to know what the weather is like in Australia, you can go there and find out. After a week or two, you can return and tell your friends about it. But suppose you want to know what death is like. Death is not like Australia (although some disappointed tourists might disagree). You cannot visit the land of the dead for two weeks, and then return to the land of the living and tell them about it.

Many people want to know what happens after they die. But we cannot apply the standard procedures to find out. We cannot make observations, conduct experiments, or take measurements. "Dead men tell no tales," as the saying goes.

Is there any other way to find answers about death, short of experiencing it oneself? Great writers have *imagined* what death is like. Homer describes Odysseus' visit to the "gibbering shades" of the underworld, and Dante paints a fascinating picture of both heaven and hell (and purgatory, too). But these are merely interesting stories. Philosophers want answers that they can believe.

The first essay in this section claims that by analyzing certain key ideas we can know what happens after we die. Or, more precisely, we can at least know what could not possibly happen. It argues that we could not possibly survive the death of our bodies. Death terminates our lives. In the second essay, the writer looks for indirect, circumstantial evidence, and tries to decide what the uncertain hints and clues add up to. The evidence is not conclusive, but it offers some support for survival, according to the second essay. If you agree with this position, you are a survivor.

NO: TERMINATOR
"Immortality"

Many people say they believe in "life after death." But how can there be *life* after *death*? Death means the end of life. Maybe what they mean to say is that no one ever dies; life continues forever. But how could anyone believe that? We see people die every day. Everyone knows that there are only two certainties: death and taxes. Actually these people do not believe in life after death, because the very idea of immortality is inconceivable. People may hope that they will never die, but they cannot believe that they will live after they die. It doesn't make sense.

The best way to begin untangling the confusion is to ask how the idea came about in the first place. It is easy to understand how people arrived at this confused notion of "life after death." You can imagine what the world will be like after you have died. You can imagine your grieving family, the people attending your funeral, the changing seasons, the daily routines that continue. Picturing the events in one's mind is very similar to imagining that one is *watching* these things. Of course imagining something is not the same as watching it, but they feel similar. But part of the situation is that one's body has been buried. So if one is watching events, then one must be invisible or insubstantial in some sense. In other words, it is easy to imagine how life goes on after one dies. Since that is a little like watching life go on, it *seems* easy to imagine also that one goes on oneself, but without a body.

But that is strictly impossible. If a person has no body, then he or she has no eyes either. But a person with no eyes cannot watch other people. With what would one watch them? Moreover, a person with no body would have no senses at all, no hearing, no sense of touch or taste or smell. How could there be any contact with the physical world if there was no way of getting information about it? There could be no interaction of any kind between the person and the world. A person without a body could not talk or affect the world in any way. He or she would be completely cut off.

From what angle would things appear to a person without a body? If there is no body, then the person is not located in space. Would one watch another person from above, or below, right or left side? The question cannot be answered, since the watcher has no body and no position relative to what he or she is watching. But if one watches or sees something, it must be from some specific point of view, from some angle. There can be no seeing except from some point of view.

Everyone agrees that our *bodies* will die and disintegrate. But some people insist that another part of themselves will continue to live, but without a body. But this makes no sense. It is impossible to think of a *person* without a body.

The concept of "person," or "human being," includes certain essential characteristics that depend on having a body. For example, "person" is defined in part as a being with senses that provide the individual with information about the environment. People (by definition) learn about their surroundings and react to them. They have minds (by definition) and their minds are filled with sights, sounds, smells, and so forth. A being with no senses whatever, no influences from the environment, would not be a person, as we understand the term.

Another essential property of persons is that they have personalities. Each one is unique. And that uniqueness depends in part on the sort of body each person has. The personality of someone who is tall, athletic, and thin will be different from that of someone who is short, awkward, and plump. It is impossible to separate the personality from the kind of body one has.

A third essential property of persons is being located in space. There may be some things that are not located in space, like the number seven or Beethoven's Fifth Symphony. But you cannot conceive of a person, who exists, but doesn't exist anywhere in particular. It is like trying to think of a table, but a table that is neither square nor round nor rectangular nor any other shape. It's impossible; it makes no sense.

Here is another essential property. If you continued to exist without a body, would you be male or female? Without a body you would be neither. But can you really conceive of yourself as neither male nor female? No, you cannot.

The problem I am describing is not that we lack imagination. Artists and writers have taken the most amazing flights of imagination in dreaming of a world of heaven and hell. Hieronymus Bosch painted fantastic creatures and scenes of the afterlife that stretch anyone's imagination. But however bizarre the inhabitants of the afterlife, they have some sort of bodies. The problem is a matter of concepts, not imagination. The concept of a person includes having a body. You cannot separate the two, just as you cannot separate the concept of a triangle and having three sides, or the concept of a bachelor and being unmarried. We know that there cannot be any bachelors who are married. There is no point in trying very hard to imagine a married bachelor. The phrase "married bachelor" doesn't make sense.

The phrase "disembodied person" is similar. You cannot conceive of yourself or any person existing without a body. It is like trying to think of a triangle with four sides. People only think that they can, because they can imagine the world continuing after they have died. But imagining the world continuing is not the same as imagining oneself without a body. They are not really imagining themselves *in* that world. They are only imagining the world by itself. What is the difference between that world *with* you in it—but with no body—and that world *without* you in it at all? There is no difference. If you have no mouth or voice or hands you cannot affect people or the world in any way. Without any sense organs, you could not be affected by the world in any way. With no interaction whatever, you are not really in the world. So people are not really imagining themselves continuing to exist without a body. They are only imagining the world after they have died.

We can imagine the world continuing after our death. But it is a mistake to think that we can imagine being in that world, but with no body. The very idea of immortality makes no sense at all.

Key Concepts

imagination	essential property	position in space
inconceivable	senses	personality

Critical Questions

1. What makes people think that they could survive their own death? What mistake are they making?
2. Why couldn't a person be aware of the world after the death of his or her body?
3. Do you agree with the first essay that one's personality depends in part on one's body type? Is being male, or female, an inseparable part of one's self?
4. How does the terminator show that people are only imagining the world after they have died, and not imagining themselves *in* that world?
5. If you cannot imagine something (e.g., being in two places at once, being your own grandfather or grandmother), does that prove that it is impossible? Can you believe that something is possible when you cannot imagine what it is?
6. Do you think the terminator has shown that immortality is *impossible*?

YES: SURVIVOR
"For and against an Afterlife"

There are three words that are very difficult to say. I'm not thinking of "I love you," although those require courage and humility. Even more difficult are "It's my fault." Hardly anyone has the strength to say those, and mean them.

I'm thinking of the difficult words "I don't know." Especially nowadays, with our information-based economy and university degrees, those words are difficult because having answers confers status. In addition, the progress of science makes us think we can know everything.

The words are most difficult to say when it comes to the most important questions, like "Does God exist?," "What is right and wrong?," and "What happens when I die?" With regard to the last question, the fact is that no one knows what happens after death. No one has experienced that state and returned to the world to tell about it. Therefore, it is *possible* that human beings survive the death of their bodies and continue to live in a different form. And it is possible that we do not. We simply don't know. Anyone who claims otherwise lacks the strength to say those three words.

Even though we can't be sure of what happens after death, we can look for evidence for and against an afterlife. And the evidence gives us a small degree of hope.

Evidence for an Afterlife

Several kinds of evidence make it probable that we will survive the death of our bodies. First, throughout history people have reported seeing apparitions of recently deceased individuals. Often groups of people have seen such beings, and even animals have reacted to them. C.J. Ducasse describes some cases in his book *A Critical Examination of Belief in a Life after Death*. The important thing is not to savor the strangeness of such cases, but to ask if they really happened, and if there is a natural explanation of them. The fact that several people have reported seeing the same apparition, and that animals—who do not lie—have reacted to them, suggests that they are real.

Second, some people report speaking with men or women who have died. Occasionally, the voice, or spirit, will inform someone of something he could not possibly have known if he had not had contact with the deceased. For example, the spirit may tell someone of the location of something that only the deceased knew.

In other cases, the spirit, who speaks through a living medium, or channel, will elaborate a profound, complex philosophical system, unlike any current philosophies or religions. The medium is often an average person, usually with a modest (perhaps high school) education. It is highly unlikely that the medium could develop such a set of beliefs and advice by himself or herself.

One of the most famous mediums was Madame Blavatsky, who founded the Theosophical Society in 1875. She said she was in spiritual contact with two long-dead Tibetan monks, who guided her writing of *The Secret Doctrine*. The book demonstrated a thorough familiarity with esoteric Tibetan religious doctrines and practices, which Blavatsky could not have known. How did she write such a book? The simplest explanation is that the deceased monks helped her.

It is true that the majority, in fact almost all, of such cases are fraudulent. The apparition was a hoax, or the person acquired the knowledge in some other way. But a few cases have been thoroughly investigated by people who know all the tricks. They defy explanation, except that some people survive the death of their bodies, and contact those they left behind.

The third kind of evidence is near-death experiences, or NDEs. Many people who have almost died, by drowning, or in surgery, report remarkably similar sights and feelings. After they have recovered, many say they felt a deep calm and sense of release. They say they left their bodies and watched the doctors trying to revive them. They were moving through a dark tunnel toward a brilliant light. They met and talked with deceased friends and relatives. Many dying, unconscious patients in hospitals have later accurately described the machines and techniques the doctors used to resuscitate them. Some even described what was happening in other rooms in the hospital.

The best known study of NDEs is *Life after Life*, by Raymond A. Moody, Jr. Moody describes numerous examples. The similarity among very different people's experiences is quite remarkable, and suggests that they are not simply hallucinating or fantasizing. After all, if twenty witnesses of an event all agree on the details, then it is probable that the event really occurred, and the witnesses are telling the truth.

Moody thinks that another fact, besides the unanimity, is even more persuasive. He asks

> How is it that the patients can give such elaborate and detailed accounts of resuscitations, explaining in their entirety what the doctors were doing to bring them back to life? How can so many people explain what was going on in other rooms of a hospital while their bodies were in the operating room being resuscitated? To me, these are the most difficult points for the NDE researchers to answer.

Skeptics can question all this evidence. Undoubtedly some patients are simply imagining things. Some writers have proposed that chemical changes in the brain, such as lack of oxygen, can explain NDEs. But while that could explain the agreement, since everyone's brain would react in a similar way, it could not explain the knowledge of other rooms that patients have.

Evidence against an Afterlife

The evidence against an afterlife is that a person's mind or consciousness is completely dependent on his or her body. Anesthetics and other drugs affect consciousness, a blow to the head can temporarily remove consciousness, light and sound impacting on the eyes and ears cause a person to have certain sensations, and so on. All this implies that if the body is destroyed, then so is the mind. Some skeptics go so far as to say that we can't imagine a mind existing without a body.

But this evidence is not persuasive. Centuries ago people probably couldn't imagine plastic surgery, or being hypnotized, or hearing a symphony thousands of miles away, or other things we take for granted. As for the body influencing the mind, there is just as much evidence that the mind influences the body. I decide to stand, and my body moves. A decision—a mental event—influences my body. If I am frightened, then my hair stands up and my heart races. Anxiety can interfere with digestion and cause ulcers. All these are cases of the mind acting on the body.

Suppose some fourth graders like to play with computers during recess instead of going outside. And suppose those computer fans get better grades and are generally better students than the kids who play outside. Should we say that playing with computers leads to being a good student, or that being a good student leads to an interest in computers? As far as we can tell, the influence goes in both directions. It's impossible to say that one is dependent on the other. And the same is true for mind and body. The influence goes in both directions.

Conclusion

It appears, then, that all the evidence that the body influences the mind is balanced by just as much evidence that the mind influences the body. Therefore, the evidence against an afterlife is neutralized. It is canceled out. As far as the evidence is concerned, it is just as reasonable to believe that there is, or that there is not, an afterlife.

But we still have the evidence *for* an afterlife. It is far from conclusive. The bottom line is that we do not know what happens when we die. But on the whole, this evidence makes it probable that we do survive the deaths of our bodies.

Key Concepts

apparition	fraudulent	evidence
medium	near-death experience	neutralized

Critical Questions

1. The survivor seems to believe in ghosts. On what grounds? Would you say this belief is rational?
2. If someone like Madame Blavatsky claimed to communicate with the dead (e.g., Tibetan monks), how would you test her claim? How would you decide whether she really could communicate with the dead?
3. Suppose someone said people near death all have similar experiences because their brains and bodies undergo similar traumas. Why wouldn't that undermine the evidence, in the survivor's view?
4. In your opinion, which of the three kinds of evidence of life after death is most plausible?
5. How is the evidence against an afterlife "neutralized," according to the second essay?
6. Does the "neutralization" test apply to the evidence *for* an afterlife?

Methods and Techniques

FACTS AND CONCEPTS

These two essays provide several contrasts. They are very different, not only in their conclusions, but also in their methods. The first essay uses a *conceptual* argument. It bases the argument entirely on the *meanings* of the crucial concepts—person, see or aware, and body. It claims that the very idea of being aware of one's surroundings is tightly connected with the idea of having a body. They are so tightly connected that they cannot be separated. That is, we cannot imagine a person who is conscious and aware, but who has no body.

The terminator would say the situation is comparable to Paul Bunyan's cook, who, the legend says, could make pancakes so thin that they had only one side. This is a cute story, but we know that one-sided pancakes are impossible. Not just extremely difficult to make, or rare, but absolutely impossible. We cannot imagine such a thing. If someone says that he seems to remember eating a one-sided pancake, or that he once had a fleeting glimpse of a one-sided pancake, we do not investigate further. We do not search for other witnesses, or conduct laboratory tests to find out more about these remarkable pancakes. We know that the person is mistaken, however sincere and honest he may be. We know he is mistaken because the concepts "pancake" and "one-sided" cannot be put together. The same is true for "conscious" and "bodyless."

The method in the second essay is completely different. The survivor admits that we cannot have any verifiable, certain knowledge of the afterlife, but thinks that various reports provide some evidence of an afterlife. The question is "How reliable are these reports?" Can we believe what people say about their experiences?

Credibility is a problem not only for philosophers, but also for journalists, scientists, and ordinary citizens during an election. Whom can you believe? Often people give conflicting reports about some event, or a person's story may be inconsistent, or the person may have some ulterior motive for telling the story. (For example, if a person says that he encountered aliens from outer space, he may become a celebrity and appear on TV. But that prospect—not respect for the truth—may be his motive for saying he encountered aliens.)

The second essay considers a variety of reports and tries to apply standards of reliability to them. One important standard is agreement. Are there several witnesses, and do the witnesses agree among themselves? Another standard is bias. Do the witnesses have any reason to lie, or would they profit from lying? Another test it applies is alternative explanations. Is there another explanation of the experience besides the one the witnesses give, and what explanation is the simplest?

The second essay also compares conflicting evidence, i.e., evidence for an afterlife and evidence against an afterlife. And it tries to weigh the two sides to decide which is more persuasive. The evidence against is the mind's dependence on the body. But the body is also dependent on the mind. The survivor argues that the evidence against is "neutralized," and so the evidence *for* an afterlife is stronger.

Philosophers search for believable answers to the most important and difficult questions we ask ourselves. They must consider many different experiences, reports, facts, and theories, all of which are in conflict. Philosophers must continually try to decide which reports are believable and what evidence is strongest. The second essay is an example of that process.

Understanding the Dilemma

TERMINATOR OR SURVIVOR?

What happens when you die? A survivor believes that you will continue to exist in some way. You will probably be conscious of your surroundings and other people, and you may interact with physical things. You will survive the death of your body. A terminator disagrees. He or she believes that dying is like going to sleep and never waking up again. You completely cease to exist. Death will terminate your existence.

Survivors believe we are immortal, because they believe a human being is a duality. They believe a human being is made up of two distinct parts. One part is the body, and the other part is the soul, or mind. The body dies, but the soul continues to live. That is possible because these two parts are completely different. The body is a physical object, with mass, shape, color, solidity, and all the characteristics of other objects. It is subject to the same physical laws as other objects. It is restrained by gravity, it can be frozen, burned, divided into smaller parts, and eventually it disintegrates, like other physical objects. But the other part of a person, the soul, is not physical and not subject to physical laws. The soul is the part that thinks, remembers, feels emotions, and enlivens the body. It is the active part of us. It is the part that is happy or sad, shy or bold, intelligent, creative, lazy, or arrogant. It has no weight, shape, or location in space. Since these two parts are so different, survivors can be called *dualists*. They believe that at death the two parts are separated. The body dies, but the soul continues to exist, separate from the body.

Terminators, on the other hand, believe a human being is just one thing, a physical body. In contrast with survivors, they are *monists*. The word "monist" comes from the Greek root *monos*, which means single, sole, or alone. We have already encountered the same root in the word "monotheism." Terminators think a human being is one complex entity, not two entities tied together. We are physical objects, but we are extremely complicated physical beings, with brains, nervous systems, sense organs, hormones, and muscles. Unlike simple tables and chairs, we are physical objects who are capable of thinking, feeling, and acting. Terminators do not deny that people think and feel. They simply say we do not need to believe in a separate, nonphysical soul to do these things. The body does them. In fact, they believe we cannot imagine a thinking, feeling person without a body. The idea of a nonphysical soul, separate from the body, does not make sense, they say. So they believe we are one thing, a complex human body. And since everyone agrees that the body dies and disintegrates, they are terminators. They believe we are mortal.

The two essays in this section are very different. They approach the issue of life after death in different ways. The second considers different kinds of evidence, or observations, that may support belief in an afterlife. But the first considers the very *idea* of an afterlife, and analyzes what the idea means. Another difference is in their assumptions about human nature. The survivor in the second essay is a dualist, while the terminator is a monist. But the main difference is in their conclusion, and that is the main decision you should make. Are you a terminator or a survivor? When you die, will you continue to exist in another form, or will death be the final end of your existence?

TERMINATOR

1. I am so intertwined with my body, and my very idea of myself is so dependent on my consciousness of my body, that I could not possibly exist without my body.
2. It is impossible to imagine (clearly, in detail) existing and interacting with the world without a body.
3. All the images and ideas of heaven or an afterlife are simply images of earthly life with the defects removed; no one has described any so-called disembodied existence.
4. All the alleged evidence of "life beyond the grave" can be explained by purely natural means (such as optical illusions, unconscious memories, etc.).

SURVIVOR

5. I use my body just as I use my car, but I am not the same thing as my body.
6. Spirits of the dead sometimes speak to people, send us messages, or move objects, start fires, break glasses, and so on.
7. Belief in life after death is not just wishful thinking, but is a rational conclusion based on a sober assessment of objective, factual evidence.
8. Life after death will be unlike anything we can possibly imagine.

FOR FURTHER STUDY

Historical Examples

TERMINATOR: Lucretius. *On the Nature of the Universe*. Penguin, 1951. First century B.C.E. In Book 3 Lucretius presents about a dozen arguments designed to show that the soul ceases to exist when the body is destroyed. Most, but not all, are based on his atomism.

SURVIVOR: Plato. *Phaedo*. Many editions. Fourth century B.C.E. Plato claims that we have a kind of knowledge that is eternal and unchanging, and that we could acquire such knowledge only if our souls existed independently of our bodies.

OTHER SOURCES

William Dudley, ed. *Death and Dying: Opposing Viewpoints*. Greenhaven Press, 1992. Chap. 5 presents short excerpts, pro and con, from books and articles on survival, near-death experiences, and the relevance of survival to the meaning of life. Easy to read.

Terence Penelhum. *Survival and Disembodied Existence*. Routledge & Kegan Paul, 1970. Penelhum argues that the existence of one's soul without a body is impossible.

Hywel D. Lewis. *The Self and Immortality*. Macmillan, 1973. Chap. 8 is an attempt to explain how one could exist without a body.

Howard P. Kainz. *The Philosophy of Man*. University Press of America, 1989. Chap. 11 discusses paranormal phenomena, and chap. 12 defends the possibility of survival, based on some careful analyses of key terms like "soul" and "existence."

Peter Carruthers. *Introducing Persons*. Croom Helm, Ltd., 1986. Chap. 7 is an imaginative (but skeptical) consideration of resurrection, reincarnation, and problems of personal identity, using science fiction thought experiments as well as other arguments.

John Hick. *The Philosophy of Religion*. 4th Edition. Prentice-Hall, 1990. Chap. 11 is an examination of the Hindu doctrine of reincarnation.

Arnold Toynbee, et al. *Man's Concern with Death*. McGraw-Hill, 1968. Part 3 includes essays on parapsychology and conceptions of a disembodied afterlife.

Raymond Moody. *Life after Life*. Mockingbird, 1975. People's stories of near-death experiences, told by a survivor.

Paul Edwards, ed. *Immortality*. Prometheus, 1997. Edwards explains the positions and issues in a long introduction, and includes thirty-four selections from Plato to Parfit.

1.5 Is Faith an Answer?
Believer or Questioner?

—————————————————— • ——————————————————

It is not easy to say what religion is, or what makes a person a religious person. Is believing in God enough? There are many ways to think about God, and some beliefs might not be enough. For example, suppose a person believes that God or the gods exist but is terribly afraid of them. Or suppose the person doesn't like God, or even hates him. Is that person religious? He believes in God, but it sounds odd to say he is a religious person.

Or imagine another example. Suppose a philosopher studies the concepts of cause and effect and time, and after careful reasoning decides that something caused the universe to exist. The nature of the world requires a Creator, or God. This philosopher also believes in God, but again, he does not seem to be a religious person.

If believing in God is not enough, then what else is necessary to be a religious person? One answer is faith. That is, a religious person is a person who has faith in God, and believes in God on the basis of faith. That is why neither of the two people in the examples above is religious. Neither has faith.

But it looks as if we have answered our question with another question. The original question was "What makes someone a religious person," and our answer was faith. But what is faith? Is faith in God like faith in your family doctor, i.e., trust that he will do the right thing? Or is it like faith in electricity, i.e., belief that it exists even though you cannot see it or understand it? Or is it something else? There is no simple answer.

The following essays explore different aspects of faith. In the first, the writer tries to explain why he has faith in God. He says it is OK to believe in God even though he has no evidence at all for his belief. We can call anyone with this position a "believer." The second essay says the believer's attitude has terrible consequences. It argues that a person should have some good reasons to back up anything he or she believes. A person who agrees with the second essay is a questioner.

YES: BELIEVER

"Accepting Limits"

I have reached the point in my life where I am beginning to feel the need to sum up what I have learned. I want to start tying up loose ends. I've had a long, full life, and now I want to take stock. What was it all about? What was it for? What has life made of me?

I could talk about my accomplishments in my work. And, to be honest, I would have to talk about some failures, too. I could spend hours thinking about the happy times with my wonderful wife, Jean, and our daughter, Chris. But should I include my first wife? Of course. That big mistake was part of my life as well.

However, I can't talk about everything at once. For the present, I want to describe one particular way that I have grown over the years. I want to explain why I believe in God. I didn't always believe. It is a part of me that has gradually changed. I am not going to discuss religion. Religion is not the same thing as belief. Actually I do worship with my congregation regularly, I work with the people there to help the less fortunate, and I try to live by our religion's principles. Religion has become more important to me in the past few years. But I want to go back to the foundations, which is belief in God. I practice religion because I believe in God, not the other way around. The belief is primary.

I will begin with an observation. It is a fact (I think) that more elderly people believe in God than young people. If you took a poll of one hundred college students and one hundred retired people, asking each group "Do you believe in God," I think that a higher percentage of retired people would answer yes than college students. Why is that? Why do more people tend to believe in God as they get older?

The most common answer is that older people are more afraid of death. They feel death approaching, it is frightening, and they believe in God because the belief is a comfort to them. It is a way of denying death. But that is not why I believe in God. To me, death is a puzzle rather than a terror. I have lived my life. I am ready for it to end. In fact, I'm a little curious about dying.

I have come to believe in God by a different route. What my life has taught me is that we human beings are not all-powerful and all-knowing. We are limited. There are some things we simply cannot understand. With all our science and technology and learning, the world is still, ultimately, a mysterious place. Elderly people have seen enough failed experiments and heard enough shallow, empty explanations that they know about limits. They have lost the blind optimism of youth.

Accepting limits is the first step toward belief in God, and it is a difficult step to take. As a young man, I denied it. I worked hard in school, and I was fascinated by the incredible wealth of knowledge and information accumulated in universities. After college, I went on to study medicine, confident that science could defeat the age-old enemies of mankind—famine, disease, war, and even death itself. For a number of years I practiced medicine, relieving pain, helping some, extending lives, and, through my research, adding a little to our medical knowledge.

But as the years passed, my doubts began to grow. I began to wonder how much of the world and man I really understood. How much did anyone really understand? The science of medicine has grown tremendously in my lifetime. But it seems that for every breakthrough we also confront new problems. Take one example. In the sixties, some brilliant surgeons developed the heart transplant technique. In those days the possibilities seemed endless. If we could transplant hearts, then perhaps we could transplant other organs. And as the transplants wore out, we could replace them with new organs from accident victims. Theoretically a person could live forever. One little problem was that the bodies of the patients kept rejecting the new hearts. They treated the new heart like a foreign invader rather than a life-saving improvement. We assumed that a few minor adjustments could solve the problem, but the adjustments didn't work. We could suppress the rejection for some time, but blocking the rejection led to other problems. We learned from our "advance" that the immune system was much more complex and subtle than we realized, and that heart transplants were not the great triumph we thought they were.

And now of course there is AIDS, an incurable, fatal disease of the immune system. Hundreds of thousands of people worldwide have already died, and many more have the infection. Why? Where did it come from, and what can stop it? We don't know. It seems almost as if nature is cruelly taunting us for challenging her. The more we learn, the more we realize we don't know.

I practiced medicine for over forty years, and I'm glad I had the opportunity to serve my community. I helped a lot of people heal themselves and get back on their feet. But there were tragic cases. Some were beyond hope, some I might have treated differently if I had a second chance, some were just baffling. During the first decade or so the deaths were very difficult to take, but I was able to snap back. I was confident that science could fight death. But a physician is in a paradoxical position. For a doctor, the greatest enemy is death. Injury and disease are challenges, but death is the ultimate defeat. And yet, every patient will eventually die. We can avoid it for some time, but death is inevitable.

As the years passed, and I witnessed more and more deaths, I began to think about death in a different way. From asking "Why did this patient die," I began asking "Why does death happen at all?" Why does everyone die? I read a good deal of the scientific literature, and I discovered that, beneath the jargon and the studies of cells and organs, the fact is that no one knows why death occurs. We can describe the process. But we don't understand why the body deteriorates to the point of collapse. It is just one of the limits we must face.

Death is a limit in two different ways. Obviously death limits each person's allotted time on earth. That was disturbing and painful to me, but I could continue living as I had with that limit. However, death is also a limit in another way. It makes no sense. We can't understand why it happens. It is a limit on our proud intellects. Even if we learn more about cell processes, we cannot answer the larger why. Why do we have such a strong will to live if we are all doomed to die in the end? Why does the world work this way? I realized I couldn't answer these questions, and that realization gradually changed my whole outlook on life. I was no longer the confident, optimistic young man I had been. I finally had to admit that we do not have answers, that there are no rational reasons for everything, and that the world is really beyond our comprehension. That was a completely new way of thinking. It made me a much more humble person.

Once I admitted some limits on our understanding, I discovered others. As a young man, I had assumed that the astronomers would eventually explain the origins of the universe. But all they talk about is the "Big Bang." They have nothing to say about what came *before* this Big Bang, or why it occurred. Here is another example. When I began my career, I thought I was in control of my life. I thought I surely understood myself and what I wanted. But somehow I found myself married to a woman I didn't love, behaving in ways I didn't want to behave. I was an overconfident, ambitious fool. Moreover, I didn't understand others any better than I understood myself. I thought expanded education and government aid would inevitably lead to a better society. But in spite of vast government programs and billions of dollars, we still have rampant crime, homelessness, broken families, and crippling debt. We seem to be in decline. One of my greatest pleasures now is music. The rhythms, harmonies, and tone colors are always delightful, and sometimes the sheer beauty is almost overwhelming. Can anyone explain that beauty? Why do I feel that way? And how did Mozart create such wonderful, inspiring sounds? No one knows. All we can do is bow our heads in the face of such mysteries.

We are like children around a campfire in the forest at night. Within the little circle of light everything is cozy and comfortable, but we are surrounded by a huge, black darkness filled with strange shapes and unidentifiable, frightening noises.

What I have learned in my threescore and ten is that the world is greater than we can know. We have a little knowledge, but we are severely limited in what we can understand. Why am I here? Why do I die? Why does the world work the way it does? Why do I do what I do? We cannot find answers to these questions through science or reason. Therefore, I have *chosen* an answer. I choose to believe in God, an all-powerful, all-knowing, all-loving Creator. He created me to worship Him. That belief provides answers to all the other questions. It tells me why I am here, why I die, why I do what I do, and why the world is the way it is.

I cannot find answers to these questions in science or philosophy, so I have *faith* that God exists. I have never been impressed by miracles (though they may occur). I have never heard a Voice of God commanding me to believe. In fact, I do not have any evidence that God exists. What I have learned is that some questions can't be decided by evidence or facts or reasons, because reality is just too complex and obscure for us to understand. For answers to these questions I rely on a different part of human nature and a different method. I have faith. I choose to believe the answer that seems best to me.

This is a two-step process. First we must admit that we cannot understand everything. Then, after recognizing our weakness and impotence, we can take the second step of freely choosing to believe in God. Where science and intellect cannot provide answers, faith and commitment can. Faith is not proof. It is not even rational. Indeed, where we have proofs and reasons, faith is out of place. But in so many areas, I have learned, we have no proofs or evidence or reasons. When we realize those limitations, faith is the next step. It is beyond proof and argument.

I am aware of my critics. Some people will say I am wrong and should not have faith. But if scientists cannot explain death or the universe or beauty, then how can they say that my answer is wrong? If they knew why we die, or how the universe began, then I would listen to them, and I would believe their answers. But they don't have the answers; they don't know what is true or what is false. They cannot prove that there is or that there isn't a God. So how can they say my belief in God is wrong?

Many people agree with me that scientists and philosophers do not have all the answers. But many refuse to take the next step and believe in God because of their pride and misplaced confidence. I am not so confident. Since we cannot find answers based on evidence and reasons, I have accepted an answer on different grounds. I believe in God on the basis of faith.

Key Concepts

limits	death	faith
understand	mystery	God

Critical Questions

1. What lesson should we learn from the heart transplant technique, according to the believer?
2. How did the believer's reflections on death lead to a basic change in his outlook on life?
3. What are some examples of things we cannot understand, according to this essay? Do you agree that no one understands these things?
4. If you agree with the essay that we do not understand these mysteries, do you also believe we will *never* understand them?
5. How does the believer reply to his critics, i.e., those who say he should not have faith? Is he right?
6. Does the believer think that he understands God? If not, but he has beliefs about God, then why couldn't he have beliefs about death, or other things he does not understand?
7. Consider an analogy. It is very difficult to know what works in education. No one knows for sure why some children succeed and some fail. Should teachers, therefore, have faith that success depends on genetics? Or diet? Or parents' income, or something else? No one knows for sure what cures cancer (if anything). Should a patient with cancer have faith in one type of cure, e.g., injections of extracts from calves' brains?

NO: QUESTIONER

"Faith and Its Consequences"

In many religions faith is held up as an important virtue. In his letter to the Corinthians, for example, St. Paul specifically lists "faith, hope, and charity" as Christian virtues. Faith may be even more central to Islam. The very word "Islam" is derived from an Arabic word that means submission, and the first of the Five Pillars of Islam is to acknowledge that there is only one God. Other religions place more or less emphasis on faith as well.

But is faith a virtue? Is someone who believes something on the basis of faith acting in a praiseworthy manner? A consideration of the *consequences* of faith shows that it is actually *not* a virtue. People should not believe things on faith. In fact, faith can be very dangerous.

To say that you believe something on the basis of faith is to say that although you do not have good *evidence*, you believe anyway. For example, many people decide to believe that an omnipotent, loving God created the universe. They have no evidence for the belief. They admit that all the "proofs" and disputes through the ages are inconclusive. The few facts we do understand can be explained by scientists using natural laws. So there is no evidence that God exists. But they decide to believe in God on the basis of faith, not on the basis of evidence.

What is evidence? To say that there is *evidence* for some belief is to say that some established facts make the belief *more probable*. For example, a prosecutor in a trial presents evidence that the defendant is guilty. The evidence might be bloodstains at the scene of the crime, which are the same blood-type as the defendant's. The two facts—blood stains and matching blood-type—make it more probable that the defendant is guilty. They aren't proof, but they are evidence of guilt. If nine out of ten patients who take a drug are cured, and all the patients who did not take the drug remain ill, those facts make it probable that similar patients who take the drug in the future will be cured. This is evidence, not faith.

Another example of faith is belief in immortality. There is no good evidence that people continue to exist after they die. The alleged "voices from beyond the grave" and other ghost stories all turn out to be hoaxes perpetrated by swindlers on desperate widows and grieving relatives. At least the cheated widows are looking for evidence, however bogus it is. But some people say they believe they will go to heaven after they die, even though there is no evidence that heaven exists. They say they do not need evidence. They simply have faith that they will never really die.

The desperate widow believes that her dead husband still exists somewhere. Why does she believe it? She has faith, people say. But that just means she decides to believe, even though she has no real evidence. *Why* does she have faith? Why do people have faith that God exists? It is a personal decision, people say. But why do they make that personal decision? The facts and objective evidence do not persuade them to believe. If they did, it would not be faith but a rational inference about probability. So why do people have faith?

There are two possible answers. One is that some *authority* tells them to have faith. For example, parents tell their children (directly or indirectly) that they should believe in God. They cannot point to convincing evidence that God exists, but they still say he does, and they expect their children to believe, too. After the children grow up, they never question what they have been told. Priests and rabbis are also looked up to as authorities. They tell people to have faith, and since people trust them, they do what the religious authorities say.

Besides authority, the other reason people have faith is comfort. The belief makes them feel better. This is obviously why the desperate widow believes her dead husband still exists. Believing that he is out there somewhere, listening or watching, makes her loss easier to bear. The same motive explains why many people believe that *they* will be immortal. The prospect of their own death is so terrifying and painful that they can't face it. So they decide to believe that they will never die. They have faith.

Both these ways of thinking lead to terrible consequences. The first way is to decide to believe something (to have faith) because an authority says it is true, even though there is no evidence to support the belief. But if people follow authorities, they will never learn to think for themselves. It is very easy to believe something because an authority says we should. We just submit, sheep-like, and avoid all responsibility. In contrast, it is very difficult to search out all the facts on some question, weigh the evidence for and against, and then make a reasonable decision. And yet the difficult path is better than the easy one. In the long run, people will be happier if they think for themselves, and society as a whole will be better if it is made up of reasonable, inquiring citizens rather than obedient sheep.

Furthermore, if people submit to authorities in matters of religion, they will soon submit in matters of politics, social policy, education, personal relationships, and other areas of life. People who habitually accept their priest's word in matters of religion will probably accept their Congressman's word in matters of foreign policy, or government expenditures. Such slavish obedience is degrading. And such tremendous power over people on the part of authorities is very dangerous, because power corrupts. In addition, if people follow authorities in matters of belief, then they will soon follow them in matters of action as well. Beliefs are the basis of action. If you decide to believe in God because your minister says you should, then what will you do when your minister says you should donate more money to the church, or convert your neighbor to the true religion, or report on any irregularities you see among your neighbors? (Literally thousands of followers of Sun Myung Moon, who lives near New York, have allowed him to choose their own spouses for them, usually complete strangers. He also decides when they should consummate the marriage.) Submitting to authorities is a bad way of thinking. Many of the horrors of history began with that seemingly innocent decision.

The consequences of this kind of faith are clear. The consequences of the other kind of faith are perhaps more difficult to see, but for that very reason they are more dangerous. The other kind of faith was when people decide to believe something because the belief makes them feel better. If people believe in God on the basis of faith, then they will believe other things on the basis of faith. It is only natural. If the method of thinking works in one area, people will use the same method in other areas, particularly when the method is comforting.

But consider the consequences. I would feel better if it were a fact that men are intellectually and emotionally superior to women. The *evidence* on the issue of men's and women's abilities is confusing. Some studies seem to support one conclusion; other studies seem to support the opposite conclusion. So there is no hard evidence one way or the other. Therefore, I will simply *choose* to believe that men are superior. Why? Because it is a very comforting belief. It makes me feel better about myself. This is the way of thinking of people who believe in God on the basis of faith. That idea makes them feel better, so they decide it must be true. But the consequences of this way of thinking are terrible. It leads to sexism. Believing that men are better than women just because it makes me feel better is blatant sexism. Of course it could just as easily lead to racism, superpatriotism, and other forms of chauvinism.

Other consequences of this kind of faith are just as bad. It is very difficult for people to accept responsibility for their actions, especially when they fail or make a mistake or do something wrong. Guilt, shame, and embarrassment are painful feelings, and everyone wants to avoid them. How easy it is to simply deny the charges. "I didn't want to do it. The system made me do it!" "I was out of my mind. I didn't know what I was doing." "The pressure from work was so intense that I had no choice but to lie." "Hey, she had it coming to her anyway." How easy it is to believe in one's own innocence, when the belief is so comforting and soothing to the conscience. The evidence may be inconclusive. It is very difficult to know why someone did something, even oneself. It is often difficult to know for sure what was right and what was wrong.

But the belief in one's innocence is sometimes a sham and a lie. Having faith because it makes one feel better is a bad way of thinking. Denying responsibility is not only false in many cases, but it also creates bad feelings among others, it sets a bad example, and it makes it easier to do even worse things in the future. If more and more people think this way, then in the long run, it will undermine society.

It comes from the practice of believing something because the belief makes one feel better. Beliefs should be based on evidence, not comfort. Our beliefs are supposed to be about the world as it really is. That is what beliefs are. Therefore, we must make every effort to find out exactly what the world is like. We do that by observing, analyzing, experimenting, and collecting information, not by obeying authorities, massaging our own egos, or letting our fantasies run wild. The consequences of basing any beliefs on faith would be disastrous.

Key Concepts

faith	authority	consequences
evidence	comfort	chauvinism

Critical Questions

1. How does the essay define "faith"? How does it define "evidence"? Can you make up an example of each?
2. Why do people have faith, in the questioner's opinion?
3. What are the consequences of trusting authorities, according to the essay?
4. Do you think accepting the authority of one's religion really would lead to the results described? Don't we all accept and believe scientific authorities?
5. How would faith lead to sexism and racism, according to the questioner?
6. Where exactly do the questioner and the believer disagree? Does a questioner think we can understand the things a believer says we cannot understand?

Methods and Techniques

CONSEQUENCES

Let's focus on the second essay for the moment. It tries to persuade you to accept a certain point of view, a thesis. The thesis is that people should not have faith in God or anything else. How does it try to get you to agree? Well, since it is a philosophical essay it tries to offer good reasons to support the thesis. Remember that if you offer reasons to believe something or do something then you are making an *argument*, in the philosophers' sense of "argument."

The essay uses a type of argument that is very common. It says you ought not to have faith, and the reason is that having faith leads to slavish obedience to authorities and stereotypical thinking. In other words, having faith leads to bad consequences. You have seen the same type of argument many times before. Some people say we ought not to show violent programs on TV. The reason is that violence on TV leads to real fighting and shooting among people who watch the violent programs. Or people say we ought not to smoke, because smoking leads to lung cancer. Your mother told you that you shouldn't leave the milk on the table all night because it will spoil. All these arguments have the same form. They try to persuade you not to do something. And their reason is that doing it leads to bad consequences. The *form* of the argument is the same in each case, even though the *content* is different.

Here is another example. A controversial topic today is euthanasia, or "mercy killing." Some people say that doctors should not help patients with terminal illnesses to die, because that would lead to terrible consequences. Once we take that first step, they say, then doctors or hospitals might want to put to death old people who are still healthy, or retarded people, or handicapped people. And that result would be horrible for society. This argument has the same form as the others. It tries to persuade you not to do something (i.e., encourage euthanasia). The reason is that doing it leads to bad consequences.

I said earlier that a big part of philosophy is the study of arguments. As you read the essays in this book you will begin to recognize the writers' arguments—their conclusions and the reasons they give to support them. And you will also begin to see *types* of arguments, that is, arguments with the same form. In other words, one philosopher might be writing about God, and another might be writing about the best society. Their conclusions and reasons will be different, since the subjects are different. But they might still use the same type of argument. The two arguments might have the same form, just as the arguments about violence, lung cancer, spoiled milk, and euthanasia all have the same form. Learning to recognize the form of an argument will help you analyze and evaluate a writer's position.

The argument in the second essay is the same type as the other examples. We can call it the "negative consequences" argument. Now the interesting question about an argument is "Is it convincing?" Should I accept the conclusion? Are the reasons strong enough to support the conclusion? Philosophers consider several factors in deciding whether or not to accept an argument, but the most important is the *truth* of the reasons. Before an argument can be convincing, the premises must be true. (Remember that reasons are also called "premises.") So, should you smoke? It depends on whether or not smoking really does lead to lung cancer. If smoking *does* have fatal consequences, then you shouldn't smoke. Should TV show violent programs? It depends on whether or not violent programs really do lead to violent behavior by those who watch.

Thus when you see a negative consequences argument, you should ask, "Does the action really lead to bad consequences?" (You probably think this way already, but it helps to be more self-conscious and methodical in your thinking.) How do you know whether smoking leads to lung cancer? How does anyone know? The best way is to find examples. If there are many examples where a person smoked, and the smoking caused the person to get lung cancer, then you can say that smoking leads to lung cancer. If there are many examples where watching violent programs on TV caused a person to commit acts of violence himself, then you can say violence on TV leads to violence in reality. (Of course, it is difficult to prove that watching TV *caused* the violent behavior.)

Finding examples is easy in some cases. Leaving milk on the table overnight really does lead to spoiled milk. I have done it myself. In other cases it is more difficult. Can we find examples of euthanasia leading to the killing of handicapped people? I don't know. You would have to do some research on medical practices around the world and throughout history. The practice of euthanasia is rare, so it is difficult to know whether the premise is true. If the premise is *not* true, then it is not a reason to accept the conclusion at all.

However, trying to evaluate a negative consequences argument can get more complicated. People who use this type of argument can modify the argument slightly to avoid the problem of proving their premise. For example, opponents of euthanasia can say that euthanasia *might* lead to the killing of handicapped people. It is *possible* that euthanasia will have terrible consequences. These consequences are so bad that we should avoid anything that even might produce them. So we should avoid euthanasia.

We could modify the smoking argument in the same way. If we did, the premise would be "It is possible that smoking leads to lung cancer," and the conclusion would still be "You should not smoke." The premise supports the conclusion because you want to keep the risk of getting lung cancer as low as possible. Now is this modified premise true? It is easier to find evidence that smoking *might* lead to lung cancer than it is to find evidence that smoking *does* lead to lung cancer. There are enough examples of people who smoke and who have lung cancer to make the modified premise believable.

What lessons can you learn from all this? Well, you should see that there is a structure common to many of the disputes and controversies you hear about. Philosophers and other people very often use a certain type of argument to convince you to believe them. (I called it the "negative consequences argument," but the name isn't important.) Second, you should see that judging the argument requires you to think carefully. It isn't so easy to decide whether or not the premises are true. And I hope you have learned that you can monitor your own thinking. Even though you encounter this type of argument all the time, you can improve your decisions and your judgment by becoming more aware of how you think. If you don't pay attention to your own thinking, it will be easy for you to make mistakes, keep bad habits, and be misled.

Understanding the Dilemma

BELIEVER OR QUESTIONER?

The essays in this section represent a fundamental contrast between two ways of thinking. The believer says his belief in God is not based on evidence; it is not rationally justified, as the beliefs in protons or dinosaurs are. The believer is acting on the general principle that we should accept some statements like "God exists" even though we have no evidence for them. Not everything is rational or explicable. In contrast, the questioner says that no one should accept beliefs on the basis of faith. That attitude will lead to very bad consequences. For example, people who believe without evidence could become overly obedient to authorities, could lose their ability to think for themselves, or could fall into stereotypical thinking because it makes them feel better. The questioner's principle is that a person should not believe something unless he or she has good evidence for it.

This is one big difference between believers and questioners: believers think that some things are beyond human comprehension. Questioners think that, sooner or later, we can find evidence to help us understand everything we can think about. But there is another difference. Let's suppose the believers are right when they say some things are beyond comprehension. Let's suppose that we have no reason whatsoever to accept either side in the debate about immortality; it is just unknowable. Then what do we do? A believer says we should *choose* the answer we want to believe. Since the two answers are equally acceptable, we can pick either one. But a questioner has a different view. If we have no good reason to accept one answer over another, then we should not accept *either* answer. We should suspend judgment until we understand the situation better.

Who is right, the believer or the questioner? Is faith a reasonable attempt to deal with a difficult, mysterious world? Does it answer questions and solve problems in the only way available? Or is faith a childish refusal to accept reality? Does faith lead to conformity, intolerance, and delusion?

Your answer to these questions depends on your confidence in human beings' abilities. If you believe we are capable of understanding the world and our place in it, through our own intellectual efforts, then you are a questioner. If you think human beings cannot understand ultimate matters by our own efforts, then you are a believer. Your answer also depends on how strongly you think we need answers. Believers want answers very badly, and in the face of conflicting evidence, they choose an answer. Questioners say that on some questions we must simply wait until we learn more. Until then, we do not have any answer.

BELIEVER

1. Faith is courageous and admirable.
2. Reality is more complex and deeper than the human mind can ever comprehend, and yet we can have opinions about things we do not understand.
3. I can separate the areas where I have faith from the areas where I look for evidence.
4. I *feel* that some things are true, and that is good enough for me.

QUESTIONER

5. The world is lawful and organized, and we can understand it.
6. Choosing beliefs for no reason is just prejudice and wishful thinking masquerading as philosophy.
7. A person who believes one thing on the basis of faith will soon believe other things on the basis of faith.
8. Hoping that something is true does not make it true, and my choices cannot make God exist.

FOR FURTHER STUDY

Historical Examples

BELIEVER: William James. "The Will to Believe." In *The Will to Believe and Other Essays*. Dover, 1956. Originally published in 1897. In this famous essay, James argues that if we cannot know the answer to an important question, and several answers are possible, then we should choose one answer and believe it.

QUESTIONER: Plato. *The Apology of Socrates*. Many editions. Fourth century B.C.E. Socrates said, "The unexamined life is not worth living." He tried to understand justice, courage, and wisdom, and refused to accept the conventional, superficial answers, even when his continual questioning endangered his life. He does not reject faith in exactly the same way as the questioner in the second essay, but he does defend a persistent and thorough reliance on reason.

OTHER SOURCES

Michael Peterson, et al. *Reason and Religious Belief: An Introduction to the Philosophy of Religion*. Oxford University Press, 1991. Clear, readable; argues for a compromise between believer and questioner.

John Hick. *The Philosophy of Religion*, 4th Edition. Prentice-Hall, 1990. Subtle, sophisticated responses to the questioner.

Baruch A. Brody. *Readings in the Philosophy of Religion: An Analytic Approach*, 2nd Edition. Prentice-Hall, 1990. Brody's book contains James' essay, as well as a famous contrary view: "The Ethics of Belief," by W.K. Clifford. Clifford is a questioner.

Hans Küng. *Does God Exist? An Answer for Today*. Trans. Edward Quinn. Crossroad Press, 1991 (1980). Chaps. 1–3 are a discussion of modern philosophers' ideas about faith.

David Cook. *Thinking about Faith: An Introductory Guide to Philosophy and Religion*. Zondervan, 1986. Simple discussion, from a Christian perspective.

Sidney Hook, ed. *Religious Experience and Truth*. New York University Press, 1961. Short articles by modern philosophers.

Ian G. Barbour. *Issues in Science and Religion*. Prentice-Hall, 1966. Discusses the methods of science, the methods of religion, and the consequences for religion of the latest discoveries in physics and biology.

Patrick Sherry, ed. *Philosophers on Religion*. Geoffrey Chapman, 1987. Short selections by great philosophers, from ancient Greece to the twentieth century.

Current Controversy

1.6 Is Buddhism Philosophy?
Buddhist or Specialist?

———————————————————•———————————————————

Tablets from ancient Mesopotamia reveal that in Sumeria five thousand years ago people speculated about the nature of the universe, our place in it, and the best way of life. Probably in the very earliest human societies people asked profound questions and searched for answers. But around 600 B.C.E., in ancient Greece, some men began giving new kinds of answers to the age-old questions, and debating the merits of their different answers. The Greeks called the creation and analysis of these new answers "philosophy," the love of wisdom.

Before 600, people had proposed religious answers to their questions. The invention of philosophy marked a turning point in Western civilization. How were the new philosophical answers different from the old religious answers?

That is an interesting question, but it isn't easy to answer. It is part of a larger question: what is the difference between religion and philosophy?

Are some ideas inherently religious ideas, and some philosophical? For example, the early religions used myths, or stories, to try to explain the nature of the world and our place in it. But stories aren't necessarily religious. Historians and even scientists tell stories as well. Religious myths are about supernatural beings who can cause storms with their breath or create living beings from mud. However, fairy tales are also stories about supernatural beings, but they aren't religious. Religious stories are about gods and goddesses, but philosophers talk about gods or God, and ask whether anyone can prove that God exists, among other things. While it isn't controversial to say that religion and philosophy are different, any attempt to explain the difference is controversial. Any attempt to explain what religion and philosophy are is controversial.

At about the same time that the Greeks were inventing philosophy, Siddhartha Gautama was proposing a new set of ideas and practices in India that grew into Buddhism. Buddhism is normally classified as a religion, but in some basic respects it is different from other religions and similar to philosophy. Examining the fundamental ideas of Buddhism forces us to ask whether it is a religion or a philosophy. Is philosophy a Western invention, like the symphony, geometry, and the assembly line? Or is it a universal human activity, like music, government, and agriculture? Even though "philosophy" is a Greek word, Asian societies could have invented their own versions of philosophy. But it is also possible that they never did, and produced only various types of religion. Could Buddhism be both? Or are religion and philosophy different from each other?

The first essay in this section argues that the Buddha's teachings are different from religious beliefs, and so Buddhism should be considered philosophy. The second essay claims that the difference between religion and philosophy is not a matter of beliefs but of attitudes. It is useful to keep the two outlooks separate, so the second writer could be called a specialist.

YES: BUDDHIST

"The Philosophy of Buddhism"

When I was in college I met an interesting woman in the cafeteria and we talked for a while. When she learned that I was thinking of majoring in philosophy, she said "I love philosophy! Alan Watts' *The Way of Zen* is one of my favorite books." At the time I smiled because I believed she had made a simple mistake. Zen Buddhism is religion, not philosophy, I thought. Since then I have changed my mind. I have learned more about Eastern thought and Buddhism in particular, and now I agree with my friend. Buddhism is philosophy, not religion.

It is impossible to summarize something as large and complex as Buddhism in a few words, but perhaps I can indicate some of the main ideas. Buddhism began with Siddhartha Gautama, who was born in the foothills of the Himalayas in Nepal in 563 B.C.E. Siddhartha's father was the ruler of the district, and by surrounding Siddhartha with servants and pleasant sights he hoped to shelter him from the pain and frustration of the world. But one day Siddhartha left the palace grounds to visit the nearby town, and he saw what Buddhists call the four signs: an old man, a sick man, a corpse, and a monk. He learned that people change and decline, that our bodies fail, and that everyone dies. He also learned how some try to reconcile themselves to these realities.

Siddhartha was so transformed by his experience that he decided to leave the comfortable life of the palace and seek wisdom wherever he could find it. He went to respected teachers and studied the ancient Hindu scriptures with them. But he decided that books and scholarship were not bringing him the wisdom he sought. He then turned to the path of the holy monks, who wandered from village to village with their begging bowl, and tried to rise above earthly pleasure and pain by fasting and disciplining the body. After the most rigorous self-denial, and at the point of starvation, Siddhartha decided he was no wiser than he had been, so he gave up the monks' way of life.

He sat under a tree and vowed that he would not move until he found genuine wisdom. After forty-nine days of profound meditation, according to the legend, he had penetrated through layer after layer of illusion to the deepest heart of reality. He had discovered the secret of our existence. The central truth of Buddhism is that *the self does not exist.* We have various perceptions, thoughts, feelings, and desires, but they change continually, and there is no "self" that holds them all together. The ego that everyone cares for so much is actually an illusion. All the working and striving and hopes and struggles for "myself" are completely futile and in vain. There is no satisfaction and peace in ordinary life because there is no stable self to satisfy.

Siddhartha discovered that no one is separate from reality. We are all integral parts of the world, and the world changes constantly, like the water in a river, or the colors of a sunset. But everyone wants to be separate and special, and everyone wants to be fixed and defined for all time. The conflict between those normal human desires and the fundamental nature of reality produces the basic quality of our lives: yearning, dissatisfaction, suffering. Siddhartha summed up his discovery in "the four noble truths."

1. Life is suffering and pain.
2. The cause of suffering is greed, or the desire to possess things, to enlarge and feed the self.
3. By understanding that the self is an illusion we can give up desire and escape from suffering and dissatisfaction.
4. The way to achieve a real, complete understanding is to follow the eight-fold path.

The eight-fold path describes the way a person should live to overcome the unhappiness of existence. The eight rules are

1. right understanding or view
2. right purpose or intention
3. right speech or conversation
4. right conduct or behavior
5. right livelihood or work
6. right effort or persistence
7. right awareness or mindfulness
8. right meditation or concentration

The first two rules concern the way one thinks, the next three concern the way one acts, and the last three concern the way one grows spiritually. By following these rules diligently, a person can understand the secret of existence fully, with more than mere intellectual comprehension. This deeper kind of understanding is called enlightenment, or "nirvana," which means "extinguished." By realizing that the self is an illusion, a person can extinguish the desire and egotism that cause dissatisfaction and achieve a state of calm, peaceful harmony with reality. When Siddhartha achieved enlightenment or nirvana, he became the Buddha, which means "the enlightened one."

Buddhism has developed and spread for thousands of years since the Buddha created it. It is practiced by millions of people all over the world, with the strongest representation in India and surrounding countries, Southeast Asia, China, and Japan. Different schools have emphasized different aspects, but the four noble truths and the goal of enlightenment are its core.

Traditionally people have called Buddhism a religion, but I believe it is really closer to philosophy, for three main reasons. First, Buddhists do not believe in God or gods. The Tibetan Dalai Lama, one of the foremost teachers in Buddhism, says that Buddhists are atheists. Therefore Buddhism is in a category different from Christianity, Hinduism, tribal religions, Islam, or any other major religion, where worshiping God or the gods is the primary focus. The Buddha taught profound truths about the nature of reality, but they are different from the stories of creation or nature spirits taught by religions. (In fact, the Buddhist view of reality is closer to modern physicists' ideas; see Fritjof Capra, *The Tao of Physics*.)

It's true that many fantastic legends and stories have grown up among some followers about the Buddha and his life—stories of demons and miraculous events—but the Buddha himself did not teach such things, and they are not part of the essential core of Buddhism. Buddhism is not a religion because it does not include supernatural elements.

The second reason that Buddhism is a philosophy is that a Buddhist's goal is enlightenment, not salvation. Enlightenment means understanding self and world, and the change in one's feelings and behavior that comes from the deepest kind of understanding. The main obstacle to enlightenment is ignorance and illusion. Through learning and meditation, one can achieve enlightenment here and now. Contrast this view with religion's emphasis on salvation and sin. A Muslim's or Christian's goal is heaven and union with God after death. A

Hindu's goal is release from the cycle of rebirth and union with Brahma. The primary means of achieving salvation is devotion, obedience to God, or loving kindness. That is, the greater emphasis is on the way one lives and acts, rather than on the way one thinks and understands. Indeed, many religions say that their truths cannot be understood by finite minds at all. Moreover, the main obstacle to salvation is sin and committing evil, not confusion as in Buddhism. Buddhism encompasses thinking, feeling, acting, and meditating, but the starting point is "right thinking." It is an intellectual philosophy, which extends to one's feelings and actions.

Of course religions value truth and belief, but the truths that religions propound are revealed, sacred truths. They are written in scriptures or uttered by holy prophets, and humbly believed by worshipers. They have an unquestionable authority. But Buddhism does not encourage obedience to authority, or faith. When the Buddha died, his last words were "Work with diligence. Be lamps unto yourselves. Betake yourselves to no external refuge. Look not for refuge to anyone beside yourself. Hold fast to the Truth as to a lamp" (Ross, 1980, p. 36). Buddhists believe the four noble truths, not because the Buddha taught them, but because they have tested them and found them to be true in their own experience. Enlightenment comes from one's own efforts, not from faith or grace or authority.

The third major difference between Buddhism and religion is Buddhism's doctrine of no self. Buddhists say we are aware of ideas, emotions, wishes, and other conscious experiences, but not aware of any additional "self." The Buddha compared the self to a chariot. A chariot is a collection of parts in a certain arrangement: wheels, front and sides, beam, harness. "And just as no part of this aggregate can be separated off and called a 'chariot,' so no part of the human creature can be set apart and called 'I'" (ibid., p. 29). If a person can fully grasp the meaning of this truth and take it to heart, then he or she can overcome the pain and suffering of existence and achieve nirvana. Religions, in contrast, preach the importance of the soul. The self or soul is the most important part of a person. Most religions teach that it is immortal, and will reside in some unearthly realm, or perhaps will be reborn in another body. The soul may need to be cleansed or purified, but it definitely exists. In ancient Egyptian religion, the gods weighed one's soul on a balance with a feather, and if the soul was heavy with sins, one would be denied entry into the afterlife. The Buddhist view is a sophisticated philosophical theory that runs counter to religion's emphasis on the soul.

In Asia people do not make a sharp distinction between religion and philosophy, so the claim that Buddhism is a philosophy doesn't surprise anyone there. But Western philosophers like to draw lines and put things in boxes. They object to classifying Buddhism as philosophy for several reasons. First, the Buddha taught that everyone will be reborn into a new life, and one's next life depends on the law of karma, that is, the law that goodness will lead to goodness and evil will lead to evil. To Westerners, this sounds like a mystical, religious belief. The doctrine raised questions even in the Buddha's own day. If the self is an illusion, people asked, how can one be reborn into a new life? What is reborn? Perhaps the best answer is that the Buddha was using the commonly accepted Hindu belief of his time and place to express his own metaphysical doctrine that a person is identical with all of reality. Since there is no "I" separate from everything else, a future person will be as much "I" as the person here and now that I call "I."

When confronted with questions like this the Buddha refused to answer. He said that if a man has been shot with a poisoned arrow, he shouldn't ask who shot the arrow or what it is made of or from where it was launched. If he tried to answer all those questions, he would die before he found the answers. It is more important to understand the basic truths than to worry about trivial details. Some Western philosophers conclude that Buddhism is anti-intellectual and closer to religion than philosophy. But Buddhists' reply is that the way to truth is not disputation but living and doing and meditating. In that they are similar to other Western philosophers such as the American pragmatists.

Of course Buddhists couldn't care less what label people put on their ideas. And the issue of "philosophy" or "religion," in the narrow sense, is merely a verbal issue. But from a broader perspective, more is at stake. By labeling Buddhism a religion many people dismiss it and do not take it seriously. They see it as another quaint custom or exotic belief from the East. But the term "philosophy" carries prestige in Western society. If people acknowledge that Buddhism is a philosophy, then they might be willing to study it more carefully and recognize its philosophical sophistication and depth. Labeling Buddhism as philosophy may be one more small step toward breaking down barriers and fostering respect among all peoples.

Key Concepts

suffering	no self	eight-fold path
enlightenment	atheism	authority

Critical Questions

1. In your opinion, is it possible to believe that the self does not exist? Is it possible for you to believe that your body is not yours?
2. Why do Buddhists believe that life is full of suffering? Can happiness outweigh suffering in a person's life, according to Buddhists?
3. If a person reads the four noble truths and believes them, is that person enlightened?
4. In your opinion, could Buddhism be a religion even if it does not involve belief in gods? Or is belief in some kind of divinity essential to religion?
5. How is enlightenment different from salvation, according to the Buddhist?
6. Why did the Buddha refuse to answer questions from his disciples about doctrines?

NO: SPECIALIST

"The Difference between Religion and Philosophy"

What is the difference between religion and philosophy? This is an important question because universities and governments and ordinary people treat the two as if they are completely different, and yet at first glance they seem very similar. Religion is concerned with God or the gods, the soul, good and evil, salvation, and belief. But philosophy is concerned with the same things: philosophers think about God and the ultimate nature of reality. They think about the relation between body and mind (or soul), right and wrong, the best way to live, and belief and reasons for believing things. Is there any difference between religion and philosophy?

Religion involves more than ideas. Many religions are based on scriptures or founding prophets. But philosophers study their "sacred" texts, such as Plato's *Republic* or Descartes' *Meditations*, just as carefully as religious people study theirs. Religions are normally organized in communities of like-minded people, such as Roman Catholics or Muslims. But philosophers organize societies devoted to the study of some great thinker, or devoted to the study of some system of ideas. The American Philosophical Association meets regularly, and many smaller societies provide opportunities for like-minded philosophers to share ideas. At these meetings philosophers even perform their "rituals" of reading scholarly papers, and examining "acolytes" (job seekers) to determine their worthiness to enter the profession.

Is Marxism a philosophy or a religion? In his *History of Western Philosophy*, Bertrand Russell points out that Marxism has its founding prophet (Marx), its sacred text (Marx's works), its future paradise (the classless society), its Satan (capitalists), its Church (the International), and even its schisms (the Soviet Union vs. China).

In spite of these similarities, which are more playful than serious, there is a fundamental and important difference between religion and philosophy. But the difference is not easy to describe because it is a difference in attitudes. Religion is based on commitment, whereas philosophy is based on criticism. Religion rests on worship and praise, whereas philosophy requires skepticism, doubt, and scrutiny. Religion begins with powerful emotions of awe, love, humility, and fear, whereas philosophy aims at the clearest possible thought and reasoning, unhindered by personal feelings. Perhaps few people reach perfection in religion or in philosophy, but the ideals are certainly different.

However, it is easy to say that philosophy and religion are very similar or that they are very different. How can one make a persuasive case for one point of view or the other? How can one support a claim about such broad, complex phenomena as religion and philosophy? That question is just as important as the original question about similarities and differences.

Before we can compare two things, we need to have a clear perception of what we are comparing. To show that religion is different from philosophy, one must first explain what religion is and what philosophy is. Probably the best

place to begin is the dictionary. Dictionaries give us a general idea of what people mean when they use the words. Some definitions of "religion" are

1. belief in and worship of God or gods;
2. the expression of humankind's belief in and reverence for a superhuman
   power recognized as the creator and governor of the universe;
3. outward acts or practices of life by which people indicate their recognition
   of and faith in God or gods;
4. any system of belief and worship based on revelation and faith.

These definitions are very general, but they are a start. They emphasize some
kind of divinity as the object of religion, faith or revelation as the means of
knowing about the divinity, worship and reverence as the response to the divinity, and certain practices as the expression of the response. Religious practices include ceremonies, which are "sets of formal acts proper to special occasions, and behavior that follows rigid etiquette," such as christenings and
funerals. And religious practices normally include adherence to moral rules.
   Some definitions of "philosophy" are

1. study of principles underlying conduct, thought, and the nature of the
   universe;
2. study and knowledge of the principles that cause, control, or explain facts
   or events;
3. study of the basic principles of a particular field of knowledge;
4. critique and analysis of fundamental beliefs as they come to be conceptual-
   ized and formulated.

As broad and vague as these definitions are, they do suggest that philosophy
is very different from religion. The objects of philosophy are basic principles
and beliefs, or the assumptions underlying thought and conduct, not divinities.
Philosophers study these principles, and even critique and analyze them; they
do not accept them on faith. These definitions do not mention any emotional
responses or expressions of reverence in ceremonies or philosophical practices.
   The words "religion" and "philosophy" can also be used as adjectives, "religious" and "philosophical." A religious person is "devout, pious, conscientiously exact, scrupulous." "Devout" means "reverent, earnest, sincere." "Pious" means "reverently observant of religion, dutiful, godly, virtuous." A
"philosophical" person is one who is "sensibly composed or calm," or "rational and serene under any circumstances." These additional definitions bring
out the difference between commitment and criticism. Being religious, in other
words, is a matter of being committed, or dedicated, or loyal. Being philosophical means putting aside one's feelings and thinking clearly.
   Where else can we find information about the nature of religion and philosophy? We can read encyclopedias and general books to get more details than
definitions provide. Encyclopedia articles on religion usually include information about particular religions, their histories, beliefs, and practices. So we can
read that Judaism was one of the first religions to emphasize ethical monothe-

ism, the belief in a single God who is just and benevolent; that the word "Islam" means peace through submission to God; that Hindus believe one's soul must be reborn again and again until it is purified; that Jainism forbids its followers to kill any living creature; and so on with other religions. Looking at articles on philosophy, we find descriptions of philosophers and their ideas, as well as accounts of areas and problems of philosophy. One area is metaphysics, the study of the nature of the universe. In metaphysics philosophers ask "What is the world made of, material objects alone, or do immaterial minds exist? Do properties of things, such as redness, exist? Numbers? Gods?" Another area is ethics, the attempt to understand the good life. Philosophers ask "What is the highest good for human beings: happiness, love, duty to the moral law, or something else? How can we know what is good or evil, right or wrong?"

The examples described in encyclopedias reinforce the conclusion that religion and philosophy promote different attitudes. Religion is oriented toward the supernatural, faith, and worship. Philosophy also deals with the nature of reality, the mind, and conduct, but the attitude is inquisitive and critical. Religious people want to believe, whereas philosophers are very reluctant to believe. They ask questions and look for problems.

Another source of information may be even better than dictionaries and encyclopedias. You can go to religious services, talk to devotees of particular religions, and try to enter into the frame of mind of religious people. If you go to a Roman Catholic service, for example, you will probably enter a large cathedral with towering columns, hear somber music, see beautiful stained glass windows and men in magnificent robes, people kneeling in prayer, and perhaps a sculpture of Christ suffering on the cross. If you participate in the service with an open mind and heart, you will begin to appreciate the real nature of religion. The images, stories, prayers, and people will create certain feelings and attitudes within yourself, and those attitudes will give you a better understanding of words like "God," "worship," and "reverence" than any dictionaries or encyclopedias can.

You can do the same with philosophy. If you take classes in a university, or attend a meeting of a philosophical society, you will hear highly abstract arguments for or against some claim. For example, a teacher might discuss the view that all our actions are determined by prior causes, and so we do not have free will. And you might see students or members of the audience raising questions or criticizing the speaker's position. It is all very theoretical and dispassionate. Philosophers have a strong desire to understand, and their disputes might even grow heated, but generally philosophers are "philosophical," i.e., calm and rational. By entering into the discussion, you can understand the desire for clarity and logical reasons that define philosophy. You will grasp philosophy's sense of critical skepticism and perhaps its sense of adventure and the unlimited possibilities opened up by fearless speculation. The attitude is almost exactly the opposite of the religious attitude.

How can we be sure that we have understood the real nature of religion and philosophy, so that we can compare them? It would probably take years of study in both areas, and even then some people may feel more affinity for one or the other. Some people might be biased toward or against religion or philosophy. For example, atheists might say the difference between religion and philosophy is the difference between soft-headed, wishful thinking and mature, objective reason. Or a religious person might say the difference is between a realistic search for answers in a mysterious universe and arrogant, sterile wordplay. Or people might have biased reasons for denying that any differences between religion and philosophy exist. But a sound comparison should be based on an objective view of the two things compared.

The fact that religion is different from philosophy doesn't imply that one is "better" than the other. Everyone needs to be committed to something, and eveyone needs to be critical at times. In fact, the real mistake is to overlook the difference and to think that one attitude or the other is enough. Ironically, recognizing the difference between religion and philosophy allows us to practice both, at different times and toward different objects. But failing to recognize the difference and trying to combine the two attitudes would make it difficult for a person to practice either religion or philosophy very well.

Key Concepts

religion	attitude	commitment	worship
philosophy	criticism	skepticism	bias

Critical Questions

1. What are some ways in which religion and philosophy are similar?
2. What is the difference between them, according to the specialist? Do you agree? Is it an important difference or a minor difference?
3. The definitions in the essay emphasize several aspects of religion. Are any aspects more important than others, in your opinion?
4. Do encyclopedias add anything important to dictionary definitions, or do they only provide illustrations of what we already know from definitions?
5. Do you think the majority of people who attended several religious services would come away with similar beliefs about the nature of religion? Would it make any difference if different people attended services of different religions?
6. The specialist claims that a philosopher can be a religious person. Do you agree? Wouldn't the attitudes come into conflict within himself or herself?

Methods and Techniques

DEFINITIONS

Philosophers are interested in definitions because they want to be as clear and precise as possible. A standard definition is an explanation of the meaning of a word. Definitions are based on usage within a linguistic community. In other words, a definition simply reports what most average speakers mean when they use a word. So writing a dictionary is like taking a sociological survey. The experts who write dictionaries base their definitions on surveys of actual usage, in books, magazines, and newspapers.

Sometimes the meanings of words change, or a word will acquire an additional meaning. For example, the word "gay" is defined as "joyous and lively, light-hearted; or bright and brilliant, as in 'gay colors.'" For centuries when English speakers used the word "gay," that's what they meant. But recently the word has also come to mean "homosexual," and dictionaries have to be revised to report this new, additional meaning.

There are different types of definitions, and the specialist's essay illustrates some of them. A report of the ordinary meaning of a word is called a "lexical definition." A *synonymous* lexical definition simply gives us one or more synonyms for the word defined. For example, "booze" means "liquor." "Genuine" means "authentic, real, not counterfeit." "Bother" means "annoy, pester." In the essay, "religious" is defined as "devout, pious, conscientiously exact, scrupulous."

An *analytic* lexical definition goes farther and breaks down the meaning into parts. It gives us the defining properties of something. The word "glower" means "to stare with sullen anger." The definition breaks down the meaning into three parts: to stare, but with anger, and not furious anger, but sullen anger. "Soul" means "an entity without material reality, regarded as the spiritual part of a person; the moral or emotional nature of man." Thus a soul is a part of a person; it is the spiritual, moral part; and it is immaterial. The specialist in the essay tries to analyze the meaning of the word "religion" into a set of attitudes and feelings toward a divinity, expressed through certain practices. "Philosophy" is analyzed into different attitudes as well.

Another way to define a word is to give examples. If someone asks me what the word "philosopher" means, I might say "Plato, Aristotle, Descartes, Hume, or a person like that." Or if someone asks what "cathedral" means, I might point to pictures of Notre Dame in Paris, Saint Paul's in London, Saint Peter's in Rome, and others. Definitions by example are called "ostensive definitions." They may be more specific and concrete than lexical definitions since they give specific examples, but there is a danger that the learner will not understand the correct meaning of a word. The person looking at pictures of Notre Dame and Saint Peter's might think that "cathedral" means "large, stone building." But in conjunction with lexical definitions, ostensive definitions are useful. The specialist refers to examples described in encyclopedia articles on religion and philosophy to supplement the lexical definitions.

In the next part of the essay, the specialist recommends going to a religious service or a philosophical lecture to understand what the words mean. This involves more than looking at examples. It requires one to do something, to go through certain steps, and see what an activity is like. A definition based on an action one performs is called an "operational definition." Scientists sometimes use operational definitions to define certain concepts. For example, the word "weight" might be defined as "the number you get when you put an object on a standard scale." "Intelligence quotient" means "one's score on a Stanford-Binet test, or another intelligence test." An operational definition does not attempt to isolate defining properties, but says the meaning of a word is whatever results from a certain procedure, so long as the procedure is performed correctly. The specialist claims that "religion" means a set of attitudes, and one way to understand the attitudes is to perform a certain operation (attend a service) and notice the resulting attitudes within oneself.

Definitions usually attempt to explain the meaning of a word on the basis of a survey of ordinary usage. The purpose is to report objectively what people mean when they use the word. But sometimes the person defining a word has strong feelings about whatever the word refers to. For example, someone might define "intelligence quotient" as "an arbitrary number used to exclude people from certain schools and jobs." People may ignore the objective meaning and insert their own positive or negative feelings into their definitions of "Communist," "conservative," "housewife," "Third World country," "technology," and so on. For example, does "technology" mean "the rampant development of machinery and electronics to further isolate people from nature," or is it "the use of science and industry to make our lives better"? When a definition is not an objective report of meaning, but is slanted to influence people's feelings about something, it is called a "persuasive definition."

It's important to distinguish persuasive definitions from emotive words. Some words include positive or negative feelings in the objective meaning of the word. "Harridan" means "a disreputable, shrewish old woman." "Crook" means "dishonest person." These are analytic, lexical definitions, not persuasive definitions. The specialist mentions persuasive definitions of "religion" and "philosophy" near the end of the essay.

Persuasive definitions do not report meanings but create new meanings in an attempt to influence people. Another type of definition that does not report meanings is called a "stipulative definition." Someone can stipulate a meaning for a word used in a special context. Thomas Hobbes was an English philosopher who wrote a book on government called *Leviathan* in 1651. There he said he would use the word "justice" to mean "the performance of covenants," that is, keeping one's agreements. This implies that when people have not made agreements, there is no justice or injustice. Hobbes didn't claim that he was reporting how people normally used the word "justice." He was stipulating a new meaning in the context of his theory of government.

The meanings of words are very important. But philosophers must not only think about the meanings of words. They must also think about the different ways of explaining the meanings of words.

Understanding the Dilemma

BUDDHIST OR SPECIALIST?

The issue in this section is the scope of philosophy. What is philosophy and what isn't? Are Eastern systems like Buddhism philosophy?

The Buddhist in this section claims that Buddhism is closer to philosophy than to religion for three reasons: Buddhists do not believe in God or gods, they seek enlightenment rather than salvation, and they do not believe in an immortal soul. Like philosophers, Buddhists value understanding more than anything, they try to live according to certain principles, and they have profound ideas about reality and human nature.

The specialist in the second essay doesn't explicitly discuss Buddhism, but argues that religion is different from philosophy because religion involves attitudes of commitment, worship, and faith, whereas philosophy requires attitudes of skepticism, questioning, and precision. The specialist would probably claim that Buddhism is closer to religion than to philosophy. So which view is more accurate, the Buddhist's or the specialist's? Is Buddhism philosophy or religion?

The issue is complex because it depends on two difficult questions: what is the essential nature of Buddhism, and what are the essential natures of religion and philosophy? The Buddhist doesn't say there is no difference between religion and philosophy. He or she only says Buddhism is more like philosophy than religion. The Buddhist is assuming that religion involves belief in God or gods, among other things. The specialist does not discuss Buddhism directly. Therefore you have to take the definitions of religion and philosophy in that essay and apply them to Buddhism yourself to see which one fits. The two points of view are connected not so much by what they say explicitly, but by what they imply.

Buddhism is normally classified as a religion, perhaps because Buddhists often behave like followers of other religions. For example, monks and monastic communities are an important part of Buddhism. Buddhist monks lead austere, pure lives, like the monks and nuns of other religions. Buddhists build temples and statues of the Buddha, and go to these holy places to worship and pray. They believe in reincarnation. And while Buddhist scholars develop and extend their ideas, Buddhists are generally not interested in "theological" sophistication or philosophical debates. Indeed, one version of Buddhism—Zen Buddhism—regards rationality and theory as obstacles to enlightenment.

The brief essay on Buddhism could not discuss every aspect of this large movement. And these "religious" practices of Buddhists lead us back to one of our central questions: what is the real nature of Buddhism? The question is difficult partly because of the difference between the Buddha's original teaching and his followers' practices. The Buddha himself did not build statues or pray to them, although later Buddhists have done so. The essay concentrates on the Buddha's original ideas rather than popular practices and beliefs of later followers, and assumes that the founders' ideas define Buddhism.

The specialist, on the other hand, in distinguishing religion and philosophy emphasizes practices and attitudes rather than ideas. Religion and philosophy deal with many of the same ideas, so the difference must lie in the attitudes toward those ideas. Religious people are devout, pious, scrupulously correct, and so on, whereas philosophers are critical, argumentative, and speculative. The actual behavior of Buddhists seems to manifest the religious attitudes rather than the philosophical attitudes.

But Buddhists do not believe in God or the soul. Can Buddhism really be a religion without those ideas? By placing so much emphasis on attitudes, the specialist runs the risk of turning everything into a religion. A person can watch football "religiously" if attitudes are sufficient: he is devoted, scrupulously correct, feels very strongly about it, practices weekly rituals, and so on. But obviously saying a person watches football "religiously" is extending the word "religion" metaphorically. It is not literally a religion. There is no God or afterlife. But there is no God or afterlife in Buddhism either.

Could Buddhism be both religion and philosophy? Could one say the ideas are philosophical but the attitudes are religious? Perhaps, but the specialist concludes by suggesting that philosophy and religion are like oil and water: they do not mix. It is impossible to be worshipful and critical at the same time about the same things. A person can be a religious scientist, for example, but she reserves her religious attitudes for God, the soul, and salvation, and applies her scientific, critical attitudes to chemistry or biology or some science. She can't have a religious attitude toward her test tubes or a scientific attitude toward the soul.

One of the deep, underlying disagreements between the Buddhist and the specialist concerns the nature of understanding or enlightenment. The Buddhist argues that Buddhism is closer to philosophy because Buddhists seek understanding. And the specialist claims that philosophers attempt to understand basic concepts and broad issues. But the two positions seem to disagree about the nature of philosophical understanding. The Buddhist believes a person achieves enlightenment through meditation and examining consciousness itself. One comes to realize that the self is an illusion, and that realization affects one's whole life. But the specialist points to examples of philosophers asking questions, formulating theories, and engaging in debates with others. Understanding comes through collaborative dialogue and explanation, not through solitary introspection. Moreover, philosophical understanding is theoretical. The effects of an explanation on one's emotions or treatment of others is irrelevant to its truth or falsity. The Buddhist and the specialist are making different assumptions about understanding.

This section is about religion and philosophy, two broad, complex phenomena. The differences in perspective between Buddhists and specialists are so numerous and so basic, that it is difficult to compare the two. And yet, developing a worldview involves deciding what you think about religion and philosophy. So, do you find yourself agreeing with the Buddhist, or with the specialist?

BUDDHIST

1. The essence of Buddhism is the four noble truths and the eight-fold path.
2. Buddhism is not a religion because it does not involve a belief in God or gods, the soul, or faith.
3. Buddhists value understanding achieved through one's own efforts, not submission to authority.

4. Eastern philosophy may be different from Western philosophy in some ways, but the two traditions can gain valuable insights from each other.

SPECIALIST

1. While religion and philosophy deal with many of the same topics, the attitudes they promote toward those topics are completely different.
2. Religion involves commitment, worship, faith, and ceremonies, whereas philosophy involves skepticism, questions, criticism, and wonder.
3. We can understand religion and philosophy by studying definitions and examples, and by participating in their activities.
4. Attempting to combine such different outlooks as religion and philosophy will lead only to confusion.

HISTORICAL SOURCES

BUDDHIST: E.A. Burtt, ed. *The Teachings of the Compassionate Buddha.* NAL, 1955. Wide range of brief selections from various sources.

SPECIALIST: A.J. Ayer. *Language, Truth, and Logic.* Gollancz, 1936. Distinguishes between scientific philosophy and soft-headed emotionalism, on the grounds that all meaningful statements must be empirically verifiable.

OTHER SOURCES

Nancy Wilson Ross. *Buddhism: A Way of Life and Thought.* Vintage, 1980. A clear, well-written account of history, doctrines, and current practice.

Ray Billington. *Understanding Eastern Philosophy.* Routledge, 1997. Survey of Hinduism, Buddhism, Taoism, and Confucianism, and in the second half, a comparison of key Eastern ideas with Western counterparts.

David J. Kalupahana. *Buddhist Philosophy: A Historical Analysis.* University Press of Hawaii, 1976. An examination of the concepts of knowledge, causality, morality, and others, as expressed in certain ancient Buddhist texts.

Eliot Deutsch, Ron Bontekoe, eds. *Companion to World Philosophy.* Blackwell, 1997. Includes brief articles on "Buddhist reality and divinity," "The Buddhist concept of self," and "Rationality in Buddhist thought," among others.

Ninian Smart. *World Philosophies.* Routledge, 1999. Broad survey of many different regions, religions, and schools of thought, describing the context, origins, and diversification of Buddhism.

Joel J. Kupperman. *Learning from Asian Philosophy.* Oxford University Press, 1999. Challenging essays on the nature of the self, and ethical choice.

Steven Collins. *Selfless Persons.* Cambridge University Press, 1982. Detailed discussion of many different aspects and interpretations of the Buddhist doctrine of "not-self" for advanced students.

Jean-Francois Revel, Matthieu Ricard. *The Monk and the Philosopher: A Father and Son Discuss the Meaning of Life.* Schocken, 1999. Wide-ranging debate/discussion on science and religion, consciousness, reality, and politics, between a secular French political philosopher and his son, a scientist who converted to Buddhism.

CONNECTIONS

TRANSCENDENTALIST OR NATURALIST?

Chapter 1 raises six very important questions and the contrasting answers that philosophers have given to them. To build your own worldview you should try to decide which answers are the most convincing. They cannot all be correct, and different people might be persuaded by different answers. The answers to these fundamental questions that you can accept will make up your worldview.

Deciding what you believe about these deep issues is not a simple matter. It takes time, reflection, and talks with other people. The answers are all yes or no, but they include more complicated ideas, too. You should think about what an answer means before you decide that you believe it. One helpful way to understand an answer is to look at the alternatives. For example, if you think that you believe God exists, you should understand what it means to believe that there is no God, and vice versa. Knowing what you do *not* believe is part of knowing what you do believe. The opposing essays should help you see the contrasts among possible answers to these questions.

Another way to understand what the answers mean is to think about how you would put them into practice. What difference would it make in your life if you are a theist or an atheist? An abstractionist or a personalist? It would make some difference in how you think about events, about your future, about religion and religious people, and about the natural world. Your choice of an answer might also affect your behavior. For example, a personalist might talk to God, but an abstractionist probably would not.

Many people know what they believe, but they don't know *why* they believe it. They have a flat, simplistic worldview. They have memorized short answers to some questions, but they cannot go farther than reciting their formulaic answers. If you want to build a solid, intricate worldview—a worldview adequate to your own complex experience and intelligence—then you should know why you accept some answers and reject others. You should be able to explain your beliefs and answer questions about them. Developing a well-grounded set of answers is like building a sturdy boat: you have chosen the best design, you have learned how to put the keel, the hull, the rudder, and other parts together, you have attended to all the little details, and now you are confident that the boat will carry you over the waves wherever you want to go. If you don't know why you hold certain beliefs you are like a person desperately clutching a few pieces of driftwood.

The image of building a boat brings us to the point of this section. If you want to build a boat you must fit the pieces together in a way that works. If the boards making the hull do not fit together exactly right, the boat will leak. If the rudder doesn't fit to the stern in the right way, you will go around in circles or zigzag like a drunken sailor. The same applies to your worldview. The different answers you accept must fit together. Otherwise your worldview won't help you, and in fact it will be a constant source of confusion, frustration, and worry for you.

Therefore you should try to understand the *connections* among the answers to the questions in Chapter 1. Some answers fit together better than others. If you are persuaded by one answer to one question, that may be a reason to accept another answer to another question.

In Section 1.1, "Does God Exist?," you read about theism and atheism. Which of the answers in the later sections fit together with theism, and which are more compatible with atheism? Probably the clearest connection is between theism and the survivor, represented in Section 1.4, "Is the Soul Immortal?" Theists believe in a transcendent being, God, who is eternal and all-powerful. Survivors believe that they will survive the death of the body and will continue to exist in a realm beyond the ever-changing natural world. The similarity between these two positions is the belief in a transcendent level of reality. The theist and the survivor both believe in a *supernatural* world, beyond the natural world. The prefix "super" means above, or over, and both God and the afterlife are above or beyond the natural world.

In contrast, atheists believe that the natural world is all there is. Reality is the world of plants and animals, men and women, buildings and machines. It is what we can see, touch, and understand. As we understand more and more, we have no reason to believe in God or the afterlife or any supernatural phenomena. An atheist is similar to a terminator because both deny that there is a transcendent level of reality, above our ordinary experience.

Let's call a person who believes in a supernatural level of reality a "transcendentalist" (because he or she believes there is a reality that "transcends" the everyday world). And we can call a person who believes that reality is what we observe and understand through ordinary experience a "naturalist." With those categories in mind, we can look at the other positions in Chapter 1 to see if they are closer to transcendentalism or naturalism. In other words, the two categories will help us look for connections, similarities and differences, among the different answers. To find connections, we should ask, "Is this answer committed to belief in a supernatural level of reality?" All the answers that say yes come from transcendentalists, and those that say no are naturalists' answers.

In Section 1.3, "Can God Allow Innocent Suffering?," you read about reconcilers and contradictors. Reconcilers believe that a loving, all-powerful God could make his creatures suffer—innocent suffering is compatible with such a God—

whereas contradictors believe that a loving God would not make his creatures suffer. If there were a God who loved us and who could prevent innocent suffering, he would do it. It is clear that a reconciler is more sympathetic with belief in God. A reconciler wants to explain how we can continue to believe in God even in the face of the terrible catastrophes we see all around us. On the other hand, most contradictors say that the fact of suffering should lead us to give up any belief in God. We know suffering occurs, and there is no way to explain how a loving God could allow it. Thus a contradictor is similar to an atheist and a terminator. They are all naturalists. But a reconciler is similar to a theist and a survivor. They are all transcendentalists.

However, these relationships can get complicated. It would be possible to believe in God, but also to accept the contradictor's argument. The way to accept the two beliefs is to deny that innocent suffering ever occurs. It may sound absurd to say that no innocent people ever suffer, but if a person believes the Christian doctrine of original sin, the person may believe that no one is completely innocent. We are all sinners in God's eyes, some people might say. We all deserve the punishments we receive. This person could agree that innocent suffering would contradict the existence of God, if it ever occurred, but it doesn't. But it is probably more common for contradictors to be atheists.

In answer to the question of Section 1.2, "Is God Like Human Beings?," an abstractionist says no, and a personalist says yes. An abstractionist believes that the word "God" refers to the abstract power of love, which courses through all things and creates harmony and unity among all things. A personalist, on the other hand, believes that God is like a parent, with a mind, with thoughts and plans and feelings, except that God is infinitely wiser, stronger, and better than a mortal parent. Both theories are about God, so both are closer to transcendentalism than naturalism.

This is clearer for the personalist than the abstractionist. A personalist says that God has human traits, but magnified far beyond anything we can grasp. God is intelligent, for example, but infinitely intelligent. God is powerful, but vastly more powerful than any natural force. God is both like, and unlike, human beings, and that is one of the mysteries surrounding God's nature.

However, an abstractionist could, just possibly, be a naturalist. It depends on how a person thinks about love. Is love a perfectly natural force, like other human emotions? Is it just gravity (mutual attraction), a force studied by physicists? If so, then an abstractionist is not saying anything that a naturalist would reject, although a naturalist would not call love "God." Or is love a supernatural force, more than merely human, more than merely natural, maybe beyond our comprehension? The essay "God Is Love" says that love is eternal, a moral guide, and all-powerful, and these characteristics go beyond purely natural forces. Its version of abstractionism, therefore, is closer to transcendentalism than naturalism.

The fifth question in Chapter 1, in Section 1.5, is "Is Faith an Answer?" A believer says that no one can know whether or not there is a God, and therefore one answer is just as good as another. The believer chooses the theist's answer. A questioner, on the other hand, argues that choosing answers that we

want to believe, or that authorities tell us to believe, leads to terrible consequences. We should base all our beliefs on evidence and good reasons.

Since a believer believes in God, he or she is a transcendentalist. A questioner's demand for evidence is similar to a naturalist's. Naturalists believe we
can observe the world and reach conclusions about it, based on our observations, i.e., evidence. But notice that while a believer is a transcendentalist, not
all transcendentalists are believers. The two theists in Section 1.1, for example,
give plausible reasons for their belief in God. Their belief is not based on faith
but on evidence, and so they are both questioners, not believers. The same is
true for the survivor and the reconciler. A survivor can be a questioner, and
vice versa.

The current controversy in Section 1.6 is about Buddhism and philosophy,
or religion and philosophy in general. The Buddhist in this section maintains
that Buddhism is closer to philosophy than to religion, because Buddhists do
not believe in God, they hold a philosophical view of the person, and they do
not rely on faith. The contrasting essay by the specialist doesn't discuss Buddhism specifically, but tries to show that religious attitudes are different from
philosophical attitudes.

The specialist is not closer to transcendentalism or to naturalism, but could
go either way. The specialist is discussing the nature of religion and philosophy in general, but is not taking a stand on any of the particular beliefs that religious people or philosophers hold. Perhaps a transcendental realm exists, or
perhaps it doesn't. The specialist is only discussing differences in the ways people think about reality—transcendent or natural.

The Buddhist in this section, on the other hand, is a naturalist. (Like all major religions, Buddhism consists of many different divisions and groups, who
disagree on various points among themselves, and some groups would reject
the version of Buddhism presented here.) The Buddhist does not believe in a
transcendent God or an immortal soul, and does not rely on faith in mysteries
that are beyond our comprehension. According to this interpretation, Buddhism
is primarily a moral doctrine. The spiritual aspect is in the development of
deeper and clearer levels of consciousness. But spiritual growth for a Buddhist
is not a supernatural process dependent upon aid from a transcendent source.

While the connections among different answers are sometimes complicated,
it is safe to say that some of the answers in Chapter 1 are similar and fit together easily, while others are mismatched. We can represent the results with
a chart.

Transcendentalist	**Naturalist**
theist	atheist
abstractionist	contradictor
personalist	terminator
reconciler	questioner
survivor	Buddhist
believer	specialist
specialist	

TRANSCENDENTALIST

1. The world is too vast, complex, and mysterious for us to understand completely.
2. There are many reasons for us to believe in a divine Creator, who is eternal, all-powerful, and good.
3. Human beings have a kinship with the Creator; essentially we are not animals but embodied spirits.
4. There are many ways to reach an understanding of reality, the mind, and truth; science shows us only one limited aspect of truth.

NATURALIST

5. The spectacular progress of science during the past four hundred years shows that science is the best way to understand the world.
6. To anyone who is willing to think, the existence of evil proves that there is no God.
7. Human beings are intelligent animals, biological systems that are born and that cease to function.
8. Believing things on the basis of faith is a dangerous practice, harmful to the individual believer and to society.

CHAPTER TWO

LIBERTY, EQUALITY, AND JUSTICE

2.1 IS SOCIETY BASED ON A CONTRACT?

CONTRACTOR OR ORGANICIST?

———————————————————— • ————————————————————

S ociety is a fascinating thing. Like everyone else, philosophers think about society and try to understand it. They try to look at it as a whole. But what kind of thing is a society? A society is a kind of abstraction. You cannot see it or touch it. It is made up of many individuals, who are not abstractions. Should we think of a society as simply a large number of individuals? Or is it something more?

Sociologists who study society never observe anything but particular individuals. On the basis of their surveys, they make generalizations about society. For example, they may say that America is becoming a more religious society. But what they actually observe is individuals going to church, or people saying that they are religious. They cannot observe a whole society.

On the other hand, societies seem to be more than just collections of individuals. We say that American society is a democracy, it is divided into economic classes, it is growing, it is one of the most violent societies in the world. But an individual is not a democracy, he or she is not divided into classes, and may not be violent. It seems that a society as a whole can have characteristics that individuals do not.

Furthermore, many people believe that society influences the individuals in it. The form of government, the educational institutions, the predominant religion, the economic activity and opportunities, the traditions, and many other aspects of society shape and mold the individuals who grow up and live in that society. If society can cause changes in individuals, it must exist and be a real thing. How can an abstraction exist and cause changes in people?

Philosophers have tried to understand society as a whole, and have divided into two main camps. Some believe that society is a real entity, existing in its own right. Societies have properties of their own, just as an animal has properties different from the properties of the individual cells in its body. Others claim that the basic reality is individuals, and the word "society" simply describes groups of individuals who live and work together. If we want to understand a society, they say, we must look at some particular individuals and their behaviors, thoughts, and feelings. Words like "class," "social role," and "collective consciousness" attempt to give reality to mental constructs that do not objectively exist.

The first essay represents the second view. It claims that society is based on a social contract, and it explains that idea. Since it emphasizes the social contract, we can call anyone with this point of view a contractor. The second essay argues that society has real properties, different from the properties of the individuals who compose it. It suggests that society is like an organism and individuals are like the cells in it. A person with this point of view is an organicist.

YES: CONTRACTOR
"The Social Contract"

In the history of political philosophy, the social contract tradition holds a prominent place. The great founders of the modern outlook, Hobbes, Locke, and Rousseau, were all contract theorists. Today the most widely discussed work in political philosophy, John Rawls' *A Theory of Justice*, employs the idea of a social contract. The theory of the social contract maintains that individuals create society when they agree among themselves to give up certain rights in return for security. The idea of a contract explains how society originated (we all agreed to form one), and why we ought to obey the laws (we all promised).

But a long tradition does not prove that a theory is true. Is this another emperor with no clothes? Another big abstraction that philosophers quarrel over that has no relevance to the real world? It is naive to think that primitive societies suddenly sprang up when some Neanderthals met together in a clearing and agreed to live together. Historically the contract very probably never happened. At the present time the theory may seem to be no more applicable. A citizen of the United States does not enter into a contract with all the other citizens or with the government. I am a citizen, but I never signed a contract. How *could* I make an agreement with all the millions of other citizens?

All of these points, about the past and the present, are well taken. But the theory of a social contract is still useful and valid. The key is to see that it is not a description of actual events at all, past or present, but is a *model* of society. What is a model? A model is a simplified structure, with just a few parts, that is like some other thing, complex and baffling, that we are trying to understand. For example, Niels Bohr said that the solar system could serve as a model of an atom. That is, we can understand an atom if we think of it as a sort of tiny solar system. The nucleus is like the sun, and the electrons are like the planets whirling around it. Everyone understood the solar system and how it worked. Bohr proposed that an atom, which people did not understand, has similar parts, related in similar ways.

The social contract is supposed to be a model of society. Its proponents say we can understand the essential features of society if we think of it *as if* people had entered a contract. A contract is a simplified structure that everyone understands. If Bob and Sue have a contract, then both agree to do something, and expect to get something in return. Bob agrees to work, and Sue agrees to pay him. Or if they are getting a divorce, Bob may agree to give up the house but keep the car, if Sue agrees to give up the car and keep the house.

But how is society like a contract? According to the social contract theorists, the most fundamental feature of society is *compromise*. Society is essentially a matter of give and take, an exchange, or rather many exchanges. Every citizen knows that we must make some sacrifices, and cannot do whatever we want. We must respect the people around us. But we also know that we benefit from the others. They build, farm, heal, teach, protect, and do all the things we cannot do for ourselves. Our relationship to them is like a contract, since we give up something and expect to get something in return. That compromise is the foundation of society, although no one ever actually makes a contract.

The social contract theory tells us what is important about the relations among people in a society. But it does more. It tells us what is important about those people who are related. It tells us about human nature. Think about the people who enter a contract. What kind of individuals must they be? Well, first they must be rational, in the sense that they think about what is good for themselves in the long term and not just the short term. They can control their impulses and therefore make sacrifices now for future gains. And they can think abstractly about benefits that are intangible and won't occur until later, like security and help in a crisis.

The second trait they must have is sociability. They must be cooperative, in the sense that they want to get along with others. They feel that life is better with other people than without. They are willing to trust others, and willing to keep their side of a bargain. Those who enter a contract must be sociable in this sense.

The social contract theory is surely correct in saying that people have these attitudes—they are rational, sociable, and willing to compromise. And it is correct in singling out these attitudes as crucial for understanding the nature of society. It is certainly an improvement over other models of society. For example, in the Middle Ages apologists for monarchs defended a "father and children" model. They wanted to emphasize the authority of the king over his subjects. Later, others offered an "organic" model, according to which society is like a living organism, and individuals are like the head, hands, eyes, and so on. They wanted to emphasize that everyone has a proper role to play, and that individuals should serve the whole society. Individuals exist for the sake of society, as arms and legs exist to serve the whole person. Today we recognize the importance of individuals, and their rationality, sociability, and willingness to compromise.

The real strength of the social contract theory lies in its ability to explain two important points. In highlighting the attitudes involved in making a contract, the theory explains the *origin* of society. It is these attitudes that create society and sustain it. Society grew up gradually, as humans became more rational and sociable and capable of making contracts. Thus the contract theory explains the origins of society by uncovering its foundations in human nature, not by hypothesizing some historical agreement.

The theory also provides a convincing answer to the most important question in political philosophy: Why should citizens obey the law? What makes a government legitimate? The theory says that living in a society and abiding by its laws is like entering a contract. And there are two reasons that people should keep their contracts. First, they have a basic, moral obligation to do what they promise to do. And second, they benefit from the contract. It would be self-defeating to break it.

In a society, citizens should obey the law because they have agreed to give up some of their liberty. They have agreed to accept the restraint of the law.

And they benefit from living in a society with stable laws. They make the sacrifice in order to win this prize in return. So it is in their long-term interest to obey the law.

In other words, we have a self-regarding reason to obey the law, and a purely moral reason. This is a powerful justification of government. When we combine it with the other explanations the social contract theory gives us, we can see why the theory has had such a long, respected career.

Key Concepts

social contract	rational	origin of society
model	sociable	obligation
compromise		

Critical Questions

1. What objections to the contract theory does the contractor mention at the beginning of the essay?
2. The essay says the social contract is a model of society. Can you give another example of a model of something?
3. What is the most fundamental feature of society, according to the essay?
4. How does the social contract theory explain the origin of society?
5. The social contract theory says we have two reasons to obey the law. What are they?
6. In your opinion, does our rationality and sociability create society, or does society create our rationality and sociability?

NO: ORGANICIST

"The Social Organism"

I went to a football game last week, and it opened my eyes to a whole new way of seeing people. The game was fun, but it was the whole experience, especially the crowd, that appeared in a new light. Sitting high in the stadium, I could see thousands of people. They all jumped to their feet together, cheered or booed at the same time, did the wave, and encouraged the team. The spectacle made me realize that the crowd was *real*. It existed, like a huge, dim-witted animal, with joys, angers, fears, and desires of its own. It was more than just a collection of people. It was just as real as the individuals, but different from them. I could see the thing move and change moods with my own eyes, as clearly as I could see my friends sitting beside me.

I first began looking at groups differently when the marching band came out on the field and lined up to spell the words "Go Bears." I had seen bands do this before, but I had never thought about it. Last week it occurred to me that the members of the band could *not* see the words. They might not even know what words they were making. From the point of view of an individual in the band, he or she was simply marching from one yard line to another, watching the person ahead, turning left and right, following instructions. The difference in perspectives was astounding. To me, the band as a whole had definite, observable properties. It had a meaningful shape, the shape of the words "Go Bears." But the properties were not visible to the individuals in the band.

"Is it possible that a whole society is like a marching band," I wondered. Is a society *more* than the individuals in it? Does a society have meaningful properties distinct from the properties of its members, properties that are only visible "from a distance"? If it does, they would be difficult to see, because we cannot "rise above" our own society, the way I could rise above the band by sitting in the stadium. And individuals are so much easier to see that they distract us from larger patterns. But I was intrigued.

After watching the marching band for a while, I began observing the crowd more carefully. The first thing I saw was the wave moving around the stadium. But I could only see it from a distance. If I looked at the individuals near me, all I saw was a person stand up and then sit down. So the crowd was like the band. It had physical properties as a whole, different from the properties of the individuals in it.

Besides shape, the crowd also had more interesting emotional properties. When our team made a long run or a pass, the crowd was thrilled and anxious for the team to do more. When we scored a touchdown, the crowd was almost delirious with joy. And it was proud, confident of winning, and a little contemptuous of the opposing team. But the game went back and forth. When the other side made a gain or a score, the crowd was dejected, confused, and a little angry. I'm not saying that *I* felt these emotions. I'm saying the crowd as a whole felt them. The crowd's emotions were just as real as the words formed by the band. They weren't as easy to see as the words, and it took a little practice to recognize them. In fact, it was the sounds more than the movements that revealed the crowd's feelings. The sounds it made when our team gained yardage were slightly different from the sounds it made when we scored. The difference was subtle, but once I began listening for it, I could hear it. It was just a matter of looking beyond the particular individuals to the properties of the whole group.

In the past I had always seen the crowd as nothing more than a collection of fans, all different from each other. But now I saw that the crowd had a life of its own, a unity, a direction, an identity, beyond the thoughts or emotions of any particular fan or group of fans. The crowd was not the same thing as the individual fans, because the crowd *influenced* the fans. When the crowd was excited I became excited, too. When the crowd felt confident and happy about the prospects of a victory, then I began feeling that way as well. The crowd had an effect on me; it imparted its emotion to me, as it did to everyone else. The energy and optimism were all around me, like the smells in the air I was breathing. It was impossible not to absorb the emotions. Watching the game in the stadium was much more intense and emotional than watching it at home on TV. The game itself was interesting, but it didn't affect me the way the crowd did.

I'm not sure exactly how the crowd was able to influence people's feelings. The combination of dramatic sights and sounds, the fact that each person was completely surrounded, and the feeling of overwhelming power from such a massive beast, all probably contributed to its effectiveness. I also saw another factor. When a couple near us cheered for the opposition, a lot of fans whistled, booed, and yelled things like "Shut up, ya bums," and "Get outa here!" The crowd enforced conformity.

Reflecting on the experience later, I realized that the crowd was a real thing, distinct from the individuals composing it. The crowd's mood was not just the sum of the fans' moods. It was made up of the individual fans' emotions, but it was something more, because it could influence the fans. The crowd had a causal power of its own, which could change the feelings of the individuals sitting in the stadium. It wasn't just an abstraction in my mind, or a generalization, or the totality of the fans. It was a real, different thing. It was created when the fans came together, but it was more than the sum of its parts.

Since the game I have been thinking about this experience, and I decided that there is an important lesson here. I have been reading about sociology, "the science of society," and I am beginning to understand what sociologists say. They say that *society* is a real thing, with its own character, and that it is not reducible to the individuals in it. Societies have "group properties," just as the marching band and the crowd do. It is a distinct entity, in the sense that it can influence and shape its members. Because of the patterns in a society and its organization, it imparts certain values and ways of thinking to its members. For example, most societies have a hierarchical structure, like a pyramid. Some people are ranked "above" others, based on their economic power, political power, military power, age, religious devotion, or something else. If we could sit in a stadium high above a society, and if we could see status relationships as easily as we can see spatial relationships, then the pyramid would be as visible as the words "Go Bears." What's more, the hierarchical pattern of a society strongly influences individuals' goals, their assumptions about other individuals, and their basic beliefs about human nature. It determines what we believe is "natural" and "right."

I hadn't understood the nature of society before now. I "couldn't see the forest for the trees." I couldn't see whole groups and their properties, but could see only individuals and their properties. I was blind because we all have an atomistic bias, in my opinion. We assume that the way to understand something is to take it apart and see how it works, see what it's made of, and reduce it to its fundamental atoms. But that tendency is shortsighted. It prevents us from seeing important aspects of the world, the aspects that only occur when parts come together to form larger wholes. The atomistic bias is partly the result of the prestige of physics and chemistry, which have been very successful in breaking things down into atoms. But it is probably even more the result of the political bias in favor of individualism in our society. People are discouraged from looking at groups and their properties because the individual is sacred in our society. But the political bias doesn't make groups any less real.

There are many examples of systems which have important properties that are not reducible to the properties of their parts. One is language. What kind of thing is a language, such as English? The atomistic bias makes us think that individual speakers and their statements at particular times are the ultimate reality. And that when linguists say, "English usually forms the plural of nouns by adding s," they are simply making a generalization about what English speakers do. But that would be a misperception of language. A language is not just the totality of the statements that individual speakers make. It exists on a different level from the particular persons who speak it. It is distinct from them in the same way that a society is distinct from its members: it influences and shapes the speakers' behavior. People speak as they do because the language requires them to. They have no choice. If someone says, "The farmer owns six cow," his error sounds so strange that people laugh, or at least correct him immediately. Something is applying tremendous pressure on the individual, and everyone else, since a violation of the grammatical rules sounds so absurd and unacceptable. That something is the language. The language is a real thing, over and above individual speakers and statements. It guides the speakers.

A language is distinct from individual speakers in another sense as well. It existed *before* any speakers alive today. English speakers do not create the language. The language came first; individual speakers learn to use it and have to conform to it. It will continue to exist after everyone living today is dead. Latin exists even though no one speaks it. Of course a language is not a physical object. We cannot touch it, as we can touch a person. But it is still real, and not the same as the person or the person's statements.

Societies consist of traditions, customs, unspoken rules, ways of behaving and thinking, and many other structures that are embodied by individuals. Think of all the obvious and subtle ways, internal and external, that Americans are different from Mexicans, Nigerians, Italians, and others. Those ways are reflections of American society. The structure *makes* individuals the way they are. American society makes a person an American, not the other way around. And the whole complex structure remains as individuals come and go.

It's true that if the individuals didn't exist, then their society wouldn't exist either. The society must be embodied in some persons. But it is also true that if the society didn't exist, then the individuals wouldn't exist. If there were no customs, traditions, rules, methods of thinking, moral values, or other social structures, then there would be no individuals. No human beings, that is. Physical organisms might exist in isolation, biologically identical to us, but they would not be human. They would have no language, no morality, no culture, no technology, no human qualities. Individuals depend on society for their existence, and societies depend on individuals. Both are equally real. But for purposes of understanding, the properties of societies are more important.

The best example of a system with group properties is a living organism. In fact the best way to understand the nature of society is to think of it as an organism. An organism, such as a fish or a bird, is made up of many smaller parts: head, tail, stomach, heart, etc. These parts can be divided into even smaller parts, until we get to individual cells. So from one point of view, a bird is a collection of cells. But obviously the bird has important—in fact, absolutely vital—properties that no single cell or group of cells has. The bird is nurturing, skillful, sometimes fearful; it flies, it forages for food, migrates in the winter, and sings to signal its territory. Stomach cells don't hunt, skin cells don't fly, and muscle cells don't sing. If we humans were the size of single cells, and if we lived inside the bird, we might never discover these important truths. We would look at other individual cells, and perhaps observe some common features ("blood cells are either red or white," "muscle cells sometimes contract"), without seeing the true reality.

But when it comes to society, we *are* like individual cells living in a larger organism. Society is the organism, and it has vital properties that affect us all. A society can be nurturing or aggressive, healthy or sick, confident or fearful. That is not to say that some individuals have these properties. The society as a whole can have them, and society is a different thing. It is much more difficult to see the properties of whole societies than it is to see the properties of an individual, especially if we are biased in favor of individuals. But they are certainly real and certainly important.

Key Concepts

society	distinct existence	atomistic bias
group properties	causal influence	organism

Critical Questions

1. What examples of group properties does the essay give? Can you think of any other examples?
2. Why does the organicist say that the football crowd is distinct from the particular fans in the stadium? Would the organicist say that the crowd is "independent" of the fans?
3. What is the atomistic bias?
4. Do you think the Latin language exists? Is it a real part of the world? If it were no longer taught in schools and colleges, would it still exist?
5. Do you think individuals and societies are *equally* dependent on each other? Don't individuals invent and change their societies?
6. In what ways are societies like organisms, according to the essay? Can you think of any important differences between societies and organisms?

Methods and Techniques

MODELS

The first essay describes the contract theory as a *model* of society. The second proposes an organism as the best model of society. Philosophers and scientists—including social scientists—often use models to try to understand things, so it will be useful to examine the idea of a model in more detail.

A model is a simpler, usually smaller, representation of something else. We are all familiar with children's models. Some children assemble wooden or plastic models of ships and planes, or play with models of cars and trucks. Other children play with dolls, which are models of people. Or they play with small representations of tea sets, kitchen utensils, or houses and furniture. Traditionally boys played with one kind of model and girls played with other kinds, but the rigid roles seem to be softening a bit. Actually almost all children's toys are models of one kind or another because children can learn a lot about the real world by practicing with these models. Playing with models is part of the long process of preparing for adulthood.

Philosophers and scientists do exactly the same thing. They build models of various things to try to learn how those things work. For example, engineers want to understand how an airplane flies, so they can make it fly better. An airplane is a very complicated machine, so engineers study different parts of it at different times. One group of engineers may study a part of one wing. They will build a model of the wing (or part of it), and a model of the atmosphere. The model of the atmosphere is called a wind tunnel, and it blows air through the tunnel like the air passing over an airplane when it is flying. They put their wing in the tunnel and study how it behaves in different conditions. It is much easier than trying to study a real airplane in flight.

The purpose of a model is to make a very complex situation simpler. The transportation departments of large cities have models of their public transportation systems. For example, each one has a model of its subway system. The model represents the lines, their intersections, the terminals, and the trains on the lines. They might also represent the passengers as well. The model is much simpler than the real subway system, with its thousands of passengers, hundreds of trains, its stops and starts, its noise and confusion, its electric currents, transit police, vagrants, and so on. The model allows the engineers to see the *main* elements and study those. The engineers must ignore much of the system if they are to understand the basic workings.

A child might have a model train, and could even have a model of the subway system. But it would look very different from the transportation department's model. The department's model would probably consist of lines and electric lights to indicate positions of trains, and perhaps other markers to show speed, number of passengers, and other information. The engineers would not have small trains and cars on little tracks moving from place to place (at least not on duty, but who knows what they do at home?). Why are the two models so different? Because the engineers and the child are interested in different aspects of the world. The child is interested in the way a train *looks*. The engineer is interested in the ways *many* trains *move* over the *whole* system relative to each other. This difference illustrates the fact that we can make different models of the same thing, and they might be equally useful.

When we think of models we usually think of physical replicas. But models can be abstract, too. For example, meteorologists make computer models of hurricanes and other weather patterns. A computer model of a storm is not physical. When a computer models a storm, you might see an image on the computer screen, or you might see only numbers. But the model is not an image. To make a model of a storm, the scientist makes a list of the main factors in the storm, like wind velocity, wind direction, humidity, barometric pressure, temperature, and so on. He also sets down certain rules regulating the relations among the factors. For example, one rule might say that when the temperature increases, the humidity also increases. Or if the barometric pressure increases, then the wind direction tends to be away from the increase. Once the scientist has noted all the factors and all the relations among them, he can manipulate the model to see how it behaves. He can tell the computer to increase the wind velocity by 50 percent, and then see what will happen to all the other factors.

Creating models is exciting and fun, but that is not why scientists do it. They want to understand what they are modeling. So the meteorologist compares the behavior of the model with real storms, to see how accurate the model is. If it is very similar to past storms, then it will allow the meteorologist to *predict* the behavior of future storms. And that is a valuable scientific accomplishment. Moreover, by manipulating the model, the meteorologist may also discover new relationships and new factors that scientists had overlooked before. Thus the real purpose of models is to enable us to understand complex phenomena in ways that we had not understood before.

The weather is a notoriously difficult phenomenon to model and predict. But societies are undoubtedly even more complex than the weather. We need a model of society to make it comprehensible. Or perhaps we need several models of the different parts of a society. Models reduce complex systems to simpler replicas. A contractor suggests that we can understand society in its essence by thinking of it as a contract among people. A contract is something that we all understand, and it is relatively simple. A contractor claims it lays bare the essential structure of society, beneath all the distracting details of individual lives, such as different styles of clothing, different types of work, different ways of relaxing, different beliefs, and different residences.

Is he right? Every model is both similar to and different from the thing modeled. How similar, and is it similar in the right ways? Is an organism a better model of society? In evaluating a model you should ask two questions: are the similarities explanatory and predictive? Are the differences unimportant or irrelevant to the behavior of the thing modeled? You might try to imagine a model of some social situation yourself. How would you model a date? A family meal? A typical class? Can you think of some physical analogue of these situations? (Some people have said two people on a date are like two magnets: the closer they get, the stronger the attraction between them.) Or can you create an abstract model of them? What are the key factors, and what rules govern the relations among the factors? You can test your model by asking the two questions I mentioned about similarities and differences.

Understanding the Dilemma

CONTRACTOR OR ORGANICIST?

Human beings live in groups. We form societies and we are formed by societies. The nature of a society, and the relation between an individual and society, are fundamental, difficult questions. Your perspective on these questions is naturally an important part of your worldview.

The contractor sees society as an artificial structure, created by individuals for their benefit. Individuals come first. It is basic human nature to be rational and cooperative, according to the contractor. All people are similar in this basic respect. These traits then give rise to society. Individuals think about their own interests, and they come together to exchange goods, defend each other, assist each other in producing food, and so on. These interactions are like contracts, although they may not be explicit or even conscious. Beginning with rational individuals, the contractor arrives at a conception of society as a set of cooperative agreements. The agreements are provisional and temporary. Individuals could change them if they wish.

The organicist claims that society is much more important than the contractor allows. In the first place, society is real in a way that the contractor ignores. Societies have properties that individuals do not have. If we make the effort to step outside of our society and look at it as a whole, then we can see features that are not just generalizations about many individuals. The organicist claims that societies are like marching bands or sports crowds, which have their own distinct properties, moods, desires, and tendencies.

But contractors have a different view. They say that the organicists have projected an abstract idea in their minds onto the real world. It's true that a society can be aggressive and interventionist, for example, but that just means that many individuals in that society are aggressive and interventionist. The social property is only a generalization in the observer's mind. It is not a distinct reality.

This disagreement cuts across many philosophical issues. The contractor has a strict standard of what is real, while the organicist has a more inclusive, flexible standard. The contractor believes that reality is made up of individual entities—human beings, trees, words—which have a shape and are located in space, that is, things one can see or touch or hear. The organicist believes reality is more complicated. It includes things that we cannot see or touch. For example, gravitational force. Gravity is not an object located at a particular point in space. It is a different kind of thing. In fact, some philosophers say that if scientific laws exist, then reality includes more than just individual entities. It includes laws, which are not just generalizations in scientists' minds. The organicist also believes that societies exist, over and above the individuals who compose them. If we agree that organisms are real, and have their own distinct properties different from properties of cells, then we can say the same about societies.

The organicist claims that societies are important in a second way. Not only are they as real as individuals, but they also influence and shape individuals. The properties of an individual—including his or her rationality and sociability—depend on the society into which he or she is born. The society comes first; it existed before the individuals who now compose it. And it molds people into the type of individuals who can fit into that society. For example, the society determines the language they speak and think with. It determines what is "rational" and "sociable." One's social class determines one's manners, goals, sense of humor, and so on.

A contractor, in contrast, believes that individuals agree among themselves to form groups. The only interactions are among individuals, not between an individual and a class or society. A contractor would say that we learn a language, of course, but we learn it from our parents, schoolmates, and teachers, not from some abstraction called a "society." We acquire goals and values, but we acquire them from our mother and father, and perhaps a few other authority figures. And when we gain maturity, we begin choosing our values for ourselves. As for rationality and sociability, they are the same everywhere.

This second disagreement, then, is about causation. Should we say that a society can influence a person, or that only other individuals can influence a person? Contractors and organicists answer this question differently.

You should also consider one last difference. To explain why people should obey the law, contractors say it is because they have promised, and because it is in their interest to obey. The organicist represented here doesn't consider that question, but he would probably have a different answer. He says a society is real, and has its own tendencies and interests, just as an organism has interests different from the interests of any particular cells in its body. A society expresses its interests in laws. Therefore, he would probably say that an individual is obligated to obey the law because it expresses something that is greater and more important than the individual. The law expresses the will of the society as a whole, made up of many individuals. The goals and needs of a whole society are obviously more important, more valuable, than the wishes of any single individual. That is why an individual should obey the law.

CONTRACTOR

1. The idea of a contract provides a model for understanding the foundations and structure of society.
2. People and their natural traits—rationality, friendliness—are basic; they create a society.
3. Individuals consider their interests and make agreements with other individuals; that web of agreements is what we call "society."
4. People are obligated to obey the laws of their society because they have implicitly promised to do so, and because it is in their interest to do so.

ORGANICIST

5. Groups have their own properties distinct from the individuals in those groups.
6. Groups are clearly distinct from individuals because groups can influence the individuals within them.
7. Virtually everything about a person is the result of living in his or her society.
8. A society exerts a moral claim on an individual because a whole society is vastly more important than a single individual.

FOR FURTHER STUDY

Historical Examples

CONTRACTOR: John Locke. *Second Treatise on Civil Government*. Many editions. Originally published in 1689. In Locke's version of the contract, rational, independent people enter into an agreement for their convenience, and can suspend the contract if they wish.

ORGANICIST: Emile Durkheim. *The Rules of Sociological Method*. Free Press, 1964. Originally published in 1895. In chap. 1, "What Is a Social Fact?," Durkheim presents his view that social facts are not reducible to individual facts.

OTHER SOURCES

Tom Campbell. *Seven Theories of Human Society*. Oxford University Press, 1981. In each chapter Campbell describes the writer's method, assumptions about human nature, and concept of society, and he adds his own assessment.

David Frisby, Derek Sayer. *Society*. Tavistock, 1986. Chap. 1 is a survey of various conceptions of society.

Michael Lessnoff. *Social Contract*. Humanities, 1986. A historical study of the idea of a social contract.

Ernest Barker. *Social Contract: Essays by Locke, Hume, and Rousseau*. Oxford University Press, 1960. Selections from writings of three famous philosophers who discuss the contract theory.

Thomas Hobbes. *Leviathan*. Macmillan, 1957. Originally published in 1651. Hobbes bases his contract theory on a strictly materialistic, egoistic theory of human nature and morality.

George Sabine. *A History of Political Theory.* Revised by Thomas Thorson. Dryden Press, 1973. The standard historical survey, with chapters on Hobbes, Locke, Rousseau, Marx, and others.

Vernon Pratt. *The Philosophy of the Social Sciences.* Methuen, 1978. A clear discussion of several issues, including the organic conception of society.

Colin Bird. *The Myth of Liberal Individualism.* Cambridge University Press, 1999. A critique of various forms of individualism, which is part of contract theory.

2.2 IS LIBERTY THE HIGHEST SOCIAL VALUE?

LIBERTARIAN OR PATERNALIST?

———————————————————•———————————————————

Most Americans have heard of the fiery speech by Patrick Henry before the Revolution, which he concluded by saying "I know not what course others may take, but as for me, give me liberty or give me death!" It was an inspiring moment. Other revolutionaries actually did sacrifice their lives for the cause of liberty, as have many Americans in the armed forces since then. Americans certainly place a great value on liberty.

But Americans value other things, too. For example, most Americans value religion. The words "In God we trust" are prominently displayed on our money and in our courts. Many parents send their children to religious schools, and others believe public schools should have regular prayers. We also value knowledge and education: a larger percentage of our population goes to college than in any other country. We value democracy and equal participation in our government.

The existence of these different political values raises a vital question: which value is the most important? What is the highest political value? Which value do people care about most, or which value *should* people care about most? Perhaps we can say they are all equally important; none takes precedence over any others. But that easy answer probably won't work in the long run. At some time the different values are going to come into conflict. When they do, we will have to decide which one is more important.

Your own political values are a significant part of your worldview. But how do you decide what you care about most? Is it just a matter of measuring your own feelings? Is it just a statement of preferences, like your taste in music?

Philosophers want a more rational basis for their political values. They want to explain what they value most highly, and why it is more important than other values. They want to have reasons for their views, reasons that might persuade another open-minded person who initially disagrees.

The following essay argues that liberty is indeed the highest political value. In defending the libertarian view, it is not merely expressing a personal feeling, but presenting points that should persuade you to agree. The second essay digs down to a deeper level. It asks what we all mean by "liberty" in the first place and says the answer is not very satisfying. It also claims that Americans value government control more than they admit. If you agree with the second essay, you are a paternalist.

YES: LIBERTARIAN

"Liberty, the Supreme Social Value"

As members of society, we all have certain social values. We all value security, prosperity, equality, justice, liberty, and perhaps other things. We want our society to have those qualities. Social values are not exactly the same as individual values. All of us want certain things for ourselves, but we also want to live in a society of a certain kind. Social values are goals that can be achieved by *groups* rather than single individuals. For example, equality can only exist among a group of people. It is not something a person can possess entirely alone. Justice is a social value because it concerns relations among people. Liberty can be social or individual. We may value individual freedom and, perhaps as a corollary, may value social arrangements that make people in our society free (whether or not we personally benefit).

We all value a variety of social goods, but we believe that the highest social good is *liberty*. That is, we Americans value liberty more than the other social goods. The same is probably true of other societies. It is relatively easy to see the priority of liberty over other values, like justice and equality. We can simply imagine a situation in which we must *choose* between liberty and equality, or liberty and justice, or liberty and some other social value, and ask what choice we would make. In each case, we would choose liberty. So liberty is the highest social value. In addition, there are some social values, such as prosperity, which upon examination turn out to be identical with liberty. There is no conflict between liberty and these "other" values.

Before comparing liberty with each of the other social values, we must clarify our concept of liberty. When we say we value liberty, what exactly are we saying? I think we all mean the same thing: liberty is the ability to make choices and act on them. If you can choose among three different places in which to live, and can then act on your choice, that is, go and live in the place you prefer, then you possess liberty. You are free with respect to places to live. (Freedom and liberty are identical.) The more choices you have, the freer you are. A person who can choose among six colleges to attend has more liberty than a person who has only three options. A person who can choose between attending one particular college or not attending any college has a small degree of freedom. A person who has only one option, that is, who must work rather than attend college, is not free at all with respect to attending college. To say that liberty is a social value is to say that we want to live in a society where the citizens have many choices, and nothing prevents us from acting on our choices.

Do we value liberty, so defined, more highly than other aspects of society? Let's consider them one by one. Take prosperity. Prosperity, for an individual, means wealth. A prosperous person is a person who has a considerable amount of money. As a characteristic of a society, prosperity means many of the citizens of the society have a considerable amount of money.

Which is more important to the well-being of the society, prosperity or liberty? When we put the question this way, we see that it is a false choice. There is no conflict, because prosperity just *is* liberty. More precisely, prosperity is a *means* of achieving liberty. In other words, having money gives a person many options. A person with money can choose among places to live, schools to attend, various entertainments, and other goods. That is why people want money. If money did not give people greater liberty (choices), they wouldn't value it. (That actually happened in the old Soviet Union. The shops were empty. There was nothing to buy, so people did not work to earn money.) Thus the value of money is *derived* from the value of liberty. Therefore liberty is higher on the scale of values than money.

Another social value is security. People want to feel safe. They want to live in a society with as little crime as possible. On the other hand, the absence of security means fear. If people are insecure they must try to protect themselves with heavy locks (or weapons), or must stay at home and never take any risks. So security is certainly a social value. But is it more valuable than liberty? Here again we have a false choice. Security is just a means of achieving liberty. It is like money. A person who feels secure is free to walk in the park at night, accept a ride from a stranger, or make other choices. If an individual feels insecure, the range of options is limited. She or he cannot go out alone at night, cannot go into certain neighborhoods, cannot leave the car unlocked. Insecurity is nothing more than the *loss* of liberty. That is why it is a terrible thing. Thus security is like prosperity. It is valuable, but its value depends on the value of liberty. Security and liberty are like the moon and the sun. The moon is a bright satellite, but its light is reflected from the sun.

The next social value we should consider is equality. The idea of equality is more complex than the idea of prosperity or security. People mean different things when they talk about equality. The two main senses of equality are equality of opportunity and equality of condition. People have equal opportunities if none of them is excluded or held back in any way. For example, the children of a town have equal opportunities to attend school because there are no arbitrary restrictions excluding anyone. People have equal opportunities to shop in all the stores so long as stores welcome all customers. But when we analyze the idea of equality of opportunity, we are led to the same conclusion we reached with security. Equality of opportunity just means liberty. It means no one prevents people from doing what they want to do. There are no arbitrary restrictions placed on people because of their race, religion, gender, political beliefs, or other personal traits. Just as security is the *absence* of threats, so equality of opportunity is the *absence* of arbitrary barriers. Thus each person is free to take advantage of the opportunities society offers. Equality of opportunity is not more or less valuable than liberty, because it is the same thing as liberty.

Equality of opportunity does not ensure equality of success. For example, in a school the students may all have an equal opportunity to play basketball. All are permitted to try out for the team, and no one is denied a chance because of irrelevant factors like hair color or musical ability. With regard to opportunity, all are equally free. But a student who is over six feet tall will have better chances to succeed than a student who is only five feet tall. The taller student has options (playing basketball) that the short student does not have. On the other hand, the short student may have talents that provide options the tall student does not have. Their *success* in different areas will not be the same. But it is still true that they have equal *opportunities*, so long as neither is restricted by irrelevant rules.

Equality of condition is different from equality of opportunity. We can imagine a society in which everyone has the same income. For example, Congress could calculate the average income of all Americans and pass a law saying that every citizen shall receive that amount in wages. No matter what work one does, all workers will receive the average salary, say, thirty thousand dollars per year. Unemployed people would be hired by the government, and other adjustments would be made. Then people's living conditions would all be equal. People would have the same amount to spend on housing, transportation, vacations, and so on. I am not saying this would ever work in practice. I am only saying we can imagine a society where people have equal living conditions.

But how many people would want to live in such a society? In particular, how many people value such equality of conditions more than liberty? I think very few. Americans value the freedom to get ahead, to make a better life for themselves. While a society of equal conditions may be comfortable, and may not have the poverty of our society, still Americans are confident that they can improve their condition, with a little luck and a lot of hard work. If the government proposed to deprive us of that liberty, and impose a strict equality of condition on us, I think it would have a revolution on its hands. Thus when we compare equality and liberty, we see that people place a higher value on liberty.

This is not to say equality is worthless. In fact, Americans pay taxes to support social programs to help the needy. The government provides low-income housing, food stamps, Medicaid, and other services to the poor, to raise their living conditions closer to the level of the middle class. They are not equal to the middle class, but they are more equal. But taxes restrict a person's liberty. A person who pays taxes has less disposable income, and therefore fewer choices, than one who does not pay taxes. So we voluntarily restrict our liberty to promote equality of condition. This seems to show that we value equality *more* than we value liberty.

This conclusion would be mistaken, however, because of the *degrees* of liberty and equality involved. We give up a very small degree of liberty to get a substantial degree of equality. Paying taxes does limit a person's liberty, but not very much. If we did not pay taxes, our lifestyle would not change very much. But social programs for the poor change their lifestyle completely. Without low-income housing, many people would be homeless. And a person living in public housing is much closer (more equal) to the middle class than a person living on the street. In other words, we get a large amount of equality in return for only a small sacrifice of liberty. Thus taxation for social programs shows that we place a greater value on liberty than on equality.

Next let's consider justice, a very important social value. Justice means giving people what they deserve. The paradigm case of justice is the arrest of a suspect, trial in a court of law, and imposition of an appropriate punishment. Or, if the suspect is judged to be innocent, setting the person free. This is the function of the criminal *justice* system, and the concern of the Federal Department of *Justice*. Now is liberty a higher social value than justice in this sense?

This is a complex issue, and we can look at it from an individual point of view and from the point of view of society as a whole. From an individual point of view, it will seem obvious that liberty is more valuable than justice. A person who commits a crime will prefer liberty over just punishment. How many criminals turn themselves in to the police and request that they be sent to jail? Given a choice between liberty and justice (jail), any criminal would choose liberty. This seems to show that people value liberty over justice. But in this case, the individual is only considering herself or himself, not society as a whole. She values her individual liberty over her just treatment. However, we are investigating social values. What kind of society do most people want?

If we think about society as a whole, rather than an individual's self-interest, it seems at first that we all value justice more than liberty. We take away people's liberty so that justice can be served. That is, we put some people in jail because that is what they deserve. We say that if people commit a serious crime, we will take away their liberty, because justice demands it. Hence, in general, justice outweighs liberty in our society.

But I believe this is only one side of the criminal justice system. The other side is its benefits for the majority. Only a small percentage of people are deprived of their liberty. And the result is that the great majority of people have *more* freedom. Taking criminals off the streets, and deterring others from committing crimes, increase the liberty of the other citizens. In fact, that benefit is at least as important as imposing justice on the criminal. Looking at justice from this point of view, it seems that liberty is more important than justice, because we impose justice on a few *for the sake of* greater liberty for the many. Justice serves liberty, so liberty is a higher value. At the very least, they are of equal value as qualities of a society.

But another fact shows that we value liberty over justice. Judges are expected to temper justice with mercy. If a person is a first offender, or if other circumstances warrant it, a judge can set aside strict justice and extend mercy to a defendant. Perhaps a suspended sentence will reform this particular criminal, whereas the just sentence would embitter him. The same is true of parents. Judges and parents use their common sense, and we often admire a merciful judge, even though she or he may be acting contrary to the demands of strict justice. A society where judges are sometimes merciful is a better society, we feel, than one where judges always exact the last ounce of justice from an offender. Now if we favor mercy in some cases, then we are actually advocating *injustice* over justice. Merciful treatment is, technically speaking, unjust, and yet there are times when a judge or a parent should be merciful.

But compare this tolerance of injustice with our attitude toward liberty. We never admire coercion. We never say that constraint is better than freedom. Of course we are speaking about a policy for average citizens. Constraint *is* better for criminals, because constraining criminals increases other people's freedom. But as a general policy for society, we never think that taking away a person's liberty is a good thing. Liberty is always better than coercion. Justice, however, is not always better than injustice, since we sometimes favor mercy. Therefore, on our scale of values liberty ranks higher than justice.

We can sum up the argument with a rhetorical question. Are we prepared to give up our liberties for the sake of X? Whatever we put in the place of X— equality, justice, prosperity—the answer is always no. Liberty is more important than anything.

Key Concepts

liberty	equality of opportunity	justice
prosperity	equality of condition	mercy
security		

Critical Questions

1. Is the libertarian definition of liberty adequate? By this definition, are you free to live on Park Avenue? Are you free to play basketball for the Knicks? Are you free to be a U.S. Senator, or a movie star?
2. Do you agree that money is a means to achieve liberty? Is it valuable *only* because it increases liberty?
3. The libertarian says opportunity means liberty and liberty means options. A tall person and a short person do not have the same options with respect to basketball. Yet the libertarian says they have equal opportunities. Isn't this a contradiction?
4. Citizens are forced to pay taxes (i.e., their liberty is restricted) to help poorer people to be more equal to the middle class. Why doesn't this show that our society values equality more than liberty, according to the essay?

5. Some citizens are deprived of their liberty completely (i.e., put in jail), because justice demands it. Why doesn't this show that our society values justice more than liberty, according to the essay?

6. Has the essay convinced you that you value liberty more than anything? If you had the power, would you sacrifice Americans' liberty for the sake of greater equality? For the sake of justice?

NO: PATERNALIST

"Empty Phrases"

A cliché is an expression that has been used so often that it has become a formula, or signal, rather than a meaningful, informative description. Examples are "as quiet as a mouse," "so hungry I could eat a horse," "he blew his top," "her heart soared," "in the national interest." Clichés are a lazy person's substitutes for observation or thought.

Some ideas are like clichés. They perform the same function in people's thinking as clichés perform in their writing. They are flattened, simplified ideas that everyone accepts automatically, but no one really examines. I would like to call your attention to one such platitude, and ask you to step back and think about it carefully and critically. I was forced to think about it myself on my recent visit to America.

The idea is this: "In a free country, a person should be allowed to do anything he (or she) wants, so long as he doesn't hurt anyone." This is known as "the harm principle." I would wager that most Americans *say* they accept this idea, as do many others around the world. You probably subscribe to it yourself. But I doubt very much that anyone could explain what the idea means in any detail. And while Americans universally praise the principle, their practice is quite different.

In particular, what does that ordinary little word "hurt" mean in this statement? When does one person hurt another? Is it when one physically damages another? Certainly one person hurts another if he gives the other a black eye, or knocks her down. If that is what "hurt" means, then the harm principle states that people should be allowed to do anything they want, so long as they don't physically damage another person.

But surely no one believes such a thing, because it would allow a person to imprison others, to force them to do things by threatening them, to steal their property, to burn down buildings, and to do other terrible things. Stealing and imprisoning do not physically damage the victims, but they should be outlawed. Therefore, this explanation of the idea allows far too much freedom.

Instead of saying "hurt" means physically damage, perhaps one can say it means *psychologically* damage. To damage someone psychologically is to cause mental pain, or emotional discomfort, or to make someone feel miserable. Now the idea is that people should be allowed to do anything they want, so long as they don't cause someone to feel miserable.

But this explanation makes the principle too restrictive. It doesn't allow enough freedom. It says a person should be forcibly prevented from making someone feel miserable. If a love affair goes sour, and the woman feels miserable, then the man could be put in jail! He was free up to the point that he hurt his lover, in the sense that he psychologically damaged her. Society may legitimately prevent him from causing emotional distress, and put him in jail as punishment for doing it. At least according to this interpretation of the idea, it may.

But this is absurd. One person's political or religious opinions may be very upsetting to other people. A person's outlandish behavior or revealing, sexy clothes may cause psychological pain in others. Bad grades may make a student miserable. But the Americans who accept the harm principle say they do not want to regulate the opinions people may have or the clothes they may wear. Whereas the physical explanation of "hurt" allowed too much freedom, this psychological explanation does not allow enough.

You may think that we are embroiled in semantics. Perhaps a society can find some way to implement the principle, without finally deciding on a strict definition of harm. But how can the principle be implemented? Who decides when someone has been harmed? Does the alleged victim decide? If the principle is implemented that way, anyone with any complaint can claim he or she has been harmed and demand legal redress. Does the alleged perpetrator decide? Then no one would ever harm anyone else. No one would decide that he or she was guilty.

The most obvious solution is to allow the *majority* in the society to decide when someone has been harmed. But notice that this "solution" is completely empty. The whole purpose of the harm principle is to extend liberty to *minorities*, to allow unusual people, unorthodox people, eccentric people, to do or say whatever they wish. The idea is to allow any behavior, including strange, bizarre, even upsetting behavior, so long as it doesn't hurt anyone. If the comfortable majority decides who has been harmed, it will suppress the people whom the principle is intended to protect.

What other explanation of the idea can its supporters offer? Probably none. I doubt that it can be explained in any useful way. It is too nebulous and vague. The problem is not that the principle is *wrong*. Rather, the problem is that it doesn't really say anything, but only seems to. It provides no real guidelines on what people should and should not be allowed to do. It is merely a mental cliché.

Not only is the harm principle empty, but most Americans are not willing to support it, however it is interpreted. They only *think* they are. Americans think that they value liberty, but actually they do not. Actually they feel much more comfortable with conformity, strict rules, moralism and public piety, a sheeplike docility. The harm principle says a person should be free to do anything he wishes, so long as he doesn't hurt anyone else. But Americans insist on imposing the majority's moral views on everyone. In America, am I free to buy and take heroin? Cocaine? No, I am not, even though taking drugs harms only myself. It is argued that someone addicted to drugs is likely to steal to support the habit. But that is certainly not always true. If I am rich, then I do not need to steal. Why not allow rich people to buy drugs?

Even if someone steals, the state can punish a person for that. Stealing does harm other people, so it should not be allowed. But buying drugs is not equivalent to stealing. If we begin to outlaw behaviors that may *lead* to crime, then we will outlaw advertising, walking by oneself at night, wearing jewelry in public, handling large amounts of money in a bank, and any number of other innocent activities.

Why do Americans forbid anyone to take recreational drugs? Because Americans, at heart, are Puritans and cannot tolerate what they regard as immorality in other people. In every state but one, prostitution is illegal. But no one is harmed by prostitution. Some say prostitution is "degrading" to the woman, but that is a moral judgment. The prostitute voluntarily sells herself. The customer voluntarily buys her services. The risk of disease is high, it is true, but that is because society will not allow prostitutes to set up an ordinary business, with health insurance, regular examinations, and so on. The real objection to prostitution is a moral objection. Americans ignore the harm principle when it interferes with the majority's moral opinions.

If you believe these kinds of laws are exceptions, just consider the latest example of official moralism. Many colleges and universities have adopted "speech codes" regulating what students may and may not say. A student may not utter anything deemed to be "offensive" to anyone else. In particular, a student may not say anything that might upset a member of some minority, such as blacks, Native Americans, Latinos, immigrants, homosexuals, handicapped people (the "physically challenged"), overweight people, women (women are included among minorities), Muslims, Jews, Buddhists, Hindus, or any other group. If a student tells a crude joke about one of these groups, he or she can be expelled from the school. No one can seriously claim that the joke actually *harms* anyone in the minority. In reality, the authorities are trying to legislate morality. They believe they can force students to conform to their own moral rules, even in speech and thought.

One can easily find many other examples of legally enforced morality. Communities decide what is obscene, and usually decide that a bare-breasted waitress is obscene. Even private clubs—a hallowed British institution—are sources of controversy in America. Apparently the official endorsement of equality is so strong that associating with one's friends in a private, relaxed setting is a grievous assault on those who cannot afford membership or those whom the club wishes to avoid. If a private club refuses to admit women or others, it is sure to be sued.

I do not want to give the impression that anything goes. Every society must have standards of moral conduct that it requires its members to meet. But the harm principle is not a viable standard, and societies should not be utterly hypocritical about their practice. Americans have a long history of attempting to enforce moral standards upon every member of society. Prohibition is only the most famous episode. The curious thing is that they insist that they really value freedom and tolerance and the harm principle.

Key Concepts

cliché   physically damage   speech code

psychologically damage   victimless crime   paternalism

Critical Questions

1. What is a cliché, and what are some additional examples of clichés?
2. What two interpretations of "hurt" does the essay consider?
3. Do you accept the harm principle? Can you explain when it applies and when it doesn't (i.e., when one person hurts another)? If you cannot, then can you still say you accept the principle?
4. Do you agree that taking someone's property, or threatening him, or imprisoning him, does not cause physical damage?
5. Consider this: One person hurts another when he makes the other miserable, *except* in those cases in which the victim voluntarily does something (e.g., falls in love) knowing that it might make him miserable. In those cases, the first person cannot be punished. Does this save the psychological interpretation?
6. Do you think all drugs should be legal? Prostitution? Available to people under age 18?
7. It is illegal in most states to drive without a seat belt. Is this law designed to prevent one person from harming another, or to prevent a person from harming himself? In your opinion, should the government force citizens to do what is good for themselves?

Methods and Techniques

GOALS

The two essays in this section illustrate an important problem-solving technique. Everyone, including doctors, engineers, business people, and housewives, tries to solve problems. Effective people—people who get things done—think in terms of problems and solutions, whatever their occupation. Philosophers are no different. The specific problems philosophers face may be different, but they try to define problems and find solutions for them. Furthermore, the standard techniques for solving problems are similar in all fields.

One of the first things problem solvers do is make a list of their goals. A doctor's goals may be to learn all the symptoms or complaints that a patient has, learn about the patient's lifestyle and diet, and then find the most likely cause of the patient's symptoms. A businesswoman's goals for one month may be to keep her customers satisfied, to find two new clients, and to train her new employee. Or a person may simply look in the kitchen and decide he needs groceries. His goals then are to go to the store and buy milk, bread, cheese, fish, and bananas. Setting goals is an important first step of problem solving, whatever you are doing.

Philosophers use this technique in trying to understand society. Societies set goals just as individuals do. Usually the government states a society's goals for the long term and the short term. For example, in the State of the Union message that the President delivers to Congress every year, he might say that the nation should be committed to improving American schools, reducing unemployment, and helping the millions of people with no health insurance. In the long term, he may say that the main goal is to preserve people's freedom from a stifling, intrusive government (if he is a Republican).

But obviously people disagree about the goals their society should have. For example, Democrats may respond that the foremost goal of our society should be to ensure that all citizens, regardless of race, gender, social class, or other factors, have opportunities to develop their fullest potential. Sometimes the disagreements over goals are basic and irreconcilable. Philosophers try to uncover and describe the basic goals of a society, and to decide which goals are better. What *should* our long-term goals be?

But more often the disagreements are not basic. Instead, people disagree over *priorities*. That is, they disagree over which goal is most important. For example, both Republicans and Democrats agree that government should not intrude into our private lives, and that all people should have opportunities. But they disagree over which goal is more important. Which goal demands more of our resources, or which should we try to achieve first? This leads to the second step in this problem-solving technique. After a problem solver has made a list of goals, he or she must *rank* the goals in order of priority. Which goal comes first, which second, which third, and so on? Priority can mean first in time (i.e., the goal one should work on first), or it can mean first in importance (i.e., the goal one wants to achieve more than any of the others). For example, a grocery shopper who has a list of five items to buy (five goals) but only three dollars to spend, must decide which item is most important, which second, and so on.

The first essay is an example of both steps. First it lists the goals our society has. But the main purpose of the essay is to rank the goals, and in particular, to show that liberty is the most important. And it offers a technique for ranking goals. It goes through the list two by two, comparing two goals and asking which of these two is more important. It argues that every time we compare liberty with another goal on the list, we see that liberty is more important. This technique could work with any list of goals.

The second essay is an example of a third step in this problem-solving technique. In trying to choose goals and rank them, it is very important to have a clear idea of exactly what the goal is. One should try to describe the goal as concretely as possible. One cannot reach a goal, or even pursue it, if one isn't sure what the goal is. For example, the goal of buying milk may seem perfectly clear. But if you send your daughter to the store to buy milk, and she sees skim milk, whole milk, two percent milk, and other choices, she will be confused. If such a simple goal can be confusing, then society's goals will be extremely difficult to describe adequately. The second essay shows just how difficult it is to explain what "liberty" means.

Understanding the Dilemma

LIBERTARIAN OR PATERNALIST?

The issues of political philosophy are probably more confusing and difficult than issues in other areas of philosophy. One reason is that the terms are not standardized; different people mean different things by the terms "liberty," "equality," "justice," and so on. Another reason is that there is less agreement about the facts in political philosophy. For example, what are the actual consequences of social programs like welfare? People disagree. And the issues are more interconnected than in other areas. Your beliefs about liberty are inseparable from your beliefs about equality, about justice, and about other questions.

Nevertheless, you should try to sort out your own beliefs about society and the way it should be organized. The topic of this section is liberty. Is it the most valuable benefit of living in a society? Or are other things even more valuable than liberty? A libertarian believes that nothing is more important than liberty. The first essay, representing the libertarian point of view, compares liberty with other social goods, and tries to show in each case that they do not outweigh liberty. It claims that several goods, like security, prosperity, and equality of opportunity, are actually the same thing as liberty.

Not everyone agrees that liberty is the highest social value. Some people think that the members of society should be compelled to do some things, such as fight in a war, even if that means they must give up some of their liberty. Others (like Plato) have argued that the majority should obey an enlightened, superior minority. They are better off following their leaders than exercising their own free judgment. A paternalist is a person who believes that the government should care for people like a wise father. (The word "paternalist" comes from the Latin word for father.) Thus Plato was a paternalist.

The second essay, representing the paternalist point of view, claims that most Americans give lip service to liberty, but they are actually paternalists themselves. It gives some examples of laws that suggest that the government knows what is best for an individual better than the individual himself or herself. You must wear a helmet on a motorcycle, wear your seat belt in your car, swim only when a lifeguard is present, contribute to social security to provide for your old age, and accept life support systems even when you are terminally ill and would like to die. In all these cases, the government restricts people's freedom "for their own good," because people are not capable of choosing what is best for themselves. It also describes cases where the government restricts people's liberty because citizens are immoral, even though the government admits that the immoral activities do not harm anyone. For example, prostitution is a crime because it is immoral, not because it harms people. Should the government protect ordinary people from themselves? Should the government promote the majority's moral values? A paternalist says yes and a libertarian says no.

Liberty is a very complex idea, and it leads to many controversies. One of the difficulties in deciding between the libertarian and the paternalist is that they cannot agree on what liberty means. The second essay shows how difficult it is to determine exactly when people are exercising their liberty, and when they are harming someone else. The most adamant libertarian does not believe people should be free to harm others against their will. But when does a person harm others? It isn't easy to say.

Disputes about liberty frequently arise over its *extent*. That is, who should be free? If everyone should be free, then should everyone have the same *degree* of freedom? If you believe that everyone should be equally free, then you must favor a large role for government, to provide people with the means to make choices—in housing, in occupations, in lifestyle, and so on. In other words, a strong belief in liberty for all may seem to lead to a belief in government regulation of people's lives. In particular, many people believe that the free market actually makes only a few people free, and restricts many others. If liberty really is valuable, then the government must restrain some people's economic activities (with taxes) to extend liberty to more people.

Neither essay in this section discusses the question of how we can promote liberty. Both address the deeper questions "What is liberty," and "Is liberty more valuable than anything else?" The disputes about how to promote liberty depend on these deeper questions. We cannot promote liberty until we know what it is, and we should not promote it until we are sure that it is more valuable than other social goods.

So this section boils down to two main questions: can a libertarian define liberty, and explain the limits on it (i.e., when a person harms another); and is individual liberty really more valuable than security and morality? A libertarian answers both questions yes, and a paternalist answers both questions no.

LIBERTARIAN

1. Liberty means having options, having real choices that one can act on, without interference from others.
2. A life of servitude, a life without liberty, is not worth living.
3. Almost all the other social goods, like security, prosperity, and equality of opportunity, are actually the same things as liberty.
4. Government can increase some people's liberty by reducing other people's liberty, but it cannot increase everyone's liberty.

PATERNALIST

5. We will never agree on how much freedom people should have, because we cannot know when a person has abused his or her liberty by harming someone else.
6. Most people do not want much liberty; they would rather let experts, supervisors, and bureaucrats make important decisions about their lives.

7. The highest social value is moral stability, and government must restrict liberty to encourage moral behavior.
8. Government makes people's lives better in many ways they aren't even aware of.

FOR FURTHER STUDY

Historical Examples

LIBERTARIAN: John Stuart Mill. *On Liberty.* Many editions. Originally published in 1859. Mill defends the famous "harm principle," and argues for complete freedom of thought and speech.

PATERNALIST: Edmund Burke. *Reflections on the Revolution in France.* Many editions. Originally published in 1792. Burke criticizes the ideals of the French Revolution, including individual liberty, equality, and innovation in politics. He believes people should rely on custom and tradition.

OTHER SOURCES

Burton M. Leiser. *Liberty, Justice, and Morals: Contemporary Value Conflicts.* 2nd Edition. Macmillan, 1979. Clear survey of many issues, easier to read than most other accounts.

Joel Feinberg. *Social Philosophy.* Prentice-Hall, 1973. Careful analysis of many social issues, including Mill's position on liberty.

Barrington Moore. *Authority and Inequality under Capitalism and Socialism.* Clarendon Press, 1987. A comparison of the institutions of authority and the resulting inequality in the United States, the Soviet Union, and China.

Milton Friedman, Rose Friedman. *Free to Choose.* Harcourt Brace Jovanovich, 1980. A defense of maximum individual freedom and minimal government in American society.

John Kleinig. *Paternalism.* Rowman and Allenheld, 1983. A cautious defense of paternalism in some areas of social life.

Rolf Sartorius, ed. *Paternalism.* University of Minnesota Press, 1983. Advanced articles analyzing different aspects of paternalism.

D.D. Raphael. *Problems of Political Philosophy.* 2nd Edition. Humanities, 1990. Chap. 3 is a discussion on an abstract level of liberty and its limits.

H.L.A. Hart. *Law, Liberty, and Morality.* Stanford University Press, 1963. Argues that the government should not try to enforce morality through law.

2.3 IS EQUALITY THE HIGHEST SOCIAL VALUE?

EGALITARIAN OR ELITIST?

———————————————————————•———————————————————————

In thinking about equality, we can ask a number of questions. Perhaps the most basic one is this: Are all people equal? Some say yes, some say no. Obviously the answer depends on what we mean by "equal." In many ways people in America clearly are not equal. And that leads to another basic question: *Should* all people be equal? Some say equality is the most important political value.

Equality, like liberty, was an important idea in the American Revolution. Thomas Jefferson wrote the Declaration of Independence to explain and justify the Revolution, and he listed the principles that guided the colonists. It is noteworthy that he placed equality first. He wrote, "We hold these truths to be self-evident: that all men are created equal; that they are endowed by their Creator with certain unalienable rights; that among these are life, liberty, and the pursuit of happiness." Jefferson not only states that people are in fact equal, but he also puts equality before liberty and other basic rights.

Even if Jefferson is right, and people are equal in some sense, he would have to admit that in other ways people in America are not equal. For example, some people have large amounts of money and others have much less money. So we still must ask ourselves, "Should all people be equal?" Jefferson is talking about human nature. Perhaps all human beings have the same basic nature, and we are all equal in that sense. But in political philosophy, the more pertinent question is, "Should people be equal?" because that is a question about how we organize society. We have no control over human nature, but it is up to us to decide how much social equality people should have.

Both of the following essays discuss equality. The first argues that making people more equal would bring about tremendous benefits in our society. The second claims that we would all be better off if we recognized the differences among people.

YES: EGALITARIAN

"Society and Property"

Sir Thomas More was the Lord Chancellor of England for several years during the reign of Henry VIII (1509–1547). He was a devout Catholic, and refused to sign a declaration stating that Henry, not the Pope, was the head of the Church of England. For this stand on principle, he had his head chopped off. But More is also famous because of a book he wrote in 1516 describing his vision of the ideal society. The book is called *Utopia*—"No Place"—and the society is ideal because it does not contain the source of most of the troubles in the world, namely, private property.

I would like to describe the main features of this ideal society, and then consider some of the reasons people give for saying it could never work. I do not think any of the reasons are conclusive, and so, as far as I can see, More is right. We ought to organize society communistically.

In More's book a character named Raphael describes the island society of Utopia, which he visited on his voyages in the South Seas. The government is a representative democracy. But the really distinctive feature of the society is that no one owns any private property. All the goods that people produce are stored in shops distributed around the island. "When the head of a household needs anything for himself or his family, he just goes to one of these shops and asks for it," writes More.[1] Food, clothing, tools, and other items are freely available to everyone. There is no need for money. Housing is free. "The houses themselves are allocated by lot, and changed round every ten years" (p. 73).

The standard objection to this system is that if goods are freely available, no one will work. But in Utopia, everyone is required to work. "The chief business of the Stywards [elected representatives]—in fact, practically their only business—is to see that nobody sits around doing nothing, but that everyone gets on with his job" (pp. 75–76). So people are legally required to work. But each person works less in Utopia than his counterpart in other societies.

> And you'll understand why it is, if you reckon up how large a proportion of the population in other countries is totally unemployed. First you have practically all the women—that gives you nearly fifty percent for a start. . . . Then there are all the priests. . . . Add all the rich. . . . Finally throw in all the beggars who are perfectly hale and hearty. (p. 77)

Furthermore, in Utopia, people produce only necessary, useful goods. They waste no time on frivolous luxuries like jewelry, furs, or banquets. Eliminating these costly and useless items reduces the workload for everyone.

By instituting these simple rules—no private property, everyone works, no expensive status symbols—the Utopians produced some marvelous consequences, according to More. First, there is no poverty, homelessness, or unemployment in their society. Obviously no one is poor because basic necessities are provided free of charge. No one is unemployed because everyone must work. Second, if there is no private property, then there will be very little crime. There would be no reason to steal, because one can easily get whatever one needs. Third, people would not be as anxious, tense, and fearful as they are now. Ask yourself this: what is your greatest fear? What do you worry about more than anything else? For most people, the answer is money and their job. But in Utopia economic insecurity does not exist. Everyone is guaranteed that his or her basic needs will be met. This is also relevant to crime. In our society it is people who live under the constant strain and pressure of poverty that commit "crimes of passion." Their anger boils over. But the pressure is removed in Utopia, so those kinds of crimes would occur far less often.

Fourth, the conflicts and anger between the rich and the poor, the haves and the have-nots, would disappear. People would not blame each other for society's problems. We could all live much more harmoniously with each other. Finally, people could develop all of their potential, and develop all sides of their personality, since they would have more free time. A person would spend less time working to produce consumer goods, and so would have more time to devote to individual interests—games, sports, hobbies, learning, socializing, or just relaxing. At least More believes these five results would follow from the abolition of private property. And he may be right.

People have been proposing ideal communistic societies since the invention of writing in ancient Egypt, and other people have always said it will never work. The critics point to five main problems. But it seems to me that More has a reasonable answer for each criticism.

PROBLEM 1. "People are lazy. If they know they can get whatever they need, they will not work."

Answer: More says that, if necessary, people will be forced to work. However, he does not think that will be necessary, because people are naturally active; they prefer to work rather than do nothing all day. Try to imagine what you would do. Suppose you won the lottery. You now have plenty of money. What would you do? Would you sit on a beach for twelve hours at a stretch? Stay in bed all day? No, you would find some meaningful, challenging work to do.

In Utopia people are not competing against each other for jobs. They are not jealous of someone's possessions. Instead, they all realize that they are working together for everyone's benefit. So they want to work for their neighbors and friends, because they care about each other.

PROBLEM 2. "Without private property, people would all be alike. No one would develop any individuality."

Answer: In Utopia people actually have *more* free time, and less worry about making money. They are free to develop their individuality. It is actually in our society that people spend all their time trying to make money and have no time to express their unique differences, or even to find out who they are. In addition, the Utopians realize that true individuality does not mean buying a blue car rather than a red car. True individuality does not depend on the particular clothes one buys. Individuality depends on a person's ideas, the unusual experiences she or he seeks out, and the ability to express oneself. It depends on imagination and the courage to follow your dreams, not the jewelry you wear. In fact, it is in our society that people have lost their individuality. Just go to an average business meeting. Businessmen and -women all look (and think) exactly alike. Or look at suburbia. People all buy the same gadgets and all watch the same shallow entertainment on TV. Where is the individuality in our society?

PROBLEM 3. "Utopia is too restrictive. In order to provide everyone with everything they need, people will have to work when they don't want to work, and will have to accept the goods society provides."

Answer: But if people learn to relate to each other as fellow citizens, instead of competitors, then they will want to work, since that benefits everybody. The sacrifices in liberty and variety of goods available are worth making, because the benefits are so great. What is the point of having leisure time if the society we live in is wrecked and dangerous? What is the point of having a gold chain if you are afraid to wear it?

PROBLEM 4. "People do not want equality. People buy expensive jewelry, designer clothing, or fancy cars, not because they think those things are more durable, reliable, or useful, but because those things make them feel superior to other people."

Answer: That might be true in most societies, but it does not *have* to be true. People do not have an inborn need to feel superior to others; they can learn to regard others as equals, with equal possessions. People can be different, as they are in Utopia, but still equal. People can feel proud of their accomplishments, without feeling that another person is a failure. In fact, I can feel that I did a better job than my neighbor, without feeling that I am a better person.

PROBLEM 5. "Equality might be possible. The problem with equality is not that it is difficult to achieve, but that we *ought not* to achieve it. It would be unjust, because different people make different contributions to society, and they ought to be rewarded in proportion to their contribution."

Answer: But in Utopia all jobs are essential. No one is doing unnecessary, useless things. Since everyone's work is essential, everyone's work is equally valuable and respectable. Everyone is entitled to the same rewards.

Why do lawyers or doctors make ten or twenty times as much as garbage collectors? Do doctors work harder? I don't think so. Lifting garbage all day is hard work. Are doctors' services more essential? No. We would not last long without garbage collection. Do doctors earn so much because they went to medical school for four years beyond college? But they wanted to go to school, and enjoyed learning. Why does doing what they wanted to do, and getting extra education, entitle them to so much money? It doesn't. Doctors' work is essential to society, but so is garbage collectors' work, and nurses' and teachers' and cooks'. People who are equally necessary for society should get equal pay. People whose work is not necessary should do something that is necessary.

These are the main criticisms of communism, and one can see that More has persuasive replies to each criticism. So why don't we set up a communistic society? There are two answers. One is that we ought to. The elimination of poverty, crime, worry, and class conflict, and the growth of individuality, are all desirable.

If we were rational we would adopt More's program. But we are not rational. The second answer is that we do not adopt it because of our insane desire to feel superior to our neighbor, and our even more insane method of achieving this feeling by trying to buy more goods than our neighbor. Perhaps if more people learn about the alternatives to this insanity, society will change. Let's hope so.

Key Concepts

utopia	communism	individuality
equality	social problems	essential to society

Critical Questions

1. Why would people work less in Utopia than in other societies?
2. Do you think that the main problems in modern society are poverty, crime, conflict between social classes, and anxiety? Has More overlooked any serious social problem? Are all these problems caused by private property?
3. In Utopia there are no luxuries. What does More mean by "luxury"? How would you define the term?
4. If people had fewer choices in the clothes, furniture, and food they could buy, but had more free time, would that increase or decrease individuality, in your opinion?
5. Do you think most people want to feel superior to their neighbors? If so, is the desire innate and ineradicable, or is it learned?
6. Do you think a sanitation worker should earn as much as a lawyer? Should a doctor earn ten or twenty times as much as a school teacher? If everyone's work is essential, then should everyone receive the same rewards?

NO: ELITIST

"What Elitists Believe"

For some people the word "elitist" is a dirty word. If someone is an elitist, then, automatically, he or she is not welcome in polite society. But many people who use the word as a term of abuse probably could not explain exactly what it means. Unfortunately, this situation is common in political philosophy. People hurl words at each other without taking the time to define their terms and principles calmly and rationally. I would like to try to explain what the word "elitist" means. And I will explain why I am an elitist.

An elitist has three beliefs that make him or her an elitist. First, an elitist believes that there is such a thing as excellence. For any job, there is a good way to do it and a poor way to do it. There is also the very best way to do it, and that is excellence. For example, an automobile salesperson's job is to sell cars. An excellent salesperson sells more cars than most other sales people. A secretary's job is to type, file documents, make appointments, and help an office run smoothly. An excellent secretary performs all these tasks very well: typing quickly with few errors, filing efficiently, and always avoiding scheduling conflicts.

Being a secretary and selling cars are occupations, but excellence exists in almost all activities. There are excellent poker players, excellent swimmers, excellent public speakers, and excellent gardeners. In fact, any time that people have some goal that they are trying to reach, excellence exists. There is an efficient way to reach the goal and an inefficient way, whether the goal is running an office, repairing a machine, replacing a kidney, teaching a class, or something else. Excellence means reaching the goal in the highest degree—for example, growing the most and the best vegetables—or reaching the goal with the least effort, or at the lowest cost, or in the shortest time, or in another efficient way.

Sometimes people do things just to relax, and then excellence doesn't apply. For example, a person may enjoy whistling. He doesn't care if anyone recognizes the tune or not. His only goal is to enjoy himself, and as long as he does that, his whistling is fine. Excellence doesn't apply. In other cases people do not agree on a goal. In dining, for example, one person may like spicy food and another may like bland food. When they go to restaurants they have different goals. Therefore, they will not be able to agree on an excellent cook. Literary critics may not agree on the excellence of an author because they have different, personal standards.

But most of the time, when we pursue a goal it is an objective goal about which many people agree. A doctor's goal is to cure her patients, and everyone knows when she has cured a patient's pneumonia and when she hasn't. As for reaching the goal most efficiently, or in the highest degree, in the least time, at the lowest cost and so on, we rely on other experts. Her fellow doctors can judge her performance and can recognize excellence. The same applies to other activities.

Elitists believe that excellence exists and is important. We also hold a second belief. We believe that for almost any job, some people will be better at it than others. Some people will be better secretaries than others. Some will be better mathematicians than others, some will be better swimmers, better marriage counselors, better auto mechanics. To say one person is better at a job than another is to say that one person achieves a higher degree of excellence than the other.

Let me state this belief more precisely. Obviously a professional auto mechanic with ten years of experience will be better at repairing cars than a novice. Elitists believe that even when many people have the same training for a job, some will be better at it than others. For example, if a group of high school seniors takes a course in auto mechanics, at the end of the course some will be better mechanics than others. If a group of college freshmen takes a lab course in chemistry, at the end of the course some will be better chemists than others. The training need not be formal education. If some grandchildren spend the summer with their grandparents on the farm, at the end of the summer some children will be better gardeners than others.

People are different. Some people are interested in auto mechanics and some aren't. Some people enjoy working with chemicals, beakers, and formulas, and others don't. Interest and enjoyment probably depend on ability. Some people learn certain things faster than others learn them, and continue to make progress at a faster rate. For example, when the grandparents tell their grandchildren how to distinguish weeds from vegetables, some kids catch on faster than others. They are ready to learn new things, while the others are still trying to recognize weeds.

Elitists believe that some people will be better at a task than others because we see it happening around us all the time, in the classroom, at the workplace, and on the playground. When people try things, some achieve excellence and others do not. Of course not everyone can recognize excellence in every field. I would not be able to distinguish an excellent chemist from an average chemist. But people with experience in chemistry can. They can even spot youngsters who have the potential to be excellent chemists. They can see the attention to detail, the extreme precision, the careful record keeping, the curiosity, and the understanding of the principles behind the messy experiments in the lab. Professional sports teams rely on scouts to spot potentially excellent ball players, and the scouts' predictions are very reliable. Differences in abilities are a fact of life.

Thus when elitists say that excellence exists, and that some people will be better at a job than others, we are being realistic. We are recognizing facts. The third belief that elitists have is not about facts but about policy. What should we as a society *do* about these facts? Elitists believe that our society should *encourage* people to do what they can do well. Society should offer incentives to channel people into careers and activities for which they have talent.

Our goal should be to find talent and to nourish it. As a first step, we should make a great effort to help people discover what they can do well and what they can't. For example, beginning in the early grades and continuing through high school, students should be encouraged to try all sorts of activities, in science, in writing, in the arts, in sports, in mechanical activities, clerical work, student government, debate, peer counseling, and so on. Good teachers can evaluate students' performances in these areas. A writing teacher can recognize an excellent writer and an experienced advisor can recognize a student's leadership skills in student government.

As a second step, we should offer incentives to guide people into the activities where they can excel. The most obvious kind of incentive is a scholarship for more training. If a student demonstrates talent in chemistry, for example, she should receive an award from the government to help her pursue her studies in college. If she is an excellent debater, she should receive a scholarship to encourage her to develop her talent, in law, or teaching, or journalism. Another kind of incentive is an internship. Students should be allowed to acquire on-the-job experience, in a bank, in a hospital, in an office, and elsewhere to discover their abilities. Furthermore, some jobs require very rare talents. It is difficult to find people who can do them well. For the most important and difficult jobs, we should offer the largest incentives, in the form of awards and social status.

If we adopted the policy of channeling people into jobs they can do well, everyone would benefit. A society in which the essential jobs are performed by people who can do them *well* is clearly more productive and better organized than a society in which the jobs are performed by people who cannot excel at their job, but who are better at something else. For any job or activity, there is an "elite" group of people who can excel at that job. Consequently, people like me are called "elitists," not because we believe we are better than anyone, but because we believe it is common sense to try to match people with the jobs they can do well, and try to avoid having people in jobs they cannot do well.

Not only would society as a whole benefit tremendously from this policy, but individuals would be happier as well. People who do what they are good at are happier than those who try to do something they cannot do well. For example, suppose a young man decides that he has to be a doctor, although what he really enjoys and excels in is business. This individual will have to struggle, he will be frustrated, and he will feel inferior to his peers and colleagues who can excel in science and medicine. He would have been happier doing what he can do well.

It is not difficult to discover what people can do well and what they can't. The difficulty is admitting the facts when we see them. Parents, mainly, refuse to admit that their child is average in most areas, and has a talent for something like clerical work or mechanical activities. Many parents want their children to be something like a brain surgeon or a famous musician. Our society cannot accept failure. If the child fails in some area, parents and others insist that schools provide more training and more "opportunities," over and over again. They assume that everyone can be excellent at every job, and if a person fails it must be due to the training and not the trainee. Elitists are more realistic. We recognize the fact that people are different.

Moreover, encouraging people to do what they do well does not limit anyone's freedom. Of course people are free to choose any occupation or any activity they wish. Elitists simply believe that we should devote our limited resources to helping people find out what they do well, and helping them develop their demonstrated talent. We waste far too much time and money striving for the false goal of complete equality. But nurturing talent does not infringe on anyone's freedom.

Elitism will never be a popular doctrine. People prefer to believe that they and their children could really be excellent in many fields, if only they had the chance. But they are deceiving themselves. In the long run, the elitist policy would actually lead to greater fulfillment and satisfaction for everyone, if only we could face the facts.

Key Concepts

elitist	better performance	training
excellence	basic abilities	incentives

Critical Questions

1. What are the three beliefs that define elitism?
2. Does excellence in teaching exist, in your opinion? Does excellence in politics exist? Don't different people have different goals and standards for evaluating *any* occupation?
3. The essay discusses differences among people with the same training. Would you say that people who take the same course (e.g., chemistry), but at different schools, have the same training or different training?
4. Doesn't our society already offer incentives (e.g., scholarships) to people with talent? Is the essay proposing anything new? Do we live in an elitist society?
5. In your opinion, would one find greater satisfaction in a job one can do very well for an average salary, or in a job one cannot do very well, but which pays a high salary?
6. Do our schools let people know what they can do well and what they can't? Should high school students be told that they are failures in some areas?

Methods and Techniques

MEANS AND ENDS

In political philosophy many of the debates concern the *means* of achieving certain ends. For example, both the essays in this section talk about the means of achieving equality in a society. It is useful, therefore, to step back and think about the general idea of means and ends.

Normally the distinction between means and ends is clear. The "end" is the same thing as the goal we are trying to reach. The "means" are the things we do, or the tools we need, to get to that goal. For example, if your goal is to be in Florida, you might use a plane, train, or automobile to get there. If your goal is to be financially secure, you might get a law degree and practice law. That is a means of achieving the end of financial security.

In political philosophy people can agree on the end, but disagree about the means. For example, everyone wants to reduce violent crime. That is an end, or goal. But some people say the best means of doing that is to impose more severe punishments on convicted criminals, while others say the best means is to provide government-funded jobs to people in poor neighborhoods. Another example is health care. Most people agree that citizens should have access to good doctors, hospitals, and treatment. But some people say competition and market mechanisms are the best means to reach that goal. Others say a universal health care program administered by the federal government is the best means. The disagreement is over means, not ends.

The disagreements about means take a variety of forms. Sometimes one group will say that a particular means simply will not produce the desired result. In the crime example, some people say severe punishments will not reduce crime; others say more jobs will not reduce crime. Here the disagreement is about causes and effects, i.e., about the consequences of implementing a certain policy. Sometimes people disagree about the costs. Some say we cannot afford to build more prisons and keep people in jail; others say we cannot afford to hire all the unemployed in poor neighborhoods. The idea is that the proposed means are just not practical, or that they are actually impossible.

Sometimes people raise moral objections to the means. For example, if "severe punishment" includes execution, then some people say these means of reducing crime are morally unacceptable. On the other side, critics say that providing government jobs destroys people's initiative and makes them dependent, and that is immoral. Various proposals of means to achieve social ends leave a lot of room for disagreements, based on consequences, costs, or morality.

The distinction between means and ends can become complicated. The terms "means" and "ends" are relative. What counts as a means in one context can be an end in another context. Take the idea of providing government-funded jobs to people in poor neighborhoods. In the example above, that was a means to reduce violent crime. But suppose we decide that it is a good idea and we want to implement it. How do we do it? That is, if our *goal* is to provide jobs, what *means* do we use to reach that goal? Does the government provide funds to local industry to hire people, or does the local congressperson set up an office to hire people directly, or does the state government relocate people to places that need workers? Or is there some other means? What was previously the means has now become an end, and we must examine new, more specific means to achieve it.

Both of the essays in this section discuss means to achieve goals. The issues are complex. But one of the best ways to keep track of the various questions, proposals, and objections—about equality or other topics in political philosophy—is to try to organize them within a framework of means and ends. Applying the concepts of means and ends will usually help you unravel the tangled disputes.

Understanding the Dilemma

EGALITARIAN OR ELITIST?

An egalitarian is a person who believes people are equal and should be treated as equals. An elitist is a person who believes people are not equal and should not be treated equally.

This is the basic issue in this section. Egalitarians disagree with elitists on the facts, and on the ideal social policies. But we can be more specific. People might be equal or unequal in certain respects, and should be treated equally or unequally in certain respects. Do egalitarians believe people are equal in every way, and that they should be treated equally in every way? And do elitists claim that people are unequal in every way? Virtually everyone today believes everyone should have the same *legal* rights and privileges. All Americans enjoy the rights laid out in the Bill of Rights in the Constitution. These rights are based on our common human nature; we are all equally human (although not too long ago many Americans believed that blacks, Native Americans, Asians, and women were not fully human).

Should every American have the same *political* rights? Egalitarians say yes, elitists say no. Of course no elitist would restrict the legal right to vote or hold office. But elitists favor placing some obstacles in people's paths. They believe that voting is a very important privilege, and that a citizen should be required to make some effort to vote. Those who are not willing to make any effort (e.g., go and register) are probably not willing to inform themselves about the candidates and their platforms, and so their vote is actually harmful. It is based on irrelevant factors like the candidate's appearance. Society is best served by having informed, thoughtful voters. Unfortunately not every citizen is informed and thoughtful, so society is not served well by having everyone vote. The same applies to holding public office. If we were really egalitarian (the elitist says), we would choose our political leaders by drawing lots. But instead we put huge obstacles in the way of anyone who wants to hold office. A politician must campaign from early to late for months, must build a large organization, work with the established party, raise large amounts of money, learn to communicate effectively, defend his or her views to the press, and so on. We assume that only the most energetic, talented, committed people will be able to surmount the obstacles.

Is this system elitist? Or is it egalitarian? After all, anyone can *try* to win public office. This shows that the terms "egalitarian" and "elitist" are hard to pin down. We have tried to clarify them on questions of legal rights and political rights. They also disagree on economic rights. One way to distinguish the two views is to think about conditions and opportunities. An egalitarian wants equality of condition. We can see that value in the first essay's discussion of More's *Utopia*. More believed that if people were equal in their material conditions—similar living conditions, similar clothes, housing, transportation, food, etc.—society would blossom in wonderful ways. Favoring equality of opportunity by itself is not enough. Equality of opportunity can exist only if people have equality of condition. The second essay argues that equality of opportunity and equality of condition would not make any difference. Many people today have equal opportunities, but some achieve excellence and others do not.

An elitist opposes equality of condition. He or she believes that some people are more talented than others, some are more intelligent than others, some are more industrious, creative, determined, or persistent than others. These individuals are extremely important and valuable to society, and therefore society must encourage and reward these people if it wants to benefit from their skills and talents. Equality of condition would harm society as a whole by reducing these people's initiative. An elitist thinks equality of opportunity is harmless, so long as it is defined narrowly. If it means that no one is prohibited from competing (for a job, a place in school, a political office, a share of the market, or a research grant) by laws or rules based on irrelevant qualities like race or gender, then it is a good thing. It is good, the elitist believes, because the more talented people will win out anyway.

What do you believe? Are people equal? Should they be treated equally? Should people be more equal than they are now, or has government gone too far in trying to enforce equality? Are you an egalitarian or an elitist?

EGALITARIAN

1. People are equal in the most important respects, and should be treated equally.
2. If people had equal property, all the major problems in society—crime, poverty, class conflict, insecurity—would disappear.
3. Real equality of opportunity requires much greater equality of condition than we have now.
4. The question isn't "Is equality popular?" but "Is equality just and right?"

ELITIST

5. Some people have the ability and the drive to achieve excellence in some field, and others do not.
6. We should be realistic enough to tell people when they are talented and when they are not.
7. If the government channeled people into the jobs they can do well, everyone would benefit tremendously.
8. People who are blessed with talent or intelligence will always be outnumbered by people who are average, and therefore elitism will always be an unpopular point of view.

FOR FURTHER STUDY

Historical Examples

EGALITARIAN: Thomas More. *Utopia*. Penguin, 1965. Originally published in 1516. A great classic in political philosophy, surprisingly contemporary, and full of fascinating ideas.

ELITIST: Plato. *The Republic*. Many editions. 4th century B.C.E. Another cornerstone of Western civilization; Plato defends an elitism of the talented, who should be carefully chosen for their merits, thoroughly educated, and given responsibility for guiding society.

OTHER SOURCES

William Ryan. *Equality*. Pantheon, 1981. A defense of social policies promoting greater equality in an easy-to-read, journalistic style.

Sidney Verba, Gary R. Owen. *Equality in America: The View from the Top*. Harvard University Press, 1985. Focuses on economic vs. political equality, current reality vs. normative ideals, individual vs. group equality, and opportunities vs. results.

Russell Kirk. *The Conservative Mind: From Burke to Eliot*. Gateway, 1978. Clear, sympathetic survey of conservative, antiegalitarian thinking over the past two hundred years.

John Rees. *Equality*. Praeger, 1971. A survey of the issues, attempting to define and make precise the ideas of "equality," "equal opportunity," "rights," and so on.

R.H. Tawney. *Equality*. 3rd Edition. Allen and Unwin, 1938. A defense of British-style socialism and equality.

William Letwin, ed. *Against Equality*. Macmillan, 1983. Critiques of various aspects of egalitarianism, by economists and social scientists.

Jonathan Wolff. *An Introduction to Political Philosophy*. Oxford University Press, 1996. Chapter 5 is a discussion of the distribution of property.

NOTE

1. Thomas More, *Utopia* (Penguin, 1965), p. 80.

2.4 IS CAPITALISM JUST?
CAPITALIST OR SOCIALIST?

———————————•———————————

People who have read some books about philosophy, or listened to philosophers talk, often decide that philosophy is too abstract and theoretical. The terms and concepts philosophers use are irrelevant to practical, real-life problems, they say. Take justice, for example. If you go to a library and look up books and articles by philosophers on the topic of justice, you will probably find some very difficult, subtle discussions. And you will wonder how all those distinctions can help you decide whether capital punishment is just, or whether raising taxes on the wealthy is just, or whether cutting aid to welfare mothers who have more children is just.

Many people would like to hear some answers to these questions about the justice or injustice of specific policies and actions. And yet the abstract theories are necessary, too. If someone told you that capital punishment is just, and so we should execute even more criminals, you would want to know why it is just. Or if a philosopher said much higher tax rates on the wealthy are just, you would want to know why. You would want to hear a general explanation of the idea of justice that leads to these answers. In other words, we all want answers to specific questions, but the answers are convincing only if they are backed up by some general principles and reasons that are also convincing.

The essays in this section try to meet both these demands. They are both about specific practices in American society. Whatever flaws they may have, they are not irrelevant to our ordinary lives. The first argues that our daily activities of buying and selling, earning a living, and the resulting distribution of income, meet the requirements of justice. In fact, it would be unjust to try to eliminate the inequalities that result. The second claims that many of our economic activities are a travesty of justice. So both essays are applicable to practical problems.

And yet both essays also try to support their answers with general principles that they believe we all accept. Both try to back up their specific recommendations with theoretical arguments. It is up to you to decide whose answers are better. The capitalist's point of view, presented in the first essay, is based on the idea that justice depends on one's contribution to society, and that capitalism recognizes this contribution. The socialist, represented in the second essay, claims that capitalism forces people to behave in immoral ways.

YES: CAPITALIST

"Capitalism, Democracy, and Justice"

A perennial question of philosophy is "What is justice?" At the beginning of Western philosophy Plato wrote his greatest work, *The Republic*, attempting to answer that question. The issue isn't merely theoretical. Everyone is interested in justice. If people believe their society is unjust, they will press for change. Perceived injustice creates instability. So the question is a practical one.

Philosophers have debated theories of justice since Plato's time, but ordinary people, in their remarkable wisdom, have worked out a practical solution. Citizens of Western democracies have put into place a system that satisfies our basic, intuitive idea of what is just and what isn't. The system is political and economic democracy, which is another way of saying "capitalism." Average citizens may not be able to explain why capitalism is just, but they know justice when they see it, and they see it in capitalism. Capitalism is a practical, not a theoretical, solution to the problem of justice. This essay is an attempt to fill in a small piece of the theory behind capitalism, and to explain why capitalism promotes justice.

First we must make sure we agree on the characteristics of capitalism. Capitalism is a complex set of institutions; it cannot be reduced to a simple formula. But several practices are essential. Probably the most basic element is private property. In a capitalistic system, people are free to buy and sell property. People are motivated to make profits, and they compete with each other in their trade. People are free to succeed, and free to fail. They are independent, and responsible for themselves.

These economic practices are closely connected with certain political practices, which also support independence and responsibility. In a capitalist system the government does not interfere with the economy. To preserve people's freedom to own property, government regulation is minimized. The government provides some services, like national defense, police and courts, large-scale transportation (roads and bridges), but only to promote free trade, not to interfere with it. Furthermore, the economic self-determination is mirrored by political self-determination. Capitalist government is democratic. All voting citizens have a voice in the government, help elect their representatives, and in that sense govern themselves.

Thus capitalism is a movement toward independence and self-reliance. It moves on two tracks, the economic track and the political track. Freedom and personal responsibility are the characteristics of each track. And neither track interferes with the other. The government does not exercise power over the economy, and economic power does not attempt to control the government. Every person has one vote, regardless of income, and bribery of elected officials is severely punished.

The popularity of capitalism around the world has grown over the past two centuries for obvious reasons. People want to be free and independent. However, freedom is not the same thing as justice. Even critics of capitalism probably agree that it gives some people some kind of freedom. But is capitalism just? Does it promote social justice? I believe that it does. To see this we must shift our attention from the idea of capitalism to the idea of justice.

On a superficial level, the question "What is justice?" is easy to answer. The *American Heritage Dictionary* defines justice as "fair handling, due reward or treatment." It says something is just if it is "properly due or merited." On this superficial level everyone can agree. Justice is being fair. It is giving people what is due to them, or what they have earned or merited. Injustice is treating people unfairly, giving some people special, unearned privileges, or unmerited punishments. In general, justice means treating people as they deserve to be treated, no better, no worse; giving them rewards if they deserve rewards, and punishments if they deserve punishments. All this is uncontroversial. The controversy begins when we ask what is due to a specific person. What is fair in a particular, complex case? What exactly does John Doe deserve? That is the difficult question.

Capitalism embodies a definite idea of justice. The moral basis of capitalism is the belief that justice depends on a person's contribution to society. If a person contributes a lot to society, in the form of building houses, or teaching kids, or healing the sick, then he or she should be rewarded. But if a person makes a negative contribution by assaulting people or robbing them or harming society in other ways, then he or she should be punished. And the rewards or punishments should be commensurate with the positive or negative contribution. Thus justice has a positive and a negative side. Philosophers call the first "distributive justice," because it concerns the distribution of goods like income and status. And they call the second "retributive justice," because it involves retribution, or punishment, for wrongdoing. The moral principle of capitalism is that both sides of justice depend on a person's contribution to society, whether it is a helpful or harmful contribution.

I think the capitalist principle agrees with our basic concept and feeling about justice. That is another reason capitalism is spreading. It not only fulfills people's desires for freedom, but it also conforms to their most basic moral feelings. But the contribution principle still doesn't answer the specific question of justice. What has a particular individual, such as John Doe or Jane Roe, contributed to society? Who decides what a specific individual deserves in capitalism?

Capitalism has created a way of answering the tough question, not with a general theory, but in the practical treatment of individuals. The ingenious solution of capitalism is to say that *no one knows* what John Doe deserves. Every individual and every case is different. No one is wise enough to understand all the details of a particular case, or impartial enough to decide in a perfectly fair way. Since there are no Godlike experts to administer justice, we will allow society as a whole to decide what John Doe, Jane Roe, and everyone else deserves. That promotes justice in a surprisingly clear way.

In capitalism the whole society determines both rewards and punishments in specific cases. First consider punishments, or retributive justice. We must have some way to decide whether or not John Doe has harmed society, and if he has, what degree of punishment he deserves. In capitalism, a jury decides who has harmed society. When a suspect is arrested, a prosecutor and a defender present their cases. A judge oversees the trial. But it is the jury that decides guilt or innocence, not the lawyer and not the judge. Now, a jury is a sort of microcosm of the whole society. It is a cross section of the community, representing society as a whole.

Once society has decided that it has been harmed by an individual, who determines the punishment? Who determines whether the harm is serious or minor? Society again decides, in the form of elected representatives in the legislature. Elected officials make the laws. They decide that some actions deserve one year in jail, while others deserve only a fine. Elected representatives are acting the way citizens want them to act, so the citizens indirectly decide what the guilty person deserves. Capitalism rests on the assumption that no single person is wise enough to decide justly. No theory is accurate enough to determine justice in each particular case. So it allows society as a whole—represented by the jury and the legislature—to decide.

Punishment is only one side of justice. The other side is rewards and benefits. Capitalism says that people who contribute positively to society deserve to be rewarded, and different contributions deserve different rewards. But who contributes, and how much do they contribute? Those are the difficult questions. And again, capitalism allows society as a whole to answer them. In capitalism people are free to buy and sell as they please. Each individual helps determine justice by spending his or her money. Thus if one person offers something that many people want to buy, that person earns a great deal of money. Earning money is society's way of saying that a person contributes to society. Consumers themselves decide who deserves to be rewarded. They decide with their pocketbook. Their votes are dollars. For example, doctors offer a service, and earn a lot of money for it. Capitalism says that doctors contribute more than receptionists, because citizens freely pay more for the service doctors offer. No experts or politicians or social workers weigh an individual's contribution to society. Society itself—innumerable people making purchases—decides how much a person contributes by paying the person for the contribution. Society rewards the person according to his or her contribution.

In capitalism some people make enormous amounts of money by offering surprising services. Sports stars like Michael Jordan make millions of dollars every year. What does he contribute to society? It might seem that an ordinary nurse or school teacher contributes more or improves society more than Michael Jordan. But the genius of capitalism is to shift the question. The question is not "What does Michael Jordan contribute?" The question is "Who decides?" Capitalism's answer is "Let the people decide." Who is better qualified to judge contributions to society than society itself, i.e., ordinary people making purchases? If people are free to buy and sell, they reward Jordan for the service he offers. It is only fair that society itself decides whether or not something benefits society, and only fair that society itself pay the reward for that contribution. Single individuals and groups are excluded from the decision, since individuals are often biased in some way.

Capitalism is radically democratic. It allows the people to determine rewards and punishments. Some intellectuals find it difficult to accept this aspect of capitalism. They assume that *they* are better qualified to decide what an individual has contributed to society. They do not believe such an important decision should be left to the uneducated masses. But this outlook is the source of all forms of totalitarianism. It is the assumption that I understand justice better than you, and better than most people, and I will force you and everyone else to be just according to my perception of justice. Capitalism is completely opposed to such an outlook, because it has faith in ordinary people.

An obvious objection to capitalist justice is that some people, through no fault of their own, cannot offer any product or service or labor that people want to buy. Some people are too old and frail. Some people are blind or paralyzed or ill. If they have nothing to offer to society, then they will receive no income at all. Is that right? Do we want these people to be completely indigent? Of course not. They should receive help. But it is compassion and kindness that demand that we help them, not justice. If it is true that they make no contribution to society, and if rewards should be proportionate to contributions, then pure justice by itself does not require that we help them. But we all have other moral feelings besides justice. We also feel compassion. Helping people who make no contribution (measured by society's willingness to pay for what they offer) is an act of compassion. Thus we can all agree that handicapped people should receive aid. But this fact is no objection to the cap-

italist practice of justice. It simply means that capitalism includes other values besides justice.

By making rewards and punishments depend on a person's contribution to
society, capitalism conforms to our basic concept of justice and fairness. And
by allowing society as a whole to decide individual cases, capitalism conforms
to our desire for democratic equality and even-handedness. It is not surprising,
therefore, that capitalism is becoming more popular all over the world.

Key Concepts

contribution	political capitalism	retributive justice
economic capitalism	distributive justice	compassion

Critical Questions

1. How is capitalist in the economy similar to capitalism in government?
2. Does the capitalist think the question "What is justice" is easy or difficult to
   answer?
3. Do you agree that in capitalism society as a whole decides who has committed a crime and how a criminal should be punished?
4. Do you think that it is just to base a person's rewards, income, and benefits
   on his or her contribution to society?
5. Do you believe that in the United States the amount of money a person
   makes is an accurate measure of his or her contribution to society? Does a
   professional basketball star contribute two hundred times as much to society as a social worker?
6. Why should society as a whole decide who contributes to society and who
   doesn't, according to the essay? Why shouldn't social scientists, or politicians, or religious leaders decide?
7. Does the capitalist think that it is unjust for the government to give financial aid to helpless or unproductive people, such as the elderly?

NO: SOCIALIST

"Capitalist Society"

The seventh century, from 600 to 700 C.E., was one of the lowest points of
European history. It was the middle of the Dark Ages, when petty barons fought
for territory, constant violence was the rule, famine was common, and most
people's minds were stupefied by ridiculous superstitions. But it is only in retrospect that we realize how horrible conditions were. Most of the people living
at that time did not think of their epoch as a Dark Age. They thought their way
of life was normal, since the decline was gradual, and they were not aware of
other times or places.

I fear that the world may be sinking into a new Dark Age. The growing
problems are not the same as the problems of the seventh century, but they are

no less severe and depressing. The discouraging trend is the worldwide spread of capitalism. The revolutions of 1989 have spread the capitalist virus like the Black Plague. But most people today are just as unaware of the threat as people in the earlier Dark Age.

Capitalism is simply immoral. It forces people to behave in callous, selfish ways, and capitalist society inevitably degenerates into an immoral war of all against all. The bedrock foundation of capitalism is the free market. People buy and sell goods and services, and negotiate the prices. Everyone's goal is to make a favorable deal. For example, if I deal in real estate, I try to buy land or buildings for one price, and then sell them for a higher price. If I manage a shoe store, I try to buy shoes from a supplier at one price, and then sell them to customers at a higher price. The difference in price is profit for me. Manufacturers have the same goal, although the process is slightly more complicated. If I manufacture automobiles, I must buy a factory, machinery and parts, and the labor of my employees. They assemble the parts, and then I must sell the automobiles for more than I spent to make them. The pursuit of profits is the heart of capitalism.

But the process is necessarily dishonest. The essence of capitalism is cheating. To make a profit, I must find someone who will pay more for an item than I paid for it myself. That is how the free market works. Capitalism is a continuous search for a sucker. It is a search for someone who will pay more for something than the seller knows it is worth. And the bigger the lie, the more "successful" the seller will be. The only skill required to get rich in real estate is the skill of manipulating someone to pay more for a property than you paid.

Dishonesty governs the relation between employers and employees, too. Employers buy people's labor, which they use to make a product or offer a service that they can sell for more than the labor costs. Employers try to squeeze more work out of their employees and pay them as little as possible. If they can cut wages or benefits they have more profit for themselves. If they can produce the same goods with part-time workers, who are paid far less than full-time workers, they will do that.

On the other side, employees sell their labor. They do not buy something at one price and sell it at a higher price. But in capitalism employees are forced to try to get more and more for their labor. They take longer breaks, use sick days for vacation, slack off on the job, and in other ways try to cheat their employer. They strike for higher wages. It is part of the climate of capitalism, where the pursuit of profits is the only goal. Dishonesty is the means. A person cannot make profits and remain honest at the same time. Capitalism not only turns people into liars; it makes them think lying is normal and respectable. They don't even realize that they are lying.

Where the free market is the basis of society, everything is for sale. In capitalism medical care must be purchased. If you are hurt in an auto accident, and you go to an emergency room at a hospital, the officials will demand to see your insurance card before they treat you. Injured people without health insurance have been turned away, and if they are allowed to stay, they will very probably not receive the same treatment as paying customers. Where medical care is for sale, the providers will naturally try to make the greatest profit they can. Medical costs will rise and rise. People will enter the medical profession with the goal of making profits. They will demand a large return on their "investment" of compassion. They will look for ways to gouge more money out of their "customers." Where medical care is for sale, providers cannot maintain their natural desire to help people for the sake of helping. They must do it for the sake of money. Capitalism destroys the basic respect and concern people have for each other.

Where the free market is the basis of society, political power is for sale. In capitalism, elections are determined by money. The candidate who spends the most on advertising, transportation, and publicity will win the election. Politicians understand this. They devote most of their time to raising funds for the next campaign, not to studying problems or looking for solutions. Special interest groups—unions, professional associations, industry representatives, the elderly, etc., etc.—are the best source of money. So in effect, politicians sell their services to the groups that pay the highest price. A politician who says that money plays no part in his or her decisions is like a car salesman who says, "just for you," he will sell you a car for less than he paid for it.

In capitalism, justice is a commodity like everything else. "Justice" in capitalism means favorable court decisions. Lawyers want the most favorable deal (the most profits) they can get. They make money by winning legal cases. Some are more skillful or unscrupulous than others, and the skillful ones will charge more for their services. Therefore, rich people who can hire the most cunning and devious lawyers will win their cases. Average or poor people, with mediocre or honest lawyers, will lose their cases. Real justice has nothing to do with it. In capitalism, justice is irrelevant.

The free market corrupts everyone and destroys all human relationships. Where everything is for sale, people are for sale, too. When capitalists hire a worker, they purchase the right to use that person for their own benefit, like a tool. They have bought the right to order the worker about, regulate his behavior, tell him when to stand, when to sit, when to eat, when to talk. The whole purpose of this degrading relationship is to wring as much profit as possible out of the worker. Of course the worker aims at the same goal; he wants to exploit the capitalist. People cannot be expected to respect each other, or see each other as free, dignified human beings, in such a situation.

Women have suffered the most under capitalism. Where everything is for sale, everything must be purchased. Medical care, political representation, justice, and of course necessities like food and clothing must be bought. But women have been deprived of the means whereby they could earn money to purchase these things. Until recently, capitalism excluded women from most jobs. Even today there is strong pressure on women to stay at home to provide full-time child care. (There is no comparable pressure on men to give up their careers to raise children.) If a woman cannot work, she has no way to earn money. But in capitalism money is a life or death issue. The only way a woman excluded from the market can survive is to marry a man and become dependent on him for money. In other words, women must sell their bodies to men. They provide sex in return for the basic necessities of life. The situation is so humiliating and dehumanizing that most women cannot admit it to themselves. They delude themselves with romantic dreams because the reality is too painful to accept. But some women are quite open about it. They freely admit that a man's income plays a large part in their attraction to him and their willingness to consider marriage. Such is the effect of capitalism on women's values and self-respect.

Women are certainly not to blame for their choices. They must survive. But most men are not to blame either. Men are trapped in the system as firmly as women. People who grow up in capitalism are bombarded with carefully selected images and messages from the day they are born. Their values are shaped by capitalism. Everywhere they look, they learn that happiness means buying things. The purpose of life is to accumulate clothes, cars, radios, houses, or other gadgets. TV, movies, parents, books, history lessons in school, all teach children to value private property and money. Even mainstream religion defends the "sanctity" of private property. Human relationships, developing one's personal potential, and cooperative work are less important. Children see the message in people's actions, if not their words. As children grow up and see what happens to people without money, how could they fail to make money their goal in life? As they see how buying and selling for a profit work, how could they value honesty? As they see how employers lay off workers, how could they learn that everyone deserves respect?

One important aspect of capitalist indoctrination is its disguise. People must not realize that they are being indoctrinated or else it will not work. Therefore capitalism loudly trumpets the value of "freedom." People are told that they are free (meaning free to buy and sell). Anyone who points to the immorality of capitalism is branded as an enemy of "freedom." But the only freedom capitalists care about is the freedom of a small minority to become fabulously wealthy. Most people in a capitalist society are enslaved to their jobs. They must work long hours, with almost no vacation, to try to make more money. In many families, both parents work, leaving children to be raised by the television. Some people hold two jobs because they believe in "freedom." What a cruel irony it is. No medieval peasant worked as many hours, or was as terrified of poverty and destitution, as a modern worker.

The oil that keeps the capitalist machine running is greed. In a free market, people must buy things. The more people buy, the faster the machine runs. Therefore everyone caught up in the system wants everyone else to buy more things. The system encourages greed. An essential part of selling is persuading someone to buy. Psychological manipulation is as important to capitalism as production of goods. People are manipulated to want more and more things. They are convinced that they need the latest fad, and that they will be miserable without it.

Capitalism must keep demand and consumption at a fever pitch. It must make people feel that they need more and more. But a person can wear only so many dresses or drive so many cars. To overcome this limitation, capitalism has transformed basic needs into relative needs. People are taught to change the definition of "need" from survival to superiority. People feel that they must be superior to their neighbors. They need to have more things and better things than other people. Otherwise they will be unhappy. They do not have a basic need for a fancy car or designer jeans or an expensive vacation. They will not starve or even be uncomfortable without these things. But they will feel inferior (or merely equal) to other people. They need the fashionable things to feel superior, so people buy more and more. This kind of relative need is boundless. Unlike hunger or fatigue, it can never be satisfied. There is no end to the pursuit of social superiority. If you rise above the people in your neighborhood, you will then compare yourself to a higher stratum of society. And then you will want to rise above them.

The psychological transformation of needs from real and basic to artificial and relative is perhaps the most pernicious and damaging aspect of capitalism. It creates economic classes in society as some people are driven to accumulate more and more superfluous goods and others are left behind. The result is envy and jealousy on one side, arrogance and contempt on the other, and hatred and resentment all around. Capitalism is a perversion of human relationships. It subverts the natural neighborliness of people and puts suspicion and conflict in its place.

It is true that capitalism produces dazzling toys for people to play with (by threatening them with homelessness if they do not work like slaves). But those consumer goods have blinded people to the more important effects. Capitalism destroys morality. It forces people to make dishonesty a way of life, it reduces all human relations to buying and selling, it reduces all aspirations to insatiable greed for material objects, and it turns people against each other. As capitalism spreads, humanity declines into materialistic selfishness, a new Dark Age. The only consolation is that the wheel of history continues to turn.

Key Concepts

capitalism	greed	relative needs
immoral	indoctrination	class divisions
dishonest		

Critical Questions

1. Do businessmen and women always charge more for their product than they paid? Do you agree with the essay that making profits is based on dishonesty?
2. What is the essay's main criticism of the capitalist health care system?
3. The essay claims that politics, the courts, and the workplace are all corrupted by capitalism. Do these three institutions all exhibit the same problem, or different problems?
4. Do you think a man's income influences a woman's desire to marry him? If so, does that make her a prostitute, in your opinion?
5. According to the essay, how does capitalism indoctrinate people?

6. How would you define "need"? Is it something one must have in order to stay alive? (Are our only needs oxygen, food, and water?) Or is it something one must have in order to be happy? (Then are the socialist's relative needs actually basic needs?)
7. How does capitalism create social classes, in the socialist's view?

Methods and Techniques

THINKING AND EMOTION

These two essays about justice are likely to stir up people's emotions, both positive and negative. As you read them, you may have found yourself feeling angry, or proud, or embarrassed. Why? Why would these essays generate strong feelings, while other articles or discussions leave people cold?

One reason is that these essays cover topics that people care about very much, like justice. We all react strongly if we think we have been treated unfairly, for example, if something was stolen from us. Most people react strongly if they see someone else treated unfairly. (Hollywood and TV understand this, and use people's sense of justice when they want to create villains.) People also care about money, and both essays are about money. Anything about having money, or getting money, or being deprived of money, automatically raises a person's emotional temperature. Both essays discuss democracy, especially the first, and people care about democracy.

Another reason for the emotional reaction is that most people feel personally involved in the topics. Most people feel that the free market directly affects their lives—their income, their rent, their entertainment budget, and their prospects for the future. Capitalism is not an irrelevant abstraction to most people but a specific set of facts in their lives. For some, the organization of society has been good, and they feel the current arrangement should be preserved. For others, the current situation is frustrating or unsatisfying or offensive. They feel that the basic organization of society should be changed.

That division points to another reason people get emotional about these topics. Both essays are implicitly accusatory. That is, the socialist says, in effect, that anyone who practices capitalism or willingly participates in the system is immoral. The capitalist says anyone who is poor deserves to be poor, and anyone who challenges the system is promoting injustice. Those are strong claims. No one likes to be called immoral or unfair. People become highly defensive and anxious when such charges are thrown around.

In reading these essays, it is tempting to go with the emotion. Some students respond with the equivalent of "So's your mother!" or a dialogue of the "Are too—Am not—Are too—Am not" variety. The normal response to being attacked is to attack back. But strong emotions are counterproductive when you are trying to understand political philosophy. They only get in the way of careful analysis. It would be futile to say one should not have emotions at all. People are going to feel strongly about these issues. But you should try to allow the other parts of your mind to work, too. You are more than just a bundle of emotions.

One way to defuse the strong feelings is to step back and be less involved. Try to think of the problem the way a scientist would. What are the facts, what are the recommendations, where are the conflicts? Another strategy is to try to isolate exactly the points that upset you. Does an author say anything that you can agree with? After you find those parts, then focus on precisely the statements or suggestions that you find disturbing. (Maybe it isn't the statements themselves that upset you, but the underlying, unwritten assumptions, or the consequences.) Once you have pinpointed the troublesome ideas, ask yourself why you find them troubling. Why do they elicit strong feelings? By using your analytical thinking, you will temporarily set aside your emotions.

This sort of analysis will help you see the reasons for a person's point of view, the pro and con, and the hidden assumptions. It is good practice, too, because most philosophical questions are like these political issues. They are questions that people care about—concerning God, right and wrong, human nature, and objective knowledge. And many people feel that they have a personal stake in the answers (in the way they lead their lives, their image of themselves, their confidence in their beliefs, and their life after death). But putting aside strong feelings so you can think clearly will help you in any task.

Understanding the Dilemma

CAPITALIST OR SOCIALIST?

When people think about justice, they might ask themselves "What is a just society?" or "What is a just person?" Or they might ask "What is a just procedure, that is, a just way of resolving disputes between people, or a just way of administering punishments and rewards?" Actually the third question, about rules and procedures, is probably the most fundamental. A just society is simply one that is based on just procedures, in the courts, in institutions like education and medical care, and in the economy. A just individual is one who acts justly, that is, who follows just procedures.

The first essay focuses on the procedure by which capitalism administers punishments and rewards. It claims the procedure is democratic, and that it leads to a just society. The second essay argues that capitalism and the free market do not produce justice and, in fact, systematically destroy people's moral sense, including their sense of justice. Which is right? Is capitalist society just, or unjust?

A capitalist believes that everyone agrees about what justice is on an abstract level: it is giving a person what he or she deserves. It is treating people fairly, in the sense of giving them what they deserve without considering irrelevant factors. But people do not agree on what a particular person deserves. Does a suspect deserve to go to jail? Does a high school graduate deserve a secure job? People have different opinions. So a society needs a way to determine what each individual deserves. It needs a procedure for administering punishments and rewards, and people must believe the procedure is just. The capi-

talist claims that in capitalism the procedure is to allow the people as a whole
to administer punishments and rewards. That is the only fair way. All experts
or authorities will be biased. The people as a whole decide what one individual's contribution to society is worth. They decide by paying her a salary, or
buying her product. The free market allows the people as a whole to spend their
money where they want, and their spending indicates their judgment of an individual's contribution. Thus administering rewards and punishments through
the free market is simply a procedure for deciding what each person deserves.
It produces a just society, according to the capitalist.

Socialists do not propose a different concept of justice, but only criticize the
capitalist concept. They point out the harmful and even immoral aspects of capitalism. They say that by making everything depend on money, capitalism undermines the judicial system, the political system, and the health care system.
In a capitalist society, people cannot think about what someone deserves, but
can think only about how much money he or she has. People cannot think about
whether a person deserves to be elected, or deserves to be convicted, or deserves decent health care, but rather they substitute money and profits for justice. The amount of money a person has is not necessarily connected with what
a person deserves, in any of these areas. Capitalism has little to do with justice,
socialists say. In capitalism people have become consumed with greed, and now
they are trying to justify their scramble for money by calling it justice.

Capitalists favor competition; they think competition brings out the best in
people, and produces benefits for everyone. Socialists think competition is not
always good. It leads to aggression and hostility between competitors. It means
a lot of people are unhappy because they are losers. There is no reason for competition; people can accomplish more by working together. Generally socialists
favor community, cooperation, and mutual help, whereas capitalists favor individualism, personal achievement, and self-reliance.

Another difference is in the attitude toward the less successful people. A
capitalist thinks they are less successful because of their own limitations. A socialist thinks that their circumstances, their educational opportunities, and the
social system in general, are to blame.

The capitalist's essay raises some other fundamental questions. Should our
income and standard of living depend on our contribution to society? Is it just
to give greater rewards to people who contribute more to society? What does
"contribution to society" mean? Should a person's contribution be determined
by his or her "marketability," that is, what others are willing to pay that person? A capitalist says yes, and a socialist says no.

In trying to decide whether you are a capitalist or a socialist, you should
also keep in mind an idea that socialists emphasize. They say that most people
will make up their minds on the basis of what serves their own economic class.
In other words, a person who is prospering in capitalism and belongs to the
upper class will believe that capitalism is a superb way to organize society. But
a person who is unsuccessful and belongs to the lower class will say the system is unjust and ought to be changed. Our position in society determines our

beliefs and judgments about society, socialists say. Are they right? Can you look at our society objectively, without simply advocating policies that will improve your own individual prospects?

CAPITALIST

1. Justice means getting what one deserves.
2. A person who contributes more to society deserves more rewards than a person who contributes less to society.
3. The only fair way to determine how much a person has contributed to society is to let the people as a whole decide, through the free market.
4. Justice is not the same thing as compassion, but if people believe society is just, they will behave compassionately.

SOCIALIST

5. In capitalism decisions are made on the basis of monetary self-interest, not justice.
6. In capitalism the emotion of greed gradually overwhelms all other emotions, until the basic institutions of society are corrupted.
7. It is essential to capitalism that it disguise its true nature, and so it works hard to make people believe it is morally neutral, or even just.
8. People in capitalism want to be better than their neighbors, without any regard for justice.

FOR FURTHER STUDY

Historical Examples

CAPITALIST: Adam Smith. *The Wealth of Nations*. Random, 1977. Book 1, chap. 10, "Of Wages and Profit in the Different Employments of Labor and Stock." Originally published in 1776. Smith explains why people in different occupations earn different amounts of money in capitalism.

SOCIALIST: Karl Marx, Friedrich Engels. *The Communist Manifesto*. Many editions. Originally published in 1848. Marx and Engels raise historical and "scientific" objections to capitalism, but their main critique is moral. Like the second essay, they claim that capitalism is dehumanizing, unjust, and immoral.

OTHER SOURCES

Irving Kristol. *Two Cheers for Capitalism*. Basic Books, 1978. See part 3, "What Is 'Social Justice'?"

Michael Harrington. *Socialism*. Saturday Review Press, 1972. A broad-ranging defense by a famous socialist.

Robert Heilbroner. *Between Capitalism and Socialism*. Random House, 1970. Essays explaining and promoting socialism by an excellent writer.

Ayn Rand. *Capitalism: The Unknown Ideal*. NAL, 1967. A collection of essays defending capitalism, mostly by Rand, a novelist.

Karen Lebacqz. *Six Theories of Justice*. Augsburg Publishing House, 1986. J.S. Mill, Rawls, Nozick, Catholic Bishops' Conference, Niebuhr (Protestantism), and Liberation Theology.

Otto Bird. *The Idea of Justice*. Praeger, 1967. An examination of three theories: justice founded on man-made law, on the social good, or on natural rights.

Bernard Cullen, "Philosophical Theories of Justice." In Klaus R. Scherer, ed. *Justice: Interdisciplinary Perspectives*. Cambridge University Press, 1992. Extensive survey and classification of contemporary theories of justice.

Robert C. Solomon, Mark C. Murphy, eds. *What Is Justice? Classic and Contemporary Readings*. Oxford University Press, 1990. Contains a wide variety of selections, including some from the two most important books on political philosophy in the past thirty years: John Rawls' *A Theory of Justice* and Robert Nozick's *Anarchy, State, and Utopia*.

Plato. *The Republic*. Penguin, 1974. Probably the most influential book in philosophy ever written. Plato set out to answer the question "What is justice," and he ended up discussing virtually every philosophical question, including justice.

Jean Hampton. *Political Philosophy*. Westview Press, 1996. Chapter 4 is an examination of utilitarian, libertarian, egalitarian, and Rawls' theories of justice.

2.5 SHOULD WE ESTABLISH A WORLD GOVERNMENT?

INTERNATIONALIST OR LOCALIST?

———————————————•———————————————

A worldview is called "worldview" because it is a perspective on the entire world. In this book the "world" includes everything: human nature, body and mind, values, God, and any other part of human experience. Building a worldview means deciding what you should believe about these basic topics. But if you asked someone, "What is your view of the world," he or she would probably think you were asking about current affairs, particularly international relations. An interesting and important part of your worldview is your beliefs about other countries in the world and America's relation to them.

Political scientists study international relations, and they try to do it scientifically. There is no sharp line between political scientists' questions and philosophers' questions. Philosophers simply try to understand the most general features of this part of human experience. For example, philosophers might ask "Are there any laws that determine the behaviors of states toward each other?" Survival of the fittest? Increasing progress toward peace and cooperation? Or is it true that there are no natural laws, no inevitable tendencies, and we are completely free to decide what kind of international relations nations will have?

Philosophers also try to understand central concepts in international relations, such as "sovereignty," "force," and "government." What exactly do these terms mean? Do they mean different things for different people? How are these important ideas related to other concepts we have, such as our concept of right and wrong, justice, and equality?

Philosophers also ask questions about policies and goals, whereas political scientists usually try to confine themselves to factual questions. In other words, philosophers ask "Should our country be the leader of the world, or should all countries treat each other as equals?" "Are there any moral rules that all people should obey?" "When is war justified, if ever?"

An important concept in international relations is the concept of world government. What does it mean? Is it possible? Is it desirable? Your answers to these questions depend partly on your beliefs about two other topics. First, do you think that the current situation in the world is new and unique, or that it is basically no different from all past eras, when attempts to form a world government failed? Second, do you think all the people in the world are basically similar and can work together, or are people in different countries so different from each other that they could not work together in one government?

The first essay in this section argues that a world government is possible and desirable. It represents the internationalist position. The second essay explains why a world government is not possible, and would not be a good thing even if it were possible. It claims that local government is better, so it represents the localist position.

YES: INTERNATIONALIST

"Choosing a Peaceful Future"

It is the business of citizens in a democracy to make choices. Some choices affect a few people in a local district. Others are more significant. The American people now face a choice that has the greatest consequences imaginable. The phrase "turning point in history" is used too often, but there is no other way to describe the present situation. Americans, together with other people around the world, have an opportunity to improve dramatically the future of humanity. We can choose to create a functioning world government, or we can choose to continue the international anarchy and war that has plagued humankind for millennia.

The idea of a world government is not new. But the remarkable conditions of the present age *are* new. The Cold War is over and the democratic West won. The world is no longer divided into two hostile blocs, each trying to exploit the weaknesses of the other. The Western powers, particularly the United States, are now supreme. Formerly Communist countries and nonaligned countries are trying to imitate the West as rapidly as possible. Every country in Latin America, with the exception of Cuba, now has a democratic government. As recently as ten years ago no one would have predicted it. The opportunity for further progress exists.

In trade and economics, nations have embraced open borders, free movements, and internationalism. The Europeans have been moving closer and closer to economic integration—common standards, common laws, even a common currency—for decades. Canada, the United States, and Mexico are following their lead with the North American Free Trade Agreement. Large corporations are completely international. Their headquarters may be located in one country, but their suppliers, factories, distribution centers, customers, and investors are spread all over the globe.

The third new development is in communications. The Internet and World Wide Web are only the most visible symbols of a broad, rapid change in modern society. International telephone connections are easy, reliable, and cheap. People today are instantly aware of major events that occur anywhere on the globe, thanks to news organizations linked by satellite. Often people can watch dramatic events as they unfold. We are living in a smaller and smaller "global village," as Marshall McLuhan said.

These political, economic, and social developments probably make some sort of world government inevitable. But we now have an opportunity to hasten the process and avoid unnecessary problems. We should proceed deliberately and gradually through several stages. The first stage is to create a federation of nations, like the United Nations, but with the military power to enforce democratic decisions. That means disarmament by powerful nations, especially nuclear disarmament, as well as support for a U.N. military force.

Nuclear disarmament is not an entirely new idea. In 1946 the United States volunteered to destroy its own nuclear weapons—the only ones in existence at that time—and to participate in an international commission to oversee all nuclear power production, so no other nation would develop nuclear weapons. The plan failed because the Soviet government would not allow international inspectors to monitor their nuclear power stations.[1] But conditions are different now.

The first stage in the creation of a world government is different from the American plan in one respect. The world federation must have teeth—military power—because its first and most important goal is to preserve the peace. If the federation, representing the will of humankind, had monopoly control of nuclear weapons and enough conventional military resources to stop local conflicts, no dictator or rogue state could challenge it. As the world became more unified and less militaristic, terrorists would have fewer places to hide. People would have to obey international law and settle their differences through negotiation.

The essential prerequisite for such a federation is democracy. Nations must have proportional representation, they must have a voice in the decision-making of the federation. Then the federation could operate like any democratic body. If serious conflicts arose and the federation decided to try to end the violence, then nations would feel that it was acting on their behalf, since they helped make the decision. Majority rule is the only principle by which people can live together peacefully, and we all live together on planet Earth. Representation must be based on population, but since different countries have reached very different levels of development, it must also take into account the financial and technological contributions each nation can make to the federation.

Once the federation established peace among nations, it could perhaps move on to stages two and three. It could begin to address global environmental problems. The environment is vitally important to everyone. But no single nation can protect the earth's air and water, although a single nation can pollute them. Preserving a clean, healthy environment requires international cooperation. The high seas, Antarctica, the ozone layer, the moon, orbital space—these are areas that affect everyone. The United States cannot take the whole responsibility for protecting them.

Global thinking would lead to a third role for the federation. It could help promote economic development among poor nations. By organizing agriculture, building infrastructure, establishing schools, and helping small industry, the federation could begin to reduce the starvation and disease that afflicts millions of people today. Of course it could make progress only in a democratic country, where the benefits would go to the people and not to the power elites. But the promise of such aid might help transform remaining corrupt governments into democracies.

The benefits of establishing such a world government are obvious: universal peace, resources devoted to development rather than to war, increased democracy, greater respect for the natural world, and an end to mass poverty and starvation. The possibilities are staggering. If all the human capital that is now wasted in conflict and poverty were employed in creative work, who can imagine the scientific and cultural advances that might occur? Humanity could very well rise to a new level of civilization.

Why, then, aren't people demanding a world government? Because some skeptics are more attuned to the past than to the future. Their reservations are of two types. First, some say a world government is impractical. It will never work, because the world is too big and people are too different. They cannot agree on anything. Second, some people say a world government would deprive their own nation of its sovereignty. Americans, for example, would lose their independence and have to obey a committee of "foreigners."

The first objection is easy to answer. A federation of nations is just like the Union of States in America. After the American Revolution, the separate states, such as New York and Pennsylvania, were reluctant to give up their independence. In fact, they tried living under a weak "Articles of Confederation" for eight years, but it didn't work. In 1789, they adopted the Constitution we have now, creating a stronger central government. Each state agreed to support a national army, which was stronger than its own state militia. The result has been a secure, prosperous nation.

The United States government implements the Constitution, even though people in America are very different. America includes people who practice different religions, who have different family customs, and who speak different languages. People from all over the world live in the United States, even though their cultural backgrounds are completely different. In spite of these differences, they all agree that they want to be safe, and they want to be represented in the government. The motto of the United States is "E Pluribus Unum": from many, one. The system works because the central government demands only tolerance of others and peaceful resolution of conflicts. It does not demand uniformity, acceptance of moral values, ideology, or any changes in one's personal affairs. If the diverse people of America can accept a central government, then so can the people of the world. All the practical objections to a world government can be answered by pointing to the United States government. It *can* work.

But other people are afraid of a world government. It might be all too possible, but it is very dangerous. They do not want to put so much power in a few people's hands who are not Americans. This fear can take several forms. Barbara Ward says that the opposition to world government is based on emotion, whereas rationality argues for it.[2] Emotional opposition is difficult to formulate precisely. Some might say that the federation could turn into a dictatorship. Since it alone would have the military means to project its power in a decisive way, it could force member states to do whatever it wanted. But the parallel with the United States applies again. Our Founding Fathers were aware of the dangers of concentrated power, so they divided power among three branches of government, they limited the terms of office, and they made the government answerable to the people through elections and recall. Similar checks and balances could apply to a world government.

Another objection is more subtle. Some people fear that their own country will lose its sovereignty (its independence or self-determination), not because of dictatorship, but because of majority rule. The federation will abide by the will of the majority. But the majority of people in the world are not Americans; they do not understand our interests, and they do not think like Americans. They will vote for some policy that harms America. (People from Italy will say the same thing about Italy, and so on.)

This fear seems to rest on several false beliefs. One is that the federation will legislate matters of individual behavior or interfere in the lives of citizens of nations. But the only concern of the federation will be to prevent war. If necessary, it will act to prevent one government from invading, attacking, or harassing the government or people of another nation. All other matters will still be the responsibilities of the national governments.

Instead of seeing other people in the world as "them," an alien majority, why can't we think of forming a federation as *joining* a majority of reasonable, peaceful people, *against* a minority of aggressive, intolerant, arrogant militarists? We will be on the majority's side, not in the minority.

Another misconception at the root of the fear of the majority is the belief that people around the world are utterly different from us, so different that they are unpredictable, or likely to favor bizarre, tyrannical policies. But while people are different in superficial ways, they are fundamentally similar. People everywhere live in families, they love their children, and they talk to their neighbors. They want the freedom to work, to play, to worship, and to learn, as we do. We aren't dealing with Martians, but with human beings like us.

Not all countries in the world today have evolved into democracies yet. And only democratic national governments could participate in a world federation. The participants must represent their people, but an authoritarian, undemocratic government would not represent its people. China, Iran, North Korea, and a few other countries would not be eligible. In fact, a country need not take part in the federation at all, so long as it did not threaten the federation with nuclear weapons or the means to produce them. But these dictatorships are dinosaurs from a bygone era. Their governments will change within a few years. We should welcome these changes, and build on them. The choice is ours.

Key Concepts

communications	environment	dictatorship
nuclear weapons	development	sovereignty
majority rule	cultural differences	

Critical Questions

1. How is the present age different from previous eras, according to the internationalist?
2. What is the internationalist's proposal? What kind of world government does the internationalist want? What is its function or purpose?
3. How does an internationalist answer the objection that people around the world are too different from each other to work together?
4. How does an internationalist answer the objection that we in America would lose our independence to a foreign majority if we joined a world federation?
5. Why does an internationalist insist that all the member states must be democracies? Doesn't that mean that the federation will never be established?
6. Do you think the United States has more to gain, or more to lose, by turning over all its nuclear weapons to an international organization?

NO: LOCALIST

"The Politics of World Government"

A perennial dream of the human race is to create a perfect society where people will all love one another and live in harmony. The Stoics, Christians, Enlightenment philosophers, socialists, and other less influential dreamers believed in a universal kinship of people, based upon reason and the inherent dignity of each human being. One version of this dream is internationalism. All these groups proposed the formation of some type of world government, whether it was the Roman Empire, the City of God, Enlightened Despotism, or the Classless Society. Liberals today change the details, but many still favor the creation of a political body with authority over all the people of the world.

The dream has a kind of charm, like a fairy tale remembered from childhood. But to realistic men and women with experience in politics, the practical proposal of a world government is a horrible idea. It is based on a completely false image of human beings, and if it were somehow put into operation, it would gradually undermine our most precious human qualities.

The world government is never described in detail, and it isn't based on real facts. When idealistic liberals get together to try to implement their vision, they soon discover that they all have different visions! Some propose a far-reaching, energetic organization to actually make every person in the world feel like a member of one community. The world government would transform education, economics, and political activity to make every person a "citizen of the world." At the other end of the spectrum is a vision of a much more limited world government, whose only function would be to prevent war. And there are variations in between.

But these different types of world governments have at least one factor in common. They are *governments*. They have some mechanism for making decisions, and they have real power to enforce their decisions. Without overwhelming power, these groups would be no different from the international organizations we have today, which any state can ignore whenever it likes. But a world government's decisions would have a real impact on people and nations.

What the idealists have failed to understand is that the world government would be a political organization. They have not understood how politics works. They seem to think that politics is a perfectly rational activity, and that it is a matter of finding the best solution to a problem. But that is engineering, not politics. Politics is not rational, it is emotional. It depends on other parts of our nature besides pure reason.

Any government must inspire loyalty and devotion among its citizens. The function of a government is to influence people to do things that they may be reluctant to do. It must call forth the people's efforts. Thus an essential element in government is leadership. Some talented individuals must be able to generate enough respect and enthusiasm among citizens that the citizens will do the difficult things that need to be done. Inspiring people and being a leader are not rational matters. The technocrat who can produce the best plan for improving the economy is not the best leader. Leadership depends on touching people's emotions. For example, there is little doubt that Jimmy Carter understood the details of government policies far better than Ronald Reagan did. But Reagan understood leadership better than Carter did.

Governments must also make decisions, usually involving a number of people. Even monarchs and dictators have advisors and councils. In democratic governments like ours, elected representatives make decisions. But that process is far from rational. Anyone who knows anything about politics knows that politicians operate on a personal level. They make deals with other politicians, compromise, do favors, call in IOUs, form coalitions, and protect each other. They try to persuade each other, but not with cold, logical arguments. They plead, cajole, threaten, make promises, and tell jokes. They appeal to their colleagues' patriotism, honor, and love of country.

Probably the most powerful technique that any politician can use on another politician is flattery. Politicians want to be regarded as Very Important Persons. In the United States we see this technique at work when the President invites members of Congress to the White House. Besides the "horse trading" that goes on, the representatives enjoy being part of the ultimate power and status that is the Presidency. It is one of the most effective techniques a President can use to promote his policies. Its effectiveness depends upon a whole set of emotions, not upon intellect and reason. Politics is personal.

How could this political process be employed in a world government? How could people from Nigeria, Russia, Honduras, and Japan get together and hammer out a policy? People from radically different cultures often cannot even communicate with each other clearly; misunderstandings are all too common. But political wheeling and dealing is far more complex and subtle than simple communication. People around the world today are simply too different to work together politically. They respond emotionally to different things. They do not know each other's cultural rituals. Should one ask about the family back home, offer a colleague a drink, offer to make a deal? Will it be perceived as a bribe? Can one confidentially criticize another representative? Different cultures have different feelings and expectations on matters like these.

On a strictly technical problem, such as scientific investigation, people from different cultures can work together (although it is difficult). But politics is not a technical problem. The decisions aren't based on mathematical calculations, and the stakes are too high.

Politics involves values more than it involves reason or intellect. A world government would inevitably run into conflicts over values. For example, what policy would a world government have toward women? Will women hold offices and supervise men? Americans will say that men and women are equal, women should have the same opportunities as men, and that both sexes should do the same jobs. But to many other people around the world—probably the majority—such an attitude is very disturbing. To some it is shocking and offensive.

What policy will the world government have toward religion? Americans say live and let live. The government should not take any actions affecting religion. But Americans are in the minority again. Most people around the world could not even imagine banning religion from public schools. They want their children to learn their religion in school. Many feel it is more important than anything else they learn. If the world government had any educational function—and how could it fail to—would it adopt the American attitude or the majority's attitude?

Who would participate in the world government? Who gets a vote? Many countries contain substantial minorities who feel that they are not represented by their official government. Gypsies in Romania, Tamils in Sri Lanka, Turks in Germany, and Basques in Spain all protest against the official government, sometimes violently. In Africa tribal loyalties are far stronger than national loyalties. The Kurds regard themselves as a legitimate nation, with their own history, traditions, culture, and language, although they live in several different countries. Which version of history will the world government adopt? Apart from who votes, where would the world government draw the boundaries between states? Violent disputes have recently occurred between Ecuador and Peru, Greece and Turkey, India and Pakistan, and Morocco and Mauritania. Governments and citizens feel very strongly about their land and borders.

People in different countries have different *basic* values. And people's values are very important to them, by definition. They are motivated to achieve and protect their values. An appeal to their values will inspire them to make sacrifices, or to fight. But reason, rational argument, and intellect do not move people. Efficient solutions are not what people care about. The idealists' mistake is to think that rationality is a larger part of human nature than emotion and tradition. But it isn't. People are influenced more by feelings than by understanding.

The idealists may be right when they say that people are all similar in being rational. And that similarity is important for scientific cooperation. But politics is not science. Politics and government involve values, personal relationships, negotiations, and emotions. When it comes to politics, the differences among people completely overshadow the similarities.

If politicians were somehow to establish a world government, that would be a disaster. It would be an expansion of big government beyond the level of national governments we have now. The American federal government has grown tremendously since the Second World War, and the main effect has been creeping dependency. Americans are losing the energy, inventiveness, initiative, and Yankee ingenuity that made us a great country. It isn't only the poor who have become dependent (and therefore doomed to remain poor). It is also big corporations, who have come to expect their "corporate welfare," their tax breaks and subsidies, and have lost the incentive to be competitive. The middle class saves almost nothing because they expect the government to care for them in their old age. Everyone calls in lawyers and goes to court over trivial, perceived slights. A world government would eventually make the member states dependent, complacent, and spiritless.

The most harmful effect of big government is to destroy personal responsibility. People should help their neighbor. Understood rightly this isn't about their metaphorical "neighbor," some distant abstraction. It is about their real, live neighbor, who lives near them. If people had the moral will to take care of their real neighbors, the world would have fewer problems. But when Americans today see someone in trouble, many of them think "the government should do something." It is much easier to put a check in the mail, write a letter to a newspaper, or serve on a committee than it is to deal with needy people face to face. Big government has undermined people's compassion and sense of responsibility, and world government would have the same effect on member states.

"That government is best which governs the least," said Thomas Jefferson. Government's natural tendency is to grow and grasp more power. That is the tendency of people who want to tell others how to live. Therefore reasonable people will restrain and check government wherever possible. Working together with neighbors and fellow citizens is useful and good. But the larger government becomes, the more removed it is from the people it affects. And relying on distant, impersonal government undermines people's best qualities. A world government would be the biggest and worst government of all.

The idealists who propose a world government are often academics and intellectuals. That might explain how they could have such an unbalanced picture of human nature. To them, reason and rational argument are wonderful, exciting activities, and the crown of human nature. But most people are not intellectuals. Most people guide their lives by love, honor, ambition, joy, and other emotions, not by rationality. That is certainly true in politics, where decisions depend on emotions and personal relationships more than rational analysis. A world government might work in a world of academics. But in the real world, with real people, it is a childish dream.

Key Concepts

government	emotion	dependency
politics	rationality	responsibility
human nature	cultural values	

Critical Questions

1. The essay says that different people have proposed different types of world governments. Which type is it criticizing?
2. Do you think egotism and vanity are important factors in the American government? Would they ever lead Congress or the President to adopt a national policy that they know is second best?
3. According to localists, why couldn't representatives from different countries work together in a world government?

4. Does a localist think all people are rational? What mistake is the supporter of world government making, in the localist's opinion?
5. What effects has the expansion of government had on people, according to the essay? Do you agree or disagree?
6. Do you think the localist's criticisms apply to the type of federation that the internationalist proposed? If the federation has only one goal—to keep the peace—then couldn't it avoid the kind of politics the localist describes?

Methods and Techniques

COMPARING

One of the most basic thinking skills we use is comparing things. Both of the essays in this section compare several things. The first compares the past with the present, when it says we are living in a new age. The main conclusion of the first essay largely depends on comparing a federation of nations with the United States. And it compares people in America with people in other countries. The second essay compares different types of world governments, science and politics, and—like the first—Americans and other people around the world.

Comparing two things means finding similarities and differences between them. To compare things effectively keep two guidelines in mind. First, you must be systematic. Observe or think about every aspect of the two items being compared: color, shape, motion, effect on people, composition, function, cost, danger, and any other feature you can imagine. It might be helpful to organize features in some way: physical, inside, outside, emotional, functional, past and future, (i.e., what is the origin of the two things, and what will their future be?), relation to other things, and so on. Being systematic will help you find similarities and differences you wouldn't otherwise find. The most interesting comparisons are the unusual, surprising ones.

To keep track of all the similarities and differences, make three columns, left, right, and center. The left column lists the characteristics of one item, and the right column lists the different characteristics of the other item. The center column lists characteristics they share, i.e., similarities. For example, in comparing apples and oranges the two outer columns might begin with differences in color: "red" on the left for apple, and "orange" on the right for orange. In the center, one might put "sweet." The use of columns organizes and directs one's thinking more effectively.

Sometimes people will argue over similarities and differences because they are looking at different *levels* of characteristics. One person is looking at a very specific feature, and the other is looking at a general feature. For example, one person might say apples and oranges are *similar* because they both have skins, or peels. But another person might say they are *different* because an apple has a thin skin while an orange has a thick skin. Both are right, of course. The disagreement arises because one person is looking at peels in general (as compared with no peel), while the other person is looking at the specific type of peel. One person might say apples and oranges are similar because they are both sweet, while another might say they are different because an apple is tart while an orange is tangy (two ways of being sweet). These two people are looking at different levels of properties, general and specific. It is best to think about both general and specific characteristics, and things will often be similar on a general level but different on a more specific level.

Besides being systematic and methodical, we should ask the *purpose* of the comparison. Any two things can be compared, and a person can find many similarities and differences between any two things. In fact, we can find too many. We need some purpose to limit the search. The purpose will help us decide which properties are relevant or important, and which ones aren't. For example, I might compare apples and oranges because I am a grocer and I need to decide which to sell. On the other hand, my purpose could be to grow them, and I need to decide which to grow. In that case, I will be interested in a different set of similarities and differences from the grocer. Or my purpose might be to eat them, or draw them, or peel them, or to persuade my children to eat more fruit, or anything else. People with different purposes will be interested in different properties. So before we begin listing similarities and differences between two things, we should think about our purpose in comparing them. If the purpose is simply to find something interesting, then anything might be relevant.

The second essay makes a point about purpose. Both essays compare Americans and other people in the world. Both agree that there are some similarities and differences; in particular, both agree that people everywhere are similar in being rational. But the second says that if the purpose is to evaluate the idea of world government, then that similarity is irrelevant. World government is a form of politics. And in politics the differences among people—differences in their values, their manners, their emotional reactions to things—are more relevant than their similarities.

Understanding the Dilemma

INTERNATIONALIST OR LOCALIST

Many people believe that citizens of one country should learn about life in another country, that countries should exchange students, and that they should cooperate on international projects. But an internationalist (as the term is used here) goes farther. He or she believes that nations should be willing to give up some of their independence. They should join a world government, in which they have a voice, but in which they do not make the final decisions. The majority in the world government makes the final decisions, and it has the power to enforce its decisions.

A localist, in contrast, believes that such a world government is not possible, because political negotiation depends on personal, emotional considerations, and people from different cultures cannot engage in that kind of give and take. They do not understand each other well enough to make the world government work.

An internationalist begins with the assumption that war is the greatest threat to every nation, and nuclear war is the worst kind of war because it could annihilate the whole country, and even destroy all life on the planet. The first essay does not mention nuclear terrorism, but an internationalist would probably say that it provides another reason to put nuclear materials under international control. Nuclear war is an obvious threat. World government is an obvious solution. People around the world can understand large, pressing problems like this, and can understand the logical means to deal with them. They can agree on the facts, the consequences of the facts, the possible actions to take, and the best course of action. Differences in diet, clothing, marriage customs, and so on do not affect people's intelligence or ability to think. Therefore people can agree to form a world government once they begin to think about the new opportunity we now have.

But a localist has a different view of people. He or she says that emotions play a much larger role than reason in determining what people decide to do. This is true in general, but it is especially true in politics. Political leadership and decision-making are very complicated. What one person calls a problem, another might not regard as a problem. What a person regards as the best solution will depend on her or his goals and values, which will be different from another person's goals and values. The differences among people around the world are not just in superficial things like clothes, but in the rules for communicating and interacting. We Americans all follow the same subtle, unspoken rules, but other people have different rules. People from different countries can negotiate on relatively minor, technical issues, but not on grave, life-or-death issues.

It is clear, then, that a fundamental disagreement between the internationalist and the localist is in their views of human nature. Are people rational, and do they make decisions based on clear perceptions and logical reasoning? Or are people swayed more by emotions, and do they make decisions based on feelings, intuition, and personal loyalties? Are they rational about some things, but emotional about other things? Your answer will help you decide whether you are an internationalist or a localist.

Internationalists and localists also have different views of government. An internationalist believes that government can exercise tremendous power wisely, for the good of all. A world government, like our national government, will be made up of representatives of the people, so it will carry out the people's wishes. There are many problems that cannot be solved by individuals, but can only be solved by governments. If a world government made every nation secure, people could devote their time and energy to productive pursuits, and create a whole new civilization.

A localist says we should look at the facts about what has actually happened, not dreams of what might happen. The fact is that growing government has made people more and more dependent on its services, a localist believes. As government takes on more responsibilities, individuals give up their own personal responsibilities and expect the government to do everything. They become more like children. Some kind of government—working together with friends and neighbors—is necessary, but the less the better, a localist believes.

Where do you stand? Are people rational? Are we all fundamentally alike? Are governments expressions of greater cooperation, or are they dangerous threats to our autonomy? Are you an internationalist or a localist?

INTERNATIONALIST

1. Current political, economic, and cultural conditions are unique in history, and make a world government possible.
2. People will accept a world government because it will have a very limited agenda, which is to keep the peace, not to interfere in people's personal lives.
3. If all the diverse people of the United States can work together in the American federal government, then the diverse people of the world can work together in a world federation.
4. There is no need to fear majority rule in a world federation because all people want the same things as Americans: peace and freedom.

LOCALIST

5. People act primarily on the basis of emotions, values, and traditions, not rational calculation.
6. Since traditions are different around the world, and the things that arouse emotions are different, it follows that people are fundamentally different.
7. Government is personal and emotional; it operates through individual relationships based on trust, bargaining, and nonverbal communication.
8. As government grows, it makes individuals more and more dependent on it.

FOR FURTHER STUDY

Historical Examples

INTERNATIONALIST: Immanuel Kant. *Perpetual Peace and Other Essays.* Hackett, 1983. Originally published in 1795. Kant proposes a limited world government, and says that its member states must be constitutional democracies.

LOCALIST: Niccolò Machiavelli. *The Prince.* Many editions. Originally written in 1512. Machiavelli, the supreme realist, says that politics is a struggle for power, and devious princes must use any means they can to maintain power.

OTHER SOURCES

Ronald J. Glossop. *World Federation? A Critical Analysis of Federal World Government.* McFarland and Co., 1993. Arguments for world government, localist objections, and internationalist replies.

Hans Morgenthau. *Politics among Nations: The Struggle for Power and Peace.* 6th Edition. Knopf, 1985. See chap. 1: "A Realist Theory of International Politics: Six Principles of Political Realism."

F.M. Stawell. *The Growth of International Thought.* H. Holt and Co., 1930. Brief, readable history of ideas about international relations, from the Greeks to 1900.

Emery Reves. *The Anatomy of Peace.* Harper, 1946. Vigorous plea for world government, written in a plain, direct style.

Inis L. Claude. *Swords into Plowshares: The Problems and Progress of International Organization.* 4th Edition. Random House, 1971. Comprehensive discussion of many types of problems facing internationalists.

James Bohman, Matthias Lutz-Bachmann, eds. *Perpetual Peace: Essays on Kant's Cosmopolitan Ideal.* MIT University Press, 1997. Positive and negative views.

John T. Rourke, ed. *Taking Sides: Clashing Views on Controversial Issues in World Politics.* 7th Edition. Dushkin Publishing Group, 1996. See Chapter 13: "Should a Permanent UN Military Force Be Established?"

NOTES

1. Samuel Eliot Morison, *The Oxford History of the American People*, vol. 3 (New American Library, 1972) p. 422.
2. Barbara Ward, *Five Ideas That Change the World* (Norton, 1959) p. 128.

Current Controversy

2.6 IS RACE ESSENTIAL TO IDENTITY?
ESSENTIALIST OR NONESSENTIALIST?

•

The fact that different races live in the United States leads to some interesting philosophical questions. In political philosophy, one can ask if democracy is fair. Racial minorities will always have fewer votes than the majority, and so will almost always be outvoted. How can they elect a candidate who represents them, or how can they promote their interests?

In ethics, the history of injustice makes people wonder about the right policy today. Do some people enjoy wealth and opportunities today because their ancestors benefitted from exploitation? Are some people disadvantaged today, not because of their own limitations, but because their ancestors were victimized and oppressed? If so, do middle-class people owe compensation to poor people, as a way of returning what was stolen in the past? Should racial minorities receive preferential treatment to make up for past injustices?

In the theory of knowledge, one can ask if people in different groups—racial groups, ethnic or linguistic groups, men and women—perceive the world in different ways. How is a black student's experience in a mostly white school with white teachers different from a white student's experience in the same school? If knowledge depends on experience, and the two students' experiences are different, will the students acquire different knowledge? To what degree will they be able to understand each other?

Philosophers have begun to think analytically about the concept of race itself. What is race? If I have one parent with light skin and one with dark skin, what does that make me?

Race is a complex phenomenon that raises many questions. The two essays in this section are about race and identity. The fact of racial differences leads people to ask how important those different characteristics are. Is a person's race an important part of the person's identity? Some say race is vitally important. Being black or Asian in America is not at all like being white. Therefore the first step in understanding another person is to recognize the person's race. Indeed, the first step in understanding oneself is to accept one's own race and all that it involves, some say.

But others say race is not important for identity. The type of person I am doesn't depend on my race. I can be black or white or yellow or red, and also intelligent or artistic, or greedy, or generous. Knowing a person's race doesn't tell us anything about the person's real nature. In fact, assuming that it does is a major problem.

The first essay below argues that race is important in understanding people. History and society play a big part in determining one's identity, and the histories of races are different. We can call this the "essentialist" point of view. The second essay takes the position that race is a physical phenomenon and not part of one's identity. Racial differences are not important. It represents the "nonessentialist" perspective.

YES: ESSENTIALIST

"The Meaning of Being Black"

What is black authenticity? Who is really black? First, blackness has no meaning outside of a system of race-conscious people and practices. After centuries of racist degradation, exploitation, and oppression in America, being black means being minimally subject to white supremacist abuse and being part of a rich culture and community that has struggled against such abuse. Hence, all black Americans have some interest in resisting racism—even if this interest is confined solely to themselves as individuals rather than to larger black communities.

This quotation is from a recent book called *Race Matters* (Vintage Press, 1994, p. 39) by Cornel West, a professor of philosophy at Princeton and an African American. It is an amazing passage. In eighty-six words West describes the multiple dimensions of black identity, and also isolates the essential core. He weaves together society, history, emotion, and refuge, concluding with an emphasis on moral commitment. By reflecting on each part of the passage, as I propose to do here, one can gain a deeper understanding of what it means to be black in America. West may not agree with my comments on his statement, but I believe he has distilled the essence of black identity. The political leaders who urge African Americans to assimilate, join the white middle class, and pretend that race does not matter, should study this passage.

"What is black authenticity? Who is really black?" West begins with questions. Before we can understand race in American, we have to step back and take a critical stance. We have to decide exactly what questions we want to ask. West's questions reveal two of his assumptions. He assumes that black authenticity is not the same as white authenticity. Being black is not like being white. One might think that point is too obvious to mention, but there are those who say that America is a color-blind society and that we have moved beyond the segregation and racism of the past. West disagrees. Race still matters.

The second assumption behind these questions is more controversial. West assumes that being black is not simple or automatic. One isn't born being black. It's possible that some black people are authentically black and some aren't; some are "really black" and some aren't. West assumes that being black is not a matter of color, but is more. What else is involved in being black besides color? Are some people closer to this "authentic blackness" than others?

"First, blackness has no meaning outside a system of race-conscious people and practices." The important word here is "system." It is essential to understand that race is not a biological or physical issue but a social issue. A person can be black only within a certain kind of society. If some people are more black than others, of course that does not mean some have darker skin than others. Being black depends upon one's position within a social system.

It may be difficult to separate race from skin color and appearance. But consider the following examples. In the 1890s Adolph Plessy, a black man living in Louisiana, sat in the white section of a train. He violated the segregation laws so he could challenge them in the Supreme Court. He lost. The Court ruled that "separate but equal" facilities for blacks and whites were constitutional. Ironically, in appearance Plessy was indistinguishable from whites, since he was seven-eighths white. But his one black ancestor meant that, in the eyes of the law—in the system—he was black. Another example shows that race doesn't depend on appearance. In the 1920s, many Jews in Germany thought of themselves as good Germans, and certainly didn't look or behave any differently from Germans. But when the Nazis instituted "a system of race-conscious people and practices," some good Germans were reclassified as Jews.

"After centuries of racist degradation, exploitation, and oppression in America. . . ." We cannot escape from the past. Being black means carrying the burden of history within oneself. We all live in the shadow of America's shameful history. History influences all of us, because it influences the society we live in now. For example, black people have rarely been able to get loans from white banks to start businesses, so it has been more difficult for them to climb the economic ladder. Black colleges made heroic efforts to educate young people, but without contributions from wealthy alumni, or income from high tuition, they could not offer the best educations. When black people began moving to cities in search of opportunity in the 1940s and 1950s, white people fled to the suburbs, perpetuating American segregation.

All these historical trends influence black and white people today. Decades of poverty, lack of education, and exclusion from white society shape children's aspirations. How could a black child plan to be a doctor or scientist or MBA, when everything she sees around her tells her it's impossible? How could white people welcome blacks into their neighborhood when they have never lived with blacks before, and the movies and press portray blacks as poor, uneducated, and prone to crime?

History influences people even more directly through parents, grandparents, aunts, and uncles. Black children hear stories of racist hatred, insults, jeering mobs, and everyday humiliation from parents and grandparents, who pass along even worse stories that they heard when they were growing up. Lived, oral history affects black children today. Individuals are part of groups, and the groups' history is part of an individual. Even if a black person has never personally been denied service in a restaurant or accused of shoplifting or insulted by white people, the person carries the group's experiences within herself. Some conservatives say that since discrimination is illegal, and colleges accept minorities now, black people are just as free as whites and have the same opportunities. They naively believe that every individual creates herself out of nothing, independently of the past. But West recognizes that no one is immune to his or her race's misfortunes or privileges. Every black person is infected by the social system, and feels the hard tumor of history within herself or himself.

"Being black means being minimally subject to white supremacist abuse. . . ." West begins his book with a story about waiting for a taxi on Park Avenue in New York City. Many empty taxis passed; none would stop for him. After a half hour, he gave up. Blacks encounter such minor abuses and discrimination all the time. Their significance is not economic or political, but psychological. They are constant reminders. Being minimally subject to white supremacist abuse means that black people are never allowed to forget that they are a small minority, not like the mainstream, and potentially victims of much greater oppression. As a result, blacks can never completely escape from fear, anger, depression, and indignation. Racial anxiety is a bigger part of being black than skin color. It's no wonder that black people suffer from hypertension and high blood pressure at much higher rates than white people.

White supremacist abuse does not only mean Klansmen in robes and hoods. It means indirect messages of inferiority. Dominant majorities feel that they are superior to conquered or enslaved minorities, and so the dominant culture—newspapers, movies, education, politics—expresses the belief. The message may be subtle, disguised, or even denied. But when black people look at schools and colleges; professional associations of doctors, lawyers, and scientists; or Fortune 500 companies, they get the message: "You are inferior, you are incompetent, you are incapable." It is a crushing assault on one's self-image, inescapable and unendurable.

Being black means being accompanied by some degree of fear and anxiety all the time. One can try to ignore these feelings, but they are always there. But beneath the constant frustrations and self-doubts is an even more painful emotion that is part of black identity. Black people feel a particular kind of powerlessness. Most black people are relatively poor and economically powerless, but being black is not a matter of class. Some white people are poor, and some black people are not. Black people are not adequately represented in government, and so lack political power. But political power would not overcome the permanent potential for supremacist abuse.

That potential leads to a special kind of powerlessness. As minorities living in a white culture, black people are powerless to define themselves. They are powerless to choose their own identity. Instead, their identity is imposed on them by the pervasive, insistent institutions of the white majority. The majority naturally takes itself as average, or the norm, and regards anything else as different, strange, or abnormal. The most insidious and crippling kind of control over people is control over their ways of defining themselves. By cutting off certain possibilities, and constantly repeating certain images, the culture drives assumptions into black people's minds and fixes their perceptions. Some black people may not even realize what has happened.

". . . part of a rich culture and community that has struggled against such abuse." People who face some hardship, such as a hurricane or famine or shipwreck, feel a bond with each other. Shared suffering brings people together. Black people form such a community. In their struggle to survive, they have created a rich culture that expresses their suffering. The themes of gospel music are travail in this life, hope for a better world, and profound sadness. The blues give voice to the everyday heartache and conflicts among oppressed people. And jazz goes beyond words to convey the black experience. Black culture includes poetry, fiction, dance, visual art, clothing, cooking, design, and every form of aesthetic expression.

By sharing this rich heritage black people may find an alternative identity to the "black identity" created by the dominant culture. The meaning of being black can be different for white people and black people, since they have such different positions and pasts. The group experience portrayed in the culture of the black community is vital; it recaptures some dignity and some self-determination for black people. Being an accepted, knowledgeable member of the black community is essential to having an authentic identity, in contrast with an artificial, imposed identity. For oppressed minorities, the group's experiences are more important than the individual's experiences, because minorities are accepted by fellow minorities but never fully accepted by the majority.

"Hence all black Americans have some interest in resisting racism—even if the interest is confined solely to themselves as individuals rather than to larger black communities." Being black means many things, based on the social system, the past, the potential for supremacist abuse, and the sense of self discovered among similar selves. But identity for anyone is mainly a matter of values and commitments. If you want to discover a person's identity, find out what he or she truly loves. Or hates and fears. Some people truly love money, and organize their lives around it. Some people truly love their children. Some people tell themselves they love their children, but actually put their career first. Some people say they love justice and equality, but send their children to exclusive, private schools. It isn't easy to be sure about one's real values.

Given the stressful, complex situation of black people in America, it is probably more difficult for them to find their true identity than white people. West concludes his incisive analysis by turning to values and interests. He suggests that all the other elements of black authenticity should give black people a purpose—to resist racism. Having suffered for centuries from racist prejudice themselves, and having survived and responded with a vibrant culture, black people are in a position to attack the disease and educate others. The tragic black experience leads naturally to a desire to eradicate racism, and therefore the deepest core of black authenticity is the commitment to justice for all. Having felt the effects of racism first hand, blacks know how terrible it is. The true meaning of being black is to love justice and hate racism.

All the pain and fear and anger in the black experience may make it difficult for black people to find their true identity. And the dominant white culture gives misleading advice. But the black spirit has endured unimaginable horrors because the moral passion at its center cannot be suppressed and cannot be denied.

Key Concepts

social phenomenon	history	white supremacist
powerlessness	community	racism

Critical Questions

1. According to the essentialist, could a society exist where some people looked black, others looked white, yellow, and red, but no races existed? Why or why not? Do you agree?
2. How does history influence people today, according to the essay? If people chose to ignore the past, could they escape from its influence?
3. If a black person is highly educated and financially successful, is he or she subject to white supremacist abuse, according to the essentialist? Why or why not?

4. Why are black people powerless to determine their own identity? If society influences everyone, then is a white person also powerless to form his or her own identity?
5. The essentialist claims that when a person belongs to a minority group, the group's collective experience is more important for that individual's identity than the individual's own particular experiences. Why?
6. Can a person say that race is essential to one's own identity, and also hate racism? Is it self-contradictory to say that an individual's race is a very important part of his or her identity, and that racism is wrong?

NO: NONESSENTIALIST
"Race and Identity"

The United States does not have a good record on race relations. The early settlers from Europe were generally suspicious and hostile toward Native Americans, and eventually killed them in large numbers and displaced the survivors from their homes. In the nineteenth century, Asian immigrants were mistreated. During the Second World War, American-born citizens of Japanese ancestry were simply assumed to be security risks, solely because of their race, and were confined to internment camps. And African Americans were enslaved, exploited, disenfranchised, segregated, and abused throughout most of America's history. Other ethnic groups were persecuted as well.

In light of this depressing history, many people today try to be more aware of race and ethnic differences. Most want to avoid the prejudice and intolerance of the past and celebrate the benefits of diversity. But people disagree on just what it means to recognize race. Granted that the attitudes of the past were wrong, what attitudes and beliefs about race should we have now and in the future? The issue is so important that every person should clarify his or her beliefs at the deepest level. I want to ask what role race plays in a person's identity.

Some say that race is vital to identity and that anyone who wants to understand himself or herself must begin by understanding his or her own race. I disagree. I believe that race is irrelevant to identity. The very attempt to avoid the mistakes of the past has led some to repeat those same mistakes.

What Is Race?

Race is a set of physical traits used by scientists to classify people. A particular race is a group of people who share certain physical traits. Physical anthropologists look at hair, skin color, facial features, the shape of the skull, blood type, resistance to some diseases, and other features. For example, some people have straight, dark hair; light skin; high cheekbones; a fold of skin over the eye (the epicanthic fold); and a round skull. Other people have curly hair; dark skin; a broad nose; and a long skull. And others have other traits.

In the nineteenth century scientists distinguished three main races: Negroid, Mongoloid, and Caucasian. But some groups did not fit any of the three categories very well, nor did they seem to be a blend of two or even three races. So now anthropologists distinguish nine or more distinct races. Moreover, some people *are* blends and do not belong definitively to one race or another. The boundaries among different races are like the boundaries among the colors of the spectrum: one shades gradually into the other.

Despite the vague boundaries, the concept of race helps us understand evolution and the influence of geography. People who live in a certain area, such as the aborigines of Australia, intermarry. Over many generations they become more similar to each other. If contact with people in other areas is limited, then differences in appearance between the separate groups may increase over time. Thus race is a function of geography.

Most of the features anthropologists study are adaptations to climate and environment. The straight hair and short limbs of the Mongoloid race are adaptations to cold. The straight hair serves to retain heat in the head, and the short limbs allow better circulation to prevent chill and frostbite. On the other hand, the curly hair and dark skin of the Negroid race are adaptations to heat. Curly hair allows air to circulate and cool the head, and dark skin gives protection from the sun.

But evolution is not perfect. In Africa, malaria is a common disease, and over the centuries Africans adapted and evolved a relative immunity to it. The adaptation involves red blood cells. Humans have two genes controlling red blood cells (like the two genes controlling eye color). Among Africans, one gene produces round red blood cells, like the other races' genes, but one produces cells shaped like a crescent, or a sickle. That gives Africans partial immunity to malaria. A problem arises, however, when a child inherits sickle genes from both parents, but no round gene. That child will have sickle cell anemia, which can be fatal. But since 50 percent of children will have immunity and only 25 percent will have sickle cell anemia, the adaptation saves more lives (from malaria) than it costs (in anemia). The details of genetics and anemia are complicated, but this simplified account illustrates how scientists can use the concept of race to help explain how people in different places evolved in different ways.

Unfortunately, some people use the concept of race for hateful purposes. *Racism* is an outlook based on the assumption that physical traits such as skin color are associated with psychological or moral traits, such as intelligence or greed. A racist is a person who believes that all or most people with certain types of hair or facial features also have certain talents or psychological tendencies or moral weaknesses. Of course there is abundant evidence to the contrary. Among all races we can find the whole range of human capacities and dispositions. Hair, skin, or shapes of noses do not help us predict anything about a child's potential. Character traits like cruelty, ambition, and empathy are learned from parents and cultural traditions.

Racists make two simple errors. First, they think that if you know a person's physical appearance, then you can know that person's mental abilities and moral character. They are like astrologers, who think that if you know a person's birthday, then you can know the person's psychological make-up, and even his or her future as well! But there is no connection. The date of people's birth doesn't determine personality or destiny. Similarly, a person's physical appearance doesn't determine his or her abilities or preferences.

The second error is different but just as silly. Racists think that if an individual belongs to a certain group, then the individual has the same qualities as other members of the group. For example, if John is Irish, and Irish people are musically gifted, then John must be musically gifted. This is stereotypical thinking. It is failing to recognize a person's individuality, but rather seeing only the qualities a person shares with other members of a group. Even if John is Irish, he may not be musical at all. In addition, it is almost always a mistake to make generalizations about large groups. Many people from Ireland are excellent musicians, but that doesn't support the statement "Irish people are musically gifted." Some are and some aren't, as with any other nation. So the racist's second error is twofold: overgeneralizing about groups, and ignoring particular individuals' uniqueness.

What Is Identity?

Identity is a complex concept, and people might disagree about its meaning. As a start, we can note that the word "identity" is related to the words "identify," "identification," and "identical." The identity of something is whatever allows people to identify it, recognize it, or pick it out of its surroundings. Thus identity is the set of properties something has that distinguish it from everything else. If two things have exactly the same properties, we say they are "identical."

Government agencies and businesses use various techniques to identify people. The FBI relies on fingerprints, since an individual's fingerprints distinguish him or her from every other person. A passport includes a photograph, and a driver's licence may mention eye color. We all use Social Security numbers and personal passwords.

But when people apply the concept of identity to themselves, they are thinking of more than these procedures. My fingerprints and Social Security number distinguish me from everyone else, but I can still wonder about my identity. Physical identity is not the same as psychological identity. Psychological identity is the set of psychological traits I have that make me the particular person I am. A person might be an introvert or an extrovert, spontaneous or cautious, romantic or practical, people oriented or task oriented, intuitive or analytical. Every person has many traits, or ways of feeling, thinking, and acting. And while two people may both be cautious and analytical, no two people will have *all* the same traits, in the same degree, expressed in the same ways. So the particular combination of curiosity, courage, determination, introspection, and so on, makes each person the unique individual he or she is.

But there is more to personal identity than this. Some of my psychological traits are important and some aren't. My tastes in breakfast cereals are a part of me, but I could change them without changing my identity. Perhaps I enjoy watching hockey, but my interest could disappear and it wouldn't matter to anyone. On the other hand, some changes would matter. They would make me "a different person." If I am a dedicated lawyer who works long hours and loves discussing cases with colleagues, and then I switch careers and become a security guard on the night shift at the mall, people will say I've changed. Someone might say "You are not the same person you were." Physically I am the same, but psychologically I am not. Some psychological traits are important, in the sense that if they change, my identity changes. Some traits are essential to me. They define me.

In fact, when people try to find their own identity, they are not trying to find the particular combination of traits that makes them unique. They are trying to find the psychological traits that are important to them. When you get to know someone well, you do not know all the person's tendencies and responses to things. Instead you learn the person's priorities, what the person cares about most deeply, what he or she could not change without becoming a different person. My identity is not only whatever makes me unique. It is whatever is most important to me about me. Identity is not a matter of uniqueness, but of value. That is why we feel so strongly about discovering our identity and having an identity. It is discovering what is valuable to us.

Is Race a Part of Identity?

If one's race were changed, would one be a different person? Is people's race a fundamental value for them? I think some do make their race central to their identity. Their race is extremely important to them. But if the present analysis of race and identity is correct, race *should not be* a part of identity. To make race a defining property of oneself is to misunderstand both race and identity.

Race is a set of physical properties, whereas identity is a set of psychological properties. Now some people are wholly preoccupied with their bodies and appearances. Judging from public interviews, some fashion models and celebrities, male and female, apparently think of little else but their appearance, and define themselves by their straight nose, their long legs, their "innocent waif" look, or whatever. Body builders look at themselves in a mirror for hours at a time, and work very hard to shape different muscles in just the right way. But models and body builders have personalities. Getting to know a model does not mean studying her portfolio. It means learning how she relates to people, how she deals with adversity, or how she imagines her future. Physical appearance changes quickly, but a person's basic personality does not change so easily. Some people may think that their body is the core of their identity, but they simply haven't found their true identity yet.

The same applies to race. A person's racial characteristics are physical, and therefore not a part of his or her personality. It is very tempting to think that physical traits are reliably connected with psychological traits, and that fat people are jolly, or redheads have fiery tempers. Physical traits are easy to see, but character is difficult to perceive. Since identity is so important to us, we sometimes slide from appearance to personality without realizing it, even when we think about ourselves. But this is racism. It is assuming that certain physical traits are associated with certain psychological or moral properties. People who feel that their race is part of their identity are unconsciously making the same mistake that racists make. What that shows, I think, is that racism is a subtle and widespread way of thinking, and will not be easy to eradicate.

Other people make race a part of their identity in a different way. All of us seem to have a basic need to belong, to be members of a group. Our first club is our family. Soon we all join a circle of friends as well. And if our group of friends rejects us or excludes us, the experience is extremely painful. We also join other groups such as sports teams, and many people feel great pride in being citizens of our country. People even define themselves by the groups they belong to. Some people might feel that being a member of a racial group is an essential part of their identity. It isn't their physical appearance in itself that is important, but the fact that they are part of a larger group—white, black, Asian, etc.—and therefore related to many others like themselves.

But this way of thinking about identity is just as misguided as the focus on physical traits. Everyone needs friends and associates, and so the desire to belong to a group is natural. Moreover, we all choose to associate with people who are similar to us. But it is a mistake to assume that if another person is of the same race as I, then she is probably similar to me in her outlook or beliefs or values. If I attend a PTA meeting of diverse parents, should I hesitate to make friends with the black parents or Asian parents, on the grounds that I probably have more in common with the white people? If I think that way, I am thinking in stereotypes. I am discounting people's individuality and treating blacks and Asians as if they are all alike. I am assuming that a person who happens to be black is similar to all other black people.

There is a terrible irony here. If I think my race is part of my identity because I am probably similar to all the other members of my race, then I am stereotyping *myself*. I am failing to recognize my own individuality. In fact, I am making the second mistake that racists make, because I am assuming that if a person is a member of a group, he or she has the characteristics of other members of the group. But I am making the racist mistake about myself. The ease with which people make this error, and even its attraction for many, shows how insidious and dangerous racist thinking is. Even the victims of racism adopt their oppressors' way of thinking.

Thinking clearly about race and identity is not easy. The ideas have been abused and distorted for centuries. Even in more enlightened times, the concept of identity is still complex and imprecise. Moreover, because of its tortured past, and its connection with our feelings about what is important, the concept of identity is charged with strong emotions. These factors make it difficult to understand. All the more reason, therefore, to approach the problem with an open mind, patience, and logic.

Key Concepts

race	geography	racist
identity	personal values	stereotype

Critical Questions

1. How do scientists explain the origin of race? How is it a useful concept?
2. What two main mistakes do racists make, according to the nonessentialist?
3. In your opinion, is psychological identity independent of physical identity? Does a person's body type—size, appearance, agility—influence his or her psychological traits?
4. Can people decide what is important to them, or is that determined by earliest experiences and unchangeable? Are little habits and beliefs I'm unaware of, such as my cruel sense of humor, or chewing my food with my mouth open, or my belief that clothing style reveals character, part of my identity?
5. The nonessentialist seems to make the following three statements:
    a. identity depends on what is really important to a person, not on all traits;
    b. a person's race can be very important to him or her;
    c. identity does not depend on race.
    Are these three statements inconsistent? Has the nonessentialist contradicted himself or herself?
6. I belong to many groups, such as my neighbors, Yankee fans, commuters, and teachers. There are others groups I do not belong to, such as out-of-towners, Cubs fans, self-employed people, and physicians. Am I stereotyping myself if I associate with people who are similar to me rather than with people who are in different groups?

Methods and Techniques

IDENTITY

Who am I? Where do I belong in the scheme of things? What makes me different from everything else? These are all questions about identity. The search for identity is one of the most powerful motives for studying philosophy. It is one of the central questions philosophers think about.

Being philosophers, they realize they cannot find any answers until they first understand the question. When people search for their identity, what is it that they are looking for? What are they asking? What would satisfy them? The Department of Motor Vehicles is satisfied with a person's name, place and date of birth, eye color, or handicaps. That is enough for a driver's license. But philosophers and others want more. What more do they want?

Perhaps we can get a clue from teenagers. Teenagers are very much concerned with identity (not to say obsessed with it). They are at a stage of life where the question "Who am I?" takes on a real urgency. They are beginning to make important decisions that will determine their whole future. And they realize that they cannot remain at home much longer, completely within the confines of their families, but must think about leaving their parents and starting their own families. So the question of identity is important to them.

If we look at teenagers we see two contradictory tendencies. On the one hand, many try to be different from everyone else, especially their parents. They wear unusual clothes; listen to new, different music; and pursue interests or hobbies that they feel set them apart from the majority of people. They seem to think that finding one's identity means finding the ways in which one is different from other people, ideally different from *every* other person. Then one is absolutely unique.

On the other hand, they also exhibit exactly the opposite tendency. They want to belong. They want to be part of the group. They want to be one of the gang, and the idea of being different, "weird," and alone is terrifying. So while they think they are choosing strange clothes and hair styles, and expressing their own unique personalities, in fact they end up looking exactly like most other teenagers, down to the precise holes in the jeans or strands of bleached hair.

We shouldn't laugh at teenagers. They are victims of logic. They are only acting out in a more pronounced way what everyone must do. Everyone must find ways in which he or she is different, and everyone must find ways in which he or she is similar to others, part of the group. Both sides are logically required to have a sense of identity, because that is what it means to identify anything.

When a person asks "Who am I?," he can answer the question in a very general way, a very specific way, or an in-between way. Some philosophers answer the question in a very general way by saying "I am a human being," and then explaining what that means. A person could also say "I am an American." That is more specific than human being. To explain what it means to be an American, she would have to say what all Americans have in common, *and* what sets Americans apart from non-Americans. Or she could be even more specific and say "I am a Democrat," "I am a college professor," "I am a philosophy teacher in California," and so on, with smaller and smaller categories. But in each case, she must explain what makes her a Democrat or college professor. And that means she must explain how she is similar to other Democrats, and how she is different from people who are not Democrats.

This duality seems to be a logical feature of identifying anything, and a necessary part of one's identity. If so, it leads to an interesting consequence. Part of one's identity consists of being a member of certain groups, some large and some small—males, the elderly, sky divers, horse lovers, people with long noses, etc. But an equally important part of one's identity consists of "the Other," of seeing the differences between oneself and others. This analysis suggests that one defines oneself in part by recognizing a group or groups who are different, who are outsiders, not like oneself. If I am male, that means there are others who are not male, different from me, set apart. If I am American, that means there must be others who are not like us Americans. If I am a human being, then there are other things that are nonhuman.

If this is true, then it is an interesting fact about human nature. In itself, it is neither good nor bad. Like atomic energy, it might be used to benefit people or to harm people. Perhaps it explains things, perhaps it is alterable. Like many conclusions in philosophy, it opens up several new questions to think about.

Understanding the Dilemma

ESSENTIALIST OR NONESSENTIALIST?

Is a person's race an essential part of his or her identity? The nonessentialist in the second essay says no. Race is a useful concept for understanding evolution and the geographical distribution of people, but it is useless for understanding identity. It tells us nothing about a person's character. Identity depends on an individual's psychological traits, especially his or her core values.

An essentialist, on the other hand, claims that race is an important part of a person's identity. Being a member of a minority group shapes one's thoughts and feelings. Even if minorities have not personally felt the effects of discrimination, they know it is always possible. They learn from their families and fellow minorities about past abuses, and present institutions remind them of their relatively powerless status. A person's race shapes the cognitive, emotional, and moral dimensions of his or her character.

Essentialists and nonessentialists disagree on several points. One difference concerns the impact of the past and social relations on one's identity. To what degree is one's identity created by one's social environment, and to what degree can one choose one's own identity independently of social influences? The essentialist believes that everyone lives in a society, and certain features of the society influence a person's identity, particularly minorities' identities. For example, black people in the United States see the distribution of wealth, the numbers of blacks in the professions, and images of blacks in movies and TV, and they may feel excluded or even powerless. The surrounding society influences blacks' self-image.

Current social realities are results of past practices, and therefore identity is shaped by history as well. Minorities learn about the prejudices and abuses of the past. The stories people hear from parents and grandparents are especially important in forming their sense of themselves, and minorities hear stories about unjust treatment of people like themselves. In addition, the essentialist argues that minorities have created distinctive subcultures and communities within the larger society, and individuals can win more respect and dignity within those communities of fellow minorities than within the society at large. The majority culture, minority culture, and history all shape people's identities in decisive ways.

The nonessentialist claims that identity depends on "what is important to you about yourself," and that people can decide for themselves what is important. It isn't easy to discover what you think is important. People sometimes say they value one thing—honesty, for example—but actually behave in a different way to get something they want. They haven't discovered, or can't admit, what they really believe is important. But the nonessentialist suggests that people can choose their values and their identity. The author doesn't explicitly address the question of what determines identity, although he argues that race does not determine it. So one difference between an essentialist and a nonessentialist is on the issue of social influences: the essentialist believes they are very strong, and the nonessentialist believes in greater self-determination.

This first disagreement rests on a deeper one. For a nonessentialist, race is a biological phenomenon. It is a set of physical characteristics that evolved over the centuries. But for an essentialist, race is a social phenomenon. It is having a minority status in a society, which means having less power—economic, political, cultural—than people in the majority.

The essentialist and nonessentialist disagree not only about the nature of race and identity, but also about attitudes or policies we *should* have about race. Specifically, the nonessentialist claims that emphasizing racial differences and race as part of identity is very dangerous. Doing so encourages the same kind of thinking that leads to racism. Racists make two false assumptions, namely that a person's abilities and qualities depend in part on his or her race, and that all the members of a race are similar to each other in important ways. But if we decide that a person's race is a key part of her identity and a good indicator of what she is really like, then we are moving back toward the first racist assumption. And if we believe that each of us has more in common with people of our own race; that we will be more comfortable and at home with fellow whites, blacks, Asians, or whatever; and that we should form racial communities, then we are moving back toward the second racist assumption.

The whole problem with race, according to the nonessentialist, comes from emphasizing differences among people instead of seeing the commonalities or universal humanity of all people. The worst thing we can do about race is to teach people that they are fundamentally different from others because of their race, and fundamentally similar to people of the same race as themselves.

The essentialist might respond to this appeal with two points. First, minorities have been treated differently for centuries. It's impossible to ignore the numerous differences in status and power among races that existed for centuries and still exist now. In fact, it would be unrealistic and lead to a false identity. Moreover, minorities do gain certain benefits in their interactions with fellow minorities in their own community. It is wrong to deny them that refuge and fulfillment.

Second, the problem with race is not difference, but hierarchy. In other words, people can recognize differences without denigrating or oppressing one group or another. We can admit differences among people and also respect those differences and even value them. Racism does not mean thinking people are different; it means thinking some people are *inferior.* If we teach respect and fairness, then there is no danger in recognizing differences among people.

So, how important is history and social status to your identity? What is race and racism? Are you an essentialist or a nonessentialist?

ESSENTIALIST

1. Race is not physical but social; it isn't appearances, but other people's reactions to appearances that are important.
2. Everyone is decisively shaped by history and by present social arrangements.
3. The basic experience of being black is feeling the permanent threat of oppression.
4. Being black is ultimately positive, because it leads to a concern for the oppressed and a desire for justice for all.

NONESSENTIALIST

5. Race is a set of physical features that evolved in different areas, mostly as adaptations to climate.
6. It is a terrible mistake to believe that race indicates anything about a person's personality, aptitudes, or character.
7. A person's identity consists of those aspects of himself or herself that are important to himself or herself.
8. A person's race should not be important to himself or herself, since physical features are irrelevant to personality, values, or talents.

FOR FURTHER STUDY

Historical Sources

ESSENTIALIST: W.E.B. Du Bois. *The Souls of Black Folk.* Edited by Henry Louis Gates, Jr. and Terri Hume Oliver. Norton, 1999. Originally published in 1903. Du Bois argues for a distinctive black identity: "One ever feels his twoness—an American, a Negro; two souls, two thoughts, two unreconciled strivings; two warring ideals in one dark body."

NONESSENTIALIST: Booker T. Washington. *Up from Slavery.* Edited by William L. Anderson. Norton, 1995. Originally published in 1901. Washington promoted very gradual assimilation of blacks into white society until, eventually, there would be no racial division.

OTHER SOURCES

Anthony Appiah. *In My Father's House.* Oxford University Press, 1992. Eloquent defense of a nonessentialist view, arguing that black people are too diverse to have a common identity.

John P. Pittman, ed. *African-American Perspectives and Philosophical Traditions.* Routledge, 1996. Readable essays on the concepts of race and identity discussing essentialist and nonessentialist views.

Lucius T. Outlaw, Jr. *On Race and Philosophy.* Routledge, 1996. Complex essays based on the essentialist belief that the characteristics of groups define the individuals in those groups.

Marvin D. Wyne, Kinnard P. White, Richard H. Coop. *The Black Self.* Prentice-Hall, 1974. Emphasizes social influences on blacks' self-image, including early peer pressure and diminished personal control.

Thomas A. Parham, Joseph L. White, Adisa Ajamu. *The Psychology of Blacks: An African-Centered Perspective.* Prentice-Hall, 1999. Rejects the idea that black identity depends on encounters (usually negative) with the white majority, and posits a black identity based on "positive (Black-oriented) institutional and social support systems."

Pyong Gap Min, Rose Kim, eds. *Struggle for Ethnic Identity: Narratives by Asian American Professionals.* Sage Publications, 1999. A spectrum of experiences, from conflicts with the white majority and strong group identity, to assimilation and weak attachments to the ethnic group.

Thomas Sowell. *Race and Culture: A World View.* Basic Books, 1994. Argues that different ethnic groups (and the individuals within them) live by different values, with the result that some groups advance economically and technologically more rapidly than others; groups can change, but slowly.

Charles W. Mills. *Blackness Visible: Essays on Philosophy and Race.* Cornell University Press, 1998. Argues for a historical, "constructivist" view of race, trying to find a middle ground between essentialism and nonessentialism.

CONNECTIONS

INDIVIDUALIST OR RELATIONIST?

If you decide that you are an egalitarian, does that mean that you should be a libertarian or a paternalist? A capitalist or a socialist? Or can an egalitarian agree with any of these positions? What connections can we find among the positions in Chapter 2?

When we looked for connections among the positions in Chapter 1 (God, Immortality, and Faith), we found that some were committed to the belief in a supernatural level of reality, and others were committed to the belief that reality is unified and accessible to observation and ordinary experience. This fundamental disagreement allowed us to organize the positions into two groups, transcendentalists and naturalists, and to see the relationships among the positions.

There is a fundamental disagreement in Chapter 2 as well. Consider Section 2.2, "Is Liberty the Highest Social Value?" You remember that a libertarian says yes and a paternalist says no. The libertarian in this section argues that many of the goals or values we have in our society seem to be different from liberty. For example, we value money, security, and equal opportunity. But actually these values are the same as liberty. So when we pursue money, for example, we are actually valuing liberty. And when we have values that really are different from liberty, such as equality of condition and justice, they are not as important to us as liberty itself. But a paternalist disagrees. He or she says that we cannot explain what liberty is, so we cannot value it. Moreover, when it comes to drugs, prostitution, wearing seat belts, saving for old age, and many other areas, we do not allow people the liberty to do whatever they want, even though they would harm no one but themselves. We value morality or security more highly than liberty.

There are several important differences between these two positions. But one difference is in the attitude toward society, or the group as a whole. The paternalist places a high value on the group and what is good for the group. The libertarian does not trust the group as much, and values the individual more than the group. That is why a libertarian claims that the most important social value is liberty (of the individual), and a paternalist claims that the group as a whole should sometimes guide an individual to do what is best (for the group and for himself or herself), even if he or she disagrees. So the question is "How much sacrifice should an individual make for the society?"

Of course the difference is a matter of emphasis; everyone values individuals and everyone values groups. But some emphasize one, and some emphasize the other. Let's call people who emphasize the group "relationists," and people who mistrust the group "individualists." These labels are merely conveniences. The word "relationist" is a made-up word, a "neologism." We can use it to talk about the similarities among some of the positions in Chapter 2. The word "individualist" has various connotations for everyone, but I am proposing that we give it a special, limited meaning here. Our goal is to find connections among the positions in Chapter 2, and we need some sort of label to attach to those similarities. "Relationist" and "individualist" can serve, but you can use different labels if you like. The important thing is the general themes running through the different positions, not the labels we use.

So, we can say that a libertarian is an individualist, because libertarians value individual liberty more than they value the moral views of the majority, and they mistrust the judgment of the group as a whole. A paternalist, on the other hand, is a relationist because paternalists think that the larger group should force an individual to do the right thing, even in cases where no one else is involved. Are any of the other positions similar to these two?

Consider Section 2.3, "Is Equality the Highest Social Value?" The two positions in this section were egalitarianism and elitism. An egalitarian believes that people in our society should be more equal. If they were, we could eliminate poverty, crime, homelessness, stress, class conflict, and conformity. In fact, if we eliminated private property, and made people equal in material standards of living, we could create a virtual utopia. We could create a society with far fewer problems than our society has today. But an elitist claims that the policy would never work. People are different, the elitist says. We might try to enforce some sort of equality among citizens, but natural talents and determination will inevitably reintroduce inequalities in a short time. Instead of denying differences, we should take advantage of them, and help people find what they can do best. Everyone would benefit in such a society.

An egalitarian is similar to a paternalist. Both trust government to improve society as a whole. Both emphasize a uniform policy applied to the whole society. An egalitarian places a great value on equality. That is similar to a paternalist insofar as a paternalist thinks that some moral rules ("don't take drugs") apply to everyone equally. And government rules designed to help people apply to everyone equally. For example, paternalists force everyone to save for their old age (through Social Security taxes), although some people have the foresight to take care of themselves.

On the other side is the elitist, who is similar to a libertarian. An elitist opposes the group's attempt to make people more equal because it would infringe on individuals' freedom to strive for excellence and surpass others. Both an elitist and a libertarian believe that people are fundamentally different and unequal. An elitist says people have different talents and abilities, and a libertarian says people have different interests and goals. The government or the group should not try to deny or suppress these individual differences. Elitists and libertarians therefore share what we are calling the individualist attitude. They do not trust society as a whole, and emphasize differences among people. In contrast, egalitarians and paternalists have the relationist attitude. They believe the whole society is more important than any individual, and they believe inequalities are the source of many of the worst problems facing us.

Section 2.5, "Should We Establish a World Government?," provides good examples of a relationist and an individualist. If you believe in a world government, then you are an internationalist. An internationalist believes that the time is ripe for nations to transfer their nuclear weapons and other military assets to an international body, which would then enforce peace. We can be confident that such a world government will work because the American government works, and America includes millions of people with very different outlooks and ethnic backgrounds. Moreover people everywhere are rational enough to do what is in their interest.

These ideas put an internationalist in the broad category of relationist. He or she clearly trusts the largest group possible—the whole world, or all nations' representatives—with absolute power. He says each nation should sacrifice some of its own independence for the sake of security that will help everyone.

On the other hand, if you are opposed to a world government, then you are a localist. A localist argues that a world government is not possible because people are not as reasonable and cooperative as an internationalist thinks. The operation of a world government would be a political process, and politics is a messy, personal business that depends on a deep understanding and sympathy between people. Representatives from different cultures could not reach that level of understanding. Their values, manners, and feelings about things are too different. The localist is suspicious of large groups and large government in general. He or she says large government is dangerous because it undermines personal responsibility. Therefore a localist is a good example of an individualist.

Where do capitalists and socialists fit in? In Section 2.4, "Is Capitalism Just?," you first read a defense of capitalism and then an attack on capitalism. A capitalist believes that it is just to reward people or punish people on the basis of their contributions to society. Some contribute positively and some contribute negatively. Capitalism embodies this moral truth. In capitalism, consumers in a free market, not the government, decide how much a person has contributed, and so determine a person's reward. But a socialist argues that capitalism is unjust because it makes people immoral. Greed corrupts the health care system, the judicial system, and the political system. Capitalism psychologically conditions people until they make money the center of their lives, and put it ahead of compassion and justice.

The socialist's essay in Section 2.4 presents a primarily negative view. It explains what socialists are against—capitalism. Socialists oppose capitalism because it destroys human relationships, in their view. But that opposition also reveals what socialists value: they value human relationships, such as compassion, generosity, and cooperation. They value these more than the free market, where individuals compete for the best profit they can get. Thus socialists are relationists because they value a harmonious society more than individual liberty. (Or they try to define "liberty" in terms of harmonious relations with others.) They want to replace the free market, so they must favor more government direction of the economy.

Capitalists are individualists because they favor an individual's self-reliance and personal responsibility. They oppose government intervention in the market, and the government's decision about what rewards (income) people should receive. Capitalists are also similar to elitists. Both believe people are different: they have different abilities, and they make different contributions to society. On the other hand, socialists oppose the inequality created by wealth in capitalism; they favor greater equality.

The first section in Chapter 2 was Section 2.1, "Is Society Based on a Contract?" The two positions were contractor, who says yes, and organicist, who says no. The organicist says no because he or she believes that society exists before any individuals living today. Everyone is born into a society that already exists. We do not make an agreement to create a society. Our ability and willingness to make agreements is created by society, not the other way around. The organicist says that society is like language. We do not create our language; it already exists, and it provides us with the tools and methods of living. Or society is like an organism, and we are like the individual cells that briefly come and go as the organism lives on.

An organicist is clearly a relationist. Like other relationists, an organicist emphasizes the whole group. He or she believes that a society as a whole has its own reality and its own character, apart from the individuals who compose it. If we only think about individuals, we will miss these important aspects of the world.

Since he emphasizes the society as a whole, an organicist places relatively less emphasis on individuals. He doesn't ignore individuals. But in attempting to understand our social existence, and therefore social policies, an organicist believes we must try to see the whole and its properties rather than focusing narrowly on individuals and their properties. From this bird's eye point of view, observing society as a whole, individuals appear more equal than from the ground level perspective. The things we all have in common and that make us similar seem more important than the things that make us different. In this respect an organicist agrees with an egalitarian, and rejects the elitist's view.

The organicist would probably be more sympathetic to the socialist's position than to the capitalist's position. An organicist believes in a common good, a goal or outcome that benefits the whole society, not just part of it. One of the most important properties of a whole society is its morality. Every society enforces certain rules, and gives them great weight. These moral rules help maintain the health and stability of the society as a whole. They promote the common good. The belief in a society-wide morality, binding on individuals, makes an organicist similar to a socialist, who criticizes capitalism for its antisocial, excessive individualism. It also creates an alliance with paternalists, who believe that by enforcing its moral rules a society can help an individual in ways the individual cannot help himself or herself.

A contractor is similar to other individualists, but the connection is not as close as the connection of an organicist with other relationists. A contractor proposes a model as a way to understand society. He or she says the model of a contract helps us see what is really fundamental in society. Two people who enter into a contract are behaving rationally and cooperatively. And those human traits—rationality and sociability—are the fundamental basis of society. They explain why society exists at all. The contract model also explains why we are all morally obligated to obey the laws. We have implicitly promised to do so when we entered the social contract.

The social contract theory is an individualistic theory. It puts individuals before society. Individuals exist first and they create society. They could exist without society. Moreover, in agreeing to help form a society, an individual is acting in his or her own interests. She is not considering the common good but her own particular good. This egoistic aspect of a contractor's view makes it similar to a capitalist's view. Both approve of capitalism, free markets, entering and keeping contracts, seeking profits for oneself. Capitalism depends on freedom as well, and a contractor believes that each person freely enters society, and could, if necessary, freely leave a society. Society rests upon free choice, not indoctrination, conditioning, or social manipulation. The social contract theory provides a foundation for the libertarian view.

So there are connections between a contractor's point of view and the other individualist positions. But, as always, the relationships are complicated. A contractor emphasizes cooperation rather than competition, and that is different from capitalism. The emphasis moves a contractor closer to socialism and relationists. Furthermore, a contractor claims that virtually everyone is rational and sociable; everyone participates in society. That moves a contractor closer to egalitarianism—another relationist position—and away from elitism. Nevertheless, it seems to me that the ties between a contractor's view and the other individualist positions are more numerous and more important than his or her ties to the relationist position.

The current controversy in Chapter 2 is the debate over race and identity. An essentialist says that your race is an important part of who you really are, your identity. The reason is that your identity depends on history and social conditions, and social conditions are strongly influenced by relations among races. In other words, a person's position in society, her chances of being exploited or abused, and her participation in minority communities, all depend to a large extent on her race. The white majority's experience is generally different from minorities' experiences. And these social experiences determine her self-image and her sense of self. Thus race is crucial to one's identity.

The nonessentialist claims that race is a set of physical traits, such as skin color, eye or nose shape, type of hair, and so on. And your physical appearance is not an essential part of your identity. Your identity is whatever you decide is important about yourself. Being white or black or brown or yellow has no impact on important qualities like honesty, ambition, creativity, and so on. What is important is your dreams for the future, your memories, your talents and abilities, your likes and dislikes. A person's skin color is irrelevant to her potential, or her decisions about what she feels is important in life.

Since the essentialist emphasizes the influence of society and history on a person's identity, he or she is a relationist. A nonessentialist emphasizes personal choices and autonomy in creating one's identity, and that means he or she is closer to other individualists.

But the relationships are debatable. These are just a few connections you might see among the positions in Chapter 2. There are certainly others, both similarities and differences. But this preliminary sketch gives us the following chart:

Individualist	**Relationist**
libertarian	paternalist
elitist	egalitarian
capitalist	socialist
contractor	organicist
localist	internationalist
nonessentialist	essentialist

INDIVIDUALIST

1. People are biologically similar, but in the most important matters—such as maturity, initiative, creativity, and drive—people are very different.

2. At the most basic level, people are self-centered and competitive.
3. Given our human nature, we all value liberty and independence, and resent restrictions on our actions.
4. The only stable society, and therefore the best society, is one that allows us freedom to work and create, and rewards those who contribute to society.

RELATIONIST

5. People are basically similar (the differences are relatively superficial compared with the similarities), and our social arrangements should recognize that fact.
6. People are normally rational, cooperative, and friendly; only danger, threats, and desperate need make us behave otherwise.
7. Everyone will benefit most in a society that promotes compromise, working together, respect, tolerance, and consideration of the common good.
8. Unrestrained individualism and competition lead to conflict, resentment, injustice, and violence.

CHAPTER THREE

HAPPINESS, OBLIGATIONS, AND VALUES

3.1 Is Pleasure the Only Value?

Hedonist or Pluralist?

E arlier (in Section 1.3) I said that the question "Can God allow innocent suffering?" probably draws more people to philosophy than any other question. But the topic of this section—"Is pleasure the only value?" or "What goals should we have?"—may be in second place. Many people assume that philosophers think a lot about how one should live, or what kind of life one should lead. So they come to philosophy looking for advice about the best way of life. Everyone would like to know what goals he or she should have, what is most important, what is less important, and what isn't important at all. We all need some guidelines to help us make important decisions, about career, marriage, friends, self-development, money, sex, children, and other concerns. And we need some sense of where it is all leading, or what it all adds up to. Everyone would like to know how to give his or her life as a whole significance, worth, and value.

The question about goals is just another way of asking what values I should have. A person's goals are the same things as the person's values. If one of your goals is to have a lot of good friends, then you value friendship. You enjoy it, you approve of it, you work to develop and keep friendships. If one of your goals is to be healthy, then you value health.

Philosophers' discussions of goals are not like psychotherapists' or counselors' discussions. People go to a psychotherapist with a specific problem. Perhaps they feel lonely, or they are unhappy with their jobs, or they get angry too easily. They want advice on how to change their lives to solve the problem. The therapist must try to discover the particular circumstances of the person's life that cause the bad feelings. Then the therapist may make some suggestions tailored to this particular client's problem.

Philosophers work differently. Philosophers think about goals that all human beings should have. Human beings are all similar in many ways. We are biologically similar, and have similar biological needs. We all grow up with families, we are all socialized by our societies, we all probably have similar psychological needs, such as self-esteem, challenging work, companionship, and perhaps others. Philosophers search for the proper goals of human life *as such*, not solutions to particular psychological problems. One can say that philosophers think about values—things that are good—and not just certain people's desires.

The first essay that follows argues that the highest goal we can have is pleasure. In fact, it is the only worthwhile goal. This view is called "hedonism." The second essay describes a wide variety of values, or goals, and rejects hedonism. Since it argues for the conclusion that there are many good things to strive for, we can call the point of view of the second essay "pluralist."

YES: HEDONIST

"Hedonism"

What makes life worthwhile? How should we live? These are the most important questions one can ask, and the most pressing questions. Before we can turn our efforts to anything—going to school, going to work, going to a movie—we should know why we are doing it, and whether we shouldn't be doing something else.

Different people propose different answers, but the most persuasive answer was put forward long ago by a school of philosophers called Epicureans (from the Greek philosopher Epicurus) or hedonists (from the Greek word for pleasure, *hedone*). They taught that the highest good is pleasure (and the absence of pain). Pleasure is what makes life worthwhile, and everyone should attempt to achieve as much pleasure as he or she can. Not only is pleasure the highest good, it is the only good.

This is not the same as "eat, drink, and be merry." Eating too much or drinking too much will result in indigestion and hangovers, or other discomfort and pain. Immediate, short-term pleasures often lead to long-term pain, so hedonism requires some restraint and self-control. A sober, disciplined person probably experiences more pleasure and less pain over a longer time than a party animal.

Some philosophers prefer the word "happiness" to "pleasure." But what is happiness? Happiness is nothing more than the experience of pleasure, or the anticipation of pleasure, or the memory of pleasure. If you will recall a time when you were happy, you will notice that you were doing something that you enjoyed. Maybe you thought of your satisfying work in the garden. Or you were anticipating some future pleasure, perhaps an evening with your special friend after you finish working. Or you were remembering the great time you had last weekend at the beach. Happiness is necessarily connected with pleasure, although the pleasure can be past, present, or future.

Critics condemn hedonism as "a pig's philosophy," suggesting that hedonists value only physical pleasures. But there are various kinds of pleasure. There is the pleasure of resting after hard work, of being loved, of interesting conversation, of learning something new, and other "mental" pleasures.

The pursuit of pleasure can take many forms. One person may find pleasure in being with her family and providing for them. Reading bedtime stories to her children makes her feel warm and delighted. Another person may derive satisfaction from fame or approval or social reputation, and pursue that. Some people enjoy art, music, or literature, and say that aesthetic appreciation is the purest pleasure. Sex is definitely pleasurable, and so are the rituals of flirting, pursuing, choosing clothes, daydreaming, and exchanging secrets that go with it. The term "pleasure" encompasses many things, but they all have that special, pleasing experience in common.

Hedonism rests on two main beliefs. First, pleasure is good. And second, pleasure is the *only* good. Are these beliefs true? Well, let's look at the first one, pleasure is good. Virtually everyone accepts this belief as true. If you have to wait at the airport for a delayed flight, is it better to stand or to sit down? Is it better to be bored or to read an interesting novel? Of course, the pleasant ways of passing the time are better than the unpleasant ways, everything else being equal.

There are some unfortunate people who will stand, or spend the whole time worrying needlessly. Some people punish themselves for no good reason. Pleasure makes some people feel guilty. It is possible to renounce and shun pleasure voluntarily, just because one has been taught that pleasure is bad. But is it wise? Is that a good way to live? If you examine your own feelings in an unprejudiced way, you will say no.

Thus virtually everyone believes that pleasure is a good thing. Such universal assent means something. But, in addition, hedonists *know* that pleasure is good. Their belief is not just a "personal value," and not just a biological instinct. They know pleasure is good in the same way they know most other things: They perceive it with their senses. For example, how do you know that the sun shines during the day, or that grass is green? You see it, obviously. How do you know that it is cold in Chicago in February? You feel it. If you haven't felt it yourself, then you believe someone who has felt it. How do you know that lemons are sour? You taste it.

Now, how do you know that a hot bath after a hard day's work is good? You feel it. As you settle into the tub and your muscles relax, you say, "This is great." You feel that pleasure is good. Or after a delightful dinner and a long talk with good friends, you say, "What a nice evening. We should do this again." The pleasure of companionship is good. It is as obvious as the fact that grass is green, and we know both facts in the same way. We feel that pleasure is good just as directly as we see, taste, and feel the other facts.

While most people will accept the first hedonist belief, that pleasure is good, few will accept the second belief, that pleasure is the *only* good. Many say that selfless love is the most wonderful experience we can have, but it is not the same thing as pleasure. And loyalty to one's community, or performing one's duty, are surely valuable, even if they require pain and sacrifice. Some say pure virtue itself makes life worthwhile. Knowledge, creativity and art, the natural world, personal growth, and many other things have been held up as valuable goals. To these people hedonists seem to have a very narrow-minded outlook. They have a one-track mind and ignore many important values in life.

Or do they? Many of the things that seem to be alternatives to pleasure in reality are not. They are valuable because they *lead to* pleasure in the long run. Hedonists can say this because they make a distinction between means and ends. They admit that some things, like hard physical exercise, are valuable, but are not enjoyable at all. But exercise is a means to achieving something else, like winning a race or looking attractive. And those things *are* pleasurable. Some people exercise so they can be healthy and live longer. Why do people want to be healthy and live longer? Because health helps one enjoy life, and a longer life means more pleasure.

Moreover, the exercise is valuable *only* because it helps a person achieve the other things. If exercising, or dieting, or going to the dentist, or studying engineering, or working to make money, did *not* lead to pleasure of some kind (or the absence of pain), no one would do them. What would be the point? Would a young woman work in a boring job if she weren't paid? No. The reason for working hard and making sacrifices is to achieve pleasure in the long run. On the other hand, pleasure is its own reward. It is an end, not a means. If something is pleasurable, people do it for its own sake. No one has to explain why she wants it.

The means we use to achieve pleasure can be complicated. Many people are devoted to their family, their community, and their country. And loyalty to the group, sacrifice for the good of the whole, public service, are good. But they are all *means*, not ends. They are ultimately means to one's own pleasure. They benefit the group by making it more stable, or secure, or prosperous. And since the person making the sacrifice is a member of the group, he or she benefits as well. Human beings are social animals. We depend on each other in countless ways. That means that often the best way for us to benefit ourselves is to help others, because they can return the favor and help us in ways that we cannot help ourselves.

Like public service, most of the other goals in life, such as knowledge, art, and conservation of nature, are valuable as means to one's own pleasure. Even obedience to God's commandments is a means of gaining the pleasures of heaven, or avoiding the pains of hell.

Pleasure is the only good. The enlightened pursuit of pleasure is the only realistic morality.

Key Concepts

pleasure	happiness	senses
highest good	mental pleasure	means and ends

Critical Questions

1. The first essay says hedonism consists of two main beliefs. What are they? In your opinion, must those two beliefs go together, or could a person accept one but not the other?
2. Why should you believe that pleasure is good, according to the essay?
3. Does a hedonist believe that individuals always do what they think will produce pleasure for themselves?
4. The hedonist makes a distinction between means and ends. Can you think of some other examples of means and ends?
5. Why are people devoted to their families and communities, according to the essay? Do you agree?

6. In your opinion, are there any things that are morally good, but do not produce any pleasure for anyone? (For example, kindness, work, knowledge, respect, love?)

NO: PLURALIST

"A World of Values"

Philosophers try to make sense of human experience. They often do this by proposing a theory to explain how diverse aspects of our lives fit together. For example, Freud claimed that all of a person's actions were, in one way or another, the expressions of the drive for sexual satisfaction. Some political philosophers have claimed that all political events—laws, elections, taxes, revolutions, ideologies, and so on—are results of a struggle for power. These kinds of theories often help us see an underlying reality, and relations among events, that we would not have seen without them. They give unity and coherence to our outlook on life.

The danger in such theories is oversimplification. We all want to understand the confusing, conflicting events in our lives so badly that sometimes we ignore facts, or distort them, to preserve a simple, familiar picture of the world. We produce "Procrustean" theories. Procrustes was a figure in Greek mythology who forced visitors to fit his bed by stretching them if they were too short or cutting off their legs if they were too long. I suspect that many people, including philosophers, act like Procrustes when they think about values.

The topic of values is complicated. But some philosophers oversimplify the issue by suggesting that there is really only one value, and that all the good things in life are somehow reflections of the one true value. Different philosophers have proposed different ultimate values. Some say it is survival, or "life," or continued existence. Some say it is devotion to God. Some say love, loyalty to loved ones, or community. Some say pleasure, or happiness.

But philosophers' should not only try to find unifying themes in human experience. Above all they should seek the truth. And to remain true to experience they should sometimes remind us just how complicated and multifarious life can be. In fact, human beings have always recognized many different values, which cannot be redefined or collapsed into each other. A survey of the main values will show just how different they are. There are personal values, which concern oneself and do not involve other people. And there are social values, which essentially involve other people. Let us begin with personal values.

Personal Values

Most personal values have to do with the preservation and development of the self, while some depend on other kinds of personal experiences. Probably the most basic and universal personal value is *survival*. Humans are living organisms, and therefore we have a drive to preserve ourselves. We want to live; we are afraid of death. Many people express this value as a desire for money. They organize their lives around the pursuit of money—for example, they seek a high-paying job—because they want to guarantee that they will always have food, clothing, and shelter. They value security.

Other people value *health*. They read and learn about proper diet, vitamins, cholesterol, fiber, and so on, and they feel that eating right is very important. Health is not exactly the same as survival. Those who value health might actually take serious risks, such as skydiving or kayaking. What they fear is not death but illness and loss of vitality.

Of course many people value other things besides survival and health. They take these for granted and look farther to see what life has to offer. They may value *personal growth*. That is, they may want new experiences, opportunities to meet different kinds of people, successes, and also failures, to feel what they are like. They may travel, change jobs, go to school, have an affair. They want to expand themselves, to add dimensions, skills, and memories to their lives.

Others think of personal development as *creativity*. People who value creativity feel that they are already full of ideas and experiences, and they want to express them. They may be inspired by creative work in the arts—film, music, novels, dance—or by creative problem solving in business or science, and they want to express their own unique talent. They want to make something new.

Another personal value is *excellence*. Excellence simply means doing something in the best way possible. For example, one house painter may slap on the paint as quickly as possible so that he or she can go on to the next job, whereas another painter will take the time to avoid painting the glass in the windows, to see that every corner is covered, and to make the coat of paint smooth and even. The two painters receive the same payment, but one values excellence. Many people admire excellence in others, such as the excellence of athletes.

However, much of the time people do not think about preserving themselves, or enlarging themselves. They just want to have *fun*. They do not worry about necessities, health, being creative, or striving for excellence. When these goals are taken for granted, or ignored, then people want to enjoy life. Enjoyment is certainly an important value. Most people watch several hours of TV every day, go to several movies every month, play games on their computers, read gossip magazines, go to restaurants, and engage in sex. People do these things because they are enjoyable. They have no other purpose. After our needs are satisfied and we feel secure, then we want some pleasant stimulation.

It's true that some people never aim higher. They think that pleasant stimulation is the ultimate goal in life, perhaps because they have never learned about other values. But I think most people have a broader outlook. After they have gained some security, and after they have had fun with movies or backyard barbecues (or sex or drugs), they look for something they think is important, not merely enjoyable. They understand that there are other values in the world, values that may be more important than pleasure, and maybe even more important than oneself.

We will turn to social values momentarily, but for now we should consider other personal values. One is *beauty*. Some people are very sensitive to their environment. They go to great lengths to surround themselves with beautiful things. They go to galleries to see paintings and sculptures, they listen to music, or they take photographs on the weekends.

People who value beauty enjoy seeing and hearing beautiful things, and therefore one could argue that beauty is really the same as enjoyment, that they are not two values but one. But that is just the kind of oversimplification that distorts experience. TV, movies, games, and magazines are not beautiful. They are too simple and superficial to be beautiful. The experience of beauty requires some effort; it takes some attentiveness, practice, and the exercise of the mind as well as the senses. Thus beautiful objects are different from entertainments, and the experience of beauty is different from the experience of having fun. For some people, it is far more valuable than simply having fun. To lump them together is to ignore important possibilities of experience.

Another important dimension of human experience is *freedom*. Many people place a great value on freedom and self-reliance. They want to lead their lives with the fewest restrictions possible. The important thing is not to have many paths open to them (as the term "freedom" might suggest), but to have *their* paths. They want to live as they think they should rather than as others think they should.

The last personal value to consider is *knowledge*, or understanding, or intelligence. Scientists, professors, counselors, economists, and many others place a great value on knowledge and understanding. They are curious about the world, they want to learn new things, to solve mysteries, and see how things work. They value knowledge itself, not the power or profits knowledge can produce. They admire others who can understand problems or who have acquired wisdom through experience.

Social Values

All the values I have mentioned so far belong in one category because they involve personal growth and development, or relaxation. They can be achieved by a single individual. But our relations with other people bring out a whole different dimension of value: the social values.

The most common social value is *love*. The word "love" encompasses many different feelings, relationships, and ideas, so when people say that love is the most important thing in their lives, they can mean different things. Some value an intimate, sharing relation with another person. Some include the warmth and trust of family relations. Some live mainly for the give and take they enjoy with their close friends. Love is not a personal value because when one person loves another, the person values the *other*. He may even value the other more than himself. At the very least, he values the relationship—the togetherness, communication, and interdependence. All the personal values are applied to the other as well as to himself.

Related to love is *compassion*. Everyone knows of people who help others. Religious groups organize soup kitchens, volunteers go to less developed countries to help build houses, executives act as big brothers to inner city children, secretaries teach illiterate people how to read. They see people who need help, and they want to help. A life that includes service is better than one that does not.

Another social value is *leadership*, or organization. Some people want to take charge, to make decisions, and to get others moving toward a common goal. Social interaction is extremely important to them, but it is a different interaction from love or service. It is interaction with groups rather than individuals. It is a kind of responsibility. However, a person who is too egotistical may mistake this value for power and control over people.

Many people value *esteem*. They want others to think well of them. They may conceive of this value in various ways, as respect, popularity, reputation, status, approval, or fame. The common factor in all these words is other people's good opinion of oneself. People have very different beliefs about how to gain esteem. Some pursue excellence, not because they value excellence itself, but because they think it will make other people think highly of them. Some try to make large amounts of money, gain knowledge, or cultivate friends for the same reason.

One of the most important social values is *justice*. Like love, justice is difficult to define. But most of us know when people are treated fairly and when they are not, and we are upset when they are not. Some people work very hard to bring about a more just society, where people's efforts and talents are rewarded, and where race, gender, and ethnic background neither help nor harm individuals in their pursuit of their values.

Justice is not exactly the same thing as *harmony*. Justice, or respect for basic rights, is perhaps the minimal condition for a good society. But many people want to go beyond justice; they want a society in which people cooperate, compromise, and enjoy each others' company. They envisage a society in which people are not only just, but even friendly and loving. Others conceive of harmony as cooperative effort, in which everyone in a community pitches in and works together for a common goal.

Another social value is *devotion to God*. All religions are founded on the cultivation of this relation. For religious people, the supreme value is God, the source of all goodness, beauty, wisdom, justice, and all other values. They value the spiritual dimension of existence—the communion with God—above everything else. The relation with God is something like the relation with another person, but much more, and the love and honor that apply to relations with people also apply to the relation with God, but in greater degree.

The last social value to consider is *nature*. Nature is not a person, but it is something outside the individual, and recognizing its value means entering into a relationship. The earth, the unspoiled forests, the streams, the massive mountains, and all the animals and plants in the natural world possess a kind of majesty that is unique. The more we experience nature first hand, the more wonderful and inspiring—and precious—it appears. It isn't only beauty, or our own need for clean air and water. Nature itself is worthy of respect.

Nature and God are probably the broadest, most inclusive values. And there may be other values that aren't included in this brief survey. In particular, we must include morality, or *moral values*. Moral values used to be called "virtues," although that word sounds old-fashioned these days. Moral values, such as courage, honesty, perseverance, and loyalty, have to do with regulating one's own behavior and being a certain kind of person. They are ideals of conduct and character. Those who value morality want to behave in certain ways—to tell the truth and to stand by their friends, for example—and want to have these traits, or virtues (honest, loyal, brave, etc.).

I have put moral values at the end of the survey because they do not fit easily into the personal or social categories. As ideals of conduct and character, they are similar to personal growth. If we value morality we try to mold ourselves into the kind of person we think we should be. Self-discipline, self-reliance, curiosity, courage, and perseverance are all "self-regarding" moral values. We can achieve them on our own. At the same time, however, some of the most important moral values essentially involve relations with other people. Honesty, trustworthiness, tolerance, compassion, and justice are ideals guiding the ways we treat others. In a way, all the values—personal and social—are moral values, since they guide our behavior. They are the bases of the choices we make.

Pleasure

These descriptions of values are far too brief, but they should make the point that there are many different values. However, some philosophers try to reduce all of them to pleasure, so I want to emphasize several ways in which this view is mistaken. The word "pleasure" refers to a physical sensation or reaction to stimuli. But some people expand the word to include personal growth, excellence, love, justice, and every other value there is. They are determined to simplify human values, but in doing so they stretch the word beyond all recognition. The word "pleasure" no longer means anything if it applies to watching TV, striving for excellence, promoting justice, and so many other things as well. A person does not feel the same ways when she or he is engaged in these activities.

Not only are people's feelings different, but feelings are not values. The philosopher who reduces all values to pleasure is mistaking personal reactions for features in the world. Pleasure is a subjective feeling in a particular person. But beauty, justice, excellence, and other values are objective qualities in the world. Many people can recognize them, describe and analyze them, reach agreement about them, and prize them. My feelings do not make an action just or unjust, or a performance excellent or average. But one individual's pleasure is that person's alone, private and personal. It is subjective, not objective, as value is.

If enjoyment were the only value, then why do people disagree on the best goals in life, or the best society, or right and wrong? We are all very similar physically, and similar stimuli produce pleasure in us. But we disagree over values. Therefore values are not the same thing as pleasure.

But even if none of these things were true, and even if philosophers could show that on some basic level pleasure was the only value, they would still face the important question: what is the best way of life? Should individuals develop their abilities or devote time to others? Should they focus on doing the best work they can, or on achieving independence, or love? The philosopher's grand theory doesn't answer any of the real questions.

Which is the highest value? Personal growth? Love? Freedom? Justice? How can we rank the different values? What happens when values come into conflict? These are some of the questions that arise when we must choose a course of action. Making choices is difficult. But it is better to wrestle with these questions, and recognize that we do have choices, than it is to ignore all the different values and try to reduce them to one or two. Health is not the same thing as justice, excellence is not the same thing as love, and none of the values can be reduced to any other. The philosophers' attempt to simplify the world is understandable, and even excusable. But we should remember that, in the end, truth is more valuable than a false simplicity.

Key Concepts

personal values	oversimplify	pleasure
social values	morality	objective quality

Critical Questions

1. Is creativity different from excellence? Isn't being creative the same as being excellent?
2. Suppose I value health and freedom because both give me pleasure. Does that show that they are the same value? Or are they still different values?
3. In your opinion, does it make sense to say that nature is valuable in itself, apart from its usefulness or beauty to mankind?
4. How does the pluralist define "moral value"? Are all values moral values, according to the pluralist?
5. The pluralist says the hedonist cannot define pleasure. Suppose the hedonist defined it in terms of *behavior*: it is "whatever leads a person to continue or repeat an experience." Is that an adequate definition, in your opinion?
6. Are the values that the essay describes objective qualities of the world? Is health objective or subjective? Creativity, excellence, compassion, justice, etc.?
7. Can you suggest a way to rank the values the essay describes? Is there any way to show that one value is more important, more valuable, than another value? By what standard is one value more important than another?

Methods and Techniques

FACTS AND VALUES

The essays in this section are about morality. Both discuss the goals we should have. I said in the introduction that your goals are the same as your values. Moral philosophy, or ethics, is concerned with values. Both essays also try to base their recommendations on certain facts, like the fact that many people sacrifice some pleasure now in order to achieve greater pleasure in the future, or the fact that people say they value many different things. So ethics is concerned with facts, too, especially the facts that may help us decide what is the best way of life.

Everyone talks about "facts and values." They are common, basic ideas, and so philosophers try to understand what they mean and clarify them, since philosophers look at all our most basic beliefs and ideas. The concepts of God, self, knowledge, freedom, and some others are the subject of philosophy. But the concepts of fact and value are not very easy to understand, just as all the basic ideas turn out to be slippery and elusive when we try to pin them down.

What is a fact and what is a value? Well, roughly speaking, we can say that a fact is something that is established as true. It is an actual state of affairs, or a real condition in the world. For example, it is a fact that Boston is north of New York. It is a fact that Socrates died in 399 B.C.E. Those are both states of affairs, or circumstances, that have been established as true. It is not a fact that Los Angeles is the capital of California. Notice that facts are complex situations, not objects. Socrates himself is not a fact, nor is the city of Boston. But Socrates' death in 399 is a fact, and Boston's location relative to New York is a fact. When we say something about something else (and our statement is true), then we are reporting facts.

How do we know that Boston is north of New York? How do we "establish" something as true? The most common way is through observation. If you travel from New York to Boston, and look at a compass along the way, you will observe that you are going north. Or if you cannot observe it yourself, you can rely on the testimony of someone else who has observed it. We often rely on other people's observations. For example, it is a fact that a mammal's heart is divided into four chambers. Most people have not cut open mammals and observed their hearts. But it is still an established fact because some qualified experts have dissected mammals and made the observation. On the other hand, I might say "The planet Pluto has a core of iron." But no one—not even an expert—has observed the interior of Pluto, and so I cannot say it is a fact that Pluto has a core of iron. It is a hypothesis, or a theory, but not a fact. Even though Socrates died twenty-four hundred years ago, that fact is established in the same way. Many people observed the event and wrote about it, and we accept their testimony.

What is a value? A value is also a state of affairs or condition, just as a fact is. But it is a state of affairs that people approve of. It is something that people desire, or pursue, or try to preserve. For example, tolerance is a value. People approve of tolerance, they try to promote it, and they admire it when they see it. They have positive feelings about it. Values arise out of our human ability to imagine a situation that is different from the actual, present situation. For example, if I am hungry, I can imagine getting food. I want food, and can try to get it. If I do this regularly over a period of time, then you could say that I value food. I can also imagine people being tolerant of each other's differences, even if they are not tolerant now. If I want tolerance and try to promote it, then I value tolerance. Tolerance is a value for me.

I can also look at a past situation, like a war, and feel regret and remorse about it. I can wish that it never happened. I can imagine what things would have been like if it had not happened, and I feel sorry about it. Then I value peace. Or I can look back on my own behavior and feel guilt or shame. For example, perhaps I remember telling a lie and I feel badly about it. If I want to be an honest person, and try to be more honest, then I value honesty.

Values are related to facts in the same way that the ideal is related to the actual. The way people actually behave is not necessarily the way they *ought* to behave. It is a fact that some people hate others; we value people respecting each other. The actual condition of our society is not necessarily the *ideal* condition. We can look at people and society and imagine a better way. Values are the better way, whether it is honesty, or tolerance, or peace, or liberty, or whatever. On the other hand, sometimes the actual *is* ideal. Sometimes we read about a cab driver who returns a wallet he found with a thousand dollars in it. The ideal is not always imaginary. What makes something a value is that people approve of it, not that it does not exist.

This preliminary analysis of facts and values is only a beginning. The concepts are central to ethics, so philosophers want to understand them as fully as possible. But many questions remain. For example, are values objective or subjective? Values are states of affairs that people approve of, but does the approval make them valuable, or do we approve of them because they are valuable in themselves? Is honesty valuable and right because we approve of it, or is it valuable whether we approve of it or not? The same question arises about facts. Do we call something a fact just because most of the people in our culture believe it? People establish facts by making observations, but observations can be mistaken. (Do we say tolerance is a value just because most people in our society value it? Can we "observe" that intolerance is evil and wrong?) You will read about some of the further questions that remain in the following sections concerning moral philosophy.

Understanding the Dilemma

HEDONIST OR PLURALIST?

The choice in this section is between hedonism and pluralism. Which is more appealing to you? Are you a hedonist or a pluralist? Is your goal in life to enjoy yourself as much as possible, or do you have other goals and values besides pleasure? Are your other goals just pleasure in disguise?

Perhaps the most important point to understand is that the hedonist and the pluralist are not arguing about psychology. The first essay, representing hedonism, does *not* say that everyone is motivated by a desire for pleasure. In fact, it says the opposite: some people deliberately do things that do not make them happy. And the second essay presents the issue in terms of values, objective qualities in the world, not motives or feelings.

The question in this section is an ethical question, not a psychological question. Philosophers distinguish between "psychological egoism" and "ethical egoism." Psychological egoism is the view that everyone always tries to benefit himself or herself. It is claimed to be a psychological fact about people. Some people accept psychological egoism and some people do not. In contrast, ethical egoism is the view that people *ought* to act in a way that benefits themselves. It is a theory about what is valuable, however people actually behave. In this section the two essays are concerned with ethical issues, not psychological issues. (You will read about psychological egoism in Section 4.5.) Note, too, that egoism—benefitting oneself—is not the same thing as hedonism—valuing pleasure. I can be an egoist but not a hedonist if, for example, I value power or knowledge for myself over pleasure. And I can be a hedonist but not an egoist if I try to promote pleasure among all people equally and not just for myself.

What does make life worthwhile after all? What kind of life do you believe you ought to live? If you live to be 70 or 80 years old, and you look back over all those years and activities, will you respect yourself and feel proud? If you spent most of your time figuring out ways to please yourself, will you respect yourself? If you spent most of your time figuring out ways to help other people, will you believe that you have missed the most valuable part of life?

The decision you must make is not about organizing your day, but about organizing your life. You are searching for an organizing principle for your life as a whole. Of course everyone needs food, clothing, and shelter. Everyone must spend some time arranging for his or her own needs to be met, usually working at a job. But how much time is enough? Do you acquire the necessities, and then go on to try to achieve something, make yourself a better person, or make the world a better place, which takes most of your time and energy? Or do you spend all of your time trying to be comfortable, to gain security, to improve your circumstances, to be entertained, to enjoy life?

How do you decide between hedonism and pluralism? Is it a "personal" choice, like your brand of clothing or hair style? Both the hedonist and the pluralist say no. They both give reasons to back up their views. They both think that their reasons are sound, convincing reasons that should persuade an open-minded reader. To decide which view you hold, you should look back at the two essays, and find the reasons the authors give to support their conclusions. Why is the first a hedonist? Why is the second a pluralist? What persuaded them? And which of their reasons are more persuasive to you?

Hedonists claim that their theory is easy to understand. They say they can explain why anything is valuable. "It gives me pleasure," they say. What's so great about health, freedom, love, or justice? They give us pleasure. And that is a good reason. If something is pleasurable, then, other things being equal, it is desirable and good. It is valuable unless some other consideration outweighs the pleasure. But pluralists do not explain why things are valuable. Pluralists say many things are valuable besides pleasure, so it is not their production of pleasure that makes them valuable. But then what is it? Why is freedom a good thing? Pluralists might say that their value is basic and ultimate. It just is good. After all, hedonists cannot explain why pleasure is valuable. It just is valuable, they say.

Hedonism is therefore a simpler theory. There is one basic principle in the theory (pleasure is valuable), and everything else is explained by reference to that basic principle. Moreover, it is a plausible principle. Pleasure is valuable, and it makes other things valuable. Pluralism is a much more complicated point of view. Pluralists make many assumptions. That is, pluralists say there are many basic, unexplained values. Another complication is the relationship among these values. What do we do when they come into conflict? How do we decide which of two basic values is *more* valuable? Pluralism has no answer.

However, pluralists say that the simplicity of hedonism is a false simplicity. Hedonists make everything depend on pleasure, but consequently they *over-simplify* matters. It is a mistake, according to pluralists, to think that all the experiences we have when we pursue all the different sorts of value are the same, namely "pleasure." Hedonists' explanation is an illusion. Pluralism remains true to our real, everyday experience.

Thus the basic issue in this section is simplicity vs. complexity, and theoretical sophistication vs. common sense. Do you want a worldview that is rigorously logical, clearly organized, and made up of a few simple axioms? Or do you think it is more important to remain close to ordinary experience, even if that means your outlook is complex, leaves loose ends dangling, and not so easy to understand?

HEDONIST

1. The ultimate reason for living (and, finally, the only reason) is to achieve happiness, which is the same as pleasure.
2. "Pleasure" is a broad term, which includes intellectual, social, and moral activities.
3. What makes anything *good* is that it helps someone, and that means it gives someone pleasure.
4. It is good to help others, but it is good because it is enjoyable, or because not helping others leads to guilt.

PLURALIST

5. Many people who think about values oversimplify matters.
6. Ordinary people recognize both personal and social values and obviously believe many things besides pleasure are good.

7. Values are objective features of the world that we pursue, not subjective feelings.
8. Values are basic and ultimate; they cannot be explained, or reduced, to something more basic (such as pleasure).

FOR FURTHER STUDY

Historical Examples

HEDONIST: Epicurus. *The Essential Epicurus*. Prometheus, 1993. Third century B.C.E. The original version of hedonism.

PLURALIST: Ralph B. Perry. *Realms of Value*. Harvard University Press, 1954. Perry develops a concept of value as "interest," and explains personal, moral, aesthetic, social, and other values.

OTHER SOURCES

William DeWitt Hyde. *The Five Great Philosophies of Life*. Macmillan, 1926. Elementary discussion of Epicurus (hedonism), the Stoics, Plato, Aristotle, and Christianity.

John Hospers. *Human Conduct: Problems of Ethics*. Shorter Edition. Harcourt Brace Jovanovich, 1972. Part 2, "Ideals of Life," surveys four ideals: epicureanism, stoicism, self-realization, and following nature.

Yi-Fu Tuan. *The Good Life*. University of Wisconsin Press, 1986. Compares different ideals from various cultures, in the context of defending a theory of happiness.

David P. Gauthier, ed. *Morality and Rational Self-Interest*. Prentice-Hall, 1970. Classical and modern writers ask "Is self-interest rational?" "Is moral motivation based on interest?" and "Is morality advantageous?"

Abraham Maslow. *Toward a Psychology of Being*. 2nd Edition. Van Nostrand Reinhold, 1982. Maslow describes a hierarchy of values, at the top of which is self-actualization.

Nell Noddings. *Caring: A Feminine Approach to Ethics and Moral Education*. University of California Press, 1984. An extensive description and analysis of caring rather than a defense.

Risieri Frondizi. *What Is Value?* 2nd Edition. Open Court, 1971. A brief, simple discussion of issues, including the objectivity/subjectivity of values.

Peter Caws. *Science and the Theory of Value*. Random House, 1967. Caws presents his definition of value in chap. 5, "Fact and Value."

M.S. Everett. *Ideals of Life: An Introduction to Ethics and the Humanities*. John Wiley and Sons, 1954. Includes chapters on basic human wants, the pursuit of happiness, traits of character, the ethics of democracy, etc.

Hunter Lewis. *A Question of Values*. HarperSanFrancisco, 1990. Lewis claims that one's method of making choices determines one's values, and discusses six methods: authority, logic, sense experience, emotion, intuition, and "science."

The books by Russell, MacIver, and Maurois listed in Section 3.2 also describe various ideals and goals in life.

3.2 CAN WE UNDERSTAND HAPPINESS?

DEFINER OR MUDDLER?

●

In Section 1.2, "Is God Like Human Beings," I raised the question of whether one can believe God exists when he or she has a very sketchy, vague (or empty) concept of God. Now we come to happiness. Can you wish for happiness if you have no clear idea of what happiness is? Can you look for something if you don't know what you are looking for? Where would you begin your search? In what direction would you look? You would be wandering aimlessly. And suppose you stumbled across your goal accidentally: how would you recognize it or realize you had found it? If you say that you are happy, how can you be sure? How do you know?

Many people will probably say that they *do* know what happiness is. "For me happiness is seeing the Giants win the Superbowl," someone will say. Or "Happiness is lying on a beach in the Virgin Islands." Is this enough? Does this person know what happiness is? It might be enough for ordinary, practical living. But some people want to step out of the day-to-day routine and try to *understand* their lives. For those who are curious about deeper questions, and who want to have a coherent worldview, it is not enough.

This kind of answer to the question "What is happiness?" faces two problems. First, different people enjoy different things. What makes one person happy will have no effect on another person. So what is happiness? The person watching the game is happy, *and* the person lying on the beach is also happy. They must have something in common, since the word "happy" applies to both. What is it? Can we understand happiness?

There is a second problem. When you say happiness is lying on a beach, you have only mentioned an activity that makes you happy. The activity is not the same thing as happiness. For example, no one would want to watch the Giants win the Superbowl three times a day, seven days a week, or lie on a beach continuously, until one dies. But one does want to be happy for the rest of one's life. Therefore happiness is not the same thing as an activity or even a set of activities. If not, then what is it?

If you want to take control of your life, you must have a clear idea of your chief goal. If you want to understand where you are going and why, you must have a concept of what you are seeking. Most people say their goal is happiness. So it makes sense to think about the nature of happiness.

The first essay below insists on the difference between the various causes of happiness and happiness itself, but it argues that we can understand and define happiness. If you agree with this essay you are a definer. In contrast, the second essay takes the skeptical view that we cannot know what happiness is. It claims that we muddle through life without understanding what goal we think we are pursuing. If you agree with the second essay you are a muddler.

YES: DEFINER

"Happiness"

Philosophers are a quarrelsome bunch. They seem to argue for the sake of arguing. But, surprisingly, they all agree on one point. They all agree on what people want. People want to be happy. Happiness is the ultimate goal of everyone's life.

Of course people try to be happy in different ways. Many want to be rich. Others pursue fame and popularity, others excitement, or security, physical vitality, and so on for different types of people. But if you asked these various people why they want these things, you would hear one answer over and over: I want to be happy. These things are all means to one end—happiness.

Maybe we should leave it at that, and enjoy the rare concord among philosophers. But at the risk of stirring up more arguments, I would like to ask a simple question. What *is* happiness? What is it that all men and women, young and old, rich and poor, seek so persistently throughout their lives? It isn't easy to say, although I believe happiness can be defined.

Happiness is not the same thing as money, no matter how many yuppies think otherwise. Obviously it's not, because many people with large amounts of money are bitterly unhappy. I am tempted to say that rich people—with their divorces, their suicides, their alcoholism—are even less happy than poor people. But it isn't true. It seems that way only because *People* magazine writes about their troubles, while no one wants to read about poor people's misery. Both rich and poor are unhappy.

Happiness is not fame. It's not a stable family life. How many housewives living quietly in suburbia with their average families are unhappy? Many. At least many say they are. Wealth, fame, and family may make some people happy, but they do not make everyone who has them happy. Therefore, we cannot *define* happiness as these things. If we defined happiness as having money, then everyone with money would be happy, by definition. There could not be a single rich person who was unhappy, if happiness were defined as having money. But it is easy to find counterexamples to that definition. The same applies to fame, stable families, or what have you.

Most books pretending to explain happiness make this mistake. They all have quite a bit to say about the *causes* of happiness, but little to say about happiness itself. One expert declares that the secret of happiness is satisfying work. A PhD in psychology takes two hundred pages to say that the secret of happiness is love. Another guru says it is health. But these are causes of happiness (so they say). What do these things cause? What is happiness itself? How do I know if I am happy or not?

We will never understand happiness itself by studying external conditions and causes. A person wouldn't get the slightest appreciation of a good meal by looking at the stove. Happiness itself is an *inner condition*, or a state of mind, not the external circumstances of one's life.

Now we are making progress. We are on the right track, although we haven't arrived yet. What sort of inner state is happiness? Some have said it is simply pleasure. Happiness, they say, is the sensation one has when one relaxes in the pool on a hot day, tastes a favorite drink, or cuddles in bed with one's partner.

But I'm afraid we just took a wrong turn again. Pleasurable sensations last only a short time. It sounds very strange to say my friend was happy for thirty seconds last week, and for five minutes yesterday. Happiness lasts longer than that. It is a condition, not just a sensation. It cannot be defined as pleasure, because even if a person is in pain, from the temporary hunger of a diet, or muscle aches from tennis, we can still say he is a happy man. An exhausted jogger can be happy precisely because she is in pain. "No pain, no gain," she thinks.

Happiness is an inner state, but not a short-term sensation or emotion. It lasts a long time. So, we have returned to the right track from the dead end of pleasure, but now the way ahead is obscure again. People can be happy in so many different ways, and their inner mental states must be very different. Both the race car driver and the homemaker can be very happy, but their mental states must be just about opposites. One thrives on danger, risks, physical exertion, noise, and grime (I mean the race car driver, not the homemaker), and the other finds happiness in security, children's laughter and miniature accomplishments, neatness, and meals together. How is the inner state of the movie buff, escaping to a fantasy world, like the inner state of the tax accountant, or the emergency room nurse?

In spite of the differences in the emotions and thoughts, crises and victories that these people must experience, I believe a single thread runs through all their lives. The thread that ties them together is that they are *achieving most of their goals*. The goals are different, just as the people are different. But they are all successful in what they are trying to do.

Happiness itself is not a matter of learning what to strive for—love, health, work, self-acceptance, or any other goal. Happiness depends upon *reaching* your goals, whatever they are. The goals can be different, but happiness is the same in each person. Happiness is dynamic, not static. It involves change, not immobility. Happy people feel that they are taking steps that bring them closer to their ultimate goals.

How wrong it is to think that happiness is pleasure, or leisure, or having drinks handed to you on your yacht. Achieving your goals will require work, and planning, and sacrifice, whatever your goals are. Human beings are active. We build things, search for answers, care for others, improve the world. Unlike amoebas, we are not happy if we are only passively absorbing food or drink, or soap operas.

I was careful to say happiness "depends upon" reaching one's goals, not "is" reaching one's goals. I did not want to make the same old mistake of confusing the cause with the thing itself. We already decided that happiness is an inner state of mind. In spite of the differences among happy people, they are all reaching their goals. They have that in common. Does that mean they have some inner mental condition in common as well?

I think it does. Everyone who reaches his or her goals must have similar feelings. A successful woman must feel satisfaction when she recalls her past accomplishments, and she must feel confidence, optimism, and a sense of competence when she looks forward to goals still to be reached. Together, these add up to self-esteem, self-respect, and calm assurance, based on objective achievements.

Happiness is this mental state. It is the feeling of accomplishment, of success, of confidence. Different people will have different goals, but all happy people will have these feelings and this perception of themselves and their place in the world. That is what it means to be happy.

Key Concepts

definition	successful	cause
counterexample	inner condition	self-esteem

Critical Questions

1. If every rich person were happy, except one, could we define happiness as being rich? Could we say the one unhappy rich person is just an abnormal exception?
2. What kind of thing is happiness, according to the essay?
3. Why can't we define happiness as pleasure, in the definer's view?
4. What external condition do all happy people have in common? What *is* happiness?
5. What would a person have to show to prove that the definer's definition is wrong? (How does the definer show that other definitions are wrong?)
6. Does the definer think that the particular goal one pursues is crucial to one's happiness, or is achieving one's goal the only requirement? Suppose my goal is to rob banks, or be a dictator of a South American country. Can I be happy by achieving those goals, in the definer's view? Do you agree or disagree?

NO: MUDDLER

"The Elusive Dream"

Writers like me stand apart from ordinary life so we can observe it. That is both good and bad. It's bad because it makes us feel different, and sometimes lonely. It's good because people's posturings and obsessions are so hilarious that once you step aside and look at them dispassionately you are endlessly entertained.

Take happiness for example. How many books have been written about it? How many fortunes made, and lost, in its name? It's even enshrined in our sacred Declaration of Independence. Americans have a legal right to it.

But the idea of happiness is an illusion. Happiness itself is real enough, but no one knows what it is. The idea is an illusion, a mere will-o-the-wisp, impossible to pin down. Just try to define this all-important concept.

Is anything absolutely essential to happiness? It would be natural to think that health is essential. But health isn't absolutely necessary, since many people have endured illness, blindness, paralysis, and other physical problems, but have still been happy. Epicurus, the Greek philosopher, suffered poor health all his life, but his letters reveal a cheerful, curious, serene man.

If not health, then perhaps love is absolutely necessary for happiness. But the stubborn fact is that many great artists and philosophers never married. They were devoted to their work, and human relationships were simply less important to them. Who is to say that none of them was happy?

It is impossible to name anything that is absolutely essential to happiness. People are just too complex and variable. Early Christians were tortured in horrible ways, but they died singing praises to God, happy in their martyrdom.

Perhaps we should approach the idea from the opposite direction. Does anything guarantee happiness? Many people say to themselves, "If only I had a million dollars, then I would be happy!" But money is no guarantee of happiness. Some rich people are happy, but others aren't.

If you put four of five male friends together for an hour, the conversation *invariably* turns to one subject: sex. (I'm not sure what women talk about.) Men fantasize about numerous partners, exotic locales, different styles and techniques. If their fantasies were realized, would they be happy? I don't think it's a sure thing. In fact, some therapists report that playboys who actually live that way feel a hollowness and lack of meaning in their lives. On the other hand, being tied to one partner is no guarantee of happiness either.

There are no guarantees. No possessions, no activities, no set of beliefs, separately or together, are sufficient for happiness. The reason is that people are too complicated, contradictory, even perverse (which is why life is so interesting).

Just think about the different things that make people happy. Some can be happy only if they are free and independent. Others are devoted to someone, incomplete by themselves, people who need people. The Roman poet Lucretius said happiness is standing on the shore watching others drown at sea. In other words, happiness is relative; it means being better off than one's neighbors, at whatever level one's neighbors live. But watching others drown, or starve, or live under tyranny, upsets many people, and makes them unhappy, not happy. There are as many kinds of happiness as there are people. Each person is happy in his or her own way.

An exasperated psychologist might step in at this point and make the following suggestion: "Instead of searching for definitions and analyzing concepts, like a philosopher, why don't you take a scientific approach? If you want to know what happiness is, just pick an example and study it. After all, if you want to know what an aardvark is you don't discuss the idea of an aardvark, you look at examples. Leave the definitions and concepts to the philosophers."

How refreshing and direct! No wonder psychology has made such great strides in this century. No wonder it is universally admired and revered. Unfortunately, in this case, the suggestion won't work. How can we pick an example of happiness if we have no idea of what it is? How can we recognize it when we see it, if we have no definition of it and can't say what it is? Can you go and study an aardvark if you don't know what it is? The psychologist's suggestion is useless without a clearer concept of happiness.

One author made an exhaustive study, and concluded that happiness is having more satisfied desires than unsatisfied desires. In other words, happiness is getting most, or many, of the things one wants. The problem with this definition is that people can want things that are bad for them. Kids want drugs; graduates want high-powered, stressful, heart-attacking jobs; women want a decisive, macho man, or a sensitive wimp, and so forth. Getting what they want makes them unhappier than they were.

Maybe we can save the definition by saying that happiness is getting most of the things one *ought* to desire, or things it is reasonable to desire, not getting the things one does desire that may be harmful. If one knows what one ought to desire—what is really important—and one satisfies those desires, then one will inevitably be happy.

But this modification of the definition only takes us around in a circle. What desires *ought* one to have? What is really important? Well, one ought to desire the things that make one happy. What is important is what leads to real happiness. That is the only way to separate beneficial desires from harmful ones.

But now the definition is circular. It defines happiness as whatever leads to happiness. We can see the circularity if we spell out each step of the proposal. The first definition was

(*a*) happiness = satisfying desires.

But we desire things that are bad for us. So we modify the definition:

(*b*) happiness = satisfying desires we *ought* to have.

How do we know which desires we ought to have?

(*c*) desires we ought to have = desires that lead to happiness.

Therefore,

(*d*) happiness = satisfying desires that lead to *happiness*.

Definition (*d*) is circular because the concept we do not understand—happiness—is itself used in the explanation of the concept. That is no help at all.

Happiness cannot be defined. People who say they are searching for happiness do not understand what they are saying. They have no idea of happiness. If people aren't driven by a desire for happiness, then why do they do what they do—work hard, take vacations, have kids? There are many explanations, of course. They do it because their parents did it, or the TV tells them they ought to do it, or they can think of nothing else to do. Or it may be sheer accident. They stumble into some job or relationship, it makes them feel a little better, so they continue. But there is no grand scheme, no ultimate goal.

If you are still caught up in the race, then you think it is all very important and you have big plans. But if you stand apart for a moment, you will see that people don't know where they are going.

Key Concepts

concept	guarantee	ultimate goal
essential condition	desires	circular

Critical Questions

1. How does the essay show that nothing is essential for happiness?
2. How does the essay show that nothing guarantees happiness?
3. Why can't we look at an example of a happy person and define happiness on the basis of that example?
4. What is wrong with the idea that happiness is having more satisfied desires than unsatisfied desires?
5. Is this idea the same as the definer's theory of happiness, or is it different? Do the muddler's criticisms invalidate the definer's theory, in your opinion?
6. The muddler says that the definition of happiness as getting most of the things one ought to desire is circular. How is the definition like a circle?

Methods and Techniques

ESSENTIAL PROPERTIES

These two writers are trying to understand the nature of happiness. They do that by trying to formulate an adequate *definition* of happiness. What is a definition? A definition is an explanation of the meaning of a term. But how do you explain the meaning of a term? For example, how do you explain the meaning of the word "owl"? You can look it up in a dictionary, of course, but how do the dictionary makers explain the meaning? Generally a definition of a word like "owl" gives the *essential characteristics* of an owl. It tries to state the properties that something has that allow people to recognize it or classify it as an owl. The dictionary definition of "owl" is "a nocturnal bird of prey (order Strigiformes) with a large head, large eyes, and a short, hooked beak." These are all characteristics of owls. If you find something with these characteristics, then you know it is an owl. And if you want to tell someone what an owl is, you can give her or him this list of characteristics.

If this definition is a good one, then these characteristics are essential. That means that all owls *must* possess these characteristics. All owls are nocturnal; there are no owls that hunt in the daytime, by definition. If we found a bird that looked like an owl but was active during the day instead of at night, we would put it in a separate category, because being nocturnal is an *essential*, defining characteristic of owls. It is just as essential as having wings or being a bird. An animal that hunts at night but is not a bird would not be an owl, because being a bird is part of the definition of "owl." It is essential.

Owls have other characteristics besides the ones in the definition. Maybe owls have four toes on their feet, three in front and one in back. But that is not an essential characteristic. If we found a bird with two toes in front and two in back, it could still be an owl, so long as it has the essential characteristics. These other traits are called *accidental* characteristics.

It is even possible that we could discover some obscure trait that *all* owls have. For example, maybe their spleens are always larger than their kidneys. But that is still an accidental characteristic, because it is not part of our *concept* of an owl, not part of our definition. A person can understand what an owl is without knowing about its spleen. But a person cannot understand what an owl is without knowing that it is a bird, or that it is nocturnal, and so on. Anyone who really understands what an owl is must know its essential properties.

Philosophers try to formulate definitions of very general terms, like "happiness," "God," "person," "liberty," "morally wrong," and so on. For example, is goodness an essential property of God? If someone says that God is evil, should we reply that she hasn't really understood what the word "God" means? Or suppose a baby is born with massive brain damage. Is it a person? Is self-consciousness or potential self-consciousness an essential property of persons? In other words, they try to determine the essential properties of these things. It is not so simple as looking in a dictionary, because different dictionaries give different lists of essential properties. And sometimes dictionaries are not perfectly accurate expressions of our concepts.

The first essay proposes a definition of "happiness." That is, it explains what the definer believes is the essential characteristic of a happy person. It is the inner state resulting from reaching most of one's goals. Is that trait really essential? Or is it accidental? Is it possible to find a person, who most people would agree is happy, but who does not have that inner state? Or is it possible to find a person who has the inner state, but who is not happy?

Definitions are not arbitrary. We cannot define words in just any way we like. Some definitions accurately state our concepts, and others do not. We test definitions by looking at examples (of owls, or happy people) to see if they really have the characteristics the definitions say they must have.

Understanding the Dilemma

DEFINER OR MUDDLER?

The first essay in this section offers a definition of happiness, and the second essay says happiness cannot be defined. So on one level, the issue is "Is the definer's definition of happiness correct?" The definer says that happiness is reaching most of your goals (whatever they are), and more precisely, it is the feelings of confidence and pride that result from accomplishing things. But the muddler claims that many people want things that are bad for them, and they are not happy when they reach their goals, so happiness cannot be defined that way.

I called a person who accepts the second essay a "muddler" because he or she says most people just muddle through each day, doing what they have to do, or what appeals to them at the moment, without having any large idea of happiness to guide them. A person who accepts the first essay is a "definer" because he or she thinks the essay has defined happiness.

Is the definer's definition correct? How can we decide? Well, a true definition of something picks out the property or properties that all those things have in common, and that nothing else has. For example, we can define "hemophiliac" as a person whose blood lacks the clotting factor. All hemophiliacs have that property (i.e., if they are cut they bleed without forming clots), and no one else has that property. Now, do all happy people have something in common? Do they have the properties the essay describes in common? And do no unhappy people have those properties? The definer says yes, and the muddler says no. What do you think?

You can think about this conflict between the definer and the muddler on a higher level as well. That is, you can ask whether or not other important concepts, like virtue, knowledge, justice, person, or love, can be defined. The essays in this section are about happiness, but a definer would probably say we can define the other general ideas, too. We need to find clear examples of something like knowledge, and then try to isolate the properties that all the examples have in common. That should not be so difficult, the definer says. And it is very important. We need a clear definition of knowledge if we are going to pursue knowledge as a goal, or give people college degrees on the grounds that they are "educated," i.e., have knowledge. We need a clear definition of justice if we are going to apply justice in our courts. How can we know if we are in love without a definition of love? Folk wisdom says "You will know it when you feel it." But that is no answer. Suppose you feel something strong and deep. Is it love or not? You cannot know without an adequate definition.

But a muddler takes the opposite point of view. Words like "knowledge" and "justice" are applied to so many different situations that we can never find something they all have in common. Different people follow different rules in applying the words. One person looks at a situation and says, "This is just," while another person says, "This is unjust." We can define "hemophiliac" because that is a specific, physical condition. But justice and knowledge are things that human beings create. They are too abstract, too vague, and too value-laden to be defined. The same is true of the other concepts. A major obstacle is our emotions. Everyone cares too much about these things. We can construct a definition, but everyone's definition will serve his or her own purposes. For example, everyone will define virtue as "the way I behave." We will use other words and examples, but that is what our definition will amount to. We will define justice in a way that proves our own claims are just, and so on. Therefore we can never formulate a correct definition. We must continue to muddle through, without knowing where we are going, or what we are doing.

Who is right? Can we formulate clear, acceptable definitions of important terms like "happiness" and "justice"? Or is all our thinking about these large abstractions confused and subjective? Are you a definer or a muddler?

DEFINER

1. Happiness is a definite inner state, which we can understand and pursue in an intelligent way.
2. The essence of happiness is the feelings of confidence, pride, and so on that result from achieving most of one's goals.
3. Understanding the nature of happiness and other key concepts is absolutely essential for social harmony and a meaningful life.
4. To define something like happiness or justice, one needs experience of a broad range of examples, and an ability to find what all the examples have in common.

MUDDLER

5. There may be such a thing as happiness, but we have no idea what it is.
6. Happiness cannot be the feelings resulting from achieving one's goals, because many people have self-destructive goals.
7. For better or worse, everyone muddles through each day, solving immediate problems, without understanding large abstractions like happiness, justice, or knowledge.
8. People use abstract words in so many different circumstances that there is no factor common to all the instances.

FOR FURTHER STUDY

Historical Examples

DEFINER: Aristotle. *Nicomachean Ethics*. Many editions. Fourth century B.C.E. In Book 1 Aristotle methodically explains his conception of happiness, and shows how it is based on human nature.

MUDDLER: Arthur Schopenhauer. "On the Suffering of the World," and "On the Vanity of Existence." In *Essays and Aphorisms*. Penguin, 1970. Originally published in 1850. Schopenhauer claims that we swing back and forth between desire and boredom, and can never achieve happiness.

OTHER SOURCES

V.J. McGill. *The Idea of Happiness*. Praeger, 1967. Historical survey followed by discussion of four issues: self-realization, happiness vs. duty, fulfillment vs. prudence, and happiness vs. pleasure.

Howard Mumford Jones. *The Pursuit of Happiness*. Cornell University Press, 1966. A historical study of the ways Americans have conceived of and pursued happiness.

Bertrand Russell. *The Conquest of Happiness*. Bantam, 1968. Originally published in 1930. Analysis of the causes of unhappiness and happiness, including (for happiness) zest, love, family, work, and impersonal interests.

R.M. MacIver. *The Pursuit of Happiness*. Simon & Schuster, 1955. Reflections on the Golden Rule, art, knowledge, love, and death, among other parts of a happy life.

Andre Maurois. *The Art of Living*. Harper, 1940. Chapters on love, family, friendship, work, leadership, and growing old.

Gordon R. Taylor. *Conditions of Happiness*. Houghton Mifflin, 1951. Discusses psychological needs, and the social conditions necessary to help people fulfill them.

Robert Nozick. *The Examined Life*. Simon & Schuster, 1989. In Chapter 10 Nozick discusses various conceptions of happiness, and argues that pleasure is not the only good.

3.3 IS MORALITY RELATIVE?
RELATIVIST OR ABSOLUTIST?

Americans have some peculiar attitudes toward America and other countries. For one thing, most Americans pride themselves on being tolerant. We say we will welcome immigrants from any other place, regardless of race, creed, or color. We say that people in America are free to do as they please. They can practice any religion, live any lifestyle, and promote any political cause. Because who is to say that one religion or lifestyle is *better* than another?

At the same time, however, Americans seem to think that the ideals of the Bill of Rights and the Constitution—freedom of speech, the right to a fair trial, a government accountable to the people, tolerance itself—are universal. They are ideals and values that *everyone* should accept, even people in foreign countries. If some dictator tyrannizes his people, we condemn him for violating basic human rights, and we might even send in the marines.

This split shows that Americans are ambivalent about values. Some say values are *relative*. That is, each society creates its own values, based on its own history, traditions, geography, and needs. And each society's values are legitimate for that society, but not necessarily legitimate for other societies. One society cannot judge another.

Other people have a different view. They say that some values are *absolute*. They are basic and universal, binding on all human beings. Americans, fortunately, have discovered these absolute values, and we have enshrined them in our political system. If another society has different values, then they are simply wrong.

Which side is correct, the absolutists or the relativists? Are there any actions that are absolutely wrong, in every society at every time? Or are human beings so diverse and flexible that no single standard can apply to all of us? This is the problem of relativism. The first essay in this section presents the relativist view. It tries to show that morality is an inextricable part of culture, and cultures are different in different societies. The second essay attacks the relativist position, and claims that it leads to logical absurdities.

YES: RELATIVIST

"Moral Relativism"

In the nineteenth century, when European missionaries and explorers encountered primitive tribes in Africa, they sometimes required the women of the tribe to dress "properly," like a Victorian lady. The women had to put on corsets and long skirts.

Today we smile at such blatant ethnocentrism. Proper attire in London is not proper in the tropics. But many people think that, when it comes to moral rules, what is proper in London *is* proper in the tropics and everywhere else. This is *moral absolutism*—the belief that some moral rules are binding on everyone, regardless of cultural differences.

The attitude supported by modern social science is *moral relativism*—the belief that morality is part of the complex web of beliefs, traditions, feelings, and practices we call "culture." One people's culture is different from another's. So their morality is different as well. People in one society might place a great value on the family and respect for ancestors. People in another society might value individuality and independence to a much greater degree.

Some tribes in New Guinea and Australia practiced cannibalism, and boasted about it. Many other cultures condemn cannibalism with the greatest vehemence. Among Bedouin tribes in Arabia, adultery on the part of a wife was grounds for execution. (They had different standards for men and women.) Among the Ituri pygmies of central Africa marital fidelity was not highly valued, and Eskimo wives slept with visitors as an act of hospitality. In the American Southwest, the Hopi ideal of behavior was sharing, avoiding conflict, and subordinating oneself for the sake of peace. Their neighbors, the Apache, expected young men to prove themselves in war.

But absolutists know about this variety in moral values and are still not convinced. They claim that some societies are more "advanced" or "civilized" than others. To make the case for relativism, we must go beyond these scattered cases and examine the nature of morality itself. If we look at some basic facts about morality, we can see that it is a part of culture. I want to emphasize three important facts. Morality is a set of rules, it is learned from cultural authorities, and it requires some standard of judgment.

1. Morality Is a Set of Rules. When an average person thinks of morality, he or she probably thinks of rules. "Thou shalt not kill." "Honesty is the best policy." "This above all: to thine own self be true." For most people, "a highly moral person" is a person who always obeys the rules. All societies have rules, although different societies have different rules.

Once we recognize that morality is a set of rules, we should acknowledge another fact. All rules—whether moral, legal, social, or the rules of games—are created, not discovered. They are invented by people as a means to coordinate their interactions with each other. They are invented, and they can be changed if people decide they are no longer useful. The rules of basketball, for example, didn't exist before human beings invented them.

Moral rules are a lot like legal rules, i.e., civil laws. Laws tell us what is permitted and what is forbidden. And no one would claim that laws are discovered or universal. They are invented, and relative to a particular society. The only difference between laws and moral rules is that moral rules are not normally written down officially and publicly by a society, as laws are. And moral rules are enforced informally by social pressure, rather than formally by the police. But they are still rules, and rules are devised, not natural.

Since all rules are artificially created, and morality is a set of rules, it follows that morality is artificially created. Moral rules are prescribed by a society to keep order and to encourage certain forms of behavior. There is nothing "absolute" or "natural" about them.

Moral rules and civil laws are very different from scientific laws. Scientific laws are descriptions of the way the natural world works. For example, Boyle's law says "Gases expand when they are heated under constant pressure." An interesting fact about this law is that we cannot violate it, even if we want to. We have no choice. If we heat a gas, it will expand. But people can and do violate moral rules all too often. One common moral rule is "Tell the truth." But people frequently violate that rule. Another interesting fact about scientific laws is that they are the same for everyone. In every society, Boyle's law holds true. In Asia, Africa, South America, and everywhere else, gases expand when they are heated. Cultural differences are irrelevant to scientific laws.

2. Each Person Is Taught a Set of Moral Rules.   The second thing we should notice is how we *know* moral rules. Why do we honor a particular set of rules? The answer is that we learn them unconsciously as we are growing up. An important part of any culture is the method of rearing children. And a large part of the supervision of small children consists of teaching them right and wrong. By the time they are grown, these basic feelings and values have become part of their personalities. Children are told "Do not hit" so often that it becomes second nature to them. They learn that hitting creates a situation in which everyone is very upset, including adults, who are their main sources of stability and security. The feeling that hitting is wrong becomes so deeply ingrained that it may even seem to be inborn.

Where else do we learn right from wrong, if not from parents and authority figures? Someone may say we rely on our conscience to know right and wrong. But people's consciences tell them what their parents and teachers taught them years earlier. Certainly small children, say 3- or 4-year-olds, do not have much of a conscience. They can be cruel, violent, deceptive, and utterly selfish. They only acquire a conscience as they grow older and are molded by the people around them.

It may be true that every adult, in every society, has a conscience. That is to be expected, since morality is an important part of every culture. All people are taught to have a conscience. But different people's consciences tell them different things about right and wrong. A Hopi's conscience said very different things from an Apache's conscience. And who is to say that one society's conscience is more authoritative than another's?

3. No One Can Step Outside All Moral Systems.   The question of which conscience is more authoritative leads to the third point. Someone might say that one society's rules are objectively "better" than another's. But that judgment implies that a person can stand outside the two societies and evaluate them on the basis of some independent standard. For example, I might say England's way of producing goods is better than China's. I am making an objective judgment because I am not involved in either society. I can look at them from outside. Of course the English would say their system is better, and the Chinese would say theirs is better, but they are both biased, because they are involved in their systems.

However, even if I am outside of their societies, I must still use *some* standard in evaluating the two economic systems. I say England's system is better than China's. That is a value judgment. But the word "better" depends on some *standard*. In fact, I am evaluating England and China by the standards of *my* culture. By "better" Americans mean more efficient. Others might use a different standard. The Chinese may define "better" as ensuring full employment, and by that definition China's way is better than England's. But everyone must have *some* standard, or else we cannot make any value judgments at all.

The important point to see is that no one can stand outside *all* cultures and decide whose morality is objectively the best. I do not want to say that a person cannot escape the strong psychological influences of his or her society. Actually people do move from one culture to another; they forget their old values, or standards, and completely adopt the different values and attitudes of their new society. Some people emigrate from one society to another, and assimilate to their new society. These transformations are psychologically possible. Rather, I want to make a logical point. No one can rise above all societies and make moral judgments about them, because every moral judgment is based on some system of values. And value systems are created by societies. If a person judges something to be good or evil, that judgment must be based on some society's moral values. Therefore it is biased, not objective. Every evaluation, every assessment, is based on *some* standard. That isn't a fact about psychology. It is a logical requirement.

We might use one set of values one day, and a different set of values on another day, but if we make moral judgments at all, then we must use some values. Values are invented by societies. So we must operate *within* some society's moral code. We cannot objectively judge *all* codes, because we always have the limited point of view of one particular code.

We can make the point by using an analogy. Culture is like language, and particular cultures are like particular languages. If we want to talk, then we have to use a language. We might move from one language to another, but we cannot talk without using some language. We cannot step outside of all language, so long as we want to talk. Just as talking requires some language, so making value judgments requires some values. If we want to make value judgments, then we must use the standards of some culture. Moral standards (like languages) are invented by societies. Therefore, it makes no sense to say some systems of morality are objectively better than others. No one can be objective in this matter, not because of psychology, but because of logic.

These three facts show that morality and our moral feelings are part of culture. Even moral absolutists admit that societies create culture, and cultures are different in different societies. These basic facts show that morality is relative to the society that creates it.

Key Concepts

moral relativism	rules	scientific law
moral absolutism	civil law	conscience
culture	biased	

Critical Questions

1. A relativist says morality is a set of rules. How does that show that morality is relative? Relative to what?
2. What are the differences between moral rules and scientific laws?
3. According to the essay, how does anyone know what is right or wrong?
4. You probably believe that cheating in school, or stealing, or taking unfair advantage of people generally, is morally wrong. Do you believe it because your parents or grandparents or someone taught you? Is that the only reason you believe it?
5. A relativist says an objective evaluation of a society is impossible. Why? Do you agree?
6. Is the relativist right? Are the moral values of a theocratic state like Iran (censorship, subordination of women, assassination of foreign critics, etc.) just as valid, just as true, as the moral values of America (the Bill of Rights, etc.)?

NO: ABSOLUTIST

"Right for You, Wrong for Me?"

In discussions of moral issues, someone always says that what is right for one person is not right for another person. I want to examine this claim, and I will begin by describing a specific case.

In many countries in Africa and Asia people practice female circumcision. The custom involves "cutting off all or part of a young girl's clitoris and labia, and in some cases stitching her vagina closed until marriage" (*New York Times*, Nov. 23, 1993). The United Nations reports that millions of women, mostly Muslim, are affected. People in these countries have followed the custom for centuries, and feel strongly about it. They say that it keeps a girl chaste and virginal. One father stated that he had his daughter circumcised "so that later she will behave herself" (ibid.). (The procedure often makes sexual intercourse joyless or painful, according to Western doctors.) Women also defend the custom. One mother said she did it for the good of the child, "to make her like the other girls so that she could find a husband" (ibid.).

Is female circumcision morally right? It is an honored tradition of long standing in these countries. The parents are doing what they believe is best for their daughters. The parents, including women who have had the operation, certainly believe it is right. On the other hand, the procedure is usually performed without anesthesia in unsanitary conditions. The girls often develop "hard scars, cysts, swellings or infections"; and it may cause lifelong health problems. A French lawyer, Linda Weil-Curiel, is emphatic: "This is butchery invented to control women," she says. "It's a form of violence we would never allow here against white girls" (ibid.). She has no doubt that the custom is morally wrong. So some say it is right and some say it is wrong.

But I am more interested in a third answer. Some people say it is morally right for the Africans and Asians, but it is wrong for us in America or Europe. These people say that the Muslims have decided that circumcision is morally proper, and so it *is* proper, for Muslims. But the same Americans or Europeans would never dream of treating their own daughters the same way. In general, some say that every person must decide what moral principles to adopt. It is a personal decision, and no one can judge another, or say another's principles are wrong. What is right for you may not be right for me, some say.

This third answer is called "moral relativism." It is a fairly popular point of view these days, but I don't think it makes sense. The problem isn't that moral relativists approve of actions that offend me (although they do). The problem is that they cannot explain what they believe in a clear, coherent way. Let's see how it applies in practice. Suppose a woman in Mali (in West Africa) named Mrs. Diarra helps circumcise her 3-month-old baby. Her moral principle is that she should help her daughter abstain from sexual intercourse until marriage, and even then realize it is not a source of pleasure. In addition, imagine that a Frenchwoman named Mrs. Robert learns of the operation. Mrs. Robert is a moral relativist, so she says Diarra did the right thing, for Diarra, although it would not be right for Robert. Robert's conscience tells her that she should not mutilate her daughter's genitals, with or without anesthesia, no matter what the traditions are. So Robert's view is that the very same action—female circumcision—was morally right for the woman in Mali, but would be morally wrong for herself in France. In fact, Diarra was admirable for doing what she believed was right. But the idea of doing the same thing to her own daughter she feels is repugnant and horrifying. She has different values and moral standards.

While this sounds reasonable, it leaves an important question unanswered. The question is "What is the crucial *difference* between Mrs. Diarra and Mrs. Robert that makes the same action right for Diarra and wrong for Robert?" There must be some very significant difference, since the very same action is right for one person but wrong for the other.

One obvious difference is that Diarra lives in Mali whereas Robert is a Frenchwoman. They live thousands of miles apart. But why is that important? Right and wrong do not depend on geography. If you want to convince someone that an action is wrong, you will not say, "It is wrong because we are located north of 20 degrees of latitude." That isn't a reason. It's irrelevant. Mali has a hot and dry climate, very different from France. But surely the different weather or geography is not a crucial moral difference. No one would say circumcision is morally right in Mali because the average temperature there is 90 degrees.

Perhaps the crucial difference between Mrs. Diarra and Mrs. Robert is simply that their values are different. They have chosen different principles. Or they were taught different principles by their parents or their cultures. That is why it is right for Diarra to circumcise her daughter, but it would be wrong for Robert to do the same.

This is probably the difference that moral relativists have in mind. But consider the consequences of this explanation. If it is right for Diarra to circumcise her daughter because she *believes* it is right, then it is right for a child molester to abuse children, so long as he *believes* it is right. In other words, the relativist says that the crucial difference between Diarra and Robert is a difference in their beliefs about what they should do. And that difference is enough to make an action right for Diarra but wrong for Robert. But then the relativist is saying that a person's *belief* that he should do something is enough to make it morally *right* that he should do it.

That makes no sense. No one thinks that it is morally right for the child molester to molest children, even if the molester, in his perverted way, does believe he ought to do it. Some societies teach their children that slavery is morally right, that people who practice a different religion aren't fit to live, that women who try to achieve equality with men are evil witches, or that criticizing the government is morally wrong. But teaching something doesn't make it right. It doesn't matter how old a custom is, because age isn't enough to make it right either. Fortunately these hateful attitudes are disappearing as literacy and education spread throughout the world. But a relativist believes all attitudes—all moral values—are equal, and so it could be just as fortunate if racism or violence gained popularity.

Thus there is *no* difference between Diarra and Robert that is important enough to justify the relativists' view. Different climates, different diets, different beliefs, different educations are not enough to make an action right in one place and wrong in another.

The idea that what is right for one person may be wrong for another person (in the same situation) is an idea that sounds attractive. It sounds very tolerant. And it would be nice if we never had to judge anyone else. But the idea makes no sense. If you believe that something is right for you, then you have to believe that it is right for anyone else in similar circumstances. Relativists cannot point to any crucial differences that make an action right for one person but wrong for another.

Relativism has another flaw. It does not recognize that people with different principles come into contact. To see how that happens, let's go back to Mrs. Diarra again. Mrs. Diarra is a real person, and in fact she was born in Mali but was living in France when she circumcised her baby. Imagine (hypothetically) that Mrs. Diarra was baby-sitting for Mrs. Robert, the French relativist, and she decided to circumcise Mrs. Robert's daughter, "for her own good." (In African countries friends and family, not only the child's mother, often perform the operation.) What would the relativist say about that?

If she follows her own principle, she will have to try to prevent Diarra from circumcising her own daughter, or have her arrested for doing so. She will tell Diarra that she should stop, that what she is doing is *wrong*. But Robert also believes that Diarra is admirable for believing in her principles. It is *right* for Diarra to circumcise girls, since that is what her principles tell her to do. She has done the same thing for her friends in Mali. Therefore in this case, the relativist must say female circumcision is right *and* wrong at the same time. Mrs. Diarra did something that was right and wrong. But that statement makes no sense. It is like saying someone is, and is not, pregnant, or the entire line is straight and also curved. The relativists' conclusion that the circumcision is both right and wrong shows that relativism is a confused and contradictory doctrine.

It doesn't help to say the action is "right from Diarra's point of view but wrong from Robert's point of view." Robert, the relativist, has to make a decision: will she applaud as Diarra applies the razor blade, will she continue to feel warmly toward Diarra, or will she protest, try to stop Diarra, and get angry at her for committing a moral evil? She cannot have it both ways. Moral relativism sounds reasonable, until two groups with different values come into contact, and an action by a person in one group affects a person in another group. When that happens, relativism collapses. The relativist who says that the action is both right and wrong isn't saying anything. It is like saying that the door is open but also closed at the same time. That is empty and uninformative.

Imagine another example. In the American South before the Civil War many people believed slavery was legitimate and even beneficial. Many people in the North believed slavery was abhorrent. Suppose a relativist says slavery was right for people in the South, but wrong in the North. But now imagine that a black man from the North crossed the border into the South and was enslaved. What does the relativist say? Was the enslavement right or wrong? The relativist should not condemn the slave owner, because slavery is morally right in the South, he says. On the other hand, the black man was not originally from the South. Where he grew up slavery was wrong, according to the relativist. In fact, the relativist has no answer. He cannot say anything about the morality of the action. His theory breaks down when two cultures come into contact.

And cultures are coming into contact more and more as the world shrinks through travel and communication. If a relativist like Mrs. Robert really believes that circumcising her own daughter would be a brutal, inhuman, domineering act, then she should tell Mrs. Diarra that what she did to her daughter was brutal and wrong. Period. Not wrong for Robert but right for Diarra. Just wrong. In fact, Diarra's daughter spent three weeks in the hospital and almost died. The mother was charged with violating French laws against harming children.

It is very difficult to tell someone that his or her action is morally wrong. But the arguments about irrelevant differences between people, and about contact between cultures, leave no alternative. If you are going to have any moral principles at all, then you are going to have to say everyone else should have the same principles. That isn't arrogant. In fact it is humbling. It means that you must work very hard and think very carefully before you adopt any beliefs about right and wrong, because those beliefs will require you to judge others.

Key Concepts

moral belief	cultural contact	tolerance
cultural differences	contradiction	universal principle

Critical Questions

1. What is the position that the essay wants to criticize? Does the moral relativist believe female circumcision is right, or that it is wrong?
2. The absolutist says the moral relativist must believe there is a big difference between Mrs. Diarra and Mrs. Robert. Why must the relativist believe this?
3. The fact that Diarra and Robert were taught different values is not enough of a difference, in the absolutist's view. Why not?
4. Do you think it is morally wrong for people in Africa to circumcise their daughters?
5. How would a relativist respond to the absolutist's example of the northern black man enslaved in the American South? Would he say the enslavement was morally right or wrong? Would it make any difference if the relativist himself or herself were the person enslaved?
6. Why is relativism attractive to many people?
7. Suppose Sue's most sacred moral principle is tolerance. In the absolutist's view, must she say that intolerant people living in an intolerant society are morally wicked? Or is that intolerance on her part?

Methods and Techniques

AD HOMINEM

Both the relativist and the absolutist present interesting arguments for their views. Both are thoughtful and balanced; both have plausible reasons to support their conclusions. But discussions of relativism are not always so cool and objective. Relativism is a sensitive issue. Often in introductory philosophy classes, when the topic of relativism comes up, the discussion degenerates into personal accusations, raised voices, hurt feelings, and stony silence.

The problem lies in the two sides' perceptions of each other. Relativists sometimes see *absolutists* as reactionaries: arrogant, self-righteous fanatics who want to impose their own narrow-minded values on everyone else, cultural imperialists, whose real goal is domination and power. Or they see absolutists as straight-laced, unhappy people living under terribly restrictive rules, who think that if they can't have any fun then no one else should either. But relativists see *themselves* as tolerant, open-minded, aware of people's basic freedoms and differences. They think that they enjoy and respect people in all their manifold diversity.

On the other side, the perceptions are entirely different. Absolutists see *relativists* as spoiled, self-indulgent egotists who only want an excuse to follow their whims and reject all standards: perpetual adolescents who cannot tolerate any rules or self-restraint. Or they see relativists as permissive, timid people who condone horrible crimes under the cloak of tolerance. Actually they are merely cowards. But absolutists see *themselves* as mature, responsible people, defending the pillars of civilization—family, civic pride, law, hard work, higher standards of literature and art, etc.—against the anarchic, degrading effects of relativism, which means no standards and no rules of any kind.

Obviously with such different images of each other, the two sides will not be able to understand each other. Nor will anyone else who wants to learn about relativism be able to get a clear picture of the real issue. The accusations are too emotional, the disputants are too involved.

Arguments like these between relativists and absolutists exemplify an important mistake that philosophers sometimes make. The mistake is called an "ad hominem." The words *ad hominem* are Latin and mean "to the man." An ad hominem is an attack on a *person* rather than a criticism of the person's *belief*. For example, suppose a Senator proposes a tax cut to stimulate the economy. One of his opponents then says, "We should not vote for the Senator's tax cut. I happen to know that he got the idea from his rich banker friends. And besides, he is a notorious womanizer." While these comments may be typical of the debates in Congress, they are completely worthless as arguments. The opponent is attacking the Senator, not the idea of a tax cut. Even if the Senator does cheat on his wife, that fact is irrelevant to the tax cut. It is no reason to believe the tax cut is a bad idea. To criticize the tax cut itself, the opponent would have to show that the government cannot afford to cut taxes, or that it would only benefit a small minority of people, or that it is undesirable for some other reason. Attacking the person who proposes it is an illogical mistake.

The opponent's other point is also an ad hominem, though perhaps it isn't so glaring. In saying the Senator got the idea from his rich banker friends, the opponent is trying to undermine the Senator's reputation, or criticize his motives. But those attacks are also irrelevant to the question of whether a tax cut would improve the economy. It may be true that the Senator is only trying to help his friends, or trying to get reelected, or that he has no idea of how the economy works. Nevertheless, pointing out these facts would be an ad hominem. They are not reasons to believe a tax cut is a bad idea. They are criticisms of the person, not the belief. (Of course criticisms of the person might be appropriate and relevant in another context, such as a reelection campaign.)

When relativists say that absolutists are intolerant bigots, the relativists are guilty of committing an ad hominem. They are criticizing people, not beliefs. It is possible that absolutists *are* bigots, but that absolutism is still true. The same goes for absolutists who say relativists are spineless cowards. Whether they are or are not is completely irrelevant to the truth of relativism. In order to decide whether relativism or absolutism is true, we must look at something besides the character or background of the people who hold those views.

Understanding the Dilemma

RELATIVIST OR ABSOLUTIST?

Everyone believes that some things are morally right and some things are morally wrong. Even the most hard-boiled cynic will become angry if his wallet is stolen. Assuming that people have beliefs about right and wrong, we can ask many questions about those beliefs. The question in this section is "Can morality be *different* in different societies?" In other words, can an action be right in one culture, but (the very same action) wrong in another culture? This is not the same as asking whether people in different societies can have different *beliefs* about right and wrong. The question is about right and wrong itself. Can an action really be right in one place and really be wrong in another? The relativist says yes, and the absolutist says no.

For example, probably everyone in the United States would say slavery is wrong. If one person tried to sell another, everyone would be outraged. But could slavery be morally right in another society, in Asia or South America or Africa? Can we say child abuse is horrible and intolerable here, but perfectly OK and maybe even a good thing in another society? The relativist says yes, and the absolutist says no. Who is right? Are you a relativist or an absolutist?

The relativist makes certain assumptions about the nature of morality and its place in society, and the absolutist makes different assumptions. According to the relativist, when we say something is morally wrong (e.g., "child abuse is wrong"), we are reporting the beliefs of our society. We are playing the role we have learned and internalized, and if we had grown up in another society, we would feel differently. But according to the absolutist, when we say something is wrong, we are talking about something in the world, something objective, like facts.

One way to look at the difference between relativists and absolutists is to focus on facts. What are facts and how do we know them? To an absolutist, it seems like an undeniable fact that beating a child is wrong. It is like seeing clearly that one line is longer than another, or that a figure is square and not round. If someone says, "Yes, it is wrong here, but in another society it is ok," the absolutist decides that the person is just ignoring the plain facts. The person has embraced a *theory* about morality and cultures, and clings to it so desperately that he can look at coal and call it white.

However, a relativist might say exactly the same thing about an absolutist. To a relativist, moral judgments are based on feelings that we all learn from our society. The words "right" and "wrong" are like the words "beautiful" and "ugly": they mean different things to different groups. They are expressions of cultural attitudes, not descriptions of objective facts. Thus if someone says beating a child is absolutely wrong for everyone, in any society, the person is expressing *his society's theory* of morality without realizing it. He is in the grip of a theory that prevents him from seeing the facts, and prevents him from seeing events the way other people see them.

Which person, the relativist or the absolutist, is most influenced by his theory? Which one is incapable of seeing the facts as they really are? Which has a more accurate perception of reality? Are you a relativist or an absolutist?

RELATIVIST

1. An action may be right in one society and wrong in another society.
2. Moral rules and moral values are invented by a society, like the customs regulating clothing, meals, and property.

3. Different societies can have different, irreconcilable values regarding basic aspects of life, such as preserving life, sexual relations, raising children, owning property, etc.
4. There is no difference between what a society *believes* is right and what *is* right.

ABSOLUTIST

5. The moral relativist cannot explain her or his position in a clear, coherent way.
6. If you believe an action is morally wrong, then you should have the courage of your convictions and say the same action is wrong everywhere.
7. The similarities among people around the world outweigh the differences; all people agree on basic moral judgments, even if they disagree about superficial styles and customs.
8. A group cannot make an action morally right or wrong simply by saying it is right or wrong.

FOR FURTHER STUDY

Historical Examples

RELATIVIST: Plato. *The Republic*. Books 1 and 2. Many editions. Fourth century B.C.E. Plato was an absolutist, but at the beginning of *The Republic* he presents the position that he wants to reject, and his presentation is one of the clearest, most striking discussions of moral relativism in the history of philosophy.

ABSOLUTIST: Cicero. *On Law*. Book 1. Harvard University Press (Loeb Classical Library). First century B.C.E. Cicero defends his belief in Natural Law largely by criticizing the relativist alternative. He points to the ways in which we are all similar, and to the similar values we all share, such as enjoyment of pleasure and fear of death.

OTHER SOURCES

Randolph M. Feezell, Curtis L. Hancock. *How Should I Live? Philosophical Conversations about Moral Life*. Paragon House, 1991. Imaginary conversations among a philosopher, Unitarian minister, environmentalist, religious fundamentalist, businessman, and others.

James Rachels. *The Elements of Moral Philosophy*. Random House, 1986. Chap. 2 is a critical examination of the factual basis of relativism and the implications of the theory by an absolutist.

John Hospers. *Human Conduct: Problems of Ethics*. Harcourt Brace Jovanovich, 1972. Brief discussion.

John Ladd, ed. *Ethical Relativism*. Wadsworth, 1973. A small anthology with a good selection, including several anthropologists.

David Wong, "Relativism." In Peter Singer, ed. *A Companion to Ethics*. Blackwell, 1991. A defense of relativism.

Abraham Edel. *Ethical Judgment: The Use of Science in Ethics*. Free Press, 1955. Chap. 1 is a discussion of the sources of relativism. Edel believes growing knowledge in social science will undermine relativism.

Shia Moser. *Absolutism and Relativism in Ethics*. Charles C. Thomas, 1968. A critique of relativism, with interesting data from various cultures.

Gilbert Harman, Judith Jarvis Thomson. *Moral Relativism and Moral Objectivity*. Blackwell, 1996. The philosophers present their views and then reply to each other.

3.4 Is Happiness the Standard of Morality?

Utilitarian or Formalist?

———————————————•———————————————

Everyone has to make moral decisions at one time or another. Some women get pregnant without intending to, and then they must decide whether or not to have an abortion. Americans in 1990 had to decide whether or not to support the war against Iraq. Students sometimes have opportunities to cheat and must decide whether or not they will be honest. People who are comfortable must decide how much of their income, if any, they should give to the poor, and so on.

One way to make these tough decisions is to go to some authority, like a priest, or perhaps a more experienced friend, and ask him or her. Or one can try to imagine what some hero or heroine would do in a certain situation. What would Gary Cooper in *High Noon* do? Or Florence Nightingale? Or your grandmother? Or one can just flip a coin.

But for many independent, reflective people none of these strategies is very satisfying. They seem too haphazard or capricious. Some people want a more systematic, methodical way of making moral decisions. Philosophers are like that. They want to sleep soundly at night with clear consciences like everyone else, so they want to make correct decisions. But they also want to understand *why* a particular decision is right. They want to see the *pattern* in moral decisions. They want to understand what unifies right actions, and sets them apart from wrong actions. In other words, they want a moral *theory*.

Having a moral theory that you can believe in is a very comforting thing. If you understand why some actions are right and others are wrong, you will feel much more confident that your decisions are right. After all, without a theory, you might misinterpret Gary Cooper. And who is to say that Cooper is the best role model anyway? Furthermore, if you have a moral theory, then you can justify and defend your decisions if anyone challenges you. You can explain yourself in a reasoned, intelligent way to others. Finally, once you step back and see the general features of moral decisions, you will be prepared for any future problems that arise. You will feel secure knowing that you will be able to make the right decision.

Moral issues are fascinating problems to think about, simply from an intellectual point of view. But philosophers are also human. The moral theories they construct not only satisfy their intellectual curiosity, but they also satisfy the need for a clear conscience and the need to feel justified.

In the following essays, you will read defenses of two famous theories of morality. The first essay argues for the utilitarian theory, and the second defends the formalist theory. Utilitarianism says that our pursuit of happiness is the basis of our moral judgments and feelings. Formalism says that a basic human characteristic is our ability to follow rules, and that unique human ability is the basis of morality.

YES: UTILITARIAN

"Utilitarianism"

"Utilitarianism" is a long, strange word, which stands for a simple, familiar idea. It is an idea about morality. Everyone must think about morality at least occasionally, because everyone must make moral decisions. "Should I volunteer down at the soup kitchen?" "Should I declare this money on my income tax form?" But utilitarianism is about morality in general. It is a theory about why we say some actions are morally right and others are morally wrong, in any context. The simple idea is that a morally right action is one that creates the greatest happiness for the greatest number of people. If you want to do the right thing in any situation, you should ask what would lead to the greatest happiness for all concerned, and do that. Wrong actions are ones that produce unhappiness. Utilitarianism, then, is a moral theory, and in fact, it is the best theory we have.

Thinking about moral theories is not exactly the same as thinking about a particular moral question. If you are wondering about volunteering at the soup kitchen, you might consider several factors: you are tired after work; but the homeless people feel worse than you do. Many of them are drug addicts; but many others are not. Volunteering is not the best way for you to help; but you aren't doing anything to help now, and so on. Thinking about moral theories requires you to step up to a higher level. Instead of debating a particular decision, you should consider a wide range of right and wrong actions. You may not know whether volunteering is right or wrong, but you do know many examples of right and wrong actions. You should try to find out *why* certain actions are right, and why others are wrong. One theory will explain the morally good deeds in one way, and another theory will explain them differently.

But then how do we choose between different moral theories? Well, a moral theory is like a sorting machine. Suppose an inventor has a machine that he says will sort apples into two groups: those that are good for eating and cooking, and those that are spoiled, bruised, wormy, and not good for anything. He puts an apple into the machine, and if it is good, a green light comes on, but if it is bad, a red light comes on. But now another inventor comes along with another apple-sorting machine, and he says his is better. How would a grocer test the two machines? The grocer would try to see which machine produces the most *correct* sorting. That is, are all the apples that the first machine says are good really good, or are some of them actually bad apples? And are all the ones it says are bad really bad, or does it throw away some good apples? Which machine makes the fewest mistakes?

A moral theory is like the imaginary apple-sorting machine, except that a moral theory sorts actions into groups of right and wrong. Sometimes a theory will put a right action into the group of wrong actions, or vice versa. For example, we all know that helping a blind person across the street is right. If a moral theory implies that such an action is wrong, then the theory is faulty. Or if the theory tells us that rape is right, then it is a very poor theory. The best theory is the one that makes the fewest errors. It is the one that agrees with our ordinary moral judgments most often.

When we step back and look at a variety of right and wrong actions, we find that utilitarianism gives us the best explanation of why they are right or wrong. Utilitarianism is the theory that all morally right actions produce the greatest possible happiness for the greatest number of people. It is the best moral theory for two main reasons. First, utilitarianism is in agreement with our ordinary feelings and judgments about right and wrong. It explains why we say certain actions are right and others are wrong. Second, it is the broadest moral theory. It incorporates the best ideas in other moral theories, but avoids their mistakes and limitations.

Examples. To see why utilitarianism is the best moral theory, let's first survey some examples, and see how well the theory explains them. Everyone agrees that murder is wrong. But why is it wrong? Because it destroys a life, it takes away a person's chances to be happy. Why is cruelty wrong? Because it creates pain and unhappiness. Take another example. Suppose a terrible accident occurs and the hospital desperately needs blood. You are healthy so there is no good reason why you cannot give blood. Utilitarianism says giving blood in this situation is morally right, because it produces a large amount of happiness in the patients, and only a little inconvenience for you. Most people would also say giving blood is the right thing to do, although they might not be able to say why it is right. Utilitarianism explains why.

Almost everyone believes that adultery is wrong. Can utilitarianism explain that judgment? The man and the woman who commit adultery may be strongly attracted to each other, and may experience real bliss in their lovemaking. Doesn't that *increase* happiness, and so shouldn't utilitarianism say it is morally *right*?

But adultery also leads to unhappy partners who are deceived, the breakup of marriages, maybe unwanted children, and less respect for vows and honesty. If we consider *all* the consequences of adultery, we see that the amount of pain and heartbreak outweighs the amount of happiness, and therefore utilitarianism agrees with common moral feelings that it is wrong.

Here is another problem case. If a right action is one that makes the most people happy, then shouldn't I withdraw my money from the bank and hand it out to people on the street? That would make hundreds of people happy, so the utilitarian theory should say the action is morally right. But no one believes that I am morally obligated to bankrupt myself. Is the theory mistaken about this action?

Actually there is no conflict between utilitarianism and ordinary moral judgment here. Utilitarianism says that a right action is one that leads to the greatest happiness for everyone, *including me*. My own happiness is just as important as other people's happiness—not more important, but not less. If I gave away all of my money, I would be homeless and starving and very unhappy. In fact, my misery would outweigh the widespread but shallow happiness created by giving a lot of people a few dollars each. Therefore utilitarianism does not say that I should sacrifice everything for others, although it does say that some sacrifices are morally required.

Why is stealing wrong? Because it leads to unhappiness for the victim, and maybe more stealing by others who follow the example. But suppose a starving man steals bread for his family from a wealthy restaurant owner, who has plenty of food and won't miss the bread. The stolen bread makes the starving man very happy, and the loss does not upset the wealthy man very much. The starving man's happiness vastly outweighs the wealthy man's irritation. In this case, stealing may lead to greater happiness for all concerned than not stealing. Utilitarianism says that stealing may be justified in this particular case, so long as it does not lead to widespread stealing in other circumstances, for example, by people who are just lazy. (The fact that it might lead others to break the law is why breaking any law is almost always wrong.) I think most people would say the same thing about the starving man. Our moral sense tells us that this particular theft was justified. All these examples show that utilitarianism explains the underlying basis of our ordinary moral judgments. We all follow (more or less) the utilitarian guideline without realizing it.

Other Moral Theories. Not only does utilitarianism explain common moral judgments, it does not have the flaws that other theories have. Many philosophers and religious leaders have tried to explain why certain actions are right and others are wrong. For example, a very widespread theory says that right actions are those that you would want others to do if they were in your place. "Do unto others as you would have them do unto you." Or "Whatever you want people to do for you, you should do for them." This theory is called the Golden Rule. Not only Jesus, but Confucius, Zoroaster, and other ancient prophets said essentially the same thing. So, for example, should you give some change to a beggar on the street? If *you* were the beggar, what would you want the passerby to do? You would want him to give you some change. Therefore the Golden Rule says you should give some money to the beggar.

But this is almost exactly the same as saying that people should do whatever creates the most happiness. Everyone wants to be happy. You want others to do things for you that make you happy. That's what "you would have them do unto you." So if you should treat others the way you want them to treat you, then you should try to make them happy. It's the same as utilitarianism.

Actually utilitarianism is a better theory. The Golden Rule can lead to actions that most people would say are not right. For example, imagine that Smith and Jones are friends. Smith comes to Jones and asks for a loan so he can market his new product: alcoholic beverages for infants. He calls it "Baby Booze." Jones tries to convince Smith that the idea is crazy, but Smith's mind is made up. He thinks Jones does not understand the baby food market. Should Jones lend his friend the money? The Golden Rule says Jones should treat Smith the way he would want Smith to treat him if he asked for a loan. If Jones had an idea for a new product, he would want Smith to lend him the money, even if Smith disagreed about the wisdom of the investment. Therefore the Golden Rule says Jones should lend Smith the money.

But that would be foolish and wrong. He would be harming himself for no good reason. He would lose his money, and Smith would gain nothing. In other words, the Golden Rule sometimes requires people to make needless sacrifices. It sometimes requires people to put others before themselves in a way that helps no one.

In contrast, utilitarianism says a person should do what creates the most happiness for all concerned, including himself. Everyone's happiness is equally important. The loan to Smith would give him a little temporary happiness, but it would make Jones unhappy for a long time. The unhappiness outweighs the happiness; therefore, it is wrong. It doesn't matter who is happy and who is unhappy. What matters is the total amount of happiness and unhappiness that results from an action.

The Golden Rule often requires one to make sacrifices, such as giving money to the poor. But there is nothing morally admirable about making oneself miserable. That is merely neurotic. There isn't even anything admirable about making oneself miserable for the sake of others, if the others benefit only a little. The only time we admire self-sacrifice is when it benefits others a lot, in fact, more than one's own loss. For instance, we admire a soldier who throws himself on a live grenade and dies to save the lives of many of his comrades. But if he did it only to protect their ears from the noise, then we would decide he had cracked up and was insane, not a hero. This shows that in making a moral judgment, we consider more than sacrifice or devotion to others. We weigh the happiness and unhappiness that results from an action, although we may not realize that we are doing so.

The Golden Rule can backfire in another way as well. Suppose Ben is a meek and timid bureaucrat. What he dislikes most is having to make a decision or take the initiative. He has always listened to his mother, and he likes his life that way. Recently he has developed an interest in Betty, his officemate, and he asks her out on a date. He respects her and wants to do the right thing. If he applied the Golden Rule, he would make all the decisions on the date, suggest what she should have in the restaurant, tell her what to think about the movie, and where they should go afterward. That is how *he* would like to be treated; so he would treat Betty that way. But dominating Betty is not morally right. It is arrogant and insensitive. And it is not likely that either of them would enjoy their date.

The Golden Rule is based on the assumption that people are all alike. It says I should treat others the way I want to be treated because what makes me happy will also make others happy. But people are different. In this case, it is morally wrong for Ben to treat Betty the way he wants to be treated.

The Golden Rule theory holds that one rule can explain all right and wrong actions. But some philosophers believe that being a good person means obeying several rules, like "Keep your promises," "Help the needy," "Don't hurt anyone," "Don't steal," and so on. We might call this the "multiple rule" theory. Right actions are those that conform to the accepted rules, and wrong actions are violations of the rules. So if you have promised not to tell anyone about your friend's illness, it would be wrong to tell. And it would be wrong because the action breaks the rule that says "Keep your promises."

But what is the purpose of these rules? They are all designed to promote happiness. The reason for obeying them is to create the greatest happiness for all concerned. The theory of utilitarianism goes beneath the surface of our thinking about morality. It explains *why* we feel the rules are important and we should obey them. Thus the multiple rule theory is just a more superficial and complicated version of utilitarianism.

There is nothing sacred about the rules themselves. In fact, as we noted above, stealing might be morally right in some circumstances. Moreover, the rules sometimes come into conflict. If a man promises to meet his wife at eight, but comes upon an automobile accident on the way, it would be better for him to stop and help than to keep his promise. Why? Not because of the rule that says "Help those in need"; another rule says "Keep your promises." It is better to stop because that action would lead to more happiness for everyone than keeping his promise. The rule theory says he should never break his promise, but most people would disagree. Thus utilitarianism is closer to our normal moral judgments.

If we want to understand morality, we must look at the feelings that most people have about right and wrong. Where else can we look? Philosophers are no better people than anyone else. They do not have a special authority on morality. Rather, they look at their own and other people's moral decisions, and try to make sense of them. They try to understand, not preach.

Utilitarianism provides the best explanation of the decisions most of us make. And it includes the correct parts of other moral theories, without making the mistakes they do. Since it explains the data, we should accept it as true.

Key Concepts

moral theory	consequences	Golden Rule
ordinary moral judgments	greatest happiness	moral rules

Critical Questions

1. What is the purpose (or purposes) of a moral theory? How can we evaluate different moral theories?
2. What does a utilitarian believe?
3. Has the utilitarian correctly interpreted the Golden Rule? In the example given, would the Golden Rule require Jones to lend Smith money? Would it require Ben to guide and control Betty?
4. Does utilitarianism ever require sacrifice, or require a person to do something painful, or something that makes him unhappy?
5. If the enslavement of 10 percent of the population of ancient Athens increased the happiness of the other 90 percent, and also freed them from labor so they could produce their magnificent drama, architecture, science, and philosophy, would the enslavement be justified, in your opinion?
6. Suppose a hotel is on fire. You can run in and help your two parents in room A, or four strangers in room B, but you can make only one trip. Which people do you think you should help? What would a utilitarian say?

NO: FORMALIST

"The Principle of Morality"

Having children is the most rewarding thing I ever did. It is also the most challenging, especially today. What I worry about the most is not my children's physical health—although that is a constant concern—but their *moral* health. Will they be honest, caring, and mature? My wife and I want to bring them up to be good people. I feel that is the most important task I have in my life. After all, I (and my wife) brought them into the world; I am responsible for them.

But how can one teach a child to be good? That would be a difficult question even in the best of times. But today, it's urgent. I used to think that I would watch the news on TV with my children, to try to make them more aware of the world and its problems, and maybe more concerned. But I can't even watch the news myself any more. The violence is sickening and numbing. Children killing children, children having babies, babies being abandoned. I don't want my children exposed to such brutality until they are much older. But they will have to go to school, and what influences will work on them there?

How can a parent make sure a child learns to tell right from wrong? How can I make my children want to do the right thing? I've been thinking about the problem for some time now, and I have decided that the best way is to teach through example. Young children learn by imitating, not by indoctrination. Four- and 5-year-olds do not understand the broad and long-term consequences of their actions. They only understand that someone is taking care of them, and they want to be like that person.

This is not new. Everyone talks about "role models" nowadays, but I think the issue is more complicated than most people realize. Who is a good role model? Children have to see more than just a few good deeds. They have to see a dedicated, conscientious person. Children are able to sense a person's inner feelings and thoughts, even if they aren't capable of abstract reasoning. They know what's in your heart. A good role model must be a good person herself or himself. And being a good person is more than doing good deeds. External behavior is too superficial. You can't fool children with pretense.

I think that being a good person means having principles. It is a matter of doing things for the right reason. Let me explain what I mean with some examples. At the kindergarten in my neighborhood I have met some of the teachers and aides. One teacher is very good; she plays games with the children, tries to attend to each one, she is sensitive to any problems that come up, and is always cheerful. Her aide does the same things. But in talking to these two women at the parent-teacher meetings I discovered that they are different. Their behavior is the same, but their motives and intentions are different. The aide has been working at the kindergarten for about a year. She began because she enjoys being with children. She laughs and plays with them almost as if she were a 4-year-old herself. The teacher, however, laughs and plays because she decided that that is the best thing for the children. She does what she believes she ought to do. Externally, the aide's behavior and the teacher's behavior are the same. But internally, the teacher is acting on her principles, whereas the aide is just doing what she enjoys.

I think the teacher is a better model for the children to follow. From the aide they will learn to do whatever they enjoy. But from the teacher they will learn to do what they believe in, what helps others, what requires dedication. I trust the teacher and I know she will always do what is best for the children. The aide is wonderful with the children now, but she may lose interest next week. She is guided by her emotions, or interests, not by her principles. She isn't a bad person. Far from it. She simply isn't the best model of moral behavior for the children to follow.

Here's another example. Imagine two young mothers with newborn babies. The babies require almost constant attention and devotion, which the mothers give them. Both mothers make sacrifices involving careers, money, time with husbands and friends, their own rest and health, and so on. But imagine that one mother does all this because she feels that is the right thing; she would prefer to do less, or hire a nurse, but she thinks that would be shirking her duty. The other mother works just as hard, but she does it because she actually enjoys it. She feels tremendous satisfaction in seeing her child grow. And she knows that eventually the child will love her and help her in return.

There are mothers of both types. But now ask yourself which mother is more admirable. Which is acting with a greater degree of moral conscientiousness? I think the answer is the first mother, who acts from a sense of duty. The second mother isn't wrong; she simply isn't acting morally. That is, we shouldn't condemn her, but we should not hold her up as an example of highly moral behavior either. She is just doing what makes her happy. The first mother, however, is an example of a person acting for moral reasons.

Consider another example. Imagine that each of the new fathers has borrowed money from his parents to cover the expenses of raising the baby. And each promised to repay the loan after two years. Each one has to give up vacations and other things to scrape up the money. Suppose that each one does repay the loan, but, like the mothers, they have different motives. One father repays the money because he promised; he feels an unbreakable obligation. He repays because it is the right thing to do. The other repays because he would feel embarrassed if he didn't; he would look irresponsible in the eyes of his wife and parents. And failure to repay might make it difficult to borrow again in the future, should the need ever arise. Although the action is exactly the same (repaying the loan), one father is thinking morally and the other is not. One is highly admirable and the other is not.

These examples suggest that the difference between a morally good person and an indifferent, neutral person (neither good nor evil) lies in their motives or intentions. The key to acting morally is *adherence to principle*. The admirable teacher, mother, and father do what their principles tell them is right. And they do it because of their principles. The aide and the other mother and father do what they feel is in their interest or will benefit themselves. That is not necessarily wrong; it just isn't acting morally. Some actions are neither moral nor immoral. If I have chocolate ice cream rather than vanilla, is that moral or immoral? It's neither. Doing what we enjoy, in most cases, is neither right nor wrong.

I want my children to have examples of moral, decent people around them. But that means more than just people doing good deeds. It means people with principles. This way of thinking about morality is based on some fundamental facts about human beings.

We are all able to act for other reasons besides self-interest. In this respect human beings are different from animals. Animals always pursue their own welfare (safety, food, mating), or they are impelled by instinct. For example, a hen that defends her chicks against a snake isn't heroic. She isn't acting morally. She is only responding instinctively to certain stimuli. She would react the same way to a garden hose or a piece of thick rope. She does not know what a snake is. She does not know what would happen if a snake bit her. Her reaction is programmed. Every time she sees a "snake" she goes through the same sequence of responses.

People are animals, too. Everyone desires safety, companionship, happiness. Humans may or may not act instinctively in some circumstances. But humans are also rational. That means (among other things) that we can follow a rule. Anyone can learn a rule, like "Knock before you enter someone's room," and apply it in new situations. We can think about when the rule applies and when it doesn't. Is this someone's room or only a closet? Would a knock wake up the child who is sleeping? Or we can decide to ignore the rule and barge in.

Animals are different. Learning to follow a rule is not the same as learning to respond to a signal. In Pavlov's famous experiment, he always rang a bell before he gave his dogs their food. Soon the dogs learned that the bell was a signal for food. When they heard the bell they automatically began salivating, anticipating the food. They were not following a rule. They did not choose to respond to the bell. The response was automatic; they could not have refrained from salivating. When seals in a circus clap their flippers they are also simply responding to a signal from their trainer, anticipating food. They have no choice but to clap. But people choose to follow a rule. When a couple goes to a formal dinner party, there are many rules they must think about. And they must decide which rules they are going to follow, and which ones are old-fashioned or inappropriate. Animals can be trained to respond to cues, but they are not following a rule.

That capacity to understand a rule and apply it distinguishes people from animals, not only intellectually, but morally as well. That is what morality is all about. Acting morally means acting on principle, or living according to rules. Acting on principle is not the same as pursuing happiness. If a person believes, for example, that stealing is wrong, and she adheres to her principles, then she will not steal. It doesn't matter how happy the stolen money or clothing or car would make her, because when a person acts on principle, she doesn't consider benefits, or harmful effects, at all. She considers only the principle involved. "Would this action be dishonest, or selfish, or cruel, or a case of stealing?" she asks. Human beings are capable of disregarding benefits or consequences of actions and acting a certain way entirely because it is the right thing to do. And that is what it means to act morally.

Evidence from history supports the same conclusion. Who are the moral heroes in history? Everyone would agree that Dr. Martin Luther King was exemplary. Dr. King did not set out to achieve security or happiness. On the contrary, he risked life and limb to live by the principle of justice. He was arrested numerous times in the fifties and sixties, roughed up, ostracized, and threatened. In Memphis he finally made the ultimate sacrifice for his beliefs. But he never wavered in his commitment to the principles of nonviolence and social justice. His actions certainly brought benefits, after much suffering. But those consequences and calculations were not why he lived as he did, and not why we admire him. We admire him for his adherence to principle.

Contrast Dr. King with Booker T. Washington. There is no doubt that Washington provided great service to blacks and Native Americans. His educational efforts, particularly at the Tuskeegee Institute, gave thousands of young men and women the vocational skills they needed to become economically productive and self-reliant. He enjoyed helping people. He was a good man, but he is not the moral hero that King is. The difference, I think, is that Washington wanted to improve people's living standards and make them happier. King wanted to force people to behave decently, whether that made them more comfortable or not. Washington was aiming at greater happiness for people, and he did it because that felt natural to him. King was aiming at justice, and he did it because he knew it was right, however difficult and costly the task was.

Who are the villains in American history? One might point to Herbert Hoover because he presided over the beginning of the Great Depression and did little to prevent it. But historians do not condemn Hoover. He did what he thought was right; he was simply mistaken. Ulysses S. Grant was probably responsible for more American deaths (probably more Union than Confederate deaths) than anyone else. But he is actually held up as a hero because he was fighting for the principles of liberty and equality. He just did it in a particularly bloody way. One American who is widely condemned is Benedict Arnold, the traitor of the Revolutionary War. Why? Not because he brought misery to people. The actual effects of his plan to surrender West Point were negligible, because the plot was discovered. But he is still regarded as thoroughly evil because he violated his oath, he betrayed his country, and he scorned all his principles.

We also admire inventors, builders, and writers, like Thomas Edison, Theodore Roosevelt, and Dr. Seuss. They improve standards of living and bring happiness to people. But they are not *moral* heroes (unless, for example, a scientist makes a discovery because of his devotion to truth). We are glad that people like Edison and the others lived, but we do not respect them in the same way that we respect moral heroes. All these examples demonstrate that moral consciousness is a separate, autonomous area of life. It is distinct from the pursuit of happiness, whether for oneself or for others. It rests on our ability to live by principles.

In this essay I have argued that acting morally means acting in accordance with one's principles, but I have said nothing about which principles one should have. That is another topic and would require a whole essay for itself. I will only conclude this essay by saying that we know which principles to follow by listening to our consciences. Everyone agrees on basic moral principles: tell the truth, do not hurt people, keep your promises, and so on. Just as humans are all more or less rational, so all have a conscience that speaks more or less clearly. It is sometimes difficult to think rationally because our ego gets in the way. In order to think rationally we must put aside our self-interest. We must do the same in order to hear what our conscience tells us. If you are facing a moral decision (e.g., should I tell a lie?), you should ask what you would expect others to do if they were in your place. You should imagine that you are not involved in any way. Then your ego will not interfere with your moral judgment, and your conscience will guide you.

Everyone accepts the same basic moral principles. Where we disagree is on the *applications* of principles to complex situations. That requires careful reflection, and reasonable people may disagree. But we can apply principles and live by them, disregarding self-interest. That is what morality is all about. My children are too young to understand this essay now, but they are not too young to understand the difference between a moral person and a person who thinks only of happiness. I hope I can teach them to imitate moral people, and to become moral people themselves.

Key Concepts

moral principle	sense of duty	instinct
self-interest	following a rule	moral heroes

Critical Questions

1. What are some examples of acting from self-interest? Is the mother who enjoys caring for her child acting from self-interest?
2. What is an instinct? Do humans have any instincts, in your opinion? Do you think humans have a "maternal instinct," or a "territorial instinct"? A "moral instinct"?
3. Is there a fundamental difference between a circus animal that has been trained to do something, and a human who is following a rule? What difference do you see?
4. Have Dr. King's actions in the struggle for civil rights increased the total amount of happiness in the United States? Would we admire him even if his actions led to greater *unhappiness* among the (white) majority of Americans?
5. The essay claims that right and wrong depend on following or not following certain principles. What evidence does it present to support the claim?
6. Do you agree with the formalist that there is a sharp difference between people we admire as moral heroes and people we admire as benefactors?
7. How do we know what our duties are, according to the formalist?

Methods and Techniques

MORAL THEORIES

Both of the essays in this section are defending moral *theories*. A theory is similar to a generalization, which you have encountered before. Remember that a generalization is a statement about all or most of the members of some class: "all insects have six legs," "most adults can read," etc. Theories are also about all the members of some class. The molecular theory of gases is about all gases. The germ theory of infectious diseases is about all infectious diseases.

But theories are different from generalizations in several ways. One difference is that theories describe things that we cannot see. They propose the existence of objects or processes that are too small to see, or that are hidden in some other way. For example, the germ theory of disease says that diseases, which we can see, are caused by tiny organisms in the body, which are too small to see. Freud's theory of the mind proposed that certain processes like repression and sublimation occur beneath the level of consciousness, so we cannot observe them. Since theories are about these hidden objects and processes, they are much more complex than generalizations. A generalization is one statement, but a theory consists of a number of statements describing the theoretical objects and their relationships.

Scientists (and philosophers) propose theories to explain generalizations. (In science generalizations are often called "laws.") The hidden objects explain why a generalization is true. For example, before Pasteur developed the germ theory, people knew that disease was associated with poor sanitation. They could state a generalization: many people who live in unsanitary conditions will get sick. But they didn't know why open sewers or untreated wounds were associated with illness. The germ theory explains the connection. Germs grow rapidly in unsanitary conditions. When that happens they are more likely to invade the body and multiply there as well. Since theories explain generalizations, they are broader or more fundamental than generalizations.

Utilitarianism is a theory of morality. Utilitarians' starting point is a set of generalizations. "All cases of murder are wrong," "All cases of adultery are wrong," "Most cases of stealing are wrong." Utilitarians take these for granted. They think everyone agrees on these statements. They are similar to the generalizations people made about diseases before Pasteur's theory appeared. Everyone could see that they were true.

Taking these statements as their data, utilitarians then propose an underlying process to explain why the statements are true. The theory of utilitarianism says that wrong actions lead to unhappiness. Most people do not realize that they are following a standard of maximizing happiness. That is why it is an "underlying process." They do not see or think about that effect of murder, adultery, or stealing. But if utilitarians are right, then utilitarianism has explained a wide variety of moral facts.

Formalists also start with a set of generalizations. They say teachers who help their children out of a sense of duty are more admirable, more moral, than other teachers who do the same thing because they enjoy it. And they give other examples of admirable behavior, and assert that everyone agrees on the cases. But their theory is different from the utilitarians'. They say moral people are acting on principle. It is the motive of remaining true to one's principles that makes an action right. We may not realize it, but the person's motive is the key. Thus formalists, too, are proposing an unseen, or unrecognized, process to explain why we say some people are acting morally.

Finally, notice that both theories attempt to unify a wide variety of judgments. We make moral judgments about all sorts of actions, in all sorts of situations. And yet utilitarians and formalists both claim to have found a single process or concept that explains them all, and therefore brings them all together. That is an important characteristic of theories.

Understanding the Dilemma

UTILITARIAN OR FORMALIST?

A utilitarian believes that what we ought to do is try to make the most people happy. The standard or test of morality is the consequences of an action. When you face a choice, and you act in a way that leads to the greatest happiness for the greatest number of people, then you have done the right thing. If you act in a way that needlessly causes pain, or that does not produce the most happiness possible, then you have done something morally wrong.

A formalist believes that we ought to obey certain rules, like "Do not lie." An action is right if it is in accordance with the rules and wrong if it breaks a rule. A formalist believes that being moral, or doing the right thing, is not the same as producing happiness. Trying to make people happy is fine, but it is not the same as thinking morally.

Now, where do you stand? What do you think is the standard of morality: the consequences, or the rules? Do we judge a person by looking at how much happiness results from his action, or by looking at his intention to obey some principle?

In thinking about your decision, you should note that utilitarianism is similar to hedonism. Both the hedonist and the utilitarian say that our goal should be happiness (or pleasure). But there is an important difference. A hedonist believes everyone should pursue his or her own pleasure, whereas a utilitarian believes a person should try to create happiness in general. All happiness is equal, so to speak. Producing happiness for others is just as good as producing happiness for myself, the utilitarian believes. Formalism is a little like pluralism. A formalist believes that being a moral person is certainly valuable, and being moral is not the same as pursuing happiness. So there are important values besides happiness. But a formalist may or may not believe in the other values described by the pluralist.

Both views in this section have the same objective, which is to *explain* moral judgments. They are not so interested in *what* we ought to do as in *why* we ought to do it. They take for granted that some actions are right and some are wrong, and they assume that most people agree on these points. But they go on to ask what do all right actions have in common, and what do all wrong actions have in common? What makes an action morally right or morally wrong? What is the standard of morality? In deciding whether you are a utilitarian or a formalist, you should decide which theory gives the best explanation of common moral judgments. The choice is not between two goals, or two ways of life, but between two ways of thinking about morality.

How can you decide? Well, formalists emphasize the unique character of moral decisions. They say that deciding to act in accordance with a principle is different from other decisions based on desires, even desires to help others. Deciding to keep a promise because it is right is different from doing it because you want to make people happy or because you would feel bad if you didn't keep it. The experience of duty, of moral obligation, of dedication to principles, is unique. If you have had this special experience, then you may think of morality as the formalist does. If you haven't, then you may be a utilitarian.

The difference in experiences is related to a broader difference. Formalists believe that morality arises out of human beings' ability to obey rules, and that ability is the fundamental difference between human beings and animals. Humans can rise above instinct, desire, and the pursuit of goals. Unlike animals, we have a moral sense. We can choose to act on principle. Of course utilitarians believe human beings are different from animals in various ways too, but the differences are not the basis of their theory of morality. Like all animals, we want to be happy. Like social animals, we want all the members of our group to be happy. So while both utilitarians and formalists recognize differences between human beings and animals, for formalists the differences are absolutely crucial to morality.

Where do you stand? Which theory provides the best explanation of why specific actions are right or wrong? Is the feeling of solemn moral obligation reducible to the desire to make people happy? Do we have a moral sense that makes us radically different from animals? Are you a utilitarian or a formalist?

UTILITARIAN

1. Being a moral person means thinking about the consequences of one's actions, and trying to make people happy.
2. Fundamentally, the rule theory of morality says the same thing as utilitarianism: make people happy.
3. If we make a list of the things a person ought *not* to do, we find that they all deny or limit happiness in some way; that is the common denominator.
4. Happiness (my own and others') is the only goal worth pursuing.

FORMALIST

5. Being a moral person means obeying certain principles, no matter what.
6. People are different from animals in that people can deliberately decide to obey rules, without being pushed by desire or instinct or calculations of interest.
7. We admire people who stick by their principles more than we admire people who try to please everybody.
8. Honesty, integrity, and fair play are valuable independently of happiness.

FOR FURTHER STUDY

Historical Examples

UTILITARIAN: John Stuart Mill. *Utilitarianism.* Many editions. Originally published in 1863. Mill explains the greatest happiness principle, different types of pleasures, and the foundations of the theory.

FORMALIST: Immanuel Kant. *Foundations of the Metaphysics of Morals.* Many editions. Originally published in 1785. Kant claims that being moral depends on following rules that everyone could and should follow.

OTHER SOURCES

James Rachels. *The Elements of Moral Philosophy.* Random House, 1986. Chaps. 7 and 8 explain and evaluate utilitarianism, and chaps. 9 and 10 do the same for Kant's version of the rule theory.

John Hospers. *Human Conduct: Problems of Ethics.* Shorter Edition. Harcourt Brace Jovanovich, 1972. Part 7, "Rules and consequences," is a discussion of the rule theory, with Hospers' attempt to reconcile that theory with utilitarianism.

J.J.C. Smart, Bernard Williams. *Utilitarianism: For and Against.* Cambridge University Press, 1973. Each philosopher defends his outlook, and then replies to the other.

Bernard Gert. *The Moral Rules.* Harper & Row, 1970. Ten basic rules and why it is rational to obey them.

Michael D. Bayles. *Contemporary Utilitarianism.* Anchor, 1968. Critiques and defenses of utilitarianism by contemporary philosophers. Difficult.

Robert Bolt. *A Man for All Seasons.* Vintage, 1990. Originally published in 1960. Interesting play (and film) about Thomas More, Henry VIII's Lord Chancellor, who lived according to his principles.

Dale Jamieson. "Method and Moral Theory." In Peter Singer, ed. *A Companion to Ethics.* Blackwell, 1991. The nature of moral theories.

Brenda Almond. *Explaining Ethics: A Traveller's Tale.* Blackwell, 1998. A readable survey of the major issues.

3.5 Is Society the Source of Values?

Functionalist or Moral Theist?

———————————————— • ————————————————

A lot of people wonder how they should live their lives, what goals they should pursue, or what makes life worth living. They wonder what values they should have. They may read some books in philosophy to find answers. Or they may get answers from psychologists, theologians, or novelists. In Section 3.1, one essay proposed pleasure, and the other proposed a variety of personal and social values, as the best goals to have.

But some people aren't satisfied with the answers they receive. They take the next step and ask *why* should anyone pursue a certain goal? Or what is the *basis* of this recommendation? These inquisitive people are not necessarily rejecting the answer. They might agree that love, or excellence, is the highest good. But they want to understand why one goal is higher than, or preferable to, another. They want to understand the sources of values, whatever values one has.

Actually, this general question about the source or basis of values is more typical of philosophy than the question of what particular values we should have. A person who recommends a way of life, or who lays down rules people should follow, is called a "moralist." A moralist tells you how you should live. Jesus and Mohammed are good examples of moralists. People who campaign against drugs are also moralists. A moral philosopher, in contrast, is a person who examines the *reasons* for adopting one way of life or another. A moral philosopher is more interested in the arguments that moralists use to back up their recommendations than in the particular values they propose. A moral philosopher might examine the assumptions a moralist makes, or the consequences of adopting the moralist's rules.

The essays in this section do include reasons to back up their claims. But they are not primarily aimed at persuading the reader to accept certain values. They are primarily interested in the sources of value. The first essay finds the source of value in society. It argues that morality has an essential function in any society, so it represents a functionalist point of view. The second essay finds the source of value in God. It represents the point of view of a moral theist.

YES: FUNCTIONALIST

"An Objective Basis for Morality"

Most people believe that they should not lie, cheat, or steal. They believe it is morally wrong to hurt others needlessly, and if they do abuse someone, they feel guilty about it. Why do people feel this way? Is there any rational basis for these moral beliefs? Or are they just personal preferences, or arbitrary, cultural traditions, with no objective foundation?

Morality has an objective basis. It is objectively true that a person ought to tell the truth, cooperate with others, and treat people fairly. But it takes a certain detachment to see the foundations of moral values. We may not know why we feel strongly about telling the truth, or respecting others' rights. Since we cannot explain the grounds for our beliefs, we may decide that there are no grounds, and that our beliefs are arbitrary.

But our perspective is too limited. We are like soldiers in the middle of a battle. To a soldier, a battle is nothing but chaos. He must run here and there, without understanding why. But to a general, a battle is highly organized, it moves according to plans, it follows a logic of warfare. Morality is like that, too.

If we were to step back and look at our whole society, and other societies as well, we could see a pattern. We could see that every society operates according to certain rules. Three particular rules are absolutely essential for any society to exist at all. Those rules are what we call morality.

No society could exist if its members did not communicate with each other. Even a society as small as a family would disintegrate if its members could not tell each other what they wanted, or intended to do. If they could not communicate, they would not be of any help to each other, and would drift apart. Now if communication is essential, then *honesty* is essential, too. Communication means truthful communication. Lying is not communicating. Thus one rule that is absolutely essential for any society to exist is "Tell the truth."

Truthfulness is essential because members of a society must communicate. They communicate because they must cooperate. Human beings learned millions of years ago that their chances of survival are better when they work together than when they try to live alone. They could find food, build shelter, and defend themselves more effectively by cooperating. Cooperation means that one person cannot think of another person as a stick, or merely an animal. If two individuals are going to work together to build a shelter, each one has to realize that each is dependent on the other, that the other has value, and that the shelter would not exist without the other. Cooperation among individuals requires a certain minimal *respect* for each other, so "respect others" is a second essential rule.

Respecting others means recognizing their property and their freedom to do what they want, sharing things with them, and listening to their ideas. It means restraining one's natural impulses to be first in line, to take a larger portion, or to act regardless of what others think. It is often frustrating. Living in society is beneficial, of course, even with the frustrations. But individuals must *believe* that they benefit, or else they will not cooperate, or will leave. They must be *motivated* to accept the restraints, and that means that their efforts must be rewarded. In other words, for any society to exist at all, the members must receive what they deserve. They must be treated fairly. The society must be just. Thus, "Treat people fairly" is the third essential rule.

Honesty, respect for others, and justice are the foundations of any society. They are also the core of morality. All the basic moral principles can be traced back to these three attitudes. For example, most people believe it is morally wrong to break a promise. That belief is an extension of the idea of being honest. If one person promises another to paint the fence and does not do it, then she or he has lied. Again, most people feel a moral obligation to help someone in trouble, such as a person in an auto accident. That is an extension of the idea of respecting the value of others.

These three basic rules must be obeyed before a society can exist. There are cases where one or more of them is temporarily broken. For example, societies with slavery break the second and third ones. But such societies inevitably break down. They cannot last. Violations like slavery lead to revolution and chaos because they are inconsistent with society itself. We have seen the gradual elimination of slavery over the course of history.

Another society may try to institutionalize lying. The citizens might be forced to lie to each other about the past, or their living standards, or their personal beliefs. But such pervasive dishonesty creates tensions and mistrust that eventually cause a breakdown.

If honesty, respect, and justice are essential for any society to exist, then every existing society must enforce these rules. Every society must make its members feel very strongly about them. They should feel more strongly about them than about inessential things, like the style of clothes people wear, or the kinds of foods they eat. Getting food is essential for society, but no particular way of getting it and no particular food is essential. That difference in seriousness, in importance, is the difference between moral rules and mere custom.

Not only must the essential rules be taken very seriously, but they must be universal as well, if they really are essential. But do not societies have different values? For example, the Eskimos used to leave their grandparents out in the cold to freeze to death. Some people said that showed they did not respect their relatives the way Europeans did. But actually the Eskimos only had different *factual* beliefs. They believed that they were helping the old people reach heaven sooner, and helping the remaining people survive. Their *moral* principle—"help others"—was the same as the Europeans'. That is true for all societies. It is their factual beliefs that are different, not their values.

Honesty, respect, and justice are absolutely essential for society. That is an objective fact. Human beings are social animals, whether we want to be or not. Every individual must live in a society. And that is an objective fact. As a social being, every person ought to obey those rules. People can quibble over the details, but the basic moral rules are built into the nature of things. They are as objective as any other facts.

Key Concepts

limited perspective	communication	moral rule
society	cooperation	objective fact
necessary condition	fairness	

Critical Questions

1. What are the three basic rules of morality, according to the essay? Are those the only moral rules?
2. A functionalist says all societies enforce those three rules. Why do they enforce the rule "Respect others"?
3. What does the functionalist mean by "justice"? Why do societies require their members to be just?
4. The functionalist admits that some societies violate the basic moral rules (e.g., tolerate slavery). How is that possible, if the rules are essential for society to exist?

5. The functionalist also admits that societies are very different from each other (e.g., Eskimos and Europeans). How is that possible, if all societies enforce the three basic rules?
6. Can I grant that the rules the essay describes are essential for society to exist, but still say that that is no reason for me to obey them?

NO: MORAL THEIST
"The Current Crisis and Its Solution"

We are living in a crisis. The house is burning around us while we sit and dawdle. In the streets we see the most horrible and revolting crimes every day. In the schools our children wander from class to class, searching for something to believe in, and not finding it. About sixteen thousand attacks, robberies, and other crimes occur in our schools *every day*. One student in five reports carrying a weapon of some type (*Newsweek*, March 9, 1992, 25). The young people of our country no longer know what is right and wrong. But adults seem just as confused. Our elected leaders are convicted of lying and taking bribes. Of all the children born in this country in 1991, 25 percent were born to unmarried mothers (among teenagers, the figure is 66 percent) (*New York Times*, Dec. 4, 1991, A, 20).

We are in a moral crisis, drifting aimlessly at sea with no landmarks in sight. But people cannot live this way, with nothing to believe in. Some will embrace any kind of ridiculous philosophy, so long as it tells them something is morally right. They will cling to it desperately, and defend it with repeated slogans and shrill shouts, trying to convince themselves it is true. (When people become angry in an argument, it is a sure sign that they don't have good reasons for their opinion.) Others feel a kind of vague nausea, being tossed back and forth by events around them, not knowing which way to go.

We need an *authority* that we can trust and obey, an authority who will tell us what we should do and why we are here. The only way out of the crisis is to rediscover the God of our fathers. Only then will we have a sense of morality again.

The reason for all the violence and confusion today is that we have forgotten the true nature of morality. We have come to believe that we can discover right and wrong by studying human needs or by studying nature. It is a fact that every person needs food, clothing, and shelter. Some say that fact implies that we ought to help everyone satisfy those needs. Others say it is a fact that we are dependent on the fragile natural world around us. They think that implies that we have a moral obligation to respect nature.

But no *fact* creates a moral obligation. The fact that we have needs or that nature is fragile does not automatically prove that anything is morally right or wrong. Let us grant that the statement "People have needs" is true. What follows? What does that fact prove? Can we draw the conclusion "We ought to help people"? No. There is no logical connection between these two statements.

A person could just as rationally draw the conclusion "People are weak and contemptible." I am not saying either conclusion is correct. I am saying that a person can go one way as easily (logically) as the other. Mere facts are not enough to believe in. Facts are not moral values. That confusion was one step toward the crisis.

Morality does not depend on facts but on *commands*. "Thou shalt not kill" is a moral principle. It tells us clearly and directly that killing is wrong. Anyone with authentic moral values has a firm commitment to obey certain commands: respect others, tell the truth, keep your promises, relieve suffering, and others. Of course we need to know the facts of a case before we can decide what we should do. We can investigate the facts; that is what trials and juries are all about. But after the facts are settled, we need a law or command in order to decide what we should do. A law has the form "Do this," or "Do not do that." No amount of facts can add up to a command.

Morality is a set of values that guides our lives. The only thing that can guide us in a principled way is commands that we are willing to obey. We are in a moral crisis because we are not willing to listen to commands anymore. We have no moral values at all.

Secular humanists tell us we can give *ourselves* commands. They admit that moral values, by their very nature, are rules to be followed, not whims or passing fancies. But they say we can decide for ourselves which rules we will follow, and which commands we will obey. The commands ultimately come from ourselves.

These humanists are deceiving themselves (and others who follow them). They see half of the truth but blindly miss the other half. Morality means commands. (They understand that.) But it makes no sense to say "a person commands himself or herself." Everyone agrees that there is a difference between obeying a command and doing whatever I want. But if I command myself, then I can also revoke the command at any time. I gave it, so I can take it back, or give another one. But if I can cancel a command whenever I want, then in what sense am I obeying commands? I am not. I am doing whatever I feel like doing at the time. That is not following rules. It is not obeying commands, and it is not morality.

We have lost sight of true moral consciousness. We have made ourselves as gods, thinking that goodness begins and ends with our own desires. But we are only gratifying our inflated self-image. We see the consequences of our arrogance all around us, in crime statistics, suicide rates, drug abuse, race relations, and the abysmal state of our society.

If morality requires commands, and if we cannot command ourselves, then where do the commands come from? The obvious answer is God. (Obvious but so hard to accept.) Only God has the authority to give commands that we can obey with confidence. Only God has the infinite wisdom, the love, the mercy, to give commands that we can trust completely. God can give us the strength to overcome our stubborn pride, submit, and do what we know is right. All we need to do is ask.

But some subtle reasoners refuse to accept the obvious. They say God cannot be the source of moral commands because that would put us in an insoluble dilemma. When God says, "Thou shalt not kill," either He has a reason for saying it, or He does not. Let's suppose He has a reason. Maybe He believes that people should not kill because all life is precious, these critics say. But then *that* is why we should not kill. God's command just reminds us of that principle—all life is precious. But He is not the source of the principle, because it is a reason for Him, too. If God has any reasons for His commands, then we can understand those reasons, and God becomes irrelevant.

On the other hand, let's suppose that God does not have reasons to justify His commands. Then He is arbitrary and capricious. If He has no reasons for giving us the commands He does, then He is just acting on impulse. But it would be insane to feel bound by commands issued that way, no matter who gave them. Therefore, whether God has reasons for His commands or does not, He is not the source of moral values.

Only certain types of people think this dilemma is a problem. Only people who have turned away from God and bowed down to Reason are disturbed. They have put rationality and having reasons above God, and attempt to test God by a standard of reason. In fact, by the standard of their own personal comprehension. This is foolish arrogance. Reason is a wonderful gift but it is not absolutely limitless. Some truths are beyond and above reason.

It is only because these people worship reason that the second option above disturbs them. "How can we obey God's commands if He has no reasons to justify them?" What a foolish question! The fact that *He* wills it is the reason. That is more than enough of a reason to obey.

Morality depends on commands, and the only commands with sufficient authority are commands from God. But what if there is no God? Then there is no morality. That is the crisis we are in today. We should try to bring people back to faith in God, for their sake, and for ours.

Key Concepts

authority	facts and values	arbitrary
commands	dilemma	reason

Critical Questions

1. What kind of crisis are we in today, according to the essay? Do you agree or disagree?
2. What relation does a moral theist see between facts and morality, e.g., the fact that people have needs, and the moral obligation to help them meet their needs?
3. Can you give some examples of commands that are issued by some authority? What makes the person or organization an authority?

4. Suppose I make a New Year's resolution. I tell myself, "From now on, I must look for some good in every single person." Would that be a moral principle, according to a moral theist?
5. Humanists say that anyone who believes that God is the source of morality faces a dilemma. What are the two sides of the dilemma?
6. Does a moral theist think that God has reasons for the commands he gives?

Methods and Techniques

NECESSARY CONDITIONS

Both of the essays in this section depend on the idea of a *necessary condition*. A necessary condition is just what it sounds like. X is a necessary condition of Y if you cannot have Y without also having X. For example, people say, "If you want to make an omelet, you have to break some eggs." They mean that broken eggs are a necessary condition of an omelet. "Where there is smoke there is fire." Fire is a necessary condition of smoke. Now, if you know that X is a necessary condition of Y, and you know that Y exists, then you can infer that X exists as well. (If you smell smoke, and you know that fire is a necessary condition of smoke, then you can infer that a fire is burning.)

A related version of the same argument goes like this: if you really want to be a doctor, and going to medical school is a necessary condition of being a doctor, then you must want to go to medical school. The inference is about what you must want, or approve of, rather than about what must exist.

Philosophers often use this sort of necessary-condition argument, but they use it in cases where the connection between X and Y isn't so clear. One example is language. Young children learn language differently from the way they learn other subjects, like geography or science. They learn their native language very quickly, without effort or teaching, and in large amounts. All children do this, regardless of their other talents. How is this possible? Some people argue that it is possible *only* if human beings have an innate language faculty. They say that the human mind must be specially wired, or evolved, to learn language. An innate language faculty is a necessary condition of such learning.

Anarchists say that a necessary condition of genuine freedom is the abolition of all government. Governments enforce laws, they employ police to harass citizens, they confiscate our earnings, they restrict us in a thousand ways. Thus if you really want to be free, you must want to abolish government.

Another example is mathematical knowledge. Everyone knows that $7 + 5 = 12$. But we know it in a peculiar way. We are absolutely certain of it. Once we understand the equation, we realize that it could not possibly be false. Nor will it ever change. We also know that if you draw a straight line through the center of a circle, you get two equal parts. We are absolutely certain of that, too. And everyone agrees that it is true. There aren't many things that *everyone* agrees on. Some philosophers who reflect upon this sort of knowledge claim that it can exist only if there is another dimension of reality—a nonphysical, eternal, perfect realm, which we can grasp when we think about mathematics. In other words, they say this nonphysical realm is a necessary condition for the existence of mathematical knowledge.

In the first essay, the functionalist claims that moral rules are a necessary condition for society. Society could not exist without the three moral rules. And since we all value society, we must value the moral rules as well. But in the second essay the moral theist claims that God's commands are a necessary condition of morality. Morality could not exist if there were no authoritative God to lay down the rules. If we believe that some things are right and other things are wrong, then we must believe in God.

Understanding the Dilemma

FUNCTIONALIST OR MORAL THEIST?

A functionalist and a moral theist agree that morality is a set of *rules*. In this respect they are both formalists and not utilitarians. But they disagree on the basis or source of the rules. A functionalist believes that morality is an organic part of society. Society, its structure, its needs and operations are basic, and morality is a natural outgrowth of society, like law.

A moral theist, however, believes that society is not enough. Social pressures cannot explain the unique power of moral rules. The moral theist says that moral commands have a profound emotional force or weight. They are absolute. They are more important than laws made by a society. The very idea of breaking them fills people with anguish. A society cannot endow its rules with the same kind of force. The only possible source of moral commands is God.

The disagreement between a functionalist and a moral theist is not about which rules are binding on us. They might both agree that lying is wrong, that we ought to keep our promises, and that we should respect other people. The disagreement is about the basis of these rules. Where do the rules come from, and why are they obligatory? The functionalist answers "society," and the moral theist says "God."

The emphasis on society makes the functionalist sound like a moral relativist. But they are different. A functionalist believes certain basic moral rules are essential to the existence and functioning of society, and every society needs the *same* rules. The first essay in this section mentions honesty, respect, and justice. A relativist, on the other hand, believes societies create moral rules (like the functionalist), but he or she believes different societies create *different* moral rules. So a functionalist is more similar to a moral absolutist than to a moral relativist. (I say "similar to" and not "is a moral absolutist" because functionalists believe morality is created by people, and depends on people's needs and desires. It is not "objective" in the sense of being part of the world independent of humanity. Most absolutists believe morality is not created by people, but is part of objective reality in some way.) The moral theist is a moral absolutist in the full sense of the word.

Are you a functionalist or a moral theist? The choice is obviously related to your beliefs about God. If you are an atheist, then you cannot be a moral theist. On the other hand, if you are a theist, then you believe that God is the source of everything, including morality. But you might not believe that God gave explicit commands to us. You might believe, instead, that moral value is implicit in human nature, or in society, or in the natural world, and it is up to us to discover it. This example shows that the relations among the various answers, like theist and moral theist, are complex and subtle.

FUNCTIONALIST

1. Society molds and shapes people in many ways, including their moral values.
2. Being a morally good person means conforming to your society's demands.
3. Some rules are absolutely essential for society to survive at all, and naturally people will have very strong feelings about those rules.
4. Morality is a human invention; it does not exist outside of human desires, agreements, and intentions.

MORAL THEIST

5. Some moral rules have an *absolute* force, and their only possible source is God, not society.
6. The best guidelines on how to live are the rules and advice given by the world's great prophets, God's messengers.
7. Moral rules are more important and more sacred than social rules or laws.
8. God has spoken clearly, in all the world's religions, about what we ought to do and ought not to do.

FOR FURTHER STUDY

Historical Examples

FUNCTIONALIST: John Rawls. *A Theory of Justice.* Harvard University Press, 1972. In chap. 1 Rawls tries to show how moral ideas are related to the fundamental structures of society.

MORAL THEIST: Hastings Rashdall. *The Theory of Good and Evil.* Clarendon Press, 1907. In vol. 2, Book 3, chap. 1, Rashdall argues that the objectivity and strict obligation of moral duties strongly suggest that God is the source of the duties.

OTHER SOURCES

Arthur L. Caplan, Bruce Jennings, eds. *Darwin, Marx, and Freud: Their Influence on Moral Theory*. Plenum Press, 1984. Essays by biologists, historians, psychologists, and philosophers.

Daniel Callahan, H. Tristram Engelhardt, Jr., eds. *The Roots of Ethics: Science, Religion, and Values*. Plenum Press, 1981. Papers by contemporary philosophers, some including responses by other philosophers.

Walter Lippmann. *A Preface to Morals*. Macmillan, 1929. Mainly historical, surveying the decline of religion-based morality and analyzing the options facing the modern world. Very well written.

Hunter Lewis. *A Question of Values*. HarperSanFrancisco, 1990. Lewis describes six types of value systems, distinguished by their methods of making moral decisions, for a popular audience.

Gilbert Harman. *The Nature of Morality: An Introduction to Ethics*. Oxford University Press, 1977. Defends a "social custom theory of morality."

Mary Midgley. "The Origin of Ethics." In Peter Singer, ed. *A Companion to Ethics*. Blackwell, 1991. Looks for clues in the social lives of other animals.

George Silberbauer. "Ethics in Small-Scale Societies." In Singer. Examination of functionalism.

Jonathan Berg. "How Could Ethics Depend on Religion?" In Singer. Berg describes a variety of ways it could.

Current Controversy

3.6 SHOULD DOCTORS EVER END PEOPLE'S LIVES?
PROTECTOR OR EUTHANIZER?

●

The word "euthanasia" comes from Greek words meaning "good death." That sounds like an oxymoron, i.e., a phrase made up of words with opposite meanings, such as "moderate extremist," or "wealthy beggar." How can death be good?

In this amazing age, many things are possible that have never been possible before. We have the technological means to keep people alive long after the heart attacks and pneumonias and accidents that would have killed them in earlier periods. We have the means to save infants born with defects that would have certainly ended their lives shortly after birth a hundred years ago.

But in the view of many people, this powerful technology is a mixed blessing. It can save lives, but it can also prolong a life beyond the point that the patient wants to live. It can keep a person alive, in the sense that the heart still beats, but the person might be permanently unconscious, completely dependent on machines for breathing, receiving nutrients, and eliminating wastes, and a demanding consumer of scarce medical resources. In cases such as these, some people argue that death can be good. A natural, peaceful passing from life's stage can be preferable to the continued pumping and draining of the organism for the sake of "life."

On the other hand, few people want to take the responsibility for killing another person. A patient may be old and sick, but would you be willing to inject the drug that stops her heart? Perhaps there is hope. Some patients recover in ways that their doctors can't explain. And if we allow doctors or others to begin killing people, where will it lead?

On its face, the act of taking an innocent life seems wrong; everyone knows it. The prohibition against killing another person—not in order to defend oneself or society—is so ancient and deeply ingrained in our moral consciousness that many people refuse to cross that line. It is the most basic moral law we know.

Nevertheless, the prospect of sinking into a confused, artificial twilight, tied to machines, severed from other people, and perhaps in great pain, makes many people approve of euthanasia. This may be a case, unusual in philosophy, where the new conditions we have created, i.e., our new power over life and death, raise fundamentally new philosophical problems. But the nature of the problem is also similar to others you have probably already encountered. We are torn between two inclinations and two ways of thinking: to respect life and preserve it, or to be merciful and rescue people from "a fate worse than death." This new philosophical dilemma is just as difficult as the oldest ones.

The first essay that follows takes the traditional view, opposing killing, and claims to be protecting innocent, vulnerable people. It can be called the protector's point of view. The second essay defends euthanasia, so it can be called the euthanizer's point of view.

NO: PROTECTOR

"Having Reasons for Moral Decisions"

In 1982 a baby boy was born in Bloomington, Indiana. Known in court documents as Infant Doe, he had Down's syndrome, which meant he would be mentally retarded and have a shorter-than-normal life span. He also had a blockage in the digestive system that prevented food from reaching the stomach. Relatively simple surgery could have solved that problem. But the parents refused to allow the surgery, or intravenous feeding, and the court supported the parents' right to make that decision. One doctor described the scene in the hospital:

> Baby Doe's shrunken, thin little body with dry cyanotic skin, extremely dehydrated, breathing shallowly and irregularly, lay passively on fresh hospital linens. Blood was running from a mouth too dry to close. Death by starvation was near. Too late for fluids. Too late for surgery. . . . (Bernards, ed., 1989, pp. 202–203)

The child died a few hours later. What was the right thing to do in this case? If you were the parent of a handicapped child, what would you do? If you were the doctor, what would you do?

Faced with such a heart-breaking image, many people feel that the child's life should have been saved and extended for as long as possible. The doctor describing the case was appealing to our feelings of pity.

But suppose the handicap is more severe. One expert in the treatment of spina bifida asks "Is it moral to encourage the survival of a child who will be a paraplegic, incontinent, and will require multiple surgical procedures for hydrocephalus, orthopedic deformity, and bladder dysfunction?" (ibid., p. 191). Besides the severe, painful, recurring physical problems, the child would have no personality and would barely be conscious during its short life. Wouldn't death be a merciful release in this case?

Another doctor describes a case of an infant born with "a skin condition similar to third degree burns over almost all of its body for which there was no cure." The slightest movement was intensely painful. "Providing basic nursing care caused tearing away of the skin. The infant could not be fed orally because of blistering in the mouth and throat." The child would live only a few days at best. "Wouldn't it have been reasonable, merciful, and justifiable," the doctor asks, "to have shortened the baby's dying by an intended direct action?" (Baird, Rosenbaum, eds., 1989, p. 121).

Descriptions such as these are very upsetting and emotional. In some cases, our feelings tell us that it is horrible to allow the child to die, and we should do whatever is necessary to save the life. But in other cases our sympathy and pity lead us to the drastic decision to end the suffering by ending the life. Unfortunately there are many cases, and so far I have described cases on both sides.

But now I want to suggest that we need to use more than our feelings. These wrenching cases do not help us make a *moral* decision. Being moral and doing the right thing requires more than feeling certain emotions, because our emotions whipsaw us in opposite directions. To be moral one must act for a good reason. A person can do the right thing accidentally, so to speak, without understanding why it is right. But to act deliberately and morally, one must have a good reason and a sound justification for one's action.

What is a good reason? For example, in the case of the child with the skin disease, what is the reason for favoring euthanasia? The doctor would say it is right to end the child's life because of the fact that the child is suffering terribly and has no chance to escape the suffering. In the case of Infant Doe, the attending physician might say it is right to save the child's life because of the fact that the surgery would be relatively easy to perform and chances of recovery are good. So when people think about moral problems, they offer relevant facts to support their decisions.

But facts aren't enough. The doctors in both these cases are also applying general principles. The first doctor is assuming a principle of mercy: one has a moral obligation to relieve pain and reduce suffering. The fact that the infant is in great pain, *together* with the principle that one should reduce suffering, leads to the decision to accelerate the end of the child's tragic life. Neither the fact by itself nor the principle by itself is enough to justify the decision. But together they are enough, in the doctor's opinion. There are exceptions, as when a doctor causes some discomfort in order to prevent greater discomfort later. But in general, reducing suffering is a basic moral principle that guides our thinking about particular cases.

The second doctor is also appealing to a general principle. The surgery to save Infant Doe is relatively simple, but that fact is relevant only because of the underlying principle: one should respect human life and never destroy it. Infant Doe may not be just like everyone else, but he is certainly human, and it is wrong to destroy human life. Therefore it is wrong to let him die, and the right thing to do is to operate and help him.

All moral reasoning depends upon determining the facts and applying principles. For example, people disagree about the morality of capital punishment. Is it morally right to execute a convicted murderer? Many people allow their feelings to guide their moral judgment. They feel pity for the victim and his or her family, and they feel anger at the criminal and want to make him or her suffer. But feelings are not good moral reasons, because they are inconsistent— we can also feel pity for the criminal whose hard life led him to commit a crime— they change from moment to moment, different people have very different feelings about things, and it is difficult to compare them or even know what we are feeling.

Making a moral decision about capital punishment means determining the facts and deciding what principles apply. That isn't easy. Some say it is a fact that capital punishment deters would-be murderers, and others say we do not know for sure if it does or doesn't. But most moral disagreements are about principles and their applications. Some say the principle of "an eye for an eye" requires execution of convicted murderers. Others say the principle of respecting human life requires the alternative sentence of life in prison. The basic disagreement is usually over the meaning and validity of certain principles, and their priority.

The issue of euthanasia is an issue of principles. Doctors try to save lives, and they try to reduce suffering. They might do other things as well, but in their role as doctors, those two principles are the most basic and fundamental commitments that guide their decisions. Normally, the two principles go hand in hand. Relieving the pain of a ruptured appendix also saves the patient's life. A heart bypass operation prevents a fatal heart attack, and also relieves chronic chest pain. But sometimes they come into conflict. Handicapped infants may face many challenges and even pain. If the pain is intense and cannot be treated—which is rare—then some people decide that the obligation to relieve suffering outweighs the obligation to respect human life. They decide to end the child's life to stop the suffering. Others believe the obligation to preserve life outweighs the duty to reduce suffering. Which principle takes priority?

A natural impulse is to reach for a compromise. One might think that sometimes respect for life takes precedence, and sometimes relieving suffering takes precedence, depending on circumstances. But this is a comforting illusion. The decision to elevate one principle over the other must be a thoughtful, reasoned decision, not a whim or momentary emotional response. But how can one justify the choice? These principles are the most basic ones doctors have. They cannot use a more basic principle to guide the decision about priority. In fact, switching from one to the other is simply relying on the strong feelings elicited by the particularities of a case, without having a principle. It is giving up on making a moral decision. One of the principles must be fundamental, if doctors are going to make moral decisions rather than respond arbitrarily.

In the rare cases when these basic obligations conflict, saving lives takes priority over relieving pain. The principle of respecting human life is the foundational principle of medicine, although it is not the only principle. Doctors can justify their decisions by using the principle of relieving pain, or the principle that medical students can learn only by practicing on real patients, and even the principle of cutting costs (by using generic drugs rather than name brands, for example). In most cases, all these principles can apply at the same time. But principles are not all equally important. Doctors agree that cutting costs never takes moral priority over saving lives. It doesn't make sense to let a person die rather than pay the cost of a prescription drug. Nor would a doctor risk a patient's life in order to let a medical student treat the patient, although if there is no risk to the patient, letting the student gain experience is morally justifiable.

While the priority of saving lives is clear in comparison with other principles, some people refuse to give it priority over the principle of reducing pain. But saving lives is more basic than this principle as well. For ending a life is final and irreversible. It destroys all hope. It ends all possibilities. So long as a person is alive, there is hope for improvement, even if the life is difficult and painful. The situation can change, and no one can be absolutely certain that it won't. But if a doctor ends a child's life, he or she can be absolutely certain that the child will never improve, and will never again experience the vital thrill of being alive.

Nancy Dubler describes the case of a college professor who learned that he had an inoperable cancer and had a short time to live. In long talks about his situation he grew even closer to his family, and he threw himself into his work with even greater intensity. He also gave his doctors clear instructions that he wanted them to do everything possible to prolong his life. Every day and even every minute was precious. Toward the end he was confined to bed and so weak he could barely speak. His heart stopped, but the medical team revived him. He had to be attached to a ventilator, which prevented him from talking to his wife at all. But on a pad of paper he was able to scrawl one word: "Hope." Ending a life is not only fundamentally wrong, it is cruel, because it deprives people of that powerful, sustaining emotion.

Another reason to give the principle of life priority is that the principle of reducing pain is so difficult to apply. How much suffering justifies the decision to end a life? What kind of suffering? No one believes that a small amount of pain justifies ending a patient's life. Amputating a leg mangled in an accident causes pain and suffering, in the recovery room, in rehabilitation, and in the frustrating adjustments to the new condition. But no one recommends letting the patient die instead of removing the leg. How much pain and frustration are enough to justify ending a life? There is no answer. There is no clear standard for deciding when relieving pain outweighs preserving life, and therefore the suggestion that the principle of relieving pain sometimes takes priority over preserving life makes no sense. When is "sometimes"? To think that it does take priority is to give up on moral thinking and to fall back on arbitrary, emotional responses to individual cases.

Doctors have always made saving lives their primary goal, and they have relieved suffering as well. Usually the two principles complement each other. But if doctors began subordinating the principle of respecting life to the goal of reducing suffering, it would be a fundamental change and would have serious, long-term consequences. It would create doubts in the public's mind about doctors. Patients have to trust their doctors. They have to provide doctors with detailed, personal information about their bodies and their lives. They have to cooperate fully, and even believe in the doctor's ability. Belief is a real factor in getting better. The foundation of their trust is the confidence that the doctor will do everything possible to save the patient. But if doctors began ending lives, even if it were only a few and in extraordinary circumstances, the seed of doubt would be planted and it would grow.

To say that respecting human life takes precedence over all of doctors' other duties is to say that the principle is an absolute. No consideration should make a doctor deliberately destroy an innocent person's life. Some people maintain that we should not have any absolute principles. The so-called postmodernists, as I understand them, reject absolute principles as unnecessary restrictions on people's freedom. It's true that absolutes are restrictions, but are they unnecessary or undesirable? There is nothing wrong with being absolutely just or absolutely good. Even postmodernists want to be absolutely free. It would be wonderful if people could be absolutely fair to each other, although we probably won't be. But saying that a principle is absolute is no criticism in itself. In fact, we must have some absolute principle as the basis for ranking and deciding among other principles.

In some circumstances, patients decide that they want to die. They may feel that they are a burden to their families, or that they have nothing to look forward to. But such depression is treatable. If patients are made to feel wanted and respected, they almost never ask for euthanasia. Most cases of physical pain are treatable as well. But if patients insist that they want to die, neither doctors nor nurses nor relatives are under any obligation to help them die. Doctors should counsel them and try to relieve their pain, but killing is wrong, and therefore helping someone kill himself or herself is also wrong. As a last resort, health professionals can withdraw from a case and let someone else take over.

The medical profession is a dignified and revered institution. Doctors have regulated themselves and made wise decisions for their patients for a long time. They handle highly emotional situations every day, and maintain their poise and clarity in very difficult circumstances. I am confident that they will continue to recognize the difference between moral decisions based on principles and emotional decisions driven by momentary pressures.

Key Concepts

feelings	principle	arbitrary
reason	hope	absolute

Critical Questions

1. According to the protector, why can't we rely on our feelings to decide whether euthanasia is right or wrong?
2. Suppose two patients need liver transplants, but we have only one liver available. I say patient A should get the liver because she is 24 years old, whereas patient B is 58 years old, and they are otherwise similar. Am I thinking morally, according to the essay?
3. Doctors save lives and they relieve suffering, but sometimes the two goals come into conflict: saving a life prolongs the suffering. Can doctors decide which goal is more important on a case-by-case basis, according to the essay? Why or why not?
4. Suppose a patient has condition XYZ, and 100 percent of the scores of patients with XYZ have died withing six months of being diagnosed. Should a doctor tell the patient he has no chance of living more than a year, according to the essay?
5. The essay says that the principle of relieving suffering cannot be applied in practice because there is no standard to follow. But suffering cannot be measured. Why can't doctors simply say that if a patient is suffering "greatly," or is in "intense pain," with no chance of recovery, then relieving pain outweighs saving lives?
6. Suppose a patient calmly and persistently wants to die. She is in pain, has only months to live, and depends on a kidney dialysis machine to stay alive. In your opinion, should her doctor grant her request, turn off the machine, and let her die? What would the protector say?

YES: EUTHANIZER
"The Complex Issue of Euthanasia"

The issue of euthanasia is complex, and the biggest mistake we can make is to oversimplify matters. That is exactly what opponents of euthanasia do. They rely on absolutes, black and white descriptions with no shades of gray, and aggressive condemnations of anyone who sees different sides. I would like to examine some of these extreme positions, and suggest more moderate alternatives. Nothing is more serious than decisions about life and death, and people have a moral obligation to save lives. But it is not an absolute obligation. We should try to save lives, but in some rare cases, it is better to help a person die.

The term "euthanasia" covers many different things. First, there is a difference between voluntary and involuntary euthanasia. In voluntary euthanasia the patient asks the doctor or provider to help him or her die. The patient may request help directly when he or she is ill, or the patient may complete a "living will" at an earlier time, asking doctors not to take extraordinary measures to prolong life, or not to resuscitate after the heart stops. Involuntary euthanasia occurs with infants or comatose patients who are unable to make their wishes known. Parents or relatives decide what is best for the patient, and may decide that ending the suffering is best.

Another complication is the distinction between active and passive euthanasia. Active euthanasia occurs when a doctor or other care-giver acts to bring about death. For example, a doctor may administer a drug that suppresses breathing or stops the heart. Passive euthanasia occurs when the doctor withdraws or withholds treatment, knowing that the result will be death. If a patient is on a respirator, for example, and cannot breathe without it, a doctor might remove the respirator. The patient will die, but the main cause of death is the disease or accident that interfered with breathing, not the doctor. In active euthanasia, the doctor is the direct cause of death. (Some philosophers deny that any real difference exists between active and passive euthanasia, and that is another complication.)

A related concept is "doctor-assisted suicide." A doctor may prepare a lethal dose of drugs and make it available to the patient with an explanation of its effect, but the patient actually administers the drugs to himself or herself. All these different scenarios raise difficult moral questions about responsibility, intentions, compassion, and killing. Simple answers cannot do justice to the whole spectrum of cases.

And yet some people take the position that no form of euthanasia is ever justified. They believe that human life is sacred, and that our most basic moral duty is to preserve life and never destroy it. For example consider "Baby Boy Houle."

> The child was born on February 9, horribly deformed. His entire left side was malformed; he had no left eye, was practically without a left ear, had a deformed left hand; some of his vertebrae were not

formed. Furthermore, he was affected with a tracheal esophageal fistula and could not be fed by mouth. Air leaked into his stomach instead of going to the lungs, and fluid from the stomach pushed up into the lungs. (Baird, Rosenbaum, eds., 1989, p. 8)

The child soon developed pneumonia, and brain damage was suspected because of poor circulation. Aggressive surgery and treatment could keep the child alive for a few days, but the parents decided against it. However, several doctors disagreed with the parents and took the case to court. Maine Superior Court Judge David G. Roberts ruled "At the moment of live birth there does exist a human being entitled to the fullest protection of the law. The most basic right enjoyed by every human being is a right to life itself" (ibid., p. 8). The doctors worked furiously, but in spite of their efforts Baby Boy Houle died after fifteen days.

It was morally wrong to keep that child alive. It accomplished nothing but to prolong the poor boy's desperate struggle and agony. Those who hold the rule "preserve human life" as an absolute cannot consider all the factors of the situation. Life is good, but it is good because of what it brings people—joy and growth and love and opportunities to share with others. Bare life itself, in the sense of a beating heart or expanding lungs, is not necessarily good, especially if it is accompanied by pain, dehumanizing dependence on machines, or a vegetative unconsciousness. In other words, it is the quality of life that people value, not simply life by itself. Unfortunately, in some cases, the quality of life is so horrible that it is wrong to extend it. Instead of thinking that "life" overrules every other factor, we should weigh the goods and the evils of each case, and recognize that sometimes the evils outweigh the goods, including life itself.

Many who oppose euthanasia do so on religious grounds, and say that "doctors cannot play God." That is, questions of life and death should be left to God, and once life exists, doctors should do whatever they can to preserve it. But who can know for sure what God wants? It is hard to believe that God wanted Baby Boy Houle to suffer for two weeks before he died. No one knows what God wants. Nevertheless, some religious leaders claim that they know, and since euthanasia is such a difficult issue, anyone who offers simple, absolute answers will attract a following. But we can find better answers if we apply our deepest moral feelings of sympathy and compassion, and think carefully about each case on its own merits.

Another absolute rule some people hold is that doctors should preserve lives and never end lives. In an article entitled "Doctors Must Not Kill," the authors say

This issue [euthanasia] touches medicine at its very moral center; if the moral center collapses, if physicians become killers or are even merely licensed to kill, the profession—and, therewith, each physician—will never again be worthy of trust and respect as healer and comforter and protector of life in all its frailty. For if medicine's power of life may be used equally to heal or kill, the doctor is no more a moral professional but rather a morally neutral technician. (Gaylin, Kass, Pellegrino, Siegler, 1988, pp. 2139–2140)

Is "doctors must not kill" an absolute rule? I don't think it is, nor do I think the profession would collapse if doctors adopted a more flexible attitude. In fact, many doctors do discretely help suffering patients die. Patients know it, ask for help, and appreciate it. Doctors' duty is to *care* for people and do whatever they can to help them. Their duty is not simply to keep people alive without considering anything else. Doctors are capable of making good decisions, in collaboration with patients and their families. They have the experience and the intelligence to weigh all factors, and do what is best for the patient. Sometimes dying sooner rather than later is best.

Some opponents of euthanasia believe in another absolute rule: "never give up hope." No matter how ill a patient is, a miracle is always possible, they say. Doctors may discover a cure, or patients may spontaneously recover. We must always hope. But euthanasia destroys all hope. It removes the possibility of recovery because it welcomes death.

This attitude is not brave. It is simply unrealistic. An intelligent person will try to estimate the probabilities and weigh the costs. A heart weakened by eighty years of work and several heart attacks is not going to become strong and healthy. An advanced and uncontrollable cancer is not going to disappear. Medical predictions may not be 100-percent reliable, but some are close. To encourage hope for a miracle in the face of such odds is misleading, not moral. It is willfully narrow-minded. And there is the cost. Should we really ask a person in terrible anguish and desperate for release to "never give up hope," and to endure the horrible pain—for how long?—because there is a one-in-a-million chance that he or she will recover? No, we should consider all the factors and do what is best in each situation. In most cases, hope is appropriate, but in other cases it isn't.

The most common argument against euthanasia is the slippery slope argument. The claim is that if society approves of euthanasia in any case at all, it will soon extend euthanasia to all sorts of unconscionable cases. If doctors decide that the right thing to do in the Baby Boy Houle case is to let the baby die peacefully, then they will soon be killing healthy babies. One writer says

Once any group of human beings is considered unworthy of living, what is to stop our society from extending this cruelty to other groups? If the mongoloid is to be deprived of his right to life, what of the blind and deaf? What of the cripple, the retarded and the senile? Or even the diabetic, or the obese individual? (Bernards, 1989, p. 28)

We must cling to our absolute rule with all the fervor of a true fanatic, this writer suggests, and resist compromise, reason, or discussion, because those will open the floodgates of moral anarchy. At this point opponents of euthanasia often describe the Nazis' policies of eliminating undesirables, and claim that we are only a short step from such depravity.

This position is more rhetoric than argument. It deliberately attempts to arouse powerful emotions of anger, fear, and indignation, and tries to substitute those responses for careful thinking. But if we put aside the strong-arm tactics, we see that the intellectual force of the argument is very weak. The argument assumes that people making decisions ten or twenty years from now will not be able to think for themselves. All they will be able to do is imitate their predecessors (us), and will even expand our policies in absurd directions. The people of the future will have no compassion, no sense of justice, no principles, unless we hold on to our absolute rule.

But this is not credible. It is hardly probable that people of the future will turn into moral monsters if we today consider different aspects of particular cases instead of sticking to a simple rule. The absolutists' mistake is to assume that everyone else is just like them. Without simple rules as guides, the world seems too overwhelming and confusing to absolutists. Without simple rules, people of the future will become monsters, they say.

But other people are not so dependent on black and white absolutes. We often recognize degrees and multiple standards with different weights. We can weigh the pain and dependence against the chances for improvement. Sometimes hope will prevail, but sometimes the need for relief will take precedence. If a person is in terrible pain and will not get better, there is no reason to prolong the agony. We can balance the belief that doctors will never harm people with the belief that they will relieve suffering. We can expect both from doctors, and can trust them to make the best decision for the patient in light of all the relevant factors.

Some people seem to be afraid to use their own intelligence. The biggest danger related to euthanasia is not a slippery slope but simple-minded rigidity.

Key Concepts

voluntary	active	quality of life	trust
involuntary	passive	playing God	slippery slope

Critical Questions

1. What is the difference between voluntary and involuntary euthanasia? Between active and passive euthanasia?
2. What does the euthanizer mean by "quality of life"? In your opinion, can doctors or relatives judge the quality of life that a handicapped infant will have in the future? Can one person ever judge another's quality of life?
3. Some say we should not "play God." Does that view imply that radical new developments in medicine, such as heart transplants or in-vitro fertilization, are morally wrong?

4. How does the euthanizer respond to those who say "doctors must not kill"? In your opinion, which would damage doctors' reputation more, their willingness to end people's lives or their unwillingness to relieve people's pain when euthanasia is the only possible relief?
5. The slippery slope argument claims that once we cross the line of killing innocent people, we will not be able to establish another clear line to restrain our killing. What is the euthanizer's response to this argument?
6. Janet Adkins, age 54, was the first person to die using Dr. Jack Kevorkian's suicide machine. She was diagnosed with Alzheimer's disease, but was in the earliest stages (if the diagnosis was correct), and was otherwise healthy. In your opinion, should a doctor have granted her request and helped her die?

Methods and Techniques

JUSTIFICATION

Imagine that your friend Jenny rushed up to you and said "There's been a terrible earthquake in California!" You would probably ask for details, but if you were a philosopher you might ask "How do you know?" Jenny says she heard it from Bob. "How does Bob know?" you ask. If Jenny is a true friend, she might explain that Bob watched the news on CNN and CNN had a reporter on the scene who saw walls sway and felt the earth move.

Philosophers and other people want to justify their beliefs, and this scenario is an example of how they might do that. Philosophers try to trace a belief back to its source, and if the source is reliable, then the belief based on it is justified. In this case, the belief depends upon an eyewitness (or several eyewitnesses), but also upon four subsequent links, from the witness to the news studio, to Bob, to Jenny, and to you. To say the belief is justified is to say one is right to believe it; it is very likely to be true.

This image or model of justification is very common. Many people think of justification as a kind of ranking of beliefs, or an arrangement of beliefs from the most reliable to less reliable ones. The eyewitness' belief is ranked first, the newsroom's report depends on the witness so it is ranked second, and so on.

Consider another scenario. You are having dinner at your favorite restaurant and you must decide what to order. You enjoy several dishes. After studying the menu, you decide that the sweet and sour pork is the dish you like more than any other, so you order that. But the waiter tells you they are out of sweet and sour pork. So you must decide which dish is second best. You choose egg foo yung, and after you order you try to rank your other favorites in case they are out of egg foo yung. This is a process of deciding on your priorities. If you know your priorities, then when you face a choice or conflict you will know what to do. This is the same kind of justification as the case of beliefs about an earthquake, except here you are ranking preferences rather than beliefs, and you are justifying your actions or decisions.

Now consider a third scenario. You have promised your friends to come over and play cards tonight, but on your way out of the office your boss asks you to give a presentation to the Board of Directors tomorrow. When you get home your spouse reminds you that tonight is your daughter's school concert. At about that time your mother calls to say your father isn't feeling well and could use a visit. What do you do? You have four obligations—keep your promise to your friends, prepare a presentation to get ahead in your career, support your daughter, and cheer up your parents.

Is it possible to rank moral obligations the way we rank preferences in food? Can we say that, as a general rule, family comes first, then work, then friends? And among family, children's needs take precedence over adult's needs? If so, then you would choose to attend your daughter's concert. The justification is the ranking of the types of obligations. But this model doesn't tell us how to produce our ranking in the first place. Does family really come before work? On the basis of what principle or obligation does one make that decision?

Or should we say the four obligations are all important and the particular facts of the situation will determine which obligation is most pressing? How ill is your father? Could you lose your job if you give a poor presentation? In the first essay above, the protector argues that if we are going to be moral, we have to rank our principles, with one at the top to supercede all others. But the euthanizer claims particular facts can justify a decision to fulfill one obligation or another.

Many people think of justification as a search for foundations. Ranking principles provides a kind of foundation, with the highest ranking principle as the solid base. You encountered another search for foundations in the moral theist's essay "The Current Crisis and its Solution." It assumes that morality consists of commands, like "Do not kill." But the force of a command depends upon its source. If a salesperson says you cannot get a refund on the dress you bought (i.e., you must keep it, a command), then you can ask to speak to the supervisor. The salesperson's command is backed up by the supervisor's command. If the supervisor issues the same command, you can go to the manager, and perhaps the owner of the store. If the owner says you must keep the dress, then you have no choice but to obey. On the other hand, if the owner agrees to a refund, then the salesperson's command is invalidated. The lower level commands depend on the higher level commands.

A moral theist assumes that moral rules are like these commands. If they have any force, they must come from some ultimate authority that cannot be questioned. The only source that cannot be questioned is God, according to a moral theist. Thus God performs the same function in morality that certainty or eyewitnesses perform in knowledge. God is the unquestionable starting point, the unshakable foundation, and no moral rules are secure until we have traced the connection between them and this ultimate authority. The protector claims that the command "preserve human life" is an absolute, but does not say the command comes from God.

Other philosophers, like hedonists and utilitarians, think that happiness, not God, is the ultimate foundation of morality. They say that an action is morally right if it leads to happiness (or pleasure). It may not lead directly to happiness.

Going to the dentist may not be enjoyable in itself, but in the long run it does lead to happiness. So for these philosophers, an action must be connected to happiness before it can be morally right. This way of thinking about morality is different from moral theists' way in several respects. For example, this way does not see morality as a matter of rules, but as a matter of goals. Moreover, it does not look back to the source of a command or an action, but it looks forward to the consequences or goal of an action. But this way, like the moral theist's approach, is an attempt to justify actions on the basis of some *foundation*. It proposes an ultimate moral justification of all actions (i.e., happiness), and the ultimate foundation, which justifies other actions, does not need further justification; it is self-justifying.

The search for foundations is probably a natural human tendency, but in Western philosophy it is also the result of the profound influence of Euclid, the Greek mathematician. Around 300 B.C.E. Euclid organized the science of geometry. He began with definitions and axioms. Axioms are basic statements that are self-evident and unquestionable. One axiom, for example, says "Two parallel lines never meet." If the lines are parallel, like railroad tracks, then no matter how long they are, they will never touch. Anyone who thinks about this statement will see that it must be true. Then, Euclid drew out the implications of these basic foundations, and proved a large number of additional truths about lines, squares, circles, angles, and so on. Each truth was shown to be based on the definitions and axioms. When you study geometry today, you are studying Euclid's ideas.

Euclid's system was so impressive that it was accepted as the perfect model of all science and indeed all knowledge. Even if you have never heard of Euclid, your way of thinking and your basic assumptions have been shaped by his book. That explains, in part, why philosophers often search for foundations.

Understanding the Dilemma

PROTECTOR OR EUTHANIZER?

The dilemma in this section is clear and urgent. If a person is suffering terribly with no real chance of relief, is it ever permissible to end the person's life? Should we stop the pain, but kill the innocent person, or should we preserve life, but allow the tormenting pain to continue? Everyone feels a strong reluctance or inability to take another person's life, but everyone also feels a strong desire or necessity to help people in terrible pain.

Our first impulse is probably to try to escape the dilemma by denying that it exists. We might say that if a person asks us for help in ending his or her life, then we are not really killing anyone. Or we might claim that pain is always manageable with the right drugs, and no one needs to suffer at the end of life. But neither of these attempts is successful. Helping a person who wants to die is not the same as other kinds of killing, but it is still killing. And unfortunately, drugs cannot work miracles on the human body. In some cases, people have to make a difficult decision about ending a life or allowing the agony to continue.

Both sides in this debate believe that they are taking the compassionate position. Both want to do what is best for people, especially people who need help the most. The protector believes that certain classes of people are particularly vulnerable: the handicapped, the very ill, unwanted infants, the elderly. Handicapped or physically challenged individuals make many healthy, busy people uncomfortable. Many don't want to take the time or make the effort to help, perhaps because they don't want to be reminded that they could easily be in the same position. But protectors believe that those who are in the greatest need deserve the most help. In addition to the physical problems, society's tendency to ignore or deny or hide the neediest people makes it even more important to preserve their basic rights. True compassion means protecting the innocent. Protectors believe that the euthanasia movement is just the latest and most extreme expression of American society's impatience with (or fear of) people who are not "successful."

However, from the point of view of euthanizers, protectors are hard and insensitive, and it is euthanizers who are taking the compassionate position. Euthanizers want to relieve pain and end suffering. They say they want to help people who need help, and sometimes patients dying of cancer need help. Stewart Alsop, the journalist, described a young man with whom he shared a hospital room when Alsop had cancer. The young man had a large, cancerous tumor in his stomach, and drugs could reduce the pain for a short time. But soon the man would begin to whimper, then moan "very low, as though he didn't want to wake me. Then he would begin to howl, like a dog" (Baird, Rosenbaum, eds., 1989, p. 7). Alsop said if the patient were an animal, he would mercifully be put to sleep. "No human being with a spark of pity could let a living thing suffer so, to no good end." Real compassion leads to euthanasia, supporters say. So protectors and euthanizers disagree over who needs help, and over the proper expression of compassion.

Another basic disagreement arises from the two sides' defenses of their views. The protector in this section argues that the duty to respect life takes priority over the duty to relieve pain. In fact, the principle of preserving human life is the highest moral principle. Since no other duty or principle can outweigh that one, it has the status of an absolute guide. Some principle has to be the most important one, and the protector says respecting human life is the best candidate for the position.

But the euthanizer in this section rejects absolutes. We all have many moral duties, including the duty to preserve human life and the duty to relieve pain. But it is a mistake to think that one always outweighs the other. In some situations one should preserve life at the cost of some pain, but in other situations the pain is so great and the time remaining is so short that the life should be ended. The decision depends on the wishes of the patient, the quality of life saved, the chances for improvement, and perhaps other factors. But life and death are too complicated to be governed by absolute rules.

Thus a protector tries to solve the dilemma by showing that the principle of respecting life should never be violated. A euthanizer tries to solve the dilemma by claiming that the particular facts of a case will indicate which side is the morally right choice. Therefore, a major disagreement between protectors and euthanizers is over absolute principles. Must we have some highest priority, or can we adapt our priorities to different circumstances?

The disagreement over absolute principles is a difficult, abstract issue. It isn't about euthanasia itself, but the nature of moral reasoning. The protector does not claim that the rule "preserve human life" is self-evident, like "the whole is greater than the part." Nor does this essay claim that the rule is a divine command and therefore absolutely binding. Rather, the claim is that if we want to think and behave in a rational, consistent way, we need some basic guiding principle that allows us to order all our other principles. Without some stable foundation, our responses to moral problems will be capricious and subjective, depending on our varying feelings of the moment. Even the euthanizer has an absolute principle. It is "Never allow a person to suffer terribly; always prevent extreme, relentless pain." The euthanizer will not violate that principle, even to save a life.

The euthanizer's response is that we should be guided by the facts of each case, and not by absolute rules. Suffering is a matter of degree, and therefore the euthanizer rejects the charge that he or she is following an absolute rule. No rule can indicate when the suffering is great enough to justify euthanasia. Only a compassionate, informed, experienced judgment can guide us.

A final basic disagreement concerns the consequences of legalizing or validating euthanasia. The protector predicts that if doctors begin practicing euthanasia, people's attitudes will change. They will regard doctors differently, and they may lose hope more easily. The basic idea is that having an absolute prohibition against destroying innocent human life gives us a clear, plausible boundary between what is morally permissible and what isn't. Once we eliminate that boundary, we cannot find another clear, plausible boundary to take its place. How much pain is necessary? Who decides? How do we define "consent?" Are financial considerations ever relevant?

These are difficult questions, the euthanizer says, but they are not impossible to answer. Of course the decisions are complex, but that just means we must gather as much information as possible and consider it carefully. It doesn't mean we should give up. People deal competently with other very complex matters without making one factor the only consideration. If euthanasia were legalized, it would lead to a whole network of laws, restrictions, clarifications, and guidelines to help us make decisions, just as divorce, adoption, organ transplants, and job termination have. Society would not collapse into anarchy, but would begin dealing with a difficult problem in a more humane way.

PROTECTOR

1. Thinking morally is not the same as feeling pity.
2. A wise moral decision must be based on a good reason, which means an acceptable principle.
3. Some principle must be paramount, and the best candidate for the ultimate principle is "respect human life."

4. The decision to euthanize patients who are in pain is not based on a workable principle, but is a return to acting arbitrarily on emotional impulses.

EUTHANIZER

5. The compassionate and right thing to do in some rare cases is to relieve a person's suffering by ending his or her life.
6. The world is too complicated for us to rely on absolute rules.
7. It isn't mere life that people value but the quality of life.
8. Allowing medical professionals to end some patients' lives will not lead to a wholesale disregard for patients' rights; to believe it will is to assume that future generations cannot think for themselves.

FOR FURTHER STUDY

Historical Examples

PROTECTOR: Albert Schweitzer. *Civilization and Ethics.* A. and C. Black, Ltd. 1923. Argues that reverence for life in all forms is the fundamental principle of morality.

EUTHANIZER: David Hume. "Of Suicide." In Stephen Copley and Andrew Edgar, eds. *David Hume: Selected Essays.* Oxford University Press, 1993. Originally written in 1757, published posthumously. Argues that suicide is natural and in no way contradicts the belief in a divine creator.

OTHER SOURCES

Neal Bernards, ed. *Euthanasia: Opposing Viewpoints.* Greenhaven, 1989. Variety of accessible articles on different aspects of euthanasia.

Robert M. Baird, Stuart E. Rosenbaum, eds. *Euthanasia: The Moral Issues.* Prometheus, 1989 Like Bernards, but slightly more advanced.

Tom L. Beauchamp, ed. *Intending Death: The Ethics of Assisted Suicide and Euthanasia.* Prentice-Hall, 1995. Sophisticated articles for more advanced students.

Gerald Dworkin, R.G. Frey, Sissela Bok. *Euthanasia and Physician-Assisted Suicide: For and Against.* Cambridge University Press, 1998. Dworkin and Frey present a variety of arguments in favor of euthanasia, Bok a variety against.

Willard Gaylin, Leon R. Kass, Edmund D. Pellegrino, Mark Siegler, "Doctors Must Not Kill." *Journal of the American Medical Association* 259, no. 14 (April 8, 1988): 2139–2140.

Nancy Dubler, David Nimmons. *Ethics on Call.* Vintage, 1993. Well-written chapters on various issues in bioethics.

Margaret Pabst Battin. *The Least Worst Death: Essays in Bioethics on the End of Life.* Oxford University Press, 1994. Defends euthanasia on the grounds of mercy and autonomy, and criticizes protector arguments.

Peter Singer. *Rethinking Life and Death: The Collapse of Our Traditional Ethics.* St. Martin's, 1995. Ambitious attempt to reinvent morality based on a notion of quality of life; defends some types of euthanasia (as well as abortion, infanticide, and respect for animals).

Herbert Hendin. *Seduced by Death: Doctors, Patients, and the Dutch Cure.* Norton, 1997. Critical report on euthanasia in the Netherlands, by a protector.

Edwin R. DuBose, Ronald P. Hamel, Laurence J. O'Connell, eds. *A Matter of Principles? Ferment in U.S. Bioethics.* Trinity Press International, 1994. Articles examining the roles of principles in reasoning about bioethics, with explorations of alternatives.

CONNECTIONS

HUMANIST OR OBJECTIVIST?

Your values are a very important part of your worldview. In this part of the book you have been reading about goals in life, obligations to others, happiness, rules, society's restraints, and other aspects of morality. One conclusion you have probably drawn is that the topic of values is complicated. But tangled areas like values are just the places you should try to find connections. In some cases, an individual's values are in conflict, and those tensions create not only confusion but often dissatisfaction on the job, anxiety over important decisions, and needless problems with others. Making connections among your values is simply unifying and integrating your character, and that benefits everyone.

What connections can we find among the positions in Chapter 3? Is there some basic issue that divides all the positions into two camps? We used that method to organize the positions in Chapters 1 and 2, where we found basic divisions between transcendentalists and naturalists, and between conservatives and liberals. Can we apply the same method here?

I think we can, so long as we remember that we are picking out only one thread in a densely woven piece of cloth. When we say in Chapter 1, for example, that atheists are similar to terminators, and both are naturalists, we are focusing on only one aspect of the two positions. Both positions believe that the natural world described by science, including the physical body, is all there is. But we could find other relationships between these two positions, and between these two and the other views presented in Chapter 1. Classifying all the positions as transcendentalist or naturalist is only one way of organizing them. You can probably think of others.

The same applies to Chapter 3. I can suggest one basic division, but you might see others. The division I am thinking of is this: does morality depend upon human desires or upon something else? In other words, are right and wrong relative to human beings and their wishes, or are they more objective than that? Are all valuable things in some way dependent upon satisfying people's desires? Or are some things valuable independently of any human being's desires? Do all obligations ultimately boil down to the duty to increase people's happiness? Or do people have duties and obligations based on conscience, or God's will, or nature, which are binding without considering the promotion of human happiness?

If you believe that all right and wrong, or good and evil, *do* depend on human desires, then you are a "humanist." But if you think morality has an *objective* basis, independent of satisfying human desires, then you are an "objectivist." This is one way of organizing the positions in Chapter 3.

Probably the clearest examples of a humanist and an objectivist are in Section 3.4, "Is Happiness the Standard of Morality?" A utilitarian believes that all right actions are actions that create the greatest happiness for the greatest number of people. That is his or her theory of morality. And it clearly makes the utilitarian a humanist: the utilitarian believes morality depends on satisfying human desires, which is the same as doing whatever makes the most people happy. However, a formalist (the opposite of a utilitarian) claims that morality depends on the fundamental difference between humans and animals. Human beings can deliberately obey rules, but animals are merely conditioned, or trained. The ability to follow rules gives us a special, *moral* way of thinking, which is different from trying to satisfy our desires. Therefore, in the formalist's view, doing the right thing is always obeying the relevant moral rule, such as "Tell the truth" and "Repay your debts." Behaving morally has nothing to do with trying to satisfy people's desires. Thus, a formalist is an objectivist.

Another example of an objectivist is in Section 3.5, "Is Society the Source of Values?" In that section you encountered a moral theist, who believes that morality depends upon God's commands. We all feel the absolute obligation of moral rules, such as "Torturing children is wrong." We are as certain about this rule as we are about anything. Many people say that they would rather die than break it. Now the only possible source of such a grave, supreme obligation is God, a perfectly wise, compassionate, all-powerful being. Only the authority of God can provide an adequate basis for such an absolute command. Thus right and wrong do not depend on human desires but on God's commands. Morality is more than merely satisfying our desires.

The opposing position in Section 3.5 is functionalism. Functionalists believe that being moral does mean obeying rules, but the rules are invented by society. They are the rules that are necessary for society to function at all, rules human beings invented to make life easier. For example, we all have a moral obligation to tell the truth. Why? Because if people did not normally tell the truth the whole fabric of society would collapse. Society depends on communication, and communication depends on trusting people to tell the truth. Society depends on other basic rules as well. But the rules are creations of human society; they exist to serve human society. Therefore functionalists are humanists. Right and wrong depend on the human desire to live together in groups. Morality is a human invention, according to functionalists.

Notice that functionalists are similar to utilitarians because both are humanists. But they are different, too, because functionalists believe being moral means obeying certain rules. Utilitarians believe being moral means calculating the amount of happiness that will result from an action, and then doing whatever produces the greatest happiness. Rules are irrelevant at best, they say, and harmful (i.e., immoral) at worst, if a person puts obeying the rules above producing happiness. The functionalist replies that obeying the rules will lead to happiness in the long run, but that is not for you to calculate; your moral duty is to obey the rules that society prescribes to you. Hence a functionalist is similar to a formalist.

This disagreement between functionalists and utilitarians illustrates the important point that two positions can be similar in one respect—being humanists, for example—and different in other respects. If we made obedience to rules the basis of our classification, then functionalists and utilitarians would have to go into opposite groups. But if we make human desires the basis, then they go into the same group, i.e., humanists.

Section 3.1, "Is Pleasure the Only Value?," contrasts hedonism with pluralism. A hedonist says pleasure is good, and it is the only good. Everything else that we value is a means to that ultimate goal. A pluralist claims that there are many different values, some personal and some social.

A hedonist is clearly a humanist: an action is right if it produces pleasure, and wrong if it produces pain. Pleasure and pain are human feelings, and so good and evil depend on human nature and human desires, according to the hedonist. On the other hand, a pluralist believes there are other values besides pleasure. Pleasure is good, but it isn't the only good. Creativity, excellence, love, compassion, and justice are only a few of the many values we all recognize. However, all these values depend on people. They do not depend on *one* person, or on pleasure, but they do depend on human beings. That suggests that a pluralist is also a humanist.

But this conclusion would be too hasty. Pluralists also believe that beauty, nature, and God are important values. Beauty, they say, is an objective quality of things in the world, not a subjective experience. Nature, of course, is independent of human desires and goals. It is an objective value. And the same applies to God. Therefore, a pluralist is an objectivist. Not all values depend on human beings or arise out of human desires, even if some do.

Another section in Chapter 3 is Section 3.3, "Is Morality Relative?" A relativist says yes and an absolutist says no. Relativists believe that every society invents its own moral laws, and the laws are different in different societies. It is impossible to make an objective judgment of the various moral codes around the world. This position is similar to humanism. It sees morality as a human invention, based on human desires. Societies invent their own morality, according to a relativist, and one society's morality is just as legitimate as another's.

Absolutists argue that none of the differences between two societies can make an action right in one but wrong in another. If child abuse is wrong in one society, it must be wrong in every other society, because there is no basis for the difference in right and wrong. Furthermore, the theory of relativism breaks down when two societies come into contact. It cannot tell us whether an action is right or wrong. It is an untenable theory.

Most absolutists are, as a matter of fact, objectivists. They believe that morality is not based on human desires, but is a matter of obeying certain rules. The rules are universal and binding on everyone. We know the rules through our consciences. And most objectivists are absolutists. If morality is based on God's commands, or on nature, or something more objective than our desires, then it is universal and absolute. Or if it is based on our rationality—which makes us different from animals—then it is absolute, because all human beings everywhere are rational.

However, an absolutist *could* be a humanist, and vice versa. An absolutist could believe that morality depends on human desires, and that the most basic human desires are the same in all societies. Everyone wants freedom from fear, freedom from hunger, and freedom of thought, she or he might say. For example, the functionalist represented in Section 3.5 is an absolutist: moral rules are the same everywhere, but also a humanist: moral rules are human inventions. Nevertheless, it is probably easier for an absolutist to be an objectivist than a humanist. The diversity in different societies' actual moral values is hard to deny. It seems that people in different societies do have different desires and values, although it is difficult to say whether or not these are "basic" desires. The conclusion is that there is no logical barrier to an absolutist being a humanist, but the factual evidence seems to suggest that absolutism is closer to objectivism.

The idea that morality depends on human desires is also relevant to Section 3.2, "Can We Understand Happiness?" A definer says that we can define happiness, and goes on to claim that happiness is an inner state of mind. It is the feelings of confidence, self-respect, and optimism that people have when they are achieving most of their goals. That is what all happy people have in common. A muddler, on the other hand, maintains that we cannot define happiness. No state of mind is common to all the people who are happy, because people are too complex and diverse. What makes some people happy makes others unhappy. We have no clear concept or definition of happiness.

Neither the definer nor the muddler represented here is talking directly about morality. They are discussing happiness, not right and wrong. The definer says that we can define happiness, but does not say happiness is the basis of morality. It may be, or it may not be. A definer could believe that morality depends on objective facts in nature, or on God's commands, or on something else. So a definer could be an objectivist or a humanist.

But a muddler would probably be an objectivist. Although the muddler is not discussing morality, he or she does say that we cannot define happiness. So it is unlikely that the muddler would go on to say that happiness is the basis of morality. If happiness is undefinable, but it is also the basis of morality, then we would not know what is right or wrong. We could not be sure that torturing babies is wrong. (The muddler argues that we cannot define happiness as pleasure or the absence of pain.) But most people *are* sure that torturing babies is wrong. We can know that some things are right and some wrong. Even a relativist admits that. Therefore, either happiness is definable, or happiness is not the basis of morality. Since the muddler rejects the first of these implications, he or she must accept the second.

In the current controversy section, "Should doctors ever end people's lives?," the protector says no and the euthanizer says yes. The protector argues that we should try to base our decision on principles rather than feelings. Moreover, we need a highest principle, or else we will go back and forth between contrasting duties, which is no better than shifting between emotional moods. The most reasonable candidate for our highest principle is "respect for life" because it allows for hope, and the principle "relieve suffering" is more vague and difficult to apply.

The opposing point of view, favoring euthanasia, claims that matters of life and death are too complicated to be reduced to a single principle. Many factors are relevant to each case, and we cannot say ahead of time which consideration will carry the most weight in a particular case. It depends on the specific circumstances. The euthanizer trusts our reasonableness and feelings of compassion.

While the two positions are clearly different, they do not fit the humanist-objectivist contrast very closely. A protector could be either a humanist or an objectivist. That is, a protector could regard the principle "respect life" as an expression of respect for humanity and human desires. We ought to abide by the principle because it is such a fundamental human drive. If that's what "respect life" means, and if that is why it is an absolute moral principle, then the protector is a humanist.

But "respect life" might mean we should respect all life, not just human life, because life itself is greater and more important than humanity. With that interpretation, the protector would be an objectivist because the basis of morality is something beyond human desires. Of course anyone who thinks the principle is a command from God is an objectivist. And protectors' emphasis on rules makes them similar to formalists, another kind of objectivist.

The euthanizer is closer to the humanist outlook, although he or she is not a perfect fit. The euthanizer says that there are no absolutes to guide our decisions about life and death, and that is different from objectivists' beliefs. Furthermore, the most important consideration for doctors and patients is the quality of life, including the joys, feelings, plans, and relationships people have. The emphasis on human experiences is similar to utilitarians' view that promoting human happiness is the foundation of moral thinking. So euthanizers are closer to humanism than objectivism. One should remember, however, that these connections are based only on selected aspects of the different positions. Emphasizing different aspects might lead to different connections.

The connections among the positions in Chapter 3 are perhaps more complicated than the ones in Chapters 1 and 2. In fact, tracing out the connections is one of the most challenging aspects of building your worldview. In practical terms it means that before you can *finally* decide on one position you must consider several other positions that are connected. For example, before you decide on utilitarianism over formalism, you should think about the definer and the muddler. If you are leaning toward utilitarianism, then you should accept the definer's view over the muddler's. (If you believe that a right action is one that increases happiness, then you should be able to explain what happiness is.) And there are other connections to keep in mind as well.

Humanist	**Objectivist**
utilitarian	formalist
functionalist	moral theist
hedonist	pluralist
relativist	absolutist
definer	definer
euthanizer	muddler
	protector

HUMANIST

1. Morality depends on human aims and desires; if people did not exist, nothing would be right or wrong.
2. Being moral means promoting happiness, one's own and others'.
3. Moral beliefs and rules seem very serious and obligatory, but that is because they are backed up by the most solemn institutions of society.
4. There is no doubt that morality is dependent upon society and its requirements; but it is difficult to determine whether all societies have the same requirements or different requirements.

OBJECTIVIST

5. Moral values are part of the objective world, built into the nature of things.
6. Being moral means following unshakable principles, which are not just guidelines for achieving happiness.
7. Human beings have a moral sense, or conscience, which makes us different from animals.
8. The concept of happiness is so broad and vague that it cannot be the foundation of morality.

CHAPTER FOUR

FREE WILL, MIND, AND HUMAN NATURE

4.1 ARE WE FREE?
HARD DETERMINIST, METAPHYSICAL
LIBERTARIAN, OR SOFT DETERMINIST?

———————————————————— • ————————————————————

The word "free" has several different meanings. When people talk about freedom they are usually talking about political freedom. We all understand what it means to be politically free, or to lack political freedom. If you are not in jail, then you are free, or freer than people who are in jail. If you can vote for government representatives, in an open and fair election, then you are free. If you can choose your own occupation, your place of residence, the ways to spend your money, then you are free. And there are other aspects of political freedom.

Philosophers discuss political freedom, but they also think about a more basic kind of freedom called "metaphysical freedom." Metaphysical freedom means freedom of choice, or the freedom to choose as you wish. The opposite of metaphysical freedom is having your choices determined. You make a choice, and no one forces you, but your choice is predetermined before you make it, perhaps by your past history, your environment, events in your brain, or something else.

Metaphysical freedom does not depend on having a wide array of options from which to choose. Some people say the North Koreans are not free because there is nothing in their stores to buy. But that is political freedom, or the lack of it. Even if you have sixteen brands of deodorant to choose from, is the choice you finally make really free, or is it determined by something (such as advertising)? That is the question of metaphysical freedom. This kind of freedom does not depend on elections, or a Bill of Rights. It depends on the basic nature of decisions and actions themselves.

The first essay in this section argues that all our actions are determined, and the second defends the view that we are free, in the metaphysical sense. The third tries to find a middle ground, and claims that we have a special kind of freedom.

NO: HARD DETERMINIST
"One World, Not Two"

According to the Judeo-Christian tradition, the natural world was created for humankind, for our nourishment and pleasure. People were made in God's image, and so we are fundamentally different from stones, plants, and animals. That difference is the basis of our self-respect and feelings of worth, so we insist on the difference adamantly. We go so far as to say that we are exempt from the laws that govern the natural world. We have free will.

But it is possible to think of ourselves as an integral part of the natural world. We feel a wonder and awe for the natural world, and so we could still respect ourselves as a part of it. In any case, we *are* part of the natural world, whether that makes us feel good or bad. Therefore we are governed by the same laws that govern everything else. Our thoughts and actions are determined, rather than free. They are caused by prior events and follow regular laws, just like everything else. We know that our thoughts and actions are determined because we know that *all* events are causally determined.

In every subject of inquiry scientists have discovered laws that explain why things happen the way they do. When we look at the sky, we see a vast mechanism of stars and planets whose movements we can predict to within seconds, over periods of thousands of years. Astronomers know exactly when the next solar eclipse will occur, and the one after that. On earth, chemists now play with the elements the way children play with building blocks. They put molecules together to create synthetic materials, such as nylon. Biologists have broken the genetic code, and with their artificially created organisms, they are beginning to rewrite it. They can make new crops that resist insects. In every domain, we continue to discover regular laws of cause and effect.

With regard to people, we understand how we are created at conception, and how we grow and change through the years. We use hundreds of different drugs to affect the body in dozens of different ways. The same is true of our minds: psychologists prescribe tranquilizers, stimulants, mood-elevating drugs. Alcohol affects the will. Many drugs affect perception and even consciousness itself. We also understand the stages in the growth of the personality and mind. We know what conditions in childhood will make a person shy as an adult, or outgoing, or competitive, ambitious, and so on.

Whether we look high or low, near or far, we find that everything is lawful and proceeds by cause and effect. The inevitable conclusion is that *all* events are causally determined. We have looked in such a variety of places—in the sky, in the earth, among living things, in the human body, even in the human mind. And the conclusion is always the same: nothing happens by chance. Everything is caused.

It is true, as some people point out, that there are events for which we have not yet found causes. One example is mutations. Sometimes two organisms produce an offspring that has a new property, unlike either parent. The genes in the two cells from the male and female simply change, and no one knows why. Another example is radio signals from several places in outer space. No one knows what is producing them. On earth, no one knows what caused the ice ages over the past half a million years. The earth became much colder, then it thawed, then it grew colder again, and so on four times. No one knows for sure why.

What are we to make of these mysteries? Should we decide that they are probably not caused at all, and no one will ever find the causes? Or should we decide that we will probably find the cause in the future? We don't want to decide blindly, without thinking. Which is the most probable statement? Two factors lead to the second belief, that we will find causes in the future. First, these unexplained events are highly unusual. There are so many events whose causes we do understand, and only a few that seem to be uncaused. In fact, it is difficult to think of examples of events that appear to be uncaused. The fact that they are so rare suggests that they are, at bottom, like all the other events. They really are causally determined. We simply haven't found the causes yet.

Second, scientists have a long record of finding the causes of events. In the past, we didn't know what caused earthquakes. Some people might even have decided they were uncaused. But now we know that movements of the huge plates covering the earth cause earthquakes. People didn't know why some elderly individuals became senile. Now we know that the loss of function is caused in many cases by Alzheimer's disease. In the twenties, some people exhibited strange symptoms like loss of hair and teeth, and brittle bones. No one knew what caused the problems. But then scientists discovered vitamins, added them to the patients' diets, and the problems disappeared. The problems were caused by vitamin deficiency.

In other words, there are many cases where we did not know the cause of something, and then we found it. It is reasonable to believe that the same process of discovering causes of things will continue in the future. Therefore, even if there are areas where events happen that we cannot explain, all the evidence suggests that those events are causally determined, and some day we will discover the causes. It is virtually certain, then, that our own thinking and behavior are causally determined.

It's true, we do not know the causes of people's actions or decisions. We cannot predict what a person will think or say at any particular time. But our ignorance shouldn't mislead us. It is still extremely likely that something—some combination of environmental influences, memories, bodily states, or past experiences—causes a person's decisions. The combination of factors brings about the person's thought; given those preceeding events, the person had to make that particular decision.

How could it be otherwise? If we recognize lawful regularities in every aspect of the universe, then we would be irrational to claim that one small area— human will—is utterly different, and not determined by prior events. It would be like saying that scientists have understood why earthquakes occur, why machines work, why blue-eyed parents have blue-eyed children, and so on and so on, except on a little island in the Pacific Ocean. There none of the laws apply. Everything that happens is a miracle.

A ridiculous attitude, to be sure. And yet when the little island is our own minds, we assume we are different, and above laws. We should be more mature, as well as more logical.

Key Concepts

part of nature	self-respect	determined
governed by law	mechanism	generalization

Critical Questions

1. What does the hard determinist mean by "determined"?
2. Suppose that the idea that all actions are determined is very upsetting. Suppose it makes some people think they can commit crimes without being responsible. What do those reactions tell us about the truth or falsity of the theory? Do they show that the theory must be false?
3. How are the hard determinist's statements about the sky and the elements relevant to the conclusion that all our thoughts and behavior are causally determined? How do they support the conclusion?
4. Suppose you want to buy a new car. You like Fords, but you also want a reliable car. So you ask ten people who already own Fords if they are reliable. They all say that they never had any trouble with their Fords, though some are as much as eight years old. Does that make it *probable* that the Ford you buy will be trouble-free? Is it possible that the Ford you buy will break down after a week? How is this argument about Fords similar to the essay's argument about determinism?
5. The essay says that people who believe in free will think that the human mind is like a small island. How is it like an island? What does the writer mean?
6. Do you think that you are part of the natural world? Does that mean that all your actions are caused and governed by natural laws?

YES: METAPHYSICAL LIBERTARIAN

"Free Will and Common Sense"

The strongest argument supporting the belief in freedom of the will is plain, old common sense. If you simply look at what is evident right under your nose, you will see that you are free. Only a person in the grip of a powerful ideology could deny the obvious facts, and assert that he or she is really merely a puppet.

By free action I mean an action that is not coerced or constrained by anything. Free actions are those that are up to you. You choose them, and you could have chosen differently, because you were not forced to choose as you did. In contrast, determinism is the belief that the world is one huge, interlocking mechanism. Your actions are the necessary results of changes in your environment. Determinism says that we are like robots, whose movements are determined by their "input," or perhaps by stored instructions, but not by their own choice.

Such a theory is false, and you can see that it is false if you observe the contents of your own mind as you deliberate. Imagine that you are considering two alternatives, like having a cheese sandwich or a tuna sandwich for lunch. And then you decide to have cheese. You begin to make your sandwich. If you recall such an incident in your own life, and *observe* the thoughts and feelings that go through your mind as you deliberate and then choose, you will see that nothing determined your choice. You can see this as clearly as you see your own hand.

You probably thought about one possibility, and then the other. You thought about the taste, the ingredients, the preparation, and some of these made you feel better than the others. After a few seconds of this kind of deliberation, you decided on cheese. But it was a free choice. The feelings didn't force you. You could just as easily have chosen tuna.

Of course this sort of observation is different from observing an external object, since in this case you are looking within your own mind. But that is something people do all the time, for example, when they say, "I just had a strange thought," or "I feel a strong craving for applesauce." Such statements are not odd or questionable. In fact, a person's reports of the contents of his own mind are extremely reliable. It might be easier for you to observe your own mind than it is for you to observe the physical world around you.

So if you do look within your self as you make a decision, and you do not see anything forcing you to go one way rather than another, that should be very reliable evidence that you are free. Moreover, I know what it is like when I am *not* free. For example, if a mugger says, "Give me your money or I'll shoot you," I know that I am being coerced. When I look within myself, I recognize the fear, and I see how it determines my behavior. In that case I am not free. But most of the time, when I observe my own deliberations, I do not find any such coercion. I can choose one thing or another.

Determinists will not admit this because they are impressed by science. Scientists look for determining causes of things, and sometimes they find them. (Actually their failures to find causes are far more numerous than their successes.) But the determinist's thinking is muddled. Science is based on observations of objects and events, as the determinist acknowledges. But the scientists' knowledge of the objects and events begins with their knowledge of their own experience, the contents of their own minds. First come observations of the way things look to them, in their own inner experience, and then, on the basis of those, they make judgments about the objects themselves, outside their mind.

Think about an example from everyday life. If you are driving on a hot, flat road with your friends, you might say, "We should slow down for that water on the road ahead." Your friends reply that there is no water on the road. It is only an illusion, a mirage, and they turn out to be right. Then you say, "Well it looked to me like there was water on the road," and you are right; it did *look* like that to you, even though there was no water. You first know how things seem to you. Then you decide whether you are right or not. "How things seem to you" refers to your inner experience, which may or may not correspond to reality. The inner experience comes first, and then you decide the world is really like that (or you decide that you were mistaken).

Every scientific observation should be prefaced with the words "It seems to me that. . . ." When a scientist conducts an experiment and checks the results, he or she should say, "It seems to me that the litmus paper is red," or "It seems to me that the scale says 368 grams," or "It seems to me that the rat has stopped." Every observation is, at the most basic level, a report of what is in one's mind. If others agree that the scale says 368 grams, then the scientist can conclude that his perception is correct. But first comes his knowledge of his own mind, or his own experience.

Our experience is an experience of freedom. The results of science tell us that everything is determined. But we should trust our experience. Determinists put the cart before the horse. They ignore the inner observation of freedom, and accept only the outer observation of a mechanical world. But inner observations are more trustworthy than outer, because inner observations are the basis of outer observations.

Key Concepts

free action	deliberation	coerce
introspection	choice	mechanism

Critical Questions

1. How does the metaphysical libertarian define "free action"?
2. According to the essay, what can we observe to know that we are free? Does the metaphysical libertarian believe that nothing causes the choices he or she makes?
3. Do you agree with the essay that the person who gives money to a mugger with a gun is *not* making a free choice? If I see a pastry in a shop window and feel a very strong desire for it, and then go in and buy it, am I acting freely?
4. Do you think I should trust my observations of myself? Is it possible that something (a fear, a desire) could influence my deliberations, and cause my choice, even if I am not aware of it?
5. A metaphysical libertarian says a person knows one of the following statements, and then knows the other on the basis of the first. Which is dependent on which?
   (*a*) The tomato is red. (*b*) The tomato looks red to me.
   (*a*) The room feels hot. (*b*) The room is hot.
   (*a*) The soup tastes salty to me. (*b*) The soup has salt in it.
6. (*a*) Suppose you listen to the horn on Joe's car and the horn on Mike's car, and Joe's is clearly louder. But several of your friends all say Mike's is louder. Would you decide Mike's is louder?
   (*b*) Suppose you trip and fall, but you aren't hurt, and you feel fine. But your friends say that you must have a headache. Would you decide that you have a headache?

YES: SOFT DETERMINIST
"Verbal Disputes, Facts, and Free Will"

The problem of free will and determinism is always confusing to people who encounter it for the first time. I think that is because they do not realize that there are actually two problems: deciding what the facts are, and deciding what the words "free will" and "determinism" mean. The words are as important as the facts. It is necessary to understand the two sides of the problem before we can answer the question "Do people have free will?"

To an outsider, philosophers often seem to be obsessed with words. They take a short statement and tease out five different interpretations of it. Or they do not give a straight answer to a simple question, but say, "Well, it depends on what you mean by ____."

But they have a good reason for putting language under a microscope. We think with words. We describe the world and our experiences with words. There are no ideas except ones expressed in particular words. There are no facts that we can know about except ones described in particular words.

Words are like rows and rows of glass jars in our heads that hold experiences or facts. Some jars are big, some small, some short and fat, some with irregular shapes, some tinted green, brown, or blue, in hundreds of different combinations. But no experiences or facts can exist for us except in those jars, i.e., words. So if we want to understand our human experience of the world, then we must examine the "containers" very carefully.

Philosophers understand the importance of language as well as poets do. Even so, philosophers sometimes do not pay as much attention to words as they should. If that happens, they can fall into a verbal dispute. A verbal dispute is a disagreement that occurs because two people use the same word but attach *different* meanings to it without realizing it.

For example, is Hamlet real? People can argue about this all day without reaching any conclusion. For one person, "real" means something you can touch, or see, something material. In this sense, Hamlet is not real. For the other, "real" means something we all know about, or something that has properties we all agree upon. For this person, Hamlet is real. One person will offer evidence and arguments that seem perfectly convincing to him. But the other person rejects them, because to her they seem to be irrelevant.

Are erotic movies art? One person will say yes, another will say no, even if they agree on all the facts. One may use the word "art" to mean an entertaining representation of some aspect of life. Paintings are art, and so is TV. To the other, the word "art" may mean something that is thought provoking, continually interesting, and beautiful. TV and erotic movies do not qualify. But if they do not realize that they mean different things by "art," they will talk past each other and argue forever.

Some disputes about free will may be merely verbal disputes. People may define "free will" in different ways. To avoid that fruitless debate, it is essential to be perfectly clear about the meaning of the term "free will." In fact, people have used the term in two different ways. I think one way is correct. That is, it is closer to what ordinary people mean when they use the word "free." But we must understand both definitions if we want to avoid confusion.

One way to define "free will" is to say a person is free so long as her choices are *not caused*. That means that nothing whatever forces her to make one choice or another. Suppose that Helen looked at two blouses and decided to buy the green blouse rather than the red one, for no particular reason. She was in a hurry, she had to choose, and she chose green. It wasn't important; she could have chosen red just as easily. Now if it really is true that she could have chosen red, then her choice must not have been caused. If it *was* caused (by a fleeting memory of a green skirt she had at home, for example), then she could not have chosen the red blouse in the same situation (with the same memories). Many people say that their choices are free, in the sense that they could have made different choices in the same situations. When they say "free," they mean uncaused, or could have been different. We can call this the *uncaused* definition of "free will."

The other definition says that a person is free so long as her choices are *caused by herself*. That means that her own thoughts or wishes cause her to choose green rather than red. She is free because she is doing what she wants, and that is what "free" means. In our example, we can imagine that Helen's brief memory of her green skirt caused her to choose the green blouse. It wasn't a salesperson, or a loud commercial on TV, or a "Sale" sign, or anything outside of herself. She made a free decision because she did what she wanted to do, not what others wanted her to do, or what some external factor forced her to do. If some external power forces her to go against her wishes and values, then she is not free. But so long as no external forces compel her, and her choices are caused by her own thoughts and values, then she is free. We can call this the *self-caused* definition of "free will."

It is necessary to decide which definition best expresses what we usually have in mind when we think of being free. If we do not decide on one definition, then we may argue endlessly because we are talking about two different things without realizing it. It seems to me that the self-caused definition is correct. When we say we are free, we mean that nothing prevents us from doing what we want. We *also* mean that we could have acted differently and made a different choice, as the uncaused definition emphasizes. But when we say that, we do not mean that we could have acted differently with the *same* thoughts and wishes. When we say we could have acted differently, we mean that we could have if our thoughts and feelings had been different. The uncaused definition ignores this point.

But choosing one definition of "free" does not end the debate. Even if people agree on the meaning of the word, they can still disagree on the facts. Is everything that happens caused, or are some events uncaused? ("Cause" means make to happen; if A causes B, then when A occurs, B must follow.) Some people believe that all events, including all our choices and decisions, are the necessary results of prior causes. Given a person's desires and thoughts and beliefs, the person *had* to choose green over red. She could not have chosen red, so long as she had the personality and tastes she had. A person who believes that everything is caused is a determinist.

Other people believe that choices are not causally determined. A person is different from the material world, according to this position. A person is not just a machine, in which one gear moves another. We have some free play in our choices. A person's desires and thoughts do not *cause* her to choose green. She could have the very same desires and thoughts, but decide on a whim to take red instead. In the human mind, prior events do not absolutely require one outcome or another. Even in physics, the old determinist view is breaking down. In the twentieth century, physicists have said that the movements of the tiniest particles in an atom may not be strictly determined. The world is unpredictable, and that is specially true of the human mind. Let's call a person who believes this a libertarian.

Here the dispute is over facts, not just words. A determinist believes the facts are one way, and a libertarian believes they are another way. Now we have two issues, about the meaning of "free," and about the extent to which events are caused. On the first issue, we distinguished the uncaused definition of "free" and the self-caused definition. I believe the self-caused definition is correct. On the second issue, we distinguished the determinist and the libertarian. I believe the determinist is right about the facts. In my opinion, it is simply inconceivable that events could be uncaused. We cannot grasp the idea. We cannot sincerely believe that it rained on Tuesday, for example, but for no reason. Or that the lamp fell, but nothing caused it to fall. Of course we often do not *know* the cause. But that is different. I think libertarians are confusing the idea that *there is no* cause with the idea that we do not know the cause.

However, I realize that some people disagree with me. Everyone must decide which definition of "free" is best, and which description of the world is best. That leads to four possible positions.

All determinists (1 and 2) agree on the fact that everything is caused. But they define "free" differently, so they disagree on free will. Hard determinists say determinism proves that we are *not* free. Soft determinists say we can be

		FACT	
		DETERMINIST	LIBERTARIAN
MEANING	UNCAUSED	**1.** Hard Determinist (not free)	**3.** Free Libertarian (free)
	SELF-CAUSED	**2.** Soft Determinist (free)	**4.** Random Libertarian (not free)

free, so long as our choices are caused by ourselves rather than by external forces. I believe the soft determinist position is the most reasonable one.

All libertarians (3 and 4) agree on the fact that some events are not caused. But again, they define "free" differently, so they disagree on free will. Free libertarians say we are free, since our choices are uncaused. But random libertarians say that our choices are uncaused, and therefore what we do is unpredictable, random, and accidental. Our choices are not caused by our own desires and plans. That is not doing what we want to do, so we are *not* free.

These four possibilities show that, while the problem of free will seems simple on the surface, it is actually very complicated. The complications cause misunderstandings among people. The average person who has not studied philosophy believes that we are free. And I think that is right; we are free. But I also believe it is important to understand exactly what that statement means. If we think carefully about the meanings of words, and about the facts, we can avoid verbal disputes and misunderstandings. More importantly, we can understand the complexities of our own beliefs.

Key Concepts

verbal dispute	self-caused	free libertarian
cause	hard determinist	random libertarian
uncaused	soft determinist	

Critical Questions

1. According to the soft determinist, why do philosophers pay close attention to words?
2. What is a verbal dispute?
3. What are the two ways in which the word "free" is usually defined?
4. How can people argue about definitions? Can't a person define a word in any way she or he pleases? What is the soft determinist's opinion on the correct meaning of "free"? Is the opinion supported?
5. What is the factual issue in the free will problem? What is the soft determinist's position on the factual question, and why does he or she hold it?
6. Suppose every part of my personality is strictly determined by my environment (e.g., smothering parents, sheltered childhood, conformist peers). My personality determines my choices later in life. Am I acting freely, according to the soft determinist? What do you think?

Methods and Techniques

INTROSPECTION

If you take a psychology course, the teacher might show you a labyrinth, with a lot of turns and dead ends, and ask you to draw an unbroken line from the outer edge to the center. After you have solved the puzzle, she or he might show you another one, and say, "This time, as you work on the puzzle, pay attention to what you are thinking and feeling *as you work*." You start, and you might talk to yourself like this: "Let's see, now I am looking at the center and at the outer edges. Should I begin with the entrance on the right, or should I begin in the center and work my way back to the edge? How to choose? Now I am being distracted by those people talking." And so on. After you finished, you could tell the teacher what went on in your mind as you worked.

The act of noticing or observing the processes of your own mind is called *introspection*. We can observe flowers and trees, listen to a lecture, and enjoy a meal, but we can also observe ourselves doing these things. I do not mean in a mirror—that would be observing our bodies—but directly, or inwardly. We observe our own thoughts, feelings, hopes, fantasies, doubts, and so on.

Introspection is an important and puzzling ability, so we should be careful in describing it. It is not the same as one of the five senses. For example, if the psychology teacher presses a cut-out letter of the alphabet on your back, you can probably identify the letter without seeing it. But you are using your sense of touch to acquire information about that physical object; you are not introspecting your own mind. Or if you taste a fine wine, and try to discover the "fresh, clear, and crisp" flavor the expert says it has, then you are using your sense of taste to acquire information about that wine. That is not introspection either.

Introspection means observing things about yourself, not objects in the world. That means your inner self, not your body. When you observe your face in a mirror, you are not introspecting. On the other hand, if you close your eyes, raise your eyebrows, and try to notice how it *feels* to raise your eyebrows, then you are using introspection. As you taste the wine, you pay close attention to the wine and try to describe it. But you can also try to notice how you search for the right words. Attending to the wine is just observation; attending to your own search for words is introspection.

In introspection you observe something that no one else could ever possibly observe. For example, suppose you have a backache from sitting and typing too long. It's a dull, constant muscle ache right in the middle of your back. If you watch TV or do something else you can almost forget about it, but if you turn your attention entirely to the soreness, it can almost fill your mind. But no one else can feel your backache. Your friend can notice that you have a backache, because you walk stiffly and hold your back. But she cannot observe it directly, as you can. She cannot feel it, or introspect it. In fact, everything that you introspect is completely beyond the reach of other people. And whatever other people can observe, like your face, you do not know through introspection. You know them through observation, like everyone else.

Our ability to introspect our own minds raises numerous philosophical questions. One is about free will: if introspection tells you that you are free, but observation tells you that everything is determined, which do you believe?

Understanding the Dilemma

HARD DETERMINIST, METAPHYSICAL LIBERTARIAN, OR SOFT DETERMINIST?

Section 4.1 is about free will. People care very much about freedom, and your image of yourself depends in part on whether or not you believe you are free. A libertarian is a person who believes we are free to make our own choices, and a hard determinist is a person who believes we aren't. A soft determinist claims that we are determined and free at the same time.

In the introduction to this section, I said that the issue is about metaphysical freedom, not political freedom. In other words, the issue is whether or not any choice or decision you make is really free. Political freedom was the topic of Section 2.2. Political freedom concerns the range of choices you have, or the variety of alternatives before you, such as the variety of news sources you may read, the range of occupations you may pursue, political candidates you may vote for, and so on. Metaphysical freedom concerns your choice of one particular alternative: was your choice free, or was it causally determined? And what do we mean by "freedom" anyway? Those are the questions these three essays consider.

They are fascinating questions. Do you think that everything you do is determined beforehand, before you do it? Is your future already fixed and set, but you just don't know what it is? Was it determined long ago that you would read this page at just this time? Was it determined by your childhood, the things you enjoyed and the things you didn't, your high school career, your parents' decisions, their income, your college counselor, other friends' remarks, the things you heard about job opportunities, interesting courses, your schedule this week, the conversation you had a half hour ago, and so on? Did all these causes lead inevitably to your actions at this moment?

Or are your choices not determined by previous events? You might believe that all these sorts of events influence you, and you may be aware of many facts and conditions, but that at the moment of choice, *you* decide which way to go. The previous events do not determine which choice you will make. If you believe your choice is not determined, then you are a metaphysical libertarian. Your view is similar to the view presented in the second essay.

A hard determinist believes that everything is caused and determined. Not only are your actions determined, but your thoughts, feelings, moods, and imaginings are also strictly determined. When you wish for something, like a cold Coke, or when you suddenly remember something, like a remark your friend made this morning, something caused that wish and that memory. There was a reason you had that wish at exactly that time, instead of a different wish. And if you decide to buy a Coke, something caused your decision. No one knows what caused your decision. A hard determinist does not claim that he or she *knows* all the causes of people's actions and choices, but says there must *be* some causes. There must be some causes for everything that happens. And therefore everything is determined.

Libertarians and determinists have different basic conceptions of the world and of people. (On the basic view of the world, hard and soft determinists line up together against libertarians.) Libertarians see the world as extremely complicated, so complicated that something completely new might happen at any time. Things are unpredictable and sometimes chaotic. Determinists see the world as orderly and governed by laws. Everything has its place, and remains in the proper relation to everything else. As for people, libertarians trust their own perceptions. They are suspicious of experts and the established "truth." They know what they see, and if scientists tell them they are mistaken, then they can go fly a kite. Determinists believe that their own perceptions are sometimes wrong, and always limited. A large group of people will probably have a better understanding of a situation than the determinist will, especially if the group is made up of trained, skillful scientists.

That is the basic issue in this section. But as you reflect on the problem you will probably soon realize that it has two dimensions, a factual dimension and a verbal dimension. That is, in deciding between determinism and libertarianism you should think about the meaning of the word "free." That is the point the third essay makes. If you are a libertarian, then you must believe that, in fact, we are free, *and* you must be able to explain what that means. It means that nothing causes your actions. We can observe our freedom within our own minds.

A hard determinist defines "free" the same way as a libertarian, but says that everything is caused, and so we are not free. A soft determinist defines "free" in a different way. He or she says free actions are caused, but they are caused by oneself. A soft determinist believes that everything is determined, but that some actions are free and some are not. The free actions are those that are caused (determined) by *oneself* rather than by something outside of oneself. A soft determinist tries to find a middle way between determinism and libertarianism, and does this by defining "free" in a special way. "Free" means self-caused. In general, to decide between libertarianism and determinism, you must make two decisions: you must decide what the words "free" and "determined" *mean*, and you must decide what the *facts* are. The third essay describes the basic options you have.

So, what is your view? Are you a hard determinist, a libertarian, or a soft determinist? Your decision on the issue of free will and determinism is an important part of your worldview. It is one of the most fundamental questions. Your belief will affect the way you think about human nature, social policies, other people, and yourself.

DETERMINIST

1. I am a product of many factors that have made me what I am, and which continue to shape all of my behavior.
2. The natural world is basically uniform and lawful, and I am part of the natural world.
3. My own personal impressions can be misleading, and if they conflict with the careful observations of many scientists, I should believe the scientists.

4. A belief in determinism will lead us to search for the causes of behavior, which eventually will enable us to help people in many ways.

METAPHYSICAL LIBERTARIAN

5. I am in control of my own life.
6. Human beings are not part of the natural world, but are different, set apart, precisely because we can choose how to live.
7. My inner experience of making a choice is proof enough that I am free, regardless of what scientists say happens elsewhere in the world.
8. If people believe all their actions are determined, they will become irresponsible, or lose all their initiative, or sink into despair.

SOFT DETERMINIST

9. The issue of free will depends on questions of meaning as much as it depends on questions of fact.
10. We should distinguish four possibilities, not two, based on different definitions of "free" and different beliefs about causation.
11. All the determinist's beliefs are correct, except for a mistaken definition of the term "free."
12. Since free actions are those that are caused by one's own thoughts and desires, rather than by external forces, we are normally free.

FOR FURTHER STUDY
Historical Examples

DETERMINIST: Thomas Hobbes. *Concerning Body.* In *The English Works of Thomas Hobbes*, translated by Sir William Molesworth. Vol. 1. John Bohn, 1839. Originally published in 1651. Chap. 9, "Of Cause and Effect," and chap. 25, "Of Sense and Animal Motion." Hobbes argues that every event is caused, including events in our minds, such as choices and decisions.

METAPHYSICAL LIBERTARIAN: Jean-Paul Sartre. *Being and Nothingness.* Pocket Books, 1993. Originally published in 1943. Part 4, chap. 1, "Freedom: the first condition of action." Sartre argues that a careful analysis of our own consciousness reveals that we are radically free.

OTHER SOURCES

Mark Thornton. *Do We Have Free Will?* St. Martin's, 1989. A clear presentation of numerous arguments for and against.

D.J. O'Connor. *Free Will.* Anchor, 1971. More complex discussion, more emphasis on science, than Thornton.

Richard Taylor. *Metaphysics*. 3rd Edition. Prentice-Hall, 1983. Defends fatalism.

Corliss Lamont. *Freedom of Choice Affirmed*. Continuum, 1990. Emphasizes the unacceptable consequences of adopting the determinist position.

Ted Honderich. *How Free Are You?* Oxford University Press, 1993. Discusses implications of modern physics, and the attitudes we should have if determinism is true.

Gerald Dworkin, ed. *Determinism, Free Will, and Moral Responsibility*. Prentice-Hall, 1970. Contemporary and historical selections, including David Hume's famous defense of a kind of soft determinism.

Sidney Hook, ed. *Determinism and Freedom in the Age of Modern Science*. New York University Press, 1958. Brief articles by modern philosophers.

Richard Kane, *The Significance of Free Will*. Oxford University Press, 1996. Excellent analysis of the context of the problem, specific issues, and a defense of a libertarian position.

4.2 ARE WE RESPONSIBLE FOR OUR ACTIONS?

EXCUSER OR JUDGE?

●

Responsibility is very important to us. The whole justice system, with its courts, its highly trained and highly paid lawyers, the extremely elaborate procedures of a trial, the right to a jury of one's peers, even the traditions going back to Magna Carta, are all aimed at determining responsibility. Our society devotes almost as much time and energy and careful investigation to assessing blame as it does to making money. We also care very much about rewarding praise. The U.S. Patent Office determines who gets credit for ideas and inventions. Often people engage in long court battles over patents and responsibility for inventions.

On a more personal level, some of the strongest emotions we ever experience are guilt, or shame. We take responsibility very seriously. Some people are even driven to end their own lives if they feel responsible for some terrible action. And on the other side, pride and self-esteem are extremely important to people. We work for years to acquire the feeling of being responsible for something good and worthwhile. Some spend years with a psychiatrist trying to develop that sense of accomplishment.

If the idea of responsibility is so important to us, then obviously we want to understand it as fully as possible. However, it is not so easy to understand. The concept is puzzling in some ways that the two essays in this section bring out. The first claims that the concept is not only puzzling, but actually senseless. It says the idea is a relict from a time when people believed in magic. If you agree that the idea is senseless, then you will excuse people who do undesirable things. You are an excuser. The second essay tries to analyze the way we actually use the concept, and argues that it is perfectly adequate, until something better appears. It says we may and should judge people, so if you agree with the second essay you are a judge.

NO: EXCUSER

"Rejecting Responsibility"

The dustbin of history is filled with beliefs and concepts that modern man has discarded. Some, like the belief in dragons and fairies, were dropped because we learned more about the world we live in. Others, like the belief that the universe is enclosed in a solid sphere, were dropped because people eventually realized they didn't make sense. (The whole universe can't be inside a sphere, because there must be an outer side of the sphere.)

People still accept unfounded, meaningless ideas. The concept of "moral responsibility" is such an idea. We want to blame someone when things go wrong, or praise someone for actions we like. But if we think carefully about how the idea of responsibility is supposed to work, we will discover that, in fact, it doesn't work at all. The whole idea is meaningless.

People who believe in moral responsibility face a dilemma. That is, they face two undesirable choices. One of them must be true; there are no other possibilities. But each one is incompatible with responsibility. No matter which they choose, they must give up their belief in responsibility.

The two possibilities are that human behavior is causally determined, or that it is not causally determined, i.e., it is free. If your action is causally determined, then you are not responsible for it. For example, if a strong man takes your hand and forces you to pull the switch of a fire alarm when there is no fire, then you are not responsible for the false alarm. Or if a dictatorship imprisons you and deprives you of food, you are not responsible for your failures due to weakness.

Nor must all causes be physical. If a doctor tells a nurse that certain pills are good medicine, when actually they are harmful, then the nurse isn't responsible for the harm done by giving the pills to patients. The nurse's actions are determined by the false belief, and ultimately by the doctor.

So if we take this side of the dilemma—human actions are causally determined—then we must conclude that people are not responsible for their actions. Now let's try the other side, and assume that your actions are *not* caused. But if your actions are *not* caused, then you aren't responsible either. If they are not caused, then they are unpredictable, random accidents, like a sudden twitch, or lurch. If your hand twitched for no reason, you would not be responsible for it. It is hard to imagine actions that aren't caused, but suppose a person could do something—hit someone, for example—that was not caused. Then the action would just happen, for no reason. The person is no more responsible for it than for other unpredictable accidents, like a sudden rain shower, or a hiccup. (When we say the action is uncaused, then we are ruling out the person's own wishes as causes. One cannot say the person *wanted* to hit someone, or else the desire to hit would be the cause.) Now surely a person is not responsible for random occurrences that happen for no reason. In sum, after looking at both possibilities, we can see the dilemma. Whether actions are causally determined, or free, a person is not responsible for them.

At this point, the believer in moral responsibility will claim that there is a middle way. You are responsible, the believer will say, when your actions are caused *by yourself*, although not when they are caused by events outside of yourself. For example, if a strong desire for money causes people to steal, then their action is causally determined, but it is determined by a part of them, i.e., their desire. No one forced them to steal, or misinformed them, so they alone are responsible. In general, then, according to this way of thinking, people are responsible for actions that are caused by themselves.

But this attempt to avoid the dilemma fails. It merely pushes the dilemma back one step, from actions to the values, or desires, or the self, that are the sources of actions. Now the dilemma applies to this inner self (instead of to actions). The two possibilities are that the *self* or values are causally determined, or they are not. Either way, the person is not responsible.

Take the example of the person who steals. If the thief's values and desires were caused by a poverty-ridden childhood, a neglectful, cruel father, and a greedy, grasping mother, then the thief would not be responsible for the kind of person he became. He didn't choose to have the desires and characteristics he has. He didn't choose to be born into that situation, he could not escape from it, and he should not be blamed for the results. On the other hand, if his personality and values are not caused at all, then he is not responsible for them. If they are not caused at all, then they are a kind of freak accident, or a so-called act of God, like a tornado, for which no one is responsible. Either way, caused or uncaused, the concept of responsibility does not apply to the self.

Believers in responsibility will try to escape this dilemma in the same way they tried to escape the dilemma about actions. They will say that people can choose the desires they have, and the traits that make up their personality. People are responsible for their own personality, because it is caused by themselves, according to this theory.

But this response makes no sense at all. It says we choose our personality, or the kind of self we want to be. But *who* chooses? We must have a personality and desires *already*, if we are able to make a choice. We must be a self, because only a self with certain desires can make choices. It makes no sense to say we choose to become a person. If we choose, then we are already a person.

It makes no sense to say we choose all our desires. We must have some basic desires already, desires that guide our choices.

This shows that a person cannot choose, or cause, the basic desires that make up the core of his or her being. So the dilemma applies to this central core, or inner self. Either it is caused (by something external to the person), or it is not. In either case, we are not responsible for the self we are. Whether we look at actions, or at the selves and values behind the actions, we find that the concept of responsibility does not apply. The whole concept of responsibility is meaningless, and should be discarded.

Our modern criminal justice system has already abandoned the archaic "eye for an eye, tooth for a tooth" concept of justice. In mental health care, we used to treat the insane as if they were criminals, but fortunately those days are past. We should now move beyond this magical belief in responsibility. When we do, we will be able to treat offenders in a more effective, humane way, by changing the causes of their destructive behavior. It is only ignorance that makes us label them as undesirables and subhuman.

Key Concepts

actions	causally determined	choices
dilemma	uncaused	self

Critical Questions

1. What are the two sides of the dilemma that the essay discusses?
2. If our actions are not caused, doesn't that mean they are free? And aren't we responsible for what we do freely?
3. If our actions are not caused, then could we have prevented them, or avoided them?
4. The excuser says that the same dilemma that applies to one's actions also applies to one's self. How is this relevant? Does it show that we are not responsible for our actions?
5. Do you agree with the excuser that a person's self (i.e., personality, values) guides his or her choices?
6. Do you think you can choose your own personality? If so, what guides your choice?

YES: JUDGE

"No Excuse"

A cop is shot and dies. Who is responsible? Who should be charged with the crime? Obviously the person who pulled the trigger. But suppose someone said that there is no difference between the perpetrator and anyone else. That the shooter is no more responsible than a bystander, or someone in another state. Anyone who said such a thing would be laughed out of town. It's absurd.

But don't laugh. Some philosophers have actually said it. They said that there is no such thing as responsibility. No one is responsible for his or her actions, so there is no moral difference between the cop's murderer and his mother.

The "no responsibility theory" may be interesting, as a theory, but it is irrelevant to the real world. In the real world we often decide that a person is responsible for something, or that she or he isn't. Our decisions are based on several factors, and if we are careful, and we consider the relevant facts, then the decisions are justified. Some people *are* responsible for their actions and the consequences.

Four main factors determine the decision that a person is responsible for something. Actually we can best understand the four if we turn the matter around and look at situations in which a person is *not* responsible for something. In other words, let's consider the *excuses* people offer when they say they are not responsible. In the case of the cop murder, a person who was in another state and was not connected with the event in any way is obviously not responsible for it. If a person shows that he did not cause an event, then he has a good excuse. That shows that a person must *cause* an event before he or she can be responsible for it.

But causing it isn't enough. People can use a different excuse, and say it was an accident. It sometimes happens that two cops enter an apartment, they are fired at, they return the fire, and in the confusion one cop accidentally shoots his partner. No one blames the cop or says he is responsible for the death. He didn't intend to shoot his partner. It was an accident. So only a person who causes an event and *intends* to cause it is responsible for it.

Another excuse comes up in court, when a person pleads insanity. If the police catch the killer, and he is positively identified by witnesses, then he or his lawyer might claim that he is insane. If he is out of his mind and doesn't know what he is doing, then he is not responsible.

Finally, a person can say he had no choice. When a bank robber points a gun at a teller and demands money, no one thinks the teller is responsible for the robber getting the money. It is true that the teller caused him to get the money, gave it to him intentionally, and knew what he was doing. But the teller was forced to do it. Therefore, in order to be responsible for something, a person must do it freely, without being forced.

These are the four standard excuses people use. If any one of these four factors (cause, intention, sanity, free choice) is *missing*, then the person is not responsible. By the same token, if all four are present, then the person *is* responsible. In other words, if a person's action causes something to happen, and he has *no excuse*, then he is responsible. He must take responsibility for his action.

It may be difficult to know whether or not the factors are present. It is notoriously difficult to decide when a person is insane. Psychiatrists for the defense and the prosecution usually disagree. But if people do agree that the four factors are present—and they often do—then they also agree that the agent is responsible.

The intention excuse is complicated in cases of negligence. Sometimes people are held responsible for something because they could have prevented it but didn't. For example, if a parked car rolls down a hill and hits another car, the owner of the rolling car will say he didn't intend for his car to roll. It was an accident. But a judge will say that he *should* have paid more attention, and could have prevented it from happening, if he had used his parking brake or parked more carefully. So even if he didn't intend for his car to roll, he is still responsible for the damage done.

The factor that philosophers have discussed the most is the last one, free choice. Sometimes a person does something intentionally, but is forced to do it, like the bank teller. That person is not responsible. But what else besides a serious threat could force someone? Could a person's environment or upbringing or education force him to do something?

Some philosophers say that the robber who robs the bank does it intentionally, but his *personality* causes him to steal. It is true that he chooses to steal, but his values and beliefs (his personality) cause him to choose that way. Even though he chooses to steal, he does not choose his personality. That is produced by his parents, his childhood experiences, his friends, his neighborhood, in short, his environment. His personality forces him to choose robbery, and he is not responsible for his personality.

Since the theft of the money is ultimately caused by things completely out of the robber's control (his environment), he is no more responsible for it than the teller. He did not choose to be the kind of person he is, and he couldn't avoid it. So he is not responsible, some philosophers say. In fact, everyone is a product of his or her environment, and therefore no one is responsible for the choices he makes and the actions he performs.

This is a common point of view among philosophers, social workers, sociologists, and others. But it is wrong. It is wrong because pointing to the robber's environment is *no excuse*. There is not a single, established law connecting a person's environment with his personality. There are scientific laws connecting a person's diet with his health. For example, if a child does not get enough calcium, he will develop rickets. But philosophers cannot say that poverty causes someone to be the kind of person who wants to steal, because most people who grow up in poverty are *not* criminal types and do not steal. On the other side, rich people steal, too. Therefore it isn't poverty that causes people to become thieves. Do children grow up to be just like their parents? Some do and some don't. So where is the reliable connection between environment and personality?

In fact, it is just an *assumption* that environment determines personality. No one really knows why some people have certain values, habits, and beliefs. Maybe it is the environment, maybe it is something else. Most likely it is a combination of dozens of things. No one knows.

What is the robber's excuse? He can't say he steals because he was deprived of toys as a child. Others were deprived, but do not have a thief's personality. It is undoubtedly true that *something* caused the thief to have the personality he has. Everything is caused. But "something" is not an excuse. Imagine a child who tells his teacher that he decided not to do his homework, but that he is not responsible for the failure, because "something" caused his decision. He doesn't know what caused him to decide not to do it, neither does his teacher nor anyone else. But everything has a cause. So he is not responsible. None of *my* teachers would have listened to such baloney, and they shouldn't have.

The robber causes the money to be given to him. He does it intentionally, and he is sane. Did he choose freely, or was he forced? The philosopher says he was forced because something—we don't know what—made him the kind of person he is. But that is not an excuse. He did cause the crime by his choice. He was not forced the way the teller was. There is no question about that. Without a more specific prior cause that made him choose the way he did (more specific than "something"), he is the obvious cause of the crime, and therefore he is responsible.

Suppose a scientist knows that gravity causes the tides, but he has no idea what causes gravity. Of course he knows that something causes gravity, since everything is caused, but he doesn't know what. The scientist does not decide that gravity is *not* the cause of the tides, just because something causes gravity.

In the same way, the philosopher knows that the robber caused the crime, but he doesn't know what caused the robber (i.e., what caused his personality). The philosopher should not decide that the robber is *not* responsible for the crime, just because something causes the robber's choice. "Something" is not an excuse. It may be true that if psychologists discovered the causes of the robber's personality, and knew for sure that they determined his choices, then we would say he was not responsible. Then he would have an excuse. But until that day arrives—and it may never arrive—the thief is responsible for his action.

Key Concepts

excuse	intention	personality
responsible	insane	environment
cause	free choice	

Critical Questions

1. According to the essay, what must we know if we know that Jones is responsible for the murder of a police officer?
2. What is the "no responsibility theory" that the judge in this essay criticizes? Does the no responsibility philosopher believe that the robber freely robbed the bank?
3. Why is the "no responsibility theory" mistaken, according to the judge? Does the judge say that the robber's personality does *not* cause his choices? Does the judge say nothing causes the robber's personality?

4. Do you think the school boy who decides not to do his homework is analogous to the bank robber? Should the school boy be excused?
5. If the robber is not responsible, does that mean that generous, heroic, or mature people are not responsible for their good deeds? Does it imply that we should not admire them or reward them?
6. If the judge admits that something causes the thief's decision to steal, then how is the thief different from the bank teller who hands over the money? Why is the thief responsible while the teller isn't?

Methods and Techniques

INFINITE REGRESS

The first essay uses several types of arguments in criticizing the concept of responsibility. One is to say that the concept leads to an *infinite regress*. "Regress" means to go backward, so "infinite regress" means to go backward forever. If a principle or explanation leads to an infinite regress, then it can never get started, or never get off the ground. It is not a real explanation.

For example, in one primitive religion the devotees believed that the earth rested on the back of a giant elephant. The elephant stood on the back of a giant tortoise. They were assuming that "everything must be held up by something." This principle seems reasonable and in conformity with everyday experience. If you stop supporting the book you are holding, it will fall. If you remove part of the foundation of a building, it will collapse. The believers simply generalized from these common observations, and extended the generalization to the world as a whole. Something must be holding it up.

The problem is that the principle leads to an infinite regress. If everything must be held up by something, then the elephant that holds up the earth must itself be supported by something. The believers decided a giant tortoise could do that. But their principle requires them to ask what holds up the tortoise. Even if their shamans and wise men could propose something to answer that question, they would have to ask what holds up *that*, and so on, ad infinitum (to infinity). There is no end to the "explanations," and therefore there is no real explanation. The principle itself is defective.

Here is another example. Some people have said that when you understand a language, you translate it into a language you already know. For example, when you take a course in French, and you understand the sentence *Il pleut*, you translate it into English: "It is raining." But if this principle is correct, then how do young children learn and understand their *native* language? Well, these philosophers say, the toddlers translate the sentences they hear into an innate, mental language, which the philosophers call "mentalese." But this is no explanation. How do the children understand "mentalese"? According to the principle, they must translate *it* into some other, deeper language they already know. There is no end to the process. The principle leads to an infinite regress, and so it must be mistaken.

In the previous section you read about introspection, and one principle concerning introspection leads to an infinite regress. Some philosophers have said consciousness is just an awareness of your own experiences. When you look at a tree, for example, you are aware of the tree, but you are also aware of your observation, or your experience, of the tree. When you remember your vacation, you are thinking about the beach, the restaurant, etc., but you are also aware that you are remembering. In general, these philosophers say, when you are aware of something, then you are also aware that you are aware. You are aware of your own mental experience. That is what it means to be conscious.

But this principle also leads to an infinite regress. It says that if I am aware of a tree, then I am also at the same time conscious of my own awareness of the tree. This consciousness is a second state of awareness. Its object is the first state of awareness (whose object is the tree). But the principle says that when a person is aware of something, then he or she must also be aware of that mental experience, that state of awareness. So I must be aware of the *second* state of awareness, too. That would be a third state, and I must be aware of that third state, which implies a fourth, and so on. There is no end of the process. But the mind cannot contain an infinite series of reflective states of consciousness, like a mirror held up before another mirror. The principle must be mistaken.

It is not always easy to see that a principle leads to an infinite regress. The example of the religious principle "everything has to be held up by something" is more obvious than the introspection principle "when you are aware of something then you are also aware that you are aware." To find an infinite regress, you should ask whether or not an explanation applies to itself. That is, when a principle says A is explained by B (e.g., the earth is held up by an elephant), then you should ask if the principle also applies to B. Is B explained by C, and C by D, and so on?

The excuser in the first essay claims that the idea of responsibility leads to an infinite regress. Responsibility is based on the principle "we are responsible for the things we freely choose." The excuser says we do not freely choose our actions because our desires and personalities determine our actions. So the defender of responsibility says we must freely choose those desires and personality. But the excuser says that won't work either. Even if we assume it is possible, the basic core self that selects values must also be freely chosen. And who makes that choice? And if something does make that choice, who chooses that something? And so on ad infinitum.

Understanding the Dilemma

EXCUSER OR JUDGE?

The two positions in this section do not have standard names. The question is fairly straightforward—Are people sometimes responsible for their actions?— but the two sides on the issue might be called different things. The view stated in the essay "No Excuse" could be called "responsibilist," or "accounter," because it says people are accountable for their actions. The opposite view, represented by "Rejecting Responsibility," could be called "antiresponsibilist," or "antiblamer," or perhaps other things. I have chosen the terms "judge" and "excuser" for the two positions because they are relatively simple and descriptive. Anyone who agrees with the second essay believes that you can judge people for their actions, and a person who agrees with the first essay wants to excuse people for their actions. The names are not important. The important thing is your beliefs. Do you believe people are sometimes responsible for their actions, or is no one ever responsible for what happens? Are you a judge or an excuser?

One way to think about this issue is to picture a line with two extreme points at each end. The point at the left end of the line represents the view that a person is responsible for everything he does, and the point at the right end represents the view that a person is not responsible for anything he does. The point in the middle represents the view that a person is responsible for about half of what he does, and the point between the middle and the left end represents the view that a person is responsible for about 75 percent of what he does, and so on. Where do you stand on that line?

The excuser stands at the right extreme: he rejects the whole idea of responsibility. Probably no one stands at the left extreme. No one says we are responsible for everything we do. Everyone accepts some excuses. The judge in the second essay even describes some excuses that relieve people of responsibility for what they do. For example, an insane person is not responsible. So the judge is not at the left extreme. He or she says we are responsible for some things we do, and not responsible for other things we do.

But *why* are we not responsible in some cases? An excuser argues that once you admit that people are not responsible in some cases, you must recognize that other cases are actually similar to those. That is, you must admit that their actions or choices were caused by something outside of their control. And you will gradually move closer and closer to the right side of the line until you reject all responsibility.

The question of responsibility is obviously related to the issue of free will and determinism, but it is not the same. In fact, both the excuser and the judge in this section are determinists, at least in the sense that both say all our actions are caused. But the judge maintains that we are still responsible for some of the things we do, even if they are caused. Apparently the way in which actions are caused is the important thing for responsibility, according to a judge. The excuser says simply that if all our actions are caused, then we are not responsible for them.

The excuser is proposing a radical point of view. Very few people have been consistent excusers. The position is not part of "common sense." It is very different from people's ordinary way of thinking. But that is not to say it is wrong. Every great idea was different from common sense at first.

When you consider your decision on this question, you might reflect on what others think and what people have usually said in the past. But that is not the real basis of your decision. The issue is not "what do most people think," or "what have people thought in the past," or even "what have I always believed up until now?" You have very likely believed that people are responsible for their actions. But now the issue is "Do you have good grounds for that belief?" Do you believe it just because others do, and because you are in the habit of thinking this way? Or is your belief sensible and based on good evidence?

Are you an excuser or a judge? Your decision will have far-reaching effects on your attitudes toward other people's actions and your own. This issue is especially important in determining your political outlook. It will influence your beliefs about wealth and poverty, about education and government aid, and particularly about crime and punishment.

EXCUSER

1. Punishing people for being born into a particular family and neighborhood is barbaric and cruel.
2. To explain all is to forgive all.
3. Many people accept the foundations of the scientific worldview, but do not think about all its implications.
4. People can change their habits and some of their values, but they cannot change the innermost core of their personality.

JUDGE

5. An individual's surroundings do not force the individual to do anything.
6. Putting the blame on parents or neighborhoods after doing something wrong is just an immature attempt to avoid taking responsibility for one's self-indulgent actions.
7. Belief in cause and effect is compatible with belief in responsibility, because individuals cause their actions and are responsible for what they cause.
8. You can be the kind of person you want to be, although it may take discipline and time to change.

FOR FURTHER STUDY

Historical Examples

EXCUSER: Clarence Darrow. *Crime: Its Causes and Treatment*. Crowell, 1922. The famous lawyer for the defense argues that people who are victims of circumstances should not be held responsible for their actions.

JUDGE: Jean-Paul Sartre. *Being and Nothingness*. Pocket Books, 1993. Originally published in 1943. Part 4, chap. 1, section 3, entitled "Freedom and Responsibility." Sartre believes that human beings have no essence, but choose what they are, and therefore are responsible for what they do.

OTHER SOURCES

Gerald Dworkin, ed. *Determinism, Free Will, and Moral Responsibility*. Prentice-Hall, 1970. Collection of classic and contemporary pieces presenting the standard positions.

Kenneth Bock. *Human Nature Mythology*. University of Illinois Press, 1994. Critical discussion of four types of determinism, based on God's will, forces of history, human instincts, and social conditioning.

Karl Menninger. *The Crime of Punishment*. Viking, 1968. A plea for a more scientific approach to the problem of crime, and a critique of the present criminal justice system.

Gertrude Ezorsky, ed. *Philosophical Perspectives on Punishment*. State University of New York Press, 1972. A large collection of classic and contemporary writings on reasons to punish someone, alternatives to punishment, and the death penalty.

Milton Goldinger, ed. *Punishment and Human Rights*. Schenkman, 1974. A collection of articles by contemporary philosophers on the justice of punishment and the various excuses that make punishment itself immoral.

Jonathan Glover. *Responsibility*. Humanities, 1970. Clear but challenging.

Herbert Fingarette. *On Responsibility*. Basic Books, 1967. Discusses what it means to live responsibly, and related concepts of self-realization and guilt.

Jennifer Trusted. *Free Will and Responsibility*. Oxford University Press, 1984. Broad survey for "readers who come fresh to philosophy," discussing many historical figures and topics.

4.3 IS THE MIND NOTHING BUT THE BRAIN?
MATERIALIST OR DUALIST?

———————————————————•———————————————————

Everyone knows what the brain is. The brain is a mass of nerve tissue weighing about three pounds, protected by the skull, and attached to the spinal cord. It is divided into left and right hemispheres, each of which is further divided into "lobes," such as the frontal lobes, the temporal lobes, and the occipital lobes. Most of the surface is covered by "gray matter," which is enfolded upon itself to create "fissures." The nerve tissue of the brain consists of cells called "neurons." Each neuron is connected to many other neurons around it. Thus, much of the brain is literally a neural net. But while scientists understand the anatomy, or components, of the brain, they do not yet understand the physiology, or functioning, very well.

The mind is even more problematical. What is a mind? It's hard to say. When we think, remember, imagine, and decide, we *use* our minds. If an accident or disease makes it impossible for someone to do these things efficiently, then we say he has "lost his mind." But what *is* a mind? What is a thought, a memory, or an image? We all have thoughts and memories, so in some sense we know what they are. But it is very difficult to describe them or categorize them. Some activities require thought, and others do not. Some memories are pleasant, and some are not. Some things we can remember easily, while we must make an effort and dig deeply to remember other things. But none of this tells us what *kind* of thing a thought, or a mind, is.

In a way, we have opposite problems in understanding the brain and the mind. We know what the mind does—it thinks, remembers, etc.—but we do not know what it is. In contrast, we know what the brain is—it is a mass of neurons, arranged in lobes, etc.—but we do not know what it does, or how it functions.

This situation, together with other considerations, has led many philosophers to decide that, in all probability, the brain *is* the mind and the mind is the brain. We do not have two organs but only one. Now, is this a plausible theory? Does this suggestion help us understand the brain, or the mind? Is there any concrete reason to say the mind is the same thing as the brain? Is there any reason to say it is not?

These are the central questions in "the mind-body problem." The first essay that follows argues that the mind and the brain are identical. It says a human being is made up entirely of matter, so it presents the point of view of a materialist. The second essay argues that the mind has some peculiar, unique properties utterly unlike any physical object. Therefore the mind cannot be the same thing as any physical object, including the brain. One who believes that the mind and the brain are two utterly different kinds of things is called a dualist.

YES: MATERIALIST
"Body and Soul"

At the present time there are two basic ways of looking at human nature. One way sees human beings as parts of the natural world, fundamentally no different from animals and even plants, except that humans are vastly more complicated. The other way sees humans as composed of two parts, a body and a soul. The body is a physical object, like animals and plants, but the soul is a different *kind* of thing, not physical, but mental, or spiritual.

The second picture, called "dualism," has prevailed throughout history and in most cultures. But now the evidence supports the first picture, called "materialism." In this view, the mind is exactly the same thing as the brain. Experiences, like thoughts, emotions, memories, and decisions, are all tiny changes in the cells that make up the brain. No nonphysical soul is required.

Several recent discoveries support materialism. For example, scientists can measure the brain's electrical activity, or brain waves, at different times. The waves are different when a person sees a familiar object and when he or she sees a strange, unfamiliar object. They are different when a person listens to someone and when he or she answers a question. This shows that different states of consciousness are closely correlated with different states of the brain. It suggests that consciousness *is* an activity of the brain.

Another dramatic piece of evidence is that changes in the brain cause changes in a person's mind. In the 1940s Wilder Penfield, a Canadian neurosurgeon, operated on the brains of patients with epilepsy. The brain has no feeling, so Penfield performed the surgery with local anesthetic, while the patients were conscious. When he touched a place in a woman's brain with a small electrode, she said she could suddenly hear a piano. Later, when he touched the same place again, she said she could hear the piano again, although this time it sounded like a phonograph record. Other patients said the probing made them relive events in their past. Clearly memory is affected by stimulating the brain. The best explanation of these facts is the theory that the mind is identical with the brain, and experiences are events in the brain.

This "identity theory" (i.e., materialism) fits in well with other discoveries and with the main trends of modern science. One trend is toward consolidation and reduction. Reduction means that physics can explain chemistry, chemistry explains biology, biology explains psychology, and psychology explains sociology. In other words, sociology is "reduced" to psychology, psychology is reduced to biology, and so on.

For example, chemists know that sodium atoms and chlorine atoms join together to form salt. They have discovered many laws governing such reactions among elements and compounds. But what *explains* the combination? For an explanation of the laws of chemistry, we must look to physics. The atoms bind together because of the electrical forces among their electrons. And electricity is a part of physics. Physics explains chemistry.

Another example is the reduction of biology to chemistry. At the turn of the century some biologists claimed that life is a unique "vital force," and fiercely resisted the idea that life is just a matter of combining the right chemicals. But then chemists artificially created amino acids—the building blocks of all living things—in a laboratory. Later they discovered DNA, the chemical code that guides every living thing. They demonstrated that chemistry explains biology.

Materialism rests on the belief that some day scientists will understand the brain well enough to explain psychology in terms of biology, i.e., the brain. Penfield's discoveries are a first step in that direction. So materialism is part of the trend of reduction.

Another trend in modern science is toward simplicity. If one basic law will explain a set of facts, then there is no reason to have two or three laws. Or if one kind of object will explain the facts, then there is no need to believe in two or three kinds of objects. The most famous example of the drive for simplicity is Newton's law of gravity. Newton studied three apparently unconnected phenomena: the orbits of the planets, the path of a cannonball, and the tides. People had gathered quite a bit of information about these things from observation, but they seemed unrelated. Newton proved that all the various rules and laws that applied to these things could be derived from one broad, fundamental law, the law of gravity.

Another example is UFOs. We could say that people see airplanes, blimps, clouds of gas, and occasionally alien space ships in the night sky. But it is simpler to say that when they think they are seeing UFOs, they are actually seeing one of the other things. That enables us to eliminate one kind of thing we have to think about, and gives us a simpler picture of the world.

Or we could say there are normal women, insane women, and there are also witches. Then we would have three basic categories of women. But it is simpler to believe that the people who are called witches are actually just insane women. There are no witches. There are only normal women and insane women. These two categories still explain all the facts. But if we take that point of view, then we have eliminated one category, and our picture of the world is much simpler. We can do the same thing with thoughts, feelings, and sensations. They are actually chemical or electrical changes in the cells of the brain, not an additional, nonphysical kind of thing.

We must be careful here. Materialism does not say that the word "sensation" *means* "brain event," or that the idea of the mind is the same as the idea of the brain. The ideas may be very different. It only says that the mind actually *is* the brain, even if we do not realize it. The situation is parallel with the witch example. Our idea of a witch includes supernatural powers, the ability to fly on a broomstick, change people into animals, and so on. That is very different from our idea of an insane woman. Nevertheless, the so-called witches were actually just insane women. People just had a lot of groundless beliefs about some of the insane women.

Materialism is in harmony with the outlook of modern science, and that is a strong reason to accept it. Another reason is that the *alternative* is so strange. Dualism says that a different kind of thing exists—a soul—and it is somehow connected very closely to a human body. What kind of thing is a soul? A spiritual thing? What does that mean? No one has ever described a soul or mind in specific terms. No one has ever defined the terms precisely. In fact, no one has a clear idea of these things.

Furthermore, how can this nonphysical soul cause my physical body to move? If the soul is nonphysical, then it is not located in space. But if it isn't, then how can my soul zero in on *my* body, but not affect another body? If it is nonphysical, how can it affect my physical nervous system? Actually, only physical things can affect other physical things.

Another problem with the alternative is that it violates the principle of the conservation of matter and energy. The principle states that the total amount of matter and energy in the universe is constant. Matter and energy are neither created nor destroyed. But if a nonphysical soul causes changes in my body, then energy has been added to the physical universe from outside. Or if I step on a tack, and my body causes big changes in my mind, then it seems that energy has flowed out of the physical world into the nonphysical realm of the soul. But a great deal of evidence proves that that is impossible.

Dualism is a strange and confusing theory. Materialism, on the other hand, is consistent with modern science, and is supported by recent discoveries. Clearly we should accept the theory that the mind is identical with the brain.

Key Concepts

materialism	correlation	simplicity
dualism	reduction	interaction

Critical Questions

1. What is materialism? What is dualism?
2. The materialist in this essay says mental events, like memories, are correlated with brain events, like stimulations of certain brain cells. What does "correlated" mean in this context? Does a materialist believe that the fact of correlation proves that mental events are the same thing as brain events?
3. According to the essay, how is the science of biology "reduced" to chemistry? How is reduction relevant to materialism?
4. The materialist says it is simpler to believe that so-called witches are just insane women. Why is it simpler?
5. The dictionary definition of "witch" is not "insane woman." When people talk about witches they do not mean insane women. Doesn't that prove that witches are not insane women?
6. How are witches relevant to memories, thoughts, and other mental events?
7. According to the materialist, why is dualism difficult to understand?

NO: DUALIST

"The Inner Life"

"Know thyself." That was the command carved in stone over the door of the temple at Delphi in ancient Greece. That was the beginning of wisdom, the Greeks believed. Do you know yourself? Are you a beast or a god? Or neither? Or both? How do you discover what you are?

It would be foolish for me to attempt to answer such large questions. All of history and literature are part of the answer. But I can say that one simplistic answer is wrong: You are not the same thing as your body. And if you want to find the correct answer, you must look within yourself. Of that I am certain.

If you set out to discover yourself, you can explore your individual personality, your quirks, preferences, habits, and all the traits that make you different from your friends. But to understand yourself, you should also ask a deeper question. You should ask what kind of being a *person* is. You are a person, a human being. What makes you and everyone else different from other things, like horses or automobiles? Since you are a human being, you will not know yourself until you know what a human being is. (When you understand that, then you can find out what particular sort of human being you are.)

One theory holds that humans are nothing more than living bodies. We understand ourselves by understanding how our bodies and brains work, according to this theory. Of course, people are different from simple objects like tables and chairs, but we are not a different *kind* of thing. We are not like ghosts, or spirits—nonmaterial beings— according to this theory.

The theory is mistaken. I am not just a living body. I *am* a different kind, or category, of thing. I am not the same as my body because I can imagine switching bodies with another person, but remaining who I am. For example, I can imagine waking up tomorrow in Bill Clinton's body, but remaining the same person I am now, with the same memories and personality. That sort of thing frequently happens in movies and fairy tales, and it strikes us as entirely possible. If I woke up in Clinton's body, and Clinton woke up in mine, there would be a lot of confusion at first, but it wouldn't take too long for people around us to realize what had happened. Therefore, I am not the same thing as my body. If I were the same thing as my body, then I could not have a different body. A different body would be a different person.

If I am not a physical body, then what am I? I believe that I am the unique set of thoughts, emotions, desires, and memories that I find within myself. A human being is a being who has such an *inner* life, a being who is not only aware of tables and chairs out in the world, but who is also aware of inner events, like suddenly having an idea, and inner states like feeling confident and optimistic. I know about these events and states through introspection. They are states that others cannot know unless I tell them. The whole, rich stream of consciousness, with its inner dialogue, its colorful images, its subtle, shifting moods, its sudden joys and pangs of regret, make up the inner life.

Why do I say that I am these inner events instead of my body? The reason is that the inner events are *mine* in a special way that my body is not. As I said, my body could change, and even change radically, while I remained exactly the same person. But my inner life could not. If my inner life changes, then I change. Suppose I woke up tomorrow with completely different desires for the future. Instead of wanting to get married, I now want to join the French Foreign Legion. After the initial shock, my friends would say that I was not the same person I used to be. This shows that the person I am depends more on my inner life than on my body.

Suppose I woke up with a different set of *memories*. Instead of remembering working at the university for the past few years, I remembered living in the Amazon rain forest capturing rare birds. Suppose I did not recognize any of the people around me. Suppose I no longer understood English, but spoke only Portuguese. Even if my body were the same, people would say that there was a different person in it.

My inner life is mine (and yours is yours) in another way as well. It is private, in the sense that no one else can know it in the way I can. If I have a toothache, I know it immediately, directly, without any doubt. You may decide that I have a toothache, if you see me grimacing and holding my jaw, but you do not know it the way I do. You do not *feel* it. You *cannot* feel my joy or anger; you cannot have my memories or thoughts. Of course, you may have a toothache, but then it is *your* toothache, not mine. You may think exactly the same thing as I, but your thought is yours, mine is mine. You cannot know what my feelings and thoughts are like, except what I tell you about them. Nor can I know what yours are like. The inner life is private.

In contrast, no parts of my body are private in this strong sense. You can know my toes as well as I can, you may know my back even better than I. But what about my brain? Are events in my brain private? You cannot see what happens in my brain, so maybe that is why you cannot know my inner life. Maybe when I have a toothache, all that is happening is that my tooth is sending a signal to my brain, and something like a red light is flashing in my brain. Of course, I do not mean a real light, but some brain event, like one special neuron is vibrating, the "toothache neuron." Maybe when I think of Bermuda a certain set of neurons begins to vibrate. When I feel angry, maybe all that happens is that a gland secretes some chemical in my brain. Being angry may be having that chemical in one's brain. Is this possible?

It sounds very scientific, but scientific theories have been wrong in the past. Thoughts and feelings are private in a stronger sense than events in my brain. Anyone can, in principle, cut into my head and observe the neurons in my brain. But no one, in principle, can feel my toothache.

Physical objects and events *cannot* be private in the way that the inner life is. Physical events are in space, so theoretically they can be perceived from different points of view, by different people. Even if only one person can perceive the event (because it occurs under a microscope with one viewer, or something like that), still *any* one person could observe it. But I am the only person in the world who could ever have my toothache. Neurons and chemicals in the brain are physical objects, and cannot be private.

On the other hand, the inner life is private and *cannot* be public, in the way physical objects are. If your inner life were public, then I should be able to feel your toothache, just as I can see your toes as well as you can. But how could I feel your toothache? Even if a brain scientist hooked me up to your brain, how would I know it was *your* toothache and not *mine*? If *I* feel it, then it is my pain. There is no difference between a pain that I have that is mine, and a pain I have that the scientist tells me is yours.

There is another problem with the hypothesis that one person might be able to feel another's toothache. If the pain I feel is really yours, then I shouldn't mind it. I shouldn't care about it. It's your problem, not mine. But if I feel it, then I do mind it. So it must be mine. Only you can experience your inner life, only I can experience mine. The idea that parts of my inner life can be experienced by anyone, as physical objects can, is incomprehensible. It's nonsense.

All events and states in the inner life are private. No events in the body are private in the same sense. Therefore, the inner life is not the same as events in my body. I have not attempted to explain what the inner life—the self—actually *is*. And it is very difficult to do so. How is the inner life related to the body? When does it begin? If a thought is not physical, what is it? I don't know the answers to these questions. I still have not fulfilled the Delphic command. But is it better to have no answer to a question, or to believe an answer that is clearly wrong? I think it is better to be aware of one's ignorance, because only then will one continue the quest for the true answer.

Key Concepts

inner life	private	brain event
a different person	public	impossible

Critical Questions

1. Does a dualist think it is really possible for a person to be transferred from one body to another?
2. Do you agree with the essay that if your desires and memories changed, then you would be a different person? Don't people often change their minds?
3. Suppose a person has a special room in his house, and he never lets anyone else in. No one but he knows what is in the room. Is the room private in the dualist's sense?
4. Why can't a person's thoughts and feelings be the same things as events in his brain?
5. I can imagine that scientists locate the emotion center of the brain, connect my brain to yours like a cordless telephone, and when something happens that makes you feel joy or sadness, the signal is amplified and routed over to my brain. Then I feel *your* emotions. Do you think this is possible?
6. The essay gives two reasons for believing that if I feel pain, then it must be mine, not yours. What are they?

Methods and Techniques

POSSIBLE AND IMPOSSIBLE

By now you have probably realized that many philosophical problems arise from simple words. Words like "God," "justice," "happiness," "right," "selfish," and "free" seem simple and straightforward but are actually very complex and hard to pin down. People disagree over the meanings of these words.

Another such word is "possible." We all use the word every day, and yet it leads to several controversies.

Both essays in this section use the ideas of possible and impossible in trying to persuade you to accept their views. But what does it mean to say something is possible or impossible? It is difficult to get people to agree about what is possible or impossible. For example, look at the following list. Do you think each one is possible or impossible? Are some "more impossible" than others?

1. It rains Oreo cookies.
2. A woman is pregnant and not pregnant at the same time.
3. You find a dog that can fly.
4. You find a round rectangle.
5. You find a one hundred dollar bill in the street.
6. It rains continuously for three weeks.
7. A spaceship travels faster than the speed of light.
8. You draw a straight line between *A* and *B* that is longer than a curved line between *A* and *B*.
9. You live to be 130 years old.
10. You experience time as moving backward instead of forward.

Could it rain cookies? Some say yes, some say no. Could a woman be pregnant and not pregnant at the same time? Almost everyone agrees that this is impossible. Flying dogs? Here people disagree again. Round rectangles? People agree on this one; it's impossible. Everyone agrees that 5 and 6 *are* possible, though unlikely. But traveling faster than the speed of light is problematic. People will argue about it. They will agree that 8 is impossible. (We will return to 9 and 10 later.)

Why do many people disagree about some of these, and agree about the others? Is it because possibility is a matter of degree? I don't think so. Is it because some people are more imaginative, more open to possibilities, than others? Probably not. That may lead to disagreements on other cases, but the problem here is different. People disagree about Oreo cookies and flying dogs because the word "possible" is *ambiguous*; that is, it has two different meanings. Some use the word to mean one thing, and others use it to mean something else. For some people, when they say something is possible, they mean it is imaginable. They can picture it in their minds. There is nothing inherently contradictory or meaningless about the situation. In this sense, it is possible that a dog could fly and that it could rain cookies. We can imagine it happening. And in the same sense, if something is impossible, that means we cannot even imagine it. The words describing the situation do not make sense. They do not fit together, like "round" and "rectangle."

Other people use the words differently. When they say something is possible, they mean it does not break any scientific laws. It conforms to nature. We could actually see it someday, or perhaps it has already happened. If that is what "possible" means, then flying dogs and raining cookies are *not* possible.

They violate known laws of nature (even if we can imagine them). Thus two people often disagree about what is possible because they are using the word with two different meanings.

Philosophers make a distinction between these two meanings. They call the first "logically possible," and the second "physically possible." Flying dogs are logically possible but not physically possible. We can imagine a flying dog, but such an animal is incompatible with laws about evolution, wings, and gravity. It is logically possible that cookies could fall to the earth out of clouds, but it is physically impossible. What is physically possible depends on what we know about the way the world works. What is logically possible depends on the meanings of words, or the concepts we use to describe the world.

While people disagree about some of these cases, they usually agree about others. For example, almost everyone agrees that a woman cannot be pregnant and not pregnant at the same time, that you cannot find a round rectangle, or a straight line between A and B that is longer than a curved line between A and B. These are all impossible. But if the word "impossible" means different things to different people, how can they agree on these cases? The answer is that logical impossibility *includes* physical impossibility. Whatever is logically impossible is also physically impossible. So if people who use the word in the logical sense say something is impossible, then people who use it in the physical sense will agree with them. However, if something is logically possible, then it may or may not be physically possible. We can also turn the relation around, and say that if something is physically possible, then it must be logically possible as well. That is why almost everyone agrees on 5 and 6.

Finally, 9 and 10 are strange cases. I'm not sure if 9 is, or is not, physically possible. And I'm not sure if 10 is, or is not, logically possible. What do you think?

Understanding the Dilemma

MATERIALIST OR DUALIST?

Is there more to you than your body and brain? Are you a soul, a mind, which inhabits your body, or dwells within your body, but is not the same thing as your body? Or are your body and brain all there is? Are you a very complex organism that can react to the environment in many different ways?

The first essay, which represents the materialist view, says that the mind is really the same thing as the brain. The second essay rejects materialism and tries to convince you that the mind is not the same as the brain, or the same as any physical object. The mind is a different kind of thing altogether. Thus the second essay represents the dualist view. A dualist believes the world is made up of *two* basic types of things: physical objects and minds. They are very different from each other.

When materialists talk about "the mind" they usually mean the whole collection of mental events and processes that we observe in ourselves and, indirectly, in others. A mind is made up of cognitive things like thoughts and ideas, memories, plans for the future, imagined scenes and events, and other parts of the stream of consciousness. It also includes emotional things like feelings of joy or regret, fear, desire, pride and shame, and so on. Materialists believe that each of these is actually some event in your brain, probably a very complicated event, but still just a physico-chemical event, not very different from electrical signals moving around in a television set. A brain is much more complex than a television set, but they are both physical objects. There is no need to believe that a brain is occupied by a spiritual "self" or nonphysical consciousness.

How can materialists prove that our minds are the same things as our brains? Well, they cannot prove their view. They simply offer it as a theory, and claim it is more reasonable in light of the evidence than dualism. The first essay summarizes the evidence supporting the theory.

The second essay does not offer evidence supporting dualism. Dualists do not say materialism is a possible theory, and dualism is another possible theory, and we must decide whether the evidence supports one or the other. That is not how dualists see the issue. Instead, dualists assert that materialism is *impossible*. It cannot be true. They point to some ordinary, commonsense facts that we can all see in our own minds, and say they prove that the mind cannot be physical. The second essay describes these facts, mainly about privacy. Dualists believe they can prove that dualism is true, because they can prove that materialism is false. So dualism must be true, since it is the only alternative.

The different ways of approaching the issue point to a basic difference between materialism and dualism. A materialist believes that science gives us the best understanding of the world. If you want to know what is real, what exists, and what the world is made of, ask the scientists. And if you ask them, they will tell you that the world is made of physical objects (including organisms).

Dualists do not reject science, or refuse to believe its discoveries, but they say we also have another way of knowing about the world. At least we have another way of knowing about one part of the world. The part is ourselves. And the way of knowing is introspection. We can look within ourselves at our own thoughts and feelings. For some people, this is a whole world to be explored, not by looking with your eyes, but by looking with "the inner eye of the mind." But introspection is not science. Others cannot see into our own minds. Not even the most brilliant psychologist can know what you are thinking at any particular moment. Introspection is a different way of knowing.

MATERIALIST

1. The world is made up of physical objects, bodies in motion, and human beings are part of the world.
2. There are no such things as ghosts, spirits, goblins, or "out of body" experiences.
3. Science tells us what the world is made of, and science depends on observation and experimentation.
4. The physical brain is complicated enough to think, feel, plan, imagine, remember, and do all the things a soul is supposed to do.

DUALIST

5. Materialism is too simple; there is more to reality than physical objects.
6. I am not the same thing as my body or brain; I am a spiritual being.
7. I can know my own mind and self better than any external observer can.
8. My thoughts, sensations, and emotions cannot be physical events inside of me; they are too different from physical events.

FOR FURTHER STUDY

Historical Examples

MATERIALIST: Julien La Mettrie. *Man a Machine.* Excerpt in Lester G. Crocker, ed. *The Age of Enlightenment.* Walker and Company, 1969. Originally published in 1748. La Mettrie supports his view that the mind is the same as the brain by pointing to numerous examples of correspondence between bodily events and mental events.

DUALIST: René Descartes. *Meditations.* Many editions. Originally published in 1641. In Meditation 6 Descartes tries to prove that the mind is distinct from the body.

OTHER SOURCES

George Graham. *Philosophy of Mind: An Introduction.* Blackwell, 1993. Graham discusses a number of topics, including mind and body, computers' minds, and animals' minds, in nontechnical language, and provides many thought-provoking examples.

Keith Campbell. *Body and Mind.* 2nd Edition. University of Notre Dame Press, 1984. A survey of issues for students with some background in philosophy.

E.R. Valentine. *Conceptual Issues in Psychology.* Allen and Unwin, 1982. Chap. 5 is good discussion of introspection and its place in a scientific psychology.

Peter Carruthers. *Introducing Persons.* Croom Helm, Ltd., 1986. Chap. 2 makes a strong case for dualism, but in chap. 5 Carruthers comes down on the side of materialism.

William H. Halverson. *A Concise Introduction to Philosophy.* Random House, 1967. Part 6 presents both sides, but Halverson thinks the arguments for dualism are stronger.

Richard Taylor. *Metaphysics.* 3rd Edition. Prentice-Hall, 1983. Clear discussion of the basic issues.

P. Smith, O.R. Jones. *The Philosophy of Mind.* Cambridge University Press, 1986. Clear discussion of contemporary approaches.

P.M.S. Hacker. *Wittgenstein.* Routledge, 1999. Very brief survey, focusing on Wittgenstein's criticisms of the idea that mental events are private.

4.4 Can Computers Think?
Mechanist or Mentalist?

———————————————————•———————————————————

This may sound like a silly question. How could computers think? How could anyone think that computers could think? Computers are nothing more than machines, pieces of metal and electric wires, maybe with a glowing screen or a printer attached. Thought, on the other hand, is the glory of mankind, the noblest and most characteristic of our human activities. "Man is but a reed," says Pascal, "the weakest thing in nature. But he is a thinking reed." Thinking makes human beings admirable. But what is admirable about a clanking machine?

Not only does thinking make us worthy of respect, but it also makes us different. Many writers throughout history have agreed that what sets human beings apart from everything else is our ability to think. Horses may be faster than us and gorillas may be stronger, birds can fly and fish can swim, but we humans are smarter than they are. It is our intelligence and thought that has made us masters of the planet and rulers over the natural world. Thinking is our specialty, our particular talent, and we are very reluctant to admit that we are not so special after all.

But if thinking is so important, then we should think about thinking. We should use our intelligence to understand intelligence. And if we can find forms of intelligence in other places, then we should investigate those forms. It would be unintelligent to do otherwise.

People have always thought that they were special, and superior to others. And they have always found, as they learned more about the others, that the differences aren't so great. In biology, investigators have been chipping away at the barrier between humans and other species. They have discovered many examples of intelligent behavior among "lower" animals. Some accomplishments, like the spider's web, may appear to be intelligent but are actually due to instinct. But others can only be described as genuinely intelligent.

As we learn more about animals' mental abilities and consciousness, our attitudes toward them change. We begin to feel more sympathy and respect for them. If animals are intelligent, then we cannot treat them as mere objects. Many people today feel very strongly that animals have basic rights, perhaps not the same rights as human beings, but some rights nevertheless.

Could the same changes occur in our attitudes toward machines? It seems preposterous, but it seemed just as preposterous to the ancient Greek that an Egyptian could be his equal, or to an American slave owner that his slave should vote and serve in Congress. What seemed preposterous to them back then does not seem preposterous to us today, because we know more about people. But still, machines aren't even alive; they are inert and constructed. But then the Greeks said barbarians did not even speak Greek or wear civilized clothes. We now see that those characteristics were irrelevant to being human. Is being alive relevant to being intelligent? Could something that isn't alive be intelligent? That is only one of the questions we must answer.

The first essay in this section points out many similarities between computers and people, and concludes that computers can think. It represents the mechanist view because it claims that thinking is basically a mechanical process, whether it occurs in machines or people. The second essay, on the other hand, claims that there are some fundamental differences between machines and people, and says thinking is not mechanical. It represents the mentalist view.

YES: MECHANIST

"Can Computers Think?"

Dear _____:

Due to the skyrocketing costs of labor, and breakthroughs in miniaturization, you will be replaced by an IBM 88XR. Pick up your check at the Payroll Office.

Dear _____:

I'm sorry, but I've met someone else. He's witty, reliable, always says the right thing, and *so* intelligent. He's a Hewlett Packard Model 1000. No hard feelings?

Could people be replaced by computers? That may be going a little too far, but it isn't far-fetched to say that one day computers may be more intelligent than people.

Most people aren't aware of what computers can do now. In the 1970s computer scientists developed "expert systems." An expert system is a computer program that can make decisions like a human expert in some field, such as medicine. One of the most successful, called "MYCIN," can take in information about the symptoms a patient has, make a diagnosis of what disease is causing the symptoms, and prescribe the best medicine for treatment. In one test, a group of doctors' answers about several cases were from 42.5 percent to 62.5 percent correct, while MYCIN's answers were 65 percent correct.

Computers can also learn and improve their performance. For example, computers play chess (and other games) extremely well. They simply follow the same rules as human players. And like human players, they have certain strategies to win, like "Try to control the center of the board," and "If you must sacrifice a knight or a bishop, sacrifice the knight." But unlike humans, computers can remember every move of every game they ever played. So they can check their strategies to see how successful they are. If a strategy is helpful only 30 percent of the time, the computer can modify it and try something new in the next game. Over time, it gets better and better.

Computers interpret complex information, learn from their mistakes, calculate, store information and retrieve it, and so forth. This evidence suggests that they are intelligent. We say they are intelligent because their performance is very similar to what *people* do, and people are intelligent. In other words, computers' output (interpretations, calculations, learning, etc.) is very similar to human output. And humans produce such things by using their intelligence, by thinking. Therefore, computers probably produce their output by thinking, too.

We make this kind of inference very frequently. For example, when you plug in your coffee pot, it produces heat to heat the water. How does it do it? Well, if you take it apart you will find a coil attached to a resistor. When an electric current passes through them, they produce heat. Now, when you plug in your electric blanket, it also produces heat, just as the coffee pot does. How does it do it? A reasonable inference is to say that, probably, there is something like a coil and a resistor in the blanket, and when electricity passes through them, they produce heat, just as they do in the coffee pot. The two items are similar in their behavior (heat), so they are probably similar in their operation (resistor) as well. The same kind of inference leads to the conclusion that computers can think.

But of course computers and people are also very different. Computers are made of wires, whereas people are made of flesh and blood. They can't talk as people can, nor can they walk, or shake hands.

But computers' wires are similar to human nerves in that they carry signals. Computers can't talk, but they can print out messages, which is similar to talking. They can't walk, perhaps, but in the form of robots they move about on wheels, and can even extend an arm in greeting. It appears that every difference can be countered by another similarity.

Some people point to deeper differences. Computers are programmed. Everything they do is planned and put into them by humans. When asked "What is 2 + 2?" a computer can be programmed to reply "5" as easily as it can be programmed to say "4." It doesn't know the difference. So it seems that any intelligence computers exhibit is the intelligence of the programmer, not their own. They are merely complicated tools that can be used intelligently (by people).

But is this fact about computers fundamentally different from humans? People must be "programmed" too, although we prefer to say "educated." We must learn a language, learn to think, to add and subtract, to solve problems. We do these things in the ways we have been taught. In fact, everything that makes us human and intelligent must be learned. Many people balk at this comparison. They feel that there is something dehumanizing about the idea of "programming" people. But it is the word that has bad connotations. If we can put our self-centered emotions aside for a moment, and look at the facts, we will see that children must be taught to talk, to read, to interact with others, to experiment, and to think. We get children to follow certain rules by rewarding some behavior and punishing other behavior, until the rules are virtually automatic, whereas we can simply type in the rules to a computer. But both people and computers must be "taught." (The basic process is the same, whether we use the word "programmed," or "taught," or "conditioned.")

Once we learn enough, we can experiment and modify what we have learned in the light of new experiences. But so can computers. The chess-playing computers can modify the rules they follow if they aren't working well. Many people think that they are not programmed, and that they can learn and change completely independently of anyone else's instructions, whereas everything in a computer was put there by the programmer. But these people are simply ignoring how much they were taught at the beginning of their lives. Later, they did inform themselves and change their behavior. But so do computers.

Perhaps the difference between people and computers is that people are creative. We are unpredictable. We write poems and paint pictures. We act in ways no one ever thought of before. But computers can surprise us, too. The chess-playing computers invent new strategies that are sometimes brilliant. They can take apart and recombine elements of different rules in ways no one ever thought of before. They can write poems that sound as interesting as much of the modern poetry one reads in journals these days. Any computer could "invent new words" by randomly selecting letters of the alphabet, combining them, and assigning meanings to the results. Isn't that creative?

But surely one difference between people and computers is clear. Computers cannot enjoy a joke, or have a good cry, or feel emotions of any kind. They might print out something a person would say, like "I'm so sad," or "I've never been happier." But a person manifests emotions with his or her eyes, tone of voice, heart rate, posture, and a hundred other subtle signs. There aren't enough similarities between people's emotional behavior and computers' output to justify the claim that computers have feelings.

So computers are different from people in that they do not have emotions. But that difference is irrelevant to the point at issue. The claim is that computers are intelligent, not that they are like people in every way. Being intelligent doesn't require emotions. Remember Mr. Spock from *Star Trek*? He was the most intelligent person on the USS *Enterprise*, but he didn't feel any emotions. One could also say that computers run on electricity, whereas humans run on calories. But that difference has no bearing on the question of their intelligence. Without some *relevant* difference, the similarities make the case: computers can think.

People still feel there *must* be some crucial difference. But none withstands careful scrutiny. Therefore, it is logical to conclude that computers can think. Now is that so bad? Actually it's exciting. It opens up a whole new world of possibilities.

Key Concepts

intelligent	creative	analogy
programmed	learn	relevant
expert system	emotions	

Critical Questions

1. The essay never defines "intelligence." On what grounds, then, can it say that computers are intelligent?
2. The essay considers several objections to the mechanist thesis. How do the critics attempt to prove that computers are *not* intelligent?
3. Computers are programmed. Why doesn't that show that they are not intelligent, according to the essay?
4. Do you agree with the mechanist that computers can be creative in the same sense that people can?
5. Do you think it would be possible to invent a machine that could take dictation, as a stenographer can? Suppose it could record someone's voice, and then type what it had recorded, the way a stenographer does. But it would never get impatient, or feel frustrated, or proud, as a real stenographer does. Would the lack of emotion show that it could not take dictation after all? How is this example relevant to the issue?
6. How do you know that your friends can think? Does your evidence *prove* that they can, or only make it very probable that they can?

NO: MENTALIST

"People vs. Machines"

One of the most popular themes in science fiction is robots. Robots are machines that have human characteristics. They are also called "androids," "cyborgs," and sometimes just "computers." Although "HAL" in Kubrick's film *2001: A Space Odyssey*, didn't move around, he had human characteristics.

But science fiction is, after all, fiction. How close to reality are these fantasies? Can we really create artificial minds, or mechanical people? I think the answer is no. Computers today do not have minds, they are not intelligent, and what's more, they never will be.

But I may be in the minority on this question. A whole industry today is based on the assumption that we can build artificial minds. Thousands of technicians and engineers spend millions of dollars and countless work-hours every year in the "artificial intelligence" industry. They are convinced that they can build machines that have minds and can think.

Their starting point was stated clearly in a research proposal written in 1956. It said:

> The study is to proceed on the basis of the conjecture that every aspect of learning or any other feature of intelligence can in principle be so precisely described that a machine can be made to simulate it.[1]

In other words, if we can describe a process, then we can build a machine that can carry it out. For example, if you watch workers assembling a car, you can describe everything they do or every move they make. Then you can build robots to take their places, according to computer scientists. The same approach applies to intelligence, they say. If you describe the steps someone takes in solving a problem or doing something intelligent, then you can build a computer that will go through the same steps, and then the computer will be intelligent.

I think this approach is much more limited than computer scientists realize. A computer cannot duplicate *every* process. Scientists can describe the steps that the atmosphere goes through to create a hurricane. But a computer cannot create a hurricane. The most it can do is "simulate" a hurricane. It goes through steps that correspond to the atmosphere's changes, and it creates something that corresponds to a hurricane, such as an image on a screen. But an image is only a weak imitation of a hurricane. As for artificial people, the most that computer scientists can do is *simulate* intelligence, or create weak imitations of minds, not real minds.

But the computer scientists will say that a mind is different from a hurricane. Minds are intangible, abstract sorts of things. Maybe a mind just *is* the process, so that when a computer goes through the process, it has a mind. Let's grant the computer scientists their assumption. Let's admit for now that if we can describe the processes of the mind, then a computer can duplicate them, and that if it duplicates them, it has a mind of its own. I do not think this assumption is true, but let's grant it for the sake of argument.

Even if we admit all of that, it is still wrong to say that computers are intelligent. The reason is that we cannot describe the processes of the mind. We do not know what intelligence consists of. So we have no steps for the computer to duplicate. We are a mystery to ourselves.

Some examples will prove this. Think of the first words of the pledge of allegiance. Remember? Now, how did you do that? You sorted through all the things you know, and hit upon those particular words, "I pledge allegiance to the flag . . ." What steps did you go through in remembering that bit of information? What is the process of remembering? No one knows. It seems that you decide to remember something, and bingo! It suddenly appears in your mind. We don't know how we do it.

What is consciousness? A tape recorder can play back the pledge of allegiance, but it isn't conscious of doing it. When you recite the pledge, you are conscious of it. What is the difference? What steps can the computer duplicate that will make it conscious, rather than just an information storage, like a tape recorder? No one knows.

You understand the meanings of words like "revolution," "marriage," and "mature." How do you do it? What makes those words meaningful to you, while "licard," "clution," and "sud" are not meaningful? What is the process of understanding the meanings for words? We don't know.

The new industry of artificial intelligence is not following its own program. Its goal was to build a computer that can duplicate the processes humans follow when they remember, understand, perceive, or do other intelligent things. But it cannot duplicate those processes because we don't know what those processes are.

If it isn't following its program, then what is it doing? It is building more complicated tape recorders. It is building machines that give the external appearance of having a mind, but that do not have the real, inner substance of intelligence.

Since we do not know how we do intelligent things, no machine can duplicate them. It may simulate intelligence by producing the same results as a human, but it does not duplicate the inner process, because we do not know what the inner process is. But that doesn't prove that we will never know. Could machines have minds in the future, if scientists discover how we remember, understand, perceive, and so forth?

Computer scientists say yes, because they view human beings one way, and I say no, because I view human beings a different way. Computer scientists think that humans and the mind are complex wholes that can be broken down into single parts, and the parts interact according to strict laws. We understand the mind the same way we understand machines.

But I believe humans are different from machines. What humans are depends in part on what they think and believe about themselves. Humans are not just cells and muscles and reflexes and habits. We have a self-image, we have knowledge about ourselves, and an ideal self. And those beliefs are more important for understanding a person than the simple, interchangeable parts.

Psychologists understand the importance of self-image, at least to some degree. If they set up an experiment with students to test, say, the ways men and women work together on common tasks, they will not tell the subjects what they are testing. Instead, they will tell them they are running an experiment on timing rats in mazes, or creativity, or something else. If they told the students the truth, the students would be self-conscious, and the men and women would not behave naturally. What people believe, especially about themselves, *changes* the way they feel and think.

Imagine that you are on a basketball team, and you are practicing shooting free throws. The coach tells you that you are bending your back, but you should keep it straight. This information about yourself will change the way you shoot the ball. Just thinking about your back as you shoot will affect the process. Eventually you will modify your technique. Whenever we think about what we are doing, or learn something about how we operate, that information changes the way we do things.

The same thing applies on a larger scale to people in general. Suppose psychologists discover something about the processes of intelligence and the ways people ordinarily think. And suppose it becomes generally known. When people learn about these processes, that knowledge will *change* them. Because what people are depends in part on what they believe about themselves.

For example, if psychologists say that memory depends on associating one thing with another (like "1492" and "Columbus sailed the ocean blue"), and if people learn about association, then they will become self-conscious about memory. Some may try to associate things, others may try to prove the psychologists wrong, others may practice more. But at any rate, the new information will *change* the way people normally remember things.

This fact about people has far-reaching implications. We cannot ever *finally* understand the processes of remembering, solving problems, or other aspects of intelligence, because as soon as we learn about them, they change. We will never be able to describe those processes so that a computer could duplicate them, and thus have a mind. As soon as we described them, and people learned about them, they would change. Then the computer would not be duplicating the processes of the human mind.

People are a mystery to themselves. They always will be. And that mystery is an essential part of our self-image. It makes us feel that we are not just machines, which are thoroughly understandable. Instead, we feel that we have within us a spark of the Divine, the ultimate mystery. We feel a kind of awe toward each human being, precisely because we cannot fully understand her or him. Most important, so long as human beings are beyond our comprehension, they are also beyond our control.

Key Concepts

simulate	computer model	blind experiment
intelligent process	self-image	mystery

Critical Questions

1. According to the essay, how do computer scientists attempt to build intelligent machines?
2. Does the mentalist believe computer scientists can build computer models of hurricanes?
3. Why can't computer scientists build computers that copy the steps people take when they remember, solve problems, and do other intelligent things?
4. In psychology experiments, why do psychologists *misinform* the people who are in the experiment?
5. Is the mentalist right to say that what we discover about ourselves changes our behavior? Have people learned anything about human nature in the past

five thousand years? If so, has that knowledge had an effect on our behavior?

6. In your opinion, if we discovered that human beings are fundamentally no different from computers, would that change our self-image? Would it change the way we behave?

Methods and Techniques

ANALOGIES

The first essay is based on an *analogy* between computers and people. Philosophers often use analogies, so it is worthwhile to examine the way they work.

An analogy is a similarity between two things. *Webster* defines the word *analogy* this way: "1. similarity in some way; 2. the inference that certain resemblances imply further similarity." So whenever you say that one thing is like another thing, you are making an analogy. The most interesting analogies are between things that *seem* to be very different. For example, when the poet e.e. cummings wants to describe his lover, he says "nobody, not even the rain, has such small hands," comparing the feel of his lover's hands to the feel of rain.

While poets use analogies in the first sense (striking similarities), philosophers use them in the second sense. That is, they make *inferences* based on similarities. To make an inference is to draw a conclusion from some evidence. An analogy in this second sense begins with a similarity between two things. That is the evidence. But then it goes a step farther: it reaches a conclusion based on the similarity. This second kind of analogy is also called an analogical argument, because it is a set of reasons to believe something. It is an attempt to persuade people that some conclusion is true.

The first essay is a perfect example of this two-step process. It says that the performance, or output, of computers is very similar to the performance of people. Computers give answers to questions, give solutions to math problems, propose good moves in games, and so on, and the answers are just like the answers people give. It describes a similarity between computers' output and people's output. But then it takes the next step. We know that people produce their answers and solutions by *thinking*. Therefore, we can infer that computers probably produce their answers by thinking, too. The essay begins with the similarity in output, and then draws an inference about the *sources* of the output.

Analogical arguments are common in philosophy and elsewhere. You have already encountered one in "Design or Chance?" an essay that attempts to prove that God exists. That essay also began with a similarity (actually several similarities): it said the natural world was similar to a machine. It then took the second step and drew an inference: it said that, since all machines are created by intelligent designers, we can conclude that the natural world was probably created by an intelligent designer as well, namely God. Like "Can Computers

Think?," the earlier essay began with a set of observable similarities between two things, and on that basis, decided the two things are probably similar in *another* way (i.e., created by an intelligent designer).

How do you decide whether analogical arguments like these are strong or weak? How do you decide whether or not to accept the conclusion? There are three main things to consider: how many similarities are there, how many differences are there, and how relevant to the conclusion are the similarities and differences?

For example, the mechanist in this section tries to strengthen the argument by describing as many similarities as possible between computers' performance and people's performance. Of course the way to *refute* an analogical argument is to point out important differences between the two things compared. The essay considers several proposed differences (computers are programmed, people aren't, people are creative, computers aren't, etc.) and claims they are illusory. Or they are not *relevant* to the conclusion. For example, the mechanist admits that people have emotions and computers do not, but says that is not relevant to the conclusion that computers think.

Analogical arguments are not proofs. A mechanist does not claim to have proven that machines can be intelligent. But analogical arguments can still be good arguments. They can provide good reasons to believe something. If the similarities outweigh the differences, then it is logical to accept the conclusion.

Understanding the Dilemma

MECHANIST OR MENTALIST?

The question at the beginning of this section—Can computers think?—seems like a simple question, but actually it involves several complex questions. When mechanists or mentalists ask "Can machines think," they are asking whether or not thinking is a mechanical process. Is the human mind like a machine: repetitive, simple, rigidly bound by rules, made of a few basic parts, and so on? Or is the process of thinking completely different from mechanical behavior: intuitive, unpredictable, unanalyzable, irreducibly mental?

One question concerns the uniqueness of humans. Thinking is a large part of what makes us human. We spend a lot of time thinking, it is essential to our survival, it is highly rewarding, and other animals do not think, at least not in the way we do. Thinking is one of the defining characteristics of being human. So if *thinking* is a mechanical process, then one might say that *people* are essentially like machines. One might say this. But there may be other human characteristics that make us different from machines. For example, the mechanist says machines can think, and human thinking is a mechanical process, but humans have emotions and machines do not. Thus our emotions make us different from machines.

Other questions concern facts and meanings. After reading the two essays, you should realize that you need as much information as you can get to answer this question. You need to know more about how people actually think and what happens when people think. And you need to know more about what machines do and what they will probably do in the future. Both essays in this section discuss interesting facts about psychology and artificial intelligence.

It is easy to get sidetracked by a semantic question. You might say, "Everything depends on what you mean by the word 'think.' If you define it one way, then machines can think, but if you define it a different way, then they cannot." But notice that the first essay does not define the word "think." The mechanist's argument does not depend on any particular definition. Neither does the second essay define the word. In fact, the mentalist says we do not know what happens when we think. So, while definitions are always useful, the issue here is not entirely about how we should define the word. It is more about what actually happens when we think, and what happens when machines process information, and how similar the two processes are. It is an issue about how the mind works, not about how we decide to define a word.

One interesting part of the issue concerns teaching. Can we teach people to think, or to think better? If thinking is a mechanical process, then it follows some basic rules. It is made up of simple, easy steps, which are combined into more complex, difficult processes. It is like an internal combustion engine. When you open the hood of your car and look at the engine, it looks complicated and confusing, and it is. But if a mechanic took it apart and explained what each part did, you would see that it is made up of simple pieces that do simple things. If thinking is a mechanical process, then we can teach people about the simplest parts and easiest steps, we can teach them to follow the rules and think more effectively. On the other hand, if thinking is a mysterious process that no one can understand, then we probably cannot teach people to improve their thinking. How could we teach them to think if we do not know how it is done?

This problem is related to the issue of freedom. Do we have free will? If thinking is a mechanical process, then it follows rules. That means it is subject to cause and effect. The way you think depends on the causes that produced your thinking. Your thinking is determined by prior conditions and inputs, just like a computer's "thinking." A mentalist rejects this idea. He or she claims that our thinking is free, and no one can control or condition us.

It is also related to the issue of nature. Is nature lawful and completely understandable, or is it too vast and complex for us to understand? In other words, is nature one huge machine, which obeys strict laws that we can discover? Or are some parts of the universe beyond our comprehension? Are we part of nature, subject to laws that we can discover? Or are we different and separate from the natural world? The mechanist says nature is mechanical and we are part of nature. We can understand how the world works, including our own minds. The mentalist says parts of nature are forever mysterious, and one of those parts is our own minds.

MECHANIST

1. The behavior (or output) of people and machines is actually very similar, if you look beyond superficial things like shape and color.
2. Human beings are made up of simple parts, and human activities like thinking are made up of simple steps, so there is no reason a machine cannot go through the same steps.
3. People believe their own thinking is different from machines' thinking because they believe they created themselves, and they ignore all the teaching and learning they had, which enabled them to think.
4. Many people let their feelings get in the way of their judgment when they ask, "Can machines think?"

MENTALIST

5. The differences between people and machines are infinitely more important than the similarities.
6. People react to the environment, but they are also conscious of *themselves*, and that quality makes them unique in the world.
7. There is a great deal about the mind that we do not understand, and will probably never understand.
8. If more knowledge means we begin to see people as machines, then we should *not* acquire more knowledge; some knowledge may be detrimental to human life.

FOR FURTHER STUDY

Historical Examples

MECHANIST: A.M. Turing. "Computing Machinery and Intelligence." *Mind* 59 (1950): 433–460. The principal inventor of the computer argues in a readable style that machines can think.

MENTALIST: Jacob Bronowski. *The Identity of Man*. Doubleday, 1972. Argues for the mentalist position on the grounds that human action cannot be reduced to a program of simple rules.

OTHER SOURCES

Keith Gunderson. *Mentality and Machines*. 2nd Edition. University of Minnesota Press, 1985. A generally skeptical survey of the issues; Gunderson points out mistakes on both sides.

Douglas R. Hofstadter, Daniel C. Dennett, eds. *The Mind's I*. Basic Books, 1981. A collection of stories, articles, personal essays, and excerpts from books on identity, the sense of self, computers, free will, and introspection.

William Barrett. *The Death of the Soul: From Descartes to the Computer*. Anchor, 1986. Historical survey of ideas about the mind since Descartes, and criticism of excessive reliance on technological images or models for understanding human nature.

Margaret Boden. *Artificial Intelligence and Natural Man*. Basic Books, 1977. A detailed survey of many aspects of artificial intelligence by a mechanist.

John Searle. *Minds, Brains, and Science*. Harvard University Press, 1984. Using his famous "Chinese Room" thought experiment, Searle argues that machines cannot think, and (with qualifications) will never be able to think.

Richard Hanley. *Is Data Human?* Basic Books, 1997. Argues that machines can be persons, and explores other questions of identity raised by science fiction; informed, detailed, thoughtful.

NOTE

1. Dorothy H. Patent, *The Quest for Artificial Intelligence* (Harcourt, Brace, Jovanovich, 1986), 1.

4.5 ARE WE ALWAYS SELFISH?
PSYCHOLOGICAL EGOIST OR
PSYCHOLOGICAL ALTRUIST?

———————————————————— • ————————————————————

Think about something you did that you believed was morally right. Maybe you returned a wallet that you found, or you visited a sick friend. Think about the experience from beginning to end. Now ask yourself this: didn't you feel good after you had done it? Didn't you feel proud, or relieved that you had resisted the temptation to sit back and do nothing? If you are like most people, the answer is yes. It does feel good to do what we know is right.

But that leads to another question. Isn't it possible that you did the good deed *because* you knew it would make you feel good afterward? Isn't it possible that you did it at least in part to benefit yourself, to make yourself feel good, or at least avoid a guilty conscience? Many people say it is not only possible, but is almost certain. We may help other people, or act in accordance with our principles, but the ultimate motive is to feel better ourselves.

They point out that a person is not always completely aware of his or her motives. You may have known someone who deceived himself, or did not fully understand herself. Maybe a man at work always laughs loudest at his employer's jokes. He says he is just being friendly and does not treat his boss any differently from anyone else. But it is obvious to you that he is trying to win his employer's approval. Or a woman wears a very short skirt. She says it is because these skirts are the fashion this year. But it is obvious to you that she likes to flirt with the men at her job.

So how can you be sure that you did the good deed for completely unselfish reasons? Isn't it possible that you can deceive yourself, just as other people deceive themselves? It is possible, and it is a problem that philosophers worry about. They worry about their understanding of themselves, since they are very concerned about their beliefs and values. They want to know what they really believe and really value. And they worry about the general problem: how can people be sure about their own motives? Is it possible that everyone's motive is always selfish?

The first essay in this section takes the view that people are always selfish. That view is called "psychological egoism." The opposite view is "psychological altruism," and it is defended in the second essay.

YES: PSYCHOLOGICAL EGOIST

"No Free Lunch"

A friend of mine told me about his grandfather's 80th birthday party. His grandfather had a fascinating life—sailed around the world in the merchant marine, sold insurance door to door, worked in vaudeville, ran his own import-export business, married three times. After the champagne, my friend asked the old man what was the most important lesson he had learned from all his varied adventures. He smiled and said, "That's easy. There is no free lunch."

My friend's grandfather may have become cynical in his old age. But he sincerely believed that everyone looks out for himself. In philosophical terms, he was a "psychological egoist." A psychological egoist believes that people are basically self-centered. He or she thinks that everything people do is designed to benefit themselves in some way.

The opposite point of view is psychological altruism. If you believe that, at least sometimes, a person will help someone else without wanting or expecting *any* reward, then you are a psychological altruist.

I have often wished that I could talk with my friend's grandfather. I wanted to ask him why he was so pessimistic. I never got the chance, but I tried to imagine what he would say. With his rich experience of people in all sorts of situations, I think he would point to examples. Look at the average business-man or woman, or the average shopper, he would say. Look at the lover pursuing his or her elusive prey. Look at the children playing. All around us we see people doing things to benefit themselves.

The examples are not completely convincing, however, because the altruist can point to many examples of people who want to help others. Look at the doctor who goes to the emergency room in the middle of the night. Look at the corporation president who gives to charity. Look at the woman who gives her friend flowers, just because her friend likes flowers. If these things happen—if just *one* person ever acts unselfishly—then the egoist is wrong.

But I have a feeling that my friend's grandfather would not give up so easily. An egoist can take the altruist's examples and *reinterpret* them, so they become examples of self-centered actions. The doctor who goes to the emergency room may do it for the money instead of for the love of humanity. Maybe the doctor does it for the admiration and respect he or she receives. Would the corporation president who gives to charity still make the donation if there was no tax break for it? Judging from the president's fierce pursuit of profits, I would say probably not.

An action that *seems* to be benevolent turns out to be self-centered. This kind of reinterpretation is a very powerful tool, but altruists may not realize how powerful it is. An egoist can point to cases where a person may not even be conscious of his or her own selfish desires, but acts on them nevertheless. The woman who gave her friend flowers may *subconsciously* want something in return—affection, loyalty—without knowing that is why she did it.

The egoist can also look for long-term benefits. A person can do things that are difficult, painful, and appear to be completely selfless. A mother works hard everyday for her baby. But she may know, in the back of her mind, that when she grows old, she herself will need help, and her child is the person she can count on to help her. Her work may not produce benefits for her now, but it is a means to *future* benefits. Or the public-spirited man may have decided early in life that a person is happier if he is concerned for his neighbor. He may have decided that, in the long run, it pays to help others unselfishly.

There is another way to reinterpret actions that seem altruistic. The egoist says a person can try to benefit himself or herself by *avoiding pain*. In other words, even if an action does not produce any benefit, conscious or unconscious, short-term or long-term, it can still be self-centered, so long as it is better than the alternative. The altruist's trump card is the example of the soldier who gives up his life for his mates. Surely that man expects no benefits from his action, the altruist says. But it is possible that the soldier thought about the prospect of *not* doing it, and living with a guilty conscience, or with a reputation of being too cautious, or even cowardly. Never being able to look anyone in the eye. Maybe he wanted to avoid that pain and embarrassment, which would last his whole life. In a crisis, just the image of such a life, occurring in a split second, might be enough to cause him to act.

So, the egoist can reinterpret actions in several ways. That makes egoism much more plausible than altruism. After all, can the altruist reinterpret *any* actions that seem self-centered, and show that they are actually benevolent? Are there any cases where a person seems to be benefiting himself, but has an unconscious desire to help others, or thinks he is helping others in the long term? I cannot think of a single example.

It is possible that every action turns out to be a self-centered action, when we go beyond appearances. My friend's grandfather lived long enough and hard enough to understand people through and through. I have no doubt that he knew all about these reinterpretations, and more. He knew that often people's actions are not what they seem. The more I think about his lesson in life and how he might explain it, the more I feel that he may be right.

Key Concepts

psychological egoist	generalization	self-centered
altruist	motive	subconscious desire

Critical Questions

1. What is it about the grandfather that makes him believable, or an authority on the question of selfishness?
2. Does the psychological egoist believe that most people are selfish most of the time, or that all people are selfish all of the time? How would he or she define the term "selfish"?
3. Why does the psychological egoist say that the corporation president probably has a self-centered motive for giving money to charity? Would the same reasoning apply to an average doctor who goes to the emergency room?
4. "Help the needy without expecting any reward. If you live by this principle, you may expect to be rewarded." Can a person believe this? Is it a contradiction?
5. The essay says a person can give up his life for his friends, but his action still might be self-centered. How? How can a person expect any advantage for himself when he will be dead?
6. The essay says it is possible to reinterpret actions that appear to be unselfish, and find selfish motives behind them. Does that prove that the actions really are selfish?
7. What would psychological egoists have to know before they would admit that an action really is altruistic? What kind of example or evidence would convince them? Would anything?

NO: PSYCHOLOGICAL ALTRUIST
"Is Love Selfish?"

November 15, 20__. I thought this relationship would last. I thought this was it, the genuine article, real love. Now I'm not sure.

We had a fight. It wasn't too bad, no broken dishes. But something else broke. My image of her is shattered. I thought I knew her, knew her real feelings, knew how she thinks. But what she said sounded so different from the woman I thought I knew.

She said people in love are in the relationship just to please themselves. Nobody cares about anyone else!

No, that's not exactly what she said. I've got to concentrate and think through this if I'm going to put things back together. Let me think.

She said that when two people are in love, each one cares about the other, of course, but each one cares so much, and does all these crazy things, because doing them makes *himself* or *herself* happy, not because it makes the other person happy. Yes, that's it. That's how it started.

I asked her if *she* felt that way. Did she make my favorite casserole and laugh at my jokes because it made *her* feel good? She tried to change the subject, but I wouldn't let her. Finally she said she likes to cook for me because I enjoy it so much, I love the food and being together, and seeing me enjoy the meal makes *her* happy. And *that's* why she did it. For herself, really.

Then I asked her if she thought *I* was in the relationship for the same reason, for myself. She said yes. Oh God! You think you know a person, and then something like this happens.

Now wait a minute. I'm a mature person, I'm intelligent. I don't want to overreact and do something I'll regret later. So what happened next? We argued, it got out of control, I said some stupid things, she went to the bedroom and slammed the door. Now I need to think about what I want to say when she comes out again. Or tomorrow at breakfast if I'm sleeping on the couch tonight.

I'm not going to sweep everything under the rug. It will just come up again. So, is she right? Is love selfish? Am I in this for *myself*? No, dammit. I would do anything for her. She's so gentle and kind, and yet strong at the same time. Smarter than I am, to tell the truth. And great with her kids in school. I love it when she talks about her work. She can mimic her students and principal so well it makes me laugh till I cry. But she's a good person. I'm really proud of her volunteer work with "America Reads." And at night, when she snuggles beside me, I feel so warm and right and protective. I really do love her.

Hmmm. When I look at what I just wrote, I realize that it's all me, me, me. I say I love her because she makes me feel good. "I feel so warm." But that's how lovers talk. Could she be right? In fact, she said that when a woman falls in love, all she thinks about is her lover, seeing him, and doing things for him. Her excitement is so strong, and her joy so intense, that she almost forgets everything else. She can talk for hours with her friends about her new lover. She is much more tied up in her own feelings and her own happiness than a person who is *not* in love.

But she's wrong. There is more to love than that. That is more like infatuation than love. When a man falls head over heels for a woman (infatuated), he wants to please her, to bring her things, to look good for her, to take her places and be proud of her. He does things *for her*. But at the same time, those things make him feel terrific, like a man. He does things for her, *because* doing things for her makes *him* feel good. Pleasing her is a means to please himself.

But that is infatuation, not love. We have grown beyond that stage. Sure I want to please her. But she's part of my life now, a part of me. What I feel about her isn't joy so much as . . . well, *love*. It's deeper, a kind of rightness, or warmth, or being part of something that is better than myself alone.

What if she doesn't agree with me? Well so what? Who does she think she is anyway? What makes her the expert? Miss Know-it-all. How does *she* know what I feel? She can't get inside my skin. Maybe *she* is in this for herself, but she doesn't know what's going on inside of *me,* or anybody else for that matter. How can she say everybody always wants to please themselves? All she knows is herself. Maybe *she* does, the rat, but she can't know why other people do what they do. What an arrogant fool!

Oh no. I lost it again. I've got to control my temper or else we'll never get anywhere. Let's see, I was thinking about love and infatuation. They aren't the same. What's the difference? How can I convince Alice that they're different?

If I take her out for pizza and a movie, but she's in a bad mood, it doesn't bother me. In fact, I'm concerned about why she's in a bad mood. I found the movie times and the restaurant because I thought she would enjoy it. But I didn't consciously plan to do something to please her because I knew that pleasing her would give *me* a thrill. I didn't think of myself at all. I know that I didn't, because when she didn't respond, I wasn't hurt or dissatisfied, but instead I was concerned for her.

Although I must admit that, in the beginning, I did think about how much fun it would be, for me, to see her enjoying the great evening I had planned. And if she didn't, I would have been hurt. But that was two years ago.

I think that is the difference between infatuation and love, between selfishness and unselfishness. In both infatuation and love, one person does something for another, to make the other happy. But when a man is infatuated, he consciously thinks of the joy and happiness he will feel when he does it. He does something for his lover and for himself, in fact, ultimately for himself. And if it doesn't work, he feels hurt. But when a man is in love, he does things for his lover, and doesn't consciously think of himself at all. That is not selfish. Even if pleasing his lover does make him happy, he doesn't plan it that way, he doesn't think of his own happiness, so he is not selfish.

It can go farther. My father cared for my mother when she was dying of cancer. He had to make a lot of tough decisions, about his career, about having her at home, about being cheerful. He could have taken an easier path, she would have understood. But he loved her. He did things for her, and he knew that they would be more difficult, more painful for him, than other things he could have done. He wasn't doing it to make himself feel better. He wasn't afraid of a guilty conscience. He did think of himself, but what he thought was that he should give that part of his life to her. She needed it more than he did.

I hope I can be like my father. I hope I can love someone that much. I know it's possible, because he did it. Love is not selfish. Maybe Alice and I aren't there yet, but we can be. We can make it if we try hard enough.

Key Concepts

selfish	love	expectation
unselfish	infatuation	sacrifice

Critical Questions

1. What is the girlfriend's point of view (not the writer's)? Does she think a person can do something to make someone else happy?
2. The psychological altruist in this essay describes why he loves his girlfriend and what it feels like to be in love. Does that description show that he is unselfish?
3. What is the crucial difference between love and infatuation? Does a person who is infatuated want to do things for his or her lover?
4. What evidence does the essay mention that one can do things for others without expecting any benefits for oneself?
5. The psychological altruist says his girlfriend does not know what is going on in his mind. Why is that important? How is it relevant to their disagreement?
6. What do you think a psychological egoist would say about the altruist's examples?
7. Can you think of any possible example that would convince psychological egoists such as the girlfriend that they are mistaken? Would anything convince them?

Methods and Techniques

GENERALIZATIONS

A psychological egoist believes that everyone always tries to gain some benefit for himself or herself. Everything we do is intended to benefit us in some way. The egoist is making a very broad *generalization*. A generalization is a statement about some or all of the members of some class. The egoist is talking about the class of people and claims that they are all selfish. Actually, if we want to be precise, we should say the psychological egoist is talking about the class of people's actions. They are all motivated by a desire for personal gain, the egoist believes. But you can make generalizations about any class of things. The statement "Most fire fighters are men" is a generalization about the class of fire fighters. "Some birds cannot fly" is about the class of birds. "All the states in the United States have two Senators" is about the class of states. The opposite of a generalization is a particular statement. It is a statement about a particular

object or event. For example, "Smith is a fire fighter" is about the particular individual, Smith.

Since philosophers are trying to understand common human experiences,
they make a lot of generalizations. From looking at the previous examples, you
can see that generalizations vary in scope, or breadth. The broadest generalizations are about *all* the members of some class, and are called "universal" generalizations. "All the states in the United States have two Senators" is a universal generalization. "Every parking place was taken" is also a universal
generalization because it is about all the parking places. Statements about *some*
members of a class of things are called "limited" generalizations. The statements
"Most fire fighters are men," "Many people are allergic to pollen," and "A few
volcanoes in Mexico are active" are all limited generalizations because they are
about some, but not all, the members of different groups.

Generalizations are very common in writing and in conversation. We may
use more generalizations than particular statements. Of course the obvious question about a generalization is "How do you know it's true?" For example, how
does a person know that *most* fire fighters are men? There are thousands of fire
departments in the United States. It would take weeks or months to visit every
one and count the men and women. If one has not visited every fire department, then should we say one cannot know that most fire fighters are men? If
a sociologist says "Sixty-five percent of women work outside the home," must
every woman be asked about her work before the sociologist can make the generalization?

Fortunately there is a way to know that a generalization is probably true
short of surveying an entire class of things. The method is to examine a *sample*
of the class. A sample is simply a part of a class. For example, the government
might write letters to two hundred fire departments around the country asking
them how many fire fighters are men and how many are women. The two hundred fire departments are a sample of the whole class of fire departments, which
may include several thousand departments. If almost all of the fire fighters in
the *sample* are men, then the government will conclude that almost all of the
fire fighters in *all* the departments are men. The government makes an inference from the sample to the whole class, on the grounds that the makeup of the
sample is like the makeup of the whole class. It makes a generalization about
the whole class of fire departments, and says "Most fire fighters in the United
States are men."

All of us make generalizations based on samples every day. But some generalizations are sound and reliable, and some aren't. It all depends on the quality of the sample. A sample can be *representative* of the whole class, or it can be
weighted, and a reliable generalization must be based on a representative sample. A representative sample is one whose makeup really is the same as the
makeup of the whole class. But a weighted sample is one whose makeup is different from the whole class. For example, if you want to make a generalization
about fire fighters, but you only talk to men over the age of 50, then your sam-

ple is weighted. The best way to make a sample representative is to make it as large as possible. Or you can try to select a sample in a way that makes it similar to the whole class. Philosophers must examine generalizations, determine the samples they are based on, and then judge whether the sample is representative, and whether it supports the generalization.

Understanding the Dilemma

PSYCHOLOGICAL EGOIST OR PSYCHOLOGICAL ALTRUIST?

Is everyone always selfish? That is the question at issue in this section. A psychological egoist says yes, and a psychological altruist says no. Where do you stand? Are you a psychological egoist or a psychological altruist? This is not just a question about your own behavior (do you ever help others without expecting any benefits whatever?), but is also a question about everyone's behavior. Does anyone ever help others without expecting any benefits?

In building this part of your worldview it is important to understand exactly what "selfish" means. A psychological egoist is not saying that everyone is selfish in the ordinary sense of the word "selfish." If you see a small child who has several toys, but who refuses to share them with any playmates, then you would say the child is being selfish. A psychological egoist does not believe that everyone always acts like the child. Obviously people sometimes share what they have and do things for others. But do they help others because they expect something in return? Do they share because they hope that others will share what they have in the future, or because they want to avoid being condemned? The egoist says yes. We all consider the costs and benefits of different actions, and do what we think will bring us the greatest rewards in the long run.

Is that true? Is that how human motivation works? The psychological altruist says no. Sometimes people are not selfish, even in this narrower sense of the word "selfish." It may be difficult, and it may be rare, but sometimes people make genuine sacrifices for others, without expecting any kind of benefits whatever. Maybe people are selfish most of the time, or much of the time, the altruist thinks, but not *all* the time.

The issue is about what motivates people and how people make decisions. It is similar to the issue of ethical egoism, which I mentioned in Section 3.1, but not the same. An ethical egoist says individuals *ought* to look out for themselves all the time and do what benefits themselves. An ethical altruist disagrees, and says people ought to help others. The two alternatives in this section are different. A psychological egoist says people *in fact* look out for themselves all the time. Maybe that is good or maybe it is bad; the psychological egoist doesn't say. He or she is just describing the way people actually behave. The ethical egoist, however, is prescribing the way people ought to behave, not the way they actually behave. Ethical altruism and psychological altruism are different in the same respect.

If you think about these two issues—how people do behave and how they ought to behave—you will see that they are necessarily connected. For example, if you are a psychological egoist then you cannot be an ethical altruist. In other words, if you believe that everyone is always selfish, then you cannot believe that people *ought* to be unselfish; because (you already believe) it is impossible to be unselfish. On the other hand, if you are a psychological altruist, then you can be an ethical altruist. Are the two issues connected in any other ways? Can a psychological altruist be an ethical egoist, for example? You should decide for yourself, and you should think about these kinds of connections in constructing your worldview.

Your beliefs about this issue are an important part of your worldview, but how can you decide who is right? You could flip a coin, but that would not satisfy you for very long. A more intelligent approach is to look at the two essays, and see how the authors decided. The first essay looks at a very wide range of experience, including the grandfather's observations over many years, and even people's unconscious desires. It examines many different kinds of cases. The egoist decides that the vast number of cases of selfishness show that everyone is selfish. In the second essay, the altruist talks about some cases, like the example of his father. And he also looks into his own mind and heart. His knowledge of his own motives seems to be what convinces him. Which method is more accurate? Which method do you trust, the egoist's or the altruist's? A wide range of examples, or your own inner experience? Remember that this is only a means of answering the main question of this section, which is, "Are you a psychological egoist or a psychological altruist?"

PSYCHOLOGICAL EGOIST

1. There is nothing "immoral," or horrible, about being selfish, since everyone is selfish in a basic sense.
2. If you didn't expect to benefit in *any* way from doing something, then you wouldn't have any reason to do it.
3. A person can do things for others and still be self-centered.
4. Since we are all members of the same species (*Homo sapiens*), we must all be psychologically similar in some ways.

PSYCHOLOGICAL ALTRUIST

5. If every individual thought only of himself or herself all the time, the world would be a dismal, terrifying place.
6. Many people are in love, many people value learning, a just society, a clean environment, and other things besides their own benefits or pleasures.
7. I know in my own case that I sometimes do things without expecting any rewards of any kind from anyone.

8. The fact that many people, or even most people, are selfish does not prove that all are.

FOR FURTHER STUDY

Historical Examples

PSYCHOLOGICAL EGOIST: Paul Henri Holbach. *The System of Nature.* Garland, 1984. Originally published in 1770. In chap. 11 of vol. 1, entitled "Of the System of Man's Free Agency," Holbach exhaustively analyzes people's motives and tries to show that they are always self-serving in some way.

PSYCHOLOGICAL ALTRUIST: Joseph Butler. *Fifteen Sermons Preached at the Rolls Chapel.* Lincoln-Rembrandt, 1986. Originally published in 1726. Butler is even more subtle and penetrating than Holbach; he paints a complex picture of human motivation, which includes altruism.

OTHER SOURCES

James Rachels. *The Elements of Moral Philosophy.* Random House, 1986. Chap. 5 is a careful, detailed critique of psychological egoism.

Alfred C. Ewing. *Ethics.* English Universities Press, 1953. Chap. 2 presents the arguments on both sides.

Michael A. Wallach. *Psychology's Sanction for Selfishness.* W.H. Freeman, 1983. A critique of egoism in contemporary psychology, emphasizing Freud and Maslow.

Paul Zweig. *The Heresy of Self-Love.* Basic Books, 1968. Historical survey of attitudes toward egoism, with an emphasis on literature.

Jane Mansbridge, ed. *Beyond Self-Interest.* University of Chicago Press, 1990. A collection of articles that defend psychological altruism and apply that view to various aspects of society and politics.

Robert Ardrey. *The Territorial Imperative.* Atheneum, 1968. An interpretation of some facts about animal behavior and evolution that suggest that mankind has a territorial instinct.

Alfie Kohn. *The Brighter Side of Human Nature.* Basic Books, 1990. See chap. 7, "Altruism Lost," and chap. 8, "Altruism Regained."

David M. Holley. *Self-Interest and Beyond.* Paragon House, 1999. Argues that self-interest depends on deep questions about the kind of self one wants to be.

Current Controversy

4.6 ARE THE DIFFERENCES BETWEEN MEN AND WOMEN PHILOSOPHICALLY SIGNIFICANT?
UNIFIER OR COMPLEMENTER?

———————————————————— • ————————————————————

A big part of philosophy is trying to organize all the questions we want to ask in some sort of order. On the topic of human nature, people ask many questions: What does it mean to be human? How are people different from animals? Can we make any broad generalizations about people? Are people basically good or basically bad? Do people have instincts, or are they entirely shaped by their environments?

Formulating the right questions is an important step in developing your worldview. In my classes students often resist the idea that we can find general laws of human nature. Many insist that every individual is unique, and any laws of human nature would overlook important features of some people's individuality. General laws restrict our freedom.

Of course they are right that everyone is unique and different from everyone else. On the other hand, all humans are human by definition, and therefore similar to other people. My students understand that people are different in some ways and similar in others. They do not want to say that we cannot find any general laws of human nature, but that differences are *more important* than similarities. Even if we find a common human nature, it doesn't matter. What matters is individuality, freedom, and self-realization.

They may be right, or they may not. But before entering that debate, it is important to recognize that we are asking a different question. We began by asking what it means to be human, or whether we can find general laws of human nature. But now we are asking whether the similarities among people are *important.* When we ask how all humans are alike, we are asking a factual, scientific question. Biologists, anthropologists, and psychologists try to answer it. But when we ask what similarities and differences are important, we are asking a more complicated, philosophical question.

Human nature is a very broad topic, and one way to narrow the focus is to think about men and women. Gender is one difference among people, but how important is it? The first essay in this section argues that it is not important. The writer wants to emphasize the unity among all people, so anyone who agrees can be called a "unifier." The second essay claims that differences between men and women are important, especially for philosophy. Men and women do not have the same talents, but complementary talents. Each can help the other. So one who accepts the second point of view can be called a "complementer."

NO: UNIFIER

"Men, Women, and People"

When I was in elementary school, my favorite part of the day was recess. All the students could go outside and play games. But one thing puzzled me. Boys and girls were always segregated. Boys played softball or soccer, and girls played volleyball or badminton, or skipped rope. I wanted to play softball. I was better at it than some of the boys, as I proved on weekends when the neighborhood kids played. I didn't look so different from boys. Boys came in all sizes and shapes, and in fact the differences between large and small boys were greater than the differences between medium boys and medium girls. When I asked why I wasn't allowed to play with the boys, I received all the usual question-begging answers: "Softball is a boys' game," "Boys and girls are different," "You wouldn't enjoy playing soccer with the boys," "Volleyball is better for girls."

Perhaps it was that experience with classifying people as boys and girls that led me to study law, because law depends so much on classifying people and actions. For example, if one person kills another, the person is guilty of homicide. But there are different types of homicide. If the person kills maliciously, the law says it is murder. But if the person kills accidentally, it is manslaughter. And there are further subdivisions within those categories.

I have always been intrigued by the ways we classify people, particularly men and women. The more I thought about it, the more it seemed to me that our classifications are socially constructed. That does not mean they are arbitrary, but it does mean they depend on choices we make as a society, and we could make other choices if we wanted to. People are similar and different in countless ways. Society decides which differences are important and which aren't, and society's decisions change over time.

To understand how gender is socially constructed, we need to think about the process of classifying in general. Classifying things is one of the most basic psychological operations. To classify means to divide a group of things into subgroups. For example, I classify the clothes in my closet into the subgroups of skirts, blouses, pants, and shoes. Colleges classify students by the number of courses they have taken: seniors have taken more than juniors, juniors more than sophomores, and sophomores more than freshmen. Librarians use the Dewey decimal system, or the Library of Congress system, to classify books by their subject matter: philosophy, religion, social science, and so on. Each of these groups can be divided even farther. The world is so complex that we must continually classify things to make sense of it all.

The same group of things can be classified in different ways. When I wash my clothes, I sort them into light and dark, not skirts and blouses. I could also classify them by color, as blue, green, brown, and yellow. Or by fabric: cotton, wool, silk, nylon, and rayon. Or size, or weight, or many other ways. Books can be classified not by subject but by difficulty or intended audience. Some are suitable for children, some for adolescents, some for adults. And students can be classified in hundreds of ways: by country or state of origin, by age, size, job experience, favorite music, hair style, and many others. Each classification is independent of the others. If I divide students into citizens and noncitizens, each of those two groups might include seniors, juniors, sophomores, and freshmen.

Everyone understands the basic process of classification, but some people have never thought about the most important point of all: none of the different ways of classifying a group of things is inherently better than another. The usefulness of a classification depends on one's purpose. If my purpose is to find clothes in the morning, then I classify them by function (skirt, blouse), but if my purpose is to wash them, a different classification is better. If my purpose is not to read books but to pack them in boxes for storage, then the best classification is by size: 5 inches long, 9 inches, 12 inches. Colleges sort students into majors to encourage them to acquire specialized knowledge in one area. If a college wants to recognize academic excellence, it can classify students by grades and place some on the Dean's list.

Which classification of students is natural, the classification based on courses taken, area of specialization, age, or grades? None is "natural." They are all legitimate. Each classification serves a particular purpose. Some classifications may be more difficult to apply than others, or may allow separate classes to overlap. For example, sorting students into those with and without work experience is not easy. What counts as "work experience"? But employers are very interested in that quality, and ask students about their work experience just so they can classify them. Their classification is just as "natural" or real as a classification based on age or courses taken.

Are *any* classifications more "natural" than others? The word "natural" makes us think of the natural world, so let's consider animals. Biologists classify animals as single-celled and multicellular, as vertebrates and invertebrates, as fish, reptiles, birds, and mammals. But a cook might classify animals as fatty or lean, a good or poor source of protein, expensive or cheap, best broiled, baked, or fried. A farmer might classify them by their fur, their skin, or the type of leather they provide. A hiker might classify them as aggressive or shy, swift or slow, poisonous or harmless. Different people are *interested* in different aspects of animals. Biologists are interested in the evolution of animals, so their classification reflects the development of animals over the centuries from simple to complex. But the characteristics biologists emphasize are no more "natural" than any other characteristics. Being poisonous or harmless is just as natural as having a backbone or not. The hiker's purpose is different from the biologist's, but both classifications are equally "natural."

Since classification is such a basic psychological operation, and since humans are social beings, we take a strong interest in classifying ourselves. The group of human beings can be divided in an infinite number of ways, by age, appearance, native language, income, and others. Our basic purposes and goals will determine which classification we use and which we take as fundamental.

One of our basic purposes is reproduction, and therefore we classify people as male and female. In fact, our drive to reproduce is so strong that we elevate a simple biological feature above all others, and even suppress others to make the biological functions stand out. Men women in most societies are taught to accentuate the physical traits that distinguish them from the opposite sex. Women have often been taught to develop their caring, nurturing, child-rearing side, and men have been taught to develop their competitive, money-making side. Women wear cosmetics and men grow facial hair. Many societies in different periods of history have encouraged this division of labor. Even in the United States, women were not allowed to vote until 1920; they were not allowed to work in many jobs until we needed their labor in the Second World War. Today women still face discrimination. Many people assume that all a women can do, or even wants to do, is bear children. All her other character-istics and talents are ignored. Men are victims of this simple-minded classifi-cation as well. They are sometimes taught that their identity is "being a real man," where that is defined as fathering a child, or engaging in sex. The abil-ity and desire for sex becomes their obsession. They are psychologically reduced to sex machines, just as women are psychologically reduced to baby-making machines.

But it is crucial to understand that we do not have to think this way. Clas-sification changes over time. Our basic purposes, such as survival and repro-duction, do not change, but our *means* of achieving those ends do change. And since no system of classification is inherently natural or better than another, the ways we sort things change as well. In the future, we may not sort people into male and female. The biological traits related to reproduction may be as unim-portant in classifications of people as the length of legs or the size of muscles are now. We won't even notice them.

In the past, people classified other people on the basis of what they could do with their hands. They were carpenters, weavers, cobblers, blacksmiths, and so on. The purpose was to organize labor in the most efficient way to increase everyone's prosperity. We still have the same goal, but our means of reaching it are different. Now we classify most people on the basis of what they can do with their minds, not their hands. We are engineers, accountants, lawyers, sales people, computer programmers. The old classification is changing and becom-ing obsolete, even though our basic purpose is the same.

Another example is transportation. Two hundred years ago if you wanted to travel you had three choices: you could walk, go by horse or carriage, or sail. Journeys were classified in those three ways: foot, horse, boat. But the steam engine created a new means of transport. Then came the internal combustion engine and the airplane. Now, if you want to travel you consider plane, train, or car (possibly ship, but probably not a sailing ship). Our means of traveling have changed, and that has inevitably changed our classifications. We think of walking more as a form of exercise and less as a practical means of travel. We can recognize a horse when we see one, but we never think of it or classify it as a way to get to work. The same radical changes in perception can occur with the categories "man" and "woman."

Our means of traveling changed gradually over many decades, but our means of having children are changing more rapidly. Humans will always want to reproduce, but like everything else, the ways in which we reproduce are changing. One of the biggest changes was the birth control pill. Before the 1960s, sexual intercourse was inextricably linked to having children. Thinking about having sex meant thinking about having children, and vice versa. But now these activities are separate. People can engage in sex without pregnancy, and can get pregnant without sexual intercourse. In vitro fertilization (i.e., in a laboratory) and artificial insemination are just two of the common techniques available. Our whole way of thinking about reproduction is changing.

Another step is surrogate mothers. Some women want to separate having children from getting pregnant, and we now have the means to do that. A woman can supply an egg and her partner can supply the sperm to fertilize it in vitro, and the fertilized egg can be implanted in another woman's uterus. The surrogate mother, or "birth mother," carries the growing embryo and fetus for nine months and gives birth to the couple's child. The genetic mother makes the same contribution to the new child as the father. She provides her sex cells containing half the genetic material. Once the child is born, she and her husband or partner could continue to share the child-rearing duties equally as well.

Soon we will have artificial wombs, just as we have artificial hearts, artificial kidneys, artificial lungs and limbs. We won't need to pay a woman to bear a child in her own womb. Then reproduction will be completely separated from sex and pregnancy, and men and women can play equal roles. Women can continue to work while the fetus grows, as men do now, and both mother and father can take maternity leave, or work part-time, during the child's early years.

Reproduction will still be important to us, but when the means of reproduction change, our ways of classifying people will change as well. Instead of focusing on the biological, reproductive features of individuals, we can attend to other characteristics, other talents, and other traits of personality. We will still recognize males and females, as we recognize physically strong and weak people now, or sharp-sighted and near-sighted people. In the distant past, when prehistoric humans were fighting for survival, those classifications were vitally important for hunting and protection. But now we have better means of protecting ourselves. Those classifications do not help us achieve our goals, and most people ignore them or are completely unaware of them. The same evolution could occur with the physical differences between men and women. In the future, being male or female may be as unimportant as being left-handed, or blonde, or over 6 feet tall.

Key Concepts

classification	means and ends	surrogate mother
categories	reproduction	artificial womb

Critical Questions

1. According to the unifier, is it better to classify students by number of courses taken, by income, or by grades?
2. Is there no difference between natural classifications and artificial or "human-made" classifications?
3. Do you think the changes in our common means of transportation have changed our ways of perceiving things such as horses, boats, or the act of walking? Could our perceptions of human males and females change fundamentally?
4. If one of your female classmates wore "men's clothes," or a male classmate wore "women's clothes," how would you feel about it? Are people who challenge traditional classifications dangerous to society?
5. If scientists developed a safe, reliable artificial womb, like the incubators hospitals use now, would the majority of women who wanted children use the machine, or would the majority get pregnant as women always have, in your opinion?
6. Do you think a unifier would approve of same-sex marriages?

YES: COMPLEMENTER

"Who's Afraid of Difference?"

Is philosophy sexist? The answer is obviously yes, in one sense of the question. All of the well-known philosophers in the Western tradition (and in other traditions as well) were men. Plato, Aristotle, Aquinas, Descartes, and so on to the twentieth century, were all men. Women were almost never permitted to study or teach philosophy, and if some natural philosophical genius appeared, her writing was not published. Female mystics and poets were permissible, but not philosophers. Thus philosophy is an exclusive male club.

But is philosophy itself sexist? Are the methods and concepts and theories in philosophy biased against women? I want to argue that the answer to this question is also yes, although it isn't as obvious. Concepts and methods cannot intentionally exclude women, or oppress them, as men can. But concepts and methods can be biased. To uncover the sexism in philosophy itself, we must first recognize some fundamental features of male and female psychology. And then we will see how those psychological tendencies biased philosophy against women.

In discussing men and women we must be very careful about making generalizations. Women have been victimized forever by unfounded generalizations, or stereotypes, that say that women in general are weak, excessively emotional, gossips, or addicted to childish fantasies of romance. History should make everyone, especially women, aware of how damaging and painful stereotypes can be. On the other hand, the fact that most generalizations are false does not imply that all are. If we are careful, we can make sound generalizations about the physical world, culture, and men and women. We simply have to base our generalizations on the broadest range of accurate data that we can, recognize exceptions, and always remember that additional observation might overturn any generalization.

With these caveats in mind, I will describe some general features of men's and women's experience that have far-reaching consequences. One feature is that women get pregnant, carry the fetus for nine months, go through labor and birth, and nurse babies. Men do none of these. In most societies—probably all societies—these biological connections lead women to interact with young children much more than men do. Until the children are weaned, women must nurse them several times a day. They continue feeding, cleaning, and comforting children more frequently then men do throughout childhood. They shape children through rewards and reprimands. Even when fathers help, most children's early, crucial experiences are primarily with their mothers. Cultures differ in small details, but everywhere women are the primary care givers for infants and toddlers.

Everyone's early experiences influence his or her personality. One vital challenge infants face is to develop an identity, or a sense of themselves as distinct beings with their own feelings and choices. A major part of creating a self is imitation. Little boys try to imitate their fathers and little girls try to imitate their mothers. Also important is learning what not to do or feel. Boys and girls distinguish themselves from the opposite parent. But these processes are different for boys and girls. The emotional ties of security and dependence between young children and their mothers are very strong. Boys must struggle to separate themselves and think of themselves as different from the mother. They must learn to suppress their natural feelings, their tendency to cling to her and depend on her for absolutely everything, including their emotions and choices. Instead, as males, they must identify with the father, who is comparatively absent and distant. The father has less physical contact, offers less comfort, less play, and less control than the mother.

Little girls, in contrast, learn to identify with the mother, who is constantly present. They do not need to separate themselves from their mothers to the degree that boys do. Consequently, their sense of self is more relational: their own thoughts, feelings, and desires are intertwined with their mother's, and later, with other people's. They do not feel the boy's need to draw sharp boundaries between self and other. On the contrary, the little girl must experience the merging with her mother as the most natural and satisfying way of finding herself. She wants to be just like her mother, and share in her mother's thoughts and feelings.

Furthermore, the emotional environment of 1- and 2-year-old children is the most intense imaginable. Living in the moment, and lacking interpretive concepts or knowledge, each experience creates the purest joy or the starkest terror, blissful contentment, or overwhelming desire, often in rapid succession. The center and source of these feelings is the mother. At this early stage of development, children do not distinguish between self, mother, and world; all are interdependent. Since the little girl identifies herself with her mother, and her mother continually elicits strong feelings in her, she accepts strong emotions and the emotional coloration of the world as normal and necessary. The little boy, on the other hand, must loosen the tie to the mother and dampen the strong emotional interactions. By shifting his focus to the father, he learns to suppress some of his feelings.

The results of these psychodynamics of family life are important. We are not discussing the fact that boys and girls internalize the values and behaviors that their culture expects of them. The process we are examining is deeper. Unlike culturally determined gender roles, it is virtually universal. In the earliest formation of a self, boys must identify with a comparatively distant parent, and girls must identify with a present parent. As a result, the structures of men's and women's personalities are different. The differences are a matter of degree, but they are important. Men see themselves as independent and self-directing; any dependency or merging with others is perceived by men as a threat. Women tend to value relationships with others, and define themselves in terms of their personal relationships. They seek interdependency. Men tend to suppress their emotional responses, whereas women regard them as a natural part of the world. To many women, men seem cold and lonely; to many men, women seem emotional and dependent. Of course there are exceptions to these generalizations. But since the mother-centered pattern of child rearing is so pervasive, and the process of forming an identity is so fundamental to personality, the generalizations probably apply in some degree to most people.

Recognizing the differences between men and women could help us improve and balance our understanding of ourselves. In particular, it could have a liberating effect in philosophy. Women's distinctive experience has been excluded from Western philosophy. In metaphysics, ethics, and the theory of knowledge, among other areas, the male perspective and masculinist assumptions have dominated. Indeed, many women have even been persuaded to accept masculinist assumptions and values as their own, and have denigrated or suppressed their distinct feminine nature. But uncovering male bias in traditional philosophy can only benefit it and remove a limitation. By adding their own contrasting voices and ideas to the dialogue, women can correct and improve our understanding of human nature, morality, and knowledge.

Modern philosophy, it is often said, began with Descartes, and Descartes held a very masculinist concept of the self. Descartes wanted to find something he could be absolutely certain of, and he began his search for certainty by discarding things he could *not* be certain of. He could not be certain that what he read in books was true, or even that what others told him directly was true. He could not be certain of what he saw with his own eyes, because sometimes his eyes tricked him. He said he couldn't even be certain that he was awake instead of dreaming, because when he was dreaming he thought that he was awake. He finally decided that the only thing he could be certain of was his own mind, or his own thinking. Even if he was dreaming, he was conscious and his mind was active. Even if he was mistaken about what he saw, at least he was thinking. "I think, therefore I am," he said. Descartes was sure of his own thinking, and decided he *was* his own thinking.

Descartes' reasoning reveals what an extremely masculinist sense of self he has. He sees himself as completely cut off from the world. Other people cannot be trusted. His senses fail to establish a firm connection. He even tries to repudiate his own body, and says he cannot be sure that he has arms and legs; maybe he is only dreaming them. The self he accepts is a sort of mathematical calculator, since he won't admit his emotions or desires as part of his self. He has taken the boy's task of separating himself from the enveloping mother to an extreme. And philosophers—almost all men—have elevated this biased sense of self to the norm. They have devalued women's ways of thinking of the self as dependent upon relations with other people, as embodied, and as emotional. No woman who has felt a child grow within her own body can take Descartes' point of view completely seriously. If women had been allowed to study philosophy, and if their ideas had been respected, Western philosophy would have a more realistic, balanced conception of the self.

Another part of philosophy skewed by a masculinist bias is ethics. A good illustration is a famous study of moral development by Harvard psychologist Lawrence Kohlberg. Kohlberg interviewed a large number of children of different ages. He described a moral problem and asked them how they would solve it. Some thought only in terms of avoiding punishment, some thought in terms of agreements and contracts among people, some thought about making the most people happy, and a few thought about universal principles of justice. According to Kohlberg, these approaches represent stages of moral growth, from the lowest egotism to the highest concern for what is right in itself. They also represent most of the major theories of morality in Western philosophy, such as egotism, social contract theories, utilitarianism, and Kantian formalism. We can disregard the details of these theories and recognize what they all have in common. All assume that being moral means finding a rule to apply in a situation. Kohlberg and others argue that as one's moral rules become more universal and more abstract, one ascends to "higher" levels of moral thinking. Moral development, therefore, means becoming more impersonal.

An interesting aspect of Kohlberg's study was that almost all his subjects were boys. Does that make any difference? Actually it was crucial. Another psychologist named Carol Gilligan noticed the imbalance in Kohlberg's study and decided to examine women's moral thinking. She presented a moral issue to a number of young women and found that they were reluctant to apply abstract rules. They assumed that every case was different, and wanted to know more specific details of each situation. They also seemed to believe that morality revolved around human relationships. They assumed that the best solution to the problem was one that preserved and strengthened caring, personal relationships among the people involved. The contrasts between Kohlberg's and Gilligan's results suggests that in moral thinking men emphasize fairness, justice, and respect for autonomous individuals, whereas women emphasize compassion, sympathy, and involvement with people. Men are more comfortable with general laws, whereas women consult their feelings about particular people and actions.

Gilligan's subjects do not fit Kohlberg's categories very well, nor do they rank very highly on his moral scale. But that only shows that Kohlberg relied on the standard moral theories of Western philosophy. The fact that boys neatly fall into the categories and girls do not suggests that the standard theories reflect masculinist values and biases. Their one-sidedness isn't surprising, since women were historically excluded from philosophy and never had the opportunity to express their distinctive approach to moral problems. If they had, we would now have a more balanced understanding of moral values and moral thinking.

Finally, in the theory of knowledge and the philosophy of science, Western philosophers have held up the ideal of objectivity. Objectivity is said to be an essential component of the proper scientific method. It is a necessary precondition of genuine knowledge of any kind. And what is objectivity? It is simply the core of the male personality structure. Being objective means separating oneself from the world, as the 1-year-old boy must separate himself from the mother. It is the attempt to eliminate or deny any connection between self and object. An objective description of something is a description of it "as it really is," without any input or influence from the person doing the describing. Philosophers have been particularly insistent that no desires or feelings can play any role in science or genuine knowledge. Being subjective, according to this tradition, means having a particular perspective, or allowing desires, goals, and emotional responses to be part of one's investigation of something.

It is difficult to describe the ideal of objectivity without realizing at once that it is unrealistic. Everyone has a personal perspective. We are all situated in a web of personal relations to the world around us. All scientists have emotions and values, which influence their choices of what phenomena to investigate and their interpretations of the results. Recognizing these facts would give us a more accurate understanding of science and the pursuit of knowledge. But as with Descartes' isolated self and Kohlberg's abstract principles, in science Western philosophers have taken the masculinist style and made it the norm, and even the ideal. Objectivity is clearly an inadequate guide in many areas, such as understanding people. To understand another person, I must be fully aware of my own thoughts and feelings. I understand another person by discovering what I would feel in similar circumstances. Understanding literature, social institutions, music, and the whole world of human culture depends upon empathy, recognizing different perspectives, and feelings. Good scientists—whether male or female—do use their feminine side in all sorts of ways: when they share ideas and hunches with colleagues, trust their intuition, use their fantasy to create novel hypotheses, indulge in the joy of discovery and understanding, and rely on friends for support and encouragement.

Men have a preferred style of thinking and women have a different style, although each gender can learn to appreciate the other's style. But in the past, men in positions of power have denigrated women's perceptions and asserted that only one way of thinking—the male way—was correct. But recognizing differences is not threatening; it is liberating. It promises a more balanced and realistic understanding of human experience.

Key Concepts

sexist	generalization	identity formation
the self	moral principles	objectivity

Critical Questions

1. Is the complementer's factual starting point correct? That is, in virtually all cultures and times, do women spend more time with small children than men do?
2. Why does a little boy try to imitate his father rather than his mother? Does the boy know he is a boy instead of a girl? If the complementer says yes, isn't she or he begging the question (i.e., assuming the boy's male identity to explain how male identity is created)?
3. Why do boys learn to suppress their emotions, according to the essay? Why don't girls learn the same thing?
4. According to the complementer, men and women have different types of personalities. Are those differences caused by genetic, biological factors or by social, historical factors, in the author's view? Could the causes be changed?
5. On the basis of Kohlberg's and Gilligan's studies, the complementer says that boys and girls think about moral issues in different ways. How does the writer get from that fact to the conclusion that Western philosophy exhibits a male bias?
6. Is objectivity a male bias, in your opinion? Can the complementer say that his or her position is subjective, in the sense that it expresses personal wishes and a limited point of view? Is the complementer being objective?

Methods and Techniques

CLASSIFICATION

Classification is one of the most basic cognitive operations. It is valuable to look into a mental mirror, so to speak, and examine our own thinking so that we can try to improve it. Psychologists call the awareness of one's own thinking "metacognition."

First we should clarify the term. To classify means to arrange a group of items into smaller subgroups. It is to take a set of things, such as people, objects, words, or anything else, and divide it into two or more subsets. For example, human beings are normally divided into the subsets of men and women. Silverware is divided into forks, knives, and spoons. Furniture can be classified by style: colonial, Mediterranean, Victorian, contemporary, and so on. The term "classify" also has a related but slightly different meaning. I can look at a single object and decide what class it belongs in. For example, a bookseller may have to decide whether to classify a new book as biography or history or travel. This second kind of classification depends on the first kind. We begin with a group and divide it into classes, and only then can we put individuals into those classes.

How do we divide a group into subsets? For example, consider the following list of ten objects: (1) rose, (2) dollar bill, (3) basketball, (4) ivy, (5) stop sign, (6) Christmas tree, (7) Mars, (8) pumpkin, (9) tiger, (10) matador's cape. Do you see any way to arrange these objects into classes? One way is by color: red (1,5,7,10); green (2,4,6); and orange (3,8,9). Or by shape: spherical (3,7,8); flat (2,5,10); and other (1,4,6,9). Or as plant (1,4,6,8); plant product (2,10); animal (9); and other (3,5,7). And there are other ways. When we classify things in this manner we are simply recognizing similarities and differences. A dollar bill, ivy, and a Christmas tree are all similar in being green. A basketball, Mars, and a pumpkin are all similar in being spherical. When we put similar things together, we form a class, and with a large group of things, we can form several classes within the group.

Seeing similarities and differences means focusing on certain properties, such as color or shape. We analyze objects in the sense that we break them down into their properties and find the same property—red, green, spherical—in different objects. The property is the key. Classification depends upon extracting the defining property, and then grouping things on the basis of whether they have the property. The term for such a defining property is "criterion," (plural, "criteria"). In other words, the property of being red can be a criterion, establishing a class of things.

Any property can be used as a criterion, and criteria can be complex. We might try to classify the ten objects into those that smell good, those that smell bad, and those that have no smell. Or a criterion might be "objects I would like to have in my living room but not in other rooms, so long as they aren't too expensive." Boxers are classified by weight, and competitive runners by the distance they run.

Recognizing the criteria that define classes is an important skill. It requires us to look at the objects in a class and extract the property they all have in common. In fact, some standardized tests use problems of this sort. They present lists of objects and ask which object doesn't belong. For example

1. moose,   2. mouse,   3. hammer,   4. cat,   5. eagle

Obviously "hammer" doesn't belong in this class because it is not an animal like the other objects. Another example:

1. Lincoln,   2. Reagan,   3. Monroe,   4. Franklin,   5. Adams

Franklin doesn't belong because all the other people were U.S. Presidents. Recognizing criteria means stepping up to a higher level of abstraction. One thinks of properties rather than particular objects.

Various problems can arise in classifying things. One problem is vagueness. The criterion that defines a class may be a matter of degree. For example, "red." Matadors' capes and American Beauty roses are definitely red, but is salmon red? Not exactly, although it is closer to red than to green or blue. Or "chubby." How much body fat must one have to be classified as chubby? There is no precise answer. The boundary between "average" and "chubby" is vague. Other vague terms are "cold," "the Midwest," "offensive," "child," "athlete," and "free." Examples of terms for classes with definite boundaries are "hydrogen," "robin," "pregnant," "state capitol," "licensed," and "metal."

Another practice that can lead to confusion is using subjective criteria. For example, I might say that most of the people in my history class in college are "likable," while most of those in my English class are "not very likable." By "likable" I simply mean that I enjoy being with them. A friend in the same classes who tries to distinguish the likable and not likable students probably wouldn't get very far, because the criterion—I enjoy being with them—is subjective and personal to me. My friend cannot apply it. He has no way of knowing whom I like and don't like. I could avoid confusion if I provide more objective criteria, such as "smiles often," "listens to people," and "has diverse interests." If those are the criteria for the class of likable people, then it will be easier to reach agreements on who is likable and who isn't.

These are only a few aspects of a fascinating topic. A final point to note is that one of the founders of Western philosophy, Socrates, believed that the essential task of philosophy was to find the underlying criteria that guide us when we classify some actions as "morally right" and others as "morally wrong." He asked what criteria define the class of just societies, the class of wise people, and the class of brave actions. In other words, he believed philosophy was the investigation of our concepts and the bases for our classifications of people and actions.

Understanding the Dilemma

UNIFIER OR COMPLEMENTER?

Are men and women fundamentally different? The unifier says no and the complementer says yes. The unifier says that even biological differences are not important, whereas the complementer says deep psychological differences divide men and women.

According to the unifier, we use biological differences as a basis for classifying people as male and female. But classifications are flexible, not written in stone. As technology provides us with more and better methods of reproduction, the biological differences will become less important, and less noticeable. In the future the categories "male" and "female" may not become obsolete, but certainly other categories, such as "creative," "ambitious," "sociable," and "generous," will become more important and receive more attention than "masculine" or "feminine."

A complementer, on the other hand, thinks it would be a tragedy if we lost sight of the differences between men and women. Women's distinctive perspective and insights have been suppressed and ignored in the past, and it's about time that we acknowledged them and recognized how valuable they are. Especially in philosophy, and in our most basic assumptions about human nature, morality, and knowledge, women's experience and the feminine point of view can correct the biases that limit our thinking.

Where do you stand? You have years of experience with many men and women. Are the differences diminishing and ultimately unimportant? Or do men and women think and feel and relate to others in fundamentally different ways?

When faced with philosophical dilemmas like this one, most people look for the middle ground. Most people would probably say some men and women are different and some aren't. We can imagine the possibilities as a horizontal line, and say there is a spectrum of types of people. On the far left, let's say, are "highly feminine women" and on the far right are "highly masculine men." In the middle are people who are both, or mixed, or feminine in some ways and masculine in others.

Is this an accurate picture of humanity? A unifier would probably say it is not. We do not need to label some behaviors as "feminine" or "masculine." In our society most women are pressured into moving toward the left side, the "feminine" side, and men are pressured into moving toward the right, the "masculine" side. But the ideal would be for most people to line up in the middle, which is neither male nor female, but "androgynous." At the present time, however, our rigid classifications of people drive them to one side or the other.

The ultimate pressure is being a mother or father. Men and women today may think and behave in similar ways—in school, in sports, in friendships, in jobs—until they start a family. Then the differences increase. The great majority of women get pregnant and give birth. Carrying the fetus, bonding with the newborn, and accepting responsibility for a helpless person pushes women to the feminine side, especially when society insists on it. Then the division of people into male and female becomes clearer and more pronounced. But it doesn't have to be that way, the unifier claims. Men and women can remain in the middle of the spectrum, with more options available to them. Alternative forms of reproduction will allow men and women to play equal roles in having children and rearing them.

A complementer disagrees, and claims that differences are valuable. Women should be proud of their differences from men. What the world needs is more caring, more communication and compromise, more empathy, and more creativity—the characteristics that are typically associated with women. The masculine traits of assertiveness, suppression of feelings, and extreme independence are nothing to envy.

At first glance, a complementer seems similar to a traditional conservative who believes men and women are very different. However, the conservative says that women are naturally suited to remain at home, support their hus-

bands, and raise children. Men are natural leaders and women are natural followers. Nothing could be further from the complementer's point of view. The
complementer says women's distinctive skills and talents belong in government,
schools, the marketplace, and everywhere. Women's concern for relationships
and understanding people make them better leaders and organizers than men.
Their antipathy to conflict and violence makes them more trustworthy citizens
than men. Their ability to work together and share things makes a more equi-
table, productive economy possible. Women are different from men, and their
differences will lead to a better world.

In thinking about the differences between men and women, many people
focus on the question of nature and nurture. Are the differences innate and unalterable, or are they culturally determined and changeable? No one who has
studied the matter takes an "either/or" view. People are products of their genes
and their environment, which constantly interact in countless ways we do not
understand.

Neither the unifier nor the complementer has a simple answer to the question of nature and nurture. The unifier claims that the important factor is not
nature or cultural roles, but human perception and classification. *Any* two
things—a pencil and a blue whale—are similar in some ways and different in
others. Human beings decide to emphasize and attend to a similarity or difference depending on their purposes and goals. There are innumerable innate similarities and differences between men and women, and innumerable cultural
similarities and differences. We decide which ones to emphasize and which to
ignore. People have always believed that the biological differences were the
most important and the basis for classifying individuals as men or women. But
it is possible to ignore biological differences and emphasize similarities, or ignore biology entirely as a basis for classifying and perceiving people. The future of the sexes doesn't depend on facts about biology or culture, but on what
we choose to make of those facts. And technology is changing the way we think
about the facts.

The complementers' view of nature and nurture is another example of looking for interactions. The complementer asserts that, because of biological facts
about pregnancy and nursing, in almost all cultures children are reared by
women. As a result, men and women form their sense of self in different ways
and have different types of personalities. Facts about pregnancy and childbirth
are biological and innate, but facts about family structure and ways of socializing children are cultural. The complementer claims these two sets of facts are
interconnected. Is the need for a sense of identity innate or learned? Is the
method of forming an identity through imitating authority figures innate or
learned? These psychological processes are probably on the border between the
inherited capacity and the acquired content. The complementer isn't so much
concerned with disentangling the interconnections of genetics and culture—
which is probably impossible—as with understanding the psychological
processes and their consequences.

The dispute between a unifier and a complementer is not just a disagreement about nature and nurture. As with many philosophical dilemmas, both facts and values are at stake. What in fact are the differences between men and women? Are they artificial, based on outdated types of classification? Or are they deeply rooted in biology and child development? And *should* we encourage women to develop their differences from men, so they can apply their superior skills to all the problems we face? If you think differences are small and should be minimized, even in family structure, then you are a unifier. If you think women are psychologically different from men, and that after centuries of oppression, allowing feminine traits to flourish is the best hope for progress, then you are a complementer.

UNIFIER

1. The classification of things depends on our purposes; categories change with changing means of achieving our purposes.
2. The only real differences between men and women are the ability to impregnate and to give birth.
3. With developments in reproductive technology, such as an artificial womb, the biological difference between men and women will become negligible.
4. When the means of reproduction are available to anyone, classifications of people as "male" and "female" will decline, and classifications based on more important traits of personality will take their place.

COMPLEMENTER

5. Identifying with the relatively absent father shapes boys' personalities, and identifying with the nurturing mother shapes girls' personalities.
6. In general, men are more independent and less emotional than women, whereas women are more social and more sensitive than men.
7. Men's competitive and alienating nature has caused many problems in economics, society, and politics, and as women gain positions of power and apply their distinctive skills, we can look forward to progress.
8. The psychological differences between men and women have influenced basic philosophical conceptions of the self, morality, and knowledge, since philosophy has been dominated by men.

FOR FURTHER STUDY

Historical Examples

UNIFIER: Mary Wollstonecraft. *A Vindication of the Rights of Woman.* Edited by Carol H. Poston. Norton. 1988. Originally published in 1792. Criticism of degrading attitudes and behavior toward women, and a plea for human rights for all humans, including women.

COMPLEMENTER: Shulamith Firestone. *The Dialectic of Sex: The Case for Feminist Revolution.* Morrow, 1970. Critique of sexism in many areas, starting from the claim that biology leads to an unjust division of labor and psychological differences (but agreeing with the unifier that the means of reproduction should be changed).

OTHER SOURCES

Nancy Holmstrom, "Human Nature." In Alison M. Jaggar, Iris Marion Young, eds. *A Companion to Feminist Philosophy.* Blackwell, 1998. Brief survey of historical and contemporary positions on the question "Does human nature take sex-differentiated forms?," showing the multiplicity of feminist ideas.

Eve Browning Cole. *Philosophy and Feminist Criticism: An Introduction.* Paragon House, 1993. Clear, basic discussion of feminist ideas in epistemology, metaphysics, ethics, and political philosophy.

Rosemarie Putnam Tong. *Feminist Thought.* 2nd Edition. Westview Press, 1998. Lively, critical presentation of various schools of feminism, including liberal, radical, Marxist, socialist, psychoanalytic, existentialist, and postmodernist feminism.

Leslie Stevenson, David L. Haberman. *Ten Theories of Human Nature.* 3rd Edition. Oxford University Press, 1998. Elementary discussion of religious, philosophical, and psychological views, including their diagnoses of the main problems we face, and their prescriptions.

Roger Trigg. *Ideas of Human Nature: An Historical Introduction.* 2nd Edition. Blackwell, 1999. Concise, informative essays on twelve great philosophers, each chapter concluding with a section on "contemporary relevance."

Peter Loptson. *Theories of Human Nature.* Broadview, 1995. Survey of eleven theories from Aristotle to Marvin Harris, considering questions of our place in nature, our malleability, our sociability, and the possibility of a science of human nature.

Jonathan Benthall, ed. *The Limits of Human Nature.* Allen Lane, 1973. Readable essays with a wide variety of perspectives, on "human universals," structuralism, animal behavior, self-images, symbol-making, artificial intelligence, and more.

Mary Midgley. *Beast and Man: The Roots of Human Nature.* Cornell University Press, 1978. Thoughtful reflections on similarities and differences between humans and animals, emphasizing our integral place in nature.

George Mandler. *Human Nature Explored.* Oxford University Press, 1997. Interesting chapters on evolution, consciousness, emotion, aggression, gender, and other topics, by a psychologist.

CONNECTIONS
REDUCTIONIST OR SPIRITUALIST?

The basic division in Chapter 4 is relatively clear. It is much simpler than the complex similarities and differences we discovered in Chapter 3, among beliefs about values. Having said that, I should also remind you that nothing in philosophy is simple. When someone claims to have a simple answer to a philosophical question, you should automatically be suspicious. However, some answers are simp*ler* than others. And the relationships among the positions in Chapter 4 are simpler than those among the positions in Chapter 3.

The basic issue regarding human nature is this: are human beings subject to natural or social laws, or are we not? Do the laws that govern the movements of physical objects also govern human beings? Or can people rise above those forces, perhaps by understanding them? Are human beings subject to social or psychological laws, applicable to us but not to physical objects? Or are the (rare) laws of the social sciences merely generalizations based on human actions, which are admittedly similar, but which are not rigidly determined beforehand? If we knew everything about an individual, could we predict what she or he would do in the future? Or is that impossible? (That is, granting that we *could* know everything, would it still be impossible to predict the person's actions?)

If you believe that human beings *are* subject to natural or social laws, then you are a "reductionist." And if you believe we are not controlled by natural or social laws, then you are a "spiritualist." I am proposing the name "reductionist" because it suggests that human actions can be "reduced" to lawful regularities. A reductionist believes that the bewildering, profuse variety of human behavior is ultimately explainable in terms of laws. The confusion and unpredictability can be reduced to order and predictability. On the other hand, a "spiritualist" believes that human beings are not just additional pieces of the world, but are different and special. People are "spiritual" beings, in the sense that some part of us is forever beyond the reach of science, measurement, prediction, complete understanding, and even lawful regularity. As the mentalist says in "People vs. Machines," we are ultimately a mystery to ourselves.

We could use different labels. If you do not like the terms "reductionist" and "spiritualist," you can find different ones. For example, you could call the first position "holism" and the second "exceptionalism" (or something like that), because the first sees human beings as integral parts of the larger whole of nature, while the second sees human beings as exceptional, fundamentally different from systems that are governed by laws. Or you could call the first group "explainers" and the second group "searchers," or something else.

But the important thing is the ideas, not the labels. I am suggesting that a certain idea runs through some of the positions in Chapter 4, and an opposite idea runs through some of the others. In other words, some of the positions are similar to each other and different from the others. Thinking about those contrasting ideas is a first step in seeing similarities and differences in the various positions. The similarities and differences are the connections among the parts of your worldview. They are the tendons, ligaments, and cartilage that hold your worldview together and allow it to function. Without them, your worldview is just a shapeless blob, like a dying jellyfish on the beach.

After reading this introduction, probably the first section of Chapter 4 that comes to mind is Section 4.1, "Are We Free?" Remember that a hard determinist says no, and a metaphysical libertarian and a soft determinist say yes. The hard determinist argues that human beings are part of the natural world, and that the whole world is governed by laws. We know it is lawful because of the many laws, in many different areas, that we have already discovered. So human behavior is subject to natural laws, too, even if we haven't yet discovered them. But a libertarian claims that we are free, and we know that we are free by simply introspecting our own thoughts and feelings as we make a decision. We can see that nothing coerces us. The libertarian is a good example of a spiritualist, while the hard determinist is a reductionist.

Does a soft determinist fit this classification? A soft determinist is a type of determinist. He or she agrees with the hard determinist about natural laws and the regularity of human behavior. Everything we do and think and feel is caused, according to the soft determinist. So he or she is a reductionist. She simply insists that we are still free, because the word "free" means caused by myself. It does not mean uncaused, or mysterious, or spiritual.

Another pair of opposites that fits the pattern is materialists and dualists. Reductionism is closely related to materialism, although they are not identical, and dualism is related to spiritualism. You read about materialists and dualists in Section 4.3, "Is the Mind Nothing but the Brain?" A materialist believes that human beings are complex organisms with remarkable brains. And that is all we are. Our minds, personalities, emotions, moods, creative insights, and consciences are just aspects of the physical brain. The remarkable correlations between brain events and mind events supports this materialistic view, as does the trend of reduction in all the sciences. Now if the human mind is just the brain—a physical organ—then the actions of the mind are all determined by physical events, because everything that happens in the brain is determined by prior physical events. Therefore materialists are reductionists.

But dualists have a different outlook. They believe that thoughts and feelings and all the experiences that make up your mind cannot be physical events because they are private. Only you can feel your toothache, but anyone (in principle) can observe events in your brain. Since mental processes are private and physical processes are public, they cannot be the same things. A human being is made of two distinct parts, mental and physical. This conclusion is relevant to the reductionist/spiritualist distinction. If the mind is not physical, then it may not be subject to laws as the physical world is. Dualists see the mind as a fundamentally different kind of entity from physical objects. So dualists are normally spiritualists.

But the connections here are not one-to-one, not perfect. A dualist *could* believe that the mind is nonphysical, but *is* subject to laws. Maybe the mind is governed by "mental laws," which are different from physical laws. In that case, the dualist would be a reductionist. It is also possible, though unlikely, that a materialist could be a spiritualist. That is, a person could believe that the mind is a physical organ, the brain, but could also believe that the physical world is *not* governed by laws. Maybe the laws that scientists have discovered are all illusions, or something like that. As I said, this is a possible belief, but not many people will hold it. It is contrary to too much evidence. Most materialists are reductionists, and most dualists are spiritualists.

While materialists try to show that the mind is the same thing as the brain, mechanists try to show that the mind works mechanically, like a computer. In Section 4.4, "Can Computers Think?," the mechanist pointed out many similarities between what people can do and what computers can do. For example, both can calculate, store information, and solve problems. Since they are similar in their output, they are probably similar in their operation as well. Computers are physical systems that operate according to instructions from a programmer. All the operations are strictly determined. If the mind works the same way as a computer, then all its operations are strictly determined, too. Therefore, mechanists are reductionists.

Mentalists, however, reject the mechanistic view of the mind. The mentalist in Section 4.4 argues that we cannot build machines that think like humans, because we do not know how humans think. We do not know any laws governing the operations of the mind, so we cannot embody them in a machine. And we never will be able to build a thinking machine, because if we do understand how we think, that knowledge will change the way we do it. So the machines can never catch up with the human way of thinking. Mentalists believe that human thought can never be captured in laws and rules. They are spiritualists.

In Section 4.5, "Are We Always Selfish?," the issue is whether or not people are subject to psychological laws. A psychological egoist believes that at least one law governs all human actions—the law of self-interest. That is, the egoist says that everything a person does is aimed at some benefit for himself or herself. No one does anything strictly for others or for any selfless principle. The evidence for this law is all the examples of actions that can be interpreted as selfish. Whenever an action appears to be altruistic, we can always find an unconscious motive, or a concern for the distant future, or a desire to avoid a greater pain, or some self-centered concern that makes the action selfish in reality.

In contrast, a psychological altruist believes that sometimes people act without any desire to benefit themselves, either in the long run or the short run or in any way. There are cases that cannot be reinterpreted as selfish, the altruist says, and therefore people are not bound by a universal law of selfishness. An altruist is a spiritualist because he or she rejects the idea of such a psychological law governing human behavior. On the other hand, an egoist accepts reductionism.

Another section in Chapter 4 is Section 4.2, "Are We Responsible for Our Actions?" The excuser says no and the judge says yes. At first glance, it might seem that an excuser is obviously a reductionist—people are not responsible because they are governed by inescapable laws—and a judge is obviously a spiritualist. But that would be too hasty. If we examine the actual details of the positions in Section 4.2, we see a more complicated picture. The excuser says people are not responsible whether their actions are caused or not. An excuser does not say people's actions are always caused, or subject to laws. Maybe actions are not caused. But the key point is that, either way, it makes no sense to say the person is responsible for the action. Thus an excuser does not necessarily hold the central belief of reductionism. But an excuser is similar to a reductionist, because most reductionists would agree that people cannot be responsible for their actions.

A judge is not simply a spiritualist either. A judge says that we have a clear and established set of rules for excusing people. We ask if the person caused an action, if the person was sane, if the person did it intentionally, and if the person did it freely. A person who does not have any of these recognized excuses is responsible, according to the judge. The judge in Section 4.2 does not say that people are outside the scope of natural or social laws. On the contrary, he says people's actions are probably caused. But we do not *know* the complex, remote causes. Since we do not know the ultimate causes, we make a decision on the basis of the causes we do know, and that is the person himself. The robber did cause the bank to be robbed, and therefore he is responsible. This position is similar to spiritualism in a practical sense because it says we do not know of any causes of human action. There may be causes, but our social and legal decisions must rest upon what we know, not upon what might be true. For all practical purposes, there are no laws governing normal human behavior.

The current controversy in Chapter 4 revolves around the question "Are the differences between men and women philosophically significant?" The unifier says no, and the complementer says yes. You will recall that a unifier claims that the process of classifying things is flexible. The categories we use, such as "mammal" and "reptile," or "dangerous" and "harmless," depend on our purposes and interests, and these change over time. The categories "male" and "female" are important because reproduction is important, but as our methods of creating new people change, these categories will matter less and less. Eventually, the biological difference between men and women will become insignificant, and other classifications of people will be more important.

The complementer in this section disagrees. Not only are men and women psychologically different, but the differences are important and we ought to take advantage of them in the future. The complementer begins with what he or she regards as basic facts about family structure and child development. In almost all families, women spend more time rearing children than men do. People can quibble over small exceptions, but the basic pattern is clear. Furthermore, children develop their personalities by imitating or identifying with the parent of the same sex. But since children interact with their mothers much more than with their fathers, the identification process is very different for boys and girls. However, the resulting strengths and assets of women have been ignored, especially in philosophy. In the future, we should celebrate these differences and benefit from them, according to the complementer.

Are these two positions similar to others in Chapter 4? The complementer's point of view is similar to other reductionist positions because the complementer believes people are subject to certain universal laws of behavior. Almost all families are organized in the same way—with female care-givers—and almost all children grow up in the same ways. We can understand ourselves and our potential for growth and happiness by understanding the forces that shape our lives. We can achieve a greater balance and harmony between men and women by recognizing the inevitable differences between them and by accepting their complementary roles.

Unifiers, in contrast, are similar to spiritualists, at least in their belief that human beings can design the kind of lives they want to have, and can even define themselves to a certain degree. Unifiers reject permanent categories, such as "male" and "female," and claim that all categories depend on our own purposes. Unifiers are not exactly like other spiritualists, such as libertarians, dualists, or mentalists, because those spiritualists believe that human nature is ultimately mysterious and irreducible to scientific law. Unifiers believe human nature is extremely complex and diverse, but that we can understand how we emphasize some qualities and not others in classifying people. The complexity, however, gives us the capacity to develop in virtually any direction we choose, including complete equality, and that faith in our open-ended future makes unifiers similar to spiritualists.

Classifying the positions in Chapter 4 as reductionist and spiritualist should help you think about the connections among your beliefs about human nature. The classification certainly isn't the last word, but it is a start. Moreover, some positions do not fit into the scheme as well as others. Hard determinists are paradigmatic reductionists, and metaphysical libertarians are perfect spiritualists, but the classification of the other positions is only approximate. These discussions of connections at the end of each chapter are not supposed to provide you with simple answers. They are intended to suggest some possible relationships among your beliefs, but you must make up your own mind about how close (or distant, or irrelevant) those relationships are. The discussions are also intended to show you a whole part of philosophy that is not covered in the rest of the book. The other parts of the book discuss particular answers to traditional questions. But you should not forget that the connections among your answers are just as important as the individual answers themselves.

Reductionist	**Spiritualist**
determinist	metaphysical libertarian
materialist	dualist
mechanist	mentalist
psychological egoist	psychological altruist
excuser	judge
complementer	unifier

REDUCTIONIST

1. Human beings are made of the same stuff as everything else and follow the same laws as everything else.
2. We can understand more and more of human behavior by learning about the physical and social causes that make each of us what we are.
3. The mind, or consciousness, is a natural phenomenon and we will eventually discover its laws of operation (perhaps by modeling the mind on a computer).
4. Since humans are animals and obey similar laws, we probably have a drive to preserve ourselves and desire what benefits us.

SPIRITUALIST

5. Human beings are not just nerves and muscle, not just objects; our consciousness sets us apart from the natural, physical world.
6. People are so complex that we cannot generalize about them; every individual is unique.
7. We can never completely understand a person.
8. We choose our own behavior; it isn't determined by anything, and therefore we should accept responsibility for it.

CHAPTER FIVE

KNOWLEDGE, SCIENCE, AND TRUTH

5.1 Can We Know about the External World?

Internalist or Perceiver?

—————————————————————•—————————————————————

Most people do not like to have tricks played on them. Especially elaborate tricks where a lot of people are in on the gag and go along with the charade, but one victim is deceived and left out. Imagine for a moment that everyone in your high school class says the spring dance is going to be a costume party. You talk about costumes with people for weeks beforehand, but when you show up in your clown costume, everyone else is dressed formally. You would feel rotten.

The really irritating thing about such an incident would be the callousness of all the other people. But we can be deceived by *things*, not people, and it is still annoying. For example, if you see your friend on the street and you call out and run up to him, but it turns out to be someone else, you feel embarrassed and annoyed. If you are watching TV, but you can't hear the sound clearly and you are confused about what people are actually saying, you will feel annoyed. Your eyes can play tricks on you: if you mistake a reflection in a mirror for the real thing, or you are driving in a fog and you can't make out the road signs, you feel annoyed. The experience of being tricked, or deceived, is itself unpleasant.

No one likes to be duped, including philosophers. But philosophers think about unusual ways of being deceived. They wonder if our eyes could play tricks on us, not just sometimes, but all the time. Or our ears or other senses. Could the whole human race be the butt of some cosmic practical joke? It would be irritating if we were, so philosophers try to discover whether or not things *are* what they *appear* to be.

Of course this issue—appearance versus reality—is interesting in its own right. Even if one does not feel irritated about being mistaken, one might be fascinated by the difference between the appearances of things and their reality, the illusions we unknowingly accept and the true state of things behind those illusions. Since philosophers' goal is to discover the truth, they are naturally very interested in anything that interferes with understanding or misleads people. They investigate particular obstacles, and they also wonder if there are any universal, systematic weaknesses built into all human beings as such. Is there anything about human nature itself that implies that we will always mistake some illusion for reality, or will never be able to comprehend the truth?

The first essay in this section argues that we *are* trapped in an illusion. We can know about our own experiences, but not about the world as it is independent of us. We can call this view internalism. The second essay says the argument for internalism fails because we cannot be mistaken about everything. It claims that we can know about the world, so we can call anyone who accepts the second essay a perceiver.

NO: INTERNALIST
"Knowledge of the External World"

The essence of philosophy is to wonder about things that everyone normally takes for granted. Why do I exist? Do other people see the world the same way I do? Why is random killing wrong? How did the universe begin?

Philosophers propose answers to these questions, and try to persuade people that their answers are correct. But sometimes philosophers must do something else before they propose an answer. They must try to get people to understand the *question* they are asking. They must show people that there really is a problem. That may not be easy, because the questions are often so odd and seem so simple.

I would like to discuss one such question, and try to explain why it really is a puzzling question. I do not have an answer, and in fact, I do not see how anyone could answer this question. But it is still a troubling question.

The question is this: How do I know that the world *is* the way it *appears* to be? In other words, when I see a yellow flower, how do I know that the flower is really yellow, or even that there is a flower there at all?

A lot of possible answers spring to mind, but before we consider answers, let's think some more about the question. One way to make the question clearer is to construct a "thought experiment." Philosophers use thought experiments in the same way scientists use physical experiments. In a physical experiment a scientist sets up an unusual situation to see what will happen. He or she might heat a metal to 1000 degrees F., or grow a corn plant in ultraviolet light, just to see what such an odd situation will lead to.

Philosophers do the same thing, but in their minds. They imagine, for example, that we were all born with green-tinted contact lenses in our eyes, and we could not remove them. Would we ever find out that our vision was distorted, and that things were not really as green as they looked to us? Or they imagine that a group of people boarded a self-supporting space ship and traveled away from Earth in a straight line. If they keep going, what would eventually happen to them?

These are examples of thought experiments, and I would like to describe two thought experiments for our question about knowing that the world is the way it appears to be. I can begin with something that actually happened. In the early seventies a boy was born in Texas who had absolutely no defenses against disease. Doctors knew from the beginning that the common germs in the air, which our bodies can handle, would kill him. So he was placed in an airtight incubator with air filters that cleaned the air. His milk had to be sterilized, and nurses had to reach in with special, long gloves to feed and change him. (*Science News*, May 25, 1974.)

Eventually he was moved to a larger incubator, but all contact with the outside world was still forbidden, because it was too dangerous. He lived in larger and larger air-conditioned compartments, until finally, when he was about 3 years old, the family and hospital built a special room for him. It had glass walls, and a secure air lock for food to go in and waste to come out. It had toys, a bed, a TV, and everything he needed. And it had some round holes with long rubber gloves attached to the inside, so his mother could reach in with both arms up to her shoulders and hold him. He lived about twelve years, but then he died of an infection.

It's a sad story. But I would like to change it slightly and ask what would happen then. Suppose the walls were not glass, but wood or metal. And suppose the only way the boy could see and hear people was on his TV. There might be cameras on the outside of his room, which show him his family and the doctors and the hospital. But all he ever sees is the TV image. He can never go outside his room to compare the TV image with the real thing.

In that case he could not know for sure that his mother really looked like the woman he saw on TV. He could not know, because he could not get outside the room to look at his mother directly. He could not look at his mother, and then look at the TV screen to see if they match. All he has are the TV images. In fact, the images on his TV might be completely artificial. They might be puppets or cartoons. He could never know if the outside world really was the way it appeared to him on his TV screen, because he could not leave his room.

The important point to understand is that all of us are in exactly the same situation *now*. But instead of TV cameras, we rely on our eyes. Instead of microphones, we rely on our ears. But all we ever see is what our eyes show us. All we have to go on are our subjective experiences, just as the boy had to rely on his TV screen. We are trapped inside our own minds. What my eyes tell me may not be exactly the same as what your eyes tell you. The boy could not get outside his room to check the accuracy of his TV, and we cannot get outside our own minds to check the accuracy of our eyes. The boy could never compare the TV image of his mother with the real woman, because he could not leave the room. *We* can never compare our experience of a flower (or anything else) with the flower itself, as it exists independently of us. So how do we know that the world really is the way it appears to us in our minds?

The thought experiment does not answer the question, but only makes it easier to grasp. It is a serious question. The second thought experiment does the same thing. To understand the experiment we must remember how we get information about the world. When I see a flower, for example, light waves bounce off the flower and enter my eye. They strike some cells on the rear wall of the eyeball (the retina), and cause those cells to send an electric impulse to the optic nerve. The optic nerve gathers all the impulses, and sends a complex signal to the brain. Then we have the experience of seeing a flower. Something similar happens in the ear when we hear a bird singing, in the nose when we smell fresh bread, and so on.

In the future, it should be possible for scientists to study the signals the optic nerve sends when I see a flower, or a dog, or a sunset. There is nothing mystical about these signals. They are electric dots and dashes, very similar to the signals that travel along the wires in a radio or TV and create sounds or images, except they move more slowly in the optic nerve. Future scientists should be able to examine my optic nerve, decode the signals, and that would tell them what I was seeing. And, in theory, they should be able to duplicate those signals.

Now suppose that, in the future, I was in a terrible accident. All of my body was destroyed, except my brain, which doctors saved and kept alive. If they knew the signals my optic nerve sent my brain when I saw a flower, couldn't they duplicate those signals themselves? Couldn't they stimulate my optic nerve directly, with microscopic electrodes? Then I would have exactly the same experience as I have when I really see a flower, but the experience would be caused by doctors and their tiny electrodes attached to my brain. In theory, couldn't they send my brain the same signals my nerves sent it when I walked through the woods, or had an excellent meal, or carried on an interesting conversation? When I awoke after my accident, I might believe that I was sitting in a chair, looking out a window, when in fact I was nothing but a brain in a jar with a lot of wires attached.

This is a bizarre thought experiment, and probably will never happen. But if all this is even *possible*, then I am faced with a real problem. How can I *know* that these experiences I am having are caused by real tables and pieces of paper, and not by ingenious doctors sending signals to my brain? Or, at least, by something very different from tables and pieces of paper? It's a real question.

The purpose of constructing these thought experiments is not to prove that we are all brains in jars. The purpose is to make us think about the grounds of our beliefs; they are a lot weaker than we assume. We cannot be certain in those areas where we feel certain. Our "common sense" is not as solid and reliable as it seems.

Key Concepts

philosophical question	thought experiment	subjective experiences
external world	sense organs	verification

Critical Questions

1. What is a thought experiment?
2. How does the internalist change the story about the boy with no defenses against disease? In what way are we like the boy, according to the internalist? Do you think he is right?
3. The internalist says I cannot *check* my experience of a flower to find out if the flower really is yellow, as it appears to me. But why can't I check my experience by asking you how it looks to you, and asking others how it looks to them? If we all agree it is yellow, then it really is yellow, isn't it?
4. Why couldn't the boy in the sealed room ask the doctor if the hospital really looked like the image on the TV screen?

5. What is the point of the story about the automobile accident? What does the internalist think it proves?
6. Is it true that all the information we get about the world comes to us via impulses through our nerves?
7. Do you think what the essay describes is really (physically) possible, and could happen someday, say, in a hundred years? If not, then is it logically possible?

YES: PERCEIVER

"The Limits of Ignorance"

Scientists and philosophers sometimes wonder if there are any limits on human knowledge. Will we eventually discover everything there is to know? Or is the amount of knowledge we can have infinite, so that no matter how much we discover, there will always be some things we do not understand?

This is a fascinating question, but some skeptical eccentrics turn it on its head and ask "Can you know anything?" Is it possible that all of our cherished "knowledge" is a delusion? This is the problem I would like to consider: not how much can we know, but how *ignorant* can we be? I want to ask a series of broader and broader questions to probe the outer limits of our ignorance. The answers will shed light on the nature of knowledge itself.

Question 1. *Can the American people be deceived?* Unfortunately the answer is yes. The Watergate conspiracy and the Iran-Contra conspiracy illustrate that sad fact. How far could such a conspiracy go? How many people could be deceived? Certainly *most* people could be kept in the dark about what the government was doing. In fact, it is possible that the President, by himself, could conduct negotiations with a foreign power, or make secret plans. Then *everyone* but the President would be ignorant.

Question 2. *Could everyone, including the President, be deceived?* We could all be fooled by Russian propaganda, or by some other country. In fact, everyone in the whole world could be deceived by one skillful leader who might set some vast plan into motion, keeping individual administrators unaware of the total design and unaware of what other administrators were doing. It would be difficult, but it is possible. It looks like there is no limit to the number of people who can be deceived about important things that affect their lives (like Iran-Contra), so long as one powerful person wants to trick them.

Question 3. *Could literally every human being be deceived?* God could deceive us all, but let's leave God out of the story for now. The answer depends on what we mean by "deceived." Normally "deceived" means tricked, or misled. It requires someone who plays the trick, or tells the lie. If we leave God out, then not everyone could be deceived. One person has to do the deceiving.

But the word "deceived" has a broader meaning, too. It can also mean mistaken. One can say, "I was deceived about the mountain. It's actually farther away than I thought." One simply means that one was mistaken, not that someone lied or played a trick.

So let's ask the broader question.

Question 4. *Could literally everyone be mistaken about something that affects our lives?* Yes, every single person in the world could believe that the earth is flat. At one time, thousands of years ago, everyone probably did believe the earth was flat. They were all mistaken. Today all of us may share some common belief that is false. It's possible.

So far we haven't found any limits on our ignorance. It is possible that everyone could be mistaken about something. But in all the examples I have given, people eventually discovered their error. Iran-Contra was exposed, people learned that the earth is round. That suggests a new question.

Question 5. *Could everyone be mistaken in such a way that they could not discover their error?* Is it possible that we all have some false belief that no one could ever correct?

I think the answer is no, but first I want to try to make the question clearer. Some people say that human sense organs might be deceptive. In other words, our eyes and ears might be giving all of us a false picture of the world. But if this is happening, there is no way we can prove it, because we have to use our eyes to see. We cannot see anything except by using our eyes, so we cannot see the alleged "real world." We could never know that we were mistaken.

Or maybe the problem goes farther than our sense organs. Maybe our *minds* are defective, these skeptics say. For example, we have to think of things existing in time, but maybe that is an illusion. Maybe time does not exist. We only think it does because of the way our minds have evolved. But we can never know the real, timeless world, because our minds are constructed to think in time. That is the skeptics' proposal.

But they have gone too far. It is not possible that we could all be mistaken, and that we could never know that we were. The reason it is impossible has nothing to do with the mind or sense organs. It depends on the meaning of the word "mistaken." We use the word to describe certain beliefs, as when we say "The belief in fairies is mistaken." By extension, we also say that a person is mistaken, as "John thinks he won, but he is mistaken." The point I want to make is that "mistaken" is the sort of word that requires an "opposite." If some beliefs are mistaken, others must be *correct*. One cannot exist without the other. "Mistaken" means wrong, off-track, defective in some way, and so we must have some standard of right, correct, or successful, which we can use to pick out the mistaken beliefs. Thus, it is not possible for every belief or every person to be mistaken. This is not because people are so smart or curious, but because that is not how we use the word "mistaken."

The word "mistaken" (or "deceived," "fooled," etc.) is like the word "tall." Could everyone be tall? No. We can only use the word "tall" when there is an opposite—short—to provide a contrast. Everyone could be over six feet in height, but not everyone could be tall. It isn't a matter of genes, or diet, or even measuring devices. It is our language that makes it impossible for everyone to be tall.

Could everyone be crazy? No. "Crazy" means abnormal. If everyone began to behave the way people in asylums behave, then that behavior would be normal, not crazy. It is possible for everyone's brain to go haywire, but it's not possible for everyone to be *crazy* because that is not what "crazy" means. Only part of the population can be crazy.

Could everyone be happy? No. To understand the meaning of the word "happiness," a person must know the meaning of the opposite, "sadness." If no one was ever sad, in the past, present, or future, then the word "happy" would be meaningless. It would make no sense to say everyone is happy.

In the same way, not everyone can be mistaken, in the peculiar way that skeptics proposed. It *is* possible for everyone to have a false belief (like the belief that the earth is flat), so long as we have an opposite to provide a contrast. The opposite is the correct belief, which we discovered. And it is possible for all of us today to be mistaken about something, so long as we *might* discover our error. But the skeptics said we may all be mistaken in such a way that we *could not* discover our error. That is not possible, because it takes away the contrast. It is like saying we might all be crazy.

The series of questions has uncovered the limits of ignorance. We cannot be hopelessly mistaken, or ignorant, about anything. Progress is always possible. But this optimistic conclusion has its sober side, too. The discussion suggests that *knowing* is linked inseparably with being ignorant. "Knowing" requires *its* opposite, just as "mistaken" does. Thus the same facts about language show that we cannot know everything. There will always be more to discover.

Key Concepts

deceived	mistaken belief	opposite
correct belief	limit	progress

Critical Questions

1. What question is the perceiver trying to answer?
2. Does the perceiver believe that every person in the world could be mistaken about something?
3. What does the essay mean when it says the word "mistaken" requires an opposite? Can you give some other examples of words that require opposites?
4. Newton said that all bodies attract each other and have weight. Everyone accepted the universal law of gravity. Later, in the space age, we discovered weightlessness. If the essay is right, how was it possible for people to believe that *everything* has weight, before they learned about weightlessness? It seems that weight did not have an opposite. Does this show that the essay is wrong?

5. Would it be possible to discover a society in which everyone was tall? Would it be possible for everyone on earth to be tall?
6. Does *language* determine what is possible and what isn't? Whether one's beliefs are mistaken or not is an objective fact, isn't it? Can our language make some objective facts impossible?

Methods and Techniques

PHILOSOPHY AND IMAGINATION

Both essays in this section illustrate the importance of imagination in philosophy. But they use imagination in slightly different ways. The first essay employs two "thought experiments," which are common in philosophy. It asks us to imagine an unusual situation (the person trapped in a room) and asks if it is any different from our own actual situation. The internalist claims it is not. The essay also asks us to imagine a future case in which a person's body is destroyed, leaving only the brain, and scientists manipulate the brain. It seems that we can imagine this, but is it really possible? The internalist claims that if it is possible, then it is also possible that our sense organs do not give us accurate information about the world, even when everything is normal.

The two thought experiments are strange and bizarre. But the highly imaginative examples serve a purpose. The internalist imagines these cases to find out how we think about our senses and our knowledge of the world. The thought experiments are intended to uncover some basic assumptions, or highlight certain aspects of our knowledge, that are not obvious in ordinary situations. The internalist's use of imagination is therefore different from a novelist's use. A novelist imagines characters, events, and settings that are realistic, normally, and the story exists for its own sake. We enjoy reading about imaginary people and places as a substitute for meeting them and being there ourselves. Literature is vicarious experience. The internalist, in contrast, wants to prove something. The strange situations aren't supposed to be interesting in themselves. They are supposed to make a point.

The second essay uses imagination, too, but in a slightly different way. Whereas the first focuses on strange medical cases, the second wonders about the meanings of key *words*, especially the word "mistaken." It says there are limits on what we can believe, limits imposed by the words we use. If we think carefully about the limits of our ideas (as embodied in words), we will see that some things cannot be true. The thesis is that it cannot be true that we are all, irredeemably, mistaken. The way to find the limits of our words is to imagine unusual situations and ask ourselves whether or not we could use a certain word in that situation. If we imagine that there are aspects of the world that no one could ever possibly know, then would we say that everyone was "mistaken"? The perceiver says no. The word cannot be used in that way because there is no opposite case. (By hypothesis, it is impossible to find out about these aspects.) But the word "mistaken" can only be used if there is the possibility of correcting the mistake.

The perceiver says there are other words that have similar limits, and imagines extreme cases to reveal their limits as well. For example, we are to imagine that everyone behaved the way people in insane asylums behave now. We could not say everyone is "crazy," because "crazy" requires a contrast with "normal," and if *everyone* behaves this way, then it is normal.

Other philosophers do the same thing. When philosophers discuss freedom, for example, they construct imaginary situations and ask if we can say a person in that situation is "free." Or "responsible." Or they imagine a strange situation and ask if we can say a certain action is "morally right." They are using their imagination to find the outer limits of these key concepts.

Understanding the Dilemma

INTERNALIST OR PERCEIVER?

Like many of the other disagreements you have read about, the disagreement in this section occurs on two levels, a specific level and a more general level. The specific disagreement is about our knowledge of the ordinary physical world, the world of tables and chairs, cats and dogs, sights and sounds. Is it possible that *all* those experiences are misleading and mistaken? Could we be mistaken about everything we see, hear, touch, taste, and smell? Is it possible that every moment of your life is like a continuous dream, created by your own mind, from which you never awaken? If you say yes, then you are an internalist. If you say no, then you are a perceiver.

An internalist believes that all you can really *know* is your own mind and your direct experiences. Everything else is merely conjecture, speculation, and guesswork. For example, let's say you seem to see a cup on the table before you. You might even pick it up. But your sense organs and your brain are only *interpreting* the complex lightwaves that enter your eye and neural impulses from your fingers. The real nature of whatever causes those lightwaves is unknown and beyond your reach. In contrast, a perceiver believes that the basic experiences we all have are the foundations of our knowledge. Experiences like seeing a cup *define* knowledge for us. Without having some examples of genuine knowledge, we would not even have any idea of ignorance or being mistaken. In the second essay, the perceiver bases the argument on the fact that the idea of an error is inseparable from the idea of being correct, and the idea of knowledge is inseparable from the idea of ignorance. Therefore not every belief can be an error.

This specific, theoretical disagreement is related to more general disagreements between the two positions. The internalist position appeals to people who trust their thinking and reasoning. Some people read step one of the argument, and it leads to step two, and then step two leads to step three, and these readers cannot find any mistakes in the reasoning. Then they accept step three, no matter how crazy it sounds. If the starting points are all true, and if the connections are all solid, then these people are willing to believe the conclusion, even if it sounds ridiculous to other people. Internalists are willing to think for themselves, even if the majority disagrees, or even if the majority thinks they are crazy.

Perceivers have a different attitude. They believe that common sense deserves more respect. If an argument or a discovery seems to turn common sense upside down, then there must be something wrong with the argument or the discovery. We just haven't found the mistake yet. Common sense is more reliable than any sophisticated philosophical argument, even if no one has uncovered the flaw in the argument yet.

The two sides disagree in another way. Anyone who believes that all of our experience is mistaken is clearly a person who is open to unusual ideas. An internalist is probably more tolerant of strange beliefs, open to any evidence, perhaps more willing to change his or her mind than most people (but not because of social pressure or majority opinion). If you cannot be sure that there is a cup in front of you, then what can you be sure about? If you are willing to accept internalism, then what theories are you going to reject as improbable?

Not many people are so flexible. Perceivers think that there are definite limits on what we can believe. Our beliefs are necessarily tied to language. Beliefs have to be expressed in language. And language imposes limits on what we can believe. We cannot make words mean anything we want them to mean. Our beliefs must make sense, they must be meaningful. This is not a moral limit on what we may believe, or a limit based on good manners. It is a limit based on meaning. What you believe must be meaningful, according to the perceiver. A perceiver says internalism isn't good, or bad, or clever, or outrageous. It is incomprehensible.

Perceivers believe that some philosophers say strange things, and they give what seem to be good reasons to back up their claims. But often they are using language in an illegitimate way. They are twisting words, or using one word with two different meanings, or playing another linguistic trick on us. If we pay careful attention to the words, we can uncover the trick. The perceiver tries to do this in "The Limits of Ignorance."

INTERNALIST

1. Each individual is trapped in his or her own perceptions.
2. The order and structure we perceive in the world may be created by our own minds, and may not be present in the world itself.
3. Most people have a very limited idea of what is possible.
4. All our ideas and knowledge come to us through our sense organs; animals with different sense organs experience an entirely different world.

PERCEIVER

5. It makes no sense to say everyone is mistaken and will always be mistaken; that is not how the word "mistaken" is used.

6. It is absurd to say that we cannot know ordinary things around us like tables and chairs.

7. If science or philosophy seems to overturn common sense, then so much the worse for science and philosophy.

8. Some writers play tricks with words and create paradoxes, but careful analysis will uncover the tricks.

FOR FURTHER STUDY

Historical Examples

INTERNALIST: George Berkeley. *Three Dialogues between Hylas and Philonous.* Many editions. Originally published in 1713. Berkeley tries to show that all we can ever know directly are the ideas and images in our own minds (and the ideas in God's mind).

PERCEIVER: John L. Austin. *Sense and Sensibilia.* Clarendon Press, 1962. Austin places great emphasis on the language we use to describe perception (e.g., the word "illusion"), and argues that illusions are not the same as delusions.

OTHER SOURCES

Bertrand Russell. *The Problems of Philosophy.* Oxford University Press, 1965. Originally published in 1912. Chap. 1, "Appearance and Reality," describes very clearly the problem of knowing the external world.

Julian Hochberg. *Perception.* 2nd Edition. Prentice-Hall, 1978. Chap. 3 includes a discussion of the physiology of vision.

C.H. Whiteley. *An Introduction to Metaphysics.* Barnes and Noble, 1964. Chap. 5 through 7 explain Berkeley's internalist position and a contemporary development of it called "phenomenalism."

Kenneth T. Gallagher. *The Philosophy of Knowledge.* Sheen and Ward, 1964. Chap. 4 presents the internalist view, and several perceiver responses based upon the careful analysis of ordinary language.

Barry R. Gross. *Analytic Philosophy: An Historical Introduction.* Pegasus, 1970. In chap. 10 Gross explains how two modern philosophers—Gilbert Ryle and J.L. Austin—appeal to the normal meanings of words to try to undermine the internalist position.

Hilary Putnam. *Reason, Truth, and History.* Cambridge University Press, 1981. See chap. 1, "Brains in a Vat," for a clear but challenging analysis of the thought experiment that the internalist uses.

Bruce Aune. *Knowledge of the External World.* Routledge, 1991. Discusses the history of the problem, with chapters on Locke, Berkeley, Hume, Kant, and Wittgenstein, and argues for a perceiver position.

5.2 DOES SCIENCE GIVE US REAL KNOWLEDGE?
POSITIVIST OR ROMANTIC?

———————————————— • ————————————————

S tudents who read about the medieval period of European history are often struck by the pervasive influence of religion at that time. People's beliefs and outlook on the world were decisively shaped by religion. Their daily routines often involved some religious function (like prayer, or giving thanks), and the important points of their lives—birth, marriage, weekly rest, etc.—were all dominated by religious rituals. Power and status in society were largely dependent on one's devotion to religion and the church. In 1200 the Pope was undoubtedly the most powerful man in Europe. The prominence and universality of religious faith is one of the things that make that period seem strange to us.

Two or three hundred years from now, future historians might look at the early twenty-first century and remark on how pervasive the influence of *science* is in our lives. Virtually everything we do is shaped by scientific discoveries, some of which occurred only recently (computers, microwave ovens, nuclear power). Our assumptions and outlook on life are shaped by science. For example, our view of human nature is largely determined by Darwin and Freud, and to some degree by Marx, a social scientist. Science and technology have a great impact on political power and social status: the United States' technological superiority in military hardware has changed the global balance of power, while Japan's technological innovations have made it an economic superpower.

The pervasive influence of science is a fact. But what should we think about that? How should we evaluate science? Is the influence good or bad? Or, to be more precise, which aspects are good and which are bad? Philosophers, social scientists, politicians, and ordinary citizens try to evaluate science from many different points of view. When most people ask "Is science a good thing or a bad thing?" they are thinking about the effects of science on our lives. For example, do the benefits of nuclear power outweigh the costs, or vice versa? Do the benefits of life-preserving technologies outweigh the costs, or vice versa?

But we can also try to evaluate science by a different standard. We can ask "Is science genuine *knowledge*?" Regardless of the effects it has, does science enable us to understand the world? What makes something knowledge, and what makes something merely opinion? The first essay in this section claims that science is real knowledge because it is objective. It presents the positivist's point of view. The second essay claims that science is not knowledge because it leaves out the lived, felt experience, which is necessary for genuine understanding. It presents the point of view of the romantic.

YES: POSITIVIST
"Science as Knowledge"

No force in the modern world is as important as science, not politics, not religion, not art. The growth of science during the past four hundred years has transformed every aspect of our lives, and even our minds. We do not think the same way as people ignorant of science, which is fortunate for us.

The reason for this overwhelming impact is that science, alone, provides us with real knowledge. Other enterprises may persuade people, and may command their fervent devotion, but they do not enable their practitioners to know and understand anything. To know (Latin *scire*) is the function of science.

In order to see this we must look at science more closely. The secret of science's power to give us knowledge lies in its method. Normally scientific method is divided into two parts, the method of discovery and the method of confirmation. The method of discovery can be discussed relatively quickly, but the method of confirmation requires more time. It is the method of confirmation that does the real work in science. But the method of discovery has its place. The method of discovery consists of observation and hypothesis. Scientific observation must be extremely thorough and precise. Many of the advances in science are simply extensions of our ability to observe the world. Galileo's telescope and van Leeuwenhoek's microscope are examples. Some scientists *noticed* things that others had overlooked. Darwin's monumental theory of evolution, for example, is based on years of patient observation (and a great deal of thinking about what he observed). Often a good scientist will see a problem where others do not. Science is founded on very careful observation. But the study of art also requires careful observation. Political progress depends upon observation as well, so thorough observation is not the key to science as knowledge.

More distinctive of scientific method is the formulation of hypotheses to explain the causes or patterns of things. The scientific investigator wants to formulate a law stating a reliable correlation between two phenomena, such as germs and disease, or oxygen and combustion, or magnetism and electricity. But there is no method of finding good hypotheses. Some people are good at imagining possible causes, and some people aren't. It is a knack that cannot be taught. Formulating hypotheses is essential to science. Science does not exist without hypotheses. But there is no *method* of finding hypotheses. It is regarded as part of the "method of discovery," but this is an imprecise use of the term "method." The ability to think of good hypotheses to explain confusing data is the surest mark of genius. In the war against ignorance, it sets apart the commanding generals from the ordinary foot soldiers. All the other parts of scientific method can be carried out by people with average talents. The observations that led Newton to formulate his law of gravity were ordinary observations which many people had made. But only Newton put them together in the right way. But again, the ability to see connections among disparate facts is not peculiar to science.

So much for the method of discovery. The method of confirmation is the vital heart of science. Once a scientist has observed some phenomena and formulated a hypothesis to explain them, then the scientist and others must decide whether or not the hypothesis is true. And then the real basis of the success of science is revealed. For how do scientists decide when a hypothesis is true? Do they appeal to the privileged authorities? Do they examine the established traditions? Do they calculate their class interests? No, they do none of these. Instead, they test it, using the method of confirmation. They set up a situation to see if the variables are really connected in the way the hypothesis says they are. Testing usually requires the deduction of certain consequences from the hypothesis. For example, if Lavoisier's hypothesis (that combustion is a mixing of oxygen with other substances) is true, then no combustion will occur in the absence of oxygen. And the hypothesis has other implications. If these are borne out in the laboratory, then the hypothesis is to some degree confirmed.

The method of confirmation yields knowledge because its results are *objective*. Real knowledge, by its very nature, is objective, not subjective, not a matter of personal taste. The objectivity of science depends on several aspects of confirmation. Perhaps the most basic aspect is repeatability. It is essential to the method of confirmation that the tests and results can be *repeated* by many investigators. Only then is a hypothesis accepted. If some scientists set up a situation in which combustion occurs without oxygen, then Lavoisier's hypothesis is rejected. But if many scientists repeat an experiment and all get the same results, then they have discovered a law. They now know something about combustion. Repeatability is essential because it demonstrates that the hypothesis is true in many different places (it isn't dependent on local conditions), and more important, it is independent of any one person's or group's biases or assumptions. It is objectively true, for anyone.

The requirement that tests be repeatable explains why scientists place so much emphasis on measurement. Measurement is simply the comparison of one thing with a second thing that is easy to observe and known to be stable and regular. For example, we measure the length of something by comparing it with the standard meter in Paris. We measure the temperature of something by comparing it with the expansion of mercury in a thermometer. We measure speed by comparing the distance covered with the movement of gears in a clock. By arbitrarily dividing the regular phenomenon into equal units (like centimeters, degrees, or seconds) we can *quantify* objects and processes. In other words, we can say the ashes weigh exactly 3 grams, or the liquid boils at exactly 99 degrees C. And quantification is essential for repeatability. Without it, scientists could never decide whether or not they got the "same" results. They could not know if their material was just as hot as Lavoisier's. With it, they have changed the world. Repeatability is the key to confirmation, then, because what is repeatable is objective.

The fact that scientific results are objective is one good reason to say that science provides us with genuine knowledge. And there are other reasons. The method of confirmation shows that scientists are *held accountable* for their beliefs. They are responsible to other scientists. Only when they can prove their hypothesis to other investigators, by explaining how they can get the same results, are the scientists entitled to accept it. Furthermore, they are held accountable by nature, so to speak. Since their hypothesis must be testable, it must be about something people can see and measure and work with. Nature is complex and subtle, and if it behaves differently, or refuses to cooperate, then the scientists must give up their hypothesis.

Another way to put this is to say that scientists must be able to make predictions that turn out true. Successful prediction is perhaps the best measure of real knowledge. A scientist who has found a law that relates X and Y will be able to predict the occurrence of Y. (It follows X.) For example, Pascal hypothesized that the atmosphere is "an ocean of air," and that the pressure of the atmosphere is weaker at higher altitudes than at sea level. X, altitude, is correlated with Y, atmospheric pressure. He then derived a prediction from his hypothesis. He predicted that if we go up on a mountain top and measure the atmospheric pressure with a barometer, it will be less than the pressure at sea level. Anyone could test this prediction. Pascal invited other scientists to try to prove him wrong. But, in fact, his prediction was correct.

Two other aspects of scientific method are important in regard to knowledge. The necessity of measurement shows that statements and laws in science must be precise and perfectly clear. There is no room for grand sounding "essences," or "forces," or "dimensions," which cannot be observed and measured. All too often people think they understand something, when in fact the words they use are so vague and shifting that they are meaningless. The scientist isn't permitted such an indulgence. Scientific knowledge is exact, and can be communicated clearly, as anything worthy of the name "knowledge" must be.

Finally, science is self-correcting. Individuals and even whole communities of scientists can be mistaken. But science has a built-in mechanism for discovering and correcting such mistakes. It is the critical, probing attitude fostered by the open-ended nature of the method of confirmation. No hypothesis is ever absolutely confirmed; some are merely more confirmed than others, if they have been more widely tested. Confirmation is never complete. That means that every law and theory is fair game to be tested in a new way, if a scientist can devise a new test. Thus scientific knowledge can never harden into a set of rigid, sacrosanct principles (which may be wrong). Continuous testing uncovers errors, and leads to new discoveries. No error can last for long under such continuous questioning and testing. Thus science corrects itself.

As a result, science changes rapidly. One of the most remarkable features of science is how quickly theories and ideas are superseded by new discoveries. Textbooks must be rewritten constantly. Professional scientists must reeducate themselves just as often. Contrast science with other areas. Our politics, religion, and art aren't much different from the ancients'. Some would say they have even declined. Only in science has there been indisputable progress.

Key Concepts

observation	objective	repeatable experiment
quantification	confirmation	self-correcting
hypothesis	accountable	

Critical Questions

1. What is a hypothesis? Can you give some examples of hypotheses, either your own or others'?
2. Why is it important for experiments to be repeated?
3. Would the positivist say that geology, botany, and astronomy are sciences? Do geologists, etc. conduct experiments to test hypotheses, or do they only make observations?
4. Exactly how does a scientist measure something? How does a scientist measure eyesight, for example? (20/20, 20/40, etc.)
5. Can you think of something that cannot be quantified, in the way the essay describes quantification? Strength? Poverty? Intelligence? Boredom? Progress? Culpability?
6. What does the positivist mean by the term "objective"? Could a person be objective about literature, or morality, in this sense?
7. How is science self-correcting, according to the essay? If scientists continually criticize each other's work, and science constantly changes, then isn't it like fashion, with one fad following another?

NO: ROMANTIC

"What Kind of Understanding?"

It is sad to see how many people today are bewitched by the mystique of Science. It is regarded with awe and reverence, a healer and a guide, the source of truth. It has its high priests and its houses of worship, and the masses repeat its catechism, with no more comprehension than the illiterate medieval peasant had of the Latin mass. But medieval religion gave the peasant an understanding of the purpose of the cosmos and his place in it. Science has nothing to say of the meaning of our existence, or our destiny.

Science limits itself to discovering the causes of certain material effects. It discovers "laws," according to which *A* will produce *B*. "An action will produce an equal and opposite reaction." "Friction produces heat." But such formulas do not provide any insight into the *significance* of these processes. What is the goal toward which all these *A*'s and *B*'s are moving? *Why* does *A* produce *B*? For what purpose? Science has no answers to these questions. It says nothing about the larger meaning of the abstract processes it studies.

Even within its own domain, Science cannot satisfy the curious mind. It only enables scientists to manipulate material objects. But manipulation is not understanding. Anyone who knows the recipe can bake a cake, without having the slightest idea of what you are doing. You put in *A*, and you take out *B*, and it doesn't matter what *A* and *B* are, or why *A* leads to *B*. All that matters is cause and effect. Examine any physics textbook. You will see an enormous number of formulas. They are reliable recipes, and if you follow them you can produce certain results, even if you don't understand all the symbols or why the recipes work. Following a formula is one thing, knowledge of nature is another. Science has mistaken control for comprehension, and manipulation for understanding. In fact, the real goal of Science is power, not knowledge.

The increasing specialization in Science is another handicap that hinders it from attaining true understanding. The power to manipulate objects has grown so much that one person can learn the recipes for only a small part of nature. No chemist would pretend to understand physics or biology. Even within chemistry, physical chemists regard organic chemists as virtually alien. Even within one narrow area, each individual chemist has his or her own esoteric specialty, which only a few other chemists can understand. Since each scientist studies only a tiny fragment of nature, no one can see the whole. No one is trained to look for the pattern of nature in its totality. And that would be knowledge truly worth having.

Another self-imposed limitation on Science is its demand for quantification. Scientists love numbers and mathematical formulas, and sometimes seem to think that if they force something into a mathematical formula, then they have understood it. The absurdities to which this leads are especially evident in "the social sciences." But how can a scientist measure love, or hope, or tragedy? Or meaning? The features of the cosmos that make it meaningful cannot be weighed and measured, like gravity or the Galvanic skin response. Science cuts itself off from all those parts of the world that we must study and absorb if we are to make sense of it. A botanist might count the number of species of plants in an area without understanding the woods as well as an observant hiker. The botanist doesn't even see the woods. He or she doesn't see the shadows, or hear the stillness, or smell the clean air. An experienced hiker knows the woods, but what does the botanist know? Nothing that I can see.

Science is literally dehumanizing. It disdains normal human responses to the world, disparaging them as "subjective." Science cannot handle human beings. It claims that we are actually just complicated computers. It must say that, because our inner experiences—which machines do not have—are completely inaccessible to Science. Only you, and you alone, can know what your experience of a fresh spring day is like. You can try to communicate your experience to a friend, but then she is only relating your words to *her* experience. She cannot feel your experience. So the real quality of your life cannot be reduced to cause and effect, cannot be measured, it cannot even be observed at all (except by yourself). Everything that makes us human is ignored and denied by Science. But if the universe is comprehensible at all, it must be comprehensible *to us*, as human beings. It must be humanly intelligible.

One tragicomic aspect of Science is that it takes great pride in precisely those rules that prevent it from reaching a higher level of understanding. Science rests on observation and experiment; its saint is the "normal observer." Its conclusions must be accessible, theoretically, to anyone. In principle, anyone should be able to perform the experiments and make the observations that Science rests on. Thus Science is radically democratic. That may or may not be good politics, but it is certainly bad philosophy. It reduces truth to the lowest common denominator. Any truths that require unusual imagination, extraordinary sensitivity, or a rare breadth of mind, are disqualified. And that is sad.

Science has given us tremendous power to change and control nature. But power corrupts. We are now beginning to see the corruption and the damage we have done to the natural world. But the corruption goes deeper. The power has blinded us to the intellectual limitations of Science. Science yields meaningless, abstract formulas rather than understanding. It restricts people to narrow specialties. Its obsession with numbers rules out most experiences. It ignores the inner world of feelings and values. And it decertifies the truths discovered by eccentric, creative people, such as poets and artists. The most frightening thought is that if people do not understand the infatuation with power and technology soon, we could blindly destroy the living earth and the human race.

Key Concepts

destiny	quantification	specialization
private experience	manipulation	lowest common denominator
scientific law	normal observer	

Critical Questions

1. Why don't scientific laws enable us to understand the natural world, according to a romantic?

2. Are control and understanding different? If scientists can control something, e.g., reproduction, malaria, or electricity, does that mean they can understand it?

3. Is specialization a bad thing, in your opinion? Does it prevent people from acquiring a unified picture of the whole world?

4. Psychology is often described as "the science of human behavior," because behavior is observable. Can there be a science of human *experience* (human emotions, imagination, intentions)?

5. What does the romantic mean by saying that science has a democratic bias?

6. Do you think there may be important insights, concepts, principles, or truths that some people will never be able to understand?

Methods and Techniques

MAKING ASSUMPTIONS

Positivists and romantics disagree because they make different *assumptions* about knowledge. Assumptions play a key role in philosophers' thinking. An assumption is a belief that someone takes for granted. It is something that a person believes is so obvious that it is not necessary to back it up, or support it with evidence. Philosophers are sometimes aware of the assumptions they are making, but sometimes they are not aware of them. In the first essay the positivist assumes that scientists make experiments, that we can know some things, and that science makes progress. In the second essay the romantic assumes that scientists are similar to each other, that we can know the forests and woods, and that people have different abilities.

To find a writer's assumptions, readers should put themselves in the writer's shoes, so to speak. They should try to see and feel the world from the writer's point of view. In fact, the concept of assumptions is similar to the concept of point of view. A person's point of view is, literally, the place from which the person sees the world. If I am sitting in the balcony at a play, and you are sitting at stage level, then our points of view are different. You will actually see the characters and the play differently from the way I see them. Speaking metaphorically, your point of view is the set of beliefs, values, and attitudes you have. My beliefs and values will influence the way I see the play, and if your beliefs and values are different from mine, then you and I will see the play differently.

For example, we may both watch Hamlet kill Polonius. But while I see a young man who has lost his mind, you see a young man who finally summons up enough courage to act decisively. I say to myself, "Hamlet killed Polonius. Therefore he is insane." You say, "Hamlet killed Polonius. Therefore he is courageous." How can our perceptions and conclusions be so different? They are different because we are making different assumptions. I am assuming that Hamlet loves and admires Polonius, since he has known Polonius for so many years. Anyone who kills someone he admires must be insane. But you are assuming that Hamlet has contempt for Polonius, since he went along with the murder of Hamlet's father. Anyone who kills an accomplice to the murder of his father is acting decisively, you think. I watch the scene and conclude that Hamlet is insane. You begin with the same evidence, but conclude that he is decisive. Our different assumptions lead us to different conclusions.

The first essay argues that science is genuine knowledge. The main evidence is that science rests upon repeatable experiments, and is therefore objective. The positivist is assuming that if an account of the world is objective, then it is real knowledge. But the romantic rejects this assumption, and claims that a strictly objective description leaves out most of what we perceive and learn about the world. It actually distorts our real experience. The romantic assumes that an objective account of the world cannot be genuine knowledge. The two writers are making opposite assumptions, so naturally they reach different conclusions.

Assumptions are extremely important because a philosopher's conclusion is only as convincing as the reasons he or she has to support it. An argument is like a chain, and a chain is only as strong as its weakest link. If philosophers make an assumption that is questionable, then their whole point of view becomes questionable. So philosophers try to be very sensitive to assumptions. They try not to take anything for granted, if possible. Or at least, they try to make assumptions that everyone agrees are true. Positivists believe that their assumption (objective results are knowledge) is obvious and accepted, but in fact, romantics reject this claim. They assert (assume) that some of our knowledge is personal and subjective.

Philosophers usually cannot avoid making some assumptions. The process of giving reasons cannot go on forever. But they can at least make all of their assumptions explicit. They can state them openly, so that everyone can see what they are assuming, and what their conclusion depends on. But it is difficult to be aware of all of one's assumptions. Sometimes philosophers will take something for granted without realizing that they are doing so. The assumption seems so obvious that they never even think about stating it explicitly. For example, the positivist assumes that we do know some things, that knowledge exists. But others have questioned even this statement. It is *hidden* assumptions that are the most dangerous. They are beliefs that a philosopher takes for granted without examining carefully. They may be true, or they may not.

As you read philosophy, or talk about the issues, you should be extremely attentive to arguments. That is, you should understand the conclusion, and the reasons that support it. And you should use your judgment to decide which reasons are good reasons, and which are not. (Some people just look at the conclusion and decide whether they agree with it or not, without examining the reasons behind it.) With a little practice, you can learn to recognize which reasons are themselves backed up by additional reasons, and which are merely assumptions. Of all the skills that philosophers develop, the ability to see assumptions—one's own and others'—is probably the most important, because assumptions are the weakest parts of a philosopher's position.

Understanding the Dilemma

POSITIVIST OR ROMANTIC?

These two essays represent two different ways of thinking about knowledge. The positivist believes knowledge must be objective. It must be about the world itself, as it really is, not about one person's idiosyncratic responses. Being objective means being independent of any individual's particular point of view or particular reactions. Whatever is objective is common to many people, in fact, to anyone who investigates the matter impartially. Scientists go to great lengths to satisfy this demanding requirement of objectivity, and when they succeed, they produce knowledge.

A romantic has a very different view of knowledge. For most people the term "romantic" means a person who easily falls in love, or a person given to dreamy fantasies. But in the early 1800s the romantic movement produced many interesting ideas about many topics, including knowledge. Here the term "romantic" means anyone who believes that real knowledge comes only from lived experience. Before you can know something, you must experience it directly. For example, a friend could tell you what it is like to ride on a roller coaster. But you would not have real knowledge of riding on a roller coaster. To have real knowledge, you must ride it yourself. And the more fully you can experience something, the more you know it. You should engage your whole mind, your senses, your feelings, your memories, your imagination, your entire being, in the experience. The more aspects or levels your encounter has, the better your knowledge will be. If you limit your experience to only one part of your mind—your intellect—then you are severely limiting your knowledge.

A positivist believes the romantic's principle is exactly backward. The degree to which you allow your personal feelings to shape your experience is the degree to which you *obstruct* knowledge. Knowledge must be objective, and the opposite of objective is subjective, that is, dependent on one person's particular reactions, colored by the individual's own emotions and desires, inward, private, incommunicable. Being subjective means mistaking your own personal feelings or imagination for reality itself. Your feelings are yours alone, but reality is common to everyone. Any understanding of the real world, therefore, must be common to everyone.

Naturally the romantic believes the positivist has everything backward. Knowledge comes from experience, but the positivist tries to suppress experience. The romantic says the positivist has taken one narrow aspect of human experience (measurement and experimentation), elevated it to the supreme position, and denigrated every other aspect. The positivist tries to deny our human nature, our other ways of knowing about the world, our emotions, and our personal responses to nature which we cannot even put into words. It is a mistake to think that we can sharply separate understanding from feeling, thought from emotion, or perception from personal reaction. To separate them is to distort our experience, and therefore our understanding of reality.

Who is right? Does science discover real knowledge? Or does a poet or artist give us a better understanding of things? Do you think knowledge must be objective? Must you suppress your personal, subjective reactions in order to understand the world? Or are your emotions and personal responses the only source of real knowledge? Are you a positivist or a romantic?

POSITIVIST

1. The best example of genuine knowledge that we have is physics.
2. Knowledge must be objective, the same for everyone, and accessible to everyone.
3. If you cannot measure something, and test it experimentally, then you cannot have real knowledge about it.
4. The best proof that science provides knowledge is that science makes progress while other endeavors (like art, politics, and religion) do not.

ROMANTIC

5. Science ignores the most important kinds of experience and knowledge.
6. We know and understand many things that cannot be measured or tested experimentally.
7. The scientific outlook is fine for some things, but it is extremist to say it is the only way to gain knowledge of anything.
8. Artists, poets, writers, and musicians can teach us more about the world and life than scientists can.

FOR FURTHER STUDY

Historical Examples

POSITIVIST: Norman Campbell. *What Is Science?* Dover, 1952. Chap. 8 is an interesting discussion of the scope and capabilities of the scientific method, as well as its limitations.

ROMANTIC: Henri Bergson. *Introduction to Metaphysics*. Roman and Allenheld, 1983. Originally published in 1903. Bergson favors what he calls "intuition" over science because science studies only classes of objects, not individuals, but through intuition we can understand the inner nature of things.

OTHER SOURCES

James H. Fetzer. *The Philosophy of Science*. Paragon House, 1993. In chap. 8 Fetzer assesses and rejects various challenges (e.g., instrumentalism, Kuhn's paradigms, sociology of knowledge, etc.) to the traditional, realist view of science as knowledge.

Martin Goldstein, Inge Goldstein. *The Experience of Science*. Plenum Press, 1984. The authors claim that the feeling of understanding is not the same as understanding, and they explain what else one must have in order to have real understanding.

Corliss Lamont. *The Philosophy of Humanism*. Frederick Ungar, 1965. Includes an explanation of scientific method, and a defense of the claim that it provides us with real knowledge.

Thomas S. Kuhn. *The Structure of Scientific Revolutions*. 2nd Edition. University of Chicago Press, 1970. A revolutionary book; extremely influential, among philosophers as well as people interested in other disciplines; introduced the concept of a "paradigm."

A.F. Chalmers. *What Is This Thing Called Science?* 3rd Edition. Hackett, 1999. Clear discussion of the issues.

Frederick E. Mosedale, ed. *Philosophy and Science: The Wide Range of Interaction*. Prentice-Hall, 1979. See selection 24, by William A. Earle, "Science and the Philosophy of Science Cannot Examine Life as It Is Lived."

P.B. Medawar. *The Limits of Science*. Harper & Row, 1984. Medawar argues that we must look to literature, religion, and philosophy, not science, for answers to questions about first and last things.

Steve Fuller. *The Philosophy of Science and Its Discontents*. 2nd Edition. The Guilford Press, 1993. Sympathetic survey of many criticisms of science by a romantic.

5.3 Is Experience the Source of All Knowledge?
Empiricist or Rationalist?

---•---

Everyone believes that knowledge is valuable and important. Look at these two sentences:

a. The doctor knows that you have disease X, and knows this treatment will help you.
b. The doctor believes that you have disease X, and believes this treatment will help you.

Sentence (*a*) is much more reassuring, much more comforting, than sentence (*b*). We contrast knowledge with mere belief. Where something important is concerned, like our own health, we insist upon knowledge rather than belief. When we are curious about something, such as the author of a book, the surface of Mars, the new tax laws, what we want is knowledge, not merely opinions. A variety of beliefs about the surface of Mars might be interesting. People used to believe the surface was covered with canals. But mere beliefs seem quaint and irrelevant beside knowledge of the same subject.

Knowledge is a kind of guarantee, or validation, or final word. If we cannot reach the high level of knowledge about something, then we are stuck with opinion, conjecture, hypothesis, hearsay, rumor, speculation, and so on. All these are assertions or states of mind that can be challenged and questioned. All these words have a faintly negative connotation. Knowledge, in contrast, brings to mind words like "proof," "certainty," "fact," "truth," and "justified."

Since knowledge is highly regarded, everyone wants to know how to get it, or where it comes from. Knowledge is like good character. Everyone agrees that good character is important. So everyone, especially parents and teachers, want to know how to produce it in children. Where does it come from, or what creates good character in a young person? What is the source of good character? People (particularly philosophers) ask the same questions about knowledge.

There are many theories about what produces good character, but the essays in this section are about knowledge, and most people have said that the main source of knowledge is *experience*. If you want to know what China is like, then go there and see it for yourself. If you want to know what the San Francisco earthquake of 1906 was like, then read accounts by people who lived through it. Ultimately knowledge derives from experience, according to this common view. One can even say that *all* knowledge must come from experience.

The first essay of this section tries to explain why many people believe all our ideas and knowledge must originate in experience. This view is called "empiricism." The second essay, on the other hand, tries to show that at least one kind of knowledge—mathematics—does not depend on experience. We will call this position "rationalism."

YES: EMPIRICST

"The Source of Knowledge"

No controversy is older or more persistent than the controversy over heredity and environment. Are people born with certain abilities, desires, and beliefs, or do they acquire them through experience? How much of a person is created by his or her surroundings, and how much would be the same no matter what the surroundings were? It is a complex issue, and I am certainly not going to settle it in this brief essay. I have a more modest aim. I want to examine one part of the question of heredity vs. environment, and ask whether *knowledge* is inherited or acquired. On this small part of the issue, the evidence points to environment as the source.

Everyone believes that both heredity and environment contribute to the formation of a human being. Some people's genes dictate that they will be athletically gifted, or musically talented, or mathematically skilled. Studies of identical twins (who have identical genes) suggest that traits like assertiveness and obedience to authority may be inherited. But at the same time, people's environment determines how they develop their inborn potential, or whether they develop it at all. The most important part of the environment is probably the social environment, including parents, siblings, friends, teachers, and other people. A person is also molded by the cultural environment, which includes resources like books, libraries, films, and TV. The physical environment includes clean or dirty air, noise, sunlight, and other things.

Psychologists argue over the amount of influence heredity and environment have. But they are arguing over the influences on *personality*. Instead of looking at such a large issue, I want to narrow the focus a little. What determines the way a person thinks? Where do people's *ideas* come from? On this question, the most popular answer is environment alone. According to this theory, our memories, thoughts, and beliefs, depend on our experiences in school, with our parents, watching movies and TV, and all the things we perceive in our particular environment.

The theory that all of our ideas originate in sensory experience is called *empiricism*. This theory makes two main claims. First, it says that a person's beliefs are complex wholes that can be broken down into simpler parts. And second, it says that all the parts must originate in experience. Let's look at the first claim: a belief can be broken down into simpler parts. An example is the belief that dogs are loyal animals. This belief is made up of the idea of dogs, the idea of loyal, and the idea of animals. In other words, we can analyze the belief into those three parts. Furthermore, each of these ideas can be broken down into simpler ideas. The idea of a dog can be analyzed into the idea of having four legs, the idea of barking, of having a certain shape, fur, a wet nose, and so on. Other ideas can be analyzed into their parts as well. The idea of loyal can be broken down into the idea of respecting, admiring, or liking something, and the idea of maintaining an attitude over a period of time. Any complex idea can be broken down into parts. The idea of a dinner plate can be broken down into the ideas of round, flat with a raised edge, and used for holding food. Most of our ideas are complex, and can be analyzed in this way. In fact, most definitions are just such analyses. A definition breaks down an idea into its parts.

Each of the constituent ideas can be analyzed even further. But eventually we get to the simplest, most basic ideas, like the idea of brown, of long shape, and of high-pitched sound. These ideas have no parts. They cannot be defined (as "dog" and "plate" can). They are the building blocks for all our more complicated ideas and beliefs.

Where do these simplest ideas come from? The answer to that question is the second main claim of empiricism. Empiricism claims that all simple ideas come from sensory experience, i.e., sight, hearing, touch, smell, and taste. When we *see* something brown then we acquire an idea of brown and understand the idea. Brown things create the idea in our minds, and we remember it. The same is true for the idea of high-pitched sound, warmth, sour taste, and so on. Sensory experience also includes inner perception. I have an idea of pain, because I sense it within myself.

Babies' senses are bombarded by thousands of qualities. The infants form simple ideas of those qualities and store them in their memories. Over time they learn which ideas go together (like the simple ideas that make up the idea "dog"), and they begin to form more complex ideas. Psychologists can study children and learn how they put their ideas together. They can observe which ideas are associated with which others, and they may discover laws of association. For example, the great Swiss psychologist, Jean Piaget, discovered that young children associate shape and volume. They believe that a short, fat glass holds less water than a tall, thin glass. Later, when they see the same amount of water poured from one glass to the other, they realize that shape and volume are independent and should not be associated. The origin of children's ideas, and the associations they make, are all based on sensory experience.

Empiricism is therefore a theory of the mind. It is an explanation of the contents of the mind and how they are arranged. In many ways it is a kind of "chemistry" of the mind. Like chemistry, it seeks the ultimate particles out of which everything else is made. A chemist analyzes substances into their component parts, or elements. He or she studies atoms, which combine to form molecules, while the empirical psychologist studies simple ideas, which combine to form complex ideas. Moreover the chemist looks for different kinds of combinations, or different laws of combination. Some elements combine easily, others hardly at all. The empirical psychologist looks for the same laws of ideas. Some ideas attract each other, some form strong bonds, some repel each other, and so on.

Empiricists present more evidence to support their theory. They point out that the *only* way a person can have a simple idea is to have a sensation of it. For example, if a woman is blind and has never seen the color brown, then she cannot imagine the color. If someone is deaf and has never heard a high-pitched sound like a train whistle, then she cannot understand another person who talks about it. Do you like the smell of cedar? If you have never smelled it, then you cannot say.

Empiricism is not only a theory of the mind and its contents but is also a theory of knowledge. It explains the difference between true knowledge and unfounded belief. The difference is experience. If a belief is grounded in experience then it is true, and qualifies as knowledge. But if a belief is not based on any experience, then it is merely belief, or imagination, not knowledge. For example, my 12-year-old son believes that some swans are black. He associates the idea of a swan with the idea of black. He makes the association because we recently visited the zoo and he actually saw black swans there. His belief counts as knowledge because it is based on experience. But if he makes the association just because he wants to, or he likes to play with ideas in his imagination, then it is not knowledge. If he believed that some swans are green, that would not be knowledge, because he has never seen green swans. Furthermore, his older sister was not with us at the zoo, but he told her that some swans are black, and now she knows about black swans, too. Her association of the ideas is based on experience, although not her own experience. It is based on her brother's experience. But if a belief cannot be traced back to someone's perceptual experience, then it is not knowledge but only fanciful speculation.

Thus empiricism is a comprehensive theory of the mind and its knowledge. But is it broad enough to cover all our ideas and knowledge? Some critics of empiricism point to ideas and beliefs that, they say, do not come from experience. The most common example is mathematical knowledge. Everyone knows that $7 + 5 = 12$, that $9 \div 3 = 3$, and that the four sides of a square are equal. How did we get the idea of equality? Mathematicians say we did *not* acquire the idea from looking at equal lines. The four sides of a square are *perfectly* equal, but we never see perfectly equal lines. All the lines we see with our eyes are slightly irregular. They may be almost equal, and we may have to look very closely to see the difference in length, but we always can. Physical lines cannot be perfectly equal. But we have an idea of perfect equality. Therefore, they conclude, we have some ideas that are not based on experience.

Empiricists are not convinced by this example. They say that we can manipulate and modify the ideas we receive through our senses. For example, we can experience a rock that is very hard and almost never breaks or crumbles. And then we can think of the same rock, but leave out completely the idea of breaking. We can imagine a rock that never breaks. We simply trim away some of the ideas that we have experienced. Then we have an idea of an "unbreakable rock." We never experience such a thing, but we can imagine it by manipulating ideas we have experienced. And we can imagine perfect equality in the same way.

Mathematicians also claim that we can know mathematical truths which are not based on experience. We know that nine divided by three is three. We *have* seen a group of nine things divided by three, but that experience is not the basis of our knowledge, they say. It cannot be the basis, because we are absolutely certain about this truth; we cannot imagine nine divided by three being anything else but three. We are never absolutely certain about something we have experienced. It is always possible that our eyes could be playing tricks on us. And we can imagine that we are wrong. I saw black swans at the zoo, but the lighting may have been bad, someone could be playing a trick on us, the swans may not look black when you look more closely, and so on. But nine divided by three is always three. Mathematical truths, then, are not based on experience.

But again, empiricists do not find these arguments persuasive. Mathematicians base their view on their feelings of certainty and on what they can imagine. But feelings of certainty are a matter of degree. One feels sure, or very sure, or completely sure. There is no sharp line between being certain and being absolutely certain. And empiricists can explain why we feel so certain about mathematical truths. They are very obvious, and very common. Anyone can see that a group of nine oranges divided by three gives us three groups of oranges.

Moreover, we can see these truths very often. They are reinforced almost everyday, and we never see the contrary. But we very rarely see black swans. Mathematicians also say we cannot imagine other answers but the true ones. But imagination is a matter of degree just as certainty is. What some people can't imagine, other people can. Some people's imaginations are more fertile than other people's. What seems unimaginable at one period of history becomes commonplace later. And it seems that students are perfectly capable of imagining wrong answers. They do it on tests all the time! Mathematical truths are no different from other kinds of truths. They must be based on experience if they are to qualify as knowledge.

All these considerations show that what we think and what we know depend on "nurture," not "nature." That is, experience is the source of all our basic ideas and is the test of our knowledge. Empiricism does not settle all the questions about inborn traits versus environment. There may still be some kinds of behavior that are inherited and unchangeable. But it does settle the question of what we think and what we know. We think and know what we have experienced.

Key Concepts

empiricist	complex idea	counterexample
simple idea	senses	experience

Critical Questions

1. Does an empiricist believe that heredity or environment is more important in the development of a person's mind?
2. Empiricism claims that ideas are either complex or simple. Is the idea of a tree complex, or is it simple? That is, can it be broken down into simpler ideas, or is it simple itself? (The idea of a grain of sand? An atom? Fire? The idea of walking?)
3. Suppose a person has never seen a gopher, or even a picture of one. Can that person have an idea of a gopher, in your opinion? If so, how? If so, does that show that the second claim of empiricism is wrong? Can a person have an idea of a dragon? How?
4. The idea of gravity is very abstract. Do people acquire the idea through sense perception (i.e., experience)?
5. Do you know that 2 + 2 = 4 because many times you have seen two things added to two other things to make a group of four things? Or do you know it is true because you think about the ideas involved, and you see that they are related?
6. Can you think of any ideas that are not acquired through sensory experience? Are moral ideas learned by observing things? How do we perceive the qualities of "morally right" or "morally wrong"? When two people disagree on a moral issue, is it because they have different perceptions?

NO: RATIONALIST

"The Strange Case of the Mathematician"

When I was in college I had a strange experience, which still puzzles me when I think about it.

It was in my senior year. I was taking a required math course, and I did poorly on the first test. That made me angry. I was really angry at myself for not studying, and at the world for not recognizing how special and brilliant I was. But at the time I thought I was angry at Professor Chang, the math teacher. I wanted a better grade. So I went up to the front of the room as everyone was leaving and said, "I have a question about my test. Are you sure this answer is incorrect?" Professor Chang looked at the red-marked paper for a moment, and said he was.

"But there are many algebra textbooks," I said. "Don't some of them give different answers to this problem? My history teacher says we should look at several texts or other sources, and try to decide who has the best answer. Why do you think this text is the best text?"

"Your history teacher is right . . . about history," Professor Chang said. "But math is different. It doesn't matter which text we use. They all agree. They might choose different topics to talk about, but on the same topic, they all give exactly the same answers. Not only that, but every math book ever written would agree on the answer to this problem."

That sounded a little fanatical to me. "It sounds like mathematicians aren't very creative. Why don't you challenge authority sometimes?"

"It's not a matter of authority," he said. "I decided for myself that this answer is correct. I'm absolutely certain of it."

"How can you be so sure?"

"Well, let's look at the problem." It was a simple equation, and he explained it. His point was that, once you understand the ideas, then you *can't imagine* being wrong. "Take a simpler case," he said. "If A is greater than B, and B is greater than C, then A is greater than C, right?"

"Right."

"Are you sure?" he asked.

"Yeah, I think so."

"I'm sure, too. In fact, I'm absolutely certain of it, because I don't even know what it would *mean* to say it is *not* true. Think about three boxes, and picture the first one as larger than the second, and the second as larger than the third. Now, can you hold that idea in your mind, and at the same time think that the first is *not* larger than the third? I can't. Or $2 + 2 = 4$. The principle is the same. Can you really believe that $2 + 2$ is equal to 5?"

"Maybe. Why not? I just say '$2 + 2 = 5$.'"

"Saying it isn't believing it. I don't think you can really believe it, once you understand the concepts. I know I can't."

By this time I was a little confused, and I wasn't sure what to say. I was trying to figure out a way to get Chang to bend a little on my test. "So you're absolutely certain about these equations, because you can't imagine being wrong. And every other mathematician agrees with you." He nodded. Then I thought of something my physics teacher said. She said the most important characteristic of a scientist is that he or she is open-minded. What he believes today might be disproved tomorrow, when we make new discoveries. I told Professor Chang that, and added "It looks like mathematicians have an unscientific attitude."

His answer surprised me. "In a way you're right," he said. "Their attitude toward math isn't exactly the same as the physicist's attitude toward physics. But the reason is that mathematicians don't make progress in the same way physicists do."

"Yeah. You mean it's sort of like an ancient religion."

"No, no," he laughed. "They discover new truths, new laws, but not in the same way physicists do. Math isn't based on observation. Mathematicians don't use microscopes or fancy technology. They just think. They think about relationships among ideas that are defined very precisely."

"I don't get it."

"Well look. You agree that physicists discover laws by looking at the way things work, conducting experiments, measuring, and so forth."

"Right."

"And if anyone asks them how they know a law is true—for example, how they know that water expands when it freezes—they point to the experiments."

"Yeah, I guess so," I said.

"Well, math isn't like that. Why do you believe $2 + 2 = 4$? Did you perform an experiment to check it? No. Why do you believe that if A is larger than B, and B is larger than C, then A is larger than C? Have you compared a lot of boxes? No. These beliefs are not based on observation. We all believe these things because we see that they *must* be true. We see, with our mind, that 2 and 2 are related to 4. We don't have to make any observations or experiments to know that."

I had to admit that the idea of mathematicians making experiments by adding up apples, or cutting a pie into quarters, did sound pretty silly.

Chang continued. "Physicists have to be open-minded because the laws of physics aren't certain. They're true, as far as we know, but they aren't *necessarily* true. The law about water expanding when it freezes just happens to be true, but the world could have been made so that water shrinks when it freezes. It just turned out differently. But the laws of math are *necessary*. No world could exist in which $2 + 2 = 5$."

By now my head was spinning, so I thanked Professor Chang for his patience and left.

I couldn't forget about what he said, though. It sounded so odd, so different from what all my other teachers kept saying, about questioning everything, and getting the facts. But when I thought about his examples, he seemed to be right. I really couldn't believe that $2 + 2 = 5$. The fact that A is larger than C seemed to be different from the fact that water expands when it freezes. How could it be absolutely certain and necessary? How could it be something everyone knows and agrees on, but not based on any observation or experience?

Over the next couple of days I decided that math was just a kind of game. It all depends on the definitions and rules. We *define* "2 + 2" as "4," just as we define "bachelor" as "unmarried male." It is true that a bachelor is an unmarried male, and we are certain about it. Once you see what the words mean, then you can be sure they are related. You can't imagine a bachelor who is *not* an unmarried male. But no one *discovered* that bachelors are unmarried. Human beings invented language, and we all decided that, so long as we speak English, those two expressions will be related.

I thought that the rules of math are like the rules of a game. If you're playing baseball, and you get three strikes, then you're out. There's no way you *can't* be out, so long as you accept the rules of baseball. But of course games and definitions are just arbitrary. We made up all of them. They don't have anything to do with the natural world.

I was proud of my theory, and I thought that if I could get Chang to accept it he might reconsider my grade. But he didn't accept it. And now, in retrospect, I think he is right. I explained my theory to him. He said, "If math depended on definitions, then we could *change* them, couldn't we? We could change the definition of "bachelor," or the rules of baseball, if we wanted to. But we can't change the fact that 2 + 2 = 4. Math isn't about *numerals*—3, III, "three," or *trois*—but about *numbers*, the things those symbols stand for."

"What do you mean?"

"Well, a numeral is a sign, or symbol, that stands for a number. For example "3" stands for the number 3. So does "three," *trois*, and other things. They are different numerals, but they all stand for the same number."

"OK."

"The numerals we use are arbitrary. We could change the word for three. We could decide that, from now on, when we mean three we will say "four," and write "4." Then "4 + 4" would equal 6. But we have only changed the symbols we use. We haven't changed the relationships among the numbers. Numbers and their relationships are independent of us."

"But how can we be absolutely certain, if it is not a matter of definition," I asked.

"That's a good question. Actually it's a philosophical question. And I'm only a mathematician, not a philosopher, so I don't have an answer. But I know that math isn't a collection of arbitrary rules. It really is about the world, because mathematicians can make predictions. If you measure some pieces of wood, and nail them together, and then add up the individual lengths, you can predict the total length of the whole structure. That's a prediction about the world, not just about our rules."

"I'll think about it," I said. "Thanks again." I did think about it, many times, but I never found an answer. It appears that math is necessarily true (true in any possible world), our knowledge of it is absolutely certain, and everyone agrees about it. Even though it's not based on observation, it is about the phys-

ical world. In mathematics, our minds seem to penetrate into the deepest structure of the universe. There seems to be some kind of harmony, or coordination,
between the way our minds work and the way the world works, so that by simply thinking, we can know about the world. It is very strange.

Key Concepts

certain	necessarily true	observation
conventional	true by definition	about the world

Critical Questions

1. Do you think everyone in your philosophy class agrees that 2 + 2 = 4? Do
   all chemists, biologists, or sociologists agree about the elementary facts and
   laws of their sciences? If so, then is math any different from science?
2. What does Chang mean by "certain"? Are you certain that the sun will rise
   tomorrow, in his sense of "certain"? Are you certain that 2 + 2 = 4, as he
   says he is?
3. In what way is math "unscientific," according to Chang?
4. What does Chang mean by "necessarily true"? Are the basic facts and laws
   of physics necessarily true?
5. The rationalist says "bachelors are unmarried males" is necessarily true, so
   long as we are speaking English. "Three strikes and you're out" is necessarily true, so long as we are playing baseball. Must we also say that "2 +
   2 = 4" is necessarily true, but *only so long as* some condition applies? Or is
   it necessarily true, no matter what?
6. What is the difference between numbers and numerals? Which do mathematicians study?
7. Do you agree that math does not depend on observation, but gives us knowledge of the physical world? If so, how is that possible, in your opinion?

Methods and Techniques

ANALYSIS

Both the essays in this section use a technique that is very important in philosophy. The technique is analysis. The word "analyze" means to take something apart or to break something down into its parts. If you analyze an essay,
for example, you try to explain how it was put together, what parts it has, and
how the parts work together. You might point out that the essay has an introduction, a main body, and a conclusion.

The first essay uses analysis when it says that beliefs can be broken down
into ideas. It analyzes the belief that dogs are loyal animals into several ideas.
And then it applies the same technique to those ideas. It analyzes the idea of
a dog into several properties. And it says that sensory properties, such as cold

or brown, cannot be broken down any further. But the technique of analysis is crucial in this point of view. In fact, the whole theory of empiricism rests on that technique. An empiricist claims that analysis of our beliefs and ideas reveals their source, and helps us understand how the mind acquires knowledge.

The second essay uses analysis, too. It begins with a simple statement in mathematics, such as $2 + 2 = 4$. By examining our understanding of the statement carefully, the essay gradually brings out its amazing characteristics. For example, it says knowledge of the statement is absolutely certain, the statement is true everywhere and at all times, everyone agrees that it is true, and it is about the world. These characteristics are not obvious at first glance. The rationalist must analyze the statement, or our understanding of it, to help us see those aspects of it.

Philosophers (and others) probably use analysis more often than any other technique. Virtually anything can be analyzed. You are analyzing these essays. That means you are doing something that philosophers do all the time, namely, analyzing arguments. In other words, you recognize that an author is trying to persuade you of something. You are faced with an argument. So you break it down into its parts. Arguments are made up of conclusions and premises, so you have been focusing on conclusions and the reasons to accept them.

In other classes you have probably analyzed works of literature, such as poems, plays, and short stories. What parts does a story have? Actually a story is a very complex work of art. You can break it down into characters, setting, plot, theme, and other parts. And then you can focus on each of these and analyze them even further. For example, you can analyze a character's personality and motives. What characteristics does she have, what goals or intentions, and what made her the way she is?

You can analyze a painting, an event like the French Revolution, an ecosystem, the federal government, a process like reproduction, and anything else. If you analyzed a painting, you would look at the different parts of the canvas; you would analyze it in space. If you analyzed the French Revolution, you would probably look at different periods and events; you would analyze it in time. If you analyzed an ecosystem, you would look at how the parts interact and depend on each other. You would analyze the functions of the parts (in space and time). If you analyzed a large organization, such as the federal government or a corporation, you might look at the places that lose money and the places that save money or make money. You would analyze the efficiencies and inefficiencies. These examples show that analysis is a very broad technique.

Philosophers analyze various things. They often analyze experiences that people have. Philosophers try to separate the complex experience into parts and look at different aspects of the experience. For example, you read about the psychological altruist's experience with her boyfriend, the metaphysical libertarian's experience making a choice, and the individualist's experiences with three friends. They want to understand what the experience means. To understand it, they try to look at the different aspects of it.

Philosophers also analyze concepts, or the meanings of words. What does the word "God" mean, for example? Or "soul," "morally right," "responsible," "free," or "knowledge"? Philosophers look at the different ways people think about these large topics, or the different ways people use the words. Can we say that we have a soul, but that the soul is just the same thing as our brain? Or does one aspect of the concept rule out the idea that the soul is a physical object? Philosophers analyze these abstract ideas to try to understand our most basic beliefs.

The technique of analysis is not difficult or complicated. It is simply a way of looking at things more carefully than we normally do. It forces us to look more closely at whatever we are analyzing. It can be applied to almost anything, and is usually very helpful.

Understanding the Dilemma

EMPIRICIST OR RATIONALIST?

An empiricist is a person who believes that experience is the original source of all our ideas and knowledge. Whatever is in your mind must have been acquired through your senses. As the first essay points out, you can take the basic ideas and put them together yourself in new ways, ways you have never experienced. But the elementary parts must have been learned through perception.

This point of view is different from rationalism, the outlook of the second essay. A rationalist begins with simple mathematical knowledge, like the knowledge that $2 + 2 = 4$, and notices that that knowledge is very different from knowledge we acquire through our senses. The second essay discusses the different characteristics it has. It is absolutely certain, everyone agrees on it, it is necessary, and it is not based on experience. Nevertheless, it applies to the world. The rationalist concludes that we have another way to know about the world, besides sense perception. We can call this other way "reason." Thus our sensory experience is not the only way we can learn about reality. There must be another way, represented by the kind of understanding we have of mathematics. We understand things like $2 + 2 = 4$ by "seeing with our mind," so to speak. Or we can say that we understand them through reason. Reason includes a kind of insight, or mental perception, which does not depend on the senses.

Empiricists and rationalists disagree over the source of knowledge. Does *all* knowledge depend on sense perception? Or can we know some things through reason? What do you think? We can get a better grip on the issue if we consider beliefs as well as ideas. Empiricists emphasize ideas, and explain how all our ideas come from sense perceptions. But they also maintain that a true belief, or knowledge, must be based on sense experience as well. For example, I believe that birds fly because I have seen them fly. I also believe that cells reproduce by division because, while I haven't actually seen them divide myself, other people have. Those are things that I know. Now I might also believe that birds reproduce by division. But I cannot *know* that, because neither I nor anyone else has ever seen birds divide. Thus sense experience is the source of all our ideas, and the source of all our knowledge. If a belief cannot be traced back to some perceptual experience (mine or someone else's), then it is not knowledge but only opinion.

A rationalist believes that we know 2 + 2 = 4 and other mathematical statements; we do not merely believe that they are true. But mathematical truths are not based on any perception. I have seen two things added to two other things to make four things, but that visual experience is not how I know 2 + 2 = 4. I know it in a different way, namely, through reason.

An empiricist says that knowledge depends on experience, but doesn't the rationalist rely on a certain experience, a feeling of certainty? That is an experience. So how are the two positions different? They are different because of the *kinds* of experience they rely on. An empiricist says the knowledge originates in *sensory* experience: seeing, hearing, touching, and so on. We might have other kinds of experiences, but they do not give us knowledge of the world, the empiricist claims. On the other hand, a rationalist believes that the basis of knowledge is a kind of insight, or feeling of certainty, and that is not like any other experience. When we examine that experience carefully, we will see how special it is. Thus both positions discuss experiences, but they are different kinds of experiences.

Probably the biggest difference between the two points of view is their attitudes toward various types of knowledge. An empiricist believes that science has harnessed and channeled our sensory experience in the most productive way, and science gives us knowledge. If you cannot see it and touch it, it isn't really knowable. Rationalists are usually more open to other kinds of knowledge. They might believe it is possible to have genuine knowledge of right and wrong (even though we cannot observe these properties), knowledge of the soul, maybe even of God. It depends on whether or not we can achieve the same kind of certainty in these areas that we do in mathematics.

But is the rationalist right? In thinking about the issue, you should not base your decision on what you *would like* to be true. You should consider the evidence and arguments for each side, and judge which most likely *is* true.

EMPIRICIST

1. Our minds (including our ideas and beliefs) are entirely products of our environments.
2. We can put simple ideas and images together in many ways, but we cannot imagine anything whose parts were not first perceived.
3. The difference between knowledge and mere opinion is that knowledge is based on sensory experience and opinion is not.
4. Mathematical truths seem so certain because they are obvious and common.

RATIONALIST

5. Mathematical truths depend on understanding with your mind (reason), not perceiving with your senses.
6. Statements like "two and two are four" cannot be empirical, because everyone agrees about them, and they could not possibly be false.
7. The mind is more than just a recorder and arranger of sensory input; it can give us deeper knowledge than that.
8. Since we can know mathematics through reason, we can probably know other aspects of reality through reason as well.

FOR FURTHER STUDY

Historical Examples

EMPIRICIST: John Locke. *Essay concerning Human Understanding*. Dover, reprint of 1894 edition. Originally published in 1689. Book 2, chap. 1, "Of Ideas in General, and Their Original." Locke claims that the mind is originally a blank tablet, and everything in the mind must enter through sensory experience.

RATIONALIST: Immanuel Kant. *Critique of Pure Reason*. St. Martin's, 1967. Originally published in 1781. Introduction, sections 1–5. Kant argues that mathematics is not just true by definition, and is not based on experience, but is a third kind of truth, which he calls "synthetic a priori."

OTHER SOURCES

Stephen Priest. *The British Empiricists, from Hobbes to Ayer*. Penguin, 1990. Clear description of the main ideas and historical development.

John Cottingham. *Rationalism*. Oxford University Press, 1988. A good discussion of many different types and applications of rationalism.

Stephen F. Barker. *The Philosophy of Mathematics*. Prentice-Hall, 1964. A challenging but readable discussion of the nature of mathematics.

Philip J. Davis, Reuben Hersh. *Descartes' Dream: The World According to Mathematics*. Houghton Mifflin, 1982. Wide-ranging chapters on various aspects of mathematics; some relatively easy, some difficult.

Bruce Aune. *Rationalism, Empiricism, and Pragmatism: An Introduction*. Random House, 1970. Theoretical, analytical, a little dense.

Roderick Chisholm. *Theory of Knowledge*. 3rd Edition. Prentice-Hall, 1989. See chap. 4 on a priori knowledge.

Jennifer Trusted. *An Introduction to the Philosophy of Knowledge*. Macmillan, 1981. A historical survey from the Greeks to the present.

5.4 IS CERTAINTY THE STANDARD OF KNOWLEDGE?

FOUNDATIONALIST OR PRAGMATIST?

───────────────── • ─────────────────

The two previous sections were about the sources of knowledge and the claim that science is knowledge. Those are both important issues, but they lead us to a deeper question: What *is* knowledge? Before we can decide what the sources of knowledge are, we must have some idea of what knowledge itself is. And we cannot decide whether or not science provides knowledge until we know what knowledge is.

This interconnection among questions is typical of philosophy. The question "Does God exist?" leads to the prior question "How should we think about God?" And the question "Is morality relative?" depends on what we mean by "morality." It is very difficult to answer any one question without having answers to many other questions. Normally the most fundamental questions are about the meanings of the basic concepts: God, justice, right and wrong, free, mind, knowledge, and a few others.

So what is knowledge? We often talk about knowledge as if it were analogous to money or wealth. We say a person "has" knowledge and "acquires" new knowledge. He or she can "accumulate" knowledge and "store" it in his or her head. We compare people on the basis of the "amount" of knowledge they have. Many people assume, perhaps unconsciously, that we can acquire knowledge (like wealth) only through effort, hard work, and maybe even suffering.

But there are differences between knowledge and wealth, too. You can *give* the knowledge you have to someone else without losing anything. When you learn something, you are changed; your outlook is different. That is, your knowledge and understanding are a central part of who you are. They are not external possessions, like money. Furthermore, no one can see or touch your knowledge, whereas money is tangible. We disagree on who has real knowledge and who really understands something, whereas everyone agrees on who has money. Perhaps the analogy with money is misleading.

One problem in trying to understand the nature of knowledge is that there are so many different types of knowledge. Just think of the different people in a university: scientific researchers, but also historians, literature teachers, musicians and music teachers, psychologists and counselors, economists and business teachers, and so on. All claim to have knowledge, but their knowledge is very different. And outside the university other people claim to know other things: mothers know their children, cab drivers know the city, cooks know their craft, connoisseurs of wine know wine, etc. Is it possible that all these different kinds of knowledge have something in common? What distinguishes one who knows from one who does not?

In the following pieces, the first essay claims that the key to knowledge is certainty. It argues that if a person knows something, that knowledge must be based on something of which he is absolutely certain. All knowledge must have this strong foundation. Anyone who accepts this view is a foundationalist. The second essay maintains that knowledge is the ability to do something. If a person can solve problems, answer questions, reach a goal, and generally manipulate the environment successfully, then that person has knowledge. If one cannot do these things, then one does not have real knowledge, however educated one seems to be. This essay represents the pragmatist position.

YES: FOUNDATIONALIST

"Certainty"

Journalists like to say that we are living in "the Age of Information," and that we are developing a "knowledge-based economy." It's a little frightening. I have a hard time remembering the date of the PTA meeting, not to mention my Social Security number, bank account number, office telephone number, zip code extension, and other essential numbers I can't recall at the moment.

But I guess the journalists are right. My grandparents worked with their hands, in the coal mines. My dad worked with machines, on the assembly line at Ford. I went to college and became a teacher. Now my kids are wild about computers. They soak up more information every day than I learned in my entire high school career. They have the Discovery Channel, the Learning Channel, the Internet, On-Line services, interactive software, teen magazines, Advanced Placement classes in school, school trips to Washington, the French Club, and Tommy across the street, who apparently knows exotic secrets about human reproduction. They are swimming in knowledge.

My kids are excellent swimmers. I prefer to lie on the beach and watch them. They come running to tell me what they have seen and heard, and I tell them not to swim out over their heads. I can't keep up with all the information. I'm not immersed in it as they are. Besides, I'm a more reflective and meditative kind of person. I've been wondering about this knowledge-based economy. If the world runs on knowledge these days, then knowledge is a pretty important commodity. But what is it? How do I recognize it when I see it? How do I know I have the real thing and not some dime-store imitation? Knowledge is more than just opinion. Opinions are cheap. As my kids say, "Opinions are like noses; everybody's got one." But opinions won't get very far in a knowledge-based economy. How can I separate real knowledge from mere opinion?

Pointing to examples doesn't answer the question. We can think about the Gross National Product of Uganda, the visual capacities of cats, casualties at the battle of Waterloo—and that's just last week's public TV schedule. But all those facts won't answer the broader question. What is knowledge in general? How do we recognize it? When can people say they *know* something, about

Uganda or cats or whatever, and when are they entitled only to say that they *believe* something?

After swimming around in a lot of examples of knowledge, I have stepped back onto the beach to gain some perspective. I've noticed a common factor in all the cases of knowledge. It's an obvious fact, but I don't think people have realized the amazing implications of this little fact. The fact is that if a person knows something, then what the person knows must be *true*. If it isn't true, then the person doesn't know it but only believes it. A person cannot know what is false. Knowledge means truth. They are connected, like kids and parents, or good ice cream and fat. You can't have the first without the second.

I want to emphasize the connection between knowledge and truth, and later draw out the implications. Suppose that Susan in New York says she knows it is raining in Seattle today, because it rains there so often. But suppose that the statement "It is raining in Seattle today" is false. In fact it is sunny for a change. Now does Susan know that it is raining in Seattle? No. We say that she only *believes* it is raining. People can believe anything. Just look at the *Jerry Springer* show. But believing is different from knowing. You can believe something that isn't true. But you cannot know it. The connection between knowledge and truth is built into the way we use the word "knowledge." It is part of our concept of knowledge.

And it doesn't matter how many people believe something. Numbers do not create knowledge. A century ago scientists said that light waves travel through a transparent "ether" that exists throughout the universe. They believed there had to be an ether to carry light waves the way air carries sound waves. The "facts" about ether were taught in all the universities. All the experts agreed about its fundamental properties. But there is no such thing as ether. Light is different from sound, and no one has ever been able to detect any sign of the ether. Did people know about the ether? No, they did not. How could they? There is nothing to know about. They certainly believed various things about the ether, but they were mistaken. They didn't have knowledge.

The fact that knowledge requires truth gives us a test to apply to all claims of knowledge. If a person knows something, it must be true. On the other hand, if it is not true, then a person only believes it. She or he has an opinion, not knowledge. But this test only rules out cases. It shows us which claims of knowledge are *not* legitimate. It doesn't "rule in" cases. That is, it doesn't show us which cases *are* legitimate. In other words, if Susan says, "I know it is raining in Seattle" when it isn't, then the truth test can show that her claim is illegitimate. But we can't say that if something is true, then it *is* knowledge.

It might seem paradoxical to say knowledge is connected with truth, but then to say that truth does not guarantee knowledge. But paradoxical or not, that's the way it is. Think again about Susan's claim to know it is raining in Seattle today. But now suppose it *is* raining in Seattle; her belief is true. Then can she say she knows it is raining? No, that is still not enough to have knowledge. Maybe she is just making a wild guess. Compare a similar case. Suppose Bill has a hunch about the amount of money Jane has in her pocket. He guesses it is fifteen dollars. Although Jane says nothing, Bill believes she has fifteen dollars. And suppose that through sheer coincidence he is right. Then does he *know* how much money Jane has? No. His guess just happens to be true, but it is still only a guess, a belief, not knowledge.

So, knowledge is connected with truth, but we have to be careful about what implications follow from this connection. The connection allows us to say this: "If you know something, then what you know is true." But it does not allow us to say this: "If what you believe is true, then you know it." Being true is not enough to make a belief into knowledge. You must have something else in addition to truth before you can have real knowledge.

What else must you have? The connection between knowledge and truth leads to the answer. You must have something that shows that you *cannot* be mistaken. Because if you can be mistaken—if what you believe can be false—then you do not have knowledge. The only way that you cannot be mistaken is to be absolutely *certain*. Absolute certainty is the test that "rules in" knowledge claims. It shows which claims are legitimate. If you are absolutely certain about something, then you know it, because your belief cannot be false. And if you aren't absolutely certain, then you only believe it.

Being absolutely certain about something means that one cannot realistically imagine it being false. For example, I can see my hand in front of me, and I can count five fingers. The light is good, my eyes aren't playing tricks on me, and I am in a normal state of mind. So I am certain that I have five fingers on my left hand. When I carefully examine my belief, I see that I cannot realistically imagine that I am mistaken. It might be possible to make up some fantastic story in which I was mistaken. I could say that I have been abducted by aliens and hypnotized. Or that I went completely insane ten years ago and all my perceptions (including the belief that I am sane) are illusions, or something like that. But those are not realistic stories. When I look at my hand, I cannot seriously imagine being wrong. I am certain that I have five fingers.

I sometimes see other things about which I am not certain. If I quickly glance at a letter, I might believe that it's addressed to me. But if someone asked, "Are you certain?" I would have to say no. I didn't look that carefully. I can imagine being mistaken. Or if I look at a couple of socks I might believe that they are the same shade of blue. But I know that the lighting in a room can affect our perception of color. So, even if I look carefully, I have to say that I am not certain that they are the same shade. I have an opinion, not knowledge. But sometimes I am certain about what I see. I can test myself to see if I am certain. In fact, visual perception is probably the most common type of knowledge we have. If we look at something very carefully—more than once, from different angles, in different conditions—then we can be certain. In those cases, we know.

The fact that knowledge means truth implies that the mark of knowledge is certainty. The way to separate real knowledge from mere opinion is to ask if the person is absolutely certain. Take any case of real knowledge, and you will find that it passes this test. Memory, for example, is an important type of knowledge. Let's say that Susan remembers that she had eggs for breakfast this morning.

She says she *knows* that she had eggs. But how does she know? She could *imagine* having anything. How does she know that she isn't just imagining that she had eggs, when in fact she had oatmeal? How does she know that she is remembering and not just imagining? In both processes she has some images in her mind. What is the difference? The difference is certainty. In other words, she considers the idea of having eggs and the idea of having oatmeal, and the first feels certain to her. It is more real, more vivid, more convincing. She cannot doubt it. She cannot realistically imagine being wrong, whereas she can easily imagine being wrong about the oatmeal. Memory is an important type of knowledge, whereas imagination isn't. And the only difference between memory and imagination is this feeling of certainty. Certainty is the standard of knowledge.

Besides perception and memory, we all rely on *reasoning* to gain knowledge. For example, I know that, by law, all the members of the School Board live in Clark County. And I know that Mr. Davidson lives in Bates County. From these two facts, I can deduce another fact: Mr. Davidson is not a legal member of the School Board. Or I might know that some snacks are very salty, and no salty foods are good for you. Putting those together, I reason that some snacks are not good for you. What I know in cases like this is that the ideas are connected. If the first statements are true, then the last one must be true as well. So if I know the two premises (about Davidson and the law), then I can know the conclusion, that Davidson is not a member of the School Board. I must know the two premises first. But if I do, then simply by thinking about them I can know the conclusion. I am certain that the ideas are connected. (However, if I only believe the premises, but do not know they are true, then I cannot know the conclusion. I cannot be certain that it is true, even if I am certain that it is connected to the premises.)

The process of reasoning is important because it is relevant to an objection some people make to the certainty standard of knowledge. These critics say that Susan can know that she has five fingers, and that she had eggs for breakfast, but not because she feels certain. She confirms her belief and makes it knowledge by asking *other people*. For example, if her sister says, "Of course you have five fingers, you moron," and her mother says, "Yes we had eggs for breakfast, dear; don't you remember?" then Susan can trust her perception and her memory. From this perspective, *consensus* is the test of knowledge, not certainty. If people agree about something, then it is knowledge.

But we've played this game before, with the scientists and their ether, and the critics lost. We cannot escape from certainty as the test of knowledge. Other people's reports are useful to me only if the others have *knowledge*. If other people are careless or misguided, then asking them isn't going to help me. For example, if Susan's mother was mistaken about breakfast, then her memory can't give Susan knowledge. Or if her mother told a fib (because she was embarrassed about serving oatmeal), then her statement doesn't give Susan knowledge. Piling up more and more witnesses is useless so long as the witnesses only have opinions. Witnesses are useful only if they are reliable, they have knowledge, they are certain, they cannot be mistaken.

In other words, if Susan seems to remember something or to perceive something, and she feels certain about it, then that is *always* a better guarantee of knowledge than any number of witnesses who agree with her. Because to rely on other people she must be certain about several things, not just one thing. She must be certain that the witnesses have real knowledge and are not mistaken. (A mistaken witness is totally worthless as far as knowledge is concerned.) She must be certain that the witnesses are truthful. And she must be certain that her own reasoning is correct and the ideas are logically connected. That's three certainties she must have. Defining knowledge as consensus (based on many people's reports) is like having to hit three bull's-eyes, whereas defining knowledge as certainty only requires us to hit one.

Perception, memory, and reasoning. These are the foundations of all knowledge, because they give us certainty. All those things on public TV about other countries, nature, and the past, rest on these foundations. All the things professors teach in universities, all that you read in a newspaper or hear from friends, are merely opinions, unless you can tie them down to a definite perception or memory through clear reasoning. To know, we must be certain. Everything else is merely belief and opinion. Maybe the journalists should say we live in the Age of Educated Guesses, and work in a belief-based economy.

Key Concepts

knowledge	certain	reasoning
truth	perception	witnesses
belief	memory	

Critical Questions

1. How does the essay try to prove that knowledge and truth are connected? What kind of evidence does it provide? Is the evidence convincing evidence?
2. Do you agree that no one can know something that is false?
3. What does a foundationalist mean by "certain"? How do you know when you are certain?
4. Consider the following statements. Can you be certain of them, in the foundationalist's sense of "certain"?
    a. If you hold this paper in contact with the fire of a lighted match, the paper will burn.
    b. Dinosaurs are extinct; they no longer exist.
    c. O.J. Simpson was acquitted at his murder trial.
    d. The ink on this page is black, not dark blue.
    e. If all *A*'s are *B*'s, and all *A*'s are *C*'s as well, then all *C*'s are *B*'s.
5. Everyone sometimes has mistaken memories. In your opinion, which is a better test of your memory of an event, your feeling of certainty or other people's agreement with you about the same event?

6. Suppose you have never had any experience with pumice, a kind of stone. But suppose that several encyclopedias, geologists, and people you know, all agree that pumice is lighter than granite. Then do you *know* that pumice is lighter than granite? How would a foundationalist answer the question?

NO: PRAGMATIST
"The Test of Knowledge"

Dear Richard,

Your mother and I were very happy to get your last letter. Although you have been in college for less than a year, it seems like you've been away forever. We're looking forward to summer vacation when you will be at home.

You seem to be anxious for a vacation, too. I know the first year is difficult. You asked some tough questions, and I'm not sure that I can answer them, but I'll try. I remember the talk we had when you were home for the winter break. You were asking what you should study. I said that you should try as many different courses as you can, because that is the only way you can find what you really like. And you should study what you enjoy and make that your career. That's the only way you can be happy. And that's what we want.

But now in your latest letter you seem to be asking a different question. You said "How do I know whom to believe?" That's a good question. You also said you are there to learn, but the different teachers tell you different things, and even in the same subject different authorities disagree. How can you sift out the gold from all the dirt? How can you tell real knowledge from pretentious assumptions? Is that what you were asking? Have I understood your questions? In other words, you aren't asking what knowledge is worth having. We talked about that last winter. Instead, you are asking what the difference is between real knowledge and fake knowledge, or between real knowledge and mere opinion.

Well, you've realized by now that your old man doesn't have all the answers. But I can tell you what I think. Believe it or not, I have asked myself the same questions you are asking now. I was once the same age you are, and it took me a long time to decide what I think about knowledge in general. But I finally found an answer that works for me. I think knowledge is practical. One of those philosophers you're reading about said "Knowledge is power," and I agree with him. Knowledge is what gives us the ability to predict the consequences of events and control our environment. Knowledge is success. It is a mistake to think of knowledge as a completely intellectual, theoretical matter.

You are taking biology and you said you enjoy it. You can see the connection between knowledge and successful action in your science courses. How do scientists discover new things? First they pose a hypothesis, then they set up an experiment to test the hypothesis, and finally they check the results. Some hypotheses are confirmed. "Confirmed" just means that a scientist's predictions about an experiment are borne out: a new drug will kill the bacteria, one group of rats will learn the maze faster, and so on. Scientists will expect the same results next time, and can produce those results if they want to. So scientists acquire knowledge in the degree that their hypotheses are confirmed. Confirmation, successful prediction, competent manipulation of the environment—these are the accepted signs of knowledge. It isn't what the scientists can tell you that counts. It's what they can *do* in their laboratory, or in the real world. You have to attend lectures and take notes and learn a lot of things. Are they knowledge? It depends on what you can or cannot do after listening to the lecture. If you can't do anything, then it isn't knowledge. But if you can dissect a frog and recognize the organs, or you can distinguish oaks from maples on campus, or you can set up a good experiment of your own, then you have gained some knowledge.

Highly general theories in science may not be so directly connected with tests and the ability to control events. The theory of relativity doesn't have many practical applications. But that characteristic of theories supports my "successful action" thesis. The lack of applications is why we call them *theories*. Theories are more like hypotheses than well-confirmed laws. They do not count as full-fledged *knowledge*. They are probably true, but we don't know for sure. And a theory must make *some* practical difference in the world, or else we can't even know it is probably true.

Knowledge is what works, and superstition or fantasy is what doesn't work. You remember how you and Carol used to fight over the newspaper because you wanted the sports section and she wanted the astrology column? Well, astrology is an example of superstition. It claims to give its followers knowledge of the future, but most educated people regard it as an entertaining game of pretend. Why? Because its predictions fail. It does not enable anyone to anticipate the actual course of events. I can predict whether or not Carol will have a good time on her date much better than her horoscope does. But she still reads it anyway. You're older. You can understand these things. The test of knowledge is this capacity to predict events and therefore act successfully.

That is the test people use not only in organized science, but in everyday affairs. Take the following example. You remember Bill Green. You and I took our lawn mower down to his shop last summer. He is a hard-working mechanic who has been repairing small motors and appliances for years. He loves his job, and has an uncanny ability to diagnose the ills of air conditioners and washing machines, and cure them. But he isn't a talkative fellow, and he can't explain very well how he does it. Nevertheless, there is no doubt that Bill is extremely knowledgeable about appliances and motors.

Well, Bill has hired an assistant named Tim Dugan, who took courses in appliance repair at the community college. Bill said he memorized the manuals and diagrams at the college, but, after weeks in the shop he hasn't actually fixed a single washing machine. He can't seem to connect the diagrams with the dark, oily chaos of wires and bolts.

Tim does not know small motors and appliances, in spite of his study, because he cannot *do* anything with the machines. The veteran Bill does have knowledge, in spite of his inarticulateness, because he can make predictions about the machines and can work successfully with them. (He may make his predictions in his imagination, if not in words.)

Tim seems like a nice kid, and he isn't entirely ignorant after taking his course. What he knows is manuals and diagrams. The criterion of knowledge—successful action—is the same. He can draw the diagram without looking at it, or answer questions about the manual. If he couldn't, he wouldn't even know those. He has simply acquired the wrong knowledge. But the test of knowledge is the same for Tim and Bill.

It may seem that some kinds of knowledge are less practical, and that we need a different test or concept of knowledge in those areas. You said you are taking a Western Civ course in the history department. I think my theory applies to history, too. Historians have knowledge, but you might say it doesn't enable them to make predictions or act successfully. But historical knowledge isn't really any different from other kinds. The basis of historical knowledge is documents, records, memoirs, and so on. If someone challenges a historian's claim to knowledge, he or she will produce these records. The historian can describe them, compare them, manipulate them successfully. That is a kind of prediction and action. What the historian knows *directly*, therefore, is the documents, and on the basis of that knowledge he or she makes credible inferences about what happened in the past and why it happened.

The capacity to make predictions and achieve one's goals is the universal test of knowledge. You know French pretty well. (I heard you talking with your high school teacher.) Is that knowledge? Sure. Studying French gave you the ability to converse with someone from France, to ask for directions in France, and to do other things you want to do there. You know France when you can find your way around, make yourself understood, and solve the little problems that arise in that country.

You will probably take an anthropology course sometime. You'll read about the Eskimos, American Indians, tribes in the Brazilian rain forest, and other primitive peoples. Is that knowledge? (Remember, we're not asking if you should or shouldn't study those things. We're asking if you acquire real knowledge when you study them.) Maybe yes, maybe no. It all depends on whether you could go to the Navaho reservation, or the rain forest, and *apply* what you have heard in the classroom. Should you barter with the Navahos, or would that offend them? If you wanted to marry a Navaho, would you talk to her father or her uncle on her mother's side? (This is just an example, of course.) If the anthropology course gave you the ability to do things like that, and to navigate successfully through their culture, then you gained some real knowledge from it. On the other hand, if you weren't able to do any more with the Navahos or other tribes after the course than you were before the course, then you haven't acquired any knowledge.

I'm sure you are meeting a lot of interesting people at college. What happens as you get to *know* someone? What's the difference between knowing some-one, and just being acquainted with someone? My theory applies here, too. One person knows another only if the first can explain why the second does what he does, or give an account of his past, or predict how he will react to some-thing. When you get to know someone, you don't have a list of essential facts. You have an ability to do something regarding that person. You are able to in-teract successfully with that person, predict what choices he will make, and be-have in a way that is satisfying to both of you.

You know yourself when you understand your own goals and priorities, and what methods of achieving them will be satisfying. In other words, when you can predict and control your own behavior and feelings successfully.

Knowledge is something that enables one to *do* something one couldn't do without it. But not everything that enables a person to do something is knowl-edge. Strength, money, and freedom give people capacities to act successfully, too. Knowledge is the *beliefs* that allow a person to do something.

I don't know if this letter will be of any help to you. I hope it will. And I hope we can talk some more. At the college I'm sure your professors will tell you a great deal about knowledge, what counts as knowledge and what doesn't. They will talk about beliefs, concepts, laws, principles, and theories. But in my opinion, all those abstractions are only *tools*. They are difficult to grasp and pin down in themselves. You can't look at a statement or theory and decide whether or not it is knowledge. There isn't any inherent characteristic that makes some of them knowledge. You have to take them out of the class-room and into the world. Do they make things easier for you, do they help you solve a problem, do they apply to the real world? That is the test. They qualify as knowledge when they enable you to manipulate your environment success-fully.

Well, there you have it. Write again soon. Mom sends her love.

Key Concepts

power	practice	belief
prediction	successful action	theory

Critical Questions

1. Why is science knowledge, according to the essay?
2. Why is astrology not knowledge? Are scientific theories knowledge? Does a pragmatist think that astrology is a scientific theory?
3. Do you think the fact that Bill can repair appliances shows that he has knowl-edge? If a person has knowledge, can't he *say* what he knows?
4. In your opinion, does anyone who can make successful predictions about something have knowledge of that thing?
5. Can you think of a kind of knowledge that does *not* give a person the abil-ity to make predictions about what he or she knows?

6. Would a pragmatist reject, or accept, a foundationalist's analysis of knowledge? Do pragmatists think knowledge is a kind of belief? Must it be true? Must it be certain?

Methods and Techniques

OBSERVATION

The foundationalist claims that observation, memory, and reasoning are all sources of certainty. If I look at my hand, I know that I have five fingers. If I see apples for sale in the supermarket, I know the store has apples for sale. Trusting our eyes is so basic that it is hard to understand that observation can be problematic. In fact, a standard joke about philosophers is that they ask "Do I really know there is a table here?"

But of course sometimes people do not see what they think they see. Psychologist have described many types of optical illusions, such as mirages and "bent pencils" standing in a glass of water. Context clues can distort our perception, as when equal lines appear to be unequal because of other lines near them.

Such illusions are rare, and ordinary observations aren't distorted in those ways. But how reliable is ordinary observation? If you were walking along the street and saw someone snatch a woman's purse and run away with it, could you identify the robber in a lineup?

As a matter of fact, ordinary observation is notoriously unreliable. Psychologist Elizabeth Loftus is an expert on perception and memory, and she wrote a fascinating book called *Eyewitness Testimony* (Harvard University Press, 1993). In it she describes various factors that affect the accuracy of observation and recall. Obviously lighting, distance, and obstructions are important. When you observed the purse snatching (let us imagine), was it during the day or at night? How far away were you? Did other people or street signs or anything else obstruct your view?

The word "observation" suggests deliberate, attentive looking, whereas "perception" means any act of becoming aware of something through the senses. Paying attention improves reliability, but only if one is paying attention to the right things, and that is a problem in itself.

Loftus mentions other "event factors" that influence perception. How long were you able to observe the robber? A brief observation is less reliable than a longer one, even though the confidence of the observer might be the same. Some details are more salient, or noticeable. When people are shown pictures of faces and then asked which features they notice, they mention eyes most often, then nose, skin, mouth, lips/chin, and hair in descending order. The feature noticed least is ears. In all situations, some details are more salient and people's observation of them is more reliable.

Another factor influencing observation is the type of fact observed. When you observed the robbery, how long did it take for the person to grab the purse and run around the corner? How far away were you? People have great difficulty in reporting accurately things like distance, the speed of a moving vehicle, or the amount of time an event takes. Loftus says there is an "invariable human tendency to overestimate the amount of time that some activity took or generally takes" (p. 29). In one experiment, people watched an individual for four seconds as he walked through a room. When asked how long they had observed the person, "Females reported that they had viewed him for an average of twenty-five seconds while males claimed it had been seven seconds, on the average" (p. 30).

Events involving violence are more difficult to observe accurately. Violence creates stress in the observer, which interferes with observation. In other words, not only do event factors influence observation, but "witness factors" play a role as well. A small degree of anxiety actually increases attention and reliable observation, but as stress increases, careful observation declines. Numerous studies have shown that if a weapon is used in a crime, witnesses observe the weapon but not much else. The danger distracts them.

The most common witness factors that interfere with observation are expectations of different types. One's past experience can predispose one to see something or not to see it. When a nonsense word is flashed on a screen, people will see it as a meaningful word they know, especially if they already have certain expectations. For example, if subjects are told that some of the words they will see are words for animals, and they are shown the nonsense word "dack," they will perceive it as "duck." Unfortunately hundreds of hunters are killed every year because other hunters are expecting to see deer. Personal values and loyalties influence perceptions at sporting events.

In our imaginary purse-snatching, are you sure it was a purse that was snatched? Was the robber male or female? Black or white? Young or old? Stereotypes and cultural expectations influence observation as well.

Loftus also describes the problems that arise after people make observations. They store the information in memory, but memory is highly selective, and as time passes and they have new experiences, those new experiences can modify their memory of the original observation. For example, if you observe the purse-snatching, and five minutes later another witness asks you "Did you notice the guy's green hat," then subsequently you are more likely to recall a green hat on the suspect, even if there was no green hat. It is fascinating, and humbling, to see how much can go wrong in something as seemingly simple as observation.

Understanding the Dilemma

FOUNDATIONALIST OR PRAGMATIST?

The question in this section is about the standard of knowledge. In asking what the standard of knowledge is we are asking how we can recognize knowledge, how we can decide who has knowledge and who doesn't, and how we can tell genuine knowledge from "false knowledge." A foundationalist says knowledge must have a firm foundation. Only someone who has this foundation can claim to know anything. And the foundation is a feeling of certainty. An example is your perception of an ordinary physical object, like a table.

A pragmatist claims there is a different standard. The test of knowledge is practice, or success. If you want to find out whether a person really knows something, put the person to the test. See if he or she can *do* something. Real knowledge of the world means that we can manipulate the world, we can achieve our goals. But if a person's beliefs are false or too vague, then he or she will not be able to apply them. They won't work in the real world. For example, if you know the formula for finding the area of a circle, then you can apply it, you can predict that the circle will be large enough to hold other figures, and so on. If you do not have real knowledge about the area of the circle, you will fail.

Who is right, the foundationalist or the pragmatist? Can they both be right? The foundationalist says nothing about success or power. He emphasizes certainty. If a person is certain about something, he may be confident that he can apply his knowledge and achieve something, but he may not have done it. Without actually proving that his belief is knowledge, he is no different from a person who has a false belief, according to the pragmatist. Nor does the pragmatist say anything about certainty. In fact, he gives the example of the repair man who cannot say how he repairs motors and appliances. He can find the trouble and fix it, so he knows appliances, but he cannot say what he knows. He does not seem to be certain of anything. Thus the two positions in this section seem to be very different.

Could you say the foundationalist is talking about one kind of knowledge and the pragmatist is talking about another? Perhaps. But how can we call certainty and power "knowledge," unless certainty and power are basically similar in some way? The problem with this approach is that if the two writers are both describing knowledge, then there must be something that the two kinds of knowledge have in common. Consider an analogy. Two biologists want to understand the nature of mammals. One looks at rats and mice, and says mammals have four legs and a long tail. Another looks at monkeys and apes, and says mammals live in trees and grasp things with their hands. Both investigators are trying to understand mammals, but they have missed the crucial characteristics. But if all the animals they examine *are* mammals, then all the animals must have something in common that makes them mammals. There must be some definition of "mammal," even if the biologists haven't found it yet. The same applies to knowledge. The foundationalist and the pragmatist both say they have found the defining characteristic of knowledge. Are they both wrong? Then there must be some *other* defining characteristic of knowledge, besides certainty or power. What could it be? Or is one right and one wrong?

Both the foundationalist and the pragmatist claim to be analyzing the nature of knowledge. Both say that they are not merely making a value judgment, or saying that one kind of knowledge is more valuable than another. The two questions are very different. One question is "What knowledge is most worth having (out of all the kinds there are)?" The other question is "What *is* knowledge (of every kind)?" Both the foundationalist and the pragmatist claim to be answering the second question. Neither says anything about why the knowledge they describe is more desirable than other kinds, so it is difficult to say that they are answering the first question.

The foundationalist believes that the mark of knowledge is an inner experience, namely, a feeling of certainty. The theory is inner-oriented, based on an intellectual apprehension. The pragmatist says the test of knowledge is power, control over one's environment. His theory is outer-oriented. It is based on action and the ability to do things. Which is a better, more reliable test of genuine knowledge? Will one test sometimes tell us that a person has knowledge when he or she really does not have knowledge (or vice versa)? Which gives us a more accurate picture of knowledge, the foundationalist or the pragmatist?

FOUNDATIONALIST

1. The difference between knowing something and only believing something is that you are certain about what you know, but you are not certain about what you believe.
2. People say they know what they remember and what they see with their eyes because they feel certain about it.
3. Knowledge must be justified, but the appeal to justification stops only when we reach the foundation of certainty.
4. The real test of your knowledge is what you can feel sure of, not what other people say you know.

PRAGMATIST

5. The proof that you know that a car has fuel is your ability to drive it, and generally the proof that you know something is your ability to apply it or use it to do something.
6. Science is the best model of knowledge, and the test of scientific knowledge is experiment, correct prediction, and successful action.
7. People can know how to do things as well as knowing that something is true.
8. The theory that knowledge is power applies to more kinds of knowledge (like knowing people, knowing yourself) than the theory that knowledge is certainty.

FOR FURTHER STUDY

Historical Examples

FOUNDATIONALIST: René Descartes. *Meditations*. Many editions. Originally published in 1641. Descartes searches for an absolutely certain foundation upon which he can base all his other beliefs.

PRAGMATIST: John Dewey. *The Quest for Certainty*. Minton, Balch and Company, 1929. In chap. 7, "The Seat of Intellectual Authority," Dewey explains how the scientific method has changed our conception of knowledge; now we conceive of knowledge as successful activity.

OTHER SOURCES

Nicholas Capaldi. *Human Knowledge: A Philosophical Analysis of Its Meaning and Scope*. Pegasus, 1969. Chap. 3, "Knowledge and Belief," is a brief survey of philosophers' quest for certainty from Plato to Kant, and the difficulties they faced.

Johathan Dancy. *An Introduction to Contemporary Epistemology*. Blackwell, 1985. Chap. 4, "Foundationalism," is a good discussion of what Dancy calls "classical foundationalism," its weaknesses, and alternative versions of foundationalism.

Roderick M. Chisholm. *Theory of Knowledge*. 3rd Edition. Prentice-Hall, 1989. Very careful, very precise definitions of key concepts in the theory of knowledge, leading to a defense of foundationalism.

Jerome A. Shaffer. *Reality, Knowledge, and Value: A Basic Introduction to Philosophy*. Random House, 1971. In the first part of the book Shaffer discusses "the problem of certainty" and its place in the theory of knowledge.

Thomas E. Hill. *Contemporary Theories of Knowledge*. The Ronald Press, 1961. Chap. 10, "Empirical Pragmatism," includes a clear account of William James' views of concepts, beliefs, and the verification of beliefs.

Beatrice H. Zedler. "Dewey's Theory of Knowledge." In John Blewett, ed. *John Dewey: His Thought and Influence*. Fordham University Press, 1960. Exposition of some main themes in Dewey's pragmatist theory of knowledge.

W.P. Montague. *The Ways of Knowing*. Allen and Unwin, 1925. Old, but easier to read than more recent books on the theory of knowledge; includes surveys of authoritarianism, mysticism, rationalism, empiricism, pragmatism, and skepticism.

Robert Audi. *Belief, Justification, and Knowledge: An Introduction to Epistemology*. Wadsworth, 1988. Survey of current issues.

Current Controversy

5.5 DOES TRUTH EXIST?
REPRESENTATIONALIST OR POSTMODERNIST?

———————————— • ————————————

What is truth? This is one of the central questions of philosophy because philosophers want to find the truth about God, morality, the mind, and so on. But they must know what they are searching for before they begin the search. How will they know when they find it? They must know what truth is. Some philosophers believe we can understand the nature of truth and can find the truth about important matters. Others claim that the whole idea of truth is confused, and that we can never really know the truth about anything.

The question "What is truth?" can mean two different things. First, it can mean the correct beliefs about something. When a person testifies in court, he or she swears to tell the truth about the alleged crime. Or if an accident happens, but the victims were all killed, the investigator might say "We will never know the whole truth about the matter." Here "the truth" means the sum total of all the facts about something. If philosophers want to know the truth about the mind, they must discover all the facts about it and discard the myths, misconceptions, and errors about it.

But the question "What is truth?" can also have a different meaning. Consider the following sentences:

1. Bananas are yellow.
2. Bananas are purple.
3. The capital of Texas is Austin.
4. The capital of Texas is Fort Worth.

Sentences 1 and 3 are true, and 2 and 4 are false. But what does it mean to say sentence 1 is true? What property does 1 have that 2 does not have? In other words, what is truth? We are not asking for the totality of correct information about bananas. Instead, we are asking what makes a particular sentence true. Some sentences are true and others aren't. What is that difference? And how are 1 and 3 similar? What do all true sentences (whatever they are about) have in common?

So the question "What is truth?" has two different meanings. In the first sense, it is a question about content, or subject matter. In the second sense, it is a question about a characteristic of certain sentences. It doesn't matter whether we are talking about bananas or state capitals.

Almost everyone is more interested in the first question than the second one. Most people would rather know the facts about bananas than the difference between sentences 1 and 2. But philosophers are different. They want to get to the bottom of things. And ask yourself this: which question is more fundamental—the question about the facts, or the question about the property of true sentences? Actually, the second question is more fundamental. Philosophers say they must understand what makes any sentence true before they can try to find "the truth" about bananas or the mind or anything. They have to know how to distinguish a true sentence from a false one before they can begin collecting true sentences, i.e., the truth. So the question about what property true sentences have in common is the more fundamental question.

The first essay in this section begins by asking whether we should value the truth. The writer says we should, and to explain why, offers an explanation of truth as a representation of the world. It is a representationalist theory. The second essay tries to show that our ordinary idea of truth is senseless. Truth as we normally think of it cannot possibly exist. This is one of the claims associated with postmodernism.

YES: REPRESENTATIONALIST
"True Beliefs and False Beliefs"

Many colleges require students to take philosophy, and students naturally wonder why. Why should anyone study philosophy? There are many reasons: philosophers have influenced the way we live and think, philosophy provides a special kind of pleasure that students should experience, and it fosters a particularly careful way of thinking.

But I want to focus on a different reason for studying philosophy. Philosophers try to find the truth about important subjects like knowledge, morality, and the self. Some students admit this, but then go on to ask a radical question. "Why should I care about the truth?" That is the question I want to consider.

Why shouldn't a person believe whatever he or she likes, without worrying about the truth? Does it really make any difference whether or not my beliefs are *true*? Wouldn't I be happier if I chose the beliefs that suit my personality? Anyway, aren't my beliefs true *for me*, and your beliefs true *for you*?

I think it makes a big difference whether or not one's beliefs are true, and I think everyone should care very much about the truth. This is not just a personal commitment of mine. I think that anyone who understands the ordinary, commonsense definitions of "belief" and "true" will agree with me. So in order to explain why people should care about the truth, I will spell out the meanings of these key words, as I think most people understand them.

The basic idea is that we all construct a model of the world within our own minds. For example, if someone asked you to draw a map of your neighborhood, you could do it, because you have an inner map of the area in your mind. You can imagine walking or driving from your house to the grocery store. And you could draw a map representing the streets, the shops, the turns, the stores or houses, and so forth. You also have a model of the actions you must perform in order to achieve something. If you are at home, and you want your daughter to type a letter, you can give her instructions. First get out the typewriter, take off the cover, place the typewriter on the table, etc. You have a model of the procedure stored in your mind.

Another word for model is "representation," and representation is defined as follows:

> representation = one thing that conveys information about another thing,
>   or one thing that stands for another thing.

Representations come in all shapes and sizes. A street sign with a curved arrow on it represents a curve in the road. A photograph of a person represents that person. Dots and lines on road maps represent cities and roads. A word, like "cat," represents cats, even though the word doesn't look anything like a cat. In each of these cases the representation carries information about the thing represented, at least for those who know how to interpret it.

Mental representations are representations that exist in someone's mind. The map of your neighborhood and the procedure for typing a letter are mental representations. They are complex symbols, in your mind, that carry information about something. People also have images or pictures in their minds—think of Mickey Mouse's face and you have a mental image. They have other kinds of mental representations, too. Think of the concept of a civil law. Everyone understands what a law is, although it is probably impossible to *picture* a law. When you think of a law the representation exists in your mind.

Mental images are like pictures, and mental concepts are like words. But other mental representations are like whole sentences. Suppose you look at Mickey's picture and think to yourself, "Mickey Mouse has big ears." Now you have a mental representation that consists of a sentence. A sentence is not exactly the same thing as a picture. Your mental representation cannot be captured by a picture. If you look at a picture of Mickey Mouse, you see many features besides the ears. The sentence is more specific than the picture. A picture of Mickey Mouse by itself might mean Mickey has big ears, or Mickey has a black nose, or Mickey is smiling, or Mickey is a cartoon character. Maybe you could draw an arrow pointing to the ears, but that still isn't enough to capture the sentence "Mickey Mouse has big ears." If you drew an arrow, then the picture might mean Mickey has an arrow near his head, or the right ear is more important than the left, or Mickey's ears are round. A sentence expresses a single thought. It has a subject (Mickey Mouse) and a verb (has), and usually an object of the verb (big ears). It focuses on specific aspects of things.

A mental sentence like "Mickey Mouse has big ears" is a *belief*. The word "belief" is defined as follows:

> belief = a mental representation consisting of a complete thought.

In other words, a belief is a representation; that means it carries information about something. It exists in someone's mind, so it is a mental representation. But unlike images and concepts, it expresses a whole thought, like "The leaves are falling," or "Milk is good for you."

So far, I have only been talking about beliefs. But I said at the beginning that I want to convince you that you should care about the truth. So now I will try to describe what an average person means when he says something is true, or something is false.

In ordinary conversation, "true" means the following:

> true = a property of a sentence that corresponds to the world, or a property of a sentence that is congruent with a fact.

A true sentence corresponds to the world. It reports something that really does exist in the world. There is a one-to-one relation between the sentence (the set of words) and the things the words are about. A false sentence, on the other hand, is one that does not correspond to any fact, or any part of the real world.

The sentence "Paul Newman has blue eyes" is true. What does "true" mean here? It means that if you find Paul Newman and look at his eyes, you will see that they are in fact blue. The sentence corresponds to the facts about Newman.

It describes Newman accurately. On the other hand, "Paul Newman has blond hair" is false. The facts about Newman are not what the sentence says they are. There is a gulf, or mismatch, between the sentence and the real world.

A newspaper is supposed to report the truth. If it says, "A fire destroyed a building on South Street," then that sentence should be true. It should correspond to what actually happened on South Street. If the newspaper goes on to describe the heroics of the Fire Department, those sentences should also correspond to the actual events that occurred. Certain events occurred, whether anyone reported them or not. The newspaper's job is to describe the actual events. Some newspapers might be more successful—more truthful—than others.

This is the difference between history and fiction. History is (or should be) true. Fiction is not. I could make up a story about a fire, and describe various people and their actions. "City Hall was turned into a towering inferno," I might write. Everyone likes to imagine things. We can create pictures in our minds, scenes, dialogues, series of events, none of which ever happened. None corresponds to the real world. If City Hall didn't burn, then the story is false, however entertaining it might be.

Notice that it makes no sense to say my beliefs are "true for me" but not "true for you." If a belief is true, then it corresponds to the world, no matter whose belief it is. So if my beliefs are true, then they are true for me and for you and for anyone. Beliefs are mental sentences, just like the sentences in a newspaper (except beliefs exist in a person's mind). If a newspaper's story is accurate, then it doesn't matter who reads the story. It is accurate for you and for me. A belief may make me happy and you sad, or I may want to believe something that you do not want to believe. But wanting does not make it true or false. Truth depends on the relation between the belief and the world.

Now we can finally come to the main point. If this is what "belief" and "true" mean, then it is clearer why a person should care about the truth. It is obvious why a person should want his or her beliefs to be true. First, we all *act* on the basis of our beliefs. If I believe it is cold outside, then I will put on my coat before I go out. Or if I believe that milk is not good for me, then I won't drink it, and so on.

Second, if my beliefs are true, then my actions will be *successful*, but if they are false, my actions will be unsuccessful. For example, if I believe it is cold outside, but my belief is false—actually it is warm—then I will put on my coat and be very uncomfortable. If my belief about milk is false—actually it is good for me—then I won't drink it, and I will harm my own health.

This is why everyone should care about the truth. Our beliefs embody the information we have about the world. That is precisely what beliefs are. All together they make up one's mental model of the world. They represent one's environment. If the information is incorrect (that is, our beliefs are false), then we will not adjust to our environment. We will act on the basis of our model, but since the real world is different from our model of it, we will fail. We will continually run into obstacles and will be incapable of achieving our goals (no matter what our goals are).

Caring about the truth, therefore, is just a matter of efficiency, and ultimately, a matter of survival. Once we understand what knowing the truth involves, of course we will want to have *true* beliefs.

Key Concepts

belief	representation	true
whole thought	mental representation	successful

Critical Questions

1. What question is the representationalist trying to answer?
2. According to the essay, what do all representations have in common? Can you give some examples of representations?
3. The essay discusses three types of mental representations. What are they?
4. What is the difference between a true sentence and a false sentence?
5. Why does everyone want his or her beliefs to be true?
6. Are representationalists right when they say a sentence cannot be true for one person but false for another person? What about the sentence "Vanilla ice cream tastes good"? Or the sentence "Chess is a very exciting game"?

NO: POSTMODERNIST
"Ten Theses on Language"

Language is a marvelous phenomenon that no one really understands. To appreciate how marvelous it is, consider the follow ten statements.

1. "Things change." The word "paradigm" means "example, or model." Thomas Kuhn used the word to describe the dominant theories in science. For example, Newton's theory of universal gravitation was a paradigm for centuries until it was replaced by Einstein's theory of relativity. Before Einstein, scientists used Newton's theory as a model to imitate, and they asked questions, looked for answers, and thought about the world in ways that were consistent with Newtonian mechanics. But after 1900 a "paradigm shift" occurred. More and more physicists began looking to Einstein's theory as a model to imitate, and consequently asked different kinds of questions and thought about the world in different ways. In the Einstein paradigm, time does not pass at a fixed rate, as it does in the Newtonian paradigm, nor is space (or distance) an absolute. In the Einstein paradigm, the world looks completely different.

A similar shift has occurred in people's thinking about language and truth. In Newton's day, language was regarded as a kind of mirror. It reflected the world, or copied the world faithfully. Or it was like a perfect painting. Language was a neutral instrument with which people could know the unblemished truth about the world. It was like a perfectly transparent window into reality. But things change. We have undergone a paradigm shift in our view of language. Now philosophers and writers think of language as a game people play, or a weapon organizations use to control people. Truth is like Newton's absolute time and space. No one believes in those things any more.

2. "'Red' is not red." Words do not resemble the things they stand for. In general, language does not correspond with reality, so how can language "reflect" or "represent" reality? It can't. Almost all the words we use are general words, like "red," "dog," and "walk," or "efficient," "democracy," and "change." But since the words are general and abstract, they omit all the concrete details of the real world. Hearing the word "red" is not at all like seeing red. The gap between language and the world is enormous.

3. "Words are defined with other words." When a person looks up a word in a dictionary to learn the meaning, what the person finds is more words. When a person goes to school and learns about democracy, what the person learns is a large number of other words. For example, the word "efficient" means "producing the desired result with a minimum of effort, expense, or waste." That definition might lead to more definitions of "minimum," "effort," and so on. In other words, understanding almost always means correlating a word or phrase with other words. It almost never means having a direct experience of the world.

In fact, there is no such thing as a "direct experience" of the world. Every person brings years of past experiences, strong expectations, countless beliefs and theories, and powerful desires and fears to every experience. All those filters and pressures exist as language in our mind. We never encounter anything except through the distorting lenses of words.

4. "I can't get inside your head." Meaning is always subjective. When I learn the word "sour," I have an experience. As we have seen, it's not a "direct experience." It is shaped and colored by my memories and thoughts, expressed in words, but it is an experience. However, I cannot possibly know what you experience when you taste something that you call "sour." What you mean depends on your private, subjective experiences and associations, which are absolutely inaccessible to me. Even if we agree on which things taste sour and which do not, we are not agreeing on the meaning of the word. The meaning, for me, is what I am aware of, and the meaning for you is what you are aware of. And I cannot taste your taste.

5. "Words have many meanings." When people talk, how well do they really understand each other? We have the illusion that we understand each other because we can manipulate physical objects and move through space more or less as expected. We can agree to meet at 5 PM and succeed. But most of what we say goes beyond physical objects and locations. "I'm concerned about Tommy's work in school." A sentence like that can mean almost anything. In fact, it doesn't have a single meaning. When you say it, the meaning depends on all the millions of connections with other words in your mind. When I hear it, the sounds call up millions of other associations in my mind, different from yours. If someone else hears it, the sentence has a different meaning for that person. Meaning depends on connections. The connections are infinitely complicated, and different for every person.

6. "I can't get outside my head." The ordinary idea of truth doesn't make sense. According to the ordinary idea, the sentence "The cat is on the mat" is true if there is a correspondence between the sentence and a fact, the fact that the cat is on the mat. I can understand the sentence, and I can look at the cat and the mat. But when I look at the cat, I have a perception. I never get into contact with the cat itself, independently of my perception of it. In fact, what I really know is my own perceptions, not the cat itself. I assume that the world out there is just like my perceptions of it, but I can never compare my perceptions with the world to see if they match. Every time I try to check the world, I have to rely on my own perceptions. "True," in the ordinary sense, means that a sentence corresponds to the world as it really is. But no one can ever know the truth in that sense.

7. "We can't talk about truth." In the ordinary sense, a sentence is true if it corresponds to a fact in the world. In other words, truth is a relation between language and the world. But think schematically. The picture is supposed to look like this:

(language) . . . . (world)

("The cat is on the mat") . . . . (the cat on the mat)

But now when I say that truth is a relation between language and the world, what is that sentence about? It isn't about the world, and it isn't about language. It is about the *relation* between those two things. So is that sentence, "truth is a relation between language and the world," true? Not according to the ordinary theory, since it doesn't correspond to a fact in the world.

Maybe we can expand our idea of "the world" to include the relation to language. So now we have

("Truth is a relation between
language and the world") . . . . ((language) . . . . (world))

But now what is this paragraph about? Not the relation between language and the world. That is represented by the right side of the diagram, but the paragraph is about the whole diagram. Someone might say "It's about the relation between the relation between language and the world and language." But that doesn't make sense. The ordinary idea of truth leads to endless paradoxes.

8. "Words affect people." The meaning of a word for a person is the host of other words, memories, images, and feelings that the word calls up in that person's mind. We like to think that most words are neutral, but actually none is. Every word and every statement elicits some kind of emotional response. The word "fish" may seem to be a perfectly bland biological term. But when I hear the word I automatically recall various meals I have had, some good, some bad, trips on a fishing boat, the wet feel of a squirming fish, and innumerable other associations creating a very complex emotional reaction. The same applies to every word everyone hears. We may not talk about the emotions or even consciously think of them, since they are different for everyone, but they are there, and we feel them.

9. "Language is power." The principal function of language is not to express an objective, public truth that is the same for everyone. We have seen that the old paradigm doesn't make sense any more for many reasons. In the new paradigm, the function of language is to exert power. People use language to control the world, including other people. If a group of people like scientists can persuade others that they have the truth, then those others will obey the scientists and do what they say. The real reason for saying a statement is true is to force others to comply. Scientists argue so vigorously about their theories because their egos depend on having the truth, and they want to defeat their rivals. No one really cares, for example, whether the mass of a star is X or Y, but grown men and women will fight like animals over the "truth" about such trivialities. Having the truth is just another way of gaining status and prestige, i.e., power over others. Besides the idea of truth, people also use the emotional meanings of words to influence others. The struggle for power never ends, and language is a major weapon in that struggle.

10. "We can watch our language." If sentences are not true, then what is the purpose of these sentences I am writing here? It isn't to express the truth, since there is no such thing. Of course it is to exercise power over readers. But people can use their influence for good or for ill. I hope I can use language for good. My goal is to change readers' minds. That is all writers' goal, although many think of it as a purely intellectual, neutral process. I hope these words will make readers think about language in new ways, and that they will become more alert to people's attempts to manipulate them and exert power over them. By recognizing the real function of "the truth," people can escape from its control. Like many of the revolutions of the past, the revolutionary new paradigm is a struggle for greater freedom.

Key Concepts

paradigm	subjective	truth
meaning	perception	power

Critical Questions

1. What does the postmodernist mean by saying that "red" is not red?
2. When you think of the meaning of a word, do you think of other words, or do you think of nonverbal objects and experiences? Is the meaning of the word "chair" a chair?
3. When you say you are happy or sad, angry or expectant, do you mean the same thing as other people when they say those words? Can you know how another person feels?

4. The postmodernist says "I can't get outside my head." Do you agree? Can you compare your perception of a cat with the cat itself?
5. "Truth is a relation between language and the world." In other words, all true sentences are accurate representations of the world. According to the postmodernist, is the sentence in quotes about the world? Is it true?
6. Do all words evoke emotions, in your opinion? Do people deliberately use words to evoke emotions in others?
7. Do you think all writers are trying to exercise power over their readers? Can writers exercise power over their readers for the readers' own good?

Methods and Techniques

PROVING A NEGATIVE

In many of the essays in this book the authors claim that something does *not* exist. An atheist claims that God does not exist; a relativist claims that absolute moral laws do not exist; a materialist claims that a spiritual soul does not exist. And in this section, the postmodernist claims that objective truth does not exist.

But it is a truism in logic that "you can't prove a negative." This means that you can't prove that something does *not* exist. You can prove that something *does* exist by observing it (e.g., white tigers, superconductivity, a cure for arthritis). But how do you prove that something does *not* exist?

For example, suppose someone says, "Unicorns do not exist." How could that statement be proved? One could say that explorers and scientists have searched the globe, but have never found any unicorns. But that does not prove there are no unicorns. Maybe the scientists just haven't looked carefully enough. In fact, no matter how thoroughly people search for unicorns without finding any, someone can always say that unicorns are very shy, there are only a few of them, they are camouflaged, and so on. No one can prove that unicorns do not exist.

The principle "you can't prove a negative" applies to general statements, not specific ones. "Unicorns exist" is a general statement, and "unicorns do not exist" is the negative form. But "There is a unicorn on display at the entrance of the zoo" is a specific statement. It is about a particular animal in a particular place. And you *can* prove the negative form of that statement (i.e., "There are *no* unicorns on display at the entrance of the zoo"). You can look at the entrance and see that there are no unicorns there. But you cannot prove that there are no unicorns anywhere.

Some philosophers use this principle to support the claim that we might find answers to philosophical questions. Skeptics say "answers do not exist." In other words, they say no one can know the answers to deep questions, or we will never find any answers. In rejecting this view, the philosopher who believes we can find answers is a little like the person who believes in unicorns. They both say maybe we haven't looked hard enough. The skeptic can never prove that answers do *not* exist, the optimistic philosopher says, or that we will *never* find them, because you can't prove a negative.

Actually, there is one way you can prove a negative, if we stretch the idea of a negative statement a little. You can show that something is self-contradictory, and if it is, then it cannot exist. For example, do square circles exist? The answer is no, there are no square circles, and you can prove it in the following way. Are these circles round? Well, if they are circles, then they must be round, but if they are square, then they are not round. So they are round and not round at the same time. This is self-contradictory and therefore senseless. The "idea" of a square circle never gets off the ground. It is inconceivable, so you can be sure that you will never find one.

The relativist uses this technique in the essay "Moral Relativism." It tries to prove that there are no objective standards of morality by arguing that the idea is self-contradictory. A standard of morality is created by a society and exists within some society. But to be objective, a standard would have to be independent of any particular society. So a so-called objective standard of morality would have to be a product of a particular social system, but at the same time independent of any social system, dependent and not dependent at the same time. As a matter of fact, the absolutist tries to use the same technique. The absolutist's essay tries to show that when two cultures come into contact, relativism must say some actions are right and are wrong at the same time. But that is meaningless.

I said this is stretching the idea of a negative because relativists and others are trying to show that some idea is senseless, that something is absolutely impossible. That is a little different from proving a negative. Skeptics don't say answers to deep questions are impossible. They just say they do not exist. Biologists do not say that the idea of unicorns is senseless, or that they are absolutely impossible. They just do not exist. But nevertheless, it cannot be proven that they do not exist.

Understanding the Dilemma

REPRESENTATIONALIST OR POSTMODERNIST?

The conflict in this section is similar to the conflict in Section 5.2, between a positivist and a romantic. A representationalist is similar to a positivist, and a postmodernist is similar to a romantic, so if you decided you were a positivist before, you will probably decide you are a representationalist now. Or if you agreed with the romantic point of view before, you will probably agree with the postmodernist point of view now.

The issue in Section 5.2 was science and knowledge, whereas the issue in this section is truth, but truth and knowledge are closely related. A representationalist analyzes the ordinary concept of truth to explain why truth is valuable to us. He or she claims that truth is a relation between a sentence and the world, or between thoughts or models in your mind and the world. If the sentence or thought is accurate, then it guides our actions successfully, but if it is inaccurate, then it leads us into problems.

A postmodernist takes the radical view that truth doesn't exist, on the basis of several considerations. First, there are problems with language. Words are highly abstract and do not convey all the rich details of things themselves. Second, there are problems with the human mind. We all have access to our own feelings and thoughts, but no direct access to other people's feelings, or to objects in the world. Consequently, we cannot know what other people mean with their words, nor can we compare our own words with things in the world to see if they match. Third, there are problems with the idea of truth. It is supposed to be a relation between language and the world. But in trying to talk about truth we seem to be trying to step outside of language and the world to talk about the relation between them. But we cannot step outside of language or the world.

The issue between the representationalist and the postmodernist is not an issue of values or preferences. Some people are more interested in their own feelings and moods and reactions to things. Others are more interested in external things, public affairs, facts, and the physical world. But that is not the main difference between the two positions in this section. Some people have a hard time seeing a situation as it really is and often project their own desires or assumptions onto the situation. Others can leave themselves and their perspective out completely, and describe what happened in a completely objective way. Both these contrasts between types of people are related to the issue in this section, but are not quite the same as the issue. A representationalist and a postmodernist disagree about whether truth really exists or not. They are not discussing types of people, what is interesting, or how accurately they can describe some event they witnessed.

In thinking about where you stand, you should notice that the two sides have different views about testing the truth of a statement. A representationalist says that in order to decide whether or not a sentence is true, you must compare it with the objective world. For example, is the sentence "Snow is white" true? The representationalist says we answer this question by comparing the sentence with the world. If we discover that there actually is something corresponding to the word "snow" and that the stuff is accurately described as "white," then the sentence is true. This process of confirming and disconfirming sentences is the main business of science, although others try to determine truth as well.

The postmodernist attacks this approach on every level. The postmodernist "problematizes" language, in the sense that he or she tries to show that representationalists overlook serious problems in language. The meaning of the word "snow" is not so simple as the representationalist assumes. Nor can we compare the sentence with reality itself, since we cannot get to reality directly, without relying on our own perceptions of reality.

The representationalist is also assuming that I can compare my belief "Snow is white" with the snow on the ground. But if my belief, my internal representation, is part of my consciousness, then who is doing the comparing? When we talk about truth, we use a picture of comparing two things, as if we could hold one in one hand and the other in the other hand. But the two things compared are "belief" (or "language"), and "the world." We cannot step outside of our beliefs or language to compare them with something else.

Finally, the postmodernist attacks the process of confirmation. It is not a completely neutral, objective procedure, as the representationalist assumes, but is a terrific struggle for power. The belief that a person possesses the truth makes that person powerful. It does not indicate that the person stands in any special relation to reality, but most people think that it does, so they defer to the person with the truth.

The postmodernist attack on the traditional way of thinking about truth is so extensive and complete that it is difficult to focus on particular disagreements. The two positions have almost nothing in common. But the representationalist can ask some critical questions of the postmodernist. The representationalist claims that knowing the truth is necessary for survival. The truth enables us to navigate through the world. If that is right, can a postmodernist really give up a belief in truth? Would a postmodernist say that there is no difference between the statements "London is in Great Britain" and "London is in France"? Of course in practical matters postmodernists behave just like representationalists. They believe some people and do not believe others.

But the postmodernist claims that while his or her behavior appears to be similar to the representationalist's, it really isn't. The postmodernist is keenly aware of people's egos and their need for power and status. Becoming aware of all the ways in which people pursue these goals, including using language and talking about truth, allows him or her to look at the world through different eyes. By becoming aware of his own drives, the postmodernist can to some degree moderate those drives, and try to use language for liberation rather than control. The minor details may seem similar to the old way of thinking, but the basic outlook is different, the postmodernist claims.

Even if we must continue to behave as if we can know the truth, that weakness doesn't necessarily imply that the postmodernist is wrong. Our ideas might still be completely confused.

Like all the other dilemmas, this one branches out into other issues. But it is useful to think about which point of view you believe is more sensible. Is truth a valuable or even essential thing to have? Should you make finding the truth one of your priorities? And by "truth" do you mean an accurate picture of the world to guide your decisions? Or is that goal riddled with untenable assumptions and self-contradictions? Are we really still instinctual animals after all, competing continuously for power and status, without realizing it, and using our intellectual tools as our weapons? Are you a representationalist or a postmodernist?

REPRESENTATIONALIST

1. If something is true, then it is true for everyone alike.

2. A belief is like a sentence in your mind.
3. A sentence is true if it corresponds to the actual world, and false if it does not.
4. Journalists, scientists, historians, and others work hard to determine the objective truth, and often succeed.

POSTMODERNIST

5. Language is too different from the world to represent it accurately.
6. The meaning of a word depends on the associations one makes between the word and one's memories, feelings, and other words, and therefore is subjective and private.
7. We cannot step outside of our minds, or our language, to compare them with the world, and so the ordinary idea of truth is a myth.
8. The real function of language is to help a person gain power over others.

FOR FURTHER STUDY

Historical Examples

REPRESENTATIONALIST: Ludwig Wittgenstein. *Tractatus Logico-Philosophicus.* Humanities, 1961. Originally published in 1922. In sections 1 through 3.1, Wittgenstein explains his "picture theory" of meaning, according to which statements are "pictures" of facts.

POSTMODERNIST: Michel Foucault. *The Foucault Reader.* Edited by Paul Rabinow. Pantheon, 1984. Foucault emphasizes the numerous, subtle forms of domination of individuals, and the effects of power on what we call knowledge.

OTHER SOURCES

Bertrand Russell. *The Problems of Philosophy.* Oxford University Press, 1912. Chap. 11 is an explanation and defense of the representationalist, or correspondence, position.

Mortimer J. Adler. *Six Great Ideas.* Macmillan, 1981. In a simple style, Adler argues that truth is objective, and that we can draw a line between matters of truth and matters of taste (which are subjective).

N.L. Gifford. *When in Rome: An Introduction to Relativism and Knowledge.* State University of New York Press, 1983. Gifford discusses, at an introductory level, various forms of subjectivism and relativism regarding knowledge, but much of his discussion applies to the question of truth as well.

Hilary Lawson, Lisa Appignanesi, eds. *Dismantling Truth: Reality in the Post-Modern World.* St. Martin's, 1989. Lawson's introduction is an interesting survey of several contemporary attacks on the representationalist position.

Alan R. White. *Truth.* Doubleday, 1970. Relatively advanced, technical discussion, beginning with the topic of what is said and what is used to say it.

Stanley J. Grenz. *A Primer on Postmodernism.* William B. Eerdmans Publishing Co., 1996. Elementary discussion of several themes.

Michael Luntley. *Reason, Truth, and Self: The Postmodern Reconditioned.* Routledge, 1995. Critique of postmodern ideas about science, knowledge, truth, self, and community.

Madan Sarup. *An Introductory Guide to Post-structuralism and Postmodernism.* 2nd Edition. University of Georgia Press, 1993. Helpful chapters on Lacan, Derrida, Foucault, Lyotard, Baudrillard, and French feminist theories, including critical assessments.

CONNECTIONS

INTUITIONIST OR EXTERNALIST?

Chapter 5 deals with some of the most abstract and difficult issues in philosophy. Philosophers call this topic "epistemology," from the Greek word for knowledge. It has perplexed reflective people for centuries, ever since Plato tried to understand how he could know about mathematics and human nature. Since philosophers want to know the truth about themselves and the world—since they are concerned with their beliefs and the grounds for their beliefs—epistemology is very important to them. It should be important to anyone with the same concerns.

Philosophers have generally divided into two camps on the questions of epistemology. Some philosophers believe that the ultimate test of knowledge is a particular kind of experience. When you have a strong feeling of certainty, for example, then you have genuine knowledge. When you see a logical connection between two statements, then you know something. For example, the statement "the two straight lines are parallel" implies the statement "the two straight lines will never cross." Seeing the relation between these ideas is a special, unique kind of experience, and that inner experience is the test of knowledge.

Other philosophers believe that knowledge has a different basis. They say that our beliefs must be tested by some external standard before the beliefs count as knowledge. People can have all kinds of ideas, experiences, and beliefs, but only some of them are real knowledge. What distinguishes knowledge from fantasy is that knowledge conforms to the real world, the world as it is outside our minds. That means we must judge an idea by an external standard, not an internal experience, before it can qualify as knowledge.

We can call the first point of view "intuitionism," because it says knowledge depends on a personal experience, or intuition. To decide whether or not I know something, I look inside, at my own mental experience. If the experience has a certain character—if it is absolutely certain, or if it is strong and vivid—then I have knowledge. The second point of view is "externalism," because it looks to the external world to validate knowledge. Knowledge is not a matter of having a particular kind of experience or intuition. Experiences are a personal matter, but knowledge is objective. It is an accurate picture of the world. Therefore to determine that I know something I must look outside my own mind to see if others agree with me, or if my ideas work in practice, or if they conform to the world. I should not trust my personal feelings. My own feelings and experiences are not reliable enough to ensure that I have knowledge.

We can see examples of intuitionists and externalists in the sections of Chapter 5. In Section 5.2, "Does Science Give Us Real Knowledge?," the positivist argues that science does produce knowledge because of its method. Scientific method is specifically designed to subject a person's belief (hypothesis) to repeatable tests. A positivist says that a person knows something only when other investigators have performed experiments and arrived at the same results. Before a belief can count as knowledge, experiments must show that it conforms to the natural world, and other scientists must agree that it does. For example, you might believe that vitamin C cures the common cold, but you could have knowledge only when experiments confirm your belief. The positivist has a demanding, external standard of knowledge.

The romantic, on the other hand, has an internal standard. He or she rejects the positivist's reliance on tests and agreement, and argues that we should rely on our own personal experiences if we want to find real knowledge. External standards only give us power, not knowledge. To really know a forest, or a roller coaster ride, for example, we must see, smell, touch, and feel it directly. That experience, or intuition, is real knowledge, and it is not dependent on experiments or agreement. In fact, it cannot even be shared at all. Each person has his or her own knowledge. To know whether or not vitamin C cures colds, I should take it when I have a cold and see how I feel.

The same division between intuitionists and externalists occurs in Section 5.4, "Is Certainty the Standard of Knowledge?" The foundationalist is an intuitionist, and the pragmatist is an externalist. The foundationalist begins with the connection between knowledge and truth, and then draws out the implications of that connection. The most important implication, he says, is that the standard of knowledge is absolute certainty. If you know something, you cannot be mistaken. The only way to be sure that you are not mistaken is to be absolutely certain. The foundationalist then defines certainty as an inner feeling or state you have when you cannot realistically imagine being wrong. Therefore the foundationalist agrees with the romantic that knowledge depends on a kind of inner experience, or intuition. He says it is a feeling of certainty.

The pragmatist, however, has an external standard. He claims that people can argue forever over their feelings of certainty. The real test of knowledge is results. A person knows something when he or she can get results. Knowledge is those beliefs and ideas that give us the ability to manipulate the world and manage successfully. People who are ignorant, or who have false beliefs, cannot manage as well as people who have knowledge. Thus successful action is the real test of knowledge. The pragmatist is like the positivist in making knowledge depend on an external standard—successful action or manipulation of the world—rather than an internal standard like intuition.

Another good example of an intuitionist is the rationalist, represented in Section 5.3, "Is Experience the Source of All Knowledge?" The rationalist discusses mathematics, and claims that it gives us a very strange but undeniable knowledge of the world. When you put two apples together with two more apples, you know for sure that you will have a total of four apples. How do you know? You know that $2 + 2 = 4$ because you see it in your mind's eye. You feel the certainty of the statement. It is puzzling that everyone agrees on this statement, that it will always be true, and that it is true in all places. But it is definitely knowledge because of the intuition you have when you understand it, the rationalist says.

In contrast, an empiricist is an externalist. An empiricist claims that all our ideas and all our knowledge depend on perception of the world. Our eyes, ears, hands, noses, and mouths are the means whereby we receive all the information we have. These sense organs are dependent on stimulation from the external world. The empiricist tries to prove this claim by showing how all our ideas and beliefs can be traced back—or analyzed into—some simple sensory quality. For example, the idea of fire can be broken down into the simpler ideas of yellow color, flickering shape, and heat. The empiricist says that if we do not have a perception of some object, then we do not have knowledge of that object. Knowledge depends on stimuli from the external world.

This disagreement over "inner" and "outer" conceptions of knowledge also divides the writers in Section 5.1, "Can We Know about the External World?" The internalist in that section used some unusual thought experiments to try to show that we are like the sick child in the sealed room: we are separated from the world by our sense organs, and we have no way to check our senses to make sure they are conveying correct information. We might have an experience of a yellow flower, but we have no way of knowing if the objective flower really is yellow, or even if a flower is causing our experience. The only real knowledge we can have is knowledge of our own subjective sensations, the appearances of things. We cannot know anything about the world outside our minds. Thus the internalist is similar to other intuitionists.

The opposite view in Section 5.1 is represented by the perceiver. The author is called a perceiver because he claims that we *can* perceive the external world. We can know that some of our perceptions are accurate, he says, because we could not be mistaken all the time. To be mistaken, one must sometimes be correct. What makes the perceiver an externalist is the reason he gives to support his claim. Why must some of my perceptions be correct? Not because of their vividness or a feeling of certainty, but because the words "mistaken" and "correct" are opposites. One requires the other because of their meaning. Thus the perceiver uses facts about language and meaning to prove something about knowledge. Our language and the words we use conform to certain objective rules. You cannot make a word mean whatever you want it to mean; its mean-

ing, and the ideas you understand when you use it, are determined by the society that uses the language. The perceiver's appeal to language and meaning
makes him an externalist.

The last section in Chapter Five is Section 5.5, "Does Truth Exist?" The representationalist says yes and the postmodernist says no. A postmodernist claims
that certain characteristics of language make the whole idea of truth incoher-
ent. We like to believe in such a thing, as we believe in nirvana or heaven or
social harmony, but it doesn't really exist. It's a comforting myth. Truth is impossible for many reasons. Language is too different from the world to represent it. Words mean different things for different people, so there is no common truth. If we try to step back and analyze the relation between language
and the world, we fail, because our analysis is in language. It impossible to
"step back." Not only that, but we try to say that our analysis of truth is, itself,
true. The analysis is part of what we are analyzing. Instead of trying to figure
out these reflexive paradoxes, we should recognize that language is just one
more tool we use to gain power and security.

All these attacks on language and truth suggest that a postmodernist is very
different from an externalist. A postmodernist rejects any external standard of
knowledge, whether it is experimental verification, or pragmatic usefulness, or
sense perception. However, that does not necessarily imply that a postmodernist is an intuitionist, or believes in an inner standard of knowledge. Actually, the postmodernist rejects all knowledge and truth, as we ordinarily think
of them. Or perhaps a better way to put it is to say the postmodernist redefines
"knowledge" and "truth" to mean labels people put on certain sentences or results or experiences to try to influence others. I will call something knowledge
if it advances my position relative to others. Ultimately, the test of knowledge
is whether or not a statement or idea promotes my own power or freedom.
Insofar as my own power is an inner experience, a postmodernist is similar to
an intuitionist. But postmodernists as represented here do not fit the classification very well.

A representationalist, on the other hand, is an externalist. He or she puts the
emphasis on the external side of things rather than the internal, personal side.
A picture of Benjamin Franklin can be true or false. What makes it true is not
my experience or feelings at all; what makes it true is that it corresponds with
the real Benjamin Franklin, an objective part of the world. The same applies to
sentences or beliefs. I might believe that Los Angeles is the capital of California. My own memories, feelings, perceptions, or experience of Los Angeles or
California have no bearing on the truth or falsity of this belief. Its truth or falsity depends on the facts about California, independently of my experience. The
belief is actually false, and no one's subjective experience can make it true. It is
not false for me but true for someone else; it's simply false, and it would be
false whether anyone thought about it or not. The external conditions of the
world make some things true and others false, and therefore our knowledge
depends on these external conditions.

At this point I should remind you of something I have said before. The connections that I have described among the positions in Chapter 5 are only a few of the connections that exist. I have classified the positions into two large groups—intuitionists and externalists—but you might see other connections. Thinking about connections among the positions is important because when you decide that you accept one position, that decision might require you to accept other positions as well. For example, if you think about Section 5.2, "Does Science Give Us Real Knowledge?," and you decide that you are a positivist, then you might also have to accept empiricism, pragmatism, representationalism, and the perceiver's view. Or you could show that the positions are not connected in the ways I have described. To do that, you must think about the connections for yourself.

Intuitionists	**Externalists**
romantic	positivist
foundationalist	pragmatist
rationalist	empiricist
internalist	perceiver
postmodernist	representationalist

INTUITIONISTS

1. The difference between genuine knowledge and mere belief is the perception, or feeling, of certainty.
2. We can know some things that we cannot communicate, even in principle.
3. Knowledge is ultimately personal; what is knowledge or truth for one person may not be knowledge or truth for another.
4. We know our own minds and inner experiences better than we know the external world, and knowledge of the world is built up from knowledge of our own experiences.

EXTERNALISTS

5. Knowledge depends on an objective, practical standard, not feelings or personal "intuitions."
6. Knowledge is a social product, achieved in cooperation with others.
7. If a person's beliefs cannot be tested, explained, and shared with others, then they are almost certainly not real knowledge.
8. If a person really knows something, then it is true and a fact for everyone.

Glossary of Contrasting Positions

absolutist. Believes that some actions are absolutely right, in all places and at all times, for anyone, and other actions are absolutely wrong, for anyone.

abstractionist. Believes that God is an abstract force, or power, such as love, and not a personal being.

atheist. Believes there is no God.

believer. Believes that when we cannot know the answers to important questions, we should choose to believe an answer that makes sense to us.

Buddhist. Believes that the only way to escape from life's continuous suffering is to recognize that the self is an illusion.

capitalist. Believes that what one contributes to society should determine the rewards one receives in society, and that capitalism ensures this relationship.

causal theist. Believes that the chain of causes cannot go back in time forever, there must be a first cause, and that proves that God (the First Cause) exists.

complementer. Believes that men and women are psychologically different due to universal patterns of parenting, and that women's distinctive strengths have been ignored.

contractor. Believes the model of a contract explains the origin of society and citizens' obligation to obey the law.

contradictor. Believes a person cannot rationally accept the existence of a loving, all-powerful God, and the existence of evil, at the same time.

definer. Believes happiness can be defined as the inner state that results from achieving most of one's goals.

design theist. Believes the order and regularity in the world proves that it was consciously designed, and therefore that God exists.

dualist. Believes the mind is a completely different kind of thing from the brain or body.

egalitarian. Believes that much more material equality among people would solve the most pressing social problems.

elitist. Believes some people are superior to others in some respect (talent, skill, virtue, drive), and that society should recognize that superiority.

empiricist. Believes all knowledge begins in, and depends on, sensory experience (i.e., sight, hearing, touch, etc.).

essentialist. Believes that identity depends on one's position with society and history, and black people's identity depends on the permanent possibility of oppression.

euthanizer. Believes that no rule applies to all the complexities of life and death, and that euthanasia is sometimes justified.

excuser. Believes that we are not responsible for our actions, whether our actions are caused or uncaused.

externalist. Believes that we acquire knowledge when we adjust our minds to the real, objective world, ideally through cooperative investigation.

formalist. Believes that being moral means obeying certain objective rules.

foundationalist. Believes that all knowledge must be based on absolute certainty, which is an inner perception or intuition.

functionalist. Believes that all societies must enforce certain basic rules in order to survive, and that these rules are what we call morality.

hard determinist. Believes that all a person's thoughts and actions are caused (i.e., determined) by previous events in her body or environment, and therefore that we are not free.

hedonist. Believes that pleasure is the only real, intrinsic value, and all other values are means to pleasure or avoidance of pain.

humanist. Believes that morality is a human creation, based ultimately on human choices and decisions, not on God or nature or some external absolute.

individualist. Believes individual liberty must be protected from group pressures toward equality.

internalist. Believes that we directly experience feelings and sensations, and that we can never prove that these inner experiences correspond to an external world.

internationalist. Believes that new conditions call for the formation of a world government, which would control all nuclear weapons and enforce world peace.

intuitionist. Believes that all knowledge ultimately rests on an inner, personal experience; a feeling of certainty; or a preverbal experience, independent of other people's experiences.

judge. Believes everyone is responsible for his or her choices, unless one of the four recognized excuses applies to the situation.

libertarian. Believes that many social goods are actually the same as liberty, and where there is a difference, liberty is more valuable.

localist. Believes a world government is impossible, because politics is a cultural art, different in different societies.

materialist. Believes the mind and mental processes are actually the same things as the brain and brain processes.

mechanist. Believes that machines can perform all the specific, intelligent operations that people can perform, and therefore that machines can think.

mentalist. Believes that machines cannot think and will never be able to think.

metaphysical libertarian. Believes that by looking at our own minds when we make a choice, we can see that we have free will.

moral theist. Believes that the only adequate basis for our sense of morality is God's commands.

muddler. Believes that we cannot define happiness because it is different for different people.

naturalist. Believes that the world and human experiences can all be explained in terms of natural, understandable processes, without any need to appeal to the supernatural.

nonessentialist. Believes that identity depends on what a person chooses to regard as important about himself or herself, and that race is not important.

objectivist. Believes that the basis of morality is something independent of human choices, not created by mankind, such as God, nature, or absolute laws.

organicist. Believes that society has a reality of its own, independent of the particular individuals within that society.

paternalist. Believes that a government should sometimes force people to do what is good for them, even if they don't want to do it.

perceiver. Believes that it makes no sense to say that all our perceptions of the world are illusions, and therefore that we can know some things.

personalist. Believes that God is similar to human beings in at least some basic ways, such as being conscious, or loving humankind.

pluralist. Believes in many personal and social values besides pleasure.

positivist. Believes that the scientific method leads to genuine knowledge because it requires people to be objective.

postmodernist. Believes truth is a myth used to preserve power and privilege among certain elites.

pragmatist. Believes the test of knowledge is the ability to manipulate the environment successfully.

protector. Believes that preserving human life is our highest moral principle, and that euthanasia is therefore wrong.

psychological altruist. Believes people sometimes act in completely unselfish ways, without expecting any benefit of any kind for themselves.

psychological egoist. Believes every human action is motivated in part by a desire for some sort of benefit for oneself.

questioner. Believes people should never believe anything without evidence or a good reason, and faith is never a good reason.

rationalist. Believes we can know some fundamental truths about the universe, such as mathematical truths, simply by thinking about them.

reconciler. Believes that evil (innocent suffering) is compatible with a loving, all-powerful God.

reductionist. Believes that natural laws regulate all human behavior, because humans are part of the natural world.

relationist. Believes that people are naturally cooperative, and that when the group as a whole prospers and benefits, then each member benefits as well.

relativist. Believes that different societies create different moral rules, and that no society's rules are objectively better than any other society's rules.

representationalist. Believes that truth is a relation between a belief and the world, whereby the belief accurately represents the world.

romantic. Believes that science distorts reality rather than revealing it, and that knowledge comes only from direct, lived experience.

socialist. Believes that capitalism makes people greedy and immoral, because in a capitalist society everything depends on money.

soft determinist. Believes that a person is free so long as his choices are caused by his own thoughts and desires, and that people are normally free in this sense.

specialist. Believes that the difference between religion and philosophy is the difference between the attitudes of commitment, faith, and devotion (religion) and skepticism, criticism, and wonder (philosophy).

spiritualist. Believes that the human mind is complex, forever mysterious, unpredictable, and not part of the physical world.

survivor. Believes that there is some evidence that the soul continues to exist after the death of the body.

terminator. Believes that we cannot conceive of a person, or soul, existing without a body.

transcendentalist. Believes that there is a higher level of reality, which includes God, the soul, and unfathomable mysteries, beyond the observable, physical world.

unifier. Believes the differences between men and women are not important, and that the biological differences will soon be obsolete.

utilitarian. Believes that the standard of right and wrong is the greatest happiness for the greatest number of people.

Index

Abilities, 128–129, 182
Absolutes, 213–225, 256–261, 265
Absolutist, 214–215, 222–225
Accidental properties, 210
Ad hominem, 222–223
Adaptation, 21
Adversity. *See* Suffering
Adultery, 229
Afterlife. *See* Immortality
Agreement, 374, 388–390, 400, 425
AIDS, 64
Altruism, 325–334
American Revolution, 109, 123, 153, 236
Analogies, 321–322
Analysis, 145–146, 384, 391–393
Androgyny, 349
Animal rights, 313–314
Animals, 234–235, 240, 338, 422
Answers, 65–66, 135–136, 361, 419–420
Apparitions, 56
Appearance vs. reality, 360
Aquinas, St. Thomas, 18
Arguments, 71, 368–369, 379, 392
Arnold, Benedict, 236
Art, 5, 190, 282
Artificial intelligence, 313–324
Artificial womb, 340
Assumptions, 367, 378–379, 422
Astronomy, 277
Atheism, 22–24, 26–28
Atomistic bias, 101
Attention, 406
Attitudes, 82–84, 87
Authenticity, 164–165, 167
Authority, 68–69, 79, 183, 245–247, 388
Axiom, 264

Beauty, 194
Belief
  consistent, 48–49
  justification of, 262
  and knowledge, 382–383, 396–405
  in mathematics, 388–391
  nature of, 412–415, 421–422
  religious, 22, 30, 35–37, 42, 62–70
Benevolence, 327
Bias, 147–148, 212, 216–217, 341, 344–346, 349
Big Bang, 65
Biology, 303
Blame. *See* Responsibility
Blavatsky, Madame, 56
Body. *See* Human body
Boyle's law, 216
Brain, 301–312, 354–355, 362

Brain waves, 303
Buddhism, 75–80, 86–89, 93
Business, 140–144

Capitalism, 136–144, 182
Categories, 337
Causal chain, 17
Cause and effect, 277–285, 287–289, 291–293, 376
Certainty, 425
  foundation of knowledge, 397–401, 407–409
  in mathematics, 386, 388–391, 393–395, 426
Chance, 21
Character, 45–48, 170
Chemistry, 277, 303, 385
Chess, 315
Child abuse, 220
Children, 245
  and conscience, 216
  early learning in, 316
  and identity, 342–343
  moral development of, 232–233
  and toys, 104
Choices, 276–289, 337
  of basic desires, 292
Christianity, 23, 36, 67
Civil laws, 215
  obedience to, 97–99
Civilization, 222
Class divisions, 125–126, 144
Classes and generalizations, 331–333, 337, 346–348
Coercion, 280, 291, 294–295
Cold War, 151
Comfort, 70
Commands, 246, 263
Common sense, 279, 311
  and the external world, 369
  and responsibility, 299
  and thought experiments, 361, 367
  and truth, 412
Communication, 151, 156, 243, 349
Communism, 124–127
Compassion, 139, 142, 158, 182, 195, 258, 261, 265, 344
Competition, 147, 182
Computers, 313–324
Concepts, 38–39, 58–59, 341
Confirmation, 372–374, 402–403, 418, 421. *See also* Verification
Confucius, 230
Conscience, 216, 236
Consciousness, 57–58, 298, 306, 313–324
  of self, 35

433

Consensus. *See* Agreement
Consequences, 68–72, 228–229, 239, 256, 342
Conservatives, 166, 349–350
Conspiracies, 364
Constitution, American, 153
Contentment, 46
Contradiction, 420
Cooperation, 243
Correspondence and truth, 412–414, 417, 421, 427
Corruption, 377
Creation, 31–32
Creativity, 190, 193, 316, 377
Crime, 124–125, 131–132, 180, 245
Criminals, 293–296
Criteria, 347
Criticism, 82, 88
Crowds, 99–101
Cruelty, 4, 228
Cultural contact, 220–221
Cultural imperialism, 222
Culture, 214–217
Customs, 214–215

Dark Ages, 140
Darwin, Charles, 24
Death, 3, 64–65, 251–261
  and faith, 68–69
  and immortality, 52–58, 60–61
Deception, 364–366, 368
Definition, 82, 84–86, 416
  and empiricism, 384
  of happiness, 203–212
  and knowledge, 390
  of knowledge, 396, 407–409
  of thinking, 318–320, 323
Dehumanization, 377
Deism, 24
Deliberation, 279–280
Democracy, 151–154
  and capitalism, 136–140
Dependency, 157, 161
Depression, 257
Descartes, René, 343–344
Designer, 20–21
Desires, 246, 249, 292–293
Destiny, 376
Determinism, 276–289, 353. *See also* Hard determinism; Soft determinism
Dilemma, 43, 247, 291
Dishonesty, 141
Doubt, 360–370
Drugs, 116–117, 277
Dualism, 301–312, 354–355
Duty, 190, 233–234, 239, 258, 265

Ego, 236
Egoism, 200, 325–334
Einstein, Albert, 415
Elections, 133, 142, 163
Elements, 20

Elitism, 127–130
Emotions, 222–223, 268
  of crowds, 100
  and happiness, 206, 211
  and identity, 342–345
  and knowledge, 380
  and meaning, 86, 417
  and morality, 224, 253–254, 259, 261
  and politics, 156–157
  and responsibility, 290
  and self-interest, 325–334
  and thinking, 145–146, 154, 316
  and understanding, 380–381
  and values, 194
Empathy, 345, 349
Empiricism, 383–387
Enjoyment, 189–191, 193
Enlightenment, 78, 88
Environment
  and identity, 350
  influences personality, 292, 295
  and knowledge, 383
  protecting, 152
Epicurus, 189, 207
Epistemology, 424
Equality, 123–134
  of condition, 111–113, 133
  mathematical, 386
  of opportunity, 111–113, 133
Error. *See* Deception
Eskimos, 244
Essential property, 53–54, 209–210, 347
Esteem, 195
Eternity, 32
Ether, 398
Ethical altruism, 333–334
Ethical egoism, 333–334
Ethics. *See* Morality
Ethnocentrism, 214
Euclid, 264
Euthanasia, 71, 251–261, 264–267
Evidence, 25–26, 67–68
  of the afterlife, 56–58
  and faith, 65–70
  of God, 36–37, 39–40
  and the mind-body problem, 310–311
  neutralized, 57
  standards of, 59
Evil, problem of, 41–51
Evolution, 21, 24
Excellence, 127–130, 193
Excuses, 294–295, 356
Exercise, 190
Expectations, 407, 416
Experiment, 425
Expert systems, 314
Explanation, 297–298
Externalists, 424–428

Facts
  and abilities, 129
  and evidence, 25–26, 58–59

and free will, 277–285
and human nature, 176, 336, 350
and morality, 215–217, 245–246, 254, 266
and philosophy, 3
and truth, 413–415, 417
and values, 198–199, 351
Factual beliefs, 244
Failure, 130. *See also* Success
Fairness. *See* Justice
Faith, 62–70, 73
Fame, 195, 204
Family life, 204
Feelings. *See* Emotions
Female circumcision, 218
Feuerbach, Ludwig, 35
First Cause, 18
Following rules, 234–235, 269
Foundations, 368, 397–401, 407–409, 425
    of morality, 241–247, 263–264
Free action, 279, 291
Free choice, 323
Free libertarian, 284–285
Free markets, 140–144, 146, 151, 182
Free will, 43
Freedom. *See also* Liberty
    metaphysical, 276–289
    political, 276
    of speech, 117, 214
Freud, Sigmund, 35–36, 192, 238
Friendship, 190
Fun, 189–191, 193
Functionalism, 242–244, 269–270

Galileo, 372
Games, 390
Gender, 337–346, 348–351
Generalizations, 171, 237, 331–333, 341–342
Genes, 277, 327, 340, 350
Genius, 372
Geometry, 264
Germ theory, 237
Gilligan, Carol, 344
Goals, 128, 131–132, 181, 188
    and classification, 340
    and happiness, 203–209
    and morality, 241
God
    as basis of morality, 245–247, 264, 269
    devotion to, 195
    existence of, 16–28
    as father figure, 35–37
    goodness of, 24, 41–51
    as love, 29–34
    nature of, 29–40
    power of, 43
Golden Rule, 230
Government, 155–158, 161
Grant, Ulysses S., 236
Gravity, 304
Great Depression, 236
Greed, 143
Greeks, ancient, 23, 75, 305, 314

Growth, 193
Guilt and shame, 290

Hamlet, 282, 378
Happiness
    in capitalism, 143–144
    causes of, 205
    as foundation of morality, 263
    nature of, 203–209
    and pleasure, 189
    requires opposite, 366
    as standard of morality, 226–232
    and worldviews, 268, 273
Hard determinism, 276–278, 287–289, 354
Harm principle, 115–118
Harmony, 195
Health, 193
Heart transplants, 64
Heaven, 44, 68, 191
Hedonism, 189–191, 239, 270
Hierarchy, 177
History, 5–6, 404
Holocaust, 24
Homelessness, 124, 180
Honesty, 196, 244
Hoover, Herbert, 236
Hope, 256, 260
Human being, 306
Human body, 53–54, 58, 301–308, 310–312
Human nature
    basis of society, 98
    and the body, 53–54, 302
    and character, 45–48
    and equality, 123, 132–133
    and identity, 176
    and immortality, 60
    and love, 33
    and reason, 156
    result of society, 107
Human rights, 9
Humanists, 246, 268–273
Humanities, 4–6
Humility, 44, 65
Hypotheses, 372–374, 402–403

Ideals, 196, 199
Ideas, 302–303, 306–307
    association of, 384–385
    simple and complex, 384–385
Identity, 163–178, 342
    and consciousness, 306
    and worldview, 10–11
Ignorance, 364–366
Illusions, 77–80, 360–370, 406. *See also* Deception
Images, 302, 306, 413
Imagination, 367–368
    and immortality, 52–55, 57–58
    and possibilities, 308–310
    and thought experiments, 361
Imitation, 342
Immortality, 36, 52–58, 68

Incentives, 129
Inconceivable, 284, 309–310
Inconsistencies, 48–50
Individualism, 125, 179–185
Indoctrination, 143–144
Inequality. *See* Equality
Infatuation, 329–330
Inference, 315, 321, 404
Infinite regress, 297–298
Infinity, 17
Innate ideas, 297
Innate potential, 128–129, 383–384. *See also* Environment
Inner experience, 279–281, 286, 306, 334, 424
Insanity, 294, 304, 366, 369, 378
Instincts, 234–235
Intelligence, 24, 65, 161, 261, 313–324
Intention, 233–234, 294
International relations, 149–162
Introspection, 279–280, 285–286, 298, 306
Intuitionists, 424–428
Irrationality, 37, 65, 126–127, 157, 278. *See also* Rationality
Islam, 23, 36

Jazz, 167
Jefferson, Thomas, 123, 158
Jesus, 230, 242
Job, 44
Judaism, 23, 36
Justice, 195, 211–212, 344
    and capitalism, 135–140, 182
    essential to society, 243
    and God, 44
    and liberty, 113–114
    and race, 168
    retributive and distributive, 137–138, 182
Justification, 262–264

King, Martin Luther, Jr., 235–236
Knowledge
    and action, 402–405, 425–426
    foundations of, 396–409
    and science, 371–381
    and skepticism, 360–370
    sources of, 382–395
    value of, 190, 194
Kohlberg, Lawrence, 344
Kuhn, Thomas, 415

Labor. *See* Work
Language, 415–418, 421
    and culture, 217
    knowledge of, 404
    reality of, 102
    shapes experience, 282
    and skepticism, 365–369
Language learning, 248, 297, 385
Lavoisier, Antoine, 373–374
Law. *See* Civil laws; Scientific laws
Lawyers, 142
Leadership, 155–156, 195

Learning, 315
Leeuwenhoek, Antony van, 372
Libertarian, 279–281
Liberty, 179–180. *See also* Freedom
    and capitalism, 136–137, 143
    defined, 110–111, 282–285
    highest social value, 109–122
    value of, 160
Life after death. *See* Immortality
Lincoln, Abraham, 46–47
Literature, 5, 367, 392
Loftus, Elizabeth, 406
Love
    definition of, 211, 329–330
    and God, 31–33
    as moral guide, 32–33
    and pleasure, 190
    power of, 32
    value of, 194
Loyalty, 190
Lucretius, 207
Luxuries, 124

Machine, 19–21, 313–324
Majority rule, 153–154
Marriage, 142–143
Materialism, 301–312, 354
Mathematics, 386–391, 393–395
    and infinity, 17
    and reality, 248–249
Matter and energy, 304–305
Maturity, 24, 33, 40, 46
McLuhan, Marshall, 151
Meaning of words, 38–39
    and arguments, 58–59
    and free will, 281–285
    and knowledge, 364–366, 426–427
    and materialism, 304
    and possibility, 309
    and science, 374
    and skepticism, 365–369
    and subjectivity, 416–417
Means and ends, 131–132, 190–191, 327, 339
Measurement, 373–374, 376, 380
Medical care, 141–142
Medicine, 64–65. *See also* Euthanasia
Memory, 302–303, 407
    and computer programs, 318
    and identity, 306–307
    and knowledge, 399–400
Mercy, 114, 252–254, 265
Mesopotamia, 75
Mind, 260, 301–312, 354, 421
Miracles, 278
Models, 97, 103–106, 264, 412–414
Money, 136, 139, 141–144, 182, 193, 204, 396
Monks, 77, 87
Monotheism, 23
Moody, Raymond A., 57
Moral consciousness, 235, 239–240, 246, 252
Moral crisis, 245–247
Moral heroes, 235–236

Moral philosopher, 242
Moral principles, 219, 233–237, 251–261, 265, 344
Moral relativism, 213–225, 249, 270–271, 420
Moral rules, 216, 231, 243, 269–271
Moral theory, 226–227, 237–238
Moral thinking, 253, 256, 266
Moral values, 196
Moralism, 117
Moralist, 242
Morality
 based on God, 245–247
 foundations of, 263
 objective judgment in, 216–217
 universality of, 221
More, Thomas, 123–127
Mothers, 233–234
 surrogate, 340
Motives, 233, 325–334
Murder, 228, 337
Mutations, 277
Mystery, 64, 66, 73
 and consciousness, 319–320
 and determinism, 277–278
Myths, 71

Naturalists, 91–94
Nature, 302, 323
 lawfulness of, 277–278, 353–358
 and mathematics, 389–391
 and mystery, 323
 order in, 19, 31–32
 totality of, 376
 value of, 195–196
Near death experience, 56–57
Necessary condition, 243–244, 248–249
Necessary truth, 388–391
Necessity. *See* Determinism
Needs, 245
 basic and relative, 144
Negative characterization, 17
Newton, Isaac, 23, 304, 415
Nirvana, 78
Nuclear weapons, 151–152, 161, 181
Numbers and numerals, 390

Obedience, 245–257. *See also* Civil laws
Objective facts, 244
Objectivists, 268–273
Objectivity
 and knowledge, 425
 and morality, 196, 249–250, 269–273
 and science, 345, 372–375, 377, 379–381
 and social class, 147–148
Obligations, 263
Observation, 286, 372, 377, 389
 of deliberation, 279–280
Old Testament, 30
Open-minded, 389
Opinion, 394, 397–399. *See also* Belief
Original sin, 92
Other, the, 175

Pain, 77
 and empiricism, 385
 and euthanasia, 251–261, 264
 and God, 45–48
 and happiness, 205
 and hedonism, 189–191
 privacy of, 307–308
 and psychological egoism, 327
Paradigm, 415
Pascal, Blaise, 374
Passion. *See* Emotions
Pasteur, Louis, 238
Paternalism, 115–118, 180
Paul, St., 67
Pavlov, Ivan, 235
Peace and war, 151–152, 161, 215
Perceptions, 222, 339, 406, 417
Person, 306
Personality, 295, 340, 342–343, 350, 354
 and the body, 54
Philosophy
 definition of, 3, 81–84
 goals of, 6, 25, 38, 59, 88, 149–150, 188, 192, 226–227, 361
 methods of, 25–26, 38, 58–59, 71–73, 83, 87–88, 210, 348, 379, 391–393
Physics, 303
Piaget, Jean, 385
Pity, 253
Pleasure, 188–191, 196–197, 199–202, 205
Pluralism, 192–197, 239
Point of view, 378
Politicians, 156–157
Polytheism, 22–23
Possible and impossible, 308–311, 420
Postmodernism, 256, 415–418, 420–423, 427
Poverty, 124, 180
Power, 142, 377, 402–405, 408, 418, 422, 425, 427
Powerlessness, 167
Pragmatists, 80
Prediction, 353, 374, 402–403
Preferential treatment, 164
President, American, 156, 364
Pride, 290
Primitive peoples, 22, 97, 214, 404
Primitive religion, 297
Principles. *See* Moral principles
Priorities, 119, 172, 255, 262
Privacy, 307–308
Problem solving, 118–119
Procrustes, 192
Profits, 136–137, 139, 141, 147, 183
Programming, 315–316
Progress, 366, 375, 389
Proof, 419–420
Property, 124–126, 136–137
Prosperity, 111
Prostitution, 117
Psychoanalysis, 35–36
Psychological damage, 115–116
Psychological manipulation, 143–144

Psychological traits, 171–172
Psychology, 303, 319–320, 323, 406
Punishment, 137–138, 293, 300, 344
Purpose, 375–376
  and classification, 338–340

Quantification. *See* Measurement

Race, 163–178
  and anxiety, 166
  and appearance, 166, 172–173
  defined, 169–170
  and history, 166, 169
Racism, 165, 168, 170–171, 173, 177
Random libertarian, 284–285
Rationalism, 388–391, 393–395
Rationality, 98
  and belief in God, 36–37
  and communism, 127
  and following rules, 235
  and society, 184
  and world government, 155–156, 161
Rawls, John, 97
Reactionaries, 222
Reality
  disagreements about, 282
  and science, 380
  of society, 106
  and truth, 410–418, 420–423
Reason, 247, 393
Reasoning, 400
Reduction, 303
Reductionists, 353–358
Reincarnation, 80, 87
Relationists, 179–185
Relativist. *See* Moral relativism
Religion
  definition of, 78, 81–84, 86–89
  and faith, 63, 66
  in medieval period, 371, 375
  and philosophy, 75–84
  and world government, 157
Repeatability, 373
Representations, 412–415
Reproduction, 338–340
Reputation, 327
Respect, 243, 313, 344
  for life, 251–257
Responsibility, 290–300, 355–356
Retribution. *See* Justice; Punishment
Revolution, 343, 418
Rights. *See* Human rights
Robots, 279, 315, 317
Role models, 233
Rules of games, 390
Russell, Bertrand, 81

Sacrifice
  and happiness, 206
  and hedonism, 191
  and psychological egoism, 327, 330, 333
  and utilitarianism, 229

Sample, 332–333
Science, 277–281, 303–305, 311, 371–381
Scientific laws
  and civil laws, 215
  discovery of, 372–377
  and human nature, 353–357
  and possibility, 309–310
  and reduction, 303–304
  universality of, 277–278, 353–357
Scientific method, 4, 372–377, 402–403
Scientific Revolution, 23
Security, 111, 193
Self
  and Buddhism, 77–80
  causally determined, 292
  and identity, 343–344, 350
  knowledge of, 305–308
Self-centered actions, 325–334
Self-correcting method, 374–375
Self-deception, 326
Self-determination, 177
Self-esteem, 206
Self-help, 11–12
Self-image, 167, 176, 319
Self-interest, 236, 355
Self-reliance, 137, 157–158, 194
Senses, 368, 384–385, 393–394, 426
  and hedonism, 190
  and immortality, 53
Sensory experience. *See* Senses
Sex, 340
Sex roles, 104
Shakespeare, William, 43
Siddhartha Gautama, 76–78
Simplicity, 192, 197, 201, 303–304
Simulation, 318
Sin, 79
Skepticism, 364, 419–420
Slavery, 221, 224, 243
Slippery slope, 260–261
Social contract, 96–99, 105
Society
  causal influence of, 100–101, 107
  contribution to, 137–140
  goals of, 119–120
  and individuals, 96–103, 106–108, 113,
    120–121, 179–185
  and justice, 137–138
  as organism, 99–103, 182, 183
  origins of, 98
  properties of, 96–103
  and values, 242–244, 269–270
Soft determinism, 281–285, 287–289
Soul, 8, 59, 79, 302
Sovereignty, 153
Specialization, 376
Speech codes, 117
Spirits, 22, 56
Spiritual thinking, 30–31
Spiritualists, 353–358
Standards
  of excellence, 127–128

of knowledge, 396–409, 424–428
of morality, 216–217, 226–240
Status, 195, 418
Stealing, 229
Stereotypes, 171, 173, 341–342
Subjective experiences, 362, 377, 380
Subjectivity, 345, 348
Success, 11, 141, 402–405
Suffering, 42–44, 46–48. *See also* Pain
Sufficient condition, 207
Suicide, 258
Superiority, feeling of, 126–127, 144
Survival
    after death, 52–58, 60
    and true beliefs, 415
    value of, 192–193

Talent, 129, 181
Taxes, 112–113, 181
Teachers, 233
Teaching
    morality, 216, 220
    thinking skills, 323
Technology, 252, 315, 350
Teenagers, 174–175
Television, 232
Theism, 26–28
Theory, 226–227, 237–238, 403
Thinking, 313–324, 343
Thought experiment, 361–362, 367
Thoughts, 302, 303, 306
Tolerance, 214, 220, 222
Tradition, 219–220
Transcendentalists, 91–94
Transportation, 339
Truth, 410–423
    and action, 402–405
    and knowledge, 398–401
    non-scientific, 377
    and values, 192

UFOs, 304
Uncaused events, 291–293, 295–296
Unconscious desires, 327
Understanding, 9
    of consciousness, 318–319, 323
    and faith, 66, 73
    limits of, 64–66
    and maturity, 31
    and science, 310, 375–377, 380
    and tragedy, 41–42

Unemployment, 124, 132
Uniqueness, 175
United Nations, 151, 218
Utilitarianism, 226–232, 263–264, 269, 344
Utopia, 123–127

Vagueness, 348
Values
    American, 109
    choice of, 292–293
    and identity, 172
    and pleasure, 188–197
    in politics, 156–157
    relativity of, 213–225
    social, 110
    source of, 241–247, 249–250
Verbal dispute, 282
Verification, 385–386, 402–403. *See also* Confirmation
Violence, 407
Virtues, 196
Vision, 362, 384–385, 399. *See also* Observation
Voting, 133

War. *See* Peace and war
Ward, Barbara, 153
Washington, Booker T., 235–236
West, Cornel, 165
Will. *See* Choices
Wisdom, 3, 305
    and character, 46
    of experts, 139
    of God, 246
    levels of, 31
    of ordinary people, 138
    value of, 194
Wishful thinking, 37
Witches, 304
Witnesses, 59, 400, 407
Women
    in capitalism, 142–143
    in world government, 156
Work, 124–125, 142
World government, 149–162
Worldview, 6–11, 74–75, 149–150, 268, 273, 288, 354

Xenophanes, 34

Zoraster, 230